Symbols and Notations

●	Any source of drinking water	⌂	Post Office
○	Seasonal water source	⊠	Will hold mail
⊏ (x)	AT Shelter and (capacity)	☽	Privy
☎	Public phone	👫	Public restroom
🛏	Hostel	🗑	Trailhead trash can
🛌	Hotel, Cabin or B&B	△	Laundry
🚿	Shower available w/o stay	🖥	Computer available
🚶	Outfitter	📶	Wireless (WiFi)
🚌	Shuttle, Bus or Taxi	🚉	Train Station
🍴	Any place that serves food	✈	Airport
🏪	Long term resupply	♗	Pharmacy
🏬	Short term resupply	✚	First Aid
⊤	Hardware store	🐕	Vet or kennel
💲	Bank or ATM	✂	Barber
📷	View	ℹ	Info center
🗼	Lookout tower	⍑	Lounge
🛶	Boating or aquablaze	🎥	Movie Theater
✳	Flora	+	Intersection
⊼	Picnic table	🏊	Swimming area

⚠ Warning: watch for trail turn or heed special rule.

■ Not categorized by other symbols; only on maps.

⊛ Locations that stamp the "AT Passport", a keepsake for hikers. Details and ordering info at ⟨www.ATPassport.com⟩

◂▸ Southbound / Northbound. Used to show distances to next shelter, and to show a transition of trails in the White Mountain National Forest.

◮ Established tentsite. On most of the AT you may camp wherever you are able; there are far more opportunties than shown by this symbol. Follow LNT principles (avoid "making" new tentsites, disperse, don't trample vegetation, stay 200' from water). Watch for camping restrictions in state & national parks, on private land, and in game lands.

🅿 Parking. Many have GPS coordinates that can be entered into a vehicle's GPS to navigate to trailhead parking lots. GPS systems are not always able to plot a course to remote locations.

✦ Treasure hunt; find answers; don't share them. Once you have them all, send them to david@awolonthetrail.com.

WFS Work For Stay

(pg.xx) More information on page xx

B/L/D Breakfast/Lunch/Dinner

$nnS, $nnD, $nnPP, $nnEAP Room prices . . . . , per- . . . . son.

Contents

C	Maildrop Guide	2
O	Book Organization	3
N	Getting to Spring . . .	5
T	Amicalola Falls . . . . Approach . . .	6
E	Great Smoky Mountain National Park	26
N	Shenandoah National Park	84
T	White Mountain National Forest	182
S	National Weather Service Wind Chill Chart	193
	Suggestions for Providing Trail Magic	213
	Equipment Manufacturers & Retailers	216
	Baxter State Park	217
	Getting to Katahdin	221
	Full Trail Map	222
	Calendar	224

D1378963

The A.T. Guide

Jerelyn Press
Titusville, FL
www.Jerelyn.com

Contributors: Bill Bancroft, Bismarck & Hopper, Tripp Clark, Chase Davidson, John Gordon (Teej), Cheryl Hadrych (Nike), Rick Hatcher (Bearfoot), Dave Hennel (Gourmet Dave), Melissa Hoppe, Dave Levy (Survivor Dave), Ryan Linn (Guthook), Frank Looper (Nightwalker), Juli Miller, Beth Robinette (Plan B), Bill Spach, John Stempa (Mechanical Man), Jeff Taussig, Pete Zuroff

Visit the Website: www.theATguide.com

The website contains updates, additions and corrections to the information contained in this book. Please let us know if there is anything we can do to improve the material or its presentation. email: david@AWOLonTheTrail.com

Directions

North/ South: At many points along the trail, a northbound hiker will be heading some direction other than compass north, but this book will always refer to "north" as the direction on the AT that ultimately leads to Katahdin. When reference is made to the true bearing, the word "compass" will precede the direction (e.g.: "compass south"). If the trail joins a section of road, enters a park, or enters a town, the "south" end is where a northbound hiker first arrives, and the "north" end is where he leaves.

East/West: "East" is to the right of the trail for a northbound hiker and "west" is to his left, regardless of the compass reading. Most east-west directions are abbreviated along with a distance in miles. For example, three-tenths of a mile east is written "0.3E."

Left/Right: If a road leads to a town that is to the west, then a northbound hiker would go to his left, and the southbound hiker to his right. Once on the road both hikers are headed in the same direction, so any additional directions are given using the words "left" and "right." "Left" and "right" are also used to describe features near a shelter, *from the perspective of a person outside of the shelter looking in*.

Maildrop Guidelines

Packages sent to post offices:

```
John Doe
C/O General Delivery
Trail Town, VA 12345

Please hold for AT hiker
ETA May 16, 2015
```

Packages sent to businesses:

```
John Doe
C/O Hiker Hostel
2176 Appalachian Way
Trail Town, VA 12345
Please hold for AT hiker
ETA May 16, 2015
```

▶ Use your real name (not a trail name), and include an ETA.

▶ Only send "General Delivery" mail to a Post office.

▶ FedEx and UPS packages cannot be addressed to PO boxes.

▶ USPS will forward unopened general delivery mail for free if it was shipped by Priority Mail.

▶ Be prepared to show an ID when you retrieve your mail.

▶ The "C/O" name is essential when mailing to a business's PO Box; without it, they may not be able to retrieve your mail.

▶ Send maildrops to a lodging facility only if you plan to stay there. If your plans change, offer to pay for the service of holding your mail.

▶ Many outfitters hold maildrops. Although none state any rules about what you send, it's bad form to buy from an on-line retailer and have it shipped to a store where you could have bought it.

Book Organization - A spread is the pair of pages seen when the book is laid open. *The A.T. Guide* contains trail data and services in alternating spreads; a spread containing trail data is followed by a spread detailing services available to hikers within that section. Occasionally the information is not distributed evenly and there are back-to-back spreads of data or services.

Data Spread - Data Spreads contain a table of landmarks, mileages and elevations. Every spread covers approximately 40.5 miles of trail (20.25 miles per page). An elevation profile is "watermarked" on the data. The lines of text that describe the landmarks are spaced so that they intersect the profile map at the approximate location of each landmark. Small triangular pointers below the profile line identify shelter locations. The vertical exaggeration of the profile maps is 8:1.

Services Spread - The Services Spreads provide resupply information in towns that the trail passes through or near. Businesses are selectively included, and maps may only show a portion of town closest to the trail.

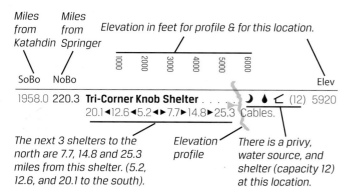

Miles from Katahdin *Miles from Springer* Elevation in feet for profile & for this location.

SoBo NoBo Elev

1958.0 220.3 **Tri-Corner Knob Shelter** . . . . . ☽ ♦ ⌐ (12) 5920
20.1◄12.6◄5.2◄►7.7►14.8►25.3 Cables.

The next 3 shelters to the north are 7.7, 14.8 and 25.3 miles from this shelter. (5.2, 12.6, and 20.1 to the south).

Elevation profile

There is a privy, water source, and shelter (capacity 12) at this location.

When a map is provided, information presented in the map is not repeated in the text unless more elaboration is needed. Post office information will be on the map and is not repeated in the text. The width of the mapped area is at the bottom of the map and maps are proportionally scaled. Places of business that appear to be adjacent may be separated by one or more unspecified buildings or roads.

Prices are listed as given in fall of 2014. **No establishment is obliged to maintain these prices.** Lodging prices are particularly volatile, but most facilities listed will do their best for hikers. Let them know if you are thru-hiking; there may be a "thru-hiker rate."

DISPOSE OF WASTE PROPERLY

Improper waste disposal can spread disease, change the habits of wildlife and spoil the scenery.

• Pack it in; pack it out. Leave any donated items at hiker boxes in town rather than at campsites or shelters.

• Walk at least 100 feet (40 steps) away from shelters, water sources and campsites to dispose of urine, toothpaste, cooking water and strained dishwater, and to wash bodies, dishes or clothing. Minimize any use of soap.

• Use the privy only for human waste and toilet paper. Pack out disposable wipes and hygiene products.

• If there is no privy, walk at least 200 feet (80 steps) away from campsites, shelters, trails and water sources to bury feces in a hole 6 to 8 inches deep. Bury or carry out toilet paper.

Read more of the Leave No Trace techniques developed for the A.T.: www.appalachiantrail.org/LNT

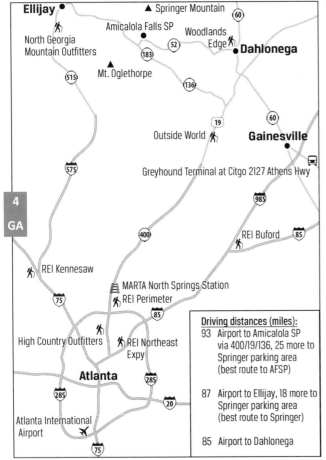

Driving distances (miles):

93 Airport to Amicalola SP via 400/19/136, 25 more to Springer parking area (best route to AFSP)

87 Airport to Ellijay, 18 more to Springer parking area (best route to Springer)

85 Airport to Dahlonega

Trail Etiquette

Avoid using a cell phone anywhere within the trail corridor, especially in shelters or within earshot of other hikers. Turn ringer off.

When hikers approach one another on the trail, the uphill hiker has the right-of-way, but the rule is irrelevant. If a hiker is approaching, look for an opportunity to step aside, regardless of your position. Be aware of hikers approaching from behind, and step aside so that they may pass.

Take only as much shelter space as you need to sleep. Shelter spaces cannot be reserved for friends who have yet to arrive. If you bring alcohol to a shelter or campsite, do so discreetly. Soon after dark is bedtime for most hikers.

The AT is liberating, and outlandish behavior is part of AT lore. Be considerate; boisterous and erratic behavior may be unsettling to strangers stuck in the woods with you. Conversely, hikers seeking a serene experience should be aware that AT hiking is, for many, a social experience. Be tolerant. Stay flexible; be prepared to move on rather than trying to convince others to conform to your expectations.

Town Etiquette

Ask permission before bringing a pack into a place of business. Assume that alcohol is not permitted in hostels & campsites until told otherwise.

Don't expect generosity, and show appreciation when it is offered. If you are granted work-for-stay, strive to provide service equal to the value of your stay.

Respect hotel room capacities; hotel owners should know how many people intend to stay in a room. Try to leave hotel rooms as clean as a car traveler would. If a shower is available, use it.

✖ Two symbols that are not in the page 1 legend are used only once in the book, on maps. What symbols are they and on what maps do they appear?

Getting to Springer Mountain

The southern terminus of the AT on Springer Mountain is accessible only by foot. The 8.8-mi. Approach Trail originating at the Visitor Center in Amicalola Falls SP is one means of getting there. Alternatively, you can drive to Springer Parking area on USFS 42, a dirt road passable by most vehicles unless there is bad-weather washout. From the gap, hike south 1 mi. on the AT to Springer Mtn. Your hike would begin by retracing your steps. (See Start of Trail map on pg. 10)

The closest major city is Atlanta, GA, 82 miles south. If you fly or take AMTRAK into Atlanta, take the MARTA rail system to the North Springs Station, and a shuttle service can pick up from there. There is also Greyhound bus service to Gainesville, GA, 38 miles from the park.

🚐 **Hiker Hostel** Package deal including shuttle, see pg. 11.

🚐 🚶 **Survivor Dave's Trail Shuttle** 678.469.0978 (No texts please) ⟨www.atsurvivordave.com⟩ Shuttle service to/from Atlanta Airport and North Springs MARTA Station to Amicalola Falls SP, Springer Mountain, and all trailheads up to Fontana Dam. Will stop at outfitter and/or supermarket for supplies (time permitting). Stove fuels available on-board. Well behaved dogs welcome. Will respond promptly to phone messages.

🚐 🚶 **Ron Brown** Cell: 706.669.0919, Home: 706.636.2825 hikershuttles@outlook.com. Flat rate shuttles to/from the A.T. or trail towns up to Fontana, including Amicalola Falls SP, Atlanta airport, and Gainesville, GA. Dogs welcome; extra stops OK. Fuel on request.

🚐 **Wes Wisson** 706.747.2671, dwisson@alltel.net Based in Suches, GA. Will shuttle year-round, up to four hikers. MARTA to Amicalola or to Big Stamp Gap.

🚐 **Sam Duke** 706.984.6633 In Blairsville; range Atlanta-Fontana.

🚐 **Henry Carter** 678.525.3497 Ranging from Atlanta-all of GA.

Outfitters Near the Southern Terminus

🚶 **Mountain Crossings** 706.745.6095 (see pg. 11)

🚶 **North Georgia Mountain Outfitters** 706.698.4453 ⟨hikeNorthGeorgia.com⟩ 583 Highland Crossing, Suite 230, East Ellijay, GA 30540 Full service outfitter. Tu-Sa 10-6

🚶 **Woodlands Edge** 706.864.5358 Open 10-5, 363 days a year (closed Easter and Christmas Day). Full service outfitter, fuel/oz, ask about shuttles. 36 North Park Street Dahlonega, GA 30533

🚶 **Outside World** 706.265.4500 471 Quill Drive, Dawsonville, GA 30534

🚶 **Half Moon Outfitters** 404.249.7921 1034 N. Highland Ave. NE, Atlanta, GA 30306

🚶 **High Country Outfitters** 404.814.0999 3906 Roswell Rd. #B, Atlanta, GA 30342

🚶 **REI** Four Atlanta area stores:
1800 Northeast Expy NE, Atlanta, GA 30329, 404.633.6508
1165 Perimeter Ctr W Suite 200, Atlanta, GA 30338, 770.901.9200
740 Barrett Parkway Suite 450, Kennesaw, GA 30144, 770.425.4480
1600 Mall of Georgia Blvd, Buford, GA 30519, 770.831.0676

1. Plan Ahead and Prepare
2. Travel and Camp on Durable Surfaces
3. Dispose of Waste Properly
4. Leave What You Find
5. Minimize Campfire Impacts
6. Respect Wildlife
7. Be Considerate of Other Visitors

leave no trace

This copyrighted information has been reprinted with permission from the Leave No Trace Center for Outdoor Ethics: ⟨www.LNT.org⟩

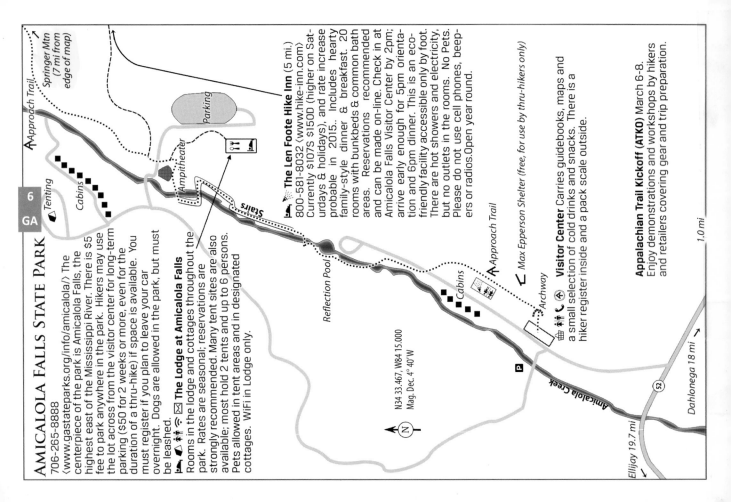

AMICALOLA FALLS STATE PARK

706-265-8888

<www.gastateparks.org/info/amicalola/> The centerpiece of the park is Amicalola Falls, the highest east of the Mississippi River. There is $5 fee to park anywhere in the park. Hikers may use the lot across from the visitor center for long-term parking ($50 for 2 weeks or more, even for the duration of a thru-hike) if space is available. You must register if you plan to leave your car overnight. Dogs are allowed in the park, but must be leashed.

The Lodge at Amicalola Falls
Rooms in the lodge and cottages throughout the park. Rates are seasonal; reservations are strongly recommended. Many tent sites are also available; most hold 2 tents and up to 6 persons. Pets allowed in tent areas and in designated cottages. WiFi in Lodge only.

The Len Foote Hike Inn (5 mi.)
800-581-8032 <www.hike-inn.com> Currently $107S $150D (higher on Saturdays & holidays), and rate increase probable in 2015.. Includes hearty family-style dinner & breakfast. 20 rooms with bunkbeds & common bath areas. Reservations recommended and can be made on-line. Check in at Amicalola Falls Visitor Center by 2pm; arrive early enough for 5pm orientation and 6pm dinner. This is an eco-friendly facility accessible only by foot. There are hot showers and electricity, but no outlets in the rooms. No Pets. Please do not use cell phones, beepers or radios.Open year round.

Max Epperson Shelter (free, for use by thru-hikers only)

Visitor Center Carries guidebooks, maps and a small selection of cold drinks and snacks. There is a hiker register inside and a pack scale outside.

Appalachian Trail Kickoff (ATKO) March 6-8.
Enjoy demonstrations and workshops by hikers and retailers covering gear and trip preparation.

Springer Mtn
(7 mi from edge of map)

Approach Trail

Tenting

Cabins

Parking

Ampitheater

Stairs

Reflection Pool

Cabins

Archway

Approach Trail

Amicalola Creek

N34 33.467, W84 15.000
Mag. Dec. 4° 40'W

N

Dahlonega 18 mi

52

Ellijay 19.7 mi

1.0 mi

The Approach Trail

SoBo	NoBo	Description	Elev
8.8	0.0	**Amicalola Falls State Park**, archway behind Visitor Center	1800
8.7	0.1	**Max Epperson Shelter**, for thru-hiker use only	1858
8.4	0.4	Reflection Pond at base of falls	2003
8.1	0.7	Staircase - 604 steps to the top of the Falls	2216
7.7	1.1	Parking, side trail to Lodge	2639
7.6	1.2	Lodge Road (lodge to east)	2642
7.5	1.3	Trail to **Len Foote Hike Inn** (5.0E) blazed lime-green	2656
7.3	1.5	USFS Road 46, steps on north side (pg. 6)	2584
5.6	3.2	High Shoals Road	2841
4.0	4.8	Frosty Mountain. Spring (0.2E) is unreliable.	3384
3.7	5.1	Frosty Mountain Road, USFS Road 46.	3178
3.4	5.4	Trail to **Len Foote Hike Inn** (1.0E) blazed lime-green. (pg. 6)	3353
3.1	5.7	Woody Knob.	3406
2.8	6.0	Nimblewill Gap, USFS Road 28	3100
2.6	6.2	Spring (left of trail), unreliable	3419
1.5	7.3	**Black Gap Shelter** (0.1W). Spring is on opposite side of the Approach Trail (0.1E).	3300
0.0	8.8	Springer Mountain	3782
SoBo	NoBo		Elev

7

GA

SoBo	NoBo	Feature	Elev
2189.2	0.0	Springer Mountain southern terminus, register on back of rock with plaque. ◉ ♦ ⌐(12)	3782
2189.0	0.2	**Springer Mountain Shelter** (0.2E) Use designated tent pads. ◖ ♦ ⌐(12)	3733
2188.2	1.0	0.0◀0.0◀0.0▶2.6▶7.9▶15.6 150 yards north, Benton MacKaye Trail to east. Big Stamp Gap, USFS 42 **P** N34 38.257 W84 11.725	3350
2187.2	2.0	Benton MacKaye Trail.	3279
2186.5	2.7	Footbridge, stream ♦◖	2947
2186.4	2.8	**Stover Creek Shelter** (0.1E) (2006) ◖♦⌐(16)	2932
		0.0◀0.0◀2.6▶5.3▶13.0▶25.3	
2186.3	2.9	Footbridge, stream ♦◖	2890
2185.8	3.4	Stream. ♦	2707
2185.0	4.2	Benton MacKaye / Duncan Ridge Trail to east	2586
2184.9	4.3	Three Forks, USFS 58, footbridge ♦	2530
2184.0	5.2	Benton MacKaye / Duncan Ridge Trail to west, Trail to Long Creek Falls ♦	2800
2183.0	6.2	Dirt road, 0.2W to Hickory Flats Cemetery, pavilion ◖	3000
2181.1	8.1	**Hawk Mountain Shelter** (0.2W) (1993) ◖♦⌐(12)	3209
		0.0◀7.9◀5.3▶7.7▶20.0▶21.2 Water south on AT and 0.1 mile behind shelter.	
2180.6	8.6	Hightower Gap, junction USFS 42 & 69 **P** N34 39.809 W84 7.779	2854

✽ **Mayapple** – White flower ball dangling under an umbrella of broad leaves. Plant is about a foot tall.

SoBo	NoBo	Feature	Elev
2178.7	10.5	Horse Gap.	2681
2177.7	11.5	Sassafras Mountain	3342
2176.9	12.3	Cooper Gap, USFS 15, 42 & 80 **P** N34 39.180 W84 5.078	2940
2176.4	12.8	Justus Mountain	3226
2175.7	13.5	Dirt road.	2743
2174.8	14.4	Justus Creek, rock-hop. Use designated campsites north of creek, to west ♦◖	2619
2174.3	14.9	Stream. ♦	2646
2173.7	15.5	Blackwell Creek. ◖♦	2674
2173.4	15.8	**Gooch Mountain Shelter** (0.1W) (200) Water behind shelter. ◖♦⌐(14)	2821
		15.6◀13.0◀7.7▶12.3▶13.5▶22.6 Designated tentsites, cables.	
2172.3	16.9	Spring to the east ◖♦	2879
2172.0	17.2	Gooch Gap, USFS 42 (gravel) **P** ♦ (pg.10-11) N34 39.1256 W84 1.9402	2837
		Suches, GA (2.7W) water north of road 0.1E on marked trail	
2171.0	18.2	Roadbed.	2969
2170.8	18.4	Liss Gap.	3064
2170.2	19.0	Ramrock Mountain ◉	3266

SoBo	NoBo	Description	Elev
2168.8	20.4	Seasonal springs.	3263
2168.4	20.8	Woody Gap, GA 60. N34 40.659 W84 0.000 P 🏛 ♟♟♦ (pg.10-11)	3235
		Suches, GA (2.0W); Hostel (6.0E); spring north of road 0.2W.	
2167.4	21.8	Preaching Rock, view to east. Woody Lake in Suches in view to west.	3589
2167.1	22.1	Big Cedar Mountain, rock ledges and views.	3737
2166.9	22.3	Spring to west	3662
2166.1	23.1	Spring to west	3305
2165.3	23.9	Dockery Lake Trail	3036
2164.9	24.3	Lance Creek, camp in designated sites north of footbridge.	2880
2164.1	25.1	Henry Gap (unmarked) is 70 yards west on side trail, woods road to GA 180. P	3080
		⚠ A hard-shell bear-resistant canister is required for hikers overnighting between Jarrard Gap and Neel Gap from Mar 1 - Jun 1. No fires (year-round) from Slaughter Creek Trail to Neel Gap.	
2162.5	26.7	Jarrard Gap, dirt road. ♦ (0.3W) (pg.10-11)	3250
2162.3	26.9	Gaddis Mountain	3394
2161.1	28.1	Turkey Stamp	3751
2161.0	28.2	**Woods Hole Shelter** (0.2W) 25.3◄20.0◄12.3◄i2►10.3►15.i ⟩ ♢ ♦ ⊏ (7)	3720
		Bird Gap, Freeman Trail east bypasses Blood Mtn & rejoins AT at Flatrock Gap	
2160.7	28.5	Slaughter Creek Trail, spring on AT, campsite 0.1 south on AT ♦ ⟨	3797
2160.3	28.9	Duncan Ridge Trail, Coosa Trail to west	4178
2159.9	29.3	**Blood Mountain Shelter** (1934) 21.2◄13.5◄1.2►9.i►13.9►21.2.. 🏛 ⟩ ⊏ (8)	4461
		Privy 50 yards south. No fires. Stream (0.8S). Many views from AT south of shelter	
2158.6	30.6	Flatrock Gap, Freeman Trail east bypasses Blood Mtn; west. P ♦ (0.2W)	3482
		to Byron Reece parking area. Balance Rock 150 yards north.	
2157.5	31.7	Neel Gap, US 19 N34 44.464 W83 55.237 P (pg.11)	3125
2156.4	32.8	Bull Gap, spring 0.1W. ♦ ⟨	3677
2155.8	33.4	Levelland Mountain, view 🏛	3831
2154.6	34.6	Swaim Gap, spring to west. ♦	3523
2153.9	35.3	Wolf Laurel Top, views to east 🏛	3764
2152.5	36.7	Cowrock Mountain 🏛	3842
2151.5	37.7	Tesnatee Gap, GA 348, Russell Hwy N34 43.570 W83 50.853 P (pg.11)	3138
2151.0	38.2	Wildcat Mountain 🏛 ⟩♦ ⟨ ⊏ (6)	3554
2150.8	38.4	**Whitley Gap Shelter** (1.2E) Spring 0.3 mile behind shelter.	3650
		22.6◄10.3◄9.i◄4.8►i2.i►20.2 Campsite 0.iE with view just beyond.	
2150.6	38.6	Hogpen Gap, GA 348, Water S of rd, E of AT. N34 43.551 W83 50.395 P ♦ (pg.11)	3468
2149.7	39.5	White Oak Stamp	3470

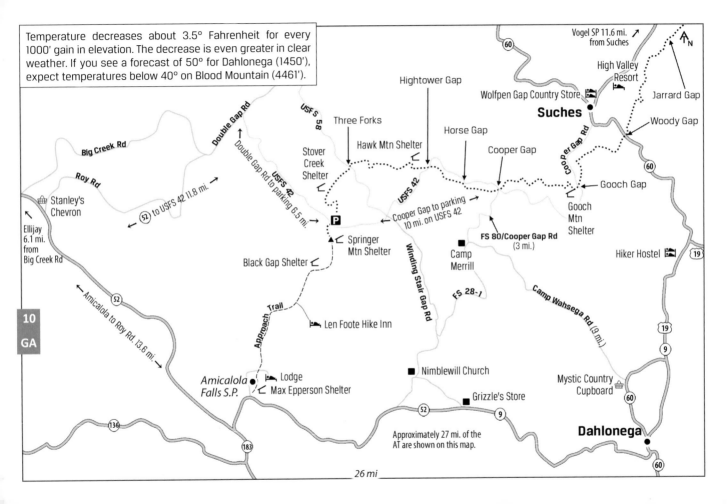

Temperature decreases about 3.5° Fahrenheit for every 1000' gain in elevation. The decrease is even greater in clear weather. If you see a forecast of 50° for Dahlonega (1450'), expect temperatures below 40° on Blood Mountain (4461').

Vogel SP 11.6 mi. from Suches

High Valley Resort

Wolfpen Gap Country Store

Suches

Jarrard Gap

Woody Gap

60

60

Cooper Gap Rd

Hightower Gap

Horse Gap

Cooper Gap

Gooch Gap

USFS 58

Three Forks

Hawk Mtn Shelter

Stover Creek Shelter

USFS 42

USFS 42

Gooch Mtn Shelter

Double Gap Rd

Double Gap Rd to parking 6.5 mi.

to USFS 42 11.8 mi.

52

Big Creek Rd

Roy Rd

Stanley's Chevron

Ellijay 6.1 mi. from Big Creek Rd

52

Cooper Gap to parking 10 mi. on USFS 42

FS 80/Cooper Gap Rd (3 mi.)

Hiker Hostel

19

P

Springer Mtn Shelter

Black Gap Shelter

Camp Merrill

Amicalola to Roy Rd. 13.6 mi.

52

Winding Stair Gap Rd

FS 28-1

Camp Wahsega Rd (9 mi.)

19

Approach Trail

Len Foote Hike Inn

9

10

GA

Amicalola Falls S.P.

Lodge

Max Epperson Shelter

Nimblewill Church

Grizzle's Store

Mystic Country Cupboard

60

136

183

52

9

Approximately 27 mi. of the AT are shown on this map.

Dahlonega

60

26 mi

17.2   Gooch Gap, USFS 42
20.8   Woody Gap, GA 60

🏕🔥⛺🚐📶🖥✉ (6.0E) **Hiker Hostel** 770.312.7342 ⟨www.hikerhostel.com⟩ hikerhostel@yahoo.com Open year-round. $18PP Bunks, $42 Private room for 2, $55-$65 Private Cabin for 2. Overnight stay includes breakfast, bed linens, towel & shower. Computer w/internet & wireless available. Laundry $3. SPECIAL(Feb 24-Apr 20): $80 pickup from Atlanta North Springs MARTA Station or Gainesville, overnight stay in bunk, breakfast, shuttle to Amicalola or Springer, 8oz of white gas/alcohol. Canister fuel and limited gear available for purchase. Feb 24-Apr 27 5pm daily pickup at Woody Gap. Shuttles from Atlanta to Blue Ridge Gap by reservation for hostel guests. Maildrops: (USPS) PO Box 802 or (FedEx/UPS) 7693 Hwy 19N, Dahlonega, GA 30533.

Suches, GA 30572 (2W)
⌂ M-F 12:15-4:15, 706.747.2611

🏕🍴♿💲 ⛺✉ **Wolfpen Gap Country Store** 706.747.2271 M-Sat 7:30-8, Su 9-6, open later in summer. Bunks $15. Laundry $5/load. Beer, soda, hiker foods, pizza and BBQ. Coleman/oz and canisters. Will pickup at Woody Gap. Accepts MC/Disc. Maildrops: 41 Wolf Pen Gap Rd, Suches, GA 30572.

🛏🏕◐ ⛺📶 **High Valley Resort** (0.7W) of PO, 404.720.0087 ⟨www.highvalleyresort.com⟩ Camping $15PP, bunkhouse $55PP. Tenters and bunkhouse have access to bathhouse, showers and lodge with satellite TV. Cabins $115/night Su-Wed; $165 Th-Sat, some sleep 4, some sleep up to 8 persons.

🛏🏕◐🍴♿ **Wildcat Lodge and Campground** 706.973.0321. (7W) $15 bunkroom, $12 camping. Lodge room sleeps 8 $100D, $25EAP. Well-stocked camp store has Coleman & canisters. Diner serves B/L.

🚐 **Wes Wisson** 706.747.2671 Shuttles cover Atlanta thru GA.
✚ **Don Pruitt** 706.747.1421, M-W 9-4, walk-ins before 10am.

26.7   Jarrard Gap

◐ 🚿 (1.0W) **Lake Winfield Scott Recreation Area** tent sites $12 for up to 5 persons, showers & bathrooms, leash dogs.

31.7   Neel Gap, US 19

🧍🏕🔥🚐🚩⛺🚐✉🖥 **Mountain Crossings** 706.745.6095 ⟨www.mountaincrossings.com⟩ Full-service outfitter, full resupply, gear shakedown, alcohol/oz., bunkroom $17PP includes shower w/towel. Shower without stay $5. No pets. Ask about shuttles. Maildrops: (USPS/UPS/FedEx) held for 2 weeks, $1 fee at pickup, 12471 Gainesville Hwy, Blairsville, GA 30512. ✘ What shoe is over the hostel door?

🛏⛺ (0.3E) **Blood Mountain Cabins** ⟨www.bloodmountain.com⟩ 800.284.6866, 706.745.9454 Thru-hiker rate $60. Cabin w/ kitchen and satellite, holds 4 adults & 2 children under the age of 13. Laundry free w/stay. WiFi at lodge. No pets.

◐ ♿🚿⛺🅿 (3W) **Vogel State Park** 706.745.2628 ⟨www.gastateparks.org⟩ Tent sites with shower $19, cabins for 2 to 10 persons $90-$160, $2 shower w/o stay. Long term parking $5.

🛏🚐 (3.5W) **Goose Creek Cabins** 706.781.8593, 706.745.5111 Cabins and shuttles available, call for details.

Blairsville, GA 30514 (14W) All major services.
🏕⛺📶 **Misty Mtn Inn** 706.745.4786 B&B rooms $98 include breakfast, cabins hold 2-7 price range $105-$125. Free pickup/return from Neel Gap, Tesnatee Gap or Hogpen Gap.

🧍 **Blairsville Hikes and Bikes** 706.745.8141 Packs, poles, fuel & hiker food. Open 10-5:30.

🚐 **Sam Duke** 706.984.6633 Shuttle range Atlanta-Fontana.
Dahlonega, GA 30597 (17E) All major services.

37.7   Tesnatee Gap,
38.6   Hogpen Gap, *Blairsville, GA 30514* (14W) listings above.

Elev

SoBo	NoBo	Description	Elev
2148.6	40.6	Poor Mountain	3620

⚠ Get the most out of your guidebook: pay attention to lines that end with a page number. The page that is referenced will list the services available at or near the trailhead.

SoBo	NoBo	Description	Elev
2146.9	42.3	Sheep Rock Top	3576
2146.0	43.2	**Low Gap Shelter** 15.1◀13.9◀4.8▶7.3▶15.4▶22.8 ☾◐◖⊂ (7)	3054
2145.6	43.6	Stream. Water 30 yards in front of shelter. Cables. Privy on steep hill beyond shelter. ◐	3216
2144.6	44.6	Poplar Stamp Gap, spring 0.1E, gap and side trail unmarked. ◐◁	3367
2143.9	45.3	Spring to west ◐	3563
2142.6	46.6	Stream with cascade, several streams in area ◐	3491
2142.1	47.1	Cold Springs Gap	3490
2141.0	48.2	Chattahoochee Gap, Jacks Knob Trail to west, spring 0.5E ◐	3480
2140.3	48.9	Red Clay Gap (pg.14) ◐	3485
2139.6	49.6	Site of former Rocky Knob Shelter ◐◖	3636
2139.4	49.8	Spring west of trail down slope	3620
2138.7	50.5	**Blue Mountain Shelter** 21.2◀12.1◀7.3▶8.1▶15.5▶23.6 ☾◐⊂ (7) Bear cables. Spring on AT (0.1S), camping west of AT, south of shelter.	3906
2137.8	51.4	Blue Mountain	4025
2136.3	52.9	Unicoi Gap, GA 75, **Helen, GA** (9.0E) N34 48.101 W83 44.570 🅿 (pg.14)	2949
		Hiawassee, GA (12.0W)	
2135.6	53.6	Stream. ◐	3514
2135.4	53.8	Rocky Mountain Trail to west ◐	3709
2134.9	54.3	Rocky Mountain, views from AT 0.1 north of summit ◁	4017
2133.6	55.6	Indian Grave Gap, USFS 283 N34 47.563 W83 42.855 📷	3113
		Andrews Cove Trail to east.	
2132.9	56.3	Tray Mountain Rd (gravel), USFS 79, piped stream east on road. ◐	3580
2132.6	56.6	Cheese factory site, water (0.1W) on blue-blazed trail ◐◁	3638
2131.9	57.3	Tray Gap, Tray Mountain Rd, USFS 79 N34 47.959 W83 41.461 🅿	3847
2131.1	58.1	Tray Mountain. 📷	4430
2130.6	58.6	**Tray Mountain Shelter** (0.2W) 20.2◀15.4◀8.1▶7.4▶15.5▶22.8 Spring 0.1 mile behind shelter. Cables. ☾◐⊂ (7)	4199
2129.4	59.8	Wolfpen Gap	3568
2128.9	60.3	Steeltrap Gap, water 0.5E ◐	3493

13 GA

SoBo	NoBo	Feature	Elev
2128.3	60.9	Young Lick Knob	3764
2127.0	62.2	Swag of the Blue Ridge	3443
2125.9	63.3	Sassafras Gap, water 0.2E on steep blue-blazed trail	3500
2125.0	64.2	Addis Gap. Campsite 0.5E down old fire road, stream to right of campsite.	3304
2124.0	65.2	Kelly Knob, trail skirts summit, water 0.1E down steep trail	4171
2123.2	66.0	**Deep Gap Shelter** (0.3E) 22.8◄15.5◄7.4◄►8.1►15.4►20.3 ⌂ (12) Water 0.1 before shelter.	3583
2122.1	67.1	"Vista" blue-blaze leads 0.1E to campsite.	3891
2121.8	67.4	Powell Mountain	3850

📶 No phone signal at Dicks Creek Gap. If you need ride, call from Shelter or Powell Mtn.

SoBo	NoBo	Feature	Elev
2120.6	68.6	Moreland Gap, water to east	2990
2119.6	69.6	Dicks Creek Gap, US 76, N34 54.728 W83 37.130 P (pg.14-15) Water, picnic tables at the gap, **Hiawassee, GA** (11.0W)	2675
2118.6	70.6	Campsite, water	3176
2117.8	71.4	Cowart Gap	2900
2116.5	72.7	Buzzard Knob	3750
2116.3	72.9	Bull Gap	3690
2115.6	73.6	Spring	3331
2115.1	74.1	**Plumorchard Gap Shelter** (0.2E) Privy 0.2 mile down steep trail ⌂ (14) 23.6◄15.5◄8.1◄►7.3►12.2►19.8 Creek on trail to shelter & spring (0.1W) of AT.	3165
2114.4	74.8	As Knob	3460
2113.9	75.3	Blue Ridge Gap, dirt road	3078
2112.9	76.3	Spring to west, campsite	3387
2112.2	77.0	Rich Cove Gap	3504
2112.0	77.2	Rocky Knob	3579
2110.7	78.5	**GA-NC** border	3833
2110.6	78.6	Bly Gap, spring west 30 yards Old and twisted tree often photographed.	3840
2109.3	79.9	Couthouse Bald, summit 0.1W	4666
2108.7	80.5	Sassafras Gap	4300
2108.4	80.8	Piped Spring	4517

48.9   Red Clay Gap

🛏️🏕️⛴️⚡🍴♨️✉️ **Enota Mountain Retreat** 706.896.9966, 1.4W from Red Clay Gap. No sign & trail not blazed; be certain of location if you walk. Marked on some maps by its previous name "Camp Pioneer." Trail is downhill to Joel's Creek and follows creek into camp. Driving from Unicoi Gap: 2.4W on Hwy 17, then left 2.4 mi. on Hwy 180. Rides sometimes available. Tentsites, cabins, bunkrooms ($25), and laundry. Store with snacks and small gear items. Dining room open when there is enough guests. Beautiful waterfall, trout pond, work for stay possible on organic farm. Maildrops (guests only): 1000 Highway 180 Hiawassee, GA 30546

52.9   Unicoi Gap, GA 75

Enota Mountain Retreat (4.8W, see listing above)

Helen, GA 30545 (9E) Lodging tax 15%

🏤 M–F 9–12:30 & 1:30-4, Sa 9-12, 706.878.2422
Tourist town with many hotels, restaurants, gift shops, ice cream shops, river rafting and tubing rentals. Visitor Center on Bruckenstrasse (near the PO) has information about places to stay and a free phone for making reservations.

🛏️🛜🖥️ **Best Western Motel** 706.878.2111 Hiker rate Mar 15-Apr 30; $50S + $5EAP up to 4. Includes breakfast buffet. Ride to/from trail weekdays only when staff is available.

🛏️⛴️🛜🖥️ **Helendorf River Inn** 800.445.2271 Prices for 1 or 2 persons Su-Th; Dec-Mar $44, Apr $54, May-Nov $84, $10EAP. Weekend rates higher. Pets $20. Includes cont B. Visa/MC/Disc accepted.

🛏️🛜 **Super 8 Motel** 706.878.2191, ask for hiker room $49+tax for 1 or 2 persons, no pets.

🛏️🛜 **Econo Lodge** 706.878.8000 Weekdays $60, weekends higher, includes cont. bfast. Pets under 20 pounds allowed with $20 fee.

🛏️🛜🖥️ **Country Inn and Suites** (706) 878-9000, indoor pool

🛒 **Betty's Country Store** 706.878.2943 open 7 days 7am-9pm.

⛴️ **laundromat**

Hiawassee, GA 30545 (12E) (see Dicks Creek Gap)

69.6   Dicks Creek Gap, US 76

🛏️⛴️⚡🏔️⛴️🚌🛜🖥️♨️✉️ (0.5W) **Top of Georgia Hostel & Hiking Center** 706.982.3252 ⟨www.topofgeorgiahostel.com⟩ Open year round 7am-7pm. Bunkroom with shower & towel $20. Overflow tenting $10pp includes shower. Free shuttles March-May to nearby town of Hiawassee, Dicks Creek Gap and Unicoi Gap for all overnight guests. Slackpacking options available and shuttles ranging from Springer to Fontana for a fee. Hearty Breakfast $8. Pizza, soft drinks, ice cream and snacks available. On-site gear shop carries backpacks, tents, sleeping bags, stoves, fuel/oz and canisters. Laundry $5/load. Computer, internet access and printer for Smoky Mtn NP permit. Thru-hiker coaching & pack shakedowns from triple crowner and guide Bob "Sir-Packs-Alot" Gabrielson. No alcohol or drugs, no pets. Guest maildrops: 7675 US Hwy 76 E, Hiawassee, GA 30546

🛏️⛴️🚌🅿️🛜🖥️✉️ **Henson Cove B&B** (5W) 800.714.5542 relax@henson-cove-place.com. Small cabin for 1-6 persons, full kitchen, 3 beds, 1.5 baths. $100 for 3 people, $120 for 6. Breakfast $8PP. Standard B&B rooms $100D, breakfast included. All stays include free ride to/from AT from Dick's Creek Gap or Unicoi Gap, or into town for provisions, free laundry & internet. Credit cards OK, well behaved pets OK. Shuttles, parking for section hikers. Mail drops: 1137 Car Miles Rd, Hiawassee, GA 30546.

Hiawassee, GA 30546 (11W)

🛏️🏔️⛴️🚌🛜🖥️✉️ **Budget Inn** 706.896.4121 ⟨hiawasseebudgetinn.com⟩ $39.99S, $5EAP, pets $10, coin laundry. For guests, free ride to/from Dick's Creek Gap or Unicoi Gap (9 & 11am) Mar-Apr. Non-guest shuttles for a fee. Three Eagles Satellite on-site. Accepts Visa/MC. Complimentary guest maildrop transfer to Franklin Budget or Sapphire Inn. Maildrops: 193 South Main Street, Hiawassee, GA 30546.

🛏️🚌🛜✉️ **Mull's Motel** 706.896.4195 $45/up, no pets, shuttles by arrangement. Guest maildrops: 213 N Main St, Hiawassee, GA 30546.

🛏🚿📶🖥✉ **Holiday Inn Express** 706.896.8884 $79/up, accepts all major credit cards. Full hot breakfast included, indoor pool and hot tub, no pets. Maildrops: 300 Big Sky Drive, Hiawassee, GA 30546.

🛏🍴🚿📶🖥 **Ramada Lake Chatuge Lodge** 706.896.5253 $89/up includes continental breakfast. **Chophouse Restaurant** on site.

🥾 **Three Eagles Satellite** (call Franklin store) Open Mar-Apr 8:30-1:30, 7 days. Footwear, hiking gear, clothing, fuel/oz, food, shipping services, free "bumps" to Franklin store.

🥾⛲🏪 **Buckhead House** 706.896.0028 Hiker friendly, carries boots, clothes and small gear, freeze-dried food, canister fuel, denatured/white gas/oz. Open year-round.

🛒🍴🏪 **Ingles** 706.896.8312 7-10, 7 days. Pharmacy, Starbucks, deli, bakery, salad bar.

■ **Goin' Postal** 706.896.1844 FedEx and UPS shipping 9-5 M-F.

85.4   Deep Gap, USFS 71
106.1   Rock Gap

🔥⛲👥🚿 **Standing Indian Campground** 828.369.0442 or 828.524.6441. 3.7W from Deep Gap and 1.5W from Rock Gap. Campsites $16, open Apr 1 - Nov 30. Camp store (season is shorter) has small selection of foods.

⚠️Many of the water sources listed in this book are springs and small streams that can go dry. Never carry just enough water to reach the next water source.

⚠️Prices are subject to change, particularly at hotels. Prices published in this guidebook were given in fall of 2014 and often represent a significant discount for hikers. Businesses *intend* to keep these prices throughout 2015, but they are not obliged to do so.

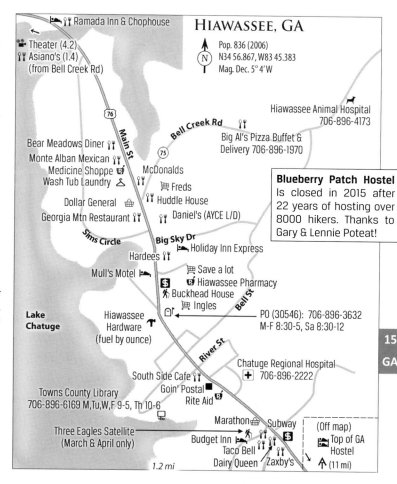

HIAWASSEE, GA

Pop. 836 (2006)
N34 56.867, W83 45.383
Mag. Dec. 5° 4'W

🛏🍴 Ramada Inn & Chophouse

🎦 Theater (4.2)
🍴 Asiano's (1.4)
(from Bell Creek Rd)

Hiawassee Animal Hospital
706-896-4173

Bell Creek Rd

Big Al's Pizza Buffet &
Delivery 706-896-1970

Blueberry Patch Hostel
Is closed in 2015 after
22 years of hosting over
8000 hikers. Thanks to
Gary & Lennie Poteat!

Bear Meadows Diner 🍴
Monte Alban Mexican 🍴
Medicine Shoppe 🏪
Wash Tub Laundry 🚿

McDonalds
🍴 Freds
🍴 Huddle House
🍴 Daniel's (AYCE L/D)

Dollar General 🏪
Georgia Mtn Restaurant 🍴

Sims Circle

Big Sky Dr

Hardees 🍴
🛏 Holiday Inn Express

Mull's Motel 🛏

🛒 Save a lot
🏪 Hiawassee Pharmacy
🥾 Buckhead House
🛒 Ingles

Lake
Chatuge

Hiawassee
Hardware
(fuel by ounce)

PO (30546): 706-896-3632
M-F 8:30-5, Sa 8:30-12

River St

Chatuge Regional Hospital
✚ 706-896-2222

South Side Cafe 🍴
Towns County Library
706-896-6169 M,Tu,W,F 9-5, Th 10-6

Goin' Postal ■
Rite Aid 🏪

Three Eagles Satellite
(March & April only)

Marathon ⛽ Subway
Budget Inn 🛏
Taco Bell
Dairy Queen Zaxby's

(Off map)
🛏 Top of GA
Hostel
🔼 (11 mi)

1.2 mi

15

GA

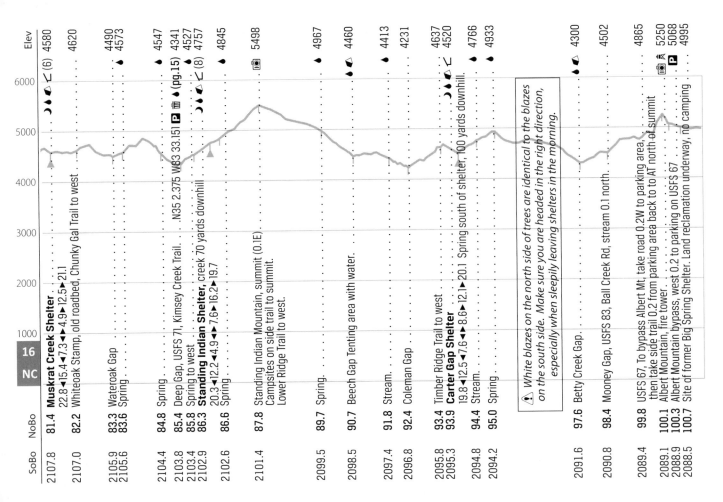

SoBo	NoBo	Description	Elev	
2107.8	81.4	**Muskrat Creek Shelter** 22.8◄15.4◄7.3◄▶4.9▶12.5▶21.1	4580	) ☽ ◢ ⌂ (6)
2107.0	82.2	Whiteoak Stamp, old roadbed, Chunky Gal Trail to west	4620	
2105.9	83.3	Wateroak Gap	4490	
2105.6	83.6	Spring	4573	◆
2104.4	84.8	Spring	4547	◆
2103.8	85.4	Deep Gap, USFS 71, Kimsey Creek Trail.	4341	P ☂
2103.4	85.8	Spring to west.	4527	◆
2102.9	86.3	**Standing Indian Shelter,** creek 70 yards downhill ...N35 2.375 W83 33.151 (pg.15)	4757	) ☽ ◢ ⌂ (8) ◆
2102.6	86.6	Spring 20.3◄12.2◄4.9▶7.6▶16.2▶19.7	4845	◆
2101.4	87.8	Standing Indian Mountain, summit (0.1E) Campsites on side trail to summit. Lower Ridge Trail to west.	5498	📷
2099.5	89.7	Spring.	4967	◆
2098.5	90.7	Beech Gap Tenting area with water.	4460	◗
2097.4	91.8	Stream.	4413	◆
2096.8	92.4	Coleman Gap	4231	
2095.8	93.4	Timber Ridge Trail to west	4637	) ☽ ◢ ⌂
2095.3	93.9	**Carter Gap Shelter** 19.8◄12.5◄7.6◄▶8.6▶12.1▶20.1 Spring south of shelter, 100 yards downhill.	4520	
2094.8	94.4	Stream.	4766	◆
2094.2	95.0	Spring	4933	◆

⚠ *White blazes on the north side of trees are identical to the blazes on the south side. Make sure you are headed in the right direction, especially when sleepily leaving shelters in the morning.*

SoBo	NoBo	Description	Elev	
2091.6	97.6	Betty Creek Gap.	4300	◢◆
2090.8	98.4	Mooney Gap, USFS 83, Ball Creek Rd, stream 0.1 north.	4502	
2089.4	99.8	USFS 67, To bypass Albert Mt, take road 0.2W to parking area, then take side trail 0.2 from parking area back to to AT north of summit	4865	
2089.1	100.1	Albert Mountain, fire tower.	5250	📷
2088.9	100.3	Albert Mountain bypass, west 0.2 to parking on USFS 67	5068	P
2088.5	100.7	Site of former Big Spring Shelter. Land reclamation underway, no camping	4995	

SoBo	NoBo	Feature	Elev
2086.7	102.5	**Long Branch Shelter** (0.1W)(2012) four tent platforms. ♦ ⊿ ⌐(16)	4503
		21.1◄16.2◄8.6▲◄3.5►11.5►18.3	
2085.9	103.3	Glassmine Gap, Long Branch Trail 2.0W to USFS 67	4202
2083.2	106.0	**Rock Gap Shelter** (1965) 19.7◄12.1◄3.5►◄8.0►14.8►19.6. ◡ ♦ ⌐(8)	3787
2083.1	106.1	Rock Gap, 0.7E to Wasalik Poplar and water.. N35 5.640 W83 31.555 P (pg.15)	3757
2082.5	106.7	Wallace Gap, W. Old Murphy Rd, stream to north.	3738

✳ **Trillium** – Three-petal flower set upon three leaves. White and pink varieties are plentiful in the southern Appalachians.

SoBo	NoBo	Feature	Elev
2079.4	109.8	Winding Stair Gap, US 64. N35 7.178 W83 32.878 P ♦ (pg.18-19)	3770
2079.2	110.0	piped spring east of steps, **Franklin, NC** (10.0E) ♦	3808
2079.1	110.1	Forest Service road, waterfall	3866
2078.8	110.4	Stream, campsite.	4066
2078.3	110.9	Logging road / Swinging Lick Gap	4100
2077.4	111.8	Panther Gap	4480
2075.2	114.0	**Siler Bald Shelter** (0.5E), south end of shelter loop trail ◡ ♦ ⊿ ⌐(8)	4786
		20.1◄11.5◄8.0▲◄6.8►11.6►17.4	
2074.8	114.4	Siler Bald, summit (0.2W), shelter (0.3E), north end of shelter loop trail	5014
2074.0	115.2	Piped spring ♦	4485
2073.7	115.5	Footbridge, stream	4376
2073.6	115.6	Wayah Crest Picnic Area (0.1W)	4257
2073.5	115.7	Wayah Gap, Wayah Rd N35 9.237 W83 34.844 P (pg.18)	4180
2073.1	116.1	AT skirts USFS 69	4351
2072.7	116.5	USFS 69, meadow	4482
2072.3	116.9	Wilson Lick Trail, 0.2W to historic site	4631
2071.8	117.4	USFS 69, piped spring to east	4992
2071.4	117.8	Bartram Trail to west	5233
2071.2	118.0	0.1E to Wine Spring Rd, meadow, campsites 0.1E, water on west side of AT	5290
2069.7	119.5	USFS 69 ♦	5193
2069.5	119.7	Paved footpath to latrines and parking N35 10.738 W83 33.729 P	5301
2069.3	119.9	Wayah Bald, stone tower and paved footpath	5342
2068.7	120.5	⚠ NoBos: AT to left, Bartram Trail to east, campsite, spring to west of trail ♦	4899
2068.4	120.8	**Wayah Bald Shelter**, east to shelter, west 0.2 to water ◡ ♦ ⌐(8)	4729
		18.3◄14.8◄6.8▲◄4.8►10.6►15.5	

Elev

109.8   Winding Stair Gap, US 64   *Franklin, NC* (10E)

Hiker Fool Bash March 27-29 at the Sapphire Inn. Food, fun & games.

🛏🏪🔧🐾♿⛺🚐🖥📫 **Haven's Budget Inn** 828.524.4403 〈www.budgetinnoffranklin.com〉 $39.99S, $5EAP, $50 pet deposit. Bunkroom $15. Owner Ron Haven makes trips at 9 & 11am Mar-Apr to drop off/pick up at Rock, Wallace & Winding Stair Gaps. Motel guests may call for free pickup Mar-Apr, and get a 4pm shuttle around town for errands. Internet and coin laundry on-site. Shower w/o stay $5. Maildrops: 433 East Palmer Street, Franklin, NC 28734.

🛏🖥📫 **Sapphire Inn** 828.524.4406, $39.99S, $5EAP Maildrops: 761 East Main Street, Bus 441, Franklin, NC 28734.

🛏🛰🖥📫 **Microtel Inn & Suites** 888.403.1700 Prices vary, cont. breakfast, pet fee $20. Maildrops: 81 Allman Dr, Franklin, NC 28734

🍴 **1st Baptist Church** Free Breakfast everyday from Mar 14 - Apr 10.

🍴 **Sunset Restaurant** Homestyle B/L/D M-Sa 6am-8pm, daily specials, 10% hiker discount.

🍸🛰♿ **Lazy Hiker Brewing Co.** Open spring 2015. Food Truck, computer/printer, pet friendly. Please sign taproom wall, ask about summit card.

🚶♿🍴🛰🖥📫 **Three Eagles Outfitters** 828.524.9061 〈www.threeeaglesoutfitters.net〉 Full-service outfitter serving AT hikers for over 20 years. 10% discount for thru-hikers & free shuttle to store from anywhere in town. Gear, footwear, clothing, hiker food, white gas/alcohol/oz. Open M-Sa 9-6, Su 12-5. **Trail Tree Cafe and Expresso Bar** inside; free coffee & internet access for hikers. UPS/USPS shipping services. Maildrops: 78 Siler Rd, Franklin, NC 28734.

🚶♿🚐🛰🖥📫 **Outdoor 76** 828.349.7676 〈www.outdoor76.com〉 Open M-Sa 10-7. Specialty AT hiking store with lightweight gear, food, fuel and draft beer, located in the center of town. Footwear experts with fully trained staff to deal with injuries and various foot issues. Spend $50 get a $10 gift card for local restaurant. 10% off for thru-hikers. Shipping services, free internet, ask about shuttles. No charge maildrops: 35 East Main Street, Franklin, NC 28734.

🍸🛰 **Rock House Lodge** Inside of Outdoor 76, M-Sa 10-7. Quality draft beers on tap and beer to go. 10% hiker discount. Live entertainment Friday and Saturday evenings. Free internet.

🚐 **Macon County Transit** 828.349.2222 Shuttle $3PP Franklin-Winding Stair Gap (either way). Open year round, call for service

🚐 **Beverly Carini** 850.572.7352 shuttle range approx 100 mi.

🚐 **Chuck Allen** 828.371.6460, Springer to Fontana, call after 1pm.

🚐 **City Taxi** 828.369.5042, by appt. after 6 pm.

🚐 **Roadrunner Driving Services** 706.201.7719 where2@mac.com Long distance shuttles covering Atlanta to Damascus.

🚐 **Larry's Taxi Service** 828.421.4987, shuttles anywhere.

🐾 **Lenzo Animal Hospital** 828.369.2635 M-F 8:30-5:00, some Sa 8:30-noon. Emergency clinic 828.665.4399.

ℹ️ **Visitor Center** (Chamber of Commerce) 828.524.3161 M-F 9-5, Sa 10-4, closed Sunday. List of hiker services and shuttles.

📫 **UPS Store** 828.524.9800, M-F 8-6, Sa 10-3.

Postal workers are present before & after the window closes at most post offices, and may retrieve a package for you. Doing so is a courtesy not an obligation. Do not impose on them unnecessarily.

115.7   Wayah Gap, Wayah Rd.
124.4   Burningtown Gap, NC 1397
129.2   Tellico Gap, Otter Creek Rd.

🛏🏪♿🍴⛺🚐🅿📫 **Nantahala Mtn Lodge** 828.321.2340 〈www.aquonecabins.com/at.html〉 Run by 2010 thru-hiker "Wiggy". Open Feb 20 - Jun 1. Bunks (clean bedding provided) $25PP, private room $50D, private cabin $100 sleeps 2 couples. Pickup or return from/to Burningtown, Wayah or Tellico $5PP per trip. Home cooked breakfast $6, 3-course evening meal $12.50. Laundry $5. Short term resupply, candy, sodas, packaged meals, some gear. Slackpacking options Rock Gap-NOC with reservations. Safe parking for section hikers. No pets. Credit cards $3 surcharge. Shipping from nearby village PO. Maildrops (guests only): 63 Britannia Dr, Aquone, NC 28781.

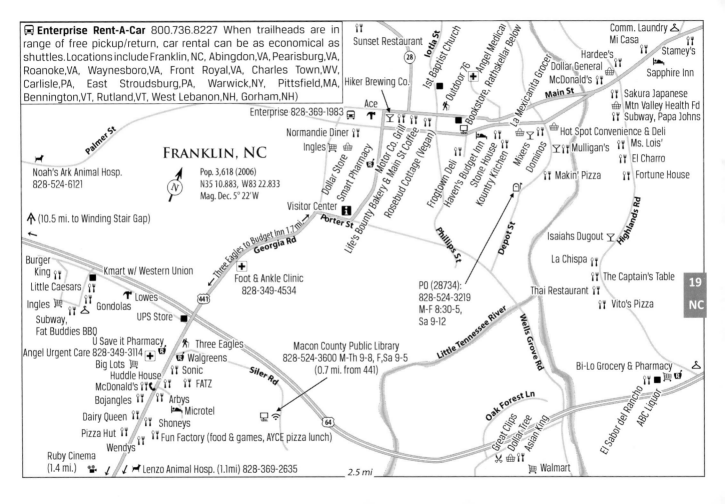

Enterprise Rent-A-Car 800.736.8227 When trailheads are in range of free pickup/return, car rental can be as economical as shuttles. Locations include Franklin, NC, Abingdon, VA, Pearisburg, VA, Roanoke, VA, Waynesboro, VA, Front Royal, VA, Charles Town, WV, Carlisle, PA, East Stroudsburg, PA, Warwick, NY, Pittsfield, MA, Bennington, VT, Rutland, VT, West Lebanon, NH, Gorham, NH)

Iotla St
Sunset Restaurant
(28)
1st Baptist Church
Outdoor 76
Angel Medical
Bookstore, Rathskellar Below
La Mexicanita Grocer
Main St

Comm. Laundry
Mi Casa
Stamey's
Hardee's
Dollar General
McDonald's
Sapphire Inn

Hiker Brewing Co.
Ace

Sakura Japanese
Mtn Valley Health Fd
Subway, Papa Johns

Enterprise 828-369-1983

Hot Spot Convenience & Deli
Ms. Lois'
Mulligan's
El Charro
Mixers
Dominos
Makin' Pizza
Fortune House

Normandie Diner
Ingles

FRANKLIN, NC

Dollar Store
Smart Pharmacy
Motor Co. Grill
Life's Bounty Bakery & Main St Coffee
Rosebud Cottage (Vegan)
Frogtown Deli
Haven's Budget Inn
Stone House
Kountry Kitchen

Pop. 3,618 (2006)
N35 10.883, W83 22.833
Mag. Dec. 5° 22'W

Noah's Ark Animal Hosp.
828-524-6121

Palmer St

⚓ (10.5 mi. to Winding Stair Gap)

Visitor Center

Porter St

Isaiahs Dugout
Highlands Rd

Phillips St

Depot St

La Chispa
The Captain's Table

19
NC

Life's Bounty to Budget Inn 1.7 mi.
Georgia Rd

Foot & Ankle Clinic
828-349-4534

Three Eagles to Budget Inn 1.7 mi.

Thai Restaurant
Vito's Pizza

Burger King
Little Caesars
Ingles
Gondolas
Subway,
Fat Buddies BBQ
U Save it Pharmacy
Angel Urgent Care 828-349-3114
Big Lots
Huddle House
McDonald's
Bojangles
Dairy Queen
Pizza Hut
Wendys
Ruby Cinema
(1.4 mi.)

Kmart w/ Western Union
Lowes

(441)

UPS Store

Three Eagles
Walgreens
Sonic
FATZ
Arbys
Microtel
Shoneys
Fun Factory (food & games, AYCE pizza lunch)

Siler Rd

PO (28734):
828-524-3219
M-F 8:30-5,
Sa 9-12

Little Tennessee River

Wells Grove Rd

Macon County Public Library
828-524-3600 M-Th 9-8, F,Sa 9-5
(0.7 mi. from 441)

(64)

Oak Forest Ln

Bi-Lo Grocery & Pharmacy

El Sabor del Rancho
ABC Liquor

Great Clips
Dollar Tree
Asian King

Walmart

Lenzo Animal Hosp. (1.1mi) 828-369-2635

2.5 mi

SoBo	NoBo	Description	Elev
2067.1	122.1	Licklog Gap	◆ (0.5W) 4440
2065.7	123.5	Intersection with old roadbed and side trails, AT turns to east	4517
2065.1	124.1	Stream.	4325
2064.8	124.4	Burningtown Gap, NC 1397 . . . . N35 13.340 W83 33.734 P (pg.18)	4236
2064.4	124.8	Spring.	◆ 4520
2063.6	125.6	**Cold Spring Shelter** . . . . ⏾ ◆ ◁ 4945
		19.6◀11.6◀4.8◀▶5.8▶10.7▶18.4 Trail to tentsites 0.1N on AT.	
2062.9	126.3	Copper Ridge Bald, views	⊙ 5080
2061.7	127.5	Side trail 0.1E to Rocky Bald, views	⊙ 5030
2060.0	129.2	Tellico Gap, NC 1365 Otter Creek Rd . . . . . N35 16.082 W83 34.353 P (pg.18)	3850
2058.6	130.6	Wesser Bald, east 40 yards to observation tower, panoramic views	⊙❄ 4627
2057.9	131.3	Spring-fed stone cistern on blue-blazed trail (0.1E)	⏾ ◆ 4224
2057.8	131.4	**Wesser Bald Shelter** (0.1W) . . . . ◁ (8) 4106
		17.4◀10.6◀5.8◀▶4.9▶12.6▶21.7 Spring 0.1S on AT (at switchback).	
		Cables. Just north of shelter trail, Wesser Creek Trail to east.	
2056.2	133.0	The Jumpoff, views	⊙ 4000
2054.5	134.7	Spring	◆ 3041
2052.9	136.3	**▲ Rufus Morgan Shelter** . . . . ◁ (6) 2201
		15.5◀10.7◀4.9◀▶7.7▶16.8▶22.9 Shelter in view to east, stream west of AT.	
2052.3	136.9	Multiple streams and footbridges	2015
2051.9	137.3	US 19 & 74, **Nantahala Outdoor Center** . . . . N35 19.873 W83 35.529 P (pg.24)	1749
2051.7	137.5	Side trail to bunkhouse	1783
2050.3	138.9	Wright Gap, dirt road	2422
2049.5	139.7	Grassy Gap, Grassy Gap Trail to west	◆ 2990
2047.9	141.3	Spring	◆ 3589

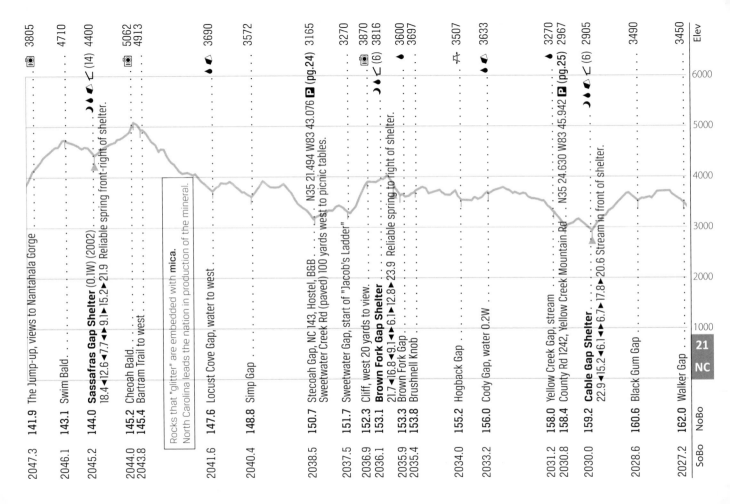

NoBo	Feature	Elev	SoBo
141.9	The Jump-up, views to Nantahala Gorge	📷 3805	2047.3
143.1	Swim Bald	4710	2046.1
144.0	**Sassafras Gap Shelter** (0.1W) (2002) ☾●▲⊆(14) 4400 18.4◀12.6◀7.7◀▶9.1▶15.2▶21.9 Reliable spring front-right of shelter.	4400	2045.2
145.2	Cheoah Bald.	📷 5062	2044.0
145.4	Bartram Trail to west	4913	2043.8
147.6	Locust Cove Gap, water to west ●▲	3690	2041.6
148.8	Simp Gap	3572	2040.4
150.7	Stecoah Gap, NC 143, Hostel, B&B . . . N35 21.494 W83 43.076 **P** (pg.24) Sweetwater Creek Rd (paved) 100 yards west to picnic tables.	3165	2038.5
151.7	Sweetwater Gap, start of "Jacob's Ladder"	3270	2037.5
152.3	Cliff, west 20 yards to view.	📷 3870	2036.9
153.1	**Brown Fork Gap Shelter** ☾●▲⊆(6) 3816 21.7◀16.8◀9.1◀▶6.1▶12.8▶23.9 Reliable spring to right of shelter.	3816	2036.1
153.3	Brown Fork Gap . ●	3600	2035.9
153.8	Brushnell Knob	3697	2035.4
155.2	Hogback Gap ⚡	3507	2034.0
156.0	Cody Gap, water 0.2W ●▲	3633	2033.2
158.0	Yellow Creek Gap, stream	3270	2031.2
158.4	County Rd 1242, Yellow Creek Mountain Rd . . . N35 24.630 W83 45.942 **P** (pg.25)	2967	2030.8
159.2	**Cable Gap Shelter** ☾●▲⊆(6) 2905 22.9◀15.2◀6.1◀▶6.7▶17.8▶20.6 Stream in front of shelter.	2905	2030.0
160.6	Black Gum Gap	3490	2028.6
162.0	Walker Gap	3450	2027.2

Rocks that "glitter" are embedded with **mica**.
North Carolina leads the nation in production of the mineral.

21
NC

| Elev | | |
| NoBo | | SoBo |

Elev				
3270				
2295				
1765				
1864 (20)				
1700				
1881				
3278				
3465				
3800 / 3597				
3680				
4520				
4381				
3842				
4602 (12)				
4775				
4120 / 4122				
4367 (14)				
4799				

NoBo	Description	SoBo
162.3	Footbridge, stream	2026.9
164.0	Spring	2025.2
164.7	NC 28 (paved). **Fontana 28 AT Crossing, Fontana Dam, NC** (2.0W) N35 26.485 W83 47.806 **P** (pg.25)	2024.5
165.9	**Fontana Dam Shelter** "Fontana Hilton" (0.1E)	2023.3
166.3	**Dam Visitor Center** 21.9◄12.8◄6.7▶11.1▶13.9▶16.8 N35 27.118 W83 48.079 **P H** (pg.25)	2022.9
167.3	Great Smoky Mountains National Park southern boundary. NoBo reenter woods, SoBo join road. (pg.26)	2021.9
169.3	Boulder jumble, throne-shaped rock	2019.9
169.6	Stream.	2019.6
170.7	Shuckstack, fire tower 0.1E.	2018.5
171.0	Sassafras Gap, Benton MacKaye Trail (BMT). The BMT reconnects with the AT at Davenport Gap. These 102 miles of the BMT on the NC side has rich cove forests and only one shelter. The high point of the BMT in the Smokies is 5843'.	2018.2
171.9	Birch Spring Gap. Campsite west 100 yards down slope, tent pads, cables, spring unreliable.	2017.3
174.2	Doe Knob, NoBo follow NC/TN border; SoBo enter NC.	2015.0
174.7	Mud Gap.	2014.5
175.6	Ekaneetlee Gap.	2013.6
177.0	**Mollies Ridge Shelter,** spring 23.9◄17.8◄11.1▶2.8▶5.7▶12.0	2012.2
177.6	Devils Tater Patch.	2011.6
179.0	Little Abrams Gap	2010.2
179.2	Big Abrams Gap	2010.0
179.8	**Russell Field Shelter,** spring 0.1W 20.6◄13.9◄2.8▶2.9▶9.2▶15.0	2009.4
181.3	Stream.	2007.9

SoBo	NoBo		Elev
2006.5	182.7	**Spence Field Shelter** (0.2E) on Eagle Creek Trail 16.8◀5.7◀2.9◀▶6.3▶12.1▶13.8 100 yards north, Bote Mountain Trail to west.	4921 ☾ △ ⊏(12)
2006.1	183.1	Jenkins Ridge trail to east	4935
2005.3	183.9	Rocky Top, views	5440 📷
2004.7	184.5	Thunderhead Mountain	5527
2004.0	185.2	Water to west.	4922 ◆

✽ **Sarvis Tree** – Also called "serviceberry." Blooms with plentiful petite white-petaled flowers.

SoBo	NoBo		Elev
2002.1	187.1	Starkey Gap	4555
2001.3	187.9	Sugar Tree Gap	4435
2000.2	189.0	**Derrick Knob Shelter** 12.0◀9.2◀6.3◀▶5.8▶7.5▶13.8 Reliable spring near shelter. Cables.	4901 ⊏(12)
1999.9	189.3	Sams Gap, Greenbrier Ridge Trail to west	4775 ◆
1997.9	191.3	Cold Spring Knob	5187
1997.6	191.6	Miry Ridge Trail to west.	4929
1997.4	191.8	Buckeye Gap	4817 ◆
1994.4	194.8	**Silers Bald Shelter**, spring 75 yard to right of shelter. 15.0◀12.1◀5.8◀▶1.7▶8.0▶15.5	5454 ⊏(12)
1994.2	195.0	Silers Bald, survey mark on boulder, AT turns to east	5607 📷
1994.0	195.2	Welch Ridge Trail to east.	5444
1992.7	196.5	**Double Spring Gap Shelter** 13.8◀7.5◀1.7◀▶6.3▶13.8▶21.2. Best water 15 yards from crest on NC side. Water is also 35 yards down TN side.	5511 ◆ ⊏(12)
1992.1	197.1	Goshen Prong Trail to west.	5768
1990.2	199.0	Mt Buckley	6585
1990.1	199.1	Trail 0.5E to Clingman's parking area (NoBo be careful at this fork).	6553
1989.8	199.4	Clingmans Tower Path, paved path between tower and parking area	6643
1989.6	199.6	Clingmans Dome, tower to east	6655 📷 🛖(pg.26)
1988.6	200.6	Mt Love	6446
1987.5	201.7	Collins Gap	5764
1986.8	202.4	Mt Collins	6182

⟨⚡⟩☀⚒ ⚐🚿🚐📞 **Nantahala Outdoor Center** 888.905.7238 ⟨www.noc.com⟩ Complex with lodging, food, gear & whitewater rafting. Coin showers available to non-guests Apr-Oct. In-season office hours 8-5. Reservations recommended, even for the hostel. If you walk in without reservation, check in at General Store; or, if store closed at River's End Restaurant.

Events at NOC: *Southern Ruck* Jan 16-19. *Founder's Bridge AT Festival* Apr 3-5 Free movies with soda and popcorn Th & Fr, thru-hiker dinner Sat. Live music, lightweight backpacking, cooking, and ATC clinics, lots of fun and giveaways, gear reps for support & repairs. Extended restaurant & store hours.

🛏 Motel rooms $57/up. Prices higher mid-summer, weekends & holidays. Baisc rooms do not have TV or phone. Rooms with more amenities at **Nantahala Inn** 1.5 miles away. For large groups, it can be economical to rent a cabin; ask about prices.

🛏 **Base Camp (hostel)** $19.38 includes tax, shower, common area & kitchen. Check in at general store.

🍴🛜 **River's End Restaurant** (B/L/D); **Big Wesser BBQ/ Pourover Pub** Live music, opens mid-April.

🚶🏪🚐✉ **NOC Outfitters** Full service outfitter, fuel/ oz. Experienced staff, gear shakedowns, Full line of gear and trail food. Open 7 days, extended hours in summer. Ask about shuttles. Maildrops: dated & marked "Hold for AT Hiker", 13077 Hwy 19W, Bryson City, NC 28713.

🏪 **Wesser General Store** Open Mar-Oct.

🏨🚐 **Nantahala Mtn Lodge** (pg.18) will pick up from NOC.
🚐 **Jude Julius** 828.736.0086 In Bryson City, NC. Shuttle range Hiawassee, GA to Newfound Gap.

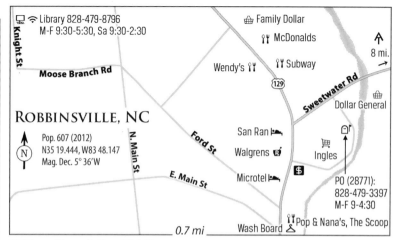

💻🛜 Library 828-479-8796
M-F 9:30-5:30, Sa 9:30-2:30

🏬 Family Dollar
🍴 McDonalds
Wendy's 🍴   🍴 Subway
🛒 Dollar General

ROBBINSVILLE, NC

Knight St
Moose Branch Rd

N. Main St
Ford St
Sweetwater Rd
129

San Ran 🍴
Walgrens 💊
Microtel 🛏
Ingles
🛒
💲
🏧
PO (28771):
828-479-3397
M-F 9-4:30

E. Main St

🅝 Pop. 607 (2012)
N35 19.444, W83 48.147
Mag. Dec. 5° 36'W

8 mi. →

0.7 mi
Wash Board ⚒   🍴 Pop & Nana's, The Scoop

150.7   Stecoah Gap, NC 143

🛏🏨🍴⚐🚐🛜✉ (3.0E) **Cabin in the Woods** Donna 828.735.1930 or Phil 828.735.3368 ⟨www.thecabininthewoods.com⟩ Hiker lodging $15PP includes ride to/from Stecoah Gap, shower, bathroom. Private cabins also available but are often booked so reserve early. $10 resupply trip to Robbinsville. For-fee shuttles ranging from Amicalola to Hot Springs or to Knoxville/Asheville bus stations & airports. Family style breakfast $5, dinner $8, laundry $3/load. Pets under 40 pounds okay. Maildrops: 301 Stecoah Heights Rd. Robbinsville, NC 28771

🛏⚐🛜✉ (20.0W) **Buffalo Creek B&B** 828.479.3892 RobMason@rocketmail. com. Hiker rate (no drive-ins) $60PP includes pickup/return from Stecoah Gap, a resupply stop in Robbinsville, laundry, breakfast. Open April-October, call for availability in other months. There is WiFi and you may print your Smokies permit here. Maildrops (guests only): 4989 W. Buffalo Rd, Robbinsville, NC 28771.

🛏⚐🛜 (1.1E) **Appalachian Inn** 828.479.8450 Luxurious log cabin with great views $130-150 double, 1.2E from Stecoah Gap. Includes pickup/return from Stecoah Gap, laundry and full country breakfast. Additional charge for lunch/ dinner. Some rooms have jacuzzi tubs.

Robbinsville, NC (8W from Stecoah Gap)

🛏🍴 **San Ran Motel** 828.479.3256 Reasonable rates, non-smoking rooms with fridge & microwave. No pets.

🛏🍴 **Microtel** 828.479.6772 $64.95D $74.95(4), rates $10 higher on weekends. Pet fee $50.

🍴 **El Pacifico** 0.4 south of Wash Board

🏪 **Ingles** 828.479.6748 7-10, 7 days

158.4   Yellow Creek Mountain Rd.

🛏🚶🚌🛜✉ **Paradise on the A.T.** 828.346.1076 Cynthia or Jeff, postandwilson@gmail.com. $50PP, $75 couple includes pickup/return from Yellow Creek Gap, Fontana Dam, or Stecoah Gap, resupply trip to Robbinsville, laundry, breakfast. Other meals $10PP. Free slackpacking. Pets welcome. Maildrops: 259 Upper Cove Rd., Robbinsville, NC, 28771.

164.7   NC 28

🚻🚌 **Fontana 28 AT Crossing** Bathrooms, vending machines, GSMNP maps ($1), and house phone to call for shuttle. More snacks & canned meats available from bait store on dock 0.1E. $3 for shuttle between here or shelter to/from Fontana Village 8:30-6 daily 2/15-5/15.

Fontana Village, NC (2W from NC 28) For all facilities contact: 800.849.2258 or 828.498.2211

🛏✉🖥💲 **Fontana Lodge** Ask for thru-hiker rate $69, room holds up to 4, no pets. Price higher on high-demand nights. Cabins $99/up. Priority Mail shipping from lobby. Maildrops: Fontana Village Resort, ATTN: Front Desk, 300 Woods Dr., Fontana Dam, NC 28733.

🏪🖥 **General Store** Grocery store, freeze-dried food, Coleman/alcohol/oz, canister fuel during thru-hiker season, small selection of gear items. 10% discount for thru-hikers on non-food items. Open Mar 7-Nov 28.

🍴 **Mountainview Bistro, Wildwood Grill** opens May 1.

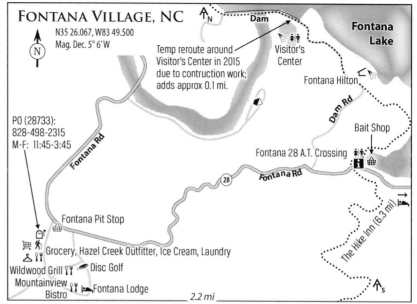

FONTANA VILLAGE, NC

N35 26.067, W83 49.500
Mag. Dec. 5° 6'W

Temp reroute around Visitor's Center in 2015 due to contruction work; adds approx 0.1 mi.

PO (28733): 828-498-2315 M-F: 11:45-3:45

Fontana Rd

Fontana Pit Stop

Grocery, Hazel Creek Outfitter, Ice Cream, Laundry

Wildwood Grill 🍴
Mountainview 🍴🛏 Fontana Lodge
Bistro

Disc Golf

Dam

Fontana Lake

Visitor's Center

Fontana Hilton

Dam Rd

Bait Shop

Fontana 28 A.T. Crossing

28

Fontana Rd

The Hike Inn (6.3 mi.)

2.2 mi

🍴 **Fontana Pit Stop** Hot dogs, nachos, microwave fare, soda & coffee. Pool table.
🚿 **Laundromat** 7 days, open year-round.

166.3   **Fontana Dam Visitor Center**

ℹ️🚿🚻 Sodas, snacks, camera supplies, free showers, GSMP self-registration permits. Open 9am-6pm daily May-Oct. Verizon and AT&T cell phones may get signal at the overlook near the shelter parking area.

🛏🚶🚌 (6.3E) **The Hike Inn** 828.479.3677 hikeinn@graham.main.nc.us www.thehikeinn.com A hiker only service for long distance & section hikers. Owned and operated by Jeff & Nancy Hoch since 1993. RESERVATION ONLY. Open year-round for accommodations & transportation. Seasonal rates. Call, e-mail or visit the website for more information, reservations & directions.

Great Smoky Mountains NP ⟨www.nps.gov/grsm⟩
Backcountry Info: 865.436.1297
Reservations: 865.436.1231

A permit is required and there is a backcountry fee - $4PP per night or $20PP flat rate fee for up to 8 nights. An on-line system allows you to pay and print a permit up to 30 days in advance ⟨www.smokiespermits.nps.gov⟩

Shelters - The only near-trail campsite is Birch Spring, otherwise hikers must stay in shelters. Reservations required for section hikers. If the shelter is full, thru-hikers must give up bunk space and tent in the vicinity of the shelter. Hikers must use bear cables to secure food.

No pets - Dogs are not permitted in the park. Below are kenneling options, vaccination records often required:

🐾 ✉ **Loving Care Kennels** 865.453.2028, 3779 ⟨www.LovingCareKennels.com⟩ Tinker Hollow Rd, Pigeon Forge, TN 37863. Pick up your dog at Fontana Dam and return him/her to Davenport Gap. $350 for one dog, $450 for two. Will deliver maildrops upon pickup or return. Call at least 2 days in advance.

🐾 **Barks and Recreation** 865.325.8245 Does not offer rides, but you can drop off/pickup from 2159 East Parkway Gatlinburg, TN. M-Sa 7am-8pm, Su 10-6.

🐾 **Standing Bear Farm** (see pg. 32)

199.6   Clingmans Dome N35 33.433 W83 29.634 🅿 👫
This is the highest point on the Appalachian Trail. Parking lot & restrooms 0.5E on a paved walkway. There are no sinks in the restrooms. Gift shop near parking area sometimes sells drinks & snacks. It's 7 mi. from the parking area to Newfound Gap on Clingmans Dome Rd; the road is closed to cars Dec 1 - Apr 1.

207.3   Newfound Gap, US 441   *Gatlinburg, TN* (15W)

🛏🚶🚗📶🖥 **Grand Prix Motel** 865.436.4561, $39, coin laundry. Shuttle up to 8 persons to Newfound Gap $30 or Clingmans Dome for $40. Maildrops: 235 Ski Mtn Rd, Gatlinburg, TN 37738.

🛏📶✉ **Microtel Gatlinburg** 865.436.0107 $44.95/up, cont B, pets $10. Maildrop with reservation: 211 Historic Nature Trail, Gatlinburg, TN 37738.

🛏📶✉ **Motel 6** 865.436.7813 Room for 2: $40 weekdays, $50 wkends, room for 4: $46 weekdays, $56 wkends. Pool, pets $10. Trolley stops at the front door. All major CC. Maildrops: 309 Ownby St, Gatlinburg, TN 37738.

🛏📶 **Days Inn** 865.436.5811

🛏📶 **Best Western** 865.436.5121

🚶 🥾 🚗 ✉ **NOC Great Outpost** 865.277.8209 Open 7 days 10-9, (Jan-May 10-6). Full line of gear, white gas/denatured/oz. Free showers & pack storage, call for shuttle schedule. Maildrops: 1138 Parkway, Gatlinburg, TN 37738.

🚶 **The Day Hiker** 865.430.0970 Small shop with shoes and fuel.

🚗 **Highlands Shuttle Service** (Ron McGaha) 423.625.0739 or 865.322.2752 mdron@bellsouth.net, shuttles from Standing Indian (NC) to Damascus, VA. Also pick up/drop off at Knoxville and Asheville airports and bus stations.

🚗 **A Walk in the Woods** 865.436.8283 ⟨www.aWalkintheWoods.com⟩ Daily pickup from NOC. Guides Vesna & Erik Plakanis resupply & shuttling (hikers & dogs). Shuttle range Springer to Damascus. Special thru-hiker rates.

🚗 **Cherokee Cab** 828.269.8621 Short and long distance shuttles 24/7 covering all trailheads in the Smokies and nearby cities.

🚗 **Cherokee Transit** 866.388.6071 ⟨www.cherokeetransit.com⟩

■ **Roger Bailey, LMT** 865.250.0676 Special thru-hiker rate $50/hr massage.

Cherokee, NC (21E) Large town, many services.

🛏🚶🚗📶🖥📞 **Microtel Inn & Suites** 828.497.7800 $65, higher on wkends, includes breakfast, free local/long distance phone. Coin laundry, pool. Adjacent supermarket, fast-food, shoe store.

Townsend, TN (22W) Large town, many services.

🛏🚶🚗 (20W) **Smoky Pearl** 865.984.4453 ⟨www.SimplyLoveHiking.com⟩ $30PP Bunk with linens, full kitchen, some resupply. Pickup from Newfound Gap or Fontana, shuttles covering all of the Smokies. Parking for section hikers.

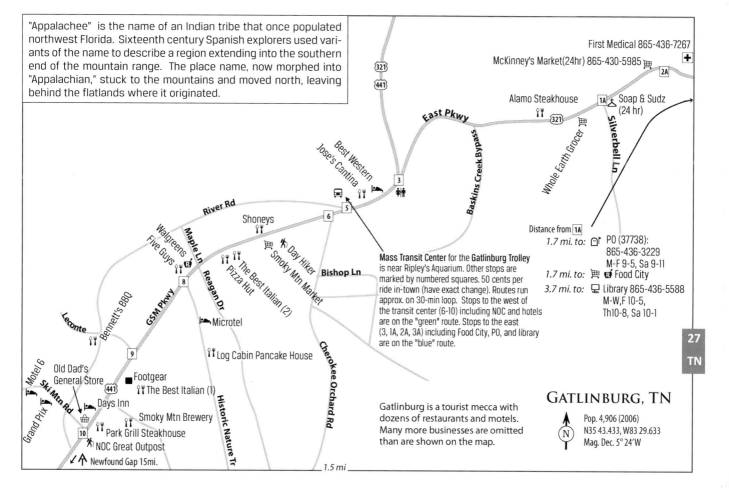

"Appalachee" is the name of an Indian tribe that once populated northwest Florida. Sixteenth century Spanish explorers used variants of the name to describe a region extending into the southern end of the mountain range. The place name, now morphed into "Appalachian," stuck to the mountains and moved north, leaving behind the flatlands where it originated.

First Medical 865-436-7267
McKinney's Market(24hr) 865-430-5985

321
441

East Pkwy

Alamo Steakhouse

321

2A

1A Soap & Sudz
(24 hr)

Whole Earth Grocer

Silverbell Ln

Best Western
Jose's Cantina

3

Baskins Creek Bypass

5

6

River Rd

Shoneys

Day Hiker

Smoky Mtn Market

Bishop Ln

Walgreens
Five Guys

Maple Ln

The Best Italian (2)
Pizza Hut

Reagan Dr

8

GSM Pkwy

Bennett's BBQ

Microtel

Leconte

9

Log Cabin Pancake House

Cherokee Orchard Rd

Motel 6

Old Dad's
General Store

441

Footgear

The Best Italian (1)

Grand Prix

Ski Mtn Rd

Days Inn

Smoky Mtn Brewery

10

Park Grill Steakhouse

NOC Great Outpost

Newfound Gap 15mi.

Historic Nature Tr

Distance from 1A

1.7 mi. to: PO (37738):
865-436-3229
M-F 9-5, Sa 9-11

1.7 mi. to: Food City

3.7 mi. to: Library 865-436-5588
M-W,F 10-5,
Th10-8, Sa 10-1

Mass Transit Center for the **Gatlinburg Trolley** is near Ripley's Aquarium. Other stops are marked by numbered squares. 50 cents per ride in-town (have exact change). Routes run approx. on 30-min loop. Stops to the west of the transit center (6-10) including NOC and hotels are on the "green" route. Stops to the east (3, 1A, 2A, 3A) including Food City, PO, and library are on the "blue" route.

27
TN

Gatlinburg is a tourist mecca with dozens of restaurants and motels. Many more businesses are omitted than are shown on the map.

GATLINBURG, TN

N Pop. 4,906 (2006)
N35 43.433, W83 29.633
Mag. Dec. 5° 24'W

1.5 mi

SoBo	NoBo	Feature	Elev
1986.4	202.8	Sugarland Mtn Trail, **Mt Collins Shelter** (0.5W) 13.8◄8.0◄6.3▲▼7.5▲14.9▶20.1 Cables. Small spring 0.1 beyond shelter.	5970 (12)
1986.1	203.1	Fork Mountain Trail east of Clingmans Dome Rd	5892
1985.3	203.9	Spring	5672
1983.6	205.6	Road Prong Trail, AT skirts Clingmans Dome Rd. N35 36.564 W83 26.799 P	5283
1983.2	206.0	Mingus Ridge, two wild hog containment bridges.	5457
1981.9	207.3	Newfound Gap, US 441 N35 36.669 W83 25.540 P 🏛 (pg.26-27) Large parking area, restrooms. There are no sinks in restrooms, and water fountain is turned off in winter. **Gatlinburg, TN** (15.0W)	5045
1980.2	209.0	Sweat Heifer Creek Trail to east	5607
1979.2	210.0	0.2W to Mt Kephart, 0.6W to Jumpoff (views), Blvd. Trail 5.5W to Mt LeConte.	6034
1978.9	210.3	**Icewater Spring Shelter** to east. 15.5◄13.8◄7.5▲▼7.4▲12.6▶20.3 Spring 75 yards north on AT.	5939 (12)
1978.0	211.2	South end of Charlies Bunion Loop Trail (0.1W)	5513
1977.9	211.3	North end of Charlies Bunion Loop Trail	5472
1977.7	211.5	Unmarked side trail 0.1W to original Charlies Bunion.	5425
1977.5	211.7	Dry Sluice Gap Trail to east	5431
1976.9	212.3	The Sawteeth	5395
1976.6	212.6	Porters Gap	5388
1973.8	215.4	View	5728
1972.8	216.4	Bradleys View	5469
1971.5	217.7	**Pecks Corner Shelter** (0.5E) on Hughes Ridge Trail 21.2◄14.9◄7.4▲▼5.2▲12.9▶20.0 Spring just south of shelter side trail.	5555 (12)
1970.6	218.6	Eagle Rocks, view.	5829
1969.8	219.4	Copper Gap	5513
1969.1	220.1	Mt Sequoyah, AT skirts summit	5941
1967.1	222.1	East ridge of Mt Chapman	6249
1966.3	222.9	**Tri-Corner Knob Shelter** 20.1◄12.6◄5.2▲▼7.7▲14.8▶25.3	5911 (12)

Page 29 NC/TN

Elevation profile — Appalachian Trail (NC/TN)

Elev	NoBo	Description	SoBo
5986	223.0	Balsam Trail to east.	1966.2
6330	224.4	Guyot Spring, trail skirts Mt Guyot	1964.8
6278	224.8	Spring	1964.4
6081	225.8	Deer Creek Gap	1963.4
5909	226.5	Yellow Creek Gap	1962.7
5912	226.6	Plane wreckage	1962.6
5796	226.7	Snake Den Ridge Trail, 5.3W to Cosby Campground	1962.5
4692	229.0	Camel Gap, Camel Gap Trail to east	1960.2
4791	230.6	**Cosby Knob Shelter,** 100 yards east 20.3◀12.9◀7.7◀▶7.1▶17.6▶25.8	1958.6
4252	231.3	Low Gap, 2.5W to Cosby Campground.	1957.9
5000	233.4	Mt Cammerer Trail, 0.6W to summit, lookout tower.	1955.8
4759	233.7	Spring	1955.5
3490	235.7	Lower Mt Cammerer Trail, Cosby Campground (7.8W)	1953.5
2869	236.7	Chestnut Branch Trail, 2.1E to parking at Big Creek Ranger Station and north end of BMT. N35 45.558 W83 6.412 **P** (2.0E)	1952.5
2826	236.9	Spring	1952.3
2572	237.7	**Davenport Gap Shelter,** spring to left of shelter 20.0◀14.8◀7.1◀▶10.5▶18.7▶23.6	1951.5
1975	238.6	TN 32, NC 284, Davenport Gap Great Smoky Mountains National Park northern boundary (pg.32)	1950.6
1728	239.6	Stateline Branch, multiple crossings	1949.6
1411	240.3	Pigeon River Bridge.	1948.9
1500	240.5	I-40 underpass (pg.32)	1948.7
1636	240.7	Stream	1948.5
1775	241.3	Green Corner Rd (gravel) hostel to west. (pg.32)	1947.9

SoBo	NoBo	Elev	Description
1945.8	243.4	2893	Painter Branch, cross branch to campsites.
1945.5	243.7	3121	Blue-blazed trail east across Painter Creek to campsite and spring. Stream.
1944.9	244.3	3489	Spanish Oak Gap, trail joins old roadbed
1943.5	245.7	4263	Snowbird Mountain, grassy bald, side trail 50 yards to FAA tower on summit.
1942.7	246.5	4075	Wildcat Spring uphill from trail
1942.1	247.1	3648	Turkey Gap
1941.2	248.0	3061	Spring
1941.0	248.2	2929	Deep Gap, **Groundhog Creek Shelter** (0.2E) 25.3◄17.6◄10.5▶8.2▶13.1▶23.0 Stone shelter with reliable spring to left. Cables.
1939.2	250.0	3577	Spring downhill, east 30 yards
1938.7	250.5	3855	Rube Rock Trail to Hawks Roost
1938.1	251.1	3500	Brown Gap, USFS 148A
1935.6	253.6	4344	Cherry Creek Trail, water 0.3E
1935.3	253.9	4262	SR 1182, Max Patch Rd., stream to north. N35 47.776 W82 57.762
1935.0	254.2	4392	Dirt road, west to parking, east to Buckeye Ridge
1934.6	254.6	4629	Max Patch Summit (campfires not permitted on bald)
1934.1	255.1	4391	Stream.
1933.7	255.5	4226	Roadbed, Buckeye Ridge Trail to east.
1933.1	256.1	4137	Stream.
1932.9	256.3	4057	Water to east (signed)
1932.8	256.4	4036	**Roaring Fork Shelter,** water 0.1S or 0.4N, cables 25.8◄18.7◄8.2▶4.9▶14.8▶29.0
1932.4	256.8	3955	Footbridge, stream
1931.7	257.5	3765	Footbridge
1931.3	257.9	3654	Stream (many in area)
1930.5	258.7	3471	Two streams about 0.1 mile apart
1929.7	259.5	3562	Footbridge
1929.4	259.8	3504	Footbridge, stream.
1929.2	260.0	3550	Lemon Gap, NC 1182, TN 107
1928.5	260.7	3963	Stream.
1928.0	261.2	4305	Walnut Mountain, grassy clearing
1927.9	261.3	4262	**Walnut Mountain Shelter** 23.6◄13.1◄4.9▶9.9▶24.1▶32.7 Walnut Mt tr. to west. Use cables, cook away from shelter. Water 0.1 behind.
1927.2	262.0	3714	Kale Gap, campsite 125 yards north on AT
1926.5	262.7	4135	Catpen Gap, 0.1 east to campsite atop small knoll
1926.1	263.1	4277	Streams
1925.8	263.4	4452	Campsite in unnamed gap.

"Max Patch" is a homophone that replaced the original name "Mack's Patch". The summit was cleared for cattle and is maintained as a bald.

NoBo	Feature	Elev	SoBo
263.7	Bluff Mountain	4686	1925.5
264.4	Spring 50 yards west.	4210	1924.8
265.0	Old roadbed, spring.	3939	1924.2
265.3	Big Rock Spring located in ravine.	3730	1923.9
265.9	Dirt road.	3427	1923.3
266.5	Brook with cascades.	2995	1922.7
266.9	Old Rd.	2715	1922.3
267.8	Garenflo Gap, Shut-In Trail to west. N35 51.206 W82 52.556 P	2500	1921.4
268.5	Taylor Hollow Gap, two footbridges, one over a stream.	2663	1920.7
271.2	**Deer Park Mountain Shelter** (0.2E) water at gap west of AT. 23.0◀14.8◀9.9◀▶14.2▶22.8▶29.6 Cables. Gragg Gap 0.1 north on AT.	2339	1918.0
272.0	Deer Park Mountain.	2583	1917.2
274.4	NC 209 + US 25/70 **Hot Springs, NC** N35 53.371 W82 49.937 P (pg.32-33)	1326	1914.8
274.8	French Broad River, US 25/70 bridge. NoBo turn east (hop guardrail) immediately after crossing river.	1326	1914.4
275.7	Lovers Leap Rock, several rock outcroppings, Silver Mine Trail to west.	1682	1913.5
277.7	Pump Gap, trail crossing.	2130	1911.5
278.4	Springs	2336	1910.8
279.3	North intersection with Pump Gap Loop Trail	2490	1909.9
279.6	Pond with boxed spring, campsite.	2529	1909.6
279.8	NoBo: AT 0.3W on dirt road. Cross Mill Ridge to gravel road. (double-blazed oak tree). Go 0.1W on gravel road and reenter woods to east.	2646	1909.4
280.1	Stream.	2454	1909.1
280.3	Tanyard Gap, US 25/70 overpass. N35 54.597 W82 47.461 P	2270	1908.9
281.7	Piped spring	3044	1907.5
282.2	Roundtop Ridge Trail west 3.5 miles to Hot Springs (former path of AT)	3246	1907.0
282.7	Side trail 0.1W to Rich Mountain Lookout Tower, piped spring and campsite north on AT.	3543	1906.5
283.2	Spring.	3218	1906.0
283.6	Hurricane Gap, northmost of two gravel road crossings.	2982	1905.6

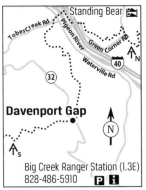

Standing Bear
TobesCreek Rd
Pigeon River
Green Corner Rd
Waterville Rd
40
N
32
Davenport Gap
N
S
Big Creek Ranger Station (1.3E)
828-486-5910 P i

238.6   Davenport Gap, **Great Smoky Mountain NP**
⛺ **(2.3E) Big Creek Campground** 865.436.1261 $14/ site, no showers or electricity. Open Apr 1 - Oct 31. Chestnut Branch Tr (2.0mi) connects campground to AT 0.1S of Davenport Gap Shelter.

240.5   I-40
🚐 🚖 **Melissa Browning** 423.608.2548 shuttles from I-40 or Davenport Gap to Newport (town has hotels, restaurants, Walmart) or other towns in 50 mi. radius. Cabins also available.
🚐 **Highlands Shuttle Service** (Ron McGaha) 423.625.0739 or 865.322.2752 mdron@bellsouth. net, shuttles from Standing Indian (NC) to Damascus, VA, Knoxville and Asheville airports and bus stations.

241.3   Green Corner Rd
🛏🍴⚡🏠♨⛺🐕🚐📞📶✉️P **Standing Bear Farm** (0.1W) 423.487.0014 curtisvowen@gmail.com; Hosted by Maria & Curtis. $25PP cabin or treehouse, $15 bunkhouse or tenting. Reasonably-priced resupply, beer, cook-yourself meals. All stove fuel. Daypacks for slackpackers. Shuttles anywhere. Kennel service & dog shuttle for hike through Smokies, $250. Directions: Green Corner Rd is gravel road 1.0 north of I-40, go west 200 yards to white farmhouse (see map). Parking $5/ car/day. Credit cards accepted. Maildrops: 4255 Green Corner Rd, Hartford, TN 37753.

274.4   NC 209, US 25/70 **Hot Springs, NC** 11.5% tax added to all Hot Springs lodging prices. **Trailfest** Apr 17-19; Friday dinner $5 at the Comm. Center, activities all day Sat & Sun pancake breakfast $4 at Still Mtn.
🛏♨✉️ **Elmers Sunnybank Inn** 828.622.7206 〈www. sunnybankretreatassociation.org〉 Long-distance hikers (100+ miles) stay for $20PP private room, includes linens, towel & shower. Guests only can purchase breakfast $6 and dinner $12; gourmet organic vegetarian meals. No pets, no smoking, no credit cards. Historic Sunnybank Inn has offered hospitality to AT hikers since 1947. Staffed by former thru-hikers, the Inn offers an extensive library & well-equipped music room. Work exchange possible. Maildrops: PO Box 233, Hot Springs, NC 28743.
🛏🚐⛺♨⛺🚿📶✉️ **Hostel at Laughing Heart Lodge** 828.206.8487 At south trailhead parking lot. $15pp bunks, $25 single private, $40D private. All rooms include shower & towel, movies, reading room, full kitchen, wireless access. Pet friendly. Tenting with shower $10, shower only $5. Laundry $5 includes wash/dry/soap. Quiet time 10pm-7am. Lodge rooms $75-100 include continental breakfast, call 828.622.0165 to reserve. Maildrops: 289 NW Hwy 25/70, Hot Springs, NC 28743.
🛏🍴📶 **Iron Horse Station** 866.402.9377 Hiker rate

HOT SPRINGS, NC

Pop. 637 (2007)
N35 53.700, W82 49.717
Mag. Dec. 5° 58'W

PO (28743):
828-622-3242
M-F 9-11:30 & 1-4,
Sa 9-10:30

Hot Springs Medical Center ✚
828-622-3245

Mountain Magnolia Inn
Hot Springs Resort and Campground
Still Mtn Restaurant
Creekside Court
Spring Creek Tavern
Hiker's Ridge Ministries
Bill Whitten Comm. Center
25 70
Wash Tub
Artisun Gallery
Harvest Moon
Iron Horse Station Inn and Restaurant
Hillbilly Market
Bridge St
Bluff Mtn Outfitter
Spring Brook Cottages
Dollar General
Gentry Hardware
Smoky Mtn Diner
Welcome Center
L&K's
Library: 828-622-3584 M,Tu,Th 10-6,
F 10-5, W,Sa 10-2
Elmer's Sunnybank Inn
Alpine Court
Spring St
Andrews Ave
French Broad River
Take OUt Grill
N
Serpentine Ave.
70
25
209
Walnut St
🛏 Hostel at Laughing Heart Lodge
P
N
S
Restrooms, WiFi.
Look for Earl Shaffer Memorial
0.7 mi

$65D. Restaurant, tavern and coffee shop. Serves L/D, and offers some vegetarian options. Live music Tu, Wed, Fri, Sat, Sun.

🛏🛰✉ **Alpine Court Motel** 828.206.3384 Hiker rate Mar-Jun $42S, $55D. No credit cards. Maildrops: 50 Bridge St, Hot Springs, NC 28743.

🛏🛰 **Creekside Court** 828.215.1261 $75D, lower on weekdays, ask for hiker discount, pets allowed.

🛏🛰◑🚿🏠🍴🛰 **Hot Springs Resort, Campground & Spa** 828.622.7267 ⟨www.nchotsprings.com⟩ Tenting $10S, $24 up to 4. Camping cabins (no TV, no linens, common bath/showers) $50 sleeps 5, $66 sleeps 8. Pets $10. Motel-style room (linens, TV, some with mineral water bath) $100-$200. Shower w/o stay $5. Mineral water spa $15S before 6pm; 3-person rate $30 before 6pm, $35 after 6pm. Camp store carries snacks & supplies. Also offers massage therapy. Accepts CC.

🛏🍴🛰 **Mountain Magnolia Inn** 800.914.9306 Discount hiker rates when rooms available $65-$130 includes AYCE breakfast. Dinner Th-M open to all. Maildrops: 204 Lawson St, Hot Springs, NC 28743.

🛏 **Creekside Court Cabins and Restaurant** 828.215.1261

🍴 **Smoky Mountain Diner** Hiker special 12 oz burger.

🍴 **Spring Creek Tavern** 50 varieties of beer, outdoor deck overlooking creek, live music Thurs-Sunday nights.

🍴🛰✉ **ArtiSun Gallery** 828.622.3573 Coffee, baked goods, ice cream, 50% off ALDHA membership, AT hiker artwork. may use phone. FedEx/UPS maildrops: 16 S. Andrews Ave, Hot Springs, NC 28743.

ℹ🚶🛰 **Visitor Center** WiFi signal accessible outside after hours.

🚶🛰🖥 **Hiker's Ridge Ministries Resource Center** Open M-Sa 9-3, Mar 15-May 15. Place to relax, coffee, drinks, doughnuts, kitchen internet, restroom.

🍴 **Harvest Moon** Coffee, fresh lemonade, tincture. Next to PO; feel free to spread out on lawn and sort through your maildrops.

🚶🏠🛒💲🖥🖥✉ **Bluff Mountain Outfitters** 828.622.7162 ⟨www.bluffmountain.com⟩ Su-Th 9-5, F-Sa 9-6 Full service outfitter, fuel/oz. Complete resupply with natural foods grocery & hiker foods. Free 30 min. computer/internet access, ask about WiFi. ATM & scale inside. Shuttles Springer-Roanoke & area airports. SoBo hikers can print Smoky Mtn NP permits here. Ships UPS packages. Maildrops: (USPS) PO Box 114 Hot Springs, NC 28743 or (FedEx/UPS) 152 Bridge St.

289.2   Allen Gap, TN 40

🏠 **Mom's Store** 828.628.3224 Just east of trail, hours vary.

290.7   Log Cabin Drive (dirt/gravel road)

🛏🚐◑🏠🍴🚶🅿🚌🛰✉ (0.7W) **Hemlock Hollow Inn & Paint Creek Cafe** 423.787.1736 ⟨www.hemlockhollowinn.com⟩ West on Log Cabin Dr. to paved Viking Mtn Rd. Bunkroom $25PP w/ linens, $20 without. Upgraded bunkroom $30 (larger mattress, linens included). Cabin for couples w/linens $60. All rooms heated. Tent site $12PP. Pets $5. All stays include shower, free return ride to trail. Non-guest shower & towel for $5. Camp store stocked with long term resupply, some gear, cold drinks, foods, fruit, stove fuels. Cafe open 7 days in hiker season, will open off-season with call-ahead reservation. Shuttles available, slack-packing welcomed. WiFi and parking free for guests, fee for non-guests. Credit cards accepted. Maildrops (ETA mandatory): 645 Chandler Circle, Greeneville, TN 37743.

310.0   Devil Fork Gap, NC 212

⚠ AT northbound is headed due south; trading post is "trail east" (to the right for northbounders) but compass west.

🚐◑🏠🚿⛺ (2.5E) **Laurel Trading Post** 828.656.2492 Open 7 days 7-7 Bunkroom $25, tenting $10, laundry $5, shower & towel w/o stay $5. Full kitchen & plenty of resupply.

318.4   Sams Gap, US 23

🍴 **Little Creek Cafe** (2.8E) 828.689.2307 M-Th&Sa 7am-2pm, F 6-3.

🏠💲 **Wolf Creek Market** (3.3E) Open 7 days

Trail work opportunities:
Apr 22-26 ALDHA Boundary work, base: Blackburn Trail Center, VA
May 17-18 Hard Core, base: Kincora, TN (sign up at Trail Days)
Jul 11-12 RPH work weekend, NY
Aug 28-30 ALDHA Boundary work, Gulf Hagas region, ME

Elev	SoBo	NoBo	Description
2997	1905.2	284.0	Grave stone
3556	1903.8	285.4	**Spring Mountain Shelter** (5) 29.0◄24.1◄14.2◄►8.6►15.4►21.8 Water 75 yards down blue-blazed trail on east side of AT. Cables.
2933	1902.0	287.2	Deep Gap, Little Paint Creek Trail, west 200 yards to spring
2777	1900.6	288.6	Spring in ravine 30 yards west
2246	1900.0	289.2	NC 208, TN 70, Allen Gap, Paint Creek 0.2W (pg.33)
2370	1899.0	290.2	AT skirts gravel road
2383	1898.5	290.7	Log Cabin Drive, private home in view 200 yards east, hostel to west (pg.33)
3670	1895.2	294.0	**Little Laurel Shelter** (5) 32.7◄22.8◄8.6◄►6.8►13.2►22.0 Boxed spring 100 yards down blue-blazed trail behind shelter. Campsites west side of AT, south of shelter. Cables.
4750	1893.9	295.3	Pounding Mill Trail to east. 0.2W to Camp Creek Bald Lookout Tower. Tower is beyond first cluster of buildings and catwalk is locked (no view)
4452	1893.1	296.1	Jones Meadow, spring 100 yards south.
4467	1892.1	297.1	Trail west to Jones Meadow, 30 yards east to Whiterock Cliff.
4503	1891.9	297.3	0.1W to Blackstack Cliffs.
4438	1891.7	297.5	Bearwallow Gap, Jerry Miller Trail to east, Firescald bypass to west reconnects.
4549	1891.0	298.2	Big Firescald Knob. AT between bypass points is rocky and strenuous. AT 1.5 miles north.
4192	1890.1	299.1	Firescald bypass to west, reconnects with AT 1.5 miles south.
4294	1889.4	299.8	Round Knob Trail to west.
4289	1888.6	300.6	Fork Ridge Trail to east.
4166	1888.4	300.8	Chestnut Log Gap, **Jerry Cabin Shelter.** (6) 29.6◄15.4◄6.8◄►6.4►15.2►25.3 Water opposite shelter. Cables.
4529	1887.6	301.6	Bald Ridge
4540	1887.2	302.0	Sarvis Cove Trail to west.
4635	1886.8	302.4	Howard C. Bassett Memorial, old roadbed before and after.
4750	1886.5	302.7	Big Butt Mountain, summit to west, short bypass trail. Squibb Creek Trail is "straight ahead," NoBo: AT east on gravel road for 1.5 mi.

34
NC/TN

⚠ AT nothbound from Flint Gap to Rice Gap is compass south.

NoBo	Description	Elev	SoBo
304.3	Shelton Gravesite.	4490	1884.9
304.6	Green Ridge Trail to east.	4488	1884.6
306.3	Flint Gap.	3469	1882.9
307.2	**Flint Mountain Shelter,** water on AT 50 yards north of shelter. 21.8◄13.2◄6.4◄▶8.8▶18.9▶29.5	3586	1882.0
307.5	Spring.	3516	1881.7
308.5	Spring	3384	1880.7
308.9	AT + roadbed south end	3293	1880.3
309.1	Spring	3284	1880.1
309.5	AT + roadbed north end.	3408	1879.7
310.0	Devil Fork Gap, NC 212, hostel & resupply 2.5E N36 0.627 W82 36.513 P (pg.33)	3115	1879.2
310.4	Rector Laurel Rd, spring north on AT. N36 0.392 W82 36.422 P	2952	1878.8
310.8	Stream	3226	1878.4
311.1	Cascade	3409	1878.1
311.3	Stream	3568	1877.9
311.8	Sugarloaf Gap.	4040	1877.4
313.2	Lick Rock	4541	1876.0
313.8	Big Flat, campsite to east	4265	1875.4
314.8	Rice Gap, dirt road	3800	1874.4
316.0	**Hogback Ridge Shelter** (0.1E) 22.0◄15.2◄8.8◄▶10.1▶20.7▶31.2 Spring 0.2 mile beyond shelter. Cables.	4332	1873.2
316.6	High Rock, view 70 yards west on blue-blazed trail	4460	1872.6
318.4	Sams Gap, US 23, I-26, trash cans N35 57.175 W82 33.636 P 🏛 (pg.33)	3850	1870.8
320.2	Meadow.	4457	1869.0
320.7	Street Gap, gravel road.	4100	1868.5
320.9	Powerline.	4161	1868.3
322.1	Low Gap, campsite downhill to west with piped spring	4300	1867.1
322.9	Spring	4624	1866.3
323.3	Powerline.	4797	1865.9
324.4	Blue-blazed trail 100 yards west to water, bypass trail to east	5060	1864.8

35
NC/
TN

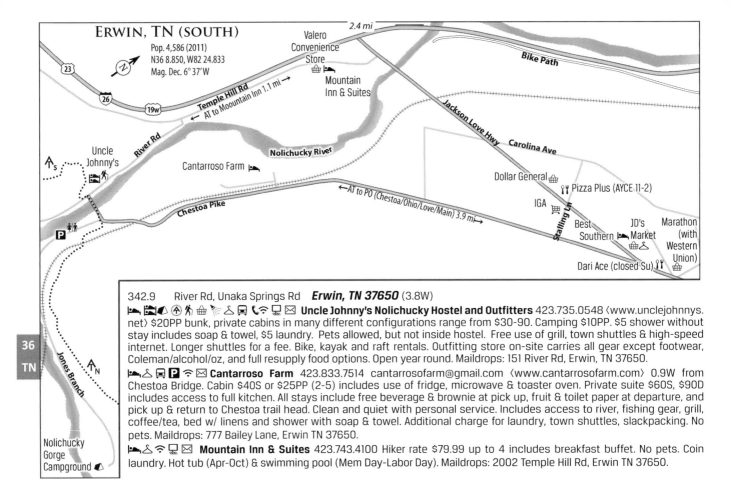

ERWIN, TN (SOUTH)

Pop. 4,586 (2011)
N36 8.850, W82 24.833
Mag. Dec. 6° 37'W

23
26
19w

Temple Hill Rd
← AT to Moountain Inn 1.1 mi →

River Rd

Uncle Johnny's

Cantarroso Farm

Nolichucky River

Chestoa Pike

Jones Branch

Nolichucky Gorge Campground

2.4 mi

Valero Convenience Store

Mountain Inn & Suites

Bike Path

Jackson Love Hwy

Carolina Ave

Dollar General

Pizza Plus (AYCE 11-2)

IGA

Stalling Ln

Best Southern

JD's Market

Marathon (with Western Union)

Dari Ace (closed Su)

← AT to PO (Chestoa/Ohio/Love/Main) 3.9 mi →

342.9   River Rd, Unaka Springs Rd *Erwin, TN 37650* (3.8W)

Uncle Johnny's Nolichucky Hostel and Outfitters 423.735.0548 ⟨www.unclejohnnys. net⟩ $20PP bunk, private cabins in many different configurations range from $30-90. Camping $10PP. $5 shower without stay includes soap & towel, $5 laundry. Pets allowed, but not inside hostel. Free use of grill, town shuttles & high-speed internet. Longer shuttles for a fee. Bike, kayak and raft rentals. Outfitting store on-site carries all gear except footwear, Coleman/alcohol/oz, and full resupply food options. Open year round. Maildrops: 151 River Rd, Erwin, TN 37650.

Cantarroso Farm 423.833.7514 cantarrosofarm@gmail.com ⟨www.cantarrosofarm.com⟩ 0.9W from Chestoa Bridge. Cabin $40S or $25PP (2-5) includes use of fridge, microwave & toaster oven. Private suite $60S, $90D includes access to full kitchen. All stays include free beverage & brownie at pick up, fruit & toilet paper at departure, and pick up & return to Chestoa trail head. Clean and quiet with personal service. Includes access to river, fishing gear, grill, coffee/tea, bed w/ linens and shower with soap & towel. Additional charge for laundry, town shuttles, slackpacking. No pets. Maildrops: 777 Bailey Lane, Erwin TN 37650.

Mountain Inn & Suites 423.743.4100 Hiker rate $79.99 up to 4 includes breakfast buffet. No pets. Coin laundry. Hot tub (Apr-Oct) & swimming pool (Mem Day-Labor Day). Maildrops: 2002 Temple Hill Rd, Erwin TN 37650.

36
TN

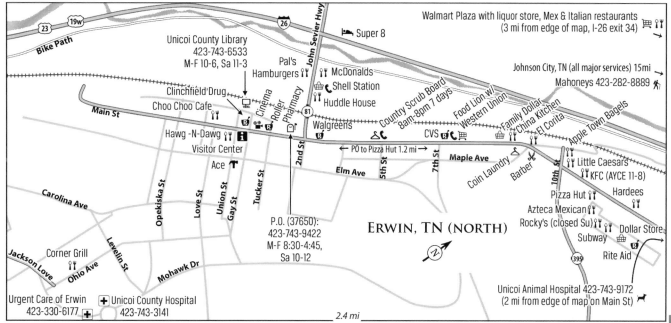

ERWIN, TN (NORTH)

Unicoi County Library
423-743-6533
M-F 10-6, Sa 11-3

Walmart Plaza with liquor store, Mex & Italian restaurants
(3 mi from edge of map, I-26 exit 34)

Johnson City, TN (all major services) 15mi
Mahoneys 423-282-8889

Super 8

Pal's Hamburgers

McDonalds

Shell Station

Huddle House

Clinchfield Drug

Choo Choo Cafe

Main St

Cinema

Roller

Pharmacy

Walgreens

Country Scrub Board
8am-8pm 7 days

Food Lion w/ Western Union

Family Dollar

China Kitchen

El Corita

Apple Town Bagels

Hawg -N-Dawg

Visitor Center

Ace

CVS

PO to Pizza Hut 1.2 mi

Maple Ave

Little Caesars

KFC (AYCE 11-8)

Hardees

Coin Laundry

Barber

Pizza Hut

Azteca Mexican

Rocky's (closed Su)

Dollar Store

Subway

Rite Aid

Elm Ave

P.O. (37650):
423-743-9422
M-F 8:30-4:45,
Sa 10-12

Carolina Ave

Opekiska St

Love St

Union St

Gay St

Tucker St

2nd St

5th St

7th St

10th St

Levelin St

Jackson Love

Corner Grill

Ohio Ave

Mohawk Dr

Unicoi Animal Hospital 423-743-9172
(2 mi from edge of map on Main St)

Urgent Care of Erwin
423-330-6177

Unicoi County Hospital
423-743-3141

2.4 mi

Best Southern 423.743.6438 $39.95S, $49.95D, no pets, Maildrops: 1315 Jackson Love Hwy, Erwin, TN 37650.

Super 8 423.743.0200, $49.99S, $59.99D includes breakfast, no pets. Coin laundry planned for 2015. Maildrops: 1101 N Buffalo St, Erwin TN 37650.

Azteca (north end of town) Serves beer.

Shuttles by Tom 423.330.7416 ⟨www.hikershuttles.com⟩ Owners Tom (10-K) and Marie (J-Walker) Bradford, icensed and insured shuttles to all area trailheads, bus stations, airports, outfitters, etc... from Springer-Harpers Ferry.

344.2   Side trail to:
Nolichucky Gorge Campground 423.743.8876, ⟨www.nolichucky.com⟩ Tent site $10, bunkroom $10 (when available), cabin $80/up. Small camp store to be added in 2015.

351.3   Indian Grave Gap, 3.3W to campground
Rock Creek Recreation Area (USFS) 423.638.4109, 423.743.4427 Tent site $12, Open May-Nov.

SoBo	NoBo	Feature	Elev
1864.7	324.5	Spring	5224
1864.5	324.7	Yellow-blazed trail to west	5368
1864.3	324.9	Big Bald, survey marker	5516
1863.7	325.5	Big Stamp, treeless saddle on ridge, bypass trail to east (0.3W)	5400
1863.4	325.8	Dirt road	5261
1863.1	326.1	**Bald Mountain Shelter** (0.1W)	5096
		25.3◄18.9◄10.1◄►10.6►21.1►33.9 Spring on side trail to shelter. Cables.	
1861.7	327.5	Little Bald (tree covered)	5220
1860.6	328.6	Spring	4403
1859.6	329.6	Whistling Gap, campsite	3889
1859.0	330.2	Trail 0.1E to High Rocks	4226
1857.9	331.3	Stream, two footbridges	3565
1857.4	331.8	Spivey Gap, US 19W. Stream south of gap. N36 1.911 W82 25.209 **P** (0.5W)	3200
1857.0	332.2	Oglesby Branch, cross twice on footbridge	3554
1856.1	333.1	Stream.	3829
1855.9	333.3	Devils Creek Gap, dirt road	3774
1853.7	335.5	Stream.	3065
1853.6	335.6	Stream.	3011
1852.8	336.4	Stream.	3064
1852.5	336.7	**No Business Knob Shelter**	3190
		29.5◄20.7◄10.6◄►10.5►23.3►32.4 Reliable water on AT 0.3S of shelter. Cables.	
1850.1	339.1	Temple Hill Gap, Temple Hill Trail	2850
1848.0	341.2	Views to Erwin	2709
1846.3	342.9	River Rd, Unaka Springs Rd. N36 6.254 W82 26.802 **P** (pg.36-37)	1720
1846.0	343.2	**Erwin, TN** (3.8W). AT to east, crossing Nolichucky River on bridge / Railroad tracks	1752
1845.0	344.2	Side trail to Nolichucky Gorge Campground before footbridge (pg.36-37)	1768

SoBo	NoBo	Description	Elev
1844.5	344.7	Footbridge, stream	1827 ◆
1844.2	345.0	Footbridge, stream	1944 ◆
1843.8	345.4	Stream.	2039 ◆
1843.5	345.7	Footbridge	2143 ◆
1843.3	345.9	Footbridge	2245 ◆
1842.0	347.2	**Curley Maple Gap Shelter**, water south of shelter △ ◆ ⌂ (14)	3083
		31.2◄21.1◄10.5▼12.8►21.9►30.3	
1841.5	347.7	Spring.	3237 ◆
1840.9	348.3	Stream	3338 ◆
1840.7	348.5	Stream	3319 ◆
1837.9	351.3	Indian Grave Gap, TN 395 N36 6.578 W82 21.696 P ◆ (pg.37)	3350
		Water 0.1E outside of curve in road.	
1837.4	351.8	Survey marker (USFS 381-28)	3703
1837.2	352.0	Powerline	3743
1836.8	352.4	USFS 230, Red Fork Rd (gravel)	3766
1834.5	354.7	Beauty Spot Gap, clearing N36 6.9796 W82 20.2321 P	4312
		Parking to west, trail parallel to USFS 230 from here north to Deep Gap.	
1834.0	355.2	Piped spring & campsites 100 yards west across USFS 230.	4114 ◗
1833.6	355.6	AT skirts Red Fork Rd	4546
1832.5	356.7	Unaka Mountain, dense spruce forest.	5180
1830.3	358.9	Low Gap, campsite, weak stream 0.1W	3900 △
1829.4	359.8	Footbridge, stream	4130 ◗
1829.2	360.0	**Cherry Gap Shelter** 33.9◄23.3◄12.8▼9.1►17.5►22.7 ⌂ (6)	4012 ◗
		Spring 120 yards on blue-blazed trail behind shelter to the left.	
1828.8	360.4	Unmarked trail crossing	3924
1827.8	361.4	Little Bald Knob, trail skirts summit	4347
1827.6	361.6	Stream.	4289
1826.1	363.1	Iron Mountain Gap, TN 107, NC 226 N36 8.600 W82 13.990 P (pg.42)	3723
1824.8	364.4	Campsite, water 0.1W from signpost near north end of clearing	4021 ◗ △

✽ **Golden ragwort** – Small flower with yellow center and small floppy petals. "Field flower" that can create a sea of yellow.

39 NC/TN

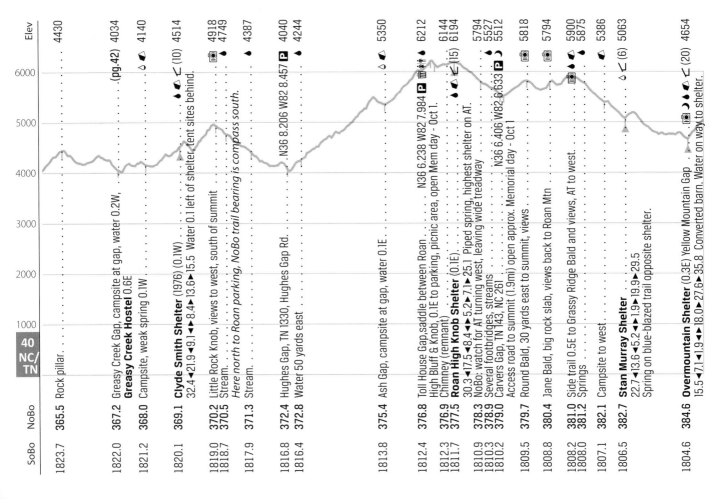

Elev	Description	NoBo	SoBo
4430	Rock pillar.	365.5	1823.7
4034	Greasy Creek Gap, campsite at gap, water 0.2W, **Greasy Creek Hostel** 0.6E (pg.42)	367.2	1822.0
4140	Campsite, weak spring 0.1W.	368.0	1821.2
4514	**Clyde Smith Shelter** (1976) (0.1W) Water 0.1 left of shelter, tent sites behind. (10) 32.4◀21.9◀9.1◀▶8.4▶13.6▶15.5	369.1	1820.1
4918	Little Rock Knob, views to west, south of summit	370.2	1819.0
4749	Stream. *Here north to Roan parking, NoBo trail bearing is compass south.*	370.5	1818.7
4387	Stream.	371.3	1817.9
4040	Hughes Gap, TN 1330, Hughes Gap Rd. N36 8.206 W82 8.457	372.4	1816.8
4244	Water 50 yards east	372.8	1816.4
5350	Ash Gap, campsite at gap, water 0.1E	375.4	1813.8
6212	Toll House Gap, saddle between Roan High Bluff & Knob, 0.1E to parking, picnic area, open Mem day - Oct 1. N36 6.238 W82 7.984	376.8	1812.4
6144	Chimney (remnant)	376.9	1812.3
6194	**Roan High Knob Shelter** (0.1E). (15) 30.3◀17.5◀8.4◀▶5.2▶7.1▶25.1 Piped spring, highest shelter on AT.	377.5	1811.7
5794	NoBo: watch for AT turning west, leaving wide treadway.	378.3	1810.9
5527	Several footbridges, streams.	378.9	1810.3
5512	Carvers Gap, TN 143, NC 261 N36 6.406 W82 6.633 Access road to summit (1.9mi) open approx. Memorial day - Oct 1	379.0	1810.2
5818	Round Bald, 30 yards east to summit, views	379.7	1809.5
5794	Jane Bald, big rock slab, views back to Roan Mtn	380.4	1808.8
5900	Side trail 0.5E to Grassy Ridge Bald and views, AT to west.	381.0	1808.2
5875	Springs	381.2	1808.0
5386	Campsite to west.	382.1	1807.1
5063	**Stan Murray Shelter** (6) 22.7◀13.6◀5.2◀▶1.9▶19.9▶29.5 Spring on blue-blazed trail opposite shelter.	382.7	1806.5
4654	**Overmountain Shelter** (0.3E) Yellow Mountain Gap (20) 15.5◀7.1◀1.9◀▶18.0▶27.6▶35.8 Converted barn. Water on way to shelter.	384.6	1804.6

Elev	NoBo	SoBo	Description
5198	385.6	1803.6	Two intersections with old roadbed
5301	385.8	1803.4	Side trail 0.1E to Big Yellow Mountain
5459	386.2	1803.0	Little Hump Mountain, clearing
5181	387.1	1802.1	Piped spring, campsites to north and south
4950	387.5	1801.7	Bradley Gap, spring east 100 yards
5410	388.1	1801.1	Fence
5587	388.4	1800.8	Hump Mountain, Stan Murray plaque, NoBo have several false summits
5199	389.2	1800.0	Fence
5009	389.8	1799.4	Spring
4866	390.1	1799.1	Spring
4600	390.8	1798.4	Doll Flats, **NC-TN** border
4322	391.1	1798.1	Stone steps, view
4097	391.4	1797.9	Spring west of trail, massive stone wall.
3269	393.0	1796.6	Stream.
3052	393.3	1796.3	Piped spring
2895	393.8	1795.9	US 19E **Elk Park, NC** (2.4E) **Roan Mtn, TN** (3.5W) N36 10.765 W82 0.767 P (pg.42-43)
2900	394.0	1795.2	Bear Branch Rd, streams north of road
3206	394.8	1794.4	AT + Jeep Path, south end, stream.
3416	395.2	1794.0	AT + Jeep Path, north end
3524	395.4	1793.8	Barbwire fence
3711	396.2	1793.0	Open ridge with views to east and west
3542	396.7	1792.5	Isaacs Cemetery
3436	397.1	1792.1	Buck Mountain Rd, water at church 0.1E N36 12.240 W81 59.847 P
3330	397.4	1791.8	Campbell Hollow Rd, streams south of road
3351	397.6	1791.6	Footbridge at bottom of ravine
3377	398.1	1791.1	Footbridge, stream
2956	399.2	1790.0	Side trail 0.1E to Jones Falls
2708	399.8	1789.4	Campsite, Elk River 0.1E
2680	400.3	1788.9	Stream.
2828	401.3	1787.9	Stream (cross twice).
3029	402.1	1787.1	Footbridge, stream.
3130	402.5	1786.7	Mountaineer Falls to west
3192	402.6	1786.6	**Mountaineer Shelter**, water 70 yards from shelter 25.1◄19.9◄18.0◄►9.6►17.8►26.4
3261	403.4	1785.8	Campsite to east
3375	403.8	1785.4	Slide Hollow Stream, footbridge
3534	404.0	1785.2	Roadbed.
3616	404.2	1785.0	Walnut Mountain Rd
3472	405.1	1784.1	Footbridge, stream (many in area)

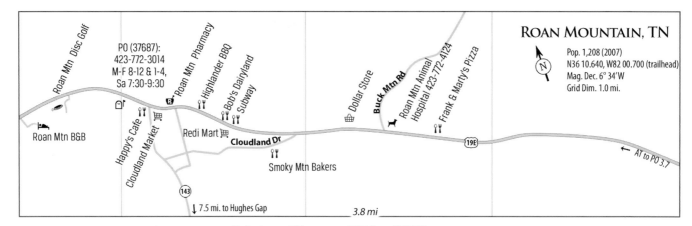

ROAN MOUNTAIN, TN

Pop. 1,208 (2007)
N36 10.640, W82 00.700 (trailhead)
Mag. Dec. 6° 34'W
Grid Dim. 1.0 mi.

Roan Mtn Disc Golf

PO (37687):
423-772-3014
M-F 8-12 & 1-4,
Sa 7:30-9:30

Roan Mtn Pharmacy

Highlander BBQ

Bob's Dairyland

Subway

Dollar Store

Buck Mtn Rd

Roan Mtn Animal Hospital 423-772-4124

Frank & Marty's Pizza

Roan Mtn B&B

Happy's Cafe

Cloudland Market

Redi Mart

Cloudland Dr

Smoky Mtn Bakers

143

↓ 7.5 mi. to Hughes Gap

3.8 mi

19E

← AT to PO 3.7

363.1   Iron Mountain Gap, TN 107, NC 226 **Buladean, NC** (4.1E)
🍴 **Mountain Grill** 828.688.9061 Large meals, cash only, closed Su.

367.2   Greasy Creek Gap
🛏🍴🔥👤🏠🛒🚿☂⛺📶🚌🅿🖥✉ (0.6E) **Greasy Creek Friendly**
828.688.9948 All room prices include tax: $10PP bunkhouse, $15PP/ up indoor accommodations, $7.50PP tenting includes shower. Shower without stay $3. Pets okay outside. Open year-round, self serve during the Sabbath (sundown Friday to sundown Saturday). Home cooked meals, including vegetarian options. Limited kitchen privileges. Store of goods for multi-day resupply including snacks, meals, Coleman/alcohol/oz. Shuttles Hot Springs to Damascus. Parking $2/night. Free long distance calls within US. No credit cards (pay by cash, check or Paypal) Directions: take old woods road east (trail east, not compass east), then take first left. You should be going downhill all the way. Hostel is first house to your right. Maildrops: 1827 Greasy Creek Rd, Bakersville, NC 28705.

393.8   US 19E
🛏🍴👤🔥🏠🛒🚿⛺📶🚌🅿✉ (0.3W) **Mountain Harbour B&B/Hiker Hostel** 866.772.9494 ⟨www.mountainharbour.net⟩ Hostel over barn overlooking creek $25PP, semi-private king bed $55, includes linens, shower, towel, full kitchen, wood burning stove, and video library. Tenting with shower $10, non-guest shower w/towel $4, laundry w/ soap $6, telephone w/calling card. Breakfast $12 available during peak hiker season. B&B rooms $125-165 includes breakfast, separate shower & fireplace, A/C, refrigerator, and cable TV/DVD. Complimentary white gas/denatured alcohol. Sells fuel canisters. Slack pack/long distance shuttles by arrangement. Secured parking $5/day or $2/day with shuttle. Open year round. Maildrops: (non-guests $5) 9151 Hwy 19E, Roan Mountain, TN 37687.

Roan Mountain, TN 37687 (3.5W)
🛏👤⛺🚌📶🅿 **Roan Mountain B&B** 423.772.3207 ⟨www.roanmtbb. com⟩ Hiker rate $65S, $85D does not include breakfast. Free return before 8am to trail at Hwy 19E, or will drop off at Happy's Cafe for breakfast and Happy's will drop off at trailhead. Free pickup after

3:30. Shuttles & slackpacking Erwin to Watauga Lake. Pets okay, no smoking inside. Do-it-yourself laundry $5. Some resupply items on-site. Parking for section hikers.

¶ Happy's Cafe 423.772.3400 7am-3pm 7 days. Hikers who come in for breakfast get ride (when staff avail) to 19E trailhead.

¶ Bob's Dairyland 423.772.3641

¶ Smoky Mountain Bakers fresh bread, wood-fired pizza

¶ Frank & Marty's Pizza 423.772.3083, closed Su & M.

Redi Mart 423.772.3032 M-Sa 8-7, closed Su.

Cloudland Market 423.772.3201

Elk Park, NC 28622 (2.4E, see services on map)

Newland, NC (7E, 19E to NC 194)

The Shady Lawn Lodge 828.733.9006, Thru-hikers get 10% off regular room rates, which are typically approx. $60. Free pickup & return when driver is available. Laundry and restaurants nearby.

AT to PO 2.4 →

Mountain Harbour

Apple House Campsite

Tennessee / North Carolina

J's Market 7-7 M-F, 7-12 Sa

19E

Betty & Carol's Ice Cream
Country House
Carolina Tobacco and Beer

Creative Grounds Coffee
Brinkley's Hardware
Elk Park Mini Market

PO (28622):
828-733-5711
M-F 7:30-12 & 1:30-4:15,
Sa 7:30-11

ELK PARK, NC
Pop. 429 (2008)
Grid Dim. 1.0 mi.

3.3 mi

405.9   (0.2W) Side trail to hostel - follow powerline.
406.5   Upper Laurel Fork. (0.3W) Blue-blazed side trail to hostel originates at the hand-railed footbridge. Follow side trail along creek.

(0.2W) **Vango/Abby Memorial Hostel** 423.772.3450, vangoabby@gmail.com. Hostel run by "Scotty," Trekkie, engineer, trail maintainer who has hiked over 14,000 trail miles. Open mid Feb - mid Nov, otherwise by arrangement, cash only. Bunkrooms with/without heat $10/$5 night. includes shower.

"Astronaut" upper private room & deck, queen bed w/linens, heat, $20S/$30D. Shower w/o stay $2. Resupply basics available daily 4-8 except Mondays: beverages, pizza, B&J ice cream, and stove fuels. Hike-in/hike-out only; no yellow-blazers and no parking. No illegal drugs, pets okay. Free tenting, WiFi, porch piano. Maildrops held free if they do not require special trip to post office: PO Box 185, Roan Mtn, TN 37687.

SoBo	NoBo	Description	Elev
1783.3	**405.9**	Bench, view, unmarked side trail west to hostel 50' north of bench. ▣ (pg.43)	3526
1782.7	**406.5**	Upper Laurel Fork, side trail to hostel ◆ (pg.43)	3335
1782.0	**407.2**	Footbridge, stream	3466
1781.8	**407.4**	USFS 293 (gravel), waterfall south on AT	3475
1781.0	**408.2**	Spring	3363
1780.8	**408.4**	Spring	3393
1780.4	**408.8**	Footbridge, stream	3463
1780.0	**409.2**	Hardcore Cascades.	3413
1779.2	**410.0**	Stream.	3648
1778.7	**410.5**	Campsite, several streams and footbridges	3581
1777.1	**412.1**	Rock outcropping, views.	3945
1777.0	**412.2**	**Moreland Gap Shelter** 29.5◄27.6◄9.6◄▶8.2▶16.8▶24.0 ⊂ (6) Water source long way downhill across from shelter.	3823
1774.8	**414.4**	Piped spring	3839
1774.4	**414.8**	Forest Service road.	3805
1773.7	**415.5**	Trail skirts White Rocks Mountain	4012
1772.4	**416.8**	Trail to Coon Den Falls 0.8E downhill	3450
1771.3	**417.9**	Stream.	2919
1770.9	**418.3**	Barn.	2647
1770.7	**418.5**	Dennis Cove Rd, USFS 50, hostels. N36 15.858 W82 7.387 **P** (pg.46-47)	2550
1769.5	**419.7**	Laurel Falls. ⚠ Do not swim close to falls, there is a dangerous whirlpool	2120
1768.8	**420.4**	**Laurel Fork Shelter** 35.8◄17.8◄8.2◄▶8.6▶15.8▶22.6 ⊂ (8)	2186
1768.5	**420.7**	Waycaster Spring, two footbridges	2048
1768.0	**421.2**	Side trail to **Hampton, TN** US 321 (1.0W) (pg.46-47) Hampton is west on 321.	1984
1765.5	**423.7**	Pond Flats, campsite, spring 0.1N on AT.	3706

NoBo	Description	SoBo	Elev
427.0	NoBo: east on Shook Branch Rd ..... N36 18.114 W82 7.738 P ⛺ (pg.46-47)	1762.2	2036
427.1	US 321, **Hampton, TN** (2.6W)	1762.1	1990
	NoBo: turn west after crossing 321		
	Shook Branch Recreation Area, picnic area, sandy beach.		
428.6	Griffith Branch	1760.6	2100
429.0	**Watauga Lake Shelter** ⚠ Likely to be closed all of 2015 (bear activity)	1760.2	2084
	26.4◄16.8◄8.6►7.2►14.0►21.6 water south of shelter on AT		
430.2	Watauga Dam, AT on road for 0.4 mile south and north of dam,	1759.0	1915
	sparsely blazed.		
431.5	Wilbur Dam Rd N36 19.726 W82 6.690 P	1757.7	2250
434.5	Spring	1754.7	3400
436.2	**Vandeventer Shelter,** views	1753.0	3579
	24.0◄15.8◄7.2►6.8►14.4►22.7		
	Water 0.3 mile down steep blue-blazed trail 0.1S of shelter.		
440.0	Campsite 0.1N, stream 100 yards east	1749.2	3867
441.3	Turkeypen Gap	1747.9	3973
442.2	Powerline	1747.0	4085
442.8	Spring	1746.4	4000
443.0	**Iron Mountain Shelter,** spring 0.3S on AT	1746.2	4118
	22.6◄14.0◄6.8►7.6►15.9►35.6		
444.3	Nick Grindstaff Monument	1744.9	4090

SoBo NoBo

45
TN

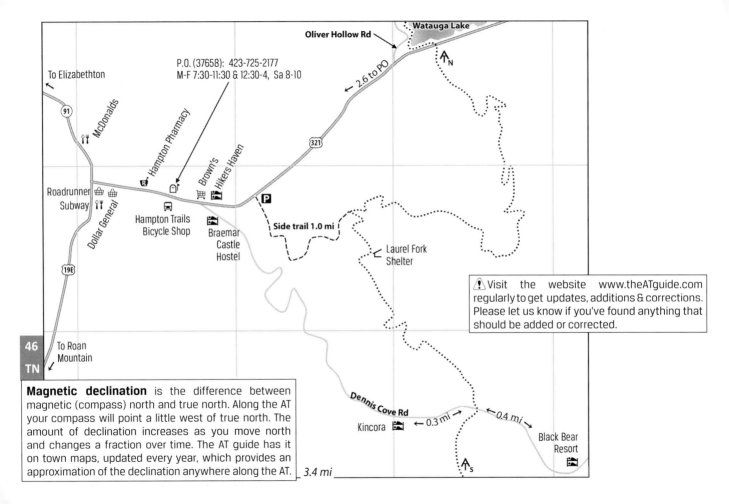

Watauga Lake

Oliver Hollow Rd

N

To Elizabethton

P.O. (37658): 423-725-2177
M-F 7:30-11:30 & 12:30-4, Sa 8-10

91

McDonalds

← 2.6 to PO

321

Hampton Pharmacy

Brown's Hikers Haven

Roadrunner
Subway

Dollar General

Hampton Trails
Bicycle Shop

P

Side trail 1.0 mi

Braemar
Castle
Hostel

Laurel Fork
Shelter

⚠ Visit the website www.theATguide.com
regularly to get updates, additions & corrections.
Please let us know if you've found anything that
should be added or corrected.

19E

46
TN

To Roan
Mountain

Dennis Cove Rd

← 0.3 mi →

0.4 mi →

Kincora

Magnetic declination is the difference between
magnetic (compass) north and true north. Along the AT
your compass will point a little west of true north. The
amount of declination increases as you move north
and changes a fraction over time. The AT guide has it
on town maps, updated every year, which provides an
approximation of the declination anywhere along the AT.

Black Bear
Resort

N
S

3.4 mi

418.5   Dennis Cove Rd, USFS 50

🏕️⬥☗⛺🚌✉ (0.3W) **Kincora Hiking Hostel** 423.725.4409 Cooking facilities, laundry, $5 per night suggested donation. No dogs, 3 night limit. Coleman/alcohol/oz. Long-time owner Bob Peoples is very active in trail maintenance; if you have interest in working on the trail, ask about opportunities. Maildrops (non-guest fee $5): 1278 Dennis Cove Rd, Hampton, TN 37658.

🏕️⬥☗🏪⛺🖥️✉ (0.4E) **Black Bear Resort** 423.725.5988 ⟨www.blackbearresorttn.com⟩ Clean and spacious creekside resort with bunkroom $18, upper bunkroom $25, tenting $10PP. Four-person cabin $45/$60, $18EAP, 6-person max. Courtesy phone, computer, movies (DVD) and free morning coffee for all guests. Camp store with long-term resupply items (freeze-dried meals), snacks, sodas, ice cream and food that can be prepared on-site with microwave or stove. Laundry $4. Fuel/oz & canister fuel. Pet friendly, accepts credit cards. Long and short distance shuttles. Parking free for section-hiking guests, $2/night for non-guests. Maildrops (non-guest fee $5): 1511 Dennis Cove Rd, Hampton, TN 37658.

421.2   Side trail to Hampton (1.0W)
427.1   US 321 (2.6W to Hampton)
         Hampton, TN

🏪🏕️⬥🚌📞 **Brown's Grocery & Braemar Castle Hostel** 423.725.2411, 423.725.2262. Both operated by Sutton Brown; check in at grocery to stay at the hostel or for shuttles. Store open M-Sa 8-6, closed Sunday.

🚲 **Hampton Trails Bicycle Shop** 423.725.5000 ⟨www.hamptontrails.com⟩ hamptontrails@embarqmail.com.

         Elizabethton, TN (services 5 mi. north of Hampton)
🏨🛜🖥️✉ **Americourt** 423.542.4466 $59.95 plus tax, up to 4 in room, includes hot breakfast. Pets $20. Not available on race weekends. Maildrops: 1515 Hwy 19 East, Elizabethton,TN 37643.

🍴 **Little Caesars, Arbys, Lone Star Steakhouse**

🛒 **Food City, Big Lots**
🎦 **State Line Drive-in** 423.542.5422 Showings F, Sa & Su
         Bulter, TN

🏨⛺🚌🛜🖥️✉ **Iron Mountain Inn** 423.768.2446 ⟨www.creeksidechalet.net⟩ 10 miles from Hampton, but you can call for pickup or for directions. Fee for pickup/return. B&B room includes breakfast for $100S/$150D. Log cabin with hot tub under the stars, $50PP no breakfast. Free laundry. Shuttles from Watauga Lake to Damascus. Maildrops: c/o Woods, 268 Moreland Dr, Butler, TN 37640.

447.6   TN 91 2.0E to Wallace Road (campground), and 4.5E to *Shady Valley* (listings below).

🏕️⬥ ⛺ (2.5E) **Switchback Creek Campground** 407.484.3388 2.0E to Wallace Rd, then turn right 0.5 mi to 570 Wallace Rd, Shady Valley, TN 37688. 2-person cabin $40, campsite $12+tax. Showers, laundry, call for ride.

454.1   Low Gap, US 421
         Shady Valley, TN 37688 (2.7E)
📮 M-F 8-12, Sa 8-10, 423.739.2173

🏪🍴 **Shady Valley Country Store & Deli** M-Sa 6am-9pm. Short term resupply, Coleman fuel. Deli serves burgers and sandwiches.
🍴 **Raceway Restaurant** Open 7am-8pm all days except W (7am-2pm) & Su (8am-2pm).

Water Sources

Be aware of trail conditions before heading out, and tune in to advice from outfitters and other hikers. The trail gets re-routed, springs dry up, streams alter their course. Be prepared to deal with changes, particularly with respect to water sources. Never plan to carry just enough water to reach the next spring.

Elevation profile — TN, page 48

SoBo	NoBo	Description	Elev
1742.4	446.8	Footbridge, stream, bog bridges north of stream.	3598
1742.1	447.1	Roadbed.	3601
1741.6	447.6	TN 91. N36 28.883 W81 57.619 🅿 (pg.47)	3525
		Shady Valley, TN (3.5E) South end of handicap-accessible trail.	
1740.8	448.4	North end of handicap-accessible trail.	3625
1738.6	450.6	**Double Springs Shelter** (6)	4225
		21.6◄14.4◄7.6◄▶8.3▶28.0▶34.3 Spring 80 yards left of shelter. Rich Knob to south, Holston Mtn Trail to north.	
1737.0	452.2	Locust Knob.	3624
1735.1	454.1	Low Gap, US 421 N36 32.316 W81 56.933 🅿 (pg.47) Piped spring on south side of road. **Shady Valley, TN** (2.7E)	3384
1733.7	455.5	Low stone wall on east side of AT	3575
1733.2	456.0	Double Spring Gap, campsite	3550
1732.8	456.4	Weak, muddy spring east side of AT.	3666
1731.8	457.4	McQueens Knob, disused shelter 0.1N.	3900
1731.4	457.8	McQueens Gap, USFS 69 N36 34.460 W81 55.921 🅿	3680
1730.3	458.9	**Abingdon Gap Shelter** (5)	3798
		22.7◄15.9◄8.3◄▶19.7▶26.0▶38.4 Piped spring 0.2 mile behind shelter on blue-blazed trail.	
1726.3	462.9	Unnamed gap.	3731
1725.2	464.0	Backbone Rock Trail leads 2.3E to USFS recreation area.	3553
1723.8	465.4	**TN-VA** border.	3302

SoBo	NoBo	Description	Elev
1722.2	467.0	Campsite, Spring 0.1E on blue-blazed trail	2825
1720.4	468.8	**Damascus, VA** (south). N36 38.162 W81 47.378 P (pg.50-51) Water St, welcome sign.	1975
1719.9	469.3	**Damascus, VA** (Laurel and Shady) (pg.50-51)	1962
1719.0	470.2	**Damascus, VA** (north). (pg.50-51) US 58, AT follows Virginia Creeper Trail for 0.4 mile.	2019
1718.5	470.7	Campsite to west	2388
1718.1	471.1	Spring	2548
1716.6	472.6	Iron Mountain Trail to west.	2933
1715.1	474.1	Beech Grove Gap Trail to west, streams and footbridges in area	2313
1714.6	474.6	Feathercamp Trail to west, stream, campsite.	2236
1714.5	474.7	US 58, Feathercamp Branch N36 38.694 W81 44.197 P	2200
1714.1	475.1	Stream.	2179
1713.7	475.5	Stream.	2206
1712.9	476.3	Footbridge, campsite.	2299
1712.2	477.0	Taylors Valley Trail	2429
1710.6	478.6	**Saunders Shelter** (0.2W) 35.6◄28.0◄19.7◄▶6.3▶18.7▶23.9. ⌐(8) Reliable spring on right behind shelter and down road.	3378
1710.2	479.0	North shelter side trail	3354
1708.3	480.9	Beartree Gap Trail, 3.0W to Beartree Recreation Area	3050
1708.2	481.0	Pond, campsite.	3012
1707.6	481.6	Stream.	2978
1707.2	482.0	Footbridge, stream	2909
1706.7	482.5	AT + Creeper Trail (south end)	2695
1706.0	483.2	Luther Hassinger Memorial Bridge, AT + Creeper Trail (north end), VA 728. N36 38.965 W81 40.345 P	2786
1705.7	483.5	Stream.	2829
1705.4	483.8	VA 859, Grassy Creek Rd (gravel)	2954
1705.3	483.9	Streams	3043
1704.3	484.9	**Lost Mountain Shelter** 34.3◄26.0◄6.3◄▶12.4▶17.6▶23.6 Water source on trail to left of shelter. ⌐(8)	3399
1703.2	486.0	US 58, footbridge, stream N36 38.389 W81 39.926 P	3160
1702.9	486.3	Stream, campsite	3253

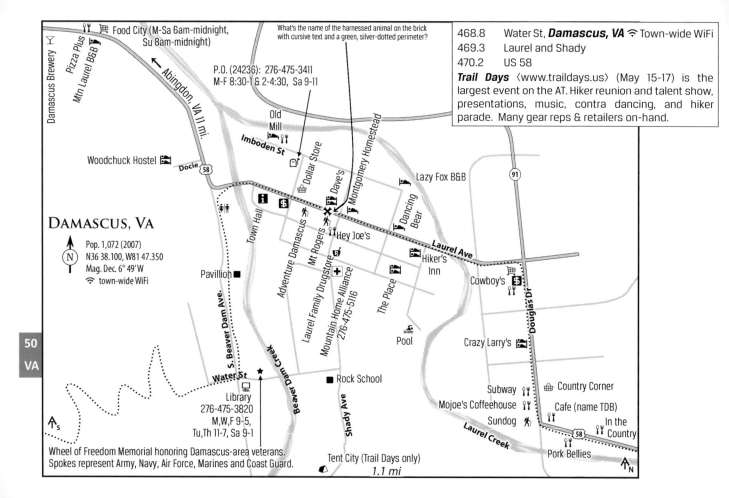

Food City (M-Sa 6am-midnight, Su 8am-midnight)

Damascus Brewery

Pizza Plus

Mtn Laurel B&B

Abingdon, VA 11 mi.

What's the name of the harnessed animal on the brick with cursive text and a green, silver-dotted perimeter?

P.O. (24236): 276-475-3411
M-F 8:30-1 & 2-4:30, Sa 9-11

Old Mill

Imboden St

Woodchuck Hostel

Docie

58

Dollar Store

Dave's

Montgomery Homestead

Lazy Fox B&B

91

DAMASCUS, VA

N

Pop. 1,072 (2007)
N36 38.100, W81 47.350
Mag. Dec. 6° 49'W
town-wide WiFi

Town Hall

Adventure Damascus

Mt Rogers

Hey Joe's

Dancing Bear

Laurel Ave

Hiker's Inn

Cowboy's

Pavillion

Laurel Family Drugstore

Mountain Home Alliance
276-475-5116

The Place

Crazy Larry's

Douglas Dr

S. Beaver Dam Ave.

Beaver Dam Creek

Pool

Water St

Library
276-475-3820
M,W,F 9-5,
Tu,Th 11-7, Sa 9-1

Shady Ave

Rock School

Subway

Mojoe's Coffeehouse

Sundog

Country Corner

Cafe (name TDB)

In the Country

Laurel Creek

58

Pork Bellies

N

Wheel of Freedom Memorial honoring Damascus-area veterans.
Spokes represent Army, Navy, Air Force, Marines and Coast Guard.

Tent City (Trail Days only)
1.1 mi

468.8	Water St, *Damascus, VA* 📶 Town-wide WiFi
469.3	Laurel and Shady
470.2	US 58

Trail Days ⟨www.traildays.us⟩ (May 15-17) is the largest event on the AT. Hiker reunion and talent show, presentations, music, contra dancing, and hiker parade. Many gear reps & retailers on-hand.

Dave's Place $20 per room per night for 1 or 2 persons, maximum stay 2 nights. All rooms private. Shower without stay $3. No alcohol, no pets, no smoking. Check in at Mount Rogers Outfitters.

Hikers Inn 276.475.3788, $25 bunks, hostel private room $50. Rooms in house $75; $65/night for multi-night stays, tax included. Guest laundry $5. Run by Lee and Paul (2010 thru-hiker "Skink"). A/C in all rooms. Smoking outside, dogs allowed in hostel, cash or check. Closed in winter.

The Place 276.475.3441 Methodist Church-run bunkrooms, tenting, pavilion, showers with towel & soap. Suggested donation $7. Seasonal caretaker, please help to keep the bunkroom clean. No pets, alcohol or smoking anywhere on the premises 2 night max unless sick/injured. Open late Mar until mid-to-late Nov. No vehicle-assisted hikers (except during Trail Days).

Crazy Larry's 276.274.3637 Hostel $20, tenting $10, Shower & morning coffee included with stay, hostel has A/C & heat. Breakfast $7, Laundry $5. No drinking or drugs. Shuttles for a fee. Maildrops: 209 Douglas Drive, Damascus, VA 24236.

Woodchuck Hostel 406.407.1272. Open Mar 15 - Nov 1. Bed w/linens $25.00. One private cabin $45.00S $55.00D. Teepee $20.00. Tent or hammock $10.00. Breakfast w/ stay. Laundry $5.00. Shower without stay $3.00. Kitchen privileges, common area, large yard, pavilion with gas grill. Dogs welcome. Alcohol/oz, cold drinks and snacks available. Free shuttles to Food City, other shuttles by arrangement. No drugs or Alcohol. Maildrops: P.O.Box 752, Damascus Va. 24236.

Montgomery Homestead Inn 276.492.6283 $70/up. No smoking, no alcohol, no pets. Guest only maildrops: (USPS) PO Box 12, (FedEx/UPS) 103 E. Laurel Ave, Damascus, VA 24236.

Dancing Bear B&B 423.571.1830, $65-$140+tax. Includes bfast. Maildrops: PO Box 252, 203 E Laurel Ave, Damascus, VA 24236.

Lazy Fox B&B 276.475.5838 $75/up includes tax & breakfast. No pets. Guest maildrops: PO Box 757, 133 Imboden St, Damascus, VA 24236.

Mountain Laurel B&B 276.475.5956

Appalachian Folk School 423.341.1843 ⟨www.warrendoyle. com⟩ Non-profit run by Warren Doyle offers work-for-stay weeknights (M-Th) only (2-3 hrs/night) for all hikers who have a spiritual/poetic connection to the trail. Open Mar-Apr and Oct-Dec. Kitchen privileges, shower, wireless, laundry and rides to/from the AT between Rt. 321 (Hampton) and VA 603 (Fox Creek).

Food City (0.5W on US 58) 276.475.3653, 7 days.

Mt. Rogers Outfitters 276.475.5416 ⟨www.mtrogersoutfitters.com⟩ Full service backpacking store, fuel/oz. Shuttle service for the Appalachian Trail, parking for section hikers $2/day. Shower only $3. Maildrops: PO Box 546, 110 W Laurel Ave, Damascus, VA 24236.

Adventure Damascus ⟨www.AdventureDamascus. com⟩ 888.595.2453 or 276.475.6262 Catering to thru-hikers with backpacking gear, hiker foods, alcohol/Coleman/oz, other fuels, bike rentals, shuttles to area trailheads by arrangement, $2 showers ($4 includes a towel), open 7 days year-round. USPS and UPS Maildrops: PO Box 1113, 128 W. Laurel Ave. Damascus, VA 24236.

Sundog Outfitter 276.475.6252 ⟨www.sundogoutfitter.com⟩ Backpacking gear and clothing, repairs, hiker food, Coleman/alcohol/oz, other fuels, shuttles to area trailheads by arrangement, open 7 days a week. Maildrops: PO Box 1113 or 331 Douglas Dr, Damascus, VA 24236.

Library 276.475.3820, M,W,F 9-5, T,Th 11-7, Sa 9-1, internet 1 hr.

Gypsy Dave Shuttles 276.492.0873, dstinnard@yahoo.com

499.8   **Grayson Highlands State Park**

276.579.7092 Blue-blazed trail (0.5E) to parking; campground 1.5 mi. farther east on road. Park closed in cold weather; call ahead if possible. Camp store with courtesy phone, tent site w/ shower $21, shower only $5. May 1 - mid Oct.

SoBo	NoBo	Description	Elev
1702.4	486.8	Spring	3397
1702.2	487.0	Fence stile	3504
1701.9	487.3	VA 601, Beech Mountain Rd N36 38.235 W81 38.425 P	3600
1701.4	487.8	Spring; Fence stile, 50 yards north of road is sign for spring to west.	3769
1699.4	489.8	Buzzard Rock, Side trail west to Whitetop Mtn Rd, summit of Whitetop Mountain..	5080
1698.6	490.6	Piped spring on east side of trail	5136
1698.5	490.7	Whitetop Mtn Rd, USFS 89 N36 37.921 W81 36.112 P; Campsites just after road.	5150
1697.8	491.4	Stream.	5235
1696.1	493.1	VA 600, Elk Garden, views, spring south on AT N36 38.769 W81 34.992 P	4511
1695.8	493.4	View, bench to west	4644
1695.5	493.7	Fence, enter Lewis Fork Wilderness	4734
1694.0	495.2	Deep Gap, spring 0.1 south and north	5076
1693.0	496.2	Brier Ridge	5276
1692.6	496.6	Spring	5252
1692.1	497.1	Side trail 0.5W to Mt Rogers, Virginia's highest peak at 5,729 ft.	5490
1691.9	497.3	Thomas Knob Shelter 38.4◄18.7◄12.4◄▶5.2▶11.2▶15.4.	5430
1691.6	497.6	Campsite	5415
1690.9	498.3	Rhododendron Gap, Pine Mountain Trail to west	5415
1690.4	498.8	Wilburn Ridge Trail 0.1E to rock outcropping, view	5465
1690.1	499.1	Fatman Squeeze (rock tunnel).	5373
1689.4	499.8	Grayson Highlands State Park (south end), fence; Horse trail crosses AT. No tenting in GHSP. (pg.51)	5017
1688.1	501.1	Massie Gap, 0.2E to parking area	4909
1687.5	501.7	GHSP boundary, two fence stiles	4616
1686.9	502.3	Stream.	4447
1686.7	502.5	Wise Shelter 23.9◄17.6◄5.2◄▶6.0▶10.2▶19.2	4429
1686.6	502.6	East fork of Big Wilson Creek, footbridge, stream, fence stile; Grayson Highlands State Park (north end)	4410
1686.2	503.0	Horse trail.	4374
1684.7	504.5	Bearpen Trail	4666
1684.1	505.1	Stone Mountain, views	4820
1683.5	505.7	The Scales livestock corral. N36 40.182 W81 29.229 P; First Peak Trail to east, Crest Trail to west.	4667

SoBo	NoBo	Description	Elev
1682.3	506.9	Fence stiles, Pine Mountain Trail to west	5000
1681.0	508.2	Spring	4269
1680.7	508.5	**Old Orchard Shelter** 23.6◄11.2◄6.0◄►4.2►13.2►23.0	4084 (6)
		Water 100 yards on blue-blazed trail to right. Privy 50 yards behind shelter.	
1679.9	509.3	Old Orchard Trail	3791
1679.0	510.2	Fox Creek, VA 603 .... N36 41.795 W81 30.398 P	3480
		Footbridges and streams 0.1 to north and to south.	
		100 yards east to parking and porta-potty.	
1677.4	511.8	Chestnut Flats, Iron Mountain Trail to west	4240
1676.5	512.7	**Hurricane Mtn Shelter** (0.1W)	3810 (8)
		15.4◄10.2◄4.2◄►9.0►18.8►25.5 Creek and tentsites opposite side of trail.	
1675.9	513.3	Hurricane Creek Trail 0.3W to USFS 84, AT to east	3469
1675.4	513.8	Spring	3160
1674.7	514.5	Powerline, stream just north on AT	3222
1674.2	515.0	Stream	3016
1673.7	515.5	Stream	2978
1673.4	515.8	Dickey Gap Trail to **USFS Hurricane Creek Campground** (0.7W)	2947
		276.783.5196 Tent site $16, shower $3. Open mid Apr-Oct.	
		Restroom & shower open Memorial Day-Labor Day.	
1672.6	516.6	Comers Creek (drinking not advised), footbridge, cascades.	3317
1671.4	517.8	Dickey Gap, AT crosses VA 650 (gravel), east 50 yards to (pg.56)	3300
		VA 16 (paved Sugar Grove Hwy), **Troutdale, VA**, 2.6 south on VA 16	
1670.6	518.6	Horse trail.	3485
1669.9	519.3	Campsite and spring on blue-blazed trail (0.2E).	3750
1667.5	521.7	**Trimpi Shelter** (0.1E)	3029 (8)
		19.2◄13.2◄9.0◄►9.8►16.5►35.4	
1666.7	522.5	Fence stiles 0.2 apart, cattle graze in area, close gates behind you	2741
1666.3	522.9	VA 672 (gravel)	2700
1665.4	523.8	VA 670, South Fork Holston River .... N36 45.784 W81 29.634 P	2450
1664.4	524.8	Stream, intermittent	2603
1663.9	525.3	Campsite on west side of trail.	2862

This is page 54 of the trail guide, showing an elevation profile for Virginia (VA).

SoBo	NoBo	Feature	Elev
1661.5	527.7	VA 601 (gravel), limited parking N36 47.963 W81 27.448 🅿	3274
1660.0	529.2	Powerline	3330
1659.1	530.1	Footbridge, stream ●	3020
1657.7	531.5	**Partnership Shelter,** showers, tenting not allowed near shelter. ♪ ☂ ☍(16) Can call for pizza from Visitor Center.	3260
1657.6	531.6	VA 16, Mt Rogers Visitor Center N36 48.682 W81 25.224 🅿 (pg.56-57)	3220
		Sugar Grove, VA, 24375 (3.2E), **Marion, VA** 24354 (5.9W) 23.0◀18.8◀9.8◀▶6.7▶25.6▶35.0	
1656.9	532.3	VA 622	3270
1653.8	535.4	USFS 86, Glade Mountain Rd N36 50.089 W81 22.246 🅿	3650
		Private road, permission required, may not be suitable for passenger cars.	
1652.5	536.7	Glade Mountain	4120
1651.5	537.7	Spring ●	3532
1651.2	538.0	Stream ●	3316
1651.0	538.2	**Chatfield Shelter** 25.5◀16.5◀6.7◀▶18.9▶28.3▶38.9 ☍(6)	3200
1650.7	538.5	USFS 644 (dirt), streams to north and south ●	3070
1650.4	538.8	Footbridge, stream ●	2959
1650.1	539.1	Stream. ●	2817
1649.4	539.4	Two powerlines	2742
1649.2	540.0	VA 615, Lindamood School N36 52.246 W81 21.461 🅿	2650
		Settlers Museum 0.1E (276.686.4401), parking available at farm. (Apr 1-Nov 15)	
1648.7	540.5	VA 729	2571
1647.9	541.3	Fence stile	2727
1647.3	541.9	Middle Fork of the Holston River, footbridge ●	2451
1646.5	542.7	VA 683, US 11, I-81, **Atkins, VA** (pg.57)	2420
1646.1	543.1	I-81 underpass	2422
1645.2	544.0	VA 617, Davis Cemetery N36 53.840 W81 22.146 🅿	2448
1644.6	544.6	Fence stile, end of field ●	2564
1644.4	544.8	Blue-blazed trail 0.1E to water at Davis Hollow ●	2540
1643.2	546.0	Davis Path campsite and privy. ●	2876

54
VA

SoBo	NoBo	Feature	Elev
1641.1	**548.1**	Little Brushy Mountain	3300
1640.7	**548.5**	Virginia Horse Trail	3190
1640.0	**549.2**	Crawfish Trail to east, campsite and stream on AT south of here	2600
1639.0	**550.2**	Stream.	3071
1638.4	**550.8**	Spring	3402
1638.2	**551.0**	Tilson Gap, crest of Walker Mtn	3500
1637.4	**551.8**	Spring, fence	2984
1636.7	**552.5**	VA 610, fence stiles here and to south.	2700
1635.9	**553.3**	Fence stile	2772
1635.3	**553.9**	VA 742, Holston River Bridge	2484
1634.8	**554.4**	Stream.	2522
1634.3	**554.9**	VA 42, O'Lystery Pavilion (private, do not use) N36 58.995 W81 24.385 P Campsite just north of trail to parking area.	2543
1633.3	**555.9**	Brushy Mountain	3200
1632.1	**557.1**	**Knot Maul Branch Shelter**, water 0.1N on AT 35.4◄25.6◄18.9▼9.4▶20.0▶35.3	2761
1631.4	**557.8**	Footbridge, stream	2614
1630.7	**558.5**	Lynn Camp Creek, footbridge, campsite	2400
1629.6	**559.6**	Lynn Camp Mountain	3024
1628.4	**560.8**	Lick Creek, footbridge	2270
1627.4	**561.8**	Stream.	2321
1627.2	**562.0**	VA 625, USFS 222 (gravel) N37 1.358 W81 25.569 P	2333
1626.0	**563.2**	Stream.	3106
1624.8	**564.4**	Chestnut Ridge, south end, start of clearing	3793
1624.5	**564.7**	Pond, spring at north end, best water source for Chestnut Knob Shelter.	3908
1623.7	**565.5**	Views from open ridgeline	4194
1622.8	**566.4**	Spring 0.1E on unmarked roadbed	4334
1622.7	**566.5**	**Chestnut Knob Shelter** 35.0◄28.3◄9.4▶10.6▶25.9▶35.6 Concrete block shelter, fully enclosed with door.	4410

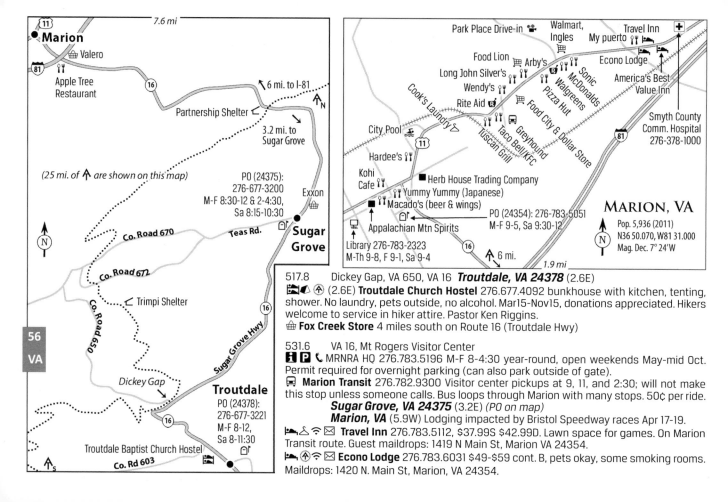

Marion 🛣11

🛣81

7.6 mi

⚑ Valero

Apple Tree Restaurant

🛣16

↑ 6 mi. to I-81

Partnership Shelter

↗N

3.2 mi. to Sugar Grove

(25 mi. of 🗡 are shown on this map)

PO (24375): 276-677-3200 M-F 8:30-12 & 2-4:30, Sa 8:15-10:30

Exxon

Co. Road 670

Teas Rd.

Sugar Grove

Co. Road 672

Trimpi Shelter

Co. Road 650

Dickey Gap

🛣16

Sugar Grove Hwy

Troutdale

PO (24378): 276-677-3221 M-F 8-12, Sa 8-11:30

Troutdale Baptist Church Hostel

Co. Rd 603

🗡s

56 VA

Park Place Drive-in

Walmart, Ingles

Travel Inn ⊞

My puerto 🍴🛏

Food Lion ⊞ Arby's 🍴🍴

Econo Lodge 🛏

Long John Silver's 🍴 Sonic McDonalds

Wendy's 🍴 Walgreens

Rite Aid 💊 Pizza Hut

America's Best Value Inn

Cook's Laundry

Food City & Dollar Store

City Pool 🏊

🛣11

Taco Bell/KFC

Tuscan Grill

Greyhound 🚌

🛣81

Smyth County Comm. Hospital 276-378-1000

Hardee's 🍴

Kohi Cafe 🍴

▪ Herb House Trading Company

🍴 Yummy Yummy (Japanese)

▪ Macado's (beer & wings)

PO (24354): 276-783-5051 M-F 9-5, Sa 9:30-12

Appalachian Mtn Spirits

🖥 Library 276-783-2323 M-Th 9-8, F 9-1, Sa 9-4

🛣16

↑ 6 mi.

MARION, VA

Ⓝ Pop. 5,936 (2011) N36 50.070, W81 31.000 Mag. Dec. 7° 24'W

1.9 mi

517.8   Dickey Gap, VA 650, VA 16 ***Troutdale, VA 24378*** (2.6E)

🏕🔌🚿 (2.6E) **Troutdale Church Hostel** 276.677.4092 bunkhouse with kitchen, tenting, shower. No laundry, pets outside, no alcohol. Mar15-Nov15, donations appreciated. Hikers welcome to service in hiker attire. Pastor Ken Riggins.

⚑ **Fox Creek Store** 4 miles south on Route 16 (Troutdale Hwy)

531.6   VA 16, Mt Rogers Visitor Center

🚻 🅿 📞 MRNRA HQ 276.783.5196 M-F 8-4:30 year-round, open weekends May-mid Oct. Permit required for overnight parking (can also park outside of gate).

🚌 **Marion Transit** 276.782.9300 Visitor center pickups at 9, 11, and 2:30; will not make this stop unless someone calls. Bus loops through Marion with many stops. 50¢ per ride.

Sugar Grove, VA 24375 (3.2E) *(PO on map)*

Marion, VA (5.9W) Lodging impacted by Bristol Speedway races Apr 17-19.

🛏🏕📶✉ **Travel Inn** 276.783.5112, $37.99S $42.99D. Lawn space for games. On Marion Transit route. Guest maildrops: 1419 N Main St, Marion VA 24354.

🛏🐾📶✉ **Econo Lodge** 276.783.6031 $49-$59 cont. B, pets okay, some smoking rooms. Maildrops: 1420 N. Main St, Marion, VA 24354.

🛏🛜 **America's Best Value Inn** 276.378.0481

🍴🛜🖥✉ **Kohi Cafe** Coffee, deli, computer w/printer. Open 7am-6pm. Maildrops: 201 E Main St Suite 102, Marion, VA 24354

■🛜 **Herb House Trading Co.** 276.356.9832 Mural on side of building. Welcomes hikers. Ice cream and local baked goods.

■ **Appalachian Mtn Spirits** Has denatured alcohol.

🚌 **Greyhound** 276.783.7114 weekdays only, four buses/day.

🍦 **Park Place Drive-In** 276.781.2222 Walk-ins welcome. Also has mini-golf, arcade, and ice cream shop.

542.7 VA 683, US 11, I-81 *Atkins, VA 24311* AT intersects with US 11 between Atkins & Rural Retreat in the township of Groseclose.

🛏⛺🚌🅿🛜✉ **Relax Inn** 276.783.5811 $40S $45D, $5EAP, pets $10. Parking $3/day. Call for shuttle availability. Maildrops for guests, limit 2 boxes) Relax Inn, 7253 Lee Hwy, Rural Retreat, VA 24368.

🍴🅿✉ **The Barn Restaurant** 276.686.6222 16oz hiker burger, Sunday buffet 11-2, parking for section hikers. Maildrops: 7412 Lee Highway Rural Retreat, VA 24368.

🏪💲 **Shell Convenience Store** 24hr, ATM inside.

■ **Rambunny & Aqua** 276.783.3754 Shuttle referrals & other help.

🚌 **Skip** 276-783-3604 By appt, covers Damascus to Pearisburg.

🛏🛜🖥✉ **Comfort Inn** (3.7W) 276.783.2144 Get hotel discount book coupon at Exxon or ask for hiker rate, usually $65. Cont. breakfast. Maildrops: 5558 Lee Hwy, Atkins, VA 24311.

582.3 VA 615, Laurel Creek

🏠◀ **Fort Bastian** 708.207.6725 Nigel "TruBrit" offers $10 bunk or tent, pickup/return & breakfast. Open all year, call after Jenkins Shelter.

590.1 US 52, North Scenic Hwy, *Bland, VA 24315* (3E to PO or Citgo, 4E to hotel & restaurants)

🏤 M-F 8:30-11:30 & 12-4, Sa 9 -11, 276.688.3751

🛏🛜✉ **Big Walker Motel** 276.688.3331 $57.89 (1 or 2), 62.18 (3 or 4), pets okay. Fridge & microwave in all rooms. Guest maildrops: 70 Skyview Lane, Bland, VA 24315.

🍴 **Subway, Dairy Queen**

🛒 **Grants Supermarket** (planned for 2015 at 615 Main St)

🏪🍴📞💲 **Citgo, Bland Square Grill** 276.688.3851 Open 6:30-7 year-round. Groceries, Canister fuel and Heet, Grill serves B/L/D.

🏪 **Dollar General**

➕ **Bland Family Clinic** 276.688.0500 M 10-6, Tu 11-7, Th 9-5, F 10-2.

🖥 **Bland County Library** 276.688.3737 M,W,F,Sa 10-4:30, T,Th 10-7:30, 697 Main Street.

🚌 **Bubba's Shuttles** 276.266.6147 barnes.james43@yahoo.com Shuttles from Damascus to Pearisburg & Roanoke Airport.

Bastian, VA 24314 (3W)

🏤 M-F 8-12, Sa 9:15-11:15, 276.688.4631

🍴 **Pizza Plus** 276.688.3332 Su-Th 11am-9pm, F-Sa 11am-10pm.

🏪💲 **Kangaroo Express** ATM

💊 **Bland Pharmacy** 276.688.4204 M,W,F 9-5, Tu,Th 9-5, Sa 9-12.

➕ **Medical Clinic** 276.688.4331 M,W 8:30-6, Tu,Th 8:30-8, F 8:30-5

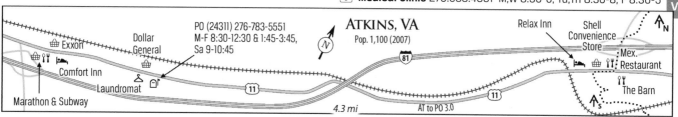

ATKINS, VA
Pop. 1,100 (2007)

Exxon

Dollar General

PO (24311) 276-783-5551
M-F 8:30-12:30 & 1:45-3:45,
Sa 9-10:45

Comfort Inn

Laundromat

Marathon & Subway

Relax Inn

Shell Convenience Store

Mex. Restaurant

The Barn

4.3 mi   AT to PO 3.0

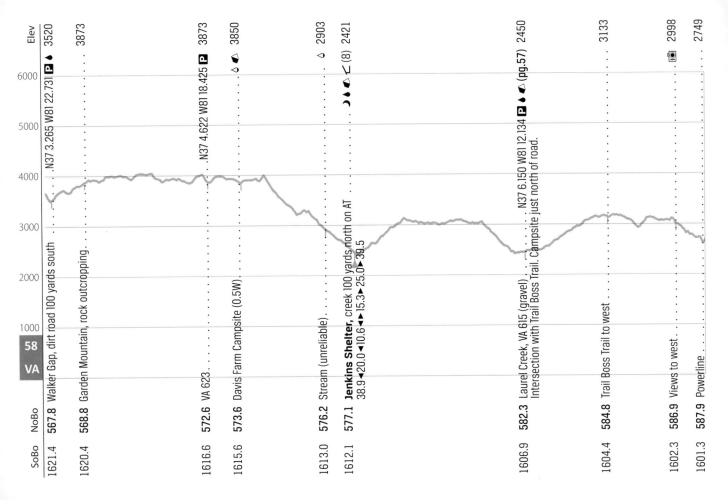

Elev

N37 3.265 W81 22.731 🅿 ♦	3520	
	3873	
N37 4.622 W81 18.425 🅿	3873	
◁ ◀	3850	
◁	2903	
☾ ♦ ◀ ⊏ (8)	2421	
N37 6.150 W81 12.134 🅿 ♦ ◀ (pg.57)	2450	
	3133	
📷	2998	
	2749	

SoBo	NoBo	
1621.4	**567.8**	Walker Gap, dirt road 100 yards south
1620.4	**568.8**	Garden Mountain, rock outcropping.
1616.6	**572.6**	VA 623.
1615.6	**573.6**	Davis Farm Campsite (0.5W)
1613.0	**576.2**	Stream (unreliable).
1612.1	**577.1**	**Jenkins Shelter,** creek 100 yards north on AT 38.9◀20.0◀10.6◀▶15.3▶25.0▶39.5
1606.9	**582.3**	Laurel Creek, VA 615 (gravel) Intersection with Trail Boss Trail. Campsite just north of road.
1604.4	**584.8**	Trail Boss Trail to west
1602.3	**586.9**	Views to west
1601.3	**587.9**	Powerline

SoBo	NoBo		Elev
1599.7	**589.5**	AT on gravel road from here north to US 52.	3101
1599.1	**590.1**	US 52 (North Scenic Hwy), **Bland, VA** (2.5E), **Bastian, VA** (3W) ..... (pg.57)	2928
1598.2	**591.0**	North end of VA 612, road walk over I-77. ..... N37 8.335 W81 7.595 **P** ♦	2620
		Water near where the AT enters woods north of road.	
1596.8	**592.4**	**Helveys Mill Shelter** (0.3E) ..... ☾ ⊏ (6)	3139
		35.3◄25.9◄15.3▼9.7►24.2►33.7	
		Water source 0.3 mile down switch-backed trail in front of shelter.	

✽ **Mountain Laurel** – Shrub similar to the rhododendron. Grows five to ten feet high and blossoms with abundant cup-shaped white flowers.

SoBo	NoBo		Elev
1590.2	**599.0**	VA 611 (gravel) ..... N37 8.7155 W81 0.561 **P** ♦	2820
1589.9	**599.3**	Stream, unreliable ◊	2685
1588.8	**600.4**	Brushy Mountain	3101
1587.1	**602.1**	**Jenny Knob Shelter,** spring near shelter ☾♦ ⊏ (6)	2684
		35.6◄25.0◄9.7▼14.5►24.0►39.7	
1586.4	**602.8**	Stream ♦	2333
1586.1	**603.1**	Stream, campsite ♦⛺	2270
1585.9	**603.3**	Lickskillet Hollow, VA 608, footbridge ..... N37 9.415 W80 57.682 **P**	2200
1584.7	**604.5**	Powerline	2775

SoBo	NoBo	Description	Elev
1580.7	608.5	Kimberling Creek, suspension bridge	2090
1580.6	608.6	VA 606, parking to east . . . N37 10.544 W80 54.500 P (pg.62) **Trent's Grocery** (0.5W), **Nature Way** (3.6E)	2105
1578.8	610.4	Dismal Falls Trail, 0.3W to waterfall, camping on side trail.	2399
1578.4	610.8	Road on other side of falls sometimes brings visitors by car. Stream, campsite.	2326
1577.6	611.6	Footbridge	2369
1577.1	612.1	Footbridge	2410
1576.9	612.3	Footbridge, stream	2434
1576.6	612.6	Two streams	2497
1576.0	613.2	Woods road	2620
1575.5	613.7	Streams	2562
1575.1	614.1	Footbridge, stream (2)	2485
1574.9	614.5	Dismal Creek, gravel road, campsite, footbridge to north	2478
1574.7	614.7	Ribble Trail 3.0W connects with AT near Big Horse Gap	2483
1574.1	615.1	Center of one-mile stretch with at least 6 stream crossings by footbridge.	2505
1573.4	615.8	Clearing, side trail to west	2536
1573.2	616.0	Footbridge, stream (2)	2538
1572.8	616.4	Dirt road	2600
1572.6	616.6	**Wapiti Shelter** (0.1E) 39.5◄24.2◄14.5◄▶9.5▶25.2▶37.8 ☾ ⊏ (5)	2622
1572.4	616.8	Stream.	2668
1572.0	617.2	Stream.	2823
1571.3	617.9	Spring	3359
1570.0	619.2	View	3899
1567.7	621.5	Side trail 0.1E to radio tower, views from ledge in front of tower	4023
1567.1	622.1	Ribble Trail west, wide grassy path, reconnects with AT south of Wapiti Shelter.	3800
1567.0	622.2	Big Horse Gap, USFS 103 ⚠ Sometimes confused with Sugar Run Gap, which is 1.5N. There is a short sign south of road, west of AT	3800
1565.8	623.4	Woods road	3549
1565.4	623.8	Sugar Run Gap, Sugar Run Rd (gravel), road fork in view to east (pg.62) **Woods Hole Hostel** (0.5E)	3450
1564.0	625.2	View, 30 yards east.	3940
1563.2	626.0	Side trail to forest service road	3576
1563.1	626.1	**Docs Knob Shelter**, reliable spring to left of shelter 33.7◄24.0◄9.5◄▶15.7▶28.3▶32.2 ☾ ⊏ (8)	3560
1561.9	627.3	Spring	3416

❀ Rhododendron – 10-15 foot tall shrubs with broad waxy leaves. Grows in thick stands that the AT sometimes tunnels through. Flowers grow in large bouquets of ruffled pink flowers.

Elev	SoBo	NoBo	Description
3161	1560.1	629.1	Spring
3443	1559.4	629.8	Powerline, view
3683	1557.3	631.9	View
3550	1556.7	632.5	Angels Rest 0.1W to view
2610	1555.5	633.7	Roadbed
2025	1554.7	634.5	Cross Ave (paved), VA 634
1650	1554.3	634.9	Lane St, **Pearisburg, VA** (0.9E), **Narrows, VA** (3.6W) . . . . . . (pg.62-63) **P** N37 20.045 W80 45.319
1654	1553.8	635.4	Side trail to Parking 0.2W on Narrows Rd
1613	1553.4	635.8	US 460, Senator Shumate Bridge, New River, Circle under north end of bridge.
1595	1552.3	636.9	Landfill Rd (dirt), don't drink from stream.
2231	1549.8	639.4	Cross Clendennin Rd (VA 641), follow Pocahontas Rd for 0.1mi
2655	1549.0	640.2	Powerline
2692	1548.8	640.4	Dirt road, Stream
3150	1547.8	641.4	Piped spring (can go dry in late summer)
3372	1547.4	641.8	**Rice Field Shelter** (0.1E) 39.7◄25.2◄15.7◄▶12.6▶16.5▶25.3 Stiles south & north. Unreliable water to left behind shelter 0.3 mile down hill.
3358	1546.7	642.5	Cell tower
3423	1546.2	643.0	Powerline, view
3300	1545.8	643.4	Campsite west, water to east
3320	1542.3	646.9	Symms Gap, campsite to west.
3419	1541.3	647.9	Groundhog Trail to west

608.6   VA 606

🔥 🏠 🍴 💲 🌿 ⛺ 🚐 ✉ **Trent's Grocery** (0.5W) 276.928.1349
Open M-Sa 7-8, Sun 9-8. Deli with pizza, hamburgers, hot dogs and more.
Camping $6, shower $3, laundry $3. Coleman/alcohol/oz and canister fuel. Soda
machines outside. Shuttles. Maildrops: 900 Wilderness Rd, Bland, VA 24315.

🛒 🍴 **Nature Way** (3.6E; 0.4E on 606, left 3.3 on 42) 540.921.1381 M-Sa 8am-
5pm Amish-run grocery with organic, locally-grown foods. Dry goods, jerky,
candy, produce, ice cream & more. 106 Nature Lane, Pearisburg, VA 24134.

🚐 **Larry Richardson** 540.921.4724 Shuttle range Bland to Pearisburg.

623.8   Sugar Run Gap, Sugar Run Rd

🛏 🛏🔥 🏠 🍴 🌿 ⛺ 🚐 💻 ✉ **Woods Hole Hostel** (0.5E) 540.921.3444
⟨www.woodsholehostel.com⟩ Open year-round. A "Slice of heaven, not to be
missed." The 1880's chestnut-log cabin was discovered by Roy & Tillie Wood,
who opened the hostel in 1986. Their granddaughter, Neville, continues the
legacy with husband Michael, with emphasis on sustainable living through
beekeeping, farming, organic gardening, yoga(free), & massage therapy.
Directions: NoBo right on dirt road at Sugar Run Gap, SoBo turn left. Bear left
at fork, go downhill 0.5 mile to hostel on right. Offers massage, healing arts, &
retreats. Bunkhouse $15PP has mattresses, electricity, hot shower, and coffee/
tea in the morning. Camping $10PP. Pet fee $3. Indoor rooms: $28PP shared
/ $55 private (thru-hiker rate). Guests often invited to share local/organic
communal meals. Dinner $13, breakfast $8. Please call to inquire or reserve.
Shuttles for a fee, computer access, laundry, smoothies, cheese & baked
goods, Coleman/alcohol/oz, fuel canisters. Credit or cash(discount). Maildrops
for guests: Woods Hole Hostel, 3696 Sugar Run Rd, Pearisburg, VA 24134.

634.9   Lane St, *Pearisburg, VA 24134* (0.9E)

🛏🚐🔥 💲 ⛺ 🛜 💻 ✉ **Holiday Motor Lodge** 540.921.1551 Prices include tax:
$20 bunkroom with WiFi, TV, pets free. Limited economy rooms $45, otherwise
rooms $67, $10 pet fee. Pool. Maildrops: 401 N Main Street, Pearisburg, VA 24134.

🛏⛺🛜 ✉ **Plaza Motel** 540.921.2591 $40S $50D plus tax, no pets, accepts
credit cards. Maildrops: 415 N. Main St, Pearisburg, VA 24134.

🛏🔥 **Holy Family Hostel** 540.626.3337 Volunteer caretaker Patrick Muldoon
please do NOT call for a ride. Check in directions posted. Donation $10PP, 2 night
max. Open Mar-Nov; otherwise call. Hot shower, fridge, grill. Keep hostel clean &

NARROWS, VA

Lurich Rd
Camp Success
Wolf Creek
MacArthur Ln
New River

Grant's
Supermarket

🛏 MacArthur Inn (first hotel in the country
to be named after the general)

Creek Side
Laundry Mat
Anna's
Barber

Town
Office

PO (24124):
540-726-3272
M-F 9-12:45 & 2-4:15, Sa 9-11

61   100

Pearisburg, VA (3.6)

Narrows Library 9-5 M-F   0.4 mi

noise down (church in residential area). No pets or alcohol.

🏠 **Pearis Mercantile** 540.921.2260 Selection of hiker
foods, small gear items, fuel.

🔧 **Harvey Electronics and Hardware** 540.921.1456 Cell
phones & supplies Canister fuel, alcohol/oz, tent repair kits.

🚐 **Don Raines** 540.921.7433 ⟨ratface20724@aol.com⟩
Anytime, anywhere

🚐 **Tom Hoffman** 540.921.1184 ⟨gopullman@aol.com⟩ mid-
range shuttles centered in Pearisburg.

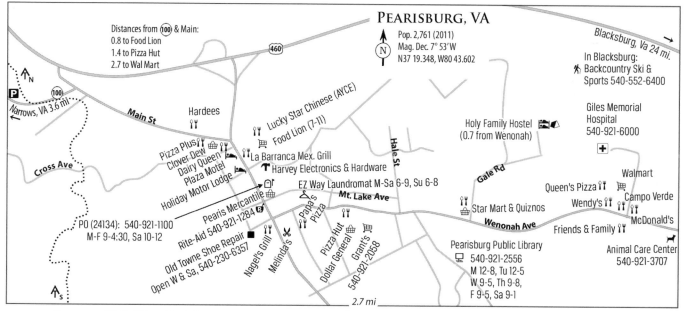

PEARISBURG, VA

Pop. 2,761 (2011)
Mag. Dec. 7° 53' W
N37 19.348, W80 43.602

Distances from (100) & Main:
0.8 to Food Lion
1.4 to Pizza Hut
2.7 to Wal Mart

Blacksburg, Va 24 mi.

In Blacksburg:
Backcountry Ski &
Sports 540-552-6400

Giles Memorial
Hospital
540-921-6000

Narrows, VA 3.6 mi.

Main St

Cross Ave

Hardees

Pizza Plus
Clover Dew
Dairy Queen
Plaza Motel
Holiday Motor Lodge

Lucky Star Chinese (AYCE)
Food Lion (7-11)

La Barranca Mex. Grill

Harvey Electronics & Hardware

Hale St

Holy Family Hostel
(0.7 from Wenonah)

Gale Rd

Walmart

Queen's Pizza

Campo Verde

Wendy's

McDonald's

Pearis Mercantile

EZ Way Laundromat M-Sa 6-9, Su 6-8

Mt. Lake Ave

Star Mart & Quiznos

Wenonah Ave

Friends & Family

PO (24134): 540-921-1100
M-F 9-4:30, Sa 10-12

Rite-Aid 540-921-1284

Old Towne Shoe Repair
Open W & Sa, 540-230-6357

Nagel's Grill

Melinda's

Papa's Pizza

Pizza Hut

Dollar General

Grant's
540-921-2058

Pearisburg Public Library
540-921-2556
M 12-8, Tu 12-5
W 9-5, Th 9-8,
F 9-5, Sa 9-1

Animal Care Center
540-921-3707

2.7 mi

Narrows, VA (3.6W on VA 100)

MacArthur Inn 540.726.7510 $45D/up. Call for ride from Pearisburg area trailheads, ride $5 each way. Longer shuttles and slackpacking can be arranged. Free long distance phone, cable TV and WiFi. In center of town with all services (restaurants, laundry, PO, grocery) in close walking distance. Shower only $8. On-site restaurant serves breakfast 6am-11am M-Sa, and dinner M & Th. Maildrops: 117 MacArthur Lane, Narrows, VA 24124.

Camp Success Camping $5, no showers. Check in at Town Office 540.726.3020 M-F 9-5. Call ahead if you will arrive on weekend or after hours.

Grants Supermarket 540.726.2303 M-Sa 8-9, Sun 9-8
Anna's Restaurant (L/D) closed Monday.

655.6   The Captain's

Camping available at 4464 Big Stony Creek Rd, 30 yards east of AT. Use zip line to cross the creek. ***This is not a hostel; do not enter the house.*** You may camp even when no one is home. Dogs bark but are friendly & are contained by an invisible electric fence. Hiker Feed two weeks after Trail Days. If it rains, you may stay on back porch.

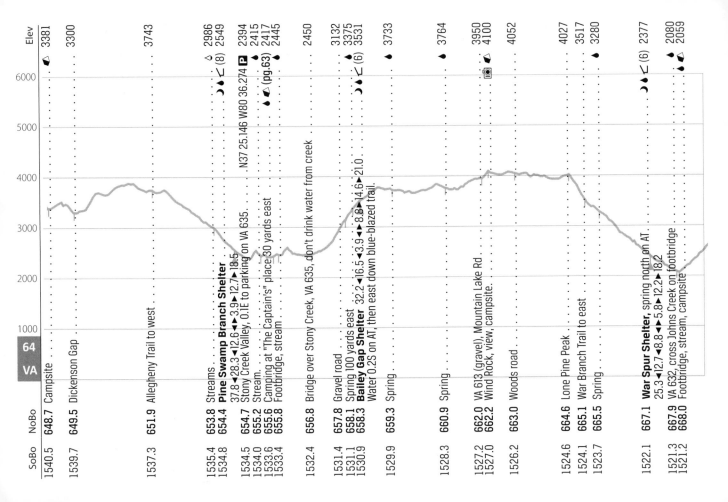

Elevation profile chart — page 64, VA (Appalachian Trail)

NoBo	SoBo	Description	Elev
648.7	1540.5	Campsite	3381
649.5	1539.7	Dickenson Gap	3300
651.9	1537.3	Allegheny Trail to west	3743
653.8	1535.4	Streams	2986
654.4	1534.8	**Pine Swamp Branch Shelter** 37.8◄28.3◄12.6◄▶3.9▶12.7▶18.5	2549
654.7	1534.5	Stony Creek Valley, 0.1E to parking on VA 635. N37 25.146 W80 36.274	2394
655.2	1534.0	Stream	2415
655.6	1533.6	Camping at "The Captain's" place 30 yards east (pg.63)	2417
655.8	1533.4	Footbridge, stream	2445
656.8	1532.4	Bridge over Stony Creek, VA 635, don't drink water from creek	2450
657.8	1531.4	Gravel road	3132
658.1	1531.1	Spring 100 yards east	3375
658.3	1530.9	**Bailey Gap Shelter** 32.2◄16.5◄3.9◄▶8.8▶14.6▶21.0 Water 0.2S on AT, then east down blue-blazed trail.	3531
659.3	1529.9	Spring	3733
660.9	1528.3	Spring	3764
662.0	1527.2	VA 613 (gravel), Mountain Lake Rd	3950
662.2	1527.0	Wind Rock, view, campsite.	4100
663.0	1526.2	Woods road	4052
664.6	1524.6	Lone Pine Peak	4027
665.1	1524.1	War Branch Trail to east	3517
665.5	1523.7	Spring	3280
667.1	1522.1	**War Spur Shelter,** spring north on AT 25.3◄12.7◄8.8◄▶5.8▶12.2▶18.2	2377
667.9	1521.3	VA 632, cross Johns Creek on footbridge	2080
668.0	1521.2	Footbridge, stream, campsite	2059

SoBo	NoBo	Description	Elev
1520.2	669.0	Spring	2638
1519.3	669.9	Rocky Gap, VA 601 (gravel)	3249
1518.7	670.5	Johns Creek Mountain Trail to west	3783
1517.5	671.7	Kelly Knob, view	3743
1516.3	672.9	**Laurel Creek Shelter** 18.5◀14.6◀5.8▶▶6.4▶12.4▶22.5. Water 60 yards north of shelter junction and west of AT.	2817
1516.1	673.1	Stream	2786
1515.7	673.5	Piney Ridge	2653
1514.3	674.9	Pasture, several fence stiles	2317
1513.9	675.3	Footbridge, Sinking Creek, VA 42, **Newport, VA** (8.0E) (pg.68) "trail east" (Nobo right, Sobo left) is compass west.	2200
1513.0	676.2	VA 630 (paved), chimney, and footbridge close together	2234
1512.6	676.6	Keffer Oak, largest oak tree on AT in south, over 18' around, over 300 yrs old Dover Oak along AT in NY is slightly larger.	2403
1512.2	677.0	Powerline	2591
1510.9	678.3	Powerline	3259
1510.1	679.1	Bruisers Knob	3435
1509.9	679.3	**Sarver Hollow Shelter** (0.4E) (2002) 21.0◀12.2◀6.4▶▶6.0▶16.1▶29.7	3418
1508.0	681.2	View	3375
1507.7	681.5	View	3350
1506.6	682.6	North end of ridge crest on Sinking Creek Mountain, Eastern Continental Divide West is old route of AT, leading 2.5 miles to Old Hall Rd.	3383
1505.0	684.2	Stream	2720
1503.9	685.3	**Niday Shelter**, water on opposite side of AT 18.2◀12.4◀6.0▶▶10.1▶23.7▶24.7 ✖ Who built the privy?	2005
1502.5	686.7	VA 621, Craig Creek Rd N37 22.755 W80 15.000	1558
1502.0	687.2	Many footbridges crossing Craig Creek and feeder streams. within a mile north of road.	1605

SoBo	NoBo	Feature	Elev
1499.6	689.6	Bench at southern crest of Brush Mountain	3064
1498.8	690.4	Audie Murphy Monument Murphy was most decorated American soldier of World War II. Monument on blue-blazed trail to west.	3100
1495.1	694.1	Footbridge, Trout Creek, VA 620 (gravel)	1559
1494.7	694.5	Powerline	1762
1493.8	695.4	**Pickle Branch Shelter** (0.3E) 22.5◀16.1◀10.1◀▶13.6▶14.6▶17.0 Tenting along trail to shelter. Water on steep trail 0.2 mile downhill from shelter.	1921
1492.8	696.4	View	2393
1489.9	699.3	View	2964
1489.6	699.6	Cove Mountain Trail 0.1E to Dragons Tooth (stone monolith), views.	3020
1488.8	700.8	Lost Spectacles Gap	2524
1488.4	700.8	Rawies Rest, view	2483
1488.2	701.0	View	2310
1487.5	701.7	Scout Trail west to Dragons Tooth Parking ▣ (pg.68)	2036
1487.1	702.1	VA 624, Newport Rd.	1810
1486.3	702.9	Footbridge	1821
1485.8	703.4	Fence stile	1845
1485.5	703.7	VA 785, Blacksburg Rd	1790
1485.2	704.0	Footbridge, Catawba Creek, fence stile, treat water	1773
1481.2	708.0	VA 311, **Catawba, VA** (1.0W) ... N37 22.808 W80 5.390 ▣ (pg.68)	1990
1480.6	708.6	Footbridge	2041
1480.2	709.0	**Johns Spring Shelter** (2003) 29.7◀23.7◀13.6◀▶1.0▶3.4▶9.4 Unreliable spring 25 yrds left front of shelter. ✖ Who built the privy?	1974

The AT is mostly on National Park Service Land from Newport Rd to Mtn Pass Rd (roughly from Catawba through Troutville). Camping permitted only in designated locations (at the shelters, Lamberts Meadow Campsite and the Pig Farm Campsite).

66
VA

SoBo	NoBo		Elev
1479.8	709.4	Footbridge	2129
1479.2	710.0	**Catawba Mountain Shelter** (1984) Camping to north ♪ ◊ ◀ (6)	2220
		24.7◀14.6◀1.0▶2.4▶8.4▶22.8 BB to water 100 yards from front of shelter.	
1477.5	711.7	McAfee Knob; excellent views, no camping. ◙	3197
1477.0	712.2	Powerline	2797
1476.9	712.3	Water to east, Pig Farm campsite, same water source as shelter ◀ ♪	2696
1476.8	712.4	**Campbell Shelter** (1989), water behind shelter ♪ ◀ ◀ (6)	2649
		17.0◀3.4◀2.4▶6.0▶20.4▶26.6	
		✽ **Fire Pink** – Scarlet-colored flower with five snake-tongued petals.	
1473.7	715.5	Brickeys Gap, Lamberts Meadow Trail to east	2250
1471.9	717.3	Tinker Cliffs, 0.5 mile cliff walk, views back to McAfee Knob. ◙	3000
1471.4	717.8	Scorched Earth Gap, Andy Layne Trail to west	2600
1470.8	718.4	**Lamberts Meadow Shelter** 9.4◀8.4◀6.0▶14.4▶20.6▶27.9 ♪ ◀ (6)	2143
1470.5	718.7	Lamberts Meadow Campsite, Sawmill Run ♪ ◀	2000
		Footbridge, stream. Trail north of footbridge to east rejoins AT at Brickeys Gap.	
1468.3	720.9	Blue-blazed trail west to view ◙	2273
1466.5	722.7	Angels Gap	1800
1466.1	723.1	Powerline	1898
1465.4	723.8	Hay Rock, view ◙	1900
1464.2	725.0	Powerline, view ◙	1915
1463.4	725.8	Powerline	1982
1462.6	726.6	Powerline	1440
1462.0	727.2	Powerline, railroad tracks, bridge	1238
1461.4	727.8	US 220, **Daleville, VA** (pg.68-69)	1350
1460.2	729.0	I-81, trail passes under on VA 779	1400
1459.9	729.3	US 11, RR tracks, **Troutville, VA** (0.8W) . N37 24.269 W79 53.369 P (pg.68-69)	1300
1459.6	729.6	Fence stile	1497

675.3   VA 42, Sinking Creek, Trail "east" here is compass west.
🛏(1.0W) **Sublett Place** 540.544.3099 ⟨www.thesublettplace.com⟩ Home and cottage for rent, prices seasonal.
🏠(1.0W) **Joe's Trees** 540.544.7303 ⟨www.joestrees.com⟩ Limited summer/fall hours (call ahead), 7 days Nov 15-Dec 21, closed Dec 22-Apr. Drinks, jerky, cheese, jams.

Newport, VA 24128 (8E)
Store, post office and restaurant near intersection of 42 and 460.
🏤 M-F 8:15-12:30 & 2:30-4:15, Sa 9-11, 540.544.7415
🛒 **Super Val-U** 540.544.7202
🍴 **Mikie's 7th** 540.544.0007 Tu-Sa 10-8.

702.1   VA 624, Newport Rd
🏕♨🚌🖥✉(0.3E) **Four Pines Hostel**   Owner Joe Mitchell cell: 540.309.8615 Hostel is a 3-bay garage with shower; please leave a donation, open year round. Pet friendly. Shuttles to/from The Homeplace Restaurant (Thurs-Sun) and to Catawba Grocery. Longer shuttles for a fee. Maildrops: 6164 Newport Rd. Catawba VA 24070
🛒🍴 **Catawba Grocery** 540.384.8050 West 0.3 mile to VA 311 and then left 0.1 mile to store, Su-Th 5am-10pm, F&Sa 5am-11pm. Grill serves breakfast, pizza, burgers, ice cream.

708.0   VA 311, **Catawba, VA 24070** (1W)
🏤 (1.0W) M-F 9-12:30 & 2:30-5, Sa 8:30-10:30, 540.384.6011
🍴 (1.4W) **Homeplace Restaurant** 540.384.7252 Th-F 4-8, Sa 3-8, Su 11-6, Popular AYCE family-style meals including drink and tax; $14 (two meats) $15 (three meats), $8 (kids 3-11).

727.8   US 220, **Daleville, VA**
729.3   US 11, **Troutville, VA**
Troutville Trail Days June 5-6 at Town Park. Food, vendors, & 5K race.
◣🚿✂⛺ **Troutville Park & Fire Station** Free camping at town park, no pets. Free laundry and showers at fire station.

🛏♨🛜🖥✉ 💲 **Howard Johnson Express** 540.992.1234 $49.95 hiker rate, cont. breakfast. Game room and pool. Maildrops: 437 Roanoke Road, Daleville, VA 24083.
🛏♨🛜🖥 **Super 8** 540.992.3000 $59.36 + tax, cont B, pool, accepts major credit cards.
🛏🛜🖥 **Comfort Inn** 540.992.5600 hiker rate $49.99D, $5EAP, continental breakfast.
🛏🛜🖥 **Quality Inn** 540.992.5335 $71/up, pets $25.
🛏♨✉ **Holiday Inn Express** 540.966.4444 $99-119. Maildrops: 3200 Lee Hwy, Troutville, VA 24175.
🛏 **Red Roof Inn** 540.992.5055
🛏♨🛜 **Stay at Inn** 540.992.6700 $38.95 $6EAP.
🍴 **Three Li'l Pigs** 540.966.0165 Summer M-Th 11-9:30, F-Sa 11-11, Su 11-9, Hiker friendly, hand-chopped BBQ ribs and wings, large selection of beer, some locally-brewed. Thru-hikers get free banana pudding dessert Mid-April to June 1.
🛒🛍 **Kroger Grocery Store and Pharmacy** 540.992.4920 24hr, pharmacy M-F 8-9, Sa 9-6, Su 12-6.
🥾♨🚌🛜🖥✉ **Outdoor Trails** 540.992.5850 Full service outfitter. White gas, denatured alcohol and Dr. Bronners soap/oz. Computer for internet use, list of shuttles. Open M-F 9-8, Sat 9-6 during hiking season (Apr 27-Jun 27); open M-F 10-8, Sat 10-6 the rest of the year. Maildrops: Botetourt Commons, 28 Kingston Dr, Daleville, VA 24083.
🚌 **Homer Witcher** 540.266.4849 Trail maintainer & 2002 thru-hiker.
🚌 **Del Schechterly** 540.529.6028 Covers Pearisburg-Waynesboro.
🍸 **Flying Mouse Brewery** Check ⟨www.flyingmousebrewery.com⟩ for beer tasting events. 0.4W to Precast Way, then right 0.1mi.

Roanoke, VA (13E)
✈ A large city with an airport approx 13 miles from the AT.
🥾 (5E) **Gander Mountain** 540.362.3658
🥾 (10E) **Sportsman's Warehouse** 540.366.9700 (3550 Ferncliff Ave NW) Full service outfitter with full line of gear including fuel, freeze dried foods, boots, clothes and trekking poles.

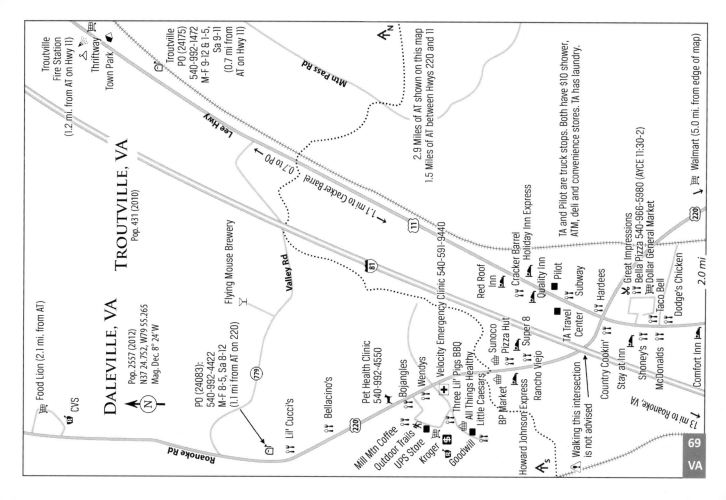

TROUTVILLE, VA

Troutville Fire Station (1.2 mi. from AT on Hwy 11)

Troutville PO (24175) 540-992-1472 M-F 9-12 & 1-5, Sa 9-11 (0.7 mi from AT on Hwy 11)

2.9 Miles of AT shown on this map
1.5 Miles of AT between Hwys 220 and 11

TA and Pilot are truck stops. Both have $10 shower, ATM, deli and convenience stores. TA has laundry.

Thriftway

Town Park

Mtn Pass Rd

Lee Hwy

1.1 mi to Cracker Barrel → 0.7 to PO ←

N

Valley Rd

Flying Mouse Brewery

81

11

Red Roof Inn

Cracker Barrel

Holiday Inn Express

Quality Inn

Pilot

Subway

Hardees

Great Impressions

Bella Pizza 540-966-5980 (AYCE 11:30-2)

Dollar General Market

Taco Bell

Dodge's Chicken

220

2.0 mi

Walmart (5.0 mi. from edge of map)

DALEVILLE, VA

Pop. 2557 (2012)
N37 24.752, W79 55.265
Mag. Dec. 8° 24'W

N

PO (24083):
540-992-4422
M-F 8-5, Sa 8-12
(1.1 mi from AT on 220)

Food Lion (2.1 mi. from AT)

CVS

Lil' Cucci's

Bellacino's

220

779

Roanoke Rd

Pet Health Clinic 540-992-4550

Bojangles

Wendys

Velocity Emergency Clinic 540-591-9440

Three Lil' Pigs BBQ

All Things Healthy

Sunoco

Pizza Hut

Super 8

BP Market

Little Caesars

Howard Johnson Express

Rancho Viejo

TA Travel Center

Country Cookin'

Stay at Inn

Shoney's

McDonalds

Comfort Inn

13 mi to Roanoke, VA

Mill Mtn Coffee

Outdoor Trails

UPS Store

Kroger

Goodwill

Walking this intersection is not advised

S

69

VA

Pop. 431 (2010)

SoBo	NoBo	Description	Elev
1459.4	729.8	VA 652, Mountain Pass Rd	1450
1459.1	730.1	Fence	1524
1456.4	732.8	**Fullhardt Knob Shelter** (0.1E) 22.8◀20.4◀14.4▶6.2▶13.5▶20.0 Treat water from cistern. ☽ ◑ ◭ ∈ (6)	2651
1453.6	735.6	Salt Pond Rd, USFS 191	2264
1452.8	736.4	Curry Creek, Curry Creek Trail to west ◑	1596
1452.0	737.2	Stream. ◑	1695
1450.7	738.5	Wilson Creek, Colliers Pit historical marker to north ◑	1568
1450.2	739.0	**Wilson Creek Shelter** 26.6◀20.6◀6.2▶7.3▶13.8▶20.8 ☽ ◑ ◭ ∈ (6)	1871
1449.7	739.5	Reliable stream 0.3 mile downhill in front of shelter. Spring ◑	2022
1447.8	741.4	Blackhorse Gap, dirt road, Blue Ridge Parkway (BRP) mile 97.7 to east.	2421
1447.1	742.1	BRP 97.0, Taylors Mountain Overlook 📷	2387
1445.3	743.9	BRP 95.3, Harveys Knob Overlook ⛭ 🏛 📷	2542
1443.6	745.6	Hammond Hollow Trail to west.	2341
1442.9	746.3	**Bobblets Gap Shelter** (0.2W) 27.9◀13.5◀7.3▶6.5▶13.5▶18.4 If spring to left of shelter dry, look farther downstream. ☽ ◑ ◭ ∈ (6)	2101
1442.1	747.1	BRP 92.5, Peaks of Otter Overlook 📷	2349
1441.5	747.7	BRP 91.8, Mills Gap Overlook 🏛 📷	2450
1439.8	749.4	Bearwallow Gap, footbridge, stream, VA 43, 0.2E to BRP 90.9. **Buchanan, VA** (5.0W) △ (pg.72)	2228

70 VA

SoBo	NoBo	Feature	Elev
1438.2	751.0	Cove Mountain	2720
1437.8	751.4	Little Cove Mountain Trail to east	2600
1436.4	752.8	**Cove Mountain Shelter** 20.0◄13.8◄6.5◄▶7.0▶11.9▶17.2	1963
1436.2	753.0	View	1986
1434.7	754.5	Buchanan Trail	1790
1433.2	756.0	Jennings Creek, VA 614 N37 31.745 W79 37.350 P ♦ (pg.72) Swimming hole, Campsites. **Buchanan, VA** (5.0W)	951
1431.6	757.6	Fork Mountain.	2042
1430.4	758.8	Stream south of powerline	1252
1430.1	759.1	Stream.	1286
1429.7	759.5	Stream.	1211
1429.4	759.8	**Bryant Ridge Shelter** 20.8◄13.5◄7.0◄▶4.9▶10.2▶22.6 Stream on trail to shelter. Blue-blazed trail 0.1N of shelter leads 0.5E to VA 714.	1302
1426.3	762.9	Campsite, 0.1W to spring (signed).	2943
1425.1	764.1	Floyd Mountain	3560
1424.5	764.7	**Cornelius Creek Shelter** (0.1E) 18.4◄11.9◄4.9◄▶5.3▶17.7▶21.6 Water on trail to shelter. Privy behind shelter.	3126
1424.2	765.0	Stream.	3045
1423.6	765.6	Black Rock Overlook, view 200' west	3450
1423.3	765.9	Footbridge, stream	3313
1423.0	766.2	Intersection with Cornelius Creek Trail	3233
1421.9	767.3	Apple Orchard Falls Trail 1.1W to 200' waterfall, 0.1E to Sunset Field, USFS 812 (Parkers Gap Rd) 0.1N on AT.	3356
1420.4	768.8	Apple Orchard Mountain, FAA tower, views	4225
1420.1	769.1	The Guillotine	4090
1419.5	769.7	BRP 76.3, spring 100 yards north, then east of AT	3900
1419.2	770.0	**Thunder Hill Shelter** 17.2◄10.2◄5.3◄▶12.4▶16.3▶25.1 Poor water source, use spring south on AT, tentsites north of shelter	3934

749.4   Bearwallow Gap, VA 43

🛏🔦🍴⛺ **(5.5E) Peaks of Otter Lodge & Restaurant**
540.586.1081 Go 0.1E on to the Blue Ridge Parkway (the overpass), then follow BRP to the left 5.0 miles. Motel rooms $126 weekdays, $136 weekends, higher in fall. Restaurant open for B/L/D. Sunday buffet breakfast. Some supplies at camp store. Dec-Mar days reduced to Th-Su. Camping managed separately, 540.586.7321, $16.

Buchanan, VA (5W) *Also see next entry.*

756.0   Jennings Creek 🔵 (0.3E), VA 614

🛏🔦🍴⛺🌿⛺📶📧 **(1.2E) Middle Creek Campground**
540.254.2550 ⟨www.middlecreekcampground.com⟩ (2014 prices) cabins $65-75, $5EAP cabin sleeps 4-6, camping $20 (2 persons), showers $5, snack bar, Ask about shuttles, limited resupply, Coleman/alcohol/oz & canisters. Laundry room (around back) is always open. Can also be reached on the northern side of Fork Mountain by taking VA 714 and VA 614 east 1.4 miles. Guest maildrops: 1164 Middle Creek Rd, Buchanan, VA 24066.

Buchanan, VA (I-81 exit 168) (5W on VA 614)

🛏🍴📶 **Wattstull Inn** 540.254.1551 Hiker rates starting at $60+tax, pets $15. **Mtn View Diner** on-site serves B/L/D.

784.6   US 501, VA 130

🛏🔦⛺🏕📧 **Lynchburg/Blue Ridge KOA** (5.0E) 434.299.5228 Hiker special $15PP includes tent site, shower w/towel, pool. Four-person cabins available. Camp store, coin laundry. Closed Dec - mid March. Maildrops: 6252 Elon Rd, Monroe ,VA 24574.

🚌 **Ken Wallace** 434.609.2704 Shuttles covering Daleville to Waynesboro and Lynchburg KOA.

Big Island, VA 24526 (5.6E)
🏤 M-F 8-12 & 1-4, Sa 8-10, 434.299.5072
⛺🍴📧 **H&H Food Market** 434.299.5153 7 days 5:30-9, B/L/D, Maildrops: 11619 Lee Jackson Hwy, Big Island, VA 24526.
➕ **Big Island Family Medical Center** 434.299.5951

Glasgow, VA 24555 (5.9W)
🅷 **Town Hall** 540.258.2246 Maintains shelter & Knick Field restrooms
🛒 **Glasgow Grocery Express** 540.258.1818 M-Sa 6-11:30pm, Su 8-1130pm, Coleman/alcohol/oz.
🐾 **Natural Bridge Animal Hospital** 540.291.1444 4.5W of Glasgow on VA 130. M,W,F 8-5:30, T,Th 8-7.
🚌 **Gary Serra** 757.681.2254 Gary has completed the AT twice in sections and is familiar with all trailheads. Pickups at Glasgow & Buena Vista trailheads. Shuttles along AT, to Roanoke, Lynchburg and Charlottesville airports, and to Amtrak station.

Library 540-254-2538
M & Th 9-7; Tu, W, F 9-5; Sa 9-1

Ransone's, Buchanan
Fountain & Grille inside

(0.2) Family Dollar

PO (24066):
540-254-2178
M-F 9-1 & 2-4,
Sa 10-12

Theater
Burger King
Exxon
🚻 43
5 mi.

BUCHANAN, VA
Pop. 1,171 (2011)
N37 31.716, W79 40.703
Mag. Dec. 8° 47'W

81
11

Shell
Mountain View Diner
Wattstull Inn
614
5 mi.

3.0 mi

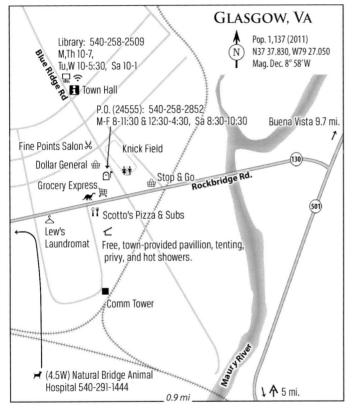

GLASGOW, VA

Pop. 1,137 (2011)
N37 37.830, W79 27.050
Mag. Dec. 8° 58'W

Library: 540-258-2509
M,Th 10-7,
Tu,W 10-5:30, Sa 10-1

Town Hall

Blue Ridge Rd

P.O. (24555): 540-258-2852
M-F 8-11:30 & 12:30-4:30, Sa 8:30-10:30

Buena Vista 9.7 mi.

Fine Points Salon ✂

Knick Field

Dollar General 🏠

Stop & Go

Grocery Express

Rockbridge Rd.

130

501

Scotto's Pizza & Subs

Lew's Laundromat

Free, town-provided pavillion, tenting, privy, and hot showers.

Comm Tower

(4.5W) Natural Bridge Animal Hospital 540-291-1444

Maury River

0.9 mi

5 mi.

Minimize Campfire Impacts

•Use stoves for cooking – if you need a fire, build one only where it's legal and in an existing fire ring. Leave hatchets and saws at home – collect dead and downed wood that you can break by hand. Burn all wood to ash.

•Do not try to burn trash, including foil, plastic, glass, cans, tea bags, food, or anything with food on it. These items do not burn thoroughly. They create noxious fumes, attract wildlife like skunks and bears, and make the area unsightly.

•Where campfires are permitted, leave the fire ring clean by removing others' trash and scattering unused wood, cold coals, and ashes 200 feet away from camp after the fire is cold and completely out.

Read more of the Leave No Trace techniques developed for the A.T.: www.appalachiantrail.org/LNT

APPALACHIAN TRAIL
CONSERVANCY®

The ATC works with the National Park Service, 31 volunteer maintaining clubs, and multiple other partners to engage the public in conserving this essential American resource. Please join or donate to the ATC.

Their website, www.AppalachianTrail.org, contains information about trail history and protection, hike planning, volunteer opportunities, and trail conditions.

Elev	Feature	NoBo	SoBo
3596	Hunting Creek Trail, BRP 74.9 🅟🏛	771.0	1418.2
3501	0.1E to BRP 74.7 Thunder Ridge Overlook	771.4	1417.8
3305	Harrison Ground Spring ◖	773.2	1416.0
2908	Spring ◗	773.8	1415.4
2369	Petites Gap, gravel road, BRP 71.0 to east.	774.7	1414.5
3030	Highcock Knob,	775.9	1413.3
2305	Marble Spring, campsite, spring 100 yards west ◖	776.9	1412.3
2400	Sulphur Spring Trail south crossing	777.4	1411.8

.ıl (NoBo) Poor cell reception at US 501, consider calling ahead if you need ride.

Elev	Feature	NoBo	SoBo
2650	Gunter Ridge Trail, Hickory Stand	779.2	1410.0
2588	Sulphur Spring Trail north crossing	779.7	1409.5
1890	Big Cove Branch, stream ◗	780.5	1408.7
869	**Matts Creek Shelter,** Matts Creek Trail 2.5E to US 501 ☽ ◗ ⌂ (6) 22.6◀17.7◀12.4►3.9►12.7►22.2	782.4	1406.8
711	AT parallels James River from here north for 1.0 mile, no camping	783.2	1406.0
678	James River footbridge, longest foot-use-only bridge on AT	784.4	1404.8
680	US 501, VA 130, **Big Island VA** (5.6E), **Glasgow VA** (5.9W) 🅟 (pg.72-73) ◗	784.6	1404.6
681	Lower Rocky Row Run Bridge, stream.	784.8	1404.4
812	VA 812, USFS 36 (gravel) N37 36.286 W79 23.295 🅿	785.7	1403.5
937	Stream.	786.1	1403.1
1036	**Johns Hollow Shelter** ☽ ◗ ◖ ⌂ (6) 21.6◀16.3◀3.9►8.8►18.3►23.9 Springs to left and right of shelter.	786.3	1402.9
2428	Little Rocky Row Trail to west, view just north on AT 🅟📷	788.2	1401.0
2992	Big Rocky Row, view 🅟📷	789.4	1399.8

.ıl (SoBo) Poor cell reception at US 501, consider calling ahead if you need ride.

SoBo	NoBo	Feature	Elev
1398.3	790.9	Saddle Gap, Saddle Gap Trail.	2600
1397.2	792.0	Saltlog Gap, Saltlog Gap Trail. (0.5W)	2573
1395.7	793.5	Bluff Mountain, Ottie Cline Powell monument, views.	3372
1394.6	794.6	Punchbowl Mountain.	2850
1394.1	795.1	**Punchbowl Shelter** (0.2W), spring front left of shelter	2504
		25.1◄12.7◄8.8◄▶9.5▶15.1▶ 25.3	
1393.7	795.5	BRP 51.7, water north of road, to the east. N37 40.426 W79 20.081	2170
1393.4	795.8	VA 607, Robinson Gap Rd (gravel) N37 40.567 W79 19.921 Water west 30 yards.	2100
1391.5	797.7	Rice Mountain	2228
1390.9	798.3	Spring.	1722
1390.5	798.7	Dirt road.	1358
1389.6	799.6	Reservoir Rd (gravel), Pedlar River Bridge. N37 40.227 W79 17.067 campsite 0.2S of road.	1002
1387.9	801.3	Spring.	1207
1387.1	802.1	Stream.	1151
1386.6	802.6	Swapping Camp Rd (gravel)	1317
1386.3	802.9	Stream.	1373
1384.6	804.6	**Brown Mountain Creek Shelter** (6)	1381
		22.2◄18.3◄9.5◄▶5.6▶15.8▶22.4 Swimming hole. Cmping opposite side of creek. In dry conditions get water from Brown Mountain Creek south of shelter.	
1382.8	806.4	US 60, **Buena Vista, VA** (9.3W) N37 43.405 W79 15.036 (pg.78-79)	2065
1381.9	807.3	USFS 507 (dirt)	2662
1380.0	809.2	Bald Knob	4059
1379.0	810.2	Hotel Trail, **Cow Camp Gap Shelter** (0.6E) (8)	3487
		23.9◄15.1◄5.6◄▶10.2▶16.8▶24.4 Water source on blue-blazed trail left of shelter before small stream crossing.	

75
VA

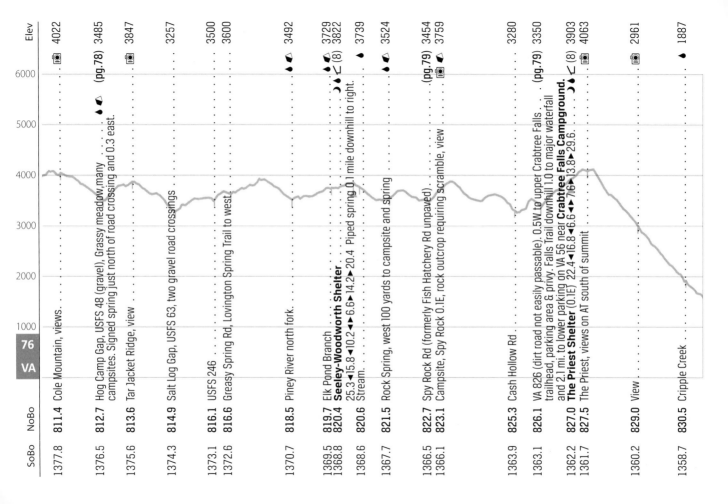

Elev	NoBo	SoBo	Feature
4022	811.4	1377.8	Cole Mountain, views.
3485	812.7	1376.5	Hog Camp Gap, USFS 48 (gravel), Grassy meadow, many campsites. Signed spring just north of road crossing and 0.3 east. (pg.78)
3847	813.6	1375.6	Tar Jacket Ridge, view
3257	814.9	1374.3	Salt Log Gap, USFS 63, two gravel road crossings
3500	816.1	1373.1	USFS 246
3600	816.6	1372.6	Greasy Spring Rd, Lovington Spring Trail to west
3492	818.5	1370.7	Piney River north fork.
3729	819.7	1369.5	Elk Pond Branch
3822	820.4	1368.8	**Seeley-Woodworth Shelter.** (8) 25.3◀15.8◀10.2◀▶6.6▶14.2▶20.4
3739	820.6	1368.6	Piped spring 0.1 mile downhill to right. Stream.
3524	821.5	1367.7	Rock Spring, west 100 yards to campsite and spring
3454	822.7	1366.5	Spy Rock Rd (formerly Fish Hatchery Rd unpaved). (pg.79)
3759	823.1	1366.1	Campsite, Spy Rock 0.1E, rock outcrop requiring scramble, view
3280	825.3	1363.9	Cash Hollow Rd.
3350	826.1	1363.1	VA 826 (dirt road not easily passable), 0.5W to upper Crabtree Falls (pg.79) trailhead, parking area & privy. Falls Trail downhill 1.0 to major waterfall and 2.1 mi. to lower parking on VA 56 near **Crabtree Falls Campground.**
3903	827.0	1362.2	**The Priest Shelter** (0.1E) (8) 22.4◀16.8◀6.6◀▶3.8▶29.6.
4063	827.5	1361.7	The Priest, views on AT south of summit
2961	829.0	1360.2	View
1887	830.5	1358.7	Cripple Creek

76
VA

NoBo	Description	Elev	SoBo
831.8	VA 56, Tye River suspension bridge . . . N37 50.305 W79 1.387 P (pg.79) 100 yards north, **Crabtree Falls Campground** (4.0W)	970	1357.4
833.0	Roadbed.	1721	1356.2
833.5	Mau-Har Trail to west, southern intersection rejoins AT at Maupin Field Shelter .	2090	1355.7
834.4	Stream.	1769	1354.8
834.6	**Harpers Creek Shelter**	1910	1354.6
	24.4◀14.2◀7.6◀▶6.2▶22.0▶34.7 Harpers Creek in front of shelter. Privy up hill.		
836.1	View.	2793	1353.1
836.6	Chimney Rock, view	3190	1352.6
837.9	Three Ridges Mountain.	3984	1351.3
838.8	Hanging Rock Overlook, view	3519	1350.4
840.8	**Maupin Field Shelter**	2765	1348.4
	20.4◀13.8◀6.2◀▶15.8▶28.5▶41.5 Piped spring behind shelter. Privy to right of shelter on unmarked path. Mau-Har Trail northern intersection. Jeep road leads 1.4mi. to BRP.		
842.5	Reeds Gap, VA 664, BRP 13.6 in view to west . N37 54.097 W78 59.115 P (pg.79)	2650	1346.7
843.0	Three Ridges Overlook, BRP 13.1. N37 54.418 W78 58.771 P 🏛	2700	1346.2
845.2	Stream	2582	1344.0
846.0	Rock Point Overlook, view to west.	2784	1343.2
846.8	Cedar Cliffs, view.	2800	1342.4
847.3	Dripping Rock, BRP 9.6, spring . . . . . . N37 56.465 W78 56.214 P	2950	1341.9
847.6	Laurel Springs Gap, spring.	2844	1341.6
848.5	Side trail 0.3W to Humpback picnic area	3210	1340.7
849.3	Campsite, view.	3483	1339.9
850.1	Humpback Mountain	3612	1339.1
851.1	Trail 0.2W to view at The Rocks	3274	1338.1

806.4   US 60

🛏🏠🍴⊞🚿🏕🅿✉ (4.0W) **Three Springs Hostel** 434.922.7069 ⟨www.threespringshostel.com⟩ $49.99 + $4.01 tax includes bunk, shower w/ towel & toiletries, laundry, pick up & return to trailhead at US 60 or Hog Camp Gap. Reservations recommended. Okay to walk from Hog Camp Gap, but not from 60 (it's dangerous and directions are needed). Free long distance calls and a family-style breakfast & dinner. Slackpacking (day packs available), and for-fee shuttles ranging Daleville-Waynesboro, VA. Parking for section hikers. Please note: this hostel is a private residence; no alcohol, drugs, smoking or firearms and no dogs. Open year round, credit cards accepted. Maildrops: 612 Wiggins Spring Road, Vesuvius, VA 24483.

Buena Vista, VA 24416 (9.3W)

◐🚿 **Glen Maury Park Campground** 540.261.7321 AT hiker special $5 tentsite. Free shower, even without stay, South end of town across river. Maury River Fiddlers Convention mid-June.

🛏🏠 **Buena Vista Motel** 540.261.2138 $44-$79 Rooms have fridge & microwave, free local calls. Shuttle to/from trail for a small fee.

🛏🏠🏕 **Budget Inn** 540.261.2156 $49-$89, pets $10 and must use smoking room.

🍴⊞ **Amish Cupboard** 540.264.0215 Deli, Ice Cream, jerky, tons of candy and dried foods. M-F 10-7, Sa 10-6.

🍴⊞ **Lewis Grocery** Short order grill with excellent burger.

🏪 **Food Lion** 540.261.7672, 7 days

🚌 **Maury Express** 800.964.5707 Area bus makes hourly loop though BV & connects with a Lexington loop bus. 50¢ per board. M-F 8-5, Sa 10-4.

🐾 **Edgewater Animal Hospital** 540.261.4114 M-F 8-7, Sa 10-12

🛈🚻🅿 **Regional Visitor Center** 540.261.8004 Multi-day parking.

Lexington, VA 24450 (15W of Buena Vista)

🛏🏕🏠✉ **Brierley Hill B&B** 540.464.8421 relax@brierleyhill.com Thru-hiker special $75PP for double occupancy room. Includes breakfast, free use of laundry facilities, and WiFi. Shuttle to/from the AT (Rt. 60) for additional fee. No Pets. Maildrops: 985 Borden Rd, Lexington, VA 24450.

🛏🏕🏠✉ **502 South Main B&B** 540.460.7353 info@ southmain.com. "Thru-hiker special" $75PP for 2 or 3 persons. Round trip to AT (Rt. 60) $10PP, free laundry, hearty breakfast. Restaurants & shops nearby. No pets, No smoking. Credit cards accepted. Maildrops: 502 S. Main St, Lexington VA 24450

🏃 **Walkabout Outfitter** 540.464.4453 Full service outfitter owned by Kirk Miller (Flying Monkey '99). Fuel canisters.

812.7   Hog Camp Gap, USFS 48

🛏 (1.5W) **Three Springs Hostel** See listing at US 60

818.9   Spy Rock Rd **Montebello, VA 24464** 2.4W to post office, general store. Go downhill on gravel road 1.1W to parking area on Fish Hatchery Rd. Watch for right turn 0.5 from AT, and watch for blue blazes. Follow F.H. Road (turn right at intersection) 0.9mi. to Crabtree Falls Hwy (VA 56). Go left on VA 56 0.4 miles to post office.

⌂ M-F 10-2, Sa 10-1, 540.377.9218

◐⊞🏕 **Montebello Camping & General Store** 540.377.2650 Store open year-round, camping & laundry Apr 1 - Oct 31. Thru-hiker rate on tentsite $14(1 person), $21(2), $28(3 or more) sometimes has fuel/oz.

826.1   VA 826 (3.7mi to campground: 0.5W on 826 to Meadows parking area, 1.0 on blue-blaze trail to top of falls, 1.7 to bottom of falls, and 0.5 right on US 56 to campground)

831.8   VA 56, Tye River (4W to campground)

🛏◐⊞🚿🏕✉ **Crabtree Falls Campground** 540.377.2066 ⟨www.crabtreefallscampground.com⟩ Cabins $50 four people, camping $26/site(2 tents). Laundry, free shower even w/o stay. Trail foods and snacks, ice cream, sodas, stove fuel. Maildrops (shoebox size or smaller): 11039 Crabtree Falls Hwy, Tyro, VA 22976.

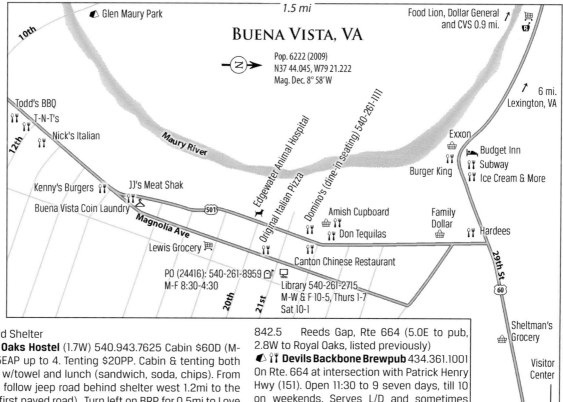

1.5 mi

BUENA VISTA, VA

Pop. 6222 (2009)
N37 44.045, W79 21.222
Mag. Dec. 8° 58'W

Glen Maury Park

Food Lion, Dollar General and CVS 0.9 mi.

6 mi. Lexington, VA

Maury River

Todd's BBQ
T-N-T's
Nick's Italian

10th

12th

Exxon
Burger King
Budget Inn
Subway
Ice Cream & More

Kenny's Burgers
JJ's Meat Shak
Buena Vista Coin Laundry

Magnolia Ave

501

Lewis Grocery

Edgewater Animal Hospital

Original Italian Pizza

Domino's (dine-in seating) 540-261-1111

Amish Cupboard
Don Tequilas

Family Dollar
Hardees

Canton Chinese Restaurant

PO (24416): 540-261-8959
M-F 8:30-4:30

Library 540-261-2715
M-W & F 10-5, Thurs 1-7
Sat 10-1

20th

21st

29th St

60

Sheltman's Grocery

Visitor Center

Buena Vista Motel

9.3 mi.

840.8   Maupin Field Shelter

🛏 ⚑ 🍴 ⛺ 📶 **Royal Oaks Hostel** (1.7W) 540.943.7625 Cabin $60D (M-Th), $85D (F-Su), $15EAP up to 4. Tenting $20PP. Cabin & tenting both include WiFi, shower w/towel and lunch (sandwich, soda, chips). From Maupin Field Shelter, follow jeep road behind shelter west 1.2mi to the Blue Ridge Parkway (first paved road). Turn left on BRP for 0.5mi to Love Rd (814). Turn right for 100 yards to Royal Oaks. From Reeds Gap, go west on 664 for a short distance to BRP. Turn left on BRP and go 2.8mi to Love Rd. Store (snacks, sodas, canned food) and deli on-site, open year round M-Sa 9-6, Su 12-6.

842.5   Reeds Gap, Rte 664 (5.0E to pub, 2.8W to Royal Oaks, listed previously)

⚑ 🍴 **Devils Backbone Brewpub** 434.361.1001 On Rte. 664 at intersection with Patrick Henry Hwy (151). Open 11:30 to 9 seven days, till 10 on weekends. Serves L/D and sometimes hiker-only breakfast for $5. Hikers welcome to camp on-site. Pickup rarely available, but morning return ride often provided.

80
VA

Elev	Feature	NoBo	SoBo
2527	Spring	852.8	1336.4
2347	Spring	853.8	1335.4
2339	Side trail 0.2W to Humpback Gap, BRP 6.0	853.9	1335.3
2267	Glass Hollow Overlook, view to east	854.8	1334.4
2303	Side trail 1.3W to Humpback Visitor Center . . . . N37 58.150 W78 53.846 **P** **H**	855.2	1334.0
2239	Albright Loop Trail to west	855.3	1333.9
1594	**Paul C. Wolfe Shelter** 29.6◄22.0◄15.8◄▶12.7▶25.7▶38.9 . . . . ☽♦⊏(10) Mill Creek 50 yards in front of shelter. Waterfall with pool 100 yards.	856.6	1332.6
1878	Small cemetery	857.4	1331.8
2085	Cabin ruins, chimney	858.1	1331.1
2058	Spring	858.3	1330.9
1883	Stream	859.7	1329.5
1745	Stream	860.5	1328.7
1912	US 250 + Blue Ridge Pkwy . . . . N38 1.864 W78 51.545 **P** **H** ♔ (pg.82-83) Rockfish Gap, **Waynesboro, VA** (3.7W), I-64 overpass, south end of Skyline Dr.	861.7	1327.5
2215	Shenandoah National Park (SNP) (pg.84) Entrance station and self-registration for overnight permits.	862.6	1326.6
2444	Skyline 102.1, McCormick Gap	865.3	1323.9
2885	Bears Den Mountain, communication towers, tractor seats	866.6	1322.6
2550	Skyline 99.5, Beagle Gap. . . . N38 4.373 W78 47.607 **P**	867.1	1322.1
2895	Little Calf Mountain	867.9	1321.3
2983	Calf Mountain	868.6	1320.6
2703	**Calf Mountain Shelter** (0.3W) 34.7◄28.5◄12.7◄▶13.0▶26.2▶34.4 ☽♦(0.2W)♦⊏(6) Spring on way to shelter. Bear pole.	869.9	1319.9
2303	Powerline	869.7	1319.5
2316	Spring	869.8	1319.4
2270	Gravel road 0.1W to Skyline 96.9, Jarman Gap	870.3	1318.9
2161	Spring, just south of woods road	870.4	1318.8

Page 81 / VA

SoBo	NoBo	Description	Elev
1317.1	872.1	Skyline 95.3, Sawmill Run Overlook. 🔭	2200
1315.7	873.5	Turk Mountain Trail to west.	2636
1315.5	873.7	Skyline 94.1, Turk Gap. . . . N38 7.740 W78 47.092 P	2600
1313.5	875.7	Skyline 92.4.	3100
1313.1	876.1	Wildcat Ridge Trail east to Skyline 92.1 . . . N38 8.904 W78 46.477 P	3000

✳ **Turks Cap Lily** – Petals of this down-facing large flower curl back to form a bun (Turk's cap) shape. Common color is flame orange and yellow, speckled with brown dots.

SoBo	NoBo	Description	Elev
1310.5	878.7	Skyline 90.0, spur trail to east leads to Riprap parking area. P	2797
1310.0	879.2	Riprap Trail branches to west	3015
1309.3	879.9	Skyline 88.9.	2639
1307.6	881.6	Skyline 87.4, Black Rock Gap, Paine Run Trail. . . . N38 12.398 W78 44.974 P	2321
1307.4	881.8	Skyline 87.2.	2385
1306.9	882.3	**Blackrock Hut** (0.2E) 41.5◀25.7◀13.0▶13.2▶21.4▶33.8)◑◐⌂⊏(6)	2758
1306.5	882.7	Trayfoot Mountain Trail to west	3087
1306.4	882.8	Blackrock, views from summit, which is skirted by the AT 🔭	3101
1305.8	883.4	Blackrock parking area. . . . N38 13.331 W78 43.992 P	2927
1305.3	883.9	Skyline 84.3.	2800
1305.2	884.0	Jones Run parking . . . N38 13.805 W78 43.577 P	2788
1304.6	884.6	Two trails west to Dundo Campground (primitive, reserved for group use)	2752
1303.9	885.3	Skyline 82.9, Browns Gap . . . N38 14.424 W78 42.653 P	2579
1303.3	885.9	Big Run Loop Trail to west	2826
1303.0	886.2	Skyline 82.2.	2775
1302.5	886.7	West to Doyles River Parking Overlook, Skyline 81.9 N38 14.806 W78 41.686 P 🔭	2838
1301.7	887.5	Doyles River Trail, west to Skyline 81.1, east to Doyles River Cabin (locked), 0.3E to spring, 1.2E to falls N38 15.254 W78 40.982 P ◆	2855
1300.9	888.3	Trail to Loft Mtn amphitheater.	3176
1300.8	888.4	Trail to **Loft Mtn Campground** (go here if camping). ◢ (pg.85)	3263
1300.2	889.0	Trail to **Loft Mtn Campground** ◢ (pg.85)	3294
1299.8	889.4	Powerline	3237
1299.6	889.6	Trail to **Loft Mtn Store** (in view to west) (pg.85)	3165
1298.4	890.8	Frazier Discovery Trail 0.3W to **Loft Mtn Wayside**	3299
1298.3	890.9	Frazier Discovery Trail to west	3306
1297.4	891.8	Trail to 0.5W to **Loft Mtn Wayside** (flatter than FDT), Ivy Creek spring 0.1W ◆	2985

861.7   Rockfish Gap

🛈 📞 🅿 Afton Mountain Visitor Center 540.943.5187 Open most days 9-5. Hiker flyers with current info about town services & trail angels. Many lodging facilities offer free pickup/return from this location. Long-term parking okay; leave contact info & return date.

🛏 Inn at Afton 540.942.5201 Hiker rate $40+tax, pets allowed, Some restaurants deliver here.

🛏 🍴 ⛺ 🛜 ✉ (0.5W   on 250) **Colony House Motel** 540.942.4156 $42-70+tax, pets $10, some snacks sold on-site, all rooms have micro & fridge. Ask about tenting on-site. Maildrops: 494 Three Notched Mtn Hwy, Waynesboro, VA 22980.

🍴 King's Gourmet Popcorn Mid-March through Nov. M-F 9am-7pm; Sa,Su 8am-8pm; Dec-Mar open Thurs-Sun. Hot dogs, sodas, ice cream, coffee, kettle corn, and gourmet popcorn.

Waynesboro, VA 22980 (4.5W on I-64)

Home to **Hiker Fest** on June 13, gather at camp area 11am for food and a movie. Camping area (bottom right corner of map) has pavilion, grill, and solar charger; shower at YMCA nearby.

🍴 ☀ YMCA 540.942.5107 Free camping and showers. Use of YMCA facilities $10. Check-in at front desk, need photo ID.

🏠 👤 🛜 🖥 Grace Hiker Hostel Supervised hostel at Lutheran Church open May 19-June 20, closed Su nights, 2-night limit. Please do not call the church office. Check-in 5-8pm, check-out 9am; hikers staying over may leave packs. Cots in air-conditioned Fellowship Hall, showers, internet, big-screen TV with DVD, kitchenette with snacks and breakfast foods in a separate hiker lounge. 20 hiker max. No pets, smoking, drugs, alcohol, firearms or foul language. Donations gratefully

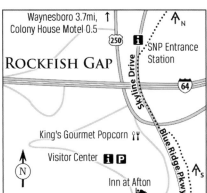

accepted. Congregation cooks free dinner Thursday nights followed by optional vespers service.

🏠 👤 ⛺ 🚐 🛜 🖥 Stanimal's 328 Hostel 540.290.4002 AdamStanley06@gmail.com $25 hiker-only hostel includes pickup/return to trail, mattress with clean linens, shower w/ towel, soap, laundry. Large private area including sunroom and finished basement, laptop, WiFi and DVDs. Fridge, freezer & microwave. Snacks, drinks, and ice cream for sale. Discounted slackpacking for multinight guests. Located in residential area but only 2 blocks from major hiker-valued businesses (grocery, restaurants). Please respect noise level. Hikers are required to call ahead and speak with owner prior to staying. Owned by Adam Stanley AT '04, PCT '10.

🛏 🛜 ✉ Tree Streets Inn 540.949.4484, $80S/D, includes breakfast, pool, snacks, no pets. Free pickup/return from Rockfish Gap with stay. Maildrops (pre-registered guests only): 421 Walnut Avenue, Waynesboro, VA 22980.

🛏 🛜 Belle Hearth B&B 540.943.1910 (www.bellehearth.com) $75S, $95D, higher on weekends, includes B, pool, pickup/return. No pets, no smoking.

🛏 🛜 🖥 Quality Inn 540.942.1171 Hiker rates $62.89S $67.14 up to 4 plus tax, pets $10. Includes continental breakfast.

🍴 Heritage on Main Hiker-friendly sports bar with variety of beer on tap, burgers, salads, sandwiches. Open 11-11. Live music Wed & Sat, trivia Thurs.

🍴 Weasie's Kitchen 5:30-8pm M-F, 5-2 weekends.

🎒 👤 Rockfish Gap Outfitters 540.943.1461 full service outfitter, Coleman/ alcohol/oz, other fuels, shuttle info. Freeze-dried foods. Located between town and trail, so ask your ride to stop on the way.

🚌 DuBose Egleston 540.487.6388 Shuttles Roanoke to Harpers Ferry.

🔧 Ace Hardware Coleman/oz.

🛶 Front Royal Outfitters 540.635.5440 Offers a variety of aquablaze options ranging from Port Republic to Snickers Gap; make arrangements from Waynesboro. Will store gear while you're on the river. Available Mar 15-Jun 25. Please learn the rules for camping on the river.

Stanimal's Hostel (1.5 mi from 340:)
540-290-4002

0.9 mi from 340:
Budget Inn:
540-942-9551
Royal Inn:
540-949-8253

McDonalds
Burger King
Gavid's
Little Caesars
Laundry Land
Dollar General
Papa Johns
Rite Aid
BP
Scotto's
CVS
Family Dollar
Tailgate Grill
Animal Hospital 540-943-3081
Hot-Spot (lounge, live music)
Ciro's
Healthy Habit
Waynesboro Area Learning Tree M-F 10-6
Green Leaf Grill
Market on Main
BZ Laundromat
Weasie's Kitchen
Arbys
Subway
LJ Silver / A&W
Pizza Hut
Hardees
Kline's Dairy Bar
Chick Peas
Broad St
Ace
Quality Inn
Jakes
Heritage on Main
Tourism Office
Constitution Park

West 2.1 mi to interstate 64
interchange where there is:

Martin's, Wal-Mart, Target,
and a dense cluster of restaurants
and motels including:

Chick-fil-A, Cracker Barrel,
Outback, Wendy's, Shoneys,
KFC, Buffalo Wild Wings,
Applebees, Ruby Tuesdays
Panera Bread

Best Western: 540-942-1100
Comfort Inn: 540-932-3060
Days Inn: 540-943-1101
Super 8: 540-943-3888
HI Express: 540-932-7170

Augusta Medical Clinic (inside
Walmart) 540-245-7329

Zeus 8 Digital Movie Theater

Magnolia Ave
Poplar Ave
Laundromat
Stone Soup
Main St
Federal St
Sam's Hot Dogs
Graham's
Shoe Services
(also repairs gear)
540-943-7463

WAYNESBORO, VA

Pop. 21,454 (2006)
N38 04.150, W78 53.367
Mag. Dec. 9° 15'W

12th St
11th St
Tree
Streets
Inn
Ming Garden AYCE L/D
Kroger (24hrs) 540-943-3172
PO (22980):
540-942-7320
M-F 9-5

Maple Ave
Walnut Ave
Belle Hearth B&B
Market Ave
Arch Ave
South River Greenway (0.9 mile)

14th St
Wayne Ave
Grace Lutheran
South River

Royal Mart
Library 540-942-6746, M-F 9-9, Sa 9-5
YMCA showers
Hiker camping with hammock posts
and solar powered charger

Tastee
Freez
Mi Rancho

A.T. 3.7 mi;
Rockfish Gap
Outfitters
0.8 mi

1.5 mi

Backcountry Permits are required for overnight hikes within the park. There is no charge for the permit and there is a fine for not having one. Permits are available from self-registration sites at the south and north entrance of the AT into SNP, from any park visitor center, or by mail (see contact information above).

Concrete 4"x4" signposts are used to mark intersections. Information is stamped into an aluminum band at the top of the post.

What is known as a "shelter" on most of the AT is called a "hut" in Shenandoah, and three-sided day-use-only structures are called "shelters." When overnighting in the park, please use the huts or designated campsites, which are usually near the huts.

Backcountry stay is limited to 14 consecutive nights; two at any one location. If you cannot tent in a designated campsite, follow LNT principles of dispersed camping. Tenting at a new location is limited to one night and must be:

- 20 yards from the trail (preferably out of view).
- One quarter mile from any park facility (roads, campgrounds, lodges, visitor centers, and picnic areas).
- 10 yards from any water source.
- 50 yards from other camping parties, building ruins, or "no camping" signs.
- Not within designated "no camping" locations.

Groups are limited to 10. Campfires are only permitted at pre-constructed fire rings at the huts. Pets must be leashed.

Lodges and campgrounds are typically full on weekends. A small number of unreserved walk-in tentsites are available on a first-come, first-served basis at all campgrounds except Lewis Mtn.

Delaware North Companies Parks & Resorts 877.247.9261 ⟨GoShenandoah.com⟩ operates the Skyland Resort, Big Meadows Lodge and Lewis Mountain Cabins, gift shops & camp stores and restaurants within Shenandoah National Park; many readily accessible from the trail.

The Park Service operates campgrounds. Call 877.444.6777 or visit ⟨www.recreation.gov⟩ to reserve campsites. All campsites accommodate 2 tents and up to 6 persons. All except Mathews Arm have coin operated laundry and showers. Many facilities are closed November-May and all are closed December-March.

🚖 **Yellow Cab of the Shenandoah** 540.692.9200 serves all of SNP (24/7). Pet friendly, accepts CC.

✖ Which Skyline Drive overlook features a display showing a couple hiking the Appalachian Trail?

If You Plan to be a 2000-Miler

The ATC recognizes hikers who have completed the trail, all at once or in sections, with a "2000-miler" certificate. Your name will be printed in the March/April issue of ATC's member magazine, *AT Journeys*, and listed on ATC's website. The honor system application states that conditional bypasses and reroutes are acceptable and that "Issues of sequence, direction, speed, length of time or whether one carries a pack are not considered." The number "2,000" is used out of tradition, and does not imply that hiking less than the full mileage qualifies. Feel free to set your own agenda on the AT, but if 2000-miler recognition is important to you keep in mind that the application will ask if you "have made an honest effort to walk the entire Trail."

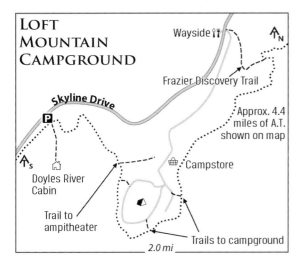

LOFT MOUNTAIN CAMPGROUND

Wayside

Frazier Discovery Trail

Skyline Drive

Approx. 4.4 miles of A.T. shown on map

Doyles River Cabin

Trail to ampitheater

Campstore

Trails to campground

2.0 mi

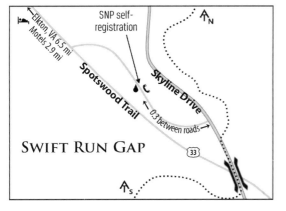

Elkton, VA 6.5 mi
Motels 2.9 mi

SNP self-registration

Spotswood Trail

Skyline Drive

0.3 between roads

33

SWIFT RUN GAP

| 888.4, 889.0 | Loft Mountain Campground |
| 889.6 | Loft Mountain Wayside |

Loft Mountain Campground Campsites $15. AT skirts the campground, and several short side trails lead to campsites and the camp store. Showers, laundry and long term resupply available from camp store. Open May-Oct.

Loft Mountain Wayside 1.1 miles from camp store, serves B/L/D, short-order menu, M-F 9-6, Sa-Su 9-7. Open 4/22 - 11/9.

907.1   US 33, Swift Run Gap. US 33 is also known as Spotswood Trail. The AT crosses over US 33 on the Skyline Drive. North of the bridge, take access road to the west to reach US 33.

(2.9W):

Country View Motel 540.298.0025 $50 most rooms hold 4. shuttle possible back to trail and to Elkton. Pets okay. Maildrops for guests: 19974 Spotswood Trail, Elkton, VA 22827.

(3.2W):

Swift Run Camping 540.298.8086, $20 campsite, laundry, pool, and snack bar.

Bear Mountain Grocery with deli, daily 6am–9pm.

(6.5W): *Elkton, VA 22827*

M-F 8:30-4:30, Sa 9-11, 540.298.7772

Food Lion, **O'Dell's Grocery**

Pizza Hut, several fast-food restaurants

Rite Aid

915.3, 915.4   Lewis Mountain Campground

Lewis Mountain Campground and Cabins 540.999.2255 Campsites $15, cabin rates seasonal, open Apr 2 - Nov 8. Reservations 877.847.1919. Lewis Mountain Camp store open in summer Su-Th 9-6, F-Sa 9-7.

SoBo	NoBo	Feature	Elev
1296.8	892.4	Cross Ivy Creek ◑	2580
1296.1	893.1	View to west ⌖	2961
1295.3	893.9	West to Skyline 77.5, Ivy Creek Overlook ⌖	2890
1293.7	895.5	**Pinefield Hut** (0.1E), Skyline Dr (0.1W) ☾ ◇ ◑ ⌂ (6) 38.9◄26.2◄13.2◄▶8.2▶20.6▶32.1 Spring on trail to shelter and 50 yards behind. Both unreliable. Campsites uphill, beyond shelter.	2493
1293.5	895.7	Skyline 75.2, Pinefield Gap. N38 17.411 W78 38.511 🅿	2590
1292.7	896.5	Weaver Mountain	2870
1291.6	897.6	Skyline 73.2, Simmons Gap ◑ Simmons Gap ranger station on paved road 0.2E from where AT crosses Skyline. Water available at pump outside buildings.	2250
1288.8	900.4	View east to Powell Gap Hollow ⌖	2577
1288.3	900.9	Skyline 69.9, Powell Gap.	2294
1286.7	902.5	Skyline 68.6, Smith Roach Gap	2600
1285.5	903.7	**Hightop Hut** (0.1W), reliable spring 0.1 from shelter ☾ ◑ ◑ (8) ⌂ (6) 34.4◄21.4◄8.2◄▶12.4▶23.9▶34.8	3200
1285.0	904.2	Spring east of AT	3534
1284.8	904.4	View to west from flank of Hightop Mtn. ⌖	3523
1283.4	905.8	Skyline 66.7 N38 20.691 W78 33.183 🅿	2650
1282.4	906.8	Stream. ◑	2509
1282.1	907.1	Skyline 65.5, Swift Run Gap, **Elkton, VA** (6.4W). Bridge over US 33, ◑ ☎ (pg.85) access rd north of bridge 0.1W to phone, water (treat), SNP self-registration	2367
1280.5	908.7	Saddleback Mtn Trail to east.	3020
1279.5	909.7	Trail 0.3E to spring at former South River Shelter site ◑	2956
1279.0	910.2	South River Picnic Area 0.1W. ◑ ⅋ N38 22.904 W78 31.151 🅿 (0.1W)	2884
1278.6	910.6	Falls Trail to east. South River Fire Road.	2880
1277.0	912.2	Baldface Mountain	3615

NoBo	Feature	Elev	SoBo
913.4	Spring, Pocosin Cabin (locked), Parking on Skyline. N38 24.813 W78 29.379 **P ◆**	3150	1275.8
913.5	Trail west to parking on Skyline **P ◆**	3147	1275.7
915.3	West to **Lewis Mtn Campground & Cabins** (pg.85)	3444	1273.9
915.4	West to **Lewis Mtn Campground.** N38 26.234 W78 28.737 **P** (pg.85)	3392	1273.8
916.1	**Bearfence Mountain Hut** (0.2E; 0.1 on gravel rd, 0.1 on side trail) 33.8◀20.6◀12.4◀▶11.5▶22.4▶26.8 **P** △ ◄ (6)	3212	1273.1
916.8	Bearfence Mountain Loop Trail, two intersections 0.2 mile apart, views 0.1E. 📷	3523	1272.4
917.3	Skyline 56.4, Bearfence Mtn Trail, parking 0.1W. N38 27.141 W78 28.015 **P**	3397	1271.9
918.7	Skyline 55.1, Bootens Gap N38 28.049 W78 27.440 **P**	3243	1270.5
919.2	Laurel Prong Trail to east. ◆	3514	1270.0
919.6	Hazeltop.	3812	1269.6
921.5	Skyline 52.8, Milam Gap, parking to east. N38 29.928 W78 26.741 **P**	3300	1267.7
922.1	Spring, No camping in Big Meadows clearing within sight of Skyline Dr ◆	3266	1267.1
922.6	Tanners Ridge Rd (gravel), cemetery	3325	1266.6
923.2	Lewis Spring & Road, Lewis Falls 0.5W. N38 27.141 W78 28.015 **P ◆** (pg.88) Gravel road 0.2E to Skyline, then left 0.2 to **Big Meadows Wayside**	3332	1266.0
923.7	Rock outcropping, view 📷	3618	1265.5
924.1	Trail to **Big Meadows Lodge**, Lewis Falls 0.5W (pg.88)	3563	1265.1
924.5	Trail east to **Big Meadows Campground** (pg.88)	3560	1264.7
924.7	David Spring 20 yards west ◆	3490	1264.5
924.9	Stream. ◆	3381	1264.3
925.7	Fishers Gap, Skyline 49.3 to east, maintenance road	3050	1263.5
925.9	Franklin Cliffs, view. 📷	3023	1263.3
927.0	Trail to Spitler Knoll parking, 4 cars N38 32.892 W78 24.828 **P**	3238	1262.2
927.6	**Rock Spring Hut** (0.2W). 32.1◀23.9◀11.5◀▶10.9▶15.3▶28.4 Locked cabin in front. ◣ ◆ ◄ (9) ◄ (8)	3530	1261.6
927.9	Trail east to Hawksbill Mountain, no camping anywhere above 3600'	3640	1261.3
928.9	Hawksbill Gap, parking to east. N38 33.776 W78 22.952 **P**	3361	1260.3
929.4	Stream, trail to Crescent Rock Overlook, parking to east. **P** 📷 ◆	3416	1259.8
930.2	Spring. ◆	3314	1259.0
931.1	Spring. ◆	3440	1258.1
931.4	Skyland stables, service road **P**	3550	1257.8
932.0	Trail to **Skyland Resort & Restaurant** (0.1W) (pg.88) **P**	3748	1257.2
932.1	Skyland service road north. **P**	3697	1257.1

923.2   Lewis Spring Rd (See map for easiest access.)
924.1   Big Meadows Lodge

♦️🏠 Big Meadows Wayside B/L/D, Fuel/oz at gas station. Open 3/17 - 11/30.

🛏️🍴🔋 Big Meadows Lodge Lodge rooms, cabins & suites, reservations required. Some pet-friendly rooms. B: 7:30-10:30, L: 12-2, D: 5:30-9. Open 5/14 - first Sun of Nov.

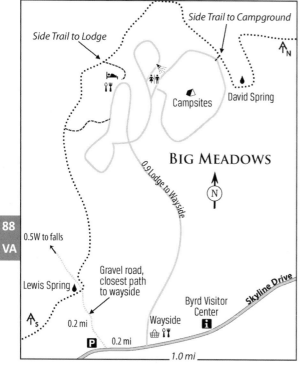

Side Trail to Lodge

Side Trail to Campground

🛏️
🍴

🚿
🚹🚺

🏕️
Campsites

💧
David Spring

BIG MEADOWS

N

0.9 Lodge to Wayside

0.5W to falls

Lewis Spring

0.2 mi

Gravel road, closest path to wayside

0.2 mi

Byrd Visitor Center ℹ️

Wayside 🏚️🍴

🅿️

Skyline Drive

1.0 mi

88
VA

924.5   Big Meadows Campground 540.999.3231

♦️🚶🏕️ Big Meadows Campground Tentsites $20 for 2 tents & 6 persons, self-register after-hours. Coin laundry & showers, Open late Mar-Oct.

932.0   Side trail to Skyland

🛏️🍴🔋🚶 Skyland Resort and Restaurant 540.999.2212 Rates seasonal, reservations required. Dining room hours B: 7:30-10:30, L: 12-2:30, D: 5:30-9, nightly entertainment. Snack foods and sodas sold at gift shop and vending machines. Open 3/27 - Sunday following Thanksgiving.

941.7   US 211, Thornton Gap

🛏️🍴📶 (4.5W on US 211) to **Brookside Cabins & Restaurant** 540.743.5698 $85-$200 cabins open year-round, range in size (2-6 persons). A few have kitchen & hot tub, no TV or phone. Restaurant AYCE on weekends, closed in winter (Dec-Mar).

🛏️♦️🍴🏧🏕️ (5.3W) **Yogi Bear's Jellystone Park** 540.743.4002 Cabins $55-$475 hold 4-19, summer weekend 3-night min. Tent sites $40-85, 2-night min. Pets at tentsites and some cabins. All stays include free water slide, paddle boat, mini golf. Memorial to Labor Day snack shop serving hamburgers, hot dogs, pizza. Coin laundry, camp store, pool.

🛏️🏕️📶🖥️ (6.9W) **Days Inn** 540.743.4521 $65-$285, pool, cont. B, pets $15.

Luray, VA 22835 (9W) Farmer's market held on Saturdays.

🛏️📶🖥️ Budget Inn 540.743.5176 $55D/up, $10EAP, pets $10. Maildrops 320 W. Main St, Luray, VA 22835.

🛏️📶 Luray Caverns Motels East & west buildings 540.743.4536, 888.941.4531, Su-Th $73, F-Sa $91. 20% discount coupon on food at Luray Caverns. No pets. Maildrops with reservation: 831 W. Main St, Luray, VA 22835.

🛏️📶 Cardinal Inn 888.648.4633 Hiker rate: winter $60, summer $75.

🛏️📶 South Court Inn B&B 540.843.0980 ⟨southcourtinn.com⟩ Discounted rate for hikers $100S/D when rooms available, includes big breakfast. No pets, smoking outside only. Wir sprechen Deutsch.

🛏️📶 Mayne View B&B 540.743.7921 ⟨mayneview.com⟩ $99-175D, includes full breakfast. 10% discount for single, $10EAP for rooms that hold 4. Outdoor hot tub w/view, movie library.

Best Western 540.743.6511 Call for rates, pet fee $20.

Woodruff House & Victorian Inn B&B 540.743.1494

Mimslyn Inn 540.743.5105 Rooms $169/up, **Speakeasy** on-site, dinner 4-11pm, full bar and W-F entertainment.

Appalachian Outdoors Adventures 540.743.7400 Full-service outfitter, Coleman/alcohol/oz, canisters, freeze-dried foods. M-Th 10-6, F-Sa 10-8, Su 1-5. Maildrops: 2 West Main St., Luray, VA 22835.

Visitor Center 540.743.3915 M-Sa 9-5, Su 12-4.
5mi. north of town on Shenandoah River:

Rock Tavern River Kamp 540.843.4232 Tentsites $45 for 4, Yurt $110 (4 person), luxury cabins hold up to 10. Canoe portage around Shenandoah River Dam, please call 24 hrs in advance.

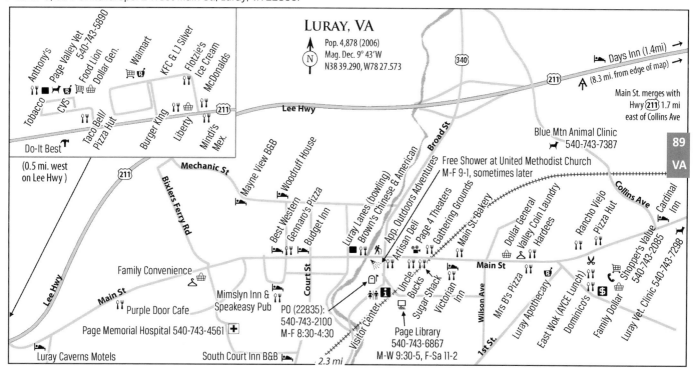

LURAY, VA
Pop. 4,878 (2006)
Mag. Dec. 9° 43'W
N38 39.290, W78 27.573

90
VA

SoBo	NoBo	Description	Elev
1256.6	932.6	Trail to Stony Man Summit (0.2W) Highest point on the AT in SNP.	3837
1256.1	933.1	Little Stony Man Cliffs, overlook to west.	3554
1255.8	933.4	Passamaquoddy Trail	3414
1255.5	933.7	Spur trail to parking N38 36.354 W78 21.983 🅿	3237
1255.1	934.1	Stony Man Overlook N38 36.735 W78 21.747 🅿	3092
1254.7	934.5	Nicholson Hollow Trail	3120
1254.6	934.6	Crusher Ridge Trail	3202
1254.0	935.2	Corbin Cabin Trail	3149
1253.5	935.7	Powerline	3333
1252.9	936.3	Pinnacles Picnic Area & Parking, restrooms, water from faucet. 🅿	3420
1252.7	936.5	East to Skyline 36.4, side trail to Jewell Hollow Overlook.	3335
1252.4	936.8	Leading Ridge Trail to west.	3409
1251.7	937.5	The Pinnacle	3730
1250.7	938.5	**Byrds Nest #3 Hut,** spring 0.4E on service road. 34.8◀22.4◀10.9▶4.4▶17.5▶28.0 (8)	3279
1250.3	938.9	View	3351
1250.0	939.2	Meadows Spring Trail to east (0.3E)	3389
1249.4	939.8	Overlook, Mary's Rock to west.	3504
1248.5	940.7	Spring	2917
1247.7	941.5	Trail to Panorama RR parking, powerline	2399
1247.5	941.7	US 211, Thornton Gap, **Luray, VA** (9W). N38 39.627 W78 19.326 🅿 (pg.88-89)	2307
1247.4	941.8	Skyline 31.2.	2413
1246.3	942.9	**Pass Mountain Hut** (1939) (0.2E) 26.8◀15.3◀4.4▶13.1▶23.6▶31.7 2 bear poles, 2 privies, and 8 tent sites. Piped spring 15 yards behind shelter. (8)	2812
1245.5	943.7	Pass Mountain	3052
1244.4	944.8	Beahms Gap Overlook, parking to east 🅿	2490
1244.0	945.2	Spring to west	2436
1243.1	946.1	Neighbor Mtn Trail, Byrds Nest #4 day use picnic area. (0.5E)	2666
1239.4	949.8	Stream, Jeremys Run Trail	2225
1238.9	950.3	**Elkwallow Wayside** (and Gap) 0.1E on side trail or on Skyline 23.9. Grill B/L/D, limited groceries, vending outside, 9-7 Early April-Early Oct. Frost-free pump at picnic area south of wayside.	2480
1238.2	951.0	Range View Cabin (locked) 0.1E (0.1E)	2971
1237.4	951.8	Skyline 21.9, Rattlesnake Point Overlook	3084
1236.8	952.4	Tuscarora Trail to **Mathews Arm Campground** (0.7W) Primitive campground open May-Oct; no services. Tent sites $14.	3400

SoBo	NoBo	Feature	Marker / Coordinates	Elev
1236.4	952.8	Skyline 21.1, Hogback parking	P	3350
1236.1	953.1	Skyline 20.8, Hogback Overlook	📷	3350
1234.9	954.3	Skyline 19.7, Little Hogback parking 50 yards east	P	3026
1234.8	954.4	Little Hogback Mountain, view	📷	3050
1234.2	955.0	Skyline 18.8		2822
1233.2	956.0	**Gravel Springs Hut** (0.2E), spring en route to shelter	☾ ◐ ⊂ (8)	2658
1233.0	956.2	28.4◄17.5◄13.1◄►10.5►18.6►24.1 Skyline 17.7, Gravel Springs Gap	N38 46.068 W78 14.010 P	2666
1232.2	957.0	View west		3063
1231.9	957.3	South Marshall Mountain	📷	3212
1231.4	957.8	Skyline 15.9, parking to west	P	3050
1230.7	958.5	North Marshall Mountain, view	📷	3368
1229.7	959.5	Hogwallow Flat		2952
1229.2	960.0	Skyline 14.2, Hogwallow Gap	N38 47.388 W78 11.319 P	2739
1227.5	961.7	Skyline 12.3, Jenkins Gap, parking to east	N38 48.389 W78 10.846 P	2400
1226.6	962.6	Compton Springs	◐	2700
1226.2	963.0	Compton Peak		2909
1225.4	963.8	Skyline 10.4, Compton Gap parking	N38 49.414 W78 10.234 P	2427
1223.6	965.6	Compton Gap Trail ("Chester Gap" post), **Front Royal Hostel** (0.5E) (pg. 94)		2350
1223.4	965.8	SNP permit self-registration station		2337
1222.7	966.5	**Tom Floyd Shelter** 28.0◄23.6◄10.5►►8.1►13.6►18.1 bear pole, trail behind shelter leads to water source, as do other side trails north of the shelter.	☾ ◐ ◐ ⊂ (6)	1961
1221.2	968.0	VA 602, stream	◐	1150
1219.8	969.4	US 522, **Front Royal, VA** (3.5W) N38 52.682 W78 9.044 P (pg.94-95) AT parallel to US 522 for 0.2mi between N & S trailheads		950
1219.0	970.2	Bear Hollow Creek	◐	1080
1216.4	972.8	Forest Service Rd		1841

Elev	NoBo	SoBo	Description
1760	973.0	1216.2	Sealock Spring, Mosby Campsite. Named after Colonel John Mosby ♦ ⚲ ◁
1668	973.7	1215.5	Powerline
1343	974.6	1214.6	**Jim & Molly Denton Shelter** Porch, chairs, solar shower,... ☽ ♦ 🚿 31.7◄18.6◄8.1◄▶5.5▶10.0▶18.4 bear pole, piped spring 100 yards south
1057	975.7	1213.5	Stream.
1081	975.8	1213.4	VA 638
800	977.6	1211.6	VA 55, Manassas Gap, RR tracks to south. . . . N38 54.550 W78 3.199 P (pg. 95); AT passes under I-66 on Tuckers Lane.
819	977.8	1211.4	Tuckers Lane parking, Footbridge, stream. N38 54.679 W78 3.178 P ♦
1431	979.1	1210.1	Stone wall.
1696	980.1	1209.1	**Manassas Gap Shelter** 24.1◄13.6◄5.5◄▶4.5▶12.9▶19.8 ☽ ♦ ◁ (6); Bear Pole. Reliable spring downhill to right of shelter on side trail. Blue-blazed trail south of shelter leads 0.9W to VA 638.
1736	981.4	1207.8	Spring ♦
2102	982.1	1207.1	Trico Tower Trail 0.4W to comm tower, some parking on VA 638.
1409	984.6	1204.6	**Dicks Dome Shelter** (0.2E) 18.1◄10.0◄4.5◄▶8.4▶15.3▶29.5. ☽ ♦ ◁ (4); Whiskey Hollow Creek in front of shelter (treat water). Stream on AT 75 yards north of shelter side trail.
1632	985.0	1204.2	Powerline
1772	985.6	1203.6	Spring ♦
1851	985.8	1203.4	Signal Knob parking on VA-638 / Fire Trail Rd 0.1W.. N38 59.112 W77 59.980 P ◁
1851	986.6	1202.6	Boundary to Sky Meadows State Park.
1821	986.9	1202.3	Bench. 1.7E to **Sky Meadows State Park Visitors Center.** 🅷 🚻 ⚲ ♦ ◁; 800-933-PARK Open W-Su, 8-5, restrooms, soda machine, 12 sites & primitive group camping, $9PP, reservation required, campers must arrive before dusk.
1598	987.7	1201.5	View 0.4E on Ambassador Whitehouse Trail 📷
914	989.3	1199.9	Two footbridges, streams ♦
960	989.4	1199.8	Ashby Gap, US 50/17
1090	989.6	1199.6	Trail 0.1E to parking on VA 601, Blueridge Mtn Rd . . . N39 0.942 W77 57.718 P
1142	990.8	1198.4	Stream. ♦
1042	991.4	1197.8	Stream. ♦
1122	991.7	1197.5	Trail west to Myron Glaser Cabin (locked)
1010	992.2	1197.0	Stream. ♦
1107	992.6	1196.6	Fishers Hill Trail to west
917	993.0	1196.2	**Rod Hollow Shelter** (0.1W) 18.4◄12.9◄8.4◄▶6.9▶21.1▶36.7 ☽ △ ◁ (8); Piped spring left of shelter. Stream on AT south of side trail.

SoBo	NoBo		Elev
1195.8	**993.4**	Stream, Fishers Hill Trail to west, south end of The Roller Coaster 13.5 miles of tightly packed ascents and descents.	824
1194.5	**994.7**	Spring at Bolden Hollow	871
1192.9	**996.3**	Footbridge, Morgan Mill Stream, campsite	800
1192.4	**996.8**	VA 605, Morgan Mill Rd (gravel) N39 4.327 W77 54.720 **P**	1060
1191.7	**997.5**	Stream.	1034
1190.8	**998.4**	Buzzard Hill, AT east of summit	1276
1190.2	**999.0**	Two streams	836
1189.3	**999.9**	**Sam Moore Shelter** (1990) 19.8◀15.3◀6.9◀▶14.2▶29.8▶33.9 Springs in front of shelter and to the left. Several tent sites to left of shelter.	931
1188.8	**1000.4**	Campsite	1305
1188.0	**1001.2**	Spout Run Ravine, stream	736
1186.8	**1002.4**	Footbridge, stream, campsite 60 yards north on AT	834
1186.3	**1002.9**	Bears Den Rocks, **Bears Den Hostel** (0.2E), view north on AT. (pg. 95)	1267
1185.7	**1003.5**	Snickers Gap, VA 7 & 679 (Pine Grove Rd).. N39 6.919 W77 50.849 **P** (pg.95)	1000
1184.9	**1004.3**	Stream.	851
1183.5	**1005.7**	Stream.	902
1183.2	**1006.0**	**VA-WV** border	1193
1183.0	**1006.2**	Raven Rocks, Crescent Rock 0.1E, view	1297
1182.8	**1006.4**	Campsite, trail east of tower	1427
1182.4	**1006.8**	The Roller Coaster (north end); 13.5 miles of ascents and descents Sand Spring to west, good water source, Devils Racecourse boulder field to north	1200
1179.5	**1009.7**	Wilson Gap	1380
1178.3	**1010.9**	Two trails 0.2E to **Blackburn AT Center** ... N39 11.259 W77 47.866 **P** (pg. 95)	1650
1176.6	**1012.6**	Laurel Springs, boardwalk.	1458

965.6 Compton Gap Trail (post labeled "VA 610/Chester Gap")

🏠🔥⛺🚐✉ **Front Royal Terrapin Station Hostel** (0.5E)
540.539.0509, Go east (straight ahead for NoBo) on Compton Gap Trail 0.5 mi. to paved road. Hostel is first house on the left on paved road. Enter around back through marked gate. Open Apr 27-July 6, 2015. Bunk only $23, shower $3, laundry $3. Hiker special $30 icludes bunk, shower, laundry, 2 sodas, 2 small pizzas & pint of ice cream. Two-night special $50 also includes slackpack. Free morning shuttle to town for groceries, PO, etc... Fuel, snacks, sodas, ice cream & oven pizza on site. Bunks have blow-up mattress, sheets, pillow & charging station. Shower includes soap & shampoo. Hikers only, picture ID required, reservations encouraged. Owned by Mike Evans (AT '95, PCT '98), ⟨gratefulgg@hotmail.com⟩. Guest maildrops: 304 Chester Gap Rd, Chester Gap, VA 22623.

🚐 **Mobile Mike's** 540.539.0509 shuttles and more (Mike Evans).

969.4 US 522 (Remount Road) *Front Royal 22630* (4W)
🏠🔥📮✉ **Mountain Home Cabbin** 540.692.6198
MountainHomeAT@gmail.com. Renovated "cabbin" at historic home of Lisa & Scott ("Possible" AT '12) Jenkins, 3471 Remount Rd (US 522). AT parallels 522 for 0.25; home with red roof on the **north** side of 522, 100 yards east of the AT. Open year-round. Walk-ins okay Apr-Sept,

94
VA

FRONT ROYAL, VA
Pop. 14,561 (2006)
N38 54.650, W78 11.083
Mag. Dec. 9° 58' W

PO (22630):
540-635-8482
M-F 8:30-5,
Sa 8:30-1

Distances from Quality Inn:
0.6 to Post office
0.7 to Martin's
0.7 to CVS
1.1 to Library
1.5 to Pizza Hut

Valley Health Urgent Care 540-635-0700

Royal Oak Animal Clinic 540-636-2000

Budget Inn 540-636-0300

Warren Memorial Hospital 540-636-0300

Library 540-645-3153
M-Th 10-8, F-Sa 10-5

4pm Fri - 6pm Sun. Other times, call/email for reservations. Sleeps up to 6, individually or as a group. $20PP includes bed, fresh linens, bath/shower, breakfast & daily town shuttle for laundry & resupply. Pizza, ice cream, snacks & canister fuel for sale on site. All hikers welcome to get free lemonade, cookies, water from faucet on SW corner of the cabbin. Dogs may stay in outdoor kennel with doghouse. Parking $3/day. No alcohol; smoking outside in designated area.

🏠 🚻 🛜 **Visitor Center** 540.635.5788 7 days, 9-5pm. Often has hiker goodie bags. Restrooms, hiker box, pack storage. Cold drinks for sale.

🛏️⛺🛜✉ **Quality Inn** 540.635.3161 $67 S/D, $10EAP (up to 4) includes continental B. Pets $15. Pool. If you need ride back to AT in the morning, let them know when you check in. 🍴**Thunwa Thai** on-site. Maildrops: 10 Commerce Avenue, Front Royal, VA 22630.

🛏️⛺🛜 **Pioneer Motel** 540.631.1153 Clean and hiker freindly: $50 single, $55 double, tax included. Mini fridge & microwave in all rooms.

🛏️🛜 **Woodward House B&B** 540.635.7010 Hiker rate Su-Th $110D + tax includes breakfast, pickup and return to trail.

🛏️🛜🖥 **Super 8** 540.636.4888 10% hiker discount, pets $10.

🛏️🛜 **Scottish Inn** 540.636.6168 $50/up, pets $10.

🛏️🛜 **Budget Inn** 540.635.2196

🍴 **Lucky Star Lounge** L/D variety, some vegetarian, live music.

🏪 **Stokes Market** Wonderfully random selection of goods & foods.

977.6   VA 55, Manassas Gap, *Linden, VA 22642* (1.2W)

📪 M-F 8-12 & 1-5, Sa 8-12, 540.636.9936, packages held only 15 days.

🍴   **Apple House Restaurant** 540.636.6329 Tu-Su 7-8, M 7-5 year-round. Hiker specials, some supplies and rides sometimes available.

🏪 **Monterey Convenience Store**

1002.9   Bears Den Rocks

🏛️🛶🚿🏪🔧⛺🅿🖥✉ **Bears Den Hostel** 540.554.8708 ⟨www.bearsdencenter.org⟩ A castle-like stone lodge, ATC owned and PATC operated. Bunk $17PP, tenting $12PP includes full house privileges. Hiker Special: Bunk, laundry, pizza, soda & pint of Ben & Jerry's ice cream $30PP. All stays include shower & self-serve pancake breakfast. Credit cards accepted. Hiker room with TV, shower, Internet & sodas, accessible all day by entering a mileage code at the hostel door. Upper lodge, kitchen, camp store & office open 5-9pm daily. Checkout 9am. Slackpacking & shuttles may be available during summer months. Parking $3/day. Hosts the **Northern Ruck** Jan 23-25, 2015. No drugs or alcohol anywhere on the property. Pets welcome, but not allowed inside. Maildrops can be picked up during office hours: Bears Den Hostel, 18393 Blue Ridge Mountain Rd, Bluemont, VA 20135. ✖ What is the Virginia license plate number?

Purcellville, VA

🥾🚐 **Appalachian Outdoor Readiness** 540.338.2437 ⟨www.appalachianreadiness.com⟩ Full service outfitter delivers gear to Bears Den, Harpers Ferry, and trailheads in-between. Store is 6mi. from Bears Den in Purcellville, VA, where there is a PO and many restaurants. Call for $20 round-trip shuttle 10am-6pm.

1003.5   Snickers Gap, VA 7 & 679 (Pine Grove Rd). AT crosses VA 7 at its intersection with Pine Grove Rd. Take Pine Grove Rd. west to anitque shop & restaurants. For PO, take VA 7 0.8E, then right on route 734 for another 0.8 mile.

Bluemont, VA 20135

📪 (1.7E) M-F 10-1 & 2-5, Sa 8:30-12, 540.554.4537

🏪🛜💧 (0.2W) **Snickers Gap Antiques** Hiker-friendly store with limited snacks & first aid items, WiFi, free water fill-up.

🍴(0.3W) **Horseshoe Curve Restaurant** 540.554.8291 Tu,W 5-9; Th-Sa 12-9, Su 12-8. Good pub food.

🍴(0.9W) **Pine Grove Restaurant** 540.554.8126 M-Sa 6:30-8, Su7-2.

1010.9 Side trails, both (0.27E) to:

🏛️🛶🔥🔌💧 **Blackburn AT Center** 540.338.9028. PATC caretaker on-site. Hiker bunks in small cabin with wood-burning stove. On porch of main building: logbook, donation box, pay phone, and electrical outlets (welcome to charge devices). Solar shower on lawn, water from hose, picnic tables. Open year-round.

SoBo	NoBo		Elev
		Buzzard Rocks	1532
1175.6	1013.6		1438
1175.1	1014.1	**David Lesser Memorial Shelter** (0.1E) · ♪ ♦ ◢ ⊏ (6)	
		29.5◀21.1◀14.2◀▶15.6▶19.7▶24.7 Overflow camping area below shelter. Spring 0.2 mile downhill from shelter.	
1173.8	1015.4	Roadbed.	1334
1172.1	1017.1	Keys Gap, WV 9, markets 0.3E or W ·········· N39 15.694 W77 45.750 **P** (pg. 98)	926
1170.6	1018.6	Powerline	923
1169.9	1019.3	Campsite ◢	1120
1168.2	1021.0	**VA-WV** border, Loudoun Heights, Loudoun Heights Trail to east	1134
1167.6	1021.6	WV 32, Chestnut Hill Rd	599
1166.7	1022.5	US 340, north end of Shenandoah River Bridge ⚠ No hitchhiking on 340 ·········· (pg.98)	336
1166.4	1022.8	Side trail to **Appalachian Trail Conservancy** (0.2W) ·········· (pg.98)	440
1166.0	1023.2	Jefferson Rock, view north to Potomac and Shenandoah Rivers ◉	450
1165.8	1023.4	**Harpers Ferry, WV,** High Street ·········· N39 18.989 W77 45.350 **P** (pg.98-99)	297
1165.5	1023.7	Potomac River, Byron Memorial Footbridge, **WV-MD** border. North of river turn east on C&O Canal Towpath. No camping on AT section of towpath.	275
1164.4	1024.8	Pass under Sandy Hook Bridge (US 340)	289
1162.9	1026.3	C&O Canal Towpath north end, RR tracks, US 340 underpass ·········· (pg.100)	266
1162.3	1026.9	From Keep Tryst Rd: **Knoxville, MD** (1.0W), **Brunswick, MD** (2.5E) Weverton Rd ·········· N39 19.977 W77 40.993 **P**	392
1161.6	1027.6	Trail east to Weverton Cliffs, view ◉	880

✽ **Poison Ivy** – Vine that can grow as ground cover or that can cling to trees or other brush. Stems redden toward the end and terminate with 3 pointed-oval leaves.

SoBo	NoBo		Elev
1159.5	1029.7	**Ed Garvey Shelter** ·········· ♪ ♦ ◢ ⊏ (12)	1100
		36.7◀29.8◀15.6◀▶4.1▶9.1▶16.6 Water on steep 0.4 mile trail in front of shelter. 2 tent sites north & south of shelter.	
1157.7	1031.5	Brownsville Gap, roadbed	1082
1155.8	1033.4	Gapland Rd, Gathland State Park, War Correspondents ·········· ♟ 🏕 ♦ (pg.100) Monument. Frost-free spigot by restrooms. No camping, no trash cans.	950

SoBo	NoBo	Description	Elev
1155.4	1033.8	**Crampton Gap Shelter** (0.3E), intermittent spring 0.1S on AT ⟍ △ △ ◀ ⊂ (6) 33.9◀19.7◀4.1◀▶5.0▶12.5▶20.7 NoBo: consider bringing water from Gathland SP in dry season.	1185
1152.8	1036.4	Spring 0.5E, trail to Bear Spring Cabin (locked)	1458
1152.2	1037.0	White Rock Cliff, view.	1606
1152.0	1037.2	Lambs Knoll 50 yards west to tower, view	1751
1150.9	1038.3	Lambs Knoll tower road (paved)	1374
1150.4	1038.8	**Rocky Run Shelter** (0.2W) 24.7◀9.1◀5.0◀▶7.5▶15.7▶20.6 ⟍ △ ◀ ⊂ (16) Left fork on side trail to better water source & old shelter. Right to new shelter.	1011
1149.4	1039.4	Fox Gap, Reno Monument Rd (paved)	1057
1148.6	1040.6	**Dahlgren Backpack Campground** (2E). ⚿ △ ◀ Large tenting area, picnic tables, restrooms; no fee. Note proximity to road.	980
1148.3	1040.9	Turners Gap, US Alt 40, restaurant 0.1W, **Boonsboro, MD** (2.5W) (pg.100-101)	1086
1147.0	1042.2	Monument Rd.	1350
1146.7	1042.5	Washington Monument State Park, picnic tables, P △△ parking and restrooms adjacent to visitor center.	1427
1146.4	1042.8	Washington Monument (0.1W)	1550
1146.1	1043.1	Powerline.	1319
1144.3	1044.9	Boonsboro Mountain Rd, residential area.	1324
1144.0	1045.2	Bartman Hill Trail 0.6W to Greenbrier SP	1409
1143.6	1045.6	I-70 footbridge, US 40 N39 32.115 W77 36.209 **P** (pg.100) Parking north end of footbridge 0.1E. Also cross Boonsboro Mtn Rd south of hwy.	1267
1142.9	1046.3	**Pine Knob Shelter** (0.1W), south end of loop trail ⟍ △ ◀ ⊂ (5) 16.6◀12.5◀7.5◀▶8.2▶13.1▶22.7 Piped spring next to shelter.	1404
1141.3	1047.9	Annapolis Rocks to west, campsite. △ ◀ (0.2W) ◀ (13) Caretaker on site. Tentsites near outstanding overlook.	1820
1140.3	1048.9	Black Rock Cliffs to west	1821
1139.9	1049.3	Black Rock Creek	1591
1139.7	1049.5	**Pogo Memorial Campsite** ⟍ △ ◀ Campsite east of AT, spring 100 yards west. Thurston Griggs Trail to west.	1500

1017.1 Keys Gap, WV 9

🛏🍴💲📫 (0.3E) **Sweet Springs Country Store** 540.668.7200 M-Sa 4am-11pm, Su 7am-11pm. Good selection of hiker foods. Stove fuel. Maildrops: 34357 Charles Town Pike, Purcellville, VA 20132.

🏠🍴 (0.3W veer left at intersection) **Mini-Mart & Torlone's Pizza**

🏠🍴⛺ (2.0E) **Stoney Brook Organic Farm** 703.622.7526, 571.442.2834, 540.668.9067 (Matt or Nathan) Spiritual Community offers WFS, meals, shower, laundry. Pickup/return from Bears Den, Blackburn Trail Center, Keys Gap, Harpers Ferry. Grocery and outfitter nearby. Maildrops: 37091 Charles Town Pike Hillsboro, VA 20132

1022.5   US 340, Shenandoah River Bridge
Go west on 340 to the Quality Hotel, KOA, or to Charles Town; east to Frederick. NoBos stay on the AT for better access to Harpers Ferry.

🛏⛺🛜🖥 **Econo Lodge** 304.535.6391 $89–$119 (peak rate mid-summer), 10% hiker discount, hot breakfast bar, no pets.

🔦🛏🍴🏠🍽⛺ (1.2W) **Harpers Ferry KOA** 304.535.6895 Camping $40/up, cabins $87/up, both prices for 2 persons, $6EAP. Coin laundry on-site, shower only $5. Cafe has limited hours.

🛏🍴⛺🛜🖥 (1.3W) **Quality Hotel** 304.535.6302 Pool, **Vista Tavern** (L/D) on-site.

Charles Town, WV 25414 (6W) All major services.

🚌🛒 **Walmart** with grocery and pharmacy 304.728.2720

✚ **Jefferson Urgent Care** 304.728.8533 M-F 9-7, Sa-Su 9-5

✚ **Winchester Foot & Ankle** 304.725.0084

🐾 **Jefferson Animal Hospital** 304.725.0428

Frederick, MD 21701 (20E) All major services.

1022.8   Side Trail to ATC HQ (0.2W)
ℹ️👤🛜📫 **ATC HQ** 304.535.6331 ⟨www.appalachiantrail.org⟩ Open year-round, 7 days 9–5, Closed Thanksgiving, Christmas, New Year's Day; extended hours in June (check appalachiantrail.org/locations for updates). If you're thru-hiking or hiking the entire trail in sections, have your photo taken for the album; a postcard version of this photo may be purchased (first one free for ATC members). Hiker lounge, register, scale, and cold & hot drinks inside, along with hats, shirts, maps, all ATC publications. Coleman/denatured alcohol/oz for donation. Information board on the front porch. Maildrops: (USPS) PO Box 807 or (FedEx/UPS) 799 Washington St, Harpers Ferry, WV 25425. ✗This tree trunk has two blazes, but they're not white. On the AT they often surround you, just out of sight. What color are they and what are they for?

1023.4   Harpers Ferry, WV 25425 *(more services on map)*
🛏👤🏠⛺🛜🖥📫 **Teahorse Hostel** 304.535.6848 0.5W of ATC ⟨www.teahorsehostel.com⟩. $33 per bunk plus tax includes waffle breakfast. Laundry $6. No pets, alcohol or smoking. Shuttle range Thornton Gap to Duncannon and Dulles Airport. Call before sending maildrops in off-season (winter). Maildrops ($2 fee for non-guests): 1312 W. Washington St., Harpers Ferry, WV 25425.

🛏 **Harpers Ferry Hostel** (in Knoxville, see pg. 100)

🛏🍴🏠⛺🚐 **Town's Inn Lodging, Dining & Supplies** 304.932.0677 ⟨www.TheTownsInn.com⟩ Room $120/$140 up to 4 persons. Walk-in rate (after noon, if avail) $40PP. Laundry $5, shuttles $1/mile, no maildrops, Visa/MC accepted. Restaurant & shop downstairs open 6am-10pm every day, stocked specifically for hiker resupply.

🛏🛜 **Laurel Lodge** 304.535.2886 $135-180 for 2 includes big breakfast, view overlooking Potomac. Call about maildrops.

🥾👤🏠 **The Outfitter at Harpers Ferry & Harpers Ferry General Store** 888.535.2087 Knowledgeable full service outfitter with good selection of shoes and trail food. Shuttle referrals. Open daily 10–6.

ℹ️🅿️ **Harpers Ferry National Historical Park** 304.535.6029 $6 entrance fee, long-term parking. Free shuttle bus to lower town.

🚐 **HostelHiker.com** 202.670.6323 Shuttles from Thorton Gap to Pen-Mar Park. Daily route to/from DC, Dulles & Baltimore. Insured.

🚐 **Mark "Strings" Cusic** 304.433.0028 mdcusic@frontier.com Shuttle range Rockfish Gap to Duncannon.

🚐 **Pan Tran** 304.263.0876 Route to Charles Town (Walmart) M-F 1:35 and 3:05, $2.50 each way.

🚆**Amtrak** 800-USA-RAIL "Capitol Limited" daily 11:25am-1:10pm HF to Washington, DC Union Station (DC to HF 4:05-5:16pm). $12 each way.

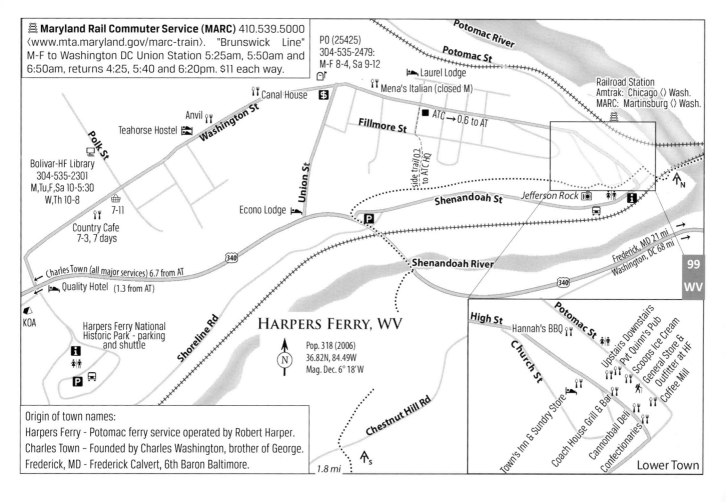

Maryland Rail Commuter Service (MARC) 410.539.5000 ⟨www.mta.maryland.gov/marc-train⟩. "Brunswick Line" M-F to Washington DC Union Station 5:25am, 5:50am and 6:50am, returns 4:25, 5:40 and 6:20pm. $11 each way.

PO (25425) 304-535-2479: M-F 8-4, Sa 9-12

⊨ Laurel Lodge

Canal House

Mena's Italian (closed M)

Anvil

Teahorse Hostel

Washington St

Railroad Station
Amtrak: Chicago ⟨⟩ Wash.
MARC: Martinsburg ⟨⟩ Wash.

Polk St

Bolivar-HF Library
304-535-2301
M,Tu,F,Sa 10-5:30
W,Th 10-8

■ ATC → 0.6 to AT

Fillmore St

side trail/0.2 to ATC HQ

7-11

Union St

Country Cafe
7-3, 7 days

Econo Lodge

P

Shenandoah St

Jefferson Rock 📷

N

340

Shenandoah River

Frederick, MD 21 mi
Washington, DC 68 mi

99
WV

← Charles Town (all major services) 6.7 from AT

← ⊨ Quality Hotel (1.3 from AT)

Shoreline Rd

KOA

Harpers Ferry National
Historic Park - parking
and shuttle

HARPERS FERRY, WV

N

Pop. 318 (2006)
36.82N, 84.49W
Mag. Dec. 6° 18'W

340

High St

Hannah's BBQ

Potomac St

Upstairs Downstairs
Pvt Quinn's Pub
Scoops Ice Cream
General Store &
Outfitter at HF
Coffee Mill

Church St

Town's Inn & Sundry Store

Coach House Grill & Bar

Cannonball Deli

Confectionaries

Chestnut Hill Rd

Origin of town names:
Harpers Ferry - Potomac ferry service operated by Robert Harper.
Charles Town - Founded by Charles Washington, brother of George.
Frederick, MD - Frederick Calvert, 6th Baron Baltimore.

1.8 mi

Lower Town

Potomac River

Potomac St

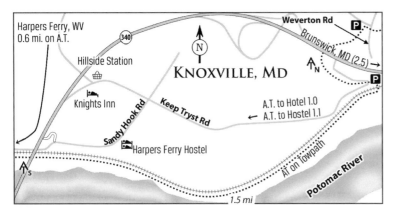

Harpers Ferry, WV
0.6 mi. on A.T.

340

Hillside Station

Knights Inn

KNOXVILLE, MD

N

Weverton Rd P

Brunswick, MD (2.5)

N

P

A.T. to Hotel 1.0
← A.T. to Hostel 1.1

Keep Tryst Rd

Sandy Hook Rd

Harpers Ferry Hostel

A.T. on Towpath

Potomac River

S

1.5 mi

1026.3 US 340, Keep Tryst Rd, *Knoxville, MD, 21758* (1W)

🏨⛵🛶⛺🏠🚌 **P** 🛜🖥✉ **Harpers Ferry Hostel** 301.834.7652
⟨www.harpersferryhostel.org⟩ Discounted thru-hiker rate $20.16 includes tax, shower, internet & WiFi, make-your-own AYCE pancakes, cupcakes, coffee & tea. Bunkroom has A/C & heat. Laundry $2 wash (soap provided), $2 dry. Tenting $6PP, pay extra $5 for shower and $3 for breakfast. Campers permitted inside only for shower, laundry or breakfast. WiFi on back porch, porta-potty, fire pits, grill. Service dogs okay inside, otherwise dogs on leash allowed only if tenting. Soda & Gatorade machine, store with hiker snacks, often free leftovers in fridge & hiker cupboard. Free pizza night on Tuesday and movie nights on request for inside guests. No drinking. Non-guest parking $5/day. Check-in 5-10pm, check out 10am. Open May 1–Nov 15 for individuals, year round for groups. Maildrops: 19123 Sandy Hook Rd, Knoxville, MD 21758.

🛏🛜 **Knights Inn** 301.660.3580 Hiker rate $59.99D, $69.99 for 3-4, includes continental breakfast.

🏠 ‖ **$** **Hillside Station** 301.834.5300 Convenience store with pizza, wings, and more. M-Sa 6am-8:30pm, Su 8-8.

Brunswick, MD 21716 (2.5E from Keep Tryst Rd)

🏠 M-F 8:30-4:30, Sa 9-12, 301.834.9944
‖ **Wing N' Pizza Shack** 301.834.5555 Delivers to HF Hostel

1033.4 Gathland SP

⛵🏠 **P** (0.4W) **Maple Tree Campground** 301.432.5585 $22 tentsite for one or two, $8EAP. Campstore has candy bars, sodas, batteries and microwavable food. Parking for section hikers. Open year-round. On Townsend road; the road to the right as you exit the park.

1040.9 Turners Gap, US Alt 40

‖ ⏷ (0.1W) **Old South Mountain Inn** 301.432.6155 Tu–F 5-9, Sa 4-close, Su brunch 10:30-2, dinner 12-7:30. Men, no sleevless shirts. Please shower first. Dining reservations preferred.

Boonsboro, MD (2.5W)

‖ **Vesta Pizzeria** 301.432.6166 M-Tu 11-9, W-Su 11-10. Delivers to Turner's Gap (Dahlgren campground).

‖ **Mountainside Deli** 301.432.6700 M-F 6am-8pm, Sa 8am-8pm, Su 11am-6pm.

🏠 **Cronise Market Place** 301.432.7377 M-Sa 9-7, Su 12-6

🛜 ‖ **Turn the Page Book Store Café** 301.432.4588

‖ 🏠 **Crawfords** 301.432.2903 M-F 7am-6pm, Sa 7am-3pm. Limited supplies.

1045.2 Bartman Hill Trail (0.6W) to:

⛵ 🚻 🧗 **Greenbrier State Park** 301.791.4767 Prices listed as MD resident/nonresident. Camping first Fri of Apr–last full weekend in October. Pets okay. Lunch concession stand open Mem-Labor Day. Entrance fee $5 not charged if camping or if you walk in on Bartman Trail. Tent sites with showers $26-28, higher weekends/holidays. Lake swimming, row boat and paddle boat rentals.

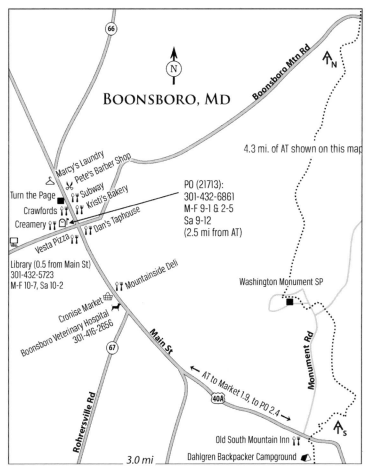

BOONSBORO, MD

66

N

Boonsboro Mtn Rd

4.3 mi. of AT shown on this map

Marcy's Laundry
Pete's Barber Shop
Turn the Page
Subway
Crawfords
Kristi's Bakery
Creamery
Dan's Taphouse
Vesta Pizza

PO (21713):
301-432-6861
M-F 9-1 & 2-5
Sa 9-12
(2.5 mi from AT)

Library (0.5 from Main St)
301-432-5723
M-F 10-7, Sa 10-2

Mountainside Deli

Washington Monument SP

Cronise Market
Boonsboro Veterinary Hospital
301-416-2656

67

Main St

Monument Rd

← AT to Market 1.9, to PO 2.4 →

40A

Rohrersville Rd

N
S

Old South Mountain Inn
Dahlgren Backpacker Campground

3.0 mi

1045.6 I-70, US 40: From US 40, it is 0.4W to entrance of **Greenbrier State Park,** (see previous entry) and an additional 0.7 to the visitor center, where the Bartman Trail enters the park. It's better to use the Bartman Trail.

1054.3 Wolfsville Rd, MD 17
💧 (0.3E) If shelter water source is dry, you may get water from ranger's house. Go 0.1 east (compass south) to a gravel road on left, then 0.2 on gravel road to first house on left.
Smithsburg, MD 21783 (1.5W)
🏤 M-F 8:30-1 & 2-4:30, Sa 8:30-12, 301.824.2828
🏬 **Dollar General Store** 301.824.6940, 7 days 8-10
🍴 **Food Lion** 301.824.7011, daily 7am-11pm
🍴 **Smithsburg Market** 301.824.2171, M-Sa 8am-8pm, Su 10am-8pm
🍴 **Rocky's Pizzeria** 301.824.2066, 7 days 11am-10pm
🍴 **Vince's New York Pizza** 301.824.3939, daily 11am-11pm
🍴 **Dixie Diner** 301.824.5334, closed M, Tu 7-2, W-F 7-8, Sa-Su 7-2
🍴 **Subway** 301.824.3826, 24 hrs
🍴 **China 88** 301.824.7300
➕ **Smithsburg Emergency Medical** 301.824.3314
🐕 **Smithsburg Veterinary Clinic** 301.416.0888
💊 **Home Care Pharmacy**
💊 **Rite Aid** 301.824.2211, store 8-9, pharmacy 9-6
� **Laundry**
🖥 **Library** 301.824.7722 M,W-F 10am-7pm, Tu 12-9pm, Sa 10am-2pm
🔨 **Ace Hardware**

101
MD

SoBo	NoBo	Description	Elev
1134.9	1054.3	Wolfsville Rd, MD17, **Smithsburg, MD** (1.5W) .... (pg.101)	1400
1134.7	1054.5	**Ensign Cowall Shelter** 20.7◄15.7◄8.2◄▶4.9▶14.5▶16.9 ≤(8) Boxed spring, somewhat stagnant, south between shelter & road.	1415
1134.5	1054.7	Powerline	1519
1133.4	1055.8	Foxville Rd, MD 77, **Smithsburg, MD** (1.7W)	1604
1132.2	1057.0	Spring	1348
1132.0	1057.2	Powerline	1369
1131.6	1057.6	Warner Gap Hollow stream, Warner Gap Rd (gravel, AT to west)	1150
1130.9	1058.3	Little Antietam Creek	1094
1130.8	1058.4	Raven Rock Rd, MD 491	1073
1130.5	1058.7	Raven Rock Cliff, view 100 yards east	1297
1129.8	1059.4	**Raven Rock Shelter** (0.1W), Ritchie Rd (0.6E) ≤(16) 20.6◄13.1◄4.9◄▶9.6▶12.0▶13.2 New "two story" shelter. Water on opposite side of AT (0.3E) on steep side trail.	1682
1128.0	1061.2	Ends of High Rock Loop Trail 0.2 apart. N39 41.690 W77 31.394 [P] 0.1E from either end to view and parking. Parking gated from dusk till 8am. 1.7 from parking area to Pen Mar Park via Pen Mar Rd.	1822
1125.2	1064.0	Pen Mar County Park N39 42.983 W77 30.433 [P] (pg.104-105)	1280
1124.9	1064.3	**Cascade, MD** (1.4E), **Waynesboro, PA** (2.1W to Walmart, downtown 4.5)	1250
1124.8	1064.4	MD-PA border, RR tracks, Mason-Dixon Line	1240
1124.3	1064.9	Pen Mar Rd	1050
1123.8	1065.4	Falls Creek, footbridge, campsite	1290
1122.6	1066.6	Buena Vista Rd	1350
1122.3	1066.9	Old PA 16	1200
1122.1	1067.1	Footbridge, stream, PA 16	1250
1121.7	1067.5	**Blue Ridge Summit, PA** (1.2E), Mentzer Gap Rd, NoBo: turn west. Rattlesnake Run Rd (gravel)	1372
1120.2	1069.0	**Deer Lick Shelters** 22.7◄14.5◄9.6◄▶2.4▶3.6▶10.2 ≤(2x5) N39 44.482 W77 29.430 [P] (pg.104-105) Spring 10 yards north on AT or (0.2E) on blue-blazed trail.	1435
1119.9	1069.3	Pipeline clearing	1502
1119.3	1069.9	Dirt road	1395
1118.0	1071.2	Orange-blazed Chickadee Snowmobile Trail	938
1117.8	1071.4	**Antietam Shelter** 16.9◄12.0◄2.4◄▶1.2▶7.8▶13.4 ≤(6) Better to get water from Old Forge Park 0.1N	911
1117.7	1071.5	Old Forge Picnic Area, Old Forge Rd N39 48.032 W77 28.760 [P]	916
1116.6	1072.6	**Tumbling Run Shelters** 13.2◄3.6◄1.2◄▶6.6▶12.2▶19.6 ≤(8) Piped water 75 yards right of shelter.	1089
1115.3	1073.9	Chimney Rocks, view to east	1900

⚠ Many springs in PA run dry in June, July & August

SoBo	NoBo	Feature	Elev
1114.4	1074.8	Pipeline clearing	1883
1113.2	1076.0	Powerline	1986
1112.6	1076.6	Snowy Mountain Rd	1687
1112.0	1077.2	Swamp Rd, **South Mountain, PA** 17261 (1.0E)	1560 (pg.105)
1111.7	1077.5	PA 233, **South Mountain, PA** 17261 (1.2E)	1600 (pg.105)
1110.0	1079.2	**Rocky Mountain Shelters** (0.2E) 10.2◄7.8◄6.6◄►5.6►13.0►19.2 Piped spring 0.5 mile on trail to road, then right 75 yards.	☾ ◗ ◭ ⊏ (8) 1660
1107.0	1082.2	US 30, **Fayetteville, PA** (3.5W). . . N39 54.352 W77 28.714 Overnight parking SW corner of US 30 & Pine Grove Rd, check in at park HQ.	960 **P** (0.6E)(pg.106)
1106.6	1082.6	Side trail to **Caledonia State Park**, pool area	939 (pg.106)
1105.8	1083.4	Locust Gap Rd, Valley Trail to west	1343
1104.4	1084.8	**Quarry Gap Shelters** 13.4◄12.2◄5.6◄►7.4►13.6►24.5	☾ ◗ ◭ ⊏ (8) 1473
1104.1	1085.1	Footbridge, stream	◗ 1547
1103.7	1085.5	Hosack Run Trail to east	1838
1102.9	1086.3	5-way gravel road intersection	2005
1102.1	1087.1	Powerline	1889
1101.7	1087.5	Woods road	2024
1100.4	1088.8	Middle Ridge Road	2075
1099.8	1089.4	3 Points (intersecting gravel roads), campsite to north	1985
1099.4	1089.8	PATC Milesburn Cabin (locked), spring 100 yards west.	◭ ◗ 1704
1099.1	1090.1	Ridge Rd (gravel), campsite north of road	◭ ◗ 1918
1098.3	1090.9	Rocky Knob Trail (orange-blazed)	1919
1097.7	1091.5	Powerline, campsite to north	☾ ◗ ◭ ⊏ (10) 1936
1097.0	1092.2	**Birch Run Shelter**, stream 75 yards north on AT 19.6◄13.0◄7.4◄►6.2►17.1►25.2	1811
1096.9	1092.3	Footbridge, stream	◗ 1805
1095.7	1093.5	Shippensburg Rd	2040 **P**
1094.6	1094.6	Dead Woman Hollow Road (gravel), **AT Midpoint** (2015) N39 59.834 W77 24.301	1952

SoBo   NoBo

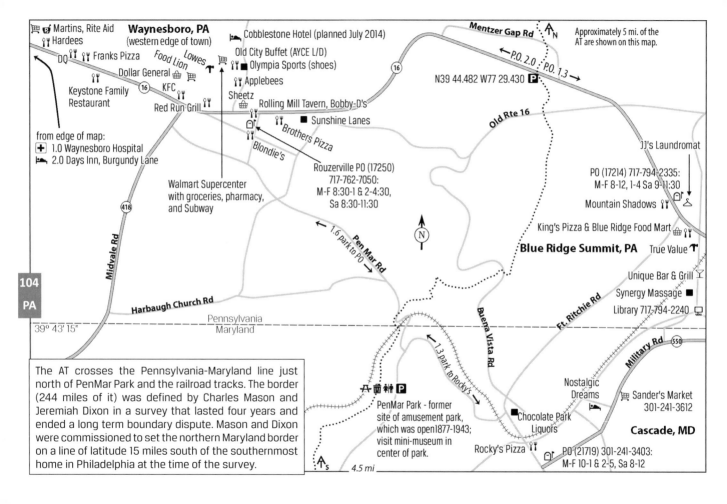

Martins, Rite Aid
Hardees
Waynesboro, PA
(western edge of town)
Cobblestone Hotel (planned July 2014)
Mentzer Gap Rd
N
Approximately 5 mi. of the
AT are shown on this map.
DQ   Franks Pizza
Food Lion
Lowes
Old City Buffet (AYCE L/D)
Olympia Sports (shoes)
16
P.O. 2.0
P.O. 1.3
Dollar General
KFC
Applebees
Sheetz
N39 44.482 W77 29.430 P
Keystone Family
Restaurant
16
Old Rte 16
Red Run Grill
Rolling Mill Tavern, Bobby-D's
Sunshine Lanes
JJ's Laundromat
Brothers Pizza
Blondie's
PO (17214) 717-794-2335:
M-F 8-12, 1-4 Sa 9-11:30
from edge of map:
+ 1.0 Waynesboro Hospital
🛏 2.0 Days Inn, Burgundy Lane
Mountain Shadows
Rouzerville PO (17250)
717-762-7050:
M-F 8:30-1 & 2-4:30,
Sa 8:30-11:30
Walmart Supercenter
with groceries, pharmacy,
and Subway
King's Pizza & Blue Ridge Food Mart
Blue Ridge Summit, PA
True Value
418
Midvale Rd
1.6 park to PO
Pen Mar Rd
N
Unique Bar & Grill
Synergy Massage
Library 717-794-2240
Harbaugh Church Rd
Buena Vista Rd
Ft. Ritchie Rd
104
PA
Pennsylvania
Maryland
39° 43' 15"
550
Military Rd
1.3 park to Rocky's
Nostalgic
Dreams
Sander's Market
301-241-3612
The AT crosses the Pennsylvania-Maryland line just
north of PenMar Park and the railroad tracks. The border
(244 miles of it) was defined by Charles Mason and
Jeremiah Dixon in a survey that lasted four years and
ended a long term boundary dispute. Mason and Dixon
were commissioned to set the northern Maryland border
on a line of latitude 15 miles south of the southernmost
home in Philadelphia at the time of the survey.
PenMar Park - former
site of amusement park,
which was open1877-1943;
visit mini-museum in
center of park.
Chocolate Park
Liquors
Rocky's Pizza
Cascade, MD
PO (21719) 301-241-3403:
M-F 10-1 & 2-5, Sa 8-12
N
S
4.5 mi

1064.0   Pen Mar County Park Open first Sun. in May to last Sun. in Oct. Vending & water; no camping. Restrooms locked when park closed. Bobby D's & other pizza places deliver. Pen Mar Rd passes in front of park, east of AT. Rouzerville PO is nearest to the AT. If intending to walk to this PO, or to Waynesboro, do so from AT/Pen Mar Rd intersection 0.3N of park. Services available in multiple directions from the park & from PA 16. See map and listings for options.

🛏🛶⛺⛺🚌📶🖥✉ **Nostalgic Dreams B&B** 717.816.5699 Caters to hikers. Hiker rate $25PP + tax includes breakfast & pickup/return from Pen Mar Park or St. Rd. 16. Call from trail for availability; no reservations at this rate. Tenting $10, additional $5 for shower or breakfast. Laundry $2. Cash, credit cards & PayPal accepted. Shuttles for a fee and parking for section hikers. Maildrops: 25321 Springdale Avenue, Cascade, MD 21719

🚌 **Dennis Sewell** 301.241.3176

   Waynesboro, PA 17214 (2.1W to Walmart and other services on edge of town, 2.0 further to center of town)

🛒 **Walmart, Food Lion**

🍴 **Bobby D's Pizza** 717.762.0388

Also: **Olympia Sports** large selection of running shoes.
   2.0W of Walmart:

🛏⛺🚌📶🖥✉ **Burgundy Lane B&B** 717.762.8112 $90-105D w/full breakfast, free laundry & shuttle to trailhead or town stop. Longer shuttles for fee. Maildrops: 128 W Main St, Waynesboro, PA 17268.

🛏📶🖥⛺ **Days Inn** 717.762.9113 $59S, $69D, $5EAP. Continental breakfast, $10 pet fee, laundry next door.

➕ **Waynesboro Hospital** 717.765.4000 501 E Main St.

🐾 **Wayne Heights Animal Hospital** 717.765.9636

🎭 **Waynesboro Theater** 717.762.7879

■ Synergy Massage 877.372.6617 〈www.synergymassage.com〉 Massage, hiker discount. Free use of outdoor shower, hot tub & pool.

   Cascade, MD (1.4E on Pen Mar/High Rock Rd)

🛒 **Sanders Market** M-Sa 8:30-8, open till 9pm Tu and Sa.

1066.9   PA 16   ***Blue Ridge Summit, PA 17214*** (1.2E)

🍴 **Unique Bar and Grill** 717.794.2565 live music, **Summit Plaza** 717.794.2500 open 7-8, B/L/D.

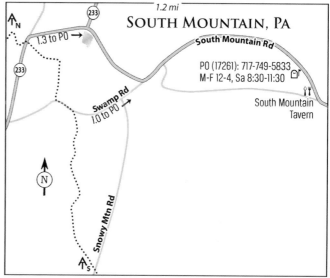

SOUTH MOUNTAIN, PA
1.2 mi
South Mountain Rd
PO (17261): 717-749-5833 M-F 12-4, Sa 8:30-11:30
South Mountain Tavern
Swamp Rd 1.0 to PO
1.3 to PO
Snowy Mtn Rd

1077.2   Swamp Rd, dirt road, walk for 0.3 before connecting with paved South Mountain Rd. (1.0E) total to PO.

1077.5   PA 233 - 0.2E of the trailhead, PA 233 veers to the north; stay to right on South Mountain Rd. (1.2E) total to PO.

   South Mountain, PA 17261 (1.0E or 1.2E)

🍴 **South Mountain Tavern**
717.749.3845 M-Sa 9am-2am

1082.2 US 30

🍴(1.5E) **Bobby A's Grill & Bar** 717.352.2252

Fayetteville, PA 17222 (spread out to west)

(0.4W)🍴 New restaurant planned for 2015.

(0.8W) 🏨🛢️⛺🛜🖥️✉️ **Trail of Hope Hostel** 717.658.7971 $22 bed or $7 camping. Coin laundry, use of kitchen, and resuppy including white gas/denatured/oz and canister fuel. Maildrops: 7798 Lincoln Way East Fayetteville, PA 17222.

(1.7W)🏪 **Rutter's Market**

(2.3W)🏪 **Dollar General**

(2.6W) 🛏️🍴⛺🛜✉️ **Scottish Inn and Suites** 717.352.2144, 800.251.1962 $59S, $69D, $15 pets. $5PP for pickup or return to trail. $10 for ride to Walmart. Coin laundry. Guest maildrops: 5651 Lincoln Way East, Fayetteville, PA 17222

(2.6W)🍴 **Flamingo Restaurant** excellent large breakfast.

(3.1W)🍴 **Vince's Pizza** 717.401.0096

(3.1W)⛺ **Squeaky Clean Laundry**

(3.2W)📮 M-F 8–4:30, Sa 8:30–12, 717.352.2022

(3.2W)💊 **Rite Aid**

(7W)🛒🍴💊 **Walmart** 24hrs w/ pharmacy and **Subway**.

🚐 **Freeman's Shuttle Service** 717.352.2513, 717.658.9185. Front Royal to DWG.

1082.6   Side trail to **Caledonia State Park**

🍴🚿📞 **Caledonia SP** 717.352.2161 Open Apr. 3 - Dec. 13. Pool & snack bar open 11-7, 7 days Jun 1 - Labor Day. Vending next to the pool & near office. Campsites, $21-23 Su-Th, $25-27 F-Sa. Discounts: $4.50 senior (62), $2 PA residents. Pet fee $2. $4 shower only. Check in at office for long term parking

1102.0   Pine Grove Furnace State Park

🏨⛺🛜🖥️✉️ **Ironmasters Mansion Hostel** 717.486.4108 ironmasterspinegrove@gmail.com. West end of park. English Tudor brick residence (with secret room) built & used by the

Ironmaster in 1829; hostel renovated in 2010. $25PP w/breakfast; 5-9pm check-in, 9 am check-out; closed during day 9am – 5pm and Tu. nights. Call/email for reservations. Laundry $3. Season Apr 1- Nov 1. Maildrops: Ironmasters Hostel, 1212 Pine Grove Rd, Gardners, PA 17324.

🏪 **Pine Grove General Store** 717.486.4920 (New concessionaire in 2015, hours & phone may change) Open 7 days Mem Day - Labor Day 9am-7pm; Open F-Su spring & fall. Food, cold drinks, short-order grill. Soda machine outside. Home of ***half gallon challenge.***

ℹ️ 🥾 **A.T. Museum** ⟨www.atmuseum.org⟩ Hikers welcome to bring food to eat outside & relax. Artifacts and photos of past hikers, signs from Springer & Katahdin. Sells halfway patch & bandana. Open Mar 28-May 3 weekends 12-4; May 9-July 19 every day 9-4; July 20-Aug 9 every day 12-4; Aug 12-Nov 1 W-Sun 12-4 **Hiker Festival** Jun 6.

✖️How many hikers are pictured in the poster between the TVs?

⛺🥾🅿️ **Pine Grove Furnace State Park** 717.486.7174 Office west of Museum. From end of Dec to end of March open weekdays only; open 7 days rest of year. Least expensive campsites $21 weekdays, $25 weekends, $2 off for PA residents. Dogs allowed in some sites. Restrooms throughout park. Check with park office before parking overnight; cars can be left for up to two weeks in lot compass south of Museum (interior of park). Beach/ swimming area at Fuller Lake.

1108.1   Side trail (0.7W) to campground

🛏️🛢️🏪⛺ **Mountain Creek Campground** 717.486.7681 Open Apr-Nov, cabins $55, tentsites $28, + tax. Either holds 2 adults/4 children. Camp store has sodas & ice cream, short-order grill on weekends.

🚐 **Gary Grant Shuttles** 717.706.2578 Rides for groups 5 to 15 hikers from Mt. Holly Springs, Boiling Springs, or Carlisle to Walmart, movie theater, restaurants & bars. Call for pickup/return. Distance shuttles for any number of hikers ranging from Caledonia SP to Duncannon.

1112.5   PA 94   ***Mt. Holly Springs, PA 17065*** (2.5W) 5mi farther to 81 interchange with Walmart and movies at Carlisle Commons.

📮 M-F 8-1 & 2-4:30, Sa 9-12, 717.486.3468

🛏️🍴🖥️🛜 **Holly Inn, Restaurant and Tavern** 717.486.3823 $50S, $55D

$10EAP, free ride to/from AT if available, $5 pick up from Pine Grove Furnace SP. Fri live music, Sa karaoke, Sun open mic. Restaurant open Su-Th 11:30-9, F-Sa 11:30-10.

🏨 **Sheetz, Dollar General**
🍴 **Laura's** breakfast, lunch, ice cream.
🍴 **Subway**, **Sicilia Pizza**
💊 **Holly Pharmacy** 717.486.5321
🧺 **Dollie's Laundromat**

1112.8   Sheet Iron Roof Rd, 0.4W to campground
🛏️🚗🍴🏨🧺 **Deer Run Campground** 717.486.8168
Tentsite $10 w/shower, Cabin $62.

1121.3   PA 174, ***Boiling Springs, PA 17007***
🌑🌙 Free hiker campsite with privy south of town. Railroad tracks pass very near campsite.
🛏️🍴🍷🏨💲🧺🛜🖥️ **Allenberry Resort Inn & Playhouse** 800.430.5468 ⟨www.allenberry.com⟩ Your zero-day oasis in PA: Hiker rate $40 double occupancy. Food service Tu-Su, bar open W-Su, general store open 7 days (snacks, beer & toiletries). Live theater $10, laundry $4, pool (in season), accepts credit cards. $5 fee for maildrops: 1559 Boiling Springs Rd, Boiling Springs, PA 17007
🛏️🧺🛜✉️ **Gelinas Manor** 717.258.6584 ⟨www.gelinasmanor.com⟩ Room w/shared bath for $99D/up. No pets, no packs inside. Full breakfast at 8:30. Laundry $6/load. Credit cards accepted. Maildrops w/reservation: MUST say "in care of Gelinas Manor", 219 Front Street, Boiling Springs, PA 17007.
🛏️🛜 **Red Cardinal B&B** 717.245.0823 Prices seasonal, queen bed room includes full breakfast & pickup/return from Boiling Springs (2mi away). No pets, no smoking.
🛒 **Karn's Quality Foods** 717.258.1458 Daily 7-10.

🏨💲 **Gettys Food Mart** 717.241.6163 ATM inside.
🛩️ **Boiling Springs Animal Hospital** 717.258.4575 M-T 8-7:30, W-F 8-6, Sa 8-1, 1.4W on Park Drive.
🍴 **Anile's Ristorante & Pizzeria** 717.258.5070 L/D subs, pizza. Su-Th 11-10, F-Sa 11-11,
🍴 **Boiling Springs Tavern** 717.258.3614 L/D 11:30-2, 5-9:30, closed Su-M.
🚿 **Boiling Springs Pool** 717.258.4121 Mem. Day-Labor Day, M-Su 11-7, $2 hot shower. If you want to swim, visit ATC Regional Office for $3 off the $12 admission.

🚌 **Mike's Shuttle Service** 717.497.6022, text-only number 717.448.5396.
🔋⚡ **ATC Mid-Atlantic Regional Office** 717.258.5771 Open wkdays 8-5. Water faucet on south side of building. Staff & bulletin board provide info on parking and trail and water conditions. Small shop with guidebooks & maps. White gas/denatured alcohol for small donation.

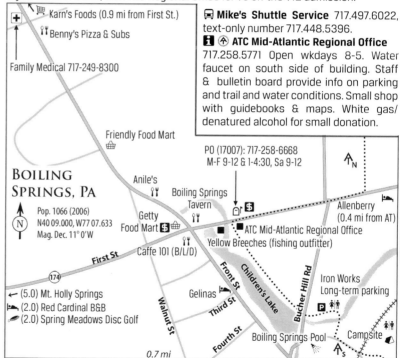

Karn's Foods (0.9 mi from First St.)
Benny's Pizza & Subs
Family Medical 717-249-8300
Friendly Food Mart

PO (17007): 717-258-6668
M-F 9-12 & 1-4:30, Sa 9-12

BOILING SPRINGS, PA
Pop. 1066 (2006)
N40 09.000, W77 07.633
Mag. Dec. 11° 0'W

Anile's
Boiling Springs Tavern
Getty Food Mart
Caffe 101 (B/L/D)
First St
174
Allenberry (0.4 mi from AT)
ATC Mid-Atlantic Regional Office
Yellow Breeches (fishing outfitter)
Children's Lake
Gelinas
Walnut St
Third St
Front St
Bucher Hill Rd
Iron Works Long-term parking
Fourth St
Boiling Springs Pool
Campsite

← (5.0) Mt. Holly Springs
🛏️ (2.0) Red Cardinal B&B
🥏 (2.0) Spring Meadows Disc Golf

0.7 mi

SoBo	NoBo		Elev
		Elev	
1093.8	1095.4	Side trail to Michener Cabin (locked) (0.3E)	1850
1093.2	1096.0	Woods road	1852
1091.9	1097.3	Woodrow Rd (gravel), campsite 0.1N	1787
1091.4	1097.8	Stream	1545
1090.9	1098.3	Sunset Rocks Trail to east, rejoins AT to north	1335
1090.8	1098.4	**Toms Run Shelters,** (one shelter burned down late in 2013). 19.2◄13.6◄6.2◄►10.9►19.0►37.2 Water behind shelter	1319
1090.6	1098.6	Stream.	1291
1090.5	1098.7	Midpoint Sign	1303
1089.6	1099.6	Michaux Rd	1330
1088.7	1100.5	Toms Run, footbridge, stream. Sunset Rocks Trail to east.	1031
1087.5	1101.7	PA 233 (paved), NoBo on road 0.1W, veer right on road into park	912
1087.2	1102.0	**Pine Grove Furnace SP, AT Museum** . . . N40 01.903 W77 18.322 P (pg.106)	874
1086.6	1102.6	Fuller Lake, free showers, snack bar 11-7 daily Mem-Labor Day	846
		No camping within one mile of PGF SP; camping within the park only at designated (paid) campsites. No overnight sleeping in pavilions.	
1084.8	1104.4	Campsite	1243
1084.6	1104.6	Pole Steeple Trail to west	1300
1083.6	1105.6	Campsite	1366
1081.4	1107.8	Roadbed	1056
1081.1	1108.1	Trail to **Mountain Creek Campground** (0.7W) signed & steep. (pg.106)	1026
1080.0	1109.2	Spring 50 yards west on marked trail	748
1079.9	1109.3	**James Fry (Tagg Run) Shelter** (0.2E), campsite west of AT 24.5◄17.1◄10.9◄►8.1►26.3►33.6 Spring uphill from shelter; water 0.2E farther.	719
1079.5	1109.7	Pine Grove Rd (paved)	685
1079.3	1109.9	Stream	660
1078.9	1110.3	Cross RR tracks; sharp east turn for NoBo, west for SoBo.	656
1078.7	1110.5	PA 34, Hunters Run Rd . . . N40 4.624 W77 11.702 P (0.5S) **Green Mountain Store** (0.2E) 7 days	632
1076.7	1112.5	PA 94, **Mt Holly Springs, PA** (2.5W) (pg.106)	880
1076.4	1112.8	Sheet Iron Roof Rd, campground 0.4W . . . N40 5.582 W77 9.846 P (pg.107)	774
1076.0	1113.2	Footbridge, stream, campsite	687
1075.7	1113.5	Footbridge, stream	675
1075.3	1113.9	Old Town Rd (gravel)	745
1074.7	1114.5	Rock maze	1179
1074.3	1114.9	Rock maze	1092

SoBo	NoBo		Elev
1073.9		Whiskey Spring Rd, reliable water from spring ... ♦	830
		🚫 No camping in Cumberland Valley between Alec Kennedy and Darlington Springs. Shelters, except at backpackers campsite south of Boiling Springs.	
1071.9	1117.3	Little Dogwood Run, campsite, orange-blazed trail 1.7E to BSA campground ... ♦ ⌂	884
1071.8	1117.4	**Alec Kennedy Shelter** (0.2E), spring behind shelter is unreliable ... ⌂ ◊ ⌐(7)	966
		25.2◄19.0◄8.1◄▶18.2▶25.5▶33.8	
1070.9	1118.3	Center Point Knob, original AT midpoint, White Rocks Trail 0.4E to view ...	1060
1069.5	1119.7	Cornfield, south end	561
1069.0	1120.2	Leidigh Dr	562
1068.4	1120.8	Backpacker's Campsite (nearby railroad tracks can be noisy) ... ⌐	514
1068.1	1121.1	Bucher Hill Rd, Iron Works Parking ... N40 8.868 W77 7.445 P	501
1067.9	1121.3	PA 174, First Street, ATC Mid-Atlantic Regional Office (pg.107) **Boiling Springs, PA**	500
1066.4	1122.8	Stone wall	618
1065.8	1123.4	PA 74, York Rd ... N40 10.385 W77 7.263 P	579
1064.8	1124.4	Lisburn Rd	555
1064.3	1124.9	Byers Rd	557
1064.2	1125.0	Footbridge, stream	511
1063.8	1125.4	Trindle Rd, PA 641, kiosk ... N40 11.700 W77 6.500 P (pg.112)	540
1062.6	1126.6	Ridge Rd, Biddle Rd ... (pg.112)	475
1062.1	1127.1	Old Stone House Rd, footbridge, stream	477
1061.4	1127.8	Appalachian Dr	514
1061.1	1128.1	PA Turnpike (I-76) overpass	497
1060.5	1128.7	Railroad tracks	475
1059.9	1129.3	US 11, **Carlisle, PA** (5.0W) ... (pg.112)	490
1059.0	1130.2	Pass over I-81 on Bernheisel Rd	485
1058.4	1130.8	Fence stile (two)	517
1057.6	1131.6	Conodoguinet Creek, footbridge alongside road N40 15.589 W77 6.221 P ⊼ ⌐ **Scott Farm Trail ATC Crew HQ** Open May–Oct, picnic table, no camping. The AT u-turns, passes under bridge, and heads north.	480
1056.5	1132.7	Sherwood Drive, parking to east. ... N40 16.439 W77 5.967 P ♦ Many footbridges, streams north and south of this road	439
1055.6	1133.6	PA 944 tunnel	480
1054.7	1134.5	Piped spring where AT crosses overgrown dirt road ... ♦ NoBo planning stay at Darlington Shelter consider getting water here.	731

SoBo	NoBo	Description	Elev
1054.0	1135.2	View	1132
1053.7	1135.5	Darlington Trail, Tuscarora Trail	1271
1053.6	1135.6	**Darlington Shelter** (0.1E) 37.2◀26.3◀18.2◀▶7.3▶15.6▶22.3 ☾ ⟁ ⊆(5)	1223
		Unreliable water on blue-blazed trail in front of shelter. Taj Mahal privy.	
1052.0	1137.2	Gravel road	750
1051.7	1137.5	Millers Gap Rd (paved)	704
1051.4	1137.8	PA 850 N40 19.308 W77 4.688 P	690
1049.9	1139.3	Service road	780
1049.7	1139.5	Footbridge, stream	883
1048.9	1140.3	Pipeline, view, trail very rocky from here north to PA 274	1335
1047.2	1142.0	Blue-blazed trail 0.4W to service road	1254
1046.3	1142.9	**Cove Mountain Shelter** (0.2E) 33.6◀25.5◀7.3◀▶8.3▶15.0▶33.0 ☾⟁⊆(8)	1268
		Spring 0.1 mile on steep side trail.	
1044.3	1144.9	Hawk Rock, view	992
1043.6	1145.6	⚠ Old trail to west, AT turns east (uphill for NoBo)	455
1043.2	1146.0	Inn Rd, trail very rocky from here south to pipeline.	384
1042.7	1146.5	PA 274, pass under US 11/15	385
1042.3	1146.9	**Duncannon, PA,** High St + Broadway (pg.112-113)	398
1040.4	1148.8	Susquehanna River N40 23.759 W77 0.512 P	402
		North end of Clarks Ferry Bridge, US 22/322, railroad tracks	
1039.6	1149.6	View	620
1038.2	1151.0	Susquehanna Trail to west.	1157
1038.0	1151.2	**Clarks Ferry Shelter** (0.1E) 33.8◀15.6◀8.3◀▶6.7▶24.7▶38.1 ☾♦⊆(8)	1258
		Reliable piped spring just beyond shelter.	
1037.7	1151.5	Powerline	1346
1035.1	1154.1	Powerline	1242
1034.2	1155.0	PA 225 N40 24.711 W76 55.796 P	1263

SoBo	NoBo		Elev
1033.6	1155.6	Powerline	1297
1032.2	1157.0	Table Rock, view	1347
1031.3	1157.9	**Peters Mountain Shelter** 22.3◀15.0◀6.7◀▶18.0▶31.4▶35.5. Weak spring 0.3 mile steeply downhill from shelter (300 rock steps).	1188
1030.3	1158.9	Victoria Trail. ⚠ See State Game Lands guidelines pg. 113	1202
1029.7	1159.5	Whitetail Trail	1325
1028.6	1160.6	Kinter View	1320
1027.2	1162.0	Shikellimy Trail 0.9E to parking area. N40 26.259 W76 49.185 🅿	1164
1026.2	1163.0	Campsite	1366
1024.9	1164.3	Spring 100 yards east on side trail	700
1024.6	1164.6	PA 325, Clarks Creek north of road. N40 27.092 W76 46.574 🅿	550
1024.3	1164.9	Spring	604
1024.2	1165.0	Henry Knauber Trail to east	682
1022.9	1166.3	Spring	1286
1021.3	1167.9	Horse-Shoe Trail to east	1650
1020.6	1168.6	Rattling Run.	1533
1018.1	1171.1	Yellow Springs Trail	1386
1017.9	1171.3	Clearing with trail register, camping Yellow Springs Village Site, old coal mining settlement (0.7W)	1450
1017.0	1172.2	Spring	1402
1015.8	1173.4	Sand Spring Trail west to "The General"	1382
1015.6	1173.6	Cold Spring Trail to east	1400

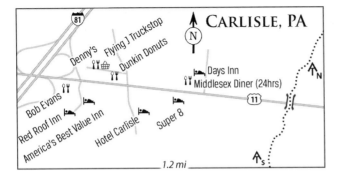

CARLISLE, PA

Flying J Truckstop · Dunkin Donuts · Denny's

Days Inn
Middlesex Diner (24hrs)

Bob Evans · Red Roof Inn · America's Best Value Inn · Hotel Carlisle · Super 8

1.2 mi

1125.4   Trindle Rd
1126.6   Ridge Rd

🛏⛺📶 **Pheasant Field B&B** (0.5W) 717.258.0717 $135/up, free pickup & return with stay, big breakfast, free laundry, behaved pets ok. Call from Trindle Rd, or from Ridge Rd, go 0.25W to Hickory Town Rd, turn left on road, B&B on right.

1129.3   US 11 (Carlisle Pike), *Carlisle, PA 17013* (0.5W to hotels)
          The AT passes over the highway on a footbridge. Side trails are bushwhacked down to the road on north end. Hotels run short of rooms (and go up in price) every other weekend when there is a car show.

🛏⛺📶🖥✉ **Super 8 Motel** 717.249.7000 $54.99S, $59.99D, cont. breakfast, $10 pet fee. Guest maildrops: 1800 Harrisburg Pike, Carlisle, PA 17013.

🛏⛺📶 **Days Inn** 717.245.2242 Hiker rate $55.95, cont B, pets $20.

🛏⛺📶🖥✉ **Red Roof Inn** 717.245.2400 call for rates. Maildrops: 1450 Harrisburg Pike, Carlisle, PA 17015.

🛏📶 **Americas Best Value Inn** 717.249.7775 $49.99/up, cont B, $15 pet fee.

🛏📶🖥⛺ **Hotel Carlisle** 717.243.1717 $15 pet fee.

🍴🏠🎒⛺ **Flying J Truckstop** 717.243.6659, 24hrs. Store, diner, pizza by the slice, showers ($12) and laundry.

Mechanicsburg, PA 17050 (7E)
Large city with many motels, restaurants, and retail.

🛏🍸 **Park Inn** 717.697.0321 Notable due to its two sizeable bars (**Legends Sports Bar & Grille** and **Blarney's Irish Pub**) and sand volleyball courts.

1146.9   High St,   *Duncannon, PA 17020*

🛏🏠🍴🖥✉ **Doyle Hotel** 717.834.6789, $25S, $35D, $7.50EAP + tax, bar serves L/D. Pool Table. Coleman/alcohol/oz and canister fuel. Accepts Visa/MC/Disc. Maildrops: (USPS/UPS) 7 North Market Street, Duncannon, PA 17020.

🛏⛺ **Stardust Motel** 717.834.3191 $45S, $55D Sometimes pickup/return rides available. No pets.

🛏📶 **Red Carpet Inn** 717.834.3320 $55S, $65D + tax.

🛶🚻 **Riverfront Campground** 717.834.5252, south of the Clarks Ferry Bridge, sites and shower $5PP, shuttles, some supplies. Note proximity of railroad tracks.

🍴 **Sorrento Pizza** 717.834.5167

🍴 **Goodies** Breakfast 6am-11am

🍴 **Ranch House Restaurant** B/L/D, near Motel Stardust has dinner buffet F-Sa, breakfast on weekends.

🛒 **Mutzabaugh's Market** 717.834.3121 Hiker-friendly, open 7 days 10-10. Pickup/return to Doyle 4pm daily.

💊 **Rite Aid** next door to market.

🏠🍴🎒⛺ **Pilot Travel Plaza** 717.834.3156, Open 24/7 $12 showers.

🐾 **Cove Mountain Animal Hospital** 717.834.5534

📶 **Store 34** M-F 12-7, Sa 10-4. High speed internet $3.00/30 min, $5/hr.

🔧 **Maguire's True Value Hardware** Coleman and Heet.

🚗🏠 **Trail Angel Mary** 717.834.4706 2 Ann St, Duncannon, PA 17020

🏃 **Blue Mountain Outfitters** 717.957.2413 8mi south in Maryville, PA

DUNCANNON, PA

N

Pop. 1503 (2006)
N40 23.683, W77 01.617
Mag. Dec. 8° 11'W

Stardust Motel (2.0 mi)
Red Carpet Inn (3.6 mi)

Pilot Travel Plaza & Subway

Riviera Tavern

Riverfront Campground

The Cabin

Butchershop Rd

High St

Market St

Susquehanna River

Municipal Building

3B Ice Cream

Cherry St

Maguire's Hardware

Cumberland St

PO (17020) (*pg.2):
717-834-3332
M-F 8-11 & 12-4:30,
Sa 8:30-12:30

William Penn Hwy

The Pub

Church / Library

Sorrento's

The Doyle

Store 34

Quick-Mart

Goodies

Two Rivers Healthcare

Sunny Daze

Zierdelli's 717-834-5167

Road Hawg BBQ (Th-Su)

Approx. 5.2 mi. of trail shown on map

Sunoco

322

22

Mutzabaugh's Market and Rite Aid (0.6 mi. from bridge)

Tubby's

1.5 mi

Harrisburg, PA
(14 mi: all services)

The AT is on **State Game Lands** in PA from north of Peters Mtn Shelter to Wind Gap, with the exception of small patches of land, mostly near major road crossings. Watch for posted regulations.

Primitive one-night camping is allowed:
- Only by hikers starting and ending at different locations.
- Within 200 feet of the AT, and
- 500 feet from water sources, trailheads, road crossings, and parking areas.
- Only small campfires are allowed, and only when the wildfire danger is less than "high."

Rausch Gap Shelter, Bake Oven Knob and George Outerbridge Shelters are on State Game Lands.

*Peter Barr ("Whippersnap" GA-ME 2010), author of **Hiking North Carolina's Lookout Towers**, recorded the track and landmarks that are the core of this book.*

SoBo	NoBo	Description	Elev
1013.4	1175.8	Spring, campsite	1113
1013.3	1175.9	**Rausch Gap Shelter** (0.3E) 33.0◄24.7◄18.0◄▶13.4▶17.5▶32.6	1094
1012.8	1176.4	AT on gravel road for 0.2 mile, bridge over Rausch Creek	925
1012.5	1176.7	Cemetery to west.	877
1012.3	1176.9	Stony Creek, footbridge	842
1011.2	1178.0	Second Mountain.	1357
1009.5	1179.7	Field	656
1009.2	1180.0	Cross two roads: Greenpoint School Rd, then PA 72	583
1008.6	1180.6	Pass under PA 72 and cross PA 443. N40 28.923 W76 33.038 P	491
1007.8	1181.4	Stream, campsite south of PA 72	
		Campsite	695
1007.2	1182.0	Swatara Gap, PA 72, **Lickdale, PA** (2.1E) (pg.116)	480
1006.8	1182.4	I-81, AT passes underneath	450
1006.5	1182.7	Gravel road	614
1002.6	1186.6	Abandoned powerline overlook, view	1382
999.9	1189.3	**William Penn Shelter** (0.1E) 38.1◄31.4◄13.4◄▶4.1▶19.2▶33.9	1421
		Water and tent sites 0.1W on blue-blazed trail.	
997.8	1191.4	PA 645, Waggoners Gap Rd, **Pine Grove, PA** (3.4W) N40 30.396 W76 22.609 P (pg.116-117)	1235
996.6	1192.6	Fisher Lookout, view	1286
995.9	1193.3	Kimmel Lookout, view	1335
995.8	1193.4	PA 501, **501 Shelter** (0.1W) N40 30.751 W76 20.664 P **Pine Grove, PA** (4.2W), **Bethel, PA** (4.1E) (pg.116-117)	1473
995.3	1193.9	Trail to Pilger Ruh (Pilgrims Rest), spring to east, Applebee Campsite to west.	1450

SoBo	NoBo	Description		Elev
992.7	1196.5	Round Head, Shower Steps Trail, campsite to south on AT. Side trail to view.	◨◉	1500
990.7	1198.5	Overlook, view.	◨◉	1402
990.3	1198.9	⚠ NoBo: AT turns east, Boulderfield Trail to west (straight ahead).		1278
990.2	1199.2	Hertline Campsite and picnic table	♦⚞	1200
989.5	1199.7	Pipeline, road paralleling pipeline, cross twice, then parallel to AT		1505
986.8	1202.4	Fort Dietrich Snyder Monument	♦(0.2W)	1424
986.5	1202.7	PA 183, Rentschler Marker on side trail 30 yards north of road		1375
986.0	1203.2	Game Commission road (gravel). N40 31.636 W76 12.888 P		1429
985.2	1204.0	Black Swatara Spring 0.3E	◇	1510
982.6	1206.6	Eagles Nest Trail to east		1580
981.4	1207.8	Sand Spring Trail 0.2E to spring	♦	1510
980.7	1208.5	**Eagles Nest Shelter** (0.3W), spring on trail to shelter 32.6◀19.2◀15.1◀▶14.7▶23.8▶31.2	☾♦⊂(8)	1593
978.8	1210.4	Shartlesville-Cross Mtn Rd (overgrown dirt road).		1450
976.1	1213.1	Phillips Canyon Spring (unmarked, unreliable).	◇	1500
974.1	1215.1	State Game Land Rd		1415
973.5	1215.7	Pipeline clearing, AT crosses multiple times		1408

LICKDALE, PA
(JONESTOWN)

N40 27.066, W76 30.822
Mag. Dec. 11° 29'W

Historic iron bridge

Swatara Creek

81

Monroe Valley Rd

Godfather's Pizza / Dunkin Donuts / Blimpie

Rail Trail 2.5 mi

72

Jonestown KOA

Comfort Inn

Days Inn

Wendy's

Subway

Best Western

McDonald's / Chester's Chicken

Love's Truck Stop: convenience store, ATM & showers

Pizza Town II

Dairy Queen

Fisher Ave

1.5 mi

1182.0   Swatara Gap, PA 72, **Lickdale, PA (Jonestown)** *(2.1E)*

Days Inn 717.865.4064 $55S/up, cont B, pets $10.

Best Western 717.865.4234 $89.99/up, cont B. Guests get 10% discount at DQ, indoor heated pool, pet fee $15.

Comfort Inn 717.865.8080 $79.95S/up, + tax includes breakfast, pool. Pets $25

Jonestown KOA 877.865.6411 Open 7 days. Summer 5am-9pm. Tentsite $31/up, cabin sleeps 4 $60/up. Pets on leash okay.

Love's Travel Stop with **McDonalds, Chesters** 717.861.7390 $10 showers, ATM, all open 24 Hrs

1191.4   PA 645,   **Pine Grove, PA** *(3.4W)* *(more services on map)*

Original Italian Pizza 570.345.5432 Delivers to 501 shelter.

Carlin's AT Shuttle Service 570.345.0474, 570.516.3447. Shuttles anywhere in PA.

    4.8W near intersection of I-81

Comfort Inn 570.345.8031 $65 includes hot breakfast. Hiker friendly, honors flat rate all season, pool, $10/pet.

Econo Lodge 570.345.4099 Hiker rate $50 when room available, includes continental breakfast. Pets $20 allowed in smoking rooms only.

Knights Inn 570.345.8095 $59-$79 + tax, Pets $10. HBO.

Pilot Travel Center 570.345.8800, shower $12. Open 24hr with **Subway, Dairy Queen** & **Auntie Anne's Pretzel**, .

1193.4   PA 501, **Bethel, PA** *(4.1E)* *(services on map)*

501 Shelter Caretaker house nearby, solar shower, water from faucet on shower, no alcohol, no smoking in shelter, pets on leash.

    Pine Grove, PA 17963 *(4.2W)*

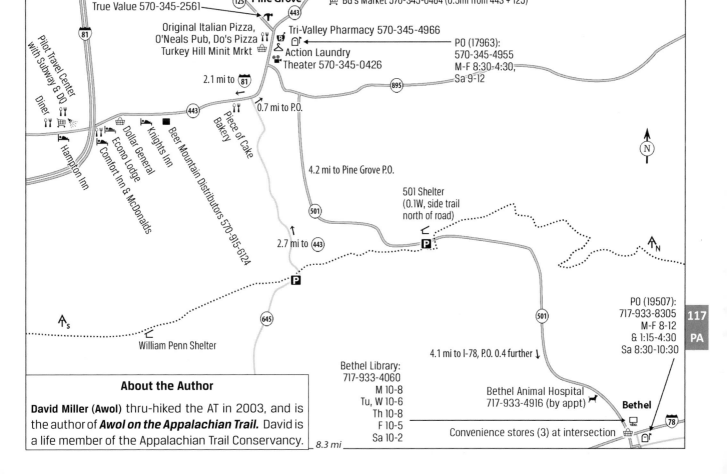

True Value 570-345-2561

Pine Grove (125) (443)

BG's Market 570-345-0464 (0.5mi from 443 + 125)

Original Italian Pizza,
O'Neals Pub, Do's Pizza
Turkey Hill Minit Mrkt

Tri-Valley Pharmacy 570-345-4966

Action Laundry
Theater 570-345-0426

PO (17963):
570-345-4955
M-F 8:30-4:30,
Sa 9-12

2.1 mi to (81)

(443)

(895)

Piece of Cake Bakery

0.7 mi to P.O.

Pilot Travel Center
with Subway & DQ
Diner

Hampton Inn

Comfort Inn & McDonalds

Econo Lodge

Dollar General

Knights Inn

Beer Mountain Distributors 570-915-6124

4.2 mi to Pine Grove P.O.

501 Shelter
(0.1W, side trail
north of road)

(N)

(501)

2.7 mi to (443)

P

A N

P

(645)

William Penn Shelter

A s

(501)

117
PA

PO (19507):
717-933-8305
M-F 8-12
& 1:15-4:30
Sa 8:30-10:30

About the Author

David Miller (Awol) thru-hiked the AT in 2003, and is
the author of **Awol on the Appalachian Trail.** David is
a life member of the Appalachian Trail Conservancy.

Bethel Library:
717-933-4060
M 10-8
Tu, W 10-6
Th 10-8
F 10-5
Sa 10-2

4.1 mi to I-78, P.O. 0.4 further

Bethel Animal Hospital
717-933-4916 (by appt)

Bethel
(78)

Convenience stores (3) at intersection

8.3 mi

SoBo	NoBo		Elev
971.9	1217.3	Schuylkill Trail 2.4E to Hamburg, parking 0.1N . . . N40 34.774 W76 1.600 P	551
971.7	1217.5	**Port Clinton, PA**, Broad St + Penn St . . . (pg.120-121)	426
971.4	1217.8	PA 61, Blue Mtn Rd, **Hamburg, PA** (1.7E) . . . (pg.120-121)	490
968.9	1220.3	Spring to west, campsite	1199
967.7	1221.5	Minnehaha Spring, frequently dry	1374
966.3	1222.9	Reservoir Rd, stream north on AT . . . N40 35.374 W75 56.659 P	889
966.0	1223.2	**Windsor Furnace Shelter** Parking 0.3E only with permission from Hamburg Borough 610.562.7821 M-F 8-5. ⊂(8)	867
965.3	1223.9	Blue-blazed trail to **Blue Rocks Campground** (1.5E) 33.9◄29.8◄14.7▲9.1►16.5►26.5 No swimming, creek south of shelter. . . . (pg.121)	1009
964.4	1224.8	Pulpit Rock, 30 yards west to privy at Pulpit Rock Astronomical Park.	1582
962.6	1226.6	Yellow-blazed trail to **Blue Rocks Campground** (1.5E) . . . (pg.121)	1594
962.2	1227.0	The Pinnacle, 0.1E to panoramic view, no camping or fires	1615
960.5	1228.7	Furnace Creek Trail to west	1448
960.3	1228.9	Gold Spring, no camping	1381
959.6	1229.6	Blue-blazed trail 1.5W reconnects with AT near Windsor Furnace Shelter	1422
959.3	1229.9	Pinnacle Spur Trail to west	1403
958.7	1230.5	Panther Creek, dependable	1074
957.8	1231.4	Parking lot 0.4E on side trail . . . N40 37.528 W75 57.208 P	838
956.9	1232.3	Hawk Mountain Rd, **Eckville Shelter** (0.2E) ⊂(6) (pg.122) 38.9◄23.8◄9.1▲7.4►17.4►24.2 Enclosed bunkroom open May-Sep, tent platforms, flush toilet, spigot at side of caretaker's house.	697
956.4	1232.8	Footbridge, stream, campsite north on AT	587
955.0	1234.2	Hawk Mtn Trail to west	1377
953.9	1235.3	Dans Pulpit, trail register.	1597
953.3	1235.9	Dans Spring 0.1E	1565

SoBo	NoBo		Elev
950.7	1238.5	Tri-County Corner, ⚠ AT to west.	1532
949.5	1239.7	**Allentown Hiking Club Shelter** . . . ☾ ◇ ◐ ⊆(8)	1500
		31.2◄16.5◄7.4◄►10.0►16.8►33.5	
949.2	1240.0	Unreliable spring downhill in front of shelter 0.2 mile, another 0.1 farther. Springs to east; Blue 100 yards, Yellow 0.3 mi ◐	1340
947.6	1241.6	Fort Franklin Rd (gravel) . . . N40 41.655 W75 50.515 **P**	1350
945.7	1243.5	Trail 0.2W to restaurant (closer to AT + PA 309)	1354
945.4	1243.8	PA 309, Blue Mountain Summit . . . N40 42.429 W75 48.516 **P** (pg.122)	1360
943.5	1245.7	Powerline, New Tripoli Campsite 0.2W. ◐ ◆	1488
942.3	1246.9	Knife Edge, view 📷	1630
941.9	1247.3	Bear Rocks, view 📷	1604
940.5	1248.7	Bake Oven Knob Rd (gravel) . . . N40 44.677 W75 44.314 **P**	1450
940.1	1249.1	Bake Oven Knob.	1560
939.5	1249.7	**Bake Oven Knob Shelter** 26.5◄17.4◄10.0◄►6.8►23.5►37.3 ◇ ◆ ⊆(6)	1404
		Trail in front leads downhill to multiple water sources, more reliable farther down.	
937.1	1252.1	Lehigh Furnace Gap, Ashfield Rd, Comm tower . . . N40 46.173 W75 41.649 **P**	1320
935.9	1253.3	South Mountain Trail 0.3E to view . ◐	1583
934.3	1254.9	North Trail (scenic route) to west, TV tower, AT is over Lehigh Valley Tunnel	1506
933.9	1255.3	Tower access road	1486
932.9	1256.3	North Trail (scenic route) to west.	1085
932.7	1256.7	**George W. Outerbridge Shelter**, reliable piped spring 0.1N. ◐ ⊆(6)	999
		24.2◄16.8◄6.8◄►16.7►30.5►61.7	

PORT CLINTON, PA

Pop. 279 (2009)
N40 34.800, W76 1.600
Mag. Dec. 11° 50'W

3C's Restaurant
1 mi from PO

Pavillion

N

Penn St.

Port Clinton Hotel
Peanut Shop

PO (19549): 610-562-3787
M-F 12:30-4:30, Sa 8-11

Broad St.

Port Clinton Fire Co.

Port Clinton Barber Shop

Union House B&B

61

N
S

**120
PA**

HAMBURG, PA

Pop. 4,211 (2008)
Many more restaurants
and services further
into town

N

AT to Library 2.9 mi.

Blue Mtn. Rd.

Schuylkill River Trail (2.4 mi from AT to 78)

61

PO (19526):
610-562-7812
M-F 9-5, Sa 9-12

Library 610-562-2843
M 10-8, Tu & Th 12-8,
W & F 10-5, Sa 9-4

Walmart superstore with
grocery & Subway

Wawa
McDonald's
Burger King

Dollar Tree
JA Buffet
Five Guys Burgers
Logan's Steakhouse
Lowe's
Subway
Wendys
Taco Bell / LJ Silver
Microtel
Red Robin
Pizza Hut
Cracker Barrel
Cigars International
Dunkin Donuts & Baskin Robbins
Cabella's & Campfire Buffet

78

Hamburg Animal
Hospital
610-562-5000

Franklin St.

4th St.

State St.

Weis Market
6am-11pm 7 days
Pharmacy M-F 9-9, Sa 8-1

2.6 mi

1217.5   Broad St, Penn St **Port Clinton, PA 19549**

🛏🍴⚠ **Port Clinton Hotel** 610.562.3354, 888.562.2626 〈www.portclintonhotel.net〉 Call for prices. $10 deposit for room key and towel, limited rooms available. Laundry, dining Tu-Th 11-9, F-Sa 11-closing, Su 11-10, closed Monday, Please shower before use of dining room, credit cards accepted.

🛏⚠ **Union House B&B** 〈www.union-house.com〉 610.562.3155 after 5pm 610.562.4076, open Friday-Sunday.

🍴📶 **3C's** 610.562.5925 M-F 5:30am-2pm, Sa, Su 6am-2pm.

🍴**Port Clinton Fire Co** Technically membership only; ask about visiting as a guest. Open 3pm-past midnight.

🏠 💲 **The Peanut Shop** soda, candy, dried fruit, trail mixes, ATM.

◐ 👫 **Pavilion Tenting** no car camping, no drive-ins.

✂**Port Clinton Barber Shop** Hikers welcome to hang out, coffee, cookies, and phone charging.

1214.0   PA 61, Blue Mtn Rd
          Hamburg, PA 19526 (1.7E)

🛏🍴⚠📶✉ **Microtel Inn** 610.562.4234 〈www.microtelinn.com〉 Hiker rate $76.05S, $90.45 up to 4 + tax, includes cont. breakfast. **Pappy T's** pub & lounge on-site. Maildrops: 100 Industrial Drive, Hamburg, PA 19526

🥾 **Cabela's** 610.929.7000, M-Sa 8-9, Su 9-8. Largest Cabela's store in the world with 250,000 sq. ft. of retail space. Full line of hiking gear, canister fuel. Pickup from trailhead if staff is available.

🍴 **Campfire Restaurant** Inside Cabela's serves B/L/D, closes a little earlier than the store.

🏠 **Turkey Hill Market**

💊 **Rite Aid** 610.562.9454, **CVS** 610.562.2454

⚠ **Hamburg Coin Laundry**

🐾 **Hamburg Animal Hospital** 610.562.5000 M-Th 9-7, Sa 9-11.

🚌 **Barta Bus Service** 610.921.0601〈www.bartabus.com〉 Routes within Hamburg $1.95 per boarding, stops at Cabellas.

Pottsville, PA 17901 (15W, compass north of AT on PA 61)

🍺 **Yuengling Brewery** 570.628.4890 America's oldest brewery; two tours on weekdays, as-needed on Sat. Closed-toe shoes required.

1220.1   Blue-blazed trail to campground
1222.8   Yellow-blazed trail to campground

🛏 ◐ 🏠 🥾 ⚠ **Blue Rocks Campground** 610.756.6366 Tentsite $30/up, cabin $55/up accommodates 2 adults, 2 children. Coin showers & laundry. Open year-round with limited days Nov-Mar. Camp store (sodas, candy bars, snacks) closed Dec-Mar.

Leave What You Find

• Leave plants, cultural artifacts and other natural objects where you found them for others to enjoy.

• Don't build structures or dig trenches around tents.

• Do not damage live trees or plants; green wood burns poorly. Collect only firewood that is dead, down, and no larger than your wrist. Leave dead standing trees and dead limbs on standing trees for the wildlife.

• Consider using rubber tips on the bottom of your trekking poles to avoid scratch marks on rocks, "clicking" sounds, and leaving holes along the trail.

• Avoid introducing or transporting non-native species by checking your boots, socks, packs, tents, and clothing for non-native seeds that you could remove before hitting the trail.

Read more of the Leave No Trace techniques developed for the A.T.:   www.appalachiantrail.org/LNT

1232.3 Hawk Mountain Rd, 1.6W to Hawk Mountain Sanctuary.

🛏🏕📶🖥🚗✉ **Common Ground Farm & Retreat** 610.756.4070 B&B on 50 acre organic farm. Hiker discount $95 for two-person stay includes breakfast & pickup/return from Eckville Shelter. Call about other trailheads. Slackpacking, parking for section hikers, longer shuttles for a fee. Mountain bike available for ride to nearby store. Open year round, no alcohol or drugs. Maildrops with reservation: 333 New Bethel Church Road, Kempton, PA 19529.

1243.8 PA 309

🛏🔔🍴🚗✉💧 **Blue Mountain Summit B&B** 570.386.2003 ⟨www.bluemountainsummit.com⟩ In view to west. $95–$125D includes breakfast. Open 7 days by appt. No pets. Help yourself to water at outside spigot at southwest corner of building. Please be respectful of non-hiking guests at the B&B and restaurant; okay to hang out in back, but please don't loiter in front or hang clothes to dry. Camping with permission, no fires. Ask about shuttles. Dining (summer) Th 12-9, F 12-10, Sa 11-9, Su 11-8; winter (after Thanksgiving) Th hours 4-9, F-Su same as summer. Live music on Fridays. All major credit cards accepted. Guest maildrops (call first): 2520 W Penn Pike, Andreas, PA 18211.

1257.0 Lehigh River, PA 873, *Slatington, PA 18080* (2E)

🏪 **Bechtel's Pharmacy** 610.767.4121

🖥 **Slatington Library** 610.767.6461 M,W: 9-7, Tu 9-3, F 9-5, Sa 8-2.

1257.5 PA 248/145, *Walnutport, PA 18088* (2E)

🛒 **Pathmark Supermarket** 610.760.8008, M-Sa 6-12pm, Su 6-10.

🏪🛒 **Kmart** 610.767.1812, Open 8-10 seven days, pharmacy hours slightly shorter. Grocery section only has dry goods (no produce).

🍴 **Valley Pizza Family Restaurant** 610.767.9000 L/D, delivers.

➕ **St Luke's Family Practice Center** 610.760.8080

🏪 **Rite Aid Pharmacy** 610.767.9595

🐕 **Blue Ridge Veterinary Clinic** 610.767.4896 Call before coming.

George Outerbridge Shelter

To Palmerton

Cross at traffic light

Woodpecker Trail

2 mi. to either town

Mountain Rd

Lehigh Dr

Riverview Dr

Lehigh River

At trailhead parking:
N40 46.981, W75 36.326
Mag. Dec. 12° 9'W

WALNUTPORT, PA

SLATINGTON

Spare Time Bowling

Kmart with Pharmacy

Walnut St

Highland Laundry

Allentown Foot Care
610-434-7000

Valley Pizza

Best Ave

PO (18080):
610-767-2182
M-F 8:30-5,
Sa 8:30-12

McDonald's

Burger King

American Legion Sunday Buffet

Bechtel's

AF Boyer

Dollar General

Rite Aid

Great Wall

Horner's Turkey Hill Library

Main St

Sals Pizza

Pathmark

Slatington Diner (B/L)

Mamma's Pizza

The Shack

PO (18088): 610-767-5191
M-F 8:30-5, Sa 8:30-12

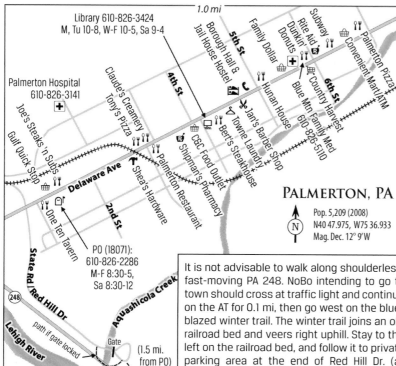

PALMERTON, PA

↑ N
Pop. 5,209 (2008)
N40 47.975, W75 36.933
Mag. Dec. 12° 9'W

Library 610-826-3424
M, Tu 10-8, W-F 10-5, Sa 9-4

1.0 mi

5th St
4th St
6th St
2nd St

Borough Hall &
Jail House Hostel

Family Dollar
Subway
Rite Aid
Dunkin' Donuts

Palmerton Pizza
Convenient Mart/ATM

Palmerton Hospital
610-826-3141

Claude's Creamery
Tony's Pizza

Joe's Steaks 'n Subs
Gulf Quick Stop

Country Harvest
Blue Mtn Family Med
610-826-5110

Hunan House
Jan's Barber Shop
Towne Laundry
Bert's Steakhouse

C&C Food Outlet
Shipman's Pharmacy

Delaware Ave
Shea's Hardware

Palmerton Restaurant

One Ten Tavern

PO (18071):
610-826-2286
M-F 8:30-5,
Sa 8:30-12

State Rd / Red Hill Dr
248

Lehigh River

path if gate locked

Gate
(1.5 mi.
from PO)

Aquashicola Creek

It is not advisable to walk along shoulderless, fast-moving PA 248. NoBo intending to go to town should cross at traffic light and continue on the AT for 0.1 mi, then go west on the blue-blazed winter trail. The winter trail joins an old railroad bed and veers right uphill. Stay to the left on the railroad bed, and follow it to private parking area at the end of Red Hill Dr. (at bottom left of town map). Cross Red Hill bridge and follow the road into town. If the bridge is gated or access is denied, hop the guardrail to PA 248, cautiously cross Aquashicola Creek on the 248 bridge, then hop the guardrail again to retun to Red Hill Drive. The total distance to town is 1.5W miles on level ground.

1257.7   Superfund Trailhead
Palmerton, PA 18071 (1.5W)
Town Ordinance: Pets must be kept on leash.

🛏️⊛ **Jail House Hostel** 610.826.2505
443 Delaware Avenue. Basement of the borough hall was never used as a jail. Hikers stay free; showers available. Check in at the borough office before 4pm on weekdays. Check in at police station after hours and on weekends. 10pm curfew. ID is required. One night limit, no vehicle-assisted hikers. No pets inside, but they can be left leashed outside. No alcohol.

🛏️◀ **Sunny Rest Resort** 610.377.2911 *Clothing optional* resort 2 miles outside of town, rides sometimes available. Weekdays: hotel rooms $118-209, camping $75, day visit $46/couple. Prices higher on weekends. Restaurant (B/L/D), nightclub, two heated pools, outdoor bar, volleyball, nature trails, 425 Sunny Rest Rd, Palmerton, PA.

🍴 **Palmerton Restaurant** 610.826.5454 Dining M-Th 4-10, F-Su 11-10.

🛒🆂 **Country Harvest** 610.824.3663 8am-9pm 7 days.

🍴🖥️ **Bert's Restaurant** B/L/D, has internet access.

🍴 **Tony's Pizzeria** L/D, no delivery.

🍴 **Joe's Place** L/D, deli sandwiches.

✚ **Palmerton Hospital** 610.826.3141

🐾 **Little Gap Animal Hospital** 610.826.2793 (3.5W) from town.

△ **Laundromat** 5am-7pm 7 days.

🚌 **Jason "SoulFlute"** 484.224.6981 Palmerton-area shuttles.

🚌 **Brenda** 484.725.9396 Local shuttles.

123
PA

Elev

SoBo	NoBo	Description		Elev
932.2	1257.0	Lehigh River South bank, PA 873, **Slatington, PA** (2.0E)	(pg.122)	437
931.7	1257.5	PA 248/145 traffic light, **Walnutport, PA** (2.0E)	(pg.122)	506
931.5	1257.7	Superfund Trailhead, **Palmerton, PA** (1.5W) N40 46.989 W75 36.247 **P**	(pg.123)	515
		Water 0.4W on blue-blazed trail to Palmerton.		
930.7	1258.5	Superfund Detour south end.		1429
		Rocky, steep trail from Lehigh Gap. Deforested ridge due to zinc smelting from 1898-1980 Palmerton Superfund site.		
928.1	1261.1	High metallic content spring 0.1W (unmarked N40 48.305 W75 33.408) emergency water source.		1383
927.9	1261.3	Superfund Detour north, powerline.	🔌	1360
		Great 360 view from pile of rocks east of trail near power line tower.		
926.8	1262.4	Little Gap Rd, **Danielsville, PA** (1.5E) N40 48.369 W75 32.077 **P**	(pg.126)	1100
926.4	1262.8	Tower access road (gravel)	🔌	1330
923.0	1266.2	Dirt road, powerline.		1571
922.0	1267.2	Delps Trail to east, △ (0.4E) N40 48.551 W75 27.073 **P** (0.7E) ◭		1580
		Campsite near trail intersection, unreliable spring 0.4E		
920.4	1268.8	Stempa Spring 0.6E	◭	1557
919.5	1269.7	Smith Gap Rd (paved) N40 49.530 W75 24.857 **P**	(pg.126)	1540
916.0	1273.2	**Leroy A. Smith Shelter** (0.2E). ⌒) ◭ ◭ ⊂ (8)		1477
		33.5◄23.5◄16.7◄►13.8►45.0►51.6 Water 0.2 mile down blue-blazed trail; second source 0.2 mile farther. Piped spring 0.5 mile down service road.		
915.8	1273.4	Powerline		1500
914.1	1275.1	Pipeline		1501
912.4	1276.8	Hahns Overlook, view.	🔌	1450

SoBo	NoBo	Description	Elev
911.6	1277.6	Powerline	1108
911.4	1277.8	PA 33, **Wind Gap, PA** (1.0E) . . . N40 51.639 W75 17.565 P (pg.126-127)	980
909.3	1279.9	Private road (gravel)	1585
905.6	1283.6	Campsite	1632
905.0	1284.2	Wolf Rocks bypass trail south end to west. Spring 100 yards west (treat)	1586
904.5	1284.7	Wolf Rocks, view	1616
903.9	1285.3	Wolf Rocks bypass trail north end to west.	1542
902.8	1286.4	Fox Gap, PA 191 (paved) N40 56.126 W75 11.815 P	1400
902.2	1287.0	**Kirkridge Shelter** 37.3◀30.5▼13.8◀▶31.2▶37.8▶43.6 ⊂ (6)	1467
		Tap 0.1 mi behind shelter, off in winter. If tap off, try Kirkridge Retreat down road.	
901.9	1287.3	Campsite, view	1505
900.3	1288.9	Totts Gap, gravel road, powerline to south	1300
900.0	1289.2	Pipeline	1381
899.7	1289.5	Roadbed.	1402
898.3	1290.9	Mt Minsi	1461
897.3	1291.9	Lookout Rock, view	800
897.1	1292.1	Stream	837
896.5	1292.7	Council Rock	600
896.4	1292.8	Turn east on gravel road	629
896.0	1293.2	Hiker parking lot N40 58.788 W75 8.518 P	549
895.8	1293.4	PA 611, **Delaware Water Gap, PA** (pg.128)	425
895.5	1293.7	**PA-NJ** border, I-80, Delaware River Bridge west bank	324
894.5	1294.7	Kittatinny Visitor Center . . . N40 58.219 W75 7.729 P H	313
		NoBo: cross under I-80 and turn left.	
894.1	1295.1	Parking, water pump (disabled in winter) V.C. is preferred for overnight parking. Sign "camping for A.T. through hikers" refers to a site 3.0N on AT.	321
893.8	1295.4	Bunnfield Trail to east	472
892.6	1296.6	Holly Spring Trail	950

1262.4   Little Gap Rd

🍴💧**Slopeside Grill** 0.2W and 0.5mi up driveway. Hikers welcome to get water from outside spigot. Grill hours: Fri 5-11pm, Sat 2-11pm, Sun 2-9pm.

Danielsville, PA 18038 (1.5E on Blue Mountain Dr, then left on Mountainview Dr to PO and B&B.)

🏤 M-F 8:30-12 & 2-4:30, Sa 8-12, 610.767.6882

🛏♿🚐🛜✉   **Filbert B&B**   610.428.3300 〈www.filbertbnb.com〉 $100S, $150D + tax. Hosted by Kathy in Victorian farmhouse with A/C includes full country breakfast. Will pickup at Little Gap (no charge). Fee for pickup at PA 309, Lehigh Gap, Smith Gap, or Wind Gap. Call ahead for reservations, no credit cards. Laundry for a fee. Parking for section hikers, ask about shuttles. Italian restaurant will deliver. Guest maildrops: 3740 Filbert Dr, Danielsville, PA 18038.

🍴💲 (0.8E) **Blue Mountain Restaurant & Ice Cream** 610.767.6379 B/L/D Tu-Su, closed M. Ask about overnighting.

🏪 (1.0E) **Miller's Market**

1269.7   Smith Gap Rd

💧⚒🚐🅿 (1.0W, blue blazes on telephone poles) Home of John "Mechanical Man" and Linda "Crayon Lady" Stempa, eponym of the spring 0.7 mile south. The Stempas (610.381.4606) welcome you to get water from spigot at rear of the house (no need to call) and to use the outside shower during daylight hours. Pet friendly, ask about dog sitting. Please sign register. For-fee shuttles ranging from Port Clinton to Delaware Water Gap, safe place to park your car. Sodas $1, ask about stoves and fuel. When they are home and *only with permission*, camp or stay in garage with hot shower, towel and ride to take out food and ATM when available, and ride back to trail for $10; call in advance. Ask about maildrops.

⛺🏪🚿♿ (2.7W) **Evergreen Lake** 610.837.6401 West 1.7 on Smith Gap Road, then left one mile on Mountain Road. Tenting $29 for up to 2 adults, 2 children. Snack shop, laundry, free showers.

Kunkletown, PA 18058 (3.0W) West on Smith Gap Rd for 2 mi to stop sign, rigtht on Lower Smith Gap Rd for 100 yards, left on Chestnut Ridge Rd for 0.9 mi to Kunkletown Rd. Pub, general store and Penny's at intersection, PO 0.5 west on Kunkletown Rd.

🏤 M-F 8-11:30 & 12:30-5, Sa 8-12, 610.381.3062

🛏🍴**Kunkletown Pub** 610.895.4253 Room $50/up, 10% discount on meals (L/D). Pool table.

🍴 **Penny's Place**

🏪💲 **General Store** 610.381.2887 Good selection of packaged foods, deli, ice cream. Summer hours 6:30-8:30 (till 7:30 in winter).

1277.8   PA 33

🛏(0.1W) **Gateway Motel** 610.863.4959 Motel temporarily closed at end of 2014, 2015 status TBD. Non-guests: please do not loiter on lawn or use hose.

🐾(4W) **Creature Comforts** 610.381.2287, 24/7 emergency care.

Wind Gap, PA 18091 (1E)

🏤 M-F 8:30-5, Sa 8:30-12, 610.863.6206

🛏🛜 **Travel Inn** 717.885.3101 $59D weekdays, $69D weekends. Room for 4 $69 weekdays, $79 weekends.

🛏🛜 **Red Carpet Inn** 610.863.7782 Stay includes cont. breakfast.

🛒 **Giant Food Store** 24hr, deli with salad bar.

🛒💊 **K-Mart** with pharmacy

🍴 **Beer Stein** Serves L/D wings, seafood.

🍴 **J&R's Smokehouse** L/D

🍴 **Sal's Pizza** 610.863.7565, delivers

🍴 **Hong Kong Chinese** L/D buffet

💊 **CVS** 610.863.5341

➕ **Priority Care** 610.654.5454 Walk-in clinic M-F 8am-8pm, Sa 10am-5pm, Su 10am-4pm.

➕ **Slate Belt Family Practice** 610.863.3019

🎦 **Gap Theatre** 610.863.3094 Movies F-Su.

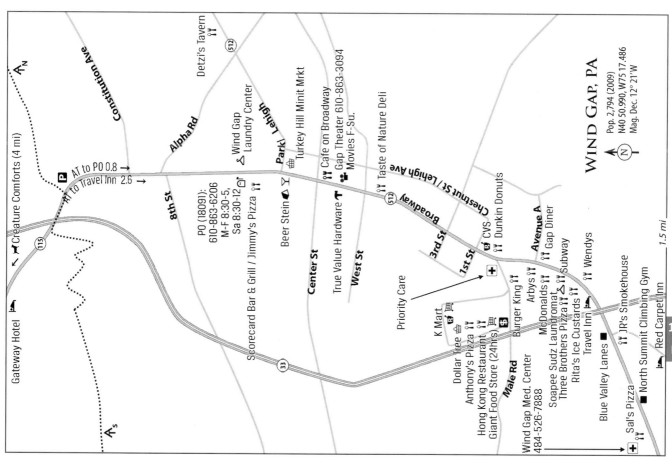

WIND GAP, PA

Pop. 2,794 (2009)
N40 50.990, W75 17.486
Mag. Dec. 12° 21'W

N

Creature Comforts (4 mi)

Constitution Ave

Detzi's Tavern

512

Alpha Rd

Wind Gap Laundry Center

Lehigh

Turkey Hill Minit Mrkt

Cafe on Broadway

Gap Theater 610-863-3094

Movies F-Su.

Taste of Nature Deli

P AT to PO 0.8 →
AT to Travel Inn 2.6 →

PO (1809):
610-863-6206
M-F 8:30-5,
Sa 8:30-12

8th St

Beer Stein

True Value Hardware

Scorecard Bar & Grill / Jimmy's Pizza

Center St

West St

Chestnut St / Lehigh Ave

512

Broadway

Dunkin Donuts

CVS

Avenue A

Gap Diner

3rd St

1st St

Subway

Wendys

Gateway Hotel

115

Priority Care

K Mart

Burger King

Arbys

McDonalds

Dollar Tree

Anthony's Pizza

Hong Kong Restaurant

Giant Food Store (24hrs)

Male Rd

Soapee Sudz Laundromat

Three Brothers Pizza

Rita's Ice Custards

Travel Inn

North Summit Climbing Gym

JR's Smokehouse

Red Carpet Inn

Blue Valley Lanes

Sal's Pizza

Wind Gap Med. Center
484-526-7888

33

N

S

1.5 mi

127
PA

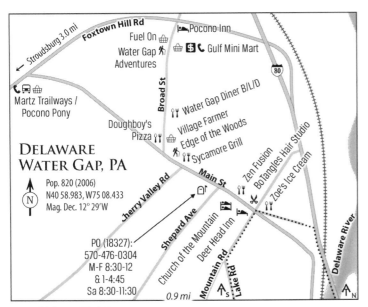

DELAWARE WATER GAP, PA

Pop. 820 (2006)
N40 58.983, W75 08.433
Mag. Dec. 12° 29'W

PO (18327):
570-476-0304
M-F 8:30-12
& 1-4:45
Sa 8:30-11:30

Stroudsburg 3.0 mi

Foxtown Hill Rd

Fuel On
Pocono Inn
Water Gap Adventures
Gulf Mini Mart

Broad St

80

Water Gap Diner B/L/D
Village Farmer
Doughboy's Pizza
Edge of the Woods
Sycamore Grill

Martz Trailways / Pocono Pony

Cherry Valley Rd

Main St

Zen Fusion
BoTangles Hair Studio
Zoe's Ice Cream

Shepard Ave

Church of the Mountain
Deer Head Inn

Mountain Rd

Lake Rd

Delaware River

0.9 mi

1293.4   PA 611

Delaware Water Gap, PA 18327

The Church of the Mountain Hostel 570.476.0345 Bunkroom, showers, overflow tenting, rides to Stroudsburg when available. Donations encouraged. 2-night max. No drive-ins, no parking, no laundry. Phone numbers of persons who can help are posted in the hostel. Thurs night hot dog dinner June-Aug.

Pocono Inn 570.476.0000 $55 weekdays, $65 F & Sa + tax. No pets.

Deer Head Inn 570.424.2000 $90/up weekdays, $120/up weekends. No pets, no TV. Restaurant & lounge open to all. Live music W-Su, hiker attire okay.

Village Farmer & Bakery 8am-8pm 7 days. Hot dog and slice of pie $2.49. Breakfast sandwich $4.99, salads, sandwiches. Credit card min. $10.

Doughboy's Pizza open 7 days in summer.

Edge of the Woods Outfitters 570.421.6681 Full line of gear, trail food, footwear. Coleman/alcohol/oz. Shuttles from Little Gap to Bear Mtn. Open 7 days, Memorial - Labor Day. Maildrops: (FedEx/UPS only) 110 Main St, Delaware Water Gap, PA 18327.

Water Gap Adventures 570.424.8533 Open Apr-Oct.

Pocono Pony 570.839.6862 ⟨gomcta.com⟩ Runs on 2hr-loop through Stroudsburg, $1.50 per boarding.

Martz Trailways 570.421.3040 $66.50 NYC roundtrip.

Pocono Cab 570.424.2800

WGM Taxi 570.223.9289

Stroudsburg, PA 18360 (3.5W)

Large town with all services, including supermarket, motels, laundry, and movie theater.

Dunkleberger's Sports 570.421.7950

Walmart 24hrs

1304.2   Camp Road

Mohican Outdoor Center (0.3W) 908.362.5670 <www.outdoors.org/lodging/mohican/> Thru-hiker rates for bunkroom $33PP, tenting $13.50. Shower/towel for tenters or w/o stay $5. Campfires only in designated areas. Welcome center & camp store hours in peak season are Su-Th 8-7, F 8-9, Sa 8-8. Open 9-5 in winter. Water available at the lodge or a spigot near the garage across the street. Deli sandwiches, sodas, candy, Coleman/alcohol/oz, and hiker supplies (footwear, packs, socks, poles). Operated by the AMC. Maildrops: 50 Camp Road, Blairstown, NJ 07825.

1321.8   US 206, Culvers Gap *(more services on map)*

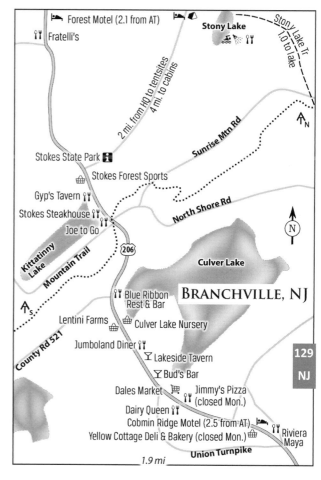

🛏 🔥 ❄ **Stokes SP** 973.948.3820 In-season (Apr-Oct). Tentsites 2 mi from SP office near Rte 206; cabins 4 mi away. Rates: tentsite 1-6 persons $30/up, cabins: $80/up. $5 transaction fee per stay. Snack bar & free showers at Stony Lake Mem-Columbus Day, accesible from 1.0 mile-long Stony Lake Tr.

🛏 ⛺ 🛰 ✉ **Forest Motel** 973.948.5456, $45S $55D + tax, pets $20, laundry $20. Guest maildrops: 104 Rte 206 N, Branchville, NJ 07826.

🛏 **Cobmin Ridge Motel** 973.948.3459, 973.652.0780 $50/up.

🍴 **Joe to Go** ⚠ Watch for posted rules, proprietor will enforce them.

🍴 **Gyps Tavern** Hikers welcome to inside or lakeside seating, charging outlets, economical food choices and packaged goods to go. Open L/D.

🍴 **Jumboland Diner** B/L/D, $2.99 breakfast, Th dinner buffet, ice cream.

🏪 (1.5E) **Dale's Market** 973.948.3078 M-F 6-9, Sa-Su 7-9

Branchville, NJ 07826 (3.4E)

🏤 M–F 8:30–5, Sa 8:30–1, 973.948.3580

1336.1   NJ 23

🔥 🚶 💧 🅿 ✉ **High Point State Park Headquarters** 973.875.4800 Office open year-round 9am-4pm, F & Sa 8-8 in summer. Bathrooms inside, water spigot outside. Overnight parking 0.25E. **Sawmill Lake Camping Area** 2.5 mile from HQ, tentsites $20 NJ resident/$25 non-resident plus $5.50 walk-in fee. Maildrops: 1480 State Rte 23, Sussex, NJ 07461.

🛏 ⛺ 🚌 🛰 ✉ (1.5E) **High Point Country Inn** 973.702.1860 $79.99D + tax, pets $5, no room phone. Laundry $7. Free pickup/return to trail from NJ 23, longer shuttles for a fee. Guest maildrops: 1328 NJ 23, Wantage, NJ 07461.

Port Jervis, NY 12785 (4.4W)

🛏 🛰 🖥 ✉ **Days Inn** 845.856.6611 $65D, $10EAP, cont B, pets $20. Guest maildrops: 2247 Greenville Turnpike, Port Jervis, NY 12771.

🍴 **Village Pizza** 973.293.3364

🛒 🎁 **Shop Rite Market**, **Price Chopper**

🎁 **Rite Aid** 845.856.8342, **Medicine Shoppe** 845.856.6681

➕ **Bon Secours Community Hospital** 845.858.7000

🐕 **Tri-States Veterinary Medical** 845.856.1914

SoBo	NoBo	Elev	Description
890.5	1298.7	1287	Backpacker Campsite, Douglas Trail to west, water south of camp. No fires, use bear boxes/poles, leash dogs.
889.7	1299.5	1382	Sunfish Pond south end, no swimming or camping.
889.1	1300.1	1384	Sunfish Pond north end, rock sculptures
888.2	1301.0	1452	Stream.
887.5	1301.7	1560	Powerline
887.4	1301.8	1513	Kittatinny Mountain, rocky summit
886.8	1302.4	1410	Kaiser Trail to west
885.0	1304.2	1111	Camp Rd (gravel), footbridge . . . N41 1.977 W75 0.237 P ◆ (pg.128) **Mohican Outdoor Center** (0.3W)
883.8	1305.4	1472	Rattlesnake Swamp Trail, view.
882.9	1306.3	1565	Catfish Lookout Tower, picnic table below the tower.
882.3	1306.9	1260	Rattlesnake Spring on dirt road about 17 yards west of AT.
882.0	1307.2	1248	Stream.
881.8	1307.4	1280	Millbrook-Blairstown Rd (paved) N41 3.567 W74 57.815 P
			Millbrook Village (1.1W) historical park with picnic area.
881.5	1307.7	1251	Swamp
881.2	1308.0	1392	Powerline
879.1	1310.1	1492	Campsite
878.0	1311.2	1350	Blue Mtn Lakes Rd, pump disabled, water 0.1E on road. No camping in zone from 0.5 mile of road to one mile north of Crater Lake.
875.9	1313.3	1454	Side trail leads 0.5E to Crater Lake. No camping.
874.9	1314.3	1560	Buttermilk Falls Trail, campsites to the north
873.6	1315.6	1306	Campsite
873.2	1316.0	1492	Rattlesnake Mountain
872.9	1316.3	1362	Spring

SoBo	NoBo	Feature	Elev
871.0	1318.2	**Brink Shelter** (0.2W)(2013) 61.7◀45.0◀31.2▲◀6.6▶12.4▶15.0 . . . ☾⟵(8) Bear box. Close to road.	1234
869.8	1319.4	Jacobs Ladder Trail	1374
868.0	1321.2	Powerline	1239
867.4	1321.8	US 206, Culvers Gap, **Branchville, NJ** (3.4E)	935
867.1	1322.1	Sunrise Mountain Rd (paved) . . . . N41 10.780 W74 47.277 P	978
865.5	1323.7	Culver Fire Tower (locked)	1526
864.5	1324.7	Stony Brook Trail 1.0W to free showers at Stony Lake . . . . . . (see map pg.129)	1348
864.4	1324.8	**Gren Anderson Shelter** (0.1W) . . . ☾ ♦ (0.1W) ⟵(8) 51.6◀37.8◀6.6▲◀5.8▶8.4▶13.0 Spring to left of shelter and downhill 70 yards.	1341
863.0	1326.2	Tinsley Trail	1454
862.0	1327.2	Sunrise Mountain, no camping at pavilion . . . . . . N41 10.780 W74 47.277 P	1653
861.3	1327.9	Roadbed.	1446
860.3	1328.9	Stream (slow outflow from pond), treatment recommended.	1391
858.6	1330.6	**Mashipacong Shelter** 43.6◀12.4◀5.8▲◀2.6▶7.2▶19.6 Close to road. ☾⟵(8)	1431
858.4	1330.8	Spring (0.6N) on red-blazed Iris Trail. Sometimes water left in bear box. Deckertown Turnpike . . . . N41 15.136 W74 41.367 P	1336
857.5	1331.7	Three intersections with red-blazed trail	1436
856.0	1333.2	**Rutherford Shelter** (0.4E) 15.0◀8.4◀2.6▲◀4.6▶17.0▶28.5 ☾ ⟵(6)	1491
855.7	1333.5	Spring 100 yards before shelter on connecting trail. Slow stream. Bear box. View	1485
854.2	1335.0	Intersection with blue-blazed trail.	1596
853.3	1335.9	Iris Trail 0.2E to parking on NJ 23	1506
853.1	1336.1	NJ 23 High Point State Park Headquarters, **Port Jervis, NY** (4.4W) . . . . . N41 18.158 W74 40.065 P ♦ (pg.129)	1500
852.1	1337.1	Wooden tower, 0.3W to beach & concessions Mem–Labor Day 12-6	1679
851.9	1337.3	Green-blazed trail 0.3W to 220' tower atop highest point in NJ	1610

Elev (6000, 5000, 4000, 3000, 2000, 1000)

SoBo	NoBo	Feature	Elev
851.4	1337.8	**High Point Shelter** (0.1E) 13.0◄7.2◄4.6◄▶12.4▶23.9▶36.0 ⟍♠⌂(8)	1310
		Streams on both sides of shelter. Road to privy to right of shelter. Bear box.	
850.1	1339.1	Greenville Rd, County 519 (paved)	1100
849.2	1340.0	Courtwright Rd (gravel), stream on AT 0.1 south of road ♠	966
848.7	1340.5	Streams. ♠	951
848.1	1341.1	Fergerson Rd (gravel), east 20 yards on road.	854
847.5	1341.7	Gemmer Rd (paved) ♠	717
847.2	1342.0	Stream. ♠	689
846.8	1342.4	Two footbridges, streams	598
846.5	1342.7	Goodrich Rd (paved)	623
846.3	1342.9	Pond	661
846.0	1343.2	Murray property 0.2W, gravel driveway (pg.135)	655
845.6	1343.6	Goldsmith Lane (gravel)	666
845.0	1344.0	Unionville Rd (paved), County Rd 651 (pg.134)	610
845.0	1344.2	Quarry Rd	607
844.3	1344.9	Lott Rd, **Unionville, NY** (0.7W) (pg.134)	590
843.2	1346.0	NJ 284, **Unionville, NY** (0.7W) N41 17.311 W74 33.141 P (pg.134)	429
842.8	1346.4	Lower Rd (Oil City Rd).	511
842.3	1346.9	Carnegie Rd; NoBo: follow road 0.2W	413
842.0	1347.2	State Line Rd, NoBo: follow road 0.5E	420
841.8	1347.4	Wallkill River, parking. N41 17.263 W74 32.042 P	410
841.5	1347.7	AT + State Line Rd north end. NoBo: turn east into Wallkill Reserve	407
840.7	1348.5	90 degree turn on Wallkill perimeter	391
840.3	1348.9	90 degree turn on Wallkill perimeter	407
839.5	1349.7	Liberty Corners Rd (paved)	440
839.4	1349.8	Water to west.	513
839.0	1350.2	**Pochuck Mtn. Shelter** (0.1W) 19.6◄17.0◄12.4◄▶11.5▶23.6▶37.9 ⟍♠⌂(6)	866
		Bear box. Spigot at vacant house at foot of Pochuck Mountain.	
838.2	1351.0	View. [📷]	1092
837.4	1351.8	Pochuck Mountain [📷]	1154
836.9	1352.3	Lovemma Lane (gravel)	897
836.7	1352.5	Stream.	822
836.3	1352.9	County Rd 565 **Glenwood, NJ** (1.1W), stream south of road ♠ (pg.135)	720
835.6	1353.6	Roadbed.	769
834.8	1354.4	County Rd 517, **Glenwood, NJ** (1.1W) N41 14.142 W74 28.830 P (pg.135)	440
834.1	1355.1	Pochuck Creek suspension footbridge.	396
833.4	1355.8	Boardwalk over swamp for (0.6S) and (0.2N) of footbridge. Canal Rd. N41 13.597 W74 28.137 P	410
833.2	1356.0	Footbridge, Wawayanda Creek. ♠	403
832.5	1356.7	NJ 94, **Vernon, NJ** (2.4E) N41 13.160 W74 27.306 P (pg.135)	450
831.5	1357.7	Spring, climb up south side of mtn known as "stairway to heaven" ♠	963
831.1	1358.1	Pinwheels vista 0.1W, Wawayanda Mountain, side trail 0.8E to views [📷]	1340

SoBo	NoBo			Elev
830.2	1359.0	Footbridge, stream		1007
829.4	1359.8	Barrett Rd (paved), **New Milford, NY** (1.8W)	(pg.135)	1140
828.3	1360.9	Cross stream on Iron Mountain Rd		1060
827.5	1361.7	**Wawayanda Shelter** (0.1W)	⌐ (6)	1189
		28.5◄23.9◄11.5▲▶12.1▶26.4▶31.7 Water from park 0.1N and 0.2E.		
827.3	1361.9	Wawayanda State Park (0.2E)	N41 11.883 W74 23.847 P 🚶	1150
827.0	1362.2	Warwick Turnpike	N41 12.085 W74 23.497 P (pg.135)	1140
826.5	1362.7	Footbridge, stream		1113
825.6	1363.6	Long House Dr / Brady Rd	N41 11.732 W74 22.290 P	1117

Camp only in designated sites; fires only in campsite fire rings. Hitchhiking is illegal in NY.

824.5	1364.7	Long House Creek, footbridge		1085
823.7	1365.5	Ernest Walter Trail (yellow-blazed) to east		1362
823.4	1365.8	**NJ-NY** border, State Line Trail 1.0E to **Lakeside, NJ**		1385
823.0	1366.2	0.1N on AT is Zig Zag Trail to west. Prospect Rock, highest point on AT in NY. Views of Greenwood Lake to east.	📷	1433
822.1	1367.1	Furnace Brook		1161
821.8	1367.4	Ladder		1243

Despite the unimposing profile, rocks, abrupt ups & downs make this section challenging.

820.4	1368.8	Cascade Brook		1184
819.6	1369.6	Village Vista Trail, 0.8E to Greenwood Lake		1276
818.0	1371.2	Powerline		1201
817.5	1371.7	NY 17A, **Bellvale, NY** (1.6W)	N41 14.658 W74 17.216 P (pg.136-137)	1180
		Greenwood Lake, NY (2.0E)		
816.9	1372.3	Pipeline clearing		1243
816.2	1373.0	Eastern Pinnacles, short bypass trail to west	📷	1184
816.0	1373.2	Brook		1053
815.7	1373.5	Cat Rocks, view	📷	1050
815.4	1373.8	**Wildcat Shelter** (0.2W) 36.0◄23.6◄12.1▲▶14.3▶19.6▶22.8	⌐ (8)	1066
		Water 0.1 south of shelter is better than water on shelter side trail.		
814.1	1375.1	Highlands Trail		774
813.9	1375.3	Lakes Rd (paved), 0.1N powerline, footbridge and stream		680
813.6	1375.6	Fitzgerald Falls		714
812.3	1376.9	Allis Trail, Sterling Fire Tower 5.0E	📷	1251
811.6	1377.6	Mombasha High Point	📷	1280

Annabele's Pizza

Unionville Rd

Horler's Store

Village Office

Wit's End Tavern

PO (10988):
845-726-3535
M-F 8-11:30 & 1-5,
Sa 9-12

Quarry Rd

Lott Rd

End of the Line Grocery

State Line Rd

Lower Rd

(284)

Carnegie Rd

UNIONVILLE, NY (N)

P

✳ Purple Looseleaf – Stalks of purple looseleaf, an invasive species, dominate swampy regions near the AT in NJ.

Wallkill River

New York
New Jersey

Wallkill Reserve

Liberty Corners Rd

1343.2   Murray property driveway
⊏⬧⬧💦︎☽ Private cabin open for the use of long distance hikers as it has been for nearly 20 years, tenting, well water, shower & privy. If you feel the need to change your brain chemistry this is probably not your stop but serious hikers welcome. No groups please.

1344.0   Unionville Rd, County Rd 651
1344.9   Lott Rd
1346.0   NJ 284   **Unionville, NY** PO is 0.5W from any road crossing.
⬧⬧👫 **Village Office** 845.726.3681 Tenters check in at office or at Horlers.
⫙⬧ **Wit's End Tavern** 845.726.3956 Darts, pool table. Open 7 days noon-midnight or later. Great ribs, burgers, wings. Music on Fri and Sat.
⫙⬧ **Horler's Store** 845.726.3210 M-Sa 6-8, Su 7-7, short-order grill.
⬧ **End of the Line Grocery** 845.726.3228 Deli, M-S 6-9, Sa-Su 6-7
⫙ **Annabelle's** 7 days 10-10, burgers, pizza by slice.

1352.9   County Rd 565
1354.4   County Rd 517 (0.9W to PO and Pochuck Valley Farm)

Glenwood, NJ 07418 (1.1W from either road)
⌂ M-F 7:30-5, Sa 10-2, 973.764.2616

🛏🛜✉ **Apple Valley Inn** 973.764.3735 $145-$160 + tax, includes country breakfast, no pets, shuttles to County Roads 517 & 565 with stay. Guest maildrops: PO Box 302, Glenwood, NJ 07418.

⛲🍴🚿🚻 **Pochuck Valley Farms Market & Deli** 973.764.4732 Open daily M-F 6am-6pm, Sa-Su 6am-5pm. B/L, produce, bakery. Water spigot and restroom.

1356.7   NJ 94

⛲🚻💲 (0.1W) **Heaven Hill Farm** 973.764.5144 Summer hours 7 days 9-7 (6 on Sundays) ice cream, bakery, seasonal fruit & vegetables, picnic tables.

🍴(0.2E) **Mitch's Roadside Grill** Hot dog stand open 11-3 Apr-Oct. Hot dogs, sodas, Italian Ice & potato knishes. Shaded picnic tables.

🛏🚿🛜✉ (1.2E) **Appalachian Motel** 973.764.6070 $70-110D, $10EAP. Call for ride. Pets $20. Laundry $10. Maildrops (guests only): 367 Route 94, Vernon, NJ 07462.

Vernon, NJ 07462 (2.4E)

🛏☀🚿🖥 **St. Thomas Episcopal Church Hostel** 973.764.7506 $10PP donation, capacity 12, one night limit. Shower/towel, fridge, micro. Hikers may have to share space with other groups and are expected to help w/cleanup. Pets outside, no alcohol, no smoking. Hikers welcome to Sunday service. Open Nov-Apr.

🛒💲 **A&P Food Store** M-Sa 7-midnight, Su 7-10, **Starbucks** Inside

VERNON, NJ
Pop. 23,943 (2010)
N41 11.906, W74 28.972
Mag. Dec. 12° 53'W

1.1 mi

Appalachian Motel 🛏

1.3 mi. from hotel
Heaven Hill Farm & Mitch's Grill near trailhead

Vernon Vet Clinic 973-764-3630

🍴 Vernon Inn

Ming's Asian Bistro

DJ's Barber Shop

China Star

Dunkin Donuts

Church St

Mixing Bowl

St. Thomas Episcopal

🍴 Paesano Pizza
🍴 Burger King

Pizza Station

McAfee Vernon Rd

Main St

Vernon Rd

⊞ Vernon Urgent Care (1.0mi)

Healthy Tyhmes Market

Rumours Hair
Rite Aid

PO (07462) 973-764-9056:
M-F 8:30-5, Sa 9:30-12:30

🍴 Lox of Bagels
🛒 A&P Grocery, Pharmacy, Starbucks

🍴 Dairy Queen

⊞ **Vernon Urgent Care** 973.209.2260 1.0mi beyond hostel, M-F 8-8, Sa-Su 9-5.
New Milford, NY (2.7W from NJ 94, listings below at Barrett Rd.)

1359.8   Barrett Rd
New Milford, NY 10959 (1.8W) 1.6W on Barret Rd, then right 0.2 on NJ 94 to shoe store and post office.
⌂ M-F 8:30-12:30, Sa 9-11:30, 845.986.3557

■ **Sneakers to Boots** 845.986.0333 314 Rt 94 South. Shoes by Merrell, Keen, Oboz and others, merino wool socks.

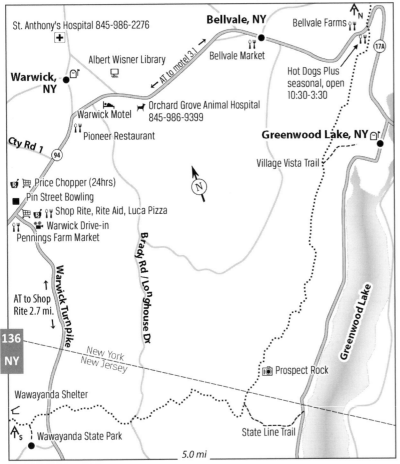

1362.2   Warwick Turnpike   *Warwick, NY 10990*
    2.7W to intersection with NY 94, 1.5N on NY 94 to downtown with many restaurants, post office & library.
🛏🛁🅿📶🖥 **Meadow Lark Farm B&B** 845.651.4286 ⟨www.meadowlarkfarm.com⟩ Weeknights $75S/D or $99 for 3-person room, includes breakfast. Rate is higher on Fri-Sa nights. Tenting $15 includes shower & breakfast. All major CC, pets welcome. Shuttles covering NJ & NY, $1 per round-trip mile; free parking for section hikers. Maildrops: 180 Union Corners Rd, Warwick, NY 10990.
🍴 **Pennings Farm Market** Harvest Grill, ice cream
🎬**Warwick Drive-In Theatre** 845.986.4440 Walk-ins welcome. $10 adults, $6 kids and seniors, no credit cards.
🏠 M-F 8:30-5, Sa 9-4, 845.986.0271
🧺 **South Street Wash & Fold**, **Warwick Laundry Center**
🖥 **Albert Wisner Public Library** 845.986.1047 M-Th 9-8, F 9-7, Sa 9-5, Su 12-4.

1371.7   NY 17A, 🍴**Hot Dog Plus** Just west of the AT.
🍴🍦📞 (0.3W) **Bellvale Farms** 845.988.1818 Ice cream, water from hose, can use phone, ask about parking.
    Bellvale, NY 10912 (1.6W)
🍴 **Bellvale Market** 845.544.7700, M-F 8-7, Sa 8-6, Su 8-4.
    Greenwood Lake, NY 10925 (2E)
🛏🍴🧺🅿📶🖥✉ **Anton's on the Lake** 845.477.0010 ⟨www.antonsonthelake.com⟩ Thru-hiker rate, two-night min, price per night: $80S/D Sunday-Thurs, $125/up Friday & Sat. All major CC, rooms with whirlpool available, no pets, no smoking, laundry small loads only, swimming, paddle boats & canoe. Free shuttles and slackpacking w/stay, longer shuttles for a fee. Open year round, hiker friendly. Maildrops for guests: (USPS) PO Box 1505 or (FedEx/UPS) 7 Waterstone Rd, Greenwood Lake, NY 10925.

Lake Lodging 845.477.0700 or 845.705.2005. Good hiker rates. No pets, no credit cards.

Breezy Point Inn 845.477.8100 ⟨www.breezypointinn.com⟩ $85+tax room with 2 double beds, no pets, no smoking, L/D dining 7 days. Closed month of January. Guest maildrops: (UPS/FedEx) 620 Jersey Ave, Greenwood Lake, NY 10925.

Cumberland Farms 24/7, deli.

Greenwood Lake Taxi 845.477.0314

Warwick, NY 10990 4.5W to downtown area, see adjacent map & more listings on pg. 135.

Warwick Motel (3.1W from NY 17A) 845.986.6656.

1383.7 NY 17 **Southfields, NY 10975** (2.1E)
M-F 9-11 & 1-5, Sa 8:30-11:30, 845.351.2628
Tuxedo Motel 845.351.4747 $54.50S, $59.50D, $10EAP. No pets, no cooking. Many food delivery options. Accepts Visa/MC. Maildrops: 985 Route 17 South, Southfields, NY, 10975.

Harriman, NY 10926 (3.7W)
Lodging, groceries, restaurants, and laundromats.

1389.2 Arden Valley Road
Lake Tiorati Beach (0.3E)
845.351.2568 Open daily mid Jun-mid Aug 9-7, weekends only spring and fall. Restrooms, free showers, vending machine, swimming.

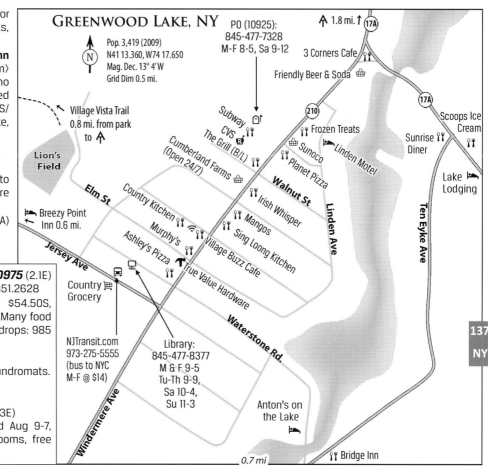

GREENWOOD LAKE, NY

Pop. 3,419 (2009)
N41 13.360, W74 17.650
Mag. Dec. 13° 4'W
Grid Dim 0.5 mi.

PO (10925):
845-477-7328
M-F 8-5, Sa 9-12

1.8 mi. ↑ 17A

3 Corners Cafe

Friendly Beer & Soda

Village Vista Trail 0.8 mi. from park to ⩓

Lion's Field

Subway
CVS
The Grill (B/L)

Cumberland Farms (Open 24/7)

210

17A

Scoops Ice Cream

Frozen Treats

Sunoco

Planet Pizza

Linden Motel

Sunrise Diner

Lake Lodging

Walnut St

Linden Ave

Ten Eyke Ave

Elm St

Country Kitchen

Irish Whisper

Breezy Point Inn 0.6 mi.

Murphy's

Ashley's Pizza

Village Buzz Cafe

Mangos

Sing Loong Kitchen

True Value Hardware

Jersey Ave

Country Grocery

NJTransit.com 973-275-5555 (bus to NYC M-F @ $14)

Library: 845-477-8377 M & F 9-5 Tu-Th 9-9, Sa 10-4, Su 11-3

Waterstone Rd.

Anton's on the Lake

Windermere Ave

0.7 mi

Bridge Inn

SoBo	NoBo	Description	Elev	Features
810.5	1378.7	Boardwalk, pond	958	◆
810.4	1378.8	West Mombasha Rd, stream just north on AT N41 16.159 W74 12.876	980	◆ **P**
809.5	1379.7	Buchanan Mountain	1142	
808.7	1380.5	East Mombasha Rd (paved)	840	
808.4	1380.8	Little Dam Lake, stepping stones over creek	758	◆
807.3	1381.9	Orange Turnpike N41 16.167 W74 10.862	780	**P** ◆ (0.5E)
806.6	1382.6	Arden Mountain	1180	
806.3	1382.9	Sapphire Trail	1140	
805.9	1383.3	View	1042	🖼
805.5	1383.7	NY 17, **Southfields, NY** (2.1E), **Harriman, NY** (3.7W), (pg.137)	550	
805.1	1384.1	AT on Arden Valley Rd for 0.4 mile, N41 15.893 W74 9.261 Passes over NY State Thruway 87.	602	**P**
803.8	1385.4	Island Pond Rd (gravel) 0.1E to pond	1045	◆
803.2	1386.0	Lemon Squeezer, Arden-Surebridge Trail to east	1150	
802.9	1386.3	Island Pond Mountain	1349	🖼
802.5	1386.7	New York Long Path 52.0E to Manhattan	1091	
801.8	1387.4	Surebridge Brook	1113	◆
801.2	1388.0	AT joins Red Dot Trail (south end)	1318	
801.1	1388.1	**Fingerboard Shelter** 37.9◄26.4◄14.3◄►5.3►8.5►40.7. Spring downhill to left unreliable. Water at Lake Tiorati 0.5E on Hurst Trail.	1348	◇ ⊏ (8)
800.5	1388.7	Fingerboard Mountain	1333	
800.0	1389.2	Arden Valley Rd (paved), Tiorati Circle (0.3E) N41 16.542 W74 5.286	1196	**P** (pg.137)
799.3	1389.9	Woods road	1039	
797.9	1391.3	Footbridge, stream	840	
797.8	1391.4	Seven Lakes Dr	850	
795.8	1393.4	**William Brien Memorial Shelter** 31.7◄19.6◄5.3◄►3.2►35.4►44.4 Unreliable spring-fed well 80 yards down blue-blazed trail to right of shelter. Yellow-blazed Menomine Trail to east.	1059	◇ ⊏ (8)
794.9	1394.3	AT joins Red Dot Trail (north end)	931	
794.5	1394.7	Black Mountain, views, can see NY City skyline	1187	🖼
793.7	1395.5	Palisades Parkway, busy 4-lane divided hwy. NY City 34E. Visitor. center in median 0.4W, soda & snack machines. ⚠ Watch blazes next 3mi. north.	680	🏠 🚻 ◆ 📞
793.4	1395.8	Beechy Bottom Brook, footbridge, parking 0.8W	607	**P** ◆
792.6	1396.6	**West Mountain Shelter** (0.6E) 22.8◄8.5◄3.2◄►32.2►41.2►49.0. Views of Hudson River & NYC.	1175	🖼 ⊏ (8)
791.9	1397.3	Views from ridge of West Mountain	1111	🖼
790.8	1398.4	Seven Lakes Dr	610	

SoBo	NoBo	Description	Elev
790.2	1399.0	Perkins Memorial Dr	805
788.4	1400.8	Bear Mountain, Perkins Memorial Tower, ... N41 18.670 W74 0.434 📷 🥾	1305
		Vending machines, view of NYC skyline.	
787.8	1401.4	Perkins Memorial Dr (south end of 0.3 mi. roadwalk)	1020
⚠ NoBo: Upon reaching the park, AT turns left through playground then follows path at edge of lake.			
786.5	1402.7	Bear Mountain Recreation Area, Hessian Lake N41 18.780 W73 59.338 P (pg.140)	175
786.1	1403.1	Tunnel under US 9, Trailside Museum, bear cage is lowest point on AT (pg.140)	163
785.6	1403.6	Bear Mountain Bridge, Hudson River, **Fort Montgomery, NY** (1.8W) (pg.140)	200
785.1	1404.1	NY 9D, Bear Mountain Bridge north end.	218
784.4	1404.8	Camp Smith Trail, 0.6E to Anthonys Nose, views of Hudson River 📷	738
783.4	1405.8	Hemlock Springs Campsite 🌢	550
783.2	1406.0	Manitou Rd (gravel). N41 19.776 W73 57.195 P	460
782.2	1407.0	Osborne Loop Trail to west (blue-blazed)	794
781.8	1407.4	Curry Pond Trail to west (yellow-blazed)	864
780.8	1408.4	Osborne Loop Trail to west (blue-blazed)	868
780.3	1408.9	Carriage Connector Trail to west (yellow-blazed)	527
779.8	1409.4	US 9 + NY 403, **Peekskill, NY** (4.5E) (pg.141)	400
779.5	1409.7	Old Highland Turnpike (paved)	451
779.2	1410.0	Franciscan Way (paved), **Graymoor Spiritual Life Center** (0.4E)	530
779.1	1410.1	Two gravel roads (pg.141)	473
777.3	1411.9	Blue-blazed trail 0.1W to Denning Hill. 📷	900
776.5	1412.7	Old Albany Post Rd (gravel), Chapman Rd	607
775.5	1413.7	Canopus Hill.	812
774.9	1414.3	Brook 🌢	393
774.8	1414.4	Canopus Hill Rd (paved) (pg.141)	420
773.8	1415.4	South Highland Rd (paved), stream north side of road. 🌢	570
773.0	1416.2	Stream. 🌢	636
772.3	1416.9	Catfish Loop Trail (red-blazed)	926
771.1	1418.1	Dennytown Rd (paved), Three Lake Trail to west ..... N41 25.234 W73 52.135 P 🌢	860
		Water on side of pump building, open late-Apr-Oct.	
770.9	1418.3	Catfish Loop Trail to east (red-blazed)	823

Elev scale: 6000 5000 4000 3000 2000 1000

1402.7 Bear Mountain Recreation Area, *Bear Mountain, NY 10911*

⚠️ Going into town? Consider passing through zoo first; hours are limited.

⌂ M–F 8–10 (8-12 June-Sept 1st wk) 845.786.3747 Limited hours not good for maildrop.

🛏🍴💲🛰🖥 **Bear Mountain Inn** 845.786.2731 $149/up+tax, continental breakfast. Multiple dining options including **1915, Blue Tapas,** and **Hiker Cafe** inside the inn and **Stand 10** seasonal concession lakeside.

🛏🛰 **Overlook Lodge** 845.786.2731 $149/up+tax, continental B, some pet rooms.

1403.1 **Trailside Museum and Zoo** ✖ Is Whitman NOBO or SOBO?
Open 10-4:30; no charge for hiking through. No dogs. Lowest elevation on the AT (124') is within the park. If closed, or if you have a dog, use bypass (see map).

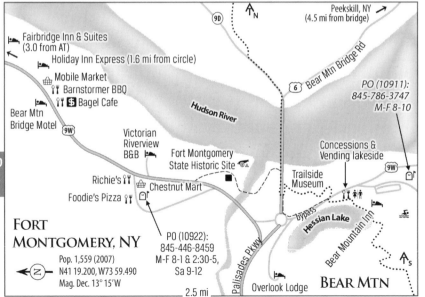

Fairbridge Inn & Suites (3.0 from AT)
Holiday Inn Express (1.6 mi from circle)
Mobile Market
🍴 Barnstormer BBQ
🍴💲 Bagel Cafe
Bear Mtn Bridge Motel
9W
Victorian Riverview B&B 🛏
Fort Montgomery State Historic Site
Richie's 🍴
Chestnut Mart
Foodie's Pizza 🍴

FORT MONTGOMERY, NY
Pop. 1,559 (2007)
N41 19.200, W73 59.490
Mag. Dec. 13° 15'W

PO (10922):
845-446-8459
M-F 8-1 & 2:30-5,
Sa 9-12

Hudson River
9D
N
Peekskill, NY (4.5 mi from bridge)
Bear Mtn Bridge Rd
6
PO (10911): 845-786-3747 M-F 8-10
Concessions & Vending lakeside
9W
Trailside Museum
Palisades Pkwy
bypass
Hessian Lake
Bear Mountain Inn
Overlook Lodge
BEAR MTN
S
2.5 mi

1403.6 Bear Mountain Bridge
Fort Montgomery, NY 10922 (1.8W)

🛏🛰✉ **Bear Mountain Bridge Motel** 845.446.2472 $75D, no pets, accepts Visa/MC, pickup/return to trail (park, zoo, or bridge) with stay. Wir sprechen Deutsch. Guest maildrops: PO Box 554, Fort Montgomery, NY 10922.

🛏⛰🛰🖥✉ **Holiday Inn Express** 845.446.4277 $120D+tax $10EAP, full B, indoor pool & sauna, coin laundry, 24-hour business center. Guest maildrops: 1106 Route 9 W, Fort Montgomery, NY 10922-0620.

🛏 **Victorian Riverview Inn** 845.446.5479 $175. $139/up. Ask for hiker rate.

🍴 **Foodies Pizza** 845.839.0383

Highland Falls, NY (3.8W)

🛏🛰 **Fairbridge Inn & Suites** 845.446.9400 $75D, continental breakfast. Pets $10.

🍴 **Dunkin' Donuts,** and many other restaurants

🏪 **My Town Market**

💊 **Rite Aid**

🖥 **Highland Falls Library** 845.446.3113 M 10-5, Tu 10-7, W-F 10-5, Sa 10-2.

Fort Montgomery State Historic Site Side trail starting from end of bridge guardrail 0.6W passes through Revolutionary War fort for which the town is named. The side trail is roughly the same length as the roadwalk but is more interesting. View the Hudson River bridge down the barrel of a cannon.

1409.4 US 9, NY 403

Appalachian Market at trailhead. Hiker-friendly, open 24hrs, deli serves B/L/D. Water from spigot on north side of building.

Stadium Sports Bar (0.8E)

Peekskill, NY 10566 (4.5E) large town

M-F 9-5, Sa 9-4, 914.737.6437

1410.0 Franciscan Way

Graymoor Spiritual Life Center (0.4E) 800.338.2620 Hikers permitted to sleep at monastery's ball field picnic shelter. Has water, privy & shower during warm months. Open all season and free. Follow signs and blue-blazes; stay to the left at both forks in the road.

1414.4 Canopus Hill Rd

(1.6E) **Putnam Valley Market** 845.528.8626 Directions: (0.3E) on Canopus Hill Rd, right on Canopus Hollow Rd for 0.1 mile, left on Sunset Hill Road for 1.2 mile. Pizza, hot food from the grill, ATM, open M-Sa 6-9, Su 6-7.

1421.8 NY 301, Canopus Lake (1E to SP)

1423.8 Side trail entry (0.2E to SP beach)

Clarence Fahnestock State Park 845.225.7207, 800.456.2267 Open mid-Apr to mid-Dec. Thru-hikers get one free night of camping. Concession at beach open weekends only Mem. Day - June 21. Open every day June 21 - Labor Day. Hours Su-F 10-4, Sa 10-5.

1428.8 Hortontown RD, **RPH Shelter** (Ralph's Peak Hiker Cabin) Trail work opportunity weekend following July 4.

Pizza delivered by **Avanti's** 845.896.6500 and **Gian Bruno's** 845.227.9276

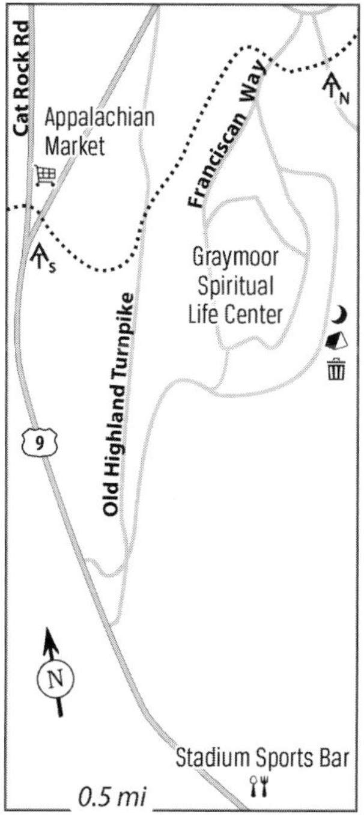

Cat Rock Rd
Appalachian Market
Franciscan Way
Graymoor Spiritual Life Center
Old Highland Turnpike
9
N
Stadium Sports Bar
0.5 mi

1433.9 NY 52

(0.4E) **Mountaintop Market Deli** 845.221.0928 Open daily 6-8, ATM and pay phone inside, welcome to water from faucet on side of building. Ask about tenting.

Danny's Pizzeria pizza by the slice.

Stormville, NY 12582 (1.9W)

M-F 8:30-5, Sa 9-12, 845.226.2627

1441.1 NY 55

(1.5W) Pleasant Ridge Plaza with **Poughquag Central Market**, **Pleasant Ridge Pizza** L/D.

(1.2W) **Total Care Pharmacy**

R's Gulf Quickmart & Deli 845.452.4040

Poughquag, NY 12570 (3.1W)

M-F 8:30-1 & 2-5, Sa 8:30-12:30, 845.724.4763

Pine Grove Motel 845.724.5151 $70S $75D, + tax, no pets, accepts Visa/MC.

Great Wall, **Clove Valley Deli & Café**

Total Care Pharmacy, Beekman Pharmacy

Beekman Animal Hospital 845.724.8387

Pawling, NY (4.0E, see pg. 144)

1446.3 County Rd 20, West Dover Rd

Dover Oak north side of road, largest oak tree on AT. Girth 20' 4" and estimated to be over 300 years old. Spigot on fence post at red house 100 yards east of the trail. Please help yourself, they would prefer that you do not interrupt them to ask permission.

Pawling, NY 12564 (3.1E, see pg. 144)

SoBo	NoBo	Feature	Elev
769.5	1419.7	Sunken Mine Rd (gravel), stream to north.	800
768.3	1420.9	Three Lakes Trail	1000
767.4	1421.8	NY 301, Canopus Lake, **Clarence Fahnestock SP** (1.0E) (pg.141)	920
766.8	1422.4	Fahnestock Trail to west	1089
765.4	1423.8	Green-blazed trail to lake, **Clarence Fahnestock SP** (0.2E) (pg.141)	974
		View of the lake from AT north of this intersection.	
764.6	1424.6	Stream	1033
763.2	1426.0	Shenandoah Mountain, view, painted 911 Memorial Flag.	1282
762.8	1426.4	Long Hill Rd (gravel)	1100
762.3	1426.9	Powerline	1029
761.7	1427.5	Shenandoah Tenting Area 0.1W, hand pump	900
761.3	1427.9	Brook	765
760.5	1428.7	Bridge over brook	374
760.4	1428.8	Hortontown Rd. N41 30.843 W73 47.509	376
760.1	1429.0	**RPH Shelter** (1982) 40.7◄35.4◄32.2▲9.0►16.8►25.6 Treat pump water.	
		Footbridge, stream, Taconic State Pkwy underpass	564
756.9	1432.3	Hosner Mountain Rd, footbridge, stream (do not drink, farm upstream)	500
755.3	1433.9	NY 52, **Stormville, NY** (1.9W). N41 32.460 W73 43.969 P (pg.141)	800
754.7	1434.5	Stream	839
754.1	1435.1	AT on Old Stormville Mountain Rd for 0.1 mile.	970
753.9	1435.3	AT on Stormville Mountain Rd for 0.1 mile, crosses over I-84	950
753.7	1435.5	Grape Hollow Rd	954
752.4	1436.8	Side trail 0.6W to Indian Pass	1167
751.5	1437.7	Mt Egbert	1329
751.4	1437.8	**Morgan Stewart Shelter**	1308
		44.4◄41.2◄9.0▲7.8►16.6►20.6	
750.3	1438.9	Depot Hill Rd, parking 0.1W. N41 34.288 W73 40.840 P	1230

Elevation profile (feet) across miles, NY section.

SoBo	NoBo	Feature	Elev
748.5	1440.7	Railroad track, Whakey Lake Stream	680
748.4	1440.8	Old Route 55	696
748.1	1441.1	NY 55, Poughquag, NY (3.1W) . . . N41 35.380 W73 39.551 P (0.1W) (pg.141)	720
747.8	1441.4	Beekman Uplands Trail to west	755
747.0	1442.2	Footbridge, stream (more streams in this area)	690
746.7	1442.5	Nuclear Lake south end, loop trail to east (yellow-blazed)	738
745.8	1443.4	Nuclear Lake north end, loop trail to east	769
745.4	1443.8	Beekman Uplands Trail to west	861
744.5	1444.7	Footbridge, swampy area	1043
744.2	1445.0	Penny Rd	1128
743.9	1445.3	West Mountain	1200
743.6	1445.6	Telephone Pioneers Shelter (0.1E), shelter trail crosses stream	977
742.9	1446.3	49.0◄16.8◄7.8◄►8.8►12.8►21.2 If dry, get water from residence 0.7N. County Rd 20, West Dover Rd, Pawling, NY (3.1E) (pg.141)	650
740.8	1448.4	Footbridge, stream, boardwalk from here north to RR track	505
740.5	1448.7	NY 22, Appalachian Trail RR Station . N41 35.629 W73 35.224 P 🏛 (pg.144) Wingdale (4W), Pawling (2.6E) hot dog stand often here in summer, deli 0.6E	480
740.3	1448.9	Hurd Corners Rd, wooden water tower	480
739.6	1449.6	Stream to west	571
738.8	1450.4	Hammersly Ridge	1032
738.6	1450.6	Red Trail	974
738.2	1451.0	Yellow Trail to east	908
737.8	1451.4	Red Trail to east, Red Trail east	951
737.7	1451.5	Green trail west, Red Trail east	966
736.8	1452.4	Pawling Nature Reserve to east	885
735.8	1453.4	Stream	805
735.2	1454.0	Leather Hill Rd (gravel), stream to south	750
734.8	1454.4	Wiley Shelter, pump 0.1N, treat water	735
734.6	1454.6	25.6◄16.6◄8.8◄►4.0►12.4►19.7	620
734.3	1454.9	Duell Hollow Rd. Footbridge, stream	472
733.6	1455.6	NY-CT border, Hoyt Rd. . . . N41 38.508 W73 31.248 P	400
733.3	1455.9	Side trail to parking, brook to north	423
733.0	1456.2	CT 55, Gaylordsville, CT (2.5E) . . . N41 38.679 W73 31.155 P (pg.144-145) Wingdale, NY (3.3W)	431
731.8	1457.4	Ten Mile Hill, Herrick Trail to east	1000
730.8	1458.4	Ten Mile River Shelter (0.1E) 20.6◄12.8◄4.0◄►8.4►15.7►25.7 Water (hand pump) to left. Group campsites across river and up trail to left.	344
730.7	1458.5	Ten Mile River, Ned Anderson Memorial Bridge	335

Pawling, NY (east from NY 55, County Rd 20, or NY 22)

⬥ ⛺ **Edward R. Murrow Memorial Park** Town allows hikers to camp in park, one night only. One mile from the center of town, park offers lake swimming, no pets.

🍴 **Vinny's Deli** 845.855.1922, **Gaudino's Pizzeria** 845.855.3200, **Mama Pizza II** 845.855.9270, **Great Wall** 845.855.9750

🍴 **Fat Guyz** Burgers, W-F dinner, Sa-Su lunch and dinner.

🍴 **McGrath Restaurant** L/D

💻 **Pawling Free Library** Closed Sundays in July and August.

🚌 **Martin and Donna Hunley** 845.505.1671 or 845.546.1832. Shuttle range RPH Shelter to Kent, CT.

🚆 **MTA Metro-North Railroad** (see pg. 145)

1448.7   NY 22, **Appalachian Trail Railroad Station**

🚆 **MTA Metro-North Railroad** (see pg. 145)

⬥ ⛺ 🚻 ⛺ 📧 **Native Landscapes & Garden Center** 845.855.7050 Open daily 9-5. Owner Pete Muroski is hiker-friendly. Allows camping on site (no fires), use of restrooms, inside shower $5, outside shower free. Drinks, snacks, freeze-dried meals and canister fuel sold at the garden center. Maildrops: 991 Route 22, Pawling, NY 12564.

🍴 🚻 ⛺ 📞 (0.6E) **Tony's Deli** sandwiches, salads, soda machine outside. Open daily 5am–midnight.

Pawling, NY (2.5E)

Wingdale, NY 12594 (4W)

🛏 ⛺ 📶 📧 **Dutchess Motor Lodge** 845.832.6400, 914.525.9276 $73S+tax. Ride for a fee when available. A/C, free long distance, guest laundry $7, one pet room. Maildrops: 1512 Route 22, Wingdale, NY 12594.

1456.2   CT 55, **Gaylordsville, CT 06755** (2.5E to bridge and country store, 0.6 further south to PO and diner)

🏤 M-F 8-1 & 2-5, Sa 8-12, 860.354.9727

⛽ 🏧 **Gaylordsville Country Store** 860.350.3802 deli, grocery M-F 6-6, Sa 6-5, Su 7-1.

🍴 **Burgerittoville Bar & Grill** 860.799.7739 Hamburger burritos, milkshakes. Big Sport bar has Saturday karaoke.

🍴 **Gaylordsville Diner**

🍴 (1.4W) **Riverview Tavern** Food, pool table, open noon-9pm.

Wingdale, NY (3.3W) see map

144
NY

PAWLING, NY

Lakeside Dr

(2.5 mi. from edge of map)

(1.7 mi. from edge of map)

N

⬥ Edward Murrow Park (1.0 from town center)

(3.0 mi. from edge of map)

Old Rte 55

County Rd 20

PO (12564): 845-855-2669 M-F 8:30-5 Sa 9-12

Pawling Free Library 845-855-3444 M & F 12-5 Tu-TH 10-8 Sa 10-4 Su 12-4

Fat Guyz

Metro-North Railroad

Coulter Ave

22

Great Wall

The Cleanery

Julia's Deli

Mamma Pizza & Pawling Tavern

McKinney & Doyle

Vinny's Deli

CVS

Gaudinos Pizzeria

1.3 mi

Hannaford (1.8mi.)

MTA Metro-North Railroad 212.532.4900
〈www.mta.info\mnr\index.html〉 Stations on the AT and in Pawling and Wingdale. Trip to NYC Grand Central Station requires a transfer, costs approx. $15 one-way, and takes about two hours. Must pay in cash when boarding at the trailhead; can purchase round trip and pay with credit card if your trip originates at Grand Central Station. Schedule varies by season. Also connects to other cities in NY and CT.

1459.7 Bulls Bridge Rd, Schaghticoke Rd
(0.4E) To covered bridge with view of the Housatonic cascading down the backside of a dam. The one-lane bridge was built in 1842. Wooden bridges are covered to protect the wood deck and trusswork from the elements.
        0.2 beyond bridge:
Country Market Fruit, ice cream, soda. M-Sa 5:30-7, Sunday 6:30-7
Bulls Bridge Inn 860.927.1000 M-Th 5-9, F 5-9:30, Sa 12-9:30, Su 12-9. American cuisine (dinners $10-26), casual atmosphere, bar.

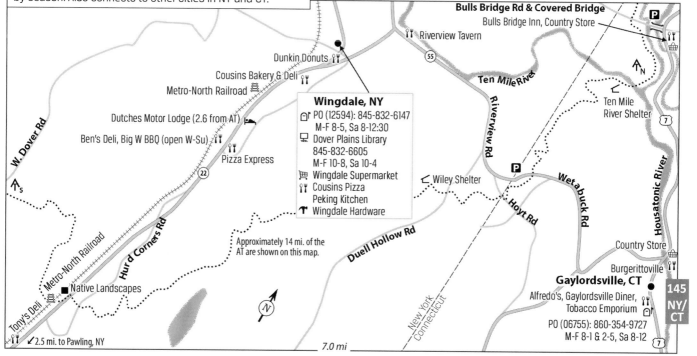

Bulls Bridge Rd & Covered Bridge

Bulls Bridge Inn, Country Store

Riverview Tavern

Dunkin Donuts

Cousins Bakery & Deli

Metro-North Railroad

Dutches Motor Lodge (2.6 from AT)

Ben's Deli, Big W BBQ (open W-Su)

Pizza Express

55

Ten Mile River

Riverview Rd

Ten Mile River Shelter

7

Wingdale, NY
PO (12594): 845-832-6147
M-F 8-5, Sa 8-12:30
Dover Plains Library
845-832-6605
M-F 10-8, Sa 10-4
Wingdale Supermarket
Cousins Pizza
Peking Kitchen
Wingdale Hardware

Wiley Shelter

Wetabuck Rd

Hoyt Rd

22

W. Dover Rd

Hurd Corners Rd

Metro-North Railroad

Tony's Deli

Native Landscapes

Approximately 14 mi. of the AT are shown on this map.

Duell Hollow Rd

New York
Connecticut

Housatonic River

Country Store

Burgerittoville

Gaylordsville, CT
Alfredo's, Gaylordsville Diner, Tobacco Emporium
PO (06755): 860-354-9727
M-F 8-1 & 2-5, Sa 8-12

145
NY/
CT

7.0 mi

2.5 mi. to Pawling, NY

146
CT

SoBo	NoBo		Elev
729.5	1459.7	Bulls Bridge Rd (paved) + Schaghticoke Rd . . N41 40.535 W73 30.610 ⓟ (pg.145) AT on Schaghticoke Rd (gravel) 0.3 mile	410
728.3	1460.9	CT-NY ⊛ Campfires prohibited in CT. Camping only in designated sites. .	1049
727.7	1461.5	View to west from exposed slab of rock, many good sitting boulders. 🖼	1227
726.3	1462.9	NY-CT, stream to north	1218
725.9	1463.3	Indian Rocks, view to east. 🖼	1232
725.3	1463.9	Schaghticoke Mountain Campsite & privy 0.1W, stream on AT.	936
724.5	1464.7	Stream.	1019
723.4	1465.8	Thayer Brook	980
722.4	1466.8	Mt Algo Shelter 21.2◄12.4◄8.4◄►7.3►17.3►28.7	694
722.1	1467.1	CT 341, Schaghticoke Rd, **Kent, CT** (0.8E) (pg.148)	350
722.0	1467.2	Macedonia Brook.	327
721.5	1467.7	Numeral Rock Trail to east.	781
719.3	1469.9	Skiff Mountain Rd (paved), stream to south	850
718.6	1470.6	Calebs Peak.	1164
718.3	1470.9	St. Johns Ledges, steep stone steps down to Housatonic River. 🖼	943
717.4	1471.3	River Rd south end, NoBo: turn west on road for 0.8 mile	480
716.6	1472.6	Kent Rd to west	443
716.4	1472.8	River Rd north end	407
715.1	1474.1	**Stewart Hollow Brook Shelter** (0.1W) 19.7◄15.7◄7.3◄►10.0►21.4►28.9 Footbridge over SH Brook.	418
714.5	1474.7	Stony Brook, campsite to west	446
713.0	1476.2	Footbridge, stream	453
712.7	1476.5	River Rd . . N41 48.342 W73 23.697 ⓟ	460
712.5	1476.7	Dawn Hill Rd (paved)	569
711.8	1477.4	Silver Hill Campsite 0.1E, pavilion, water from pump (may take many pumps to get water flowing)	934
711.0	1478.2	CT 4, Guinea Brook, **Cornwall Bridge, CT** (0.9E) (pg.149) High water bypass 0.5E on CT 4, then left on unpaved Old Sharon Rd for 0.5 mi.	700
710.8	1478.4	Old Sharon Rd (gravel)	758
710.7	1478.5	Breadloaf Trail 0.1E, view.	932
709.6	1479.6	Hatch Brook.	880

SoBo	NoBo		Elev
709.4	1479.8	Pine Knob Loop Trail 1.0E to Housatonic Meadows State Park	967
708.7	1480.5	Another intersection with Pine Knob Loop Trail to east.	1014
708.4	1480.8	Caesar Rd, Caesar Brook Campsite, stream to north.	774
706.9	1482.3	Stream.	890
706.3	1482.5	Carse Brook, footbridge	810
706.2	1483.0	West Cornwall Rd, **West Cornwall, CT** (2.2E), **Sharon, CT** (4.7W) (pg.149)	852
705.9	1483.3	Pass through cracked boulder similar to Lemon Squeezer.	1126
705.1	1484.1	**Pine Swamp Brook Shelter** 25.7◄17.3◄10.0◄►11.4►18.9►20.1	1100
704.2	1485.0	Sharon Mountain Rd	1150
703.6	1485.6	Woods road	1304
703.4	1485.8	Woods road	1311
702.7	1486.5	Sharon Mountain Campsite 0.1W, stream nearby.	1200
699.8	1489.4	Belters Campsite 0.2W, view.	757
699.5	1489.7	US 7, CT 112	520
699.1	1490.1	US 7, parking, bridge over Housatonic River ◆N41 55.960 W73 21.810 **P** (pg.150)	511
698.5	1490.7	Mohawk Trail 0.5E to view.	543
697.9	1491.3	Warren Turnpike, footbridge, stream to north.	518
697.0	1492.2	Water St parking: **Falls Village, CT**(0.3E) N41 57.352 W73 22.056 **P** (pg.150)	530
696.7	1492.5	Iron Mtn Bridge over Housatonic River	528
696.4	1492.8	Housatonic River Rd, AT crosses road twice 0.2 mi. N41 57.736 W73 22.442 **P**	604
695.8	1493.4	Spring. apart. In between are two short trails east to views of great falls.	804
694.4	1494.8	Mt Prospect	1475
693.7	1495.5	**Limestone Spring Shelter** (0.5W), road 0.25 farther. 28.7◄21.4◄11.4◄►7.5►8.7►17.5	1339
693.6	1495.6	Rands View (field)	1250
693.2	1496.0	Giants Thumb	1288
692.4	1496.8	Stream.	993
690.3	1498.9	AT on US 44 for 0.2W (pg.150-151)	700
690.0	1499.2	AT on Cobble Rd 0.2E, **Salisbury, CT** (0.5W)	701
689.6	1499.6	Undermountain Rd (paved) N41 59.645 W73 25.615 **P** (pg.150-151)	720
689.3	1499.9	**Salisbury, CT** (0.8W) Stream.	836

SoBo   NoBo   Elev

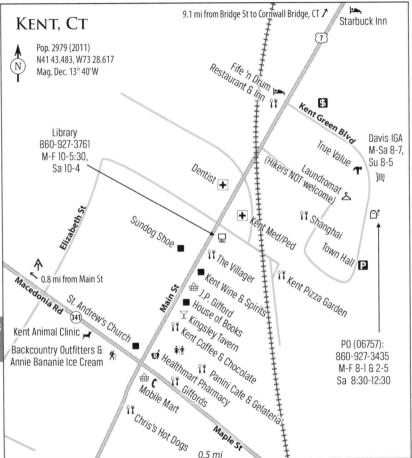

Kent, Ct

Pop. 2979 (2011)
N41 43.483, W73 28.617
Mag. Dec. 13° 40'W

9.1 mi from Bridge St to Cornwall Bridge, CT ↗

Starbuck Inn

Fife 'n Drum Restaurant & Inn

Kent Green Blvd

Library
860-927-3761
M-F 10-5:30,
Sa 10-4

Davis IGA
M-Sa 8-7,
Su 8-5

True Value

Laundromat
(Hikers NOT welcome!)

Dentist

Elizabeth St

Sundog Shoe

Kent Med/Ped

Shanghai

Town Hall

Macedonia Rd

0.8 mi from Main St

St. Andrew's Church

Main St

The Villager

Kent Wine & Spirits

J.P. Gifford

House of Books

Kingsley Tavern

Kent Coffee & Chocolate

Kent Pizza Garden

PO (06757):
860-927-3435
M-F 8-1 & 2-5
Sa 8:30-12:30

Kent Animal Clinic

Backcountry Outfitters &
Annie Bananie Ice Cream

Healthmart Pharmacy

Panini Cafe & Gelateria

Giffords

Mobile Mart

Chris's Hot Dogs

Maple St

0.5 mi

1467.1   CT 341, Schaghticoke Rd

Kent, CT 06757 (0.8E) (15% lodging tax)

Fife 'n Drum Inn & Restaurant

860.927.3509 ⟨www.fifendrum.com⟩ hiker room rates $116D+tax wkdays, $140D+tax wkends, $25EAP+tax, no pets. Call for reservations, front desk closed Tu (can make prior arrangements for room access). Guest maildrops: (USPS) PO Box 188 or (FedEx/UPS) 53 N Main Street, Kent, CT 06757.

Cooper Creek B&B 860.927.4334 Hiker rate Su-Th $95D. Weekend rates seasonal & considerably higher. 2.5mi. north of town on US 7. Shuttles to/from Kent w/stay, longer shuttles for a fee.

Starbuck Inn 860.927.1788 $207D/up + tax, includes full breakfast & afternoon tea. Sometimes discounted mid-week, accepts credit cards, no pets.

Newbury Inn 203.775.0220 About 20 miles from Kent, Gaylordsville, or Pawling (1030 Federal Rd, Brookfield, CT 06804) but has affordable hiker rate ($60D + tax, $10EAP), includes hot breakfast. Shuttle can be arranged from Backcountry Outfitters.

Backcountry Outfitters

860.927.3377 ⟨www.bcoutfitters.com⟩ M–Sa 9–6, Su 10–4. In summer hours extended 6am till 8pm weekdays, 9pm Fri & Sat, 6pm Sunday. Flat rate mail services. Fuel/oz, canisters, selection of gear. Farmer's market F 4-7. **Annie Bananie** ice cream & grill inside serving hot dogs, coffee, snacks, barrels of candy, chocolates. Shuttles anywhere. Maildrops: 5 Bridge Street, Kent, CT 06757.

JP Gifford Breakfast sandwiches, salads, bakery, coffee and supplies.

■ **Sundog Shoe** 860.927.0009 10% hiker discount

on footwear (Salomon, Merrell, High-Tech, Keen), socks (Darn Tough), Dirty Girl Gaiters and footbeds (Superfeet, Power Step).
■ **House of Books** UPS services, open daily 10-5:30.

1478.2 CT 4, ***Cornwall Bridge, CT 06754*** (0.9E)

Hitching Post Motel 860.672.6219 $65/up weekdays, $85/up weekends. Pets $10, laundry $5, shuttles $2/mi. Maildrops: 45 Kent Road, Cornwall Bridge, CT 06754.

The Amselhaus 860.248.3155 $85S, $100 for couple, $50 EAP. 2-3 bedroom apartments includes laundry, sat. TV, local and long-distance phone. Rides available. Located behind carpet store, check in at grey house next door to apartments. Maildrops: C/O Tyler, 7 River Road South, Cornwall Bridge, CT 06754.

Housatonic Meadows State Park 860.672.6772 Camping and Cabins 1.3 mi. north of town on US 7. Campsite $17 for CT residents, $27 non-residents, $3 walk-in fee for first night. Cabins $60 with 2 night minimum. No hammocks. Open mid-May to Oct, registration at main cabin by gate, no alcohol.

Cornwall Inn 860.672.6884 Su-Th $129D + tax, includes cont. breakfast. Weekends 10% hiker discount. 2.2 miles south on US 7. Pickup/return to trailhead and other shuttles for a fee. Pet friendly. Maildrops with reservation.

Cornwall Country Market 860.619.8199 M-F 6am-7pm, Sa-Su 7-5. Hiker friendly, hot meals, breakfast, groceries, charging stations.

Housatonic River Outfitters 860.672.1010 ⟨www.dryflies.com⟩ Some hiker gear, Aquamira, white gas/alcohol/oz (no canisters).

Cornwall Package Store 860.672.6645 closed Su, water spigot outside. Stopping to sign their register can be refreshing.

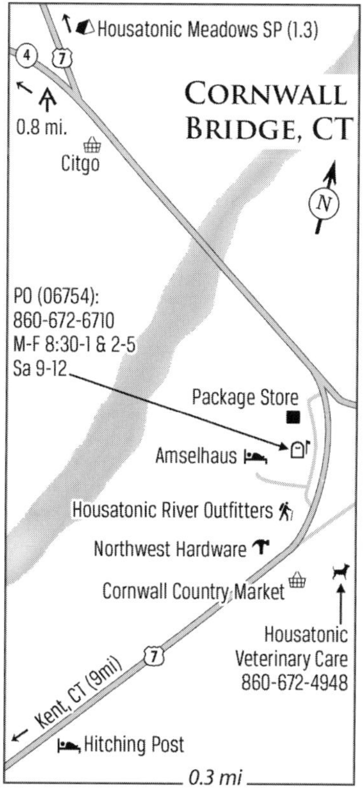

Housatonic Meadows SP (1.3)
4
7
CORNWALL BRIDGE, CT
0.8 mi.
Citgo
N
PO (06754):
860-672-6710
M-F 8:30-1 & 2-5
Sa 9-12
Package Store
Amselhaus
Housatonic River Outfitters
Northwest Hardware
Cornwall Country Market
Housatonic Veterinary Care
860-672-4948
Kent, CT (9mi)
7
Hitching Post
0.3 mi

1483.0 West Cornwall Rd

Bearded Woods One-of-a-Kind Bunk & Dine Will pick up from Falls Village or Salisbury. See details on pg. 150.

West Cornwall, CT 06796 (2.2E)

M-F 8:30-12 & 2-4:30, Sa 9-12, 860.672.6791

Wandering Moose Café 860.672.0178

Buck's Ice Cream

Sharon, CT 06069 (4.7W)

M-F 9:30-4:30, Sa 9:30-12:30, 860.364.5306

Sharon Farm Market

Sharon Hospital 860.364.4141

Sharon Pharmacy

Stacked Kitchen

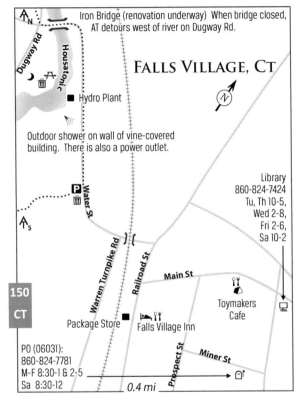

Iron Bridge (renovation underway) When bridge closed, AT detours west of river on Dugway Rd.

FALLS VILLAGE, CT

Dugway Rd

Housatonic

N

■ Hydro Plant

Outdoor shower on wall of vine-covered building. There is also a power outlet.

Library
860-824-7424
Tu, Th 10-5,
Wed 2-8,
Fri 2-6,
Sa 10-2

P Water St

Warren Turnpike Rd

Railroad St

Main St

Package Store

Falls Village Inn

Toymakers Cafe

Prospect St

Miner St

PO (06031):
860-824-7781
M-F 8:30-1 & 2-5
Sa 8:30-12

0.4 mi

1490.1   US 7, bridge over Housatonic River

🏠🕐⊕⛺🚐🖥 **Bearded Woods One-of-a-Kind Bunk & Dine** 860.480.2966 (www.beardedwoods.com) Hudson & BIG Lu offer accommodations in their home to hikers $50pp. Includes: clean bunk with linens, shower with amenities, communal laundry, shuttle to/from trail and PO. Cash only. All guests invited at no cost for family style dinner & breakfast. Call or text Hudson for *pickup from West Cornwall Rd, Falls Village or Salisbury* between 12:00 - 5:30. Resupplies available, stove fuel & Aquamira. Well behaved pets $10. Free slackpacking between W. Cornwall Rd and Salisbury with second night stay. Longer shuttles for fee. Not a party place. Open May 1-Sept 1. Limited services (no dinners) before May 1 & after Sept. 1 reservations required. Relax and let your AT experience be fulfilled!

1492.2   Water Street Parking Area *Falls Village, CT 06031*

🍴🌀 **Toymakers Café** 860.824.8168 B/L Thursday-Sunday (Th–F 7-2, Sa-Su 7-4) free tent sites, hiker friendly, knock on upstairs door if closed. Cash only.

🛏🍴 **Falls Village Inn** 860.824.0033 $229/up hiker discounts. Restaurant & bar.

1499.2   Cobble Rd (0.5W)
1499.6   Undermountain Rd (0.8W) *Salisbury, CT 06068*

🏠✉ **Maria McCabe** 860.435.0593 Beds in home $35PP includes shower, use of living room, shuttle to coin laundry, cash only. Guest maildrops: 4 Grove Street.

🏠⛺🚐✉ **Vanessa Breton** 860.435.9577 Beds in home $40PP, pets $5, laundry $5. Shuttle range 100 mi. Guest maildrops: 7 The Lock Up Rd, Salisbury, CT 06068.

🛏🍴 **White Hart Inn** 860.435.0030 Rooms $250/up.

🍴 **Chaiwalla** 860.435.9758 W-Su 10-6. Hiker friendly tea room. Closed in Mar, open weekends only in winter.

🥾✉ **Peter Becks Village Store** 860.596.4217 ⟨www.peterbecks.com⟩ M-Sa 10-6, Su 10-4, full line of gear, denatured alcohol/oz and canisters. Maildrops: 19 Main Street, Salisbury, CT 06068.

🛒🍴 **LaBonne's Market** M-Sa 8-7, Sun. till 6pm. Grocery, deli, bakery, pizza.

ℹ **Town Hall** 860.435.5170 M-F 8:30-4 Hikers welcome to use bathrooms and phone (local calls only).

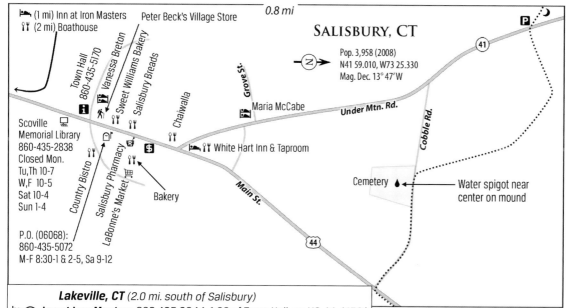

0.8 mi

SALISBURY, CT

(1 mi) Inn at Iron Masters
(2 mi) Boathouse
Peter Beck's Village Store

Pop. 3,958 (2008)
N41 59.010, W73 25.330
Mag. Dec. 13° 47'W

Town Hall 860-435-5170
Vanessa Breton
Sweet Williams Bakery
Salisbury Breads
Grove St.
Chaiwalla
Maria McCabe
Under Mtn. Rd.
Cobble Rd.

Scoville
Memorial Library
860-435-2838
Closed Mon.
Tu,Th 10-7
W,F 10-5
Sat 10-4
Sun 1-4

Country Bistro
Salisbury Pharmacy
LaBonne's Market
Bakery
White Hart Inn & Taproom

Main St.

Cemetery
Water spigot near
center on mound

P.O. (06068):
860-435-5072
M-F 8:30-1 & 2-5, Sa 9-12

44

Lakeville, CT *(2.0 mi. south of Salisbury)*

Inn at Iron Masters 860.435.9844 1.0S of Town Hall, on US 44. $159/up Apr - midNov, $131 midNov-Mar, cont B, non-smoking, some pet rooms.

Boathouse 860.435.2111 Sports bar/restaurant

Mizza's Pizza 860.435.6266

Washboard Laundromat Behind Mizza's

1513.7   Elbow Trailhead on MA 41

Racebrook Lodge 413.229.2916 ⟨www.rblodge.com⟩ Rates lowest off-season (Nov-May). M-Th $85-$160, F-Su $115-170. Stay includes breakfast. Pets $15/night. **Stagecoach Tavern** on-site open Th-Su for dinner. Accepts Visa/MC/Disc, open year-round.

1517.4   MA 41   **South Egremont, MA 01258** (1.2W)
M–F 8:15–12 & 12:30–4, Sa 9–11:30, 413.528.1571

(0.1W) **ATC New England Regional Office** 413.528.8002 in Kellogg Conservation Center.

Egremont Market 413.528.0075 Market & deli 6:30am-7pm 7 days (6pm in winter). Ice cream, trail mix, sodas.

Mom's Country Cafe 413.528.2414 Breakfast/Lunch restaurant open 6:30-3 every day and 5-9pm F-Su. Breakfast all day, free coffee refills, outdoor water spigot, hikers welcome.

152
MA

SoBo	NoBo	Feature	Elev
688.1	1501.1	Streams (multiple).	1114
687.3	1501.9	Lions Head Trail 0.5W to Bunker Hill Rd.	1493
687.0	1502.2	Lions Head, view, bypass trail to west.	1712
686.2	1503.0	**Riga Shelter,** spring, Tent platform behind shelter. 28.9◀18.9◀7.5◀1.2▶10.0▶10.1	1653
685.6	1503.6	Ball Brook Campsite, stream.	1743
685.0	1504.2	**Brassie Brook Shelter,** stream 20 yards north on AT. 20.1◀8.7◀1.2▶8.8▶9.▶23.2	1770
684.5	1504.7	Undermountain Trail 1.9E to CT 41.	1841
684.3	1504.9	Bear Mountain Rd to west.	1920
683.6	1505.6	Bear Mountain, rock observation tower, view. North side steep & rocky.	2316
683.2	1506.0	Unmarked trail 0.6W to Mt Washington Rd	1828
683.0	1506.2	Paradise Lane Trail to east, **CT-MA** border 50 yards north (not marked)	1739
682.8	1506.4	Sages Ravine Campsite to west.	1576
682.4	1506.8	Sages Ravine, Misplaced border sign at footbridge. AT parallel to stream for 0.3 mile, swimming holes.	1535
681.1	1508.1	Laurel Ridge Campsite 0.1W, spring to south.	1649
680.9	1508.3	Stream.	1685
679.1	1510.1	Mt Race, views along ridgeline for 0.6S.	2365
678.0	1511.2	Race Brook Falls Trail 0.3E to campsite.	1950
677.3	1511.9	Mt Everett.	2602
676.6	1512.6	Guilder Pond Picnic Area, Mt Everett Rd.	2130
676.2	1513.0	**The Hemlocks Shelter** (0.1E) 17.5◀10.0◀8.8▶0.1▶14.4▶19.7	1975
676.1	1513.1	**Glen Brook Shelter** (0.1E) 10.1◀8.9◀0.1▶14.3▶19.6▶21.4	1932
675.5	1513.7	Elbow Trail 1.5E to MA 41 near **Racebrook Lodge** (pg.151)	1746
674.5	1514.7	Mt Bushnell.	1822
673.4	1515.8	Jug End, view.	1464
672.7	1516.5	Jug End Rd, unreliable piped spring 0.2E. N42 8.665 W73 25.893 P	876
671.8	1517.4	MA 41, **South Egremont, MA** (1.2W). (pg.151)	810
670.8	1518.4	Footbridge, stream (2 close together).	707
670.2	1519.0	Footbridge, stream.	702
670.0	1519.2	Sheffield Egremont Rd, Shays Rebellion Monument. N42 8.828 W73 23.200 P	700
669.2	1520.0	Gravel road.	750

SoBo	NoBo	Feature	Elev
668.9	1520.3	West Rd (paved)	714
668.2	1521.0	US 7, RR to south, soda vending 0.2E at repair shop . . . (pg.154-155)	694
		Sheffield, MA (3.0E), **Great Barrington, MA** (3.0W)	
668.0	1521.2	Footbridge, stream	682
667.3	1521.9	Housatonic River, cross on Kellogg Rd Bridge . . . N42 8.637 W73 21.572 **P**	720
666.9	1522.3	Boardman St.	728
665.5	1523.7	June Mtn	1238
665.3	1523.9	Homes Rd (paved)	1150
664.5	1524.7	Footbridge, spring at bottom of cleft	1577
663.9	1525.3	East Mountain, view	1800
663.5	1525.7	Woods road	1829
661.8	1527.4	Ice Gulch, **Tom Leonard Shelter** . . . ⌷ ◗ ⟍ ◢ ⊏ (10)	1617
		23.2◀14.4◀14.3◀▶5.3▶7.1▶21.1 Campsite overlooking ravine north of shelter.	
660.7	1528.5	Stream 0.2 on path to left or 0.3 on path to right.	1150
		Lake Buel Rd (paved), parking area with kiosk . . . N42 10.471 W73 17.639 **P**	
659.8	1529.4	MA 23 (paved)	1050
		East Mountain Retreat Center (1.0W) . . . N42 11.065 W73 17.444 **P** (pg.155)	
658.6	1530.6	Blue Hill Rd (paved), Stony Brook Rd	1550
657.9	1531.3	Beartown Mtn Rd, Benedict Pond, 0.5W on blue-blazed trail to	1621
657.7	1531.5	**Beartown State Forest**, beach, picnic area, phone, tent sites, $10.	1641
		Benedict Pond Loop Trail to west, footbridge and stream east of AT	
657.2	1532.0	The Ledges	1820
656.8	1532.4	Stream.	1683
656.5	1532.7	**Mt Wilcox South Shelters**	1852
		19.7◀19.6◀5.3◀▶1.8▶15.8▶24.6 Old shelter 0.1E (6), newer shelter 0.2E (12).	
655.6	1533.6	Stream (several)	1839
655.5	1533.7	Pond, Swann Brook outlet at south end.	1844
654.7	1534.5	**Mt Wilcox North Shelter** (0.3E)	2136
		21.4◀7.1◀1.8◀▶14.0▶22.8▶3.6	
654.0	1535.2	Motorcycle path	1879
653.8	1535.4	Beartown Mountain Rd, NoBo: turn east	1839
653.5	1535.7	East Brook, footbridge, more streams north and south	1755
650.9	1538.3	Fernside Rd / Jerusalem Rd (gravel).	1200
650.6	1538.6	Shaker Campsite to east; platforms, bear box, water north on AT	910
648.9	1540.3	Cobble Hill.	1233

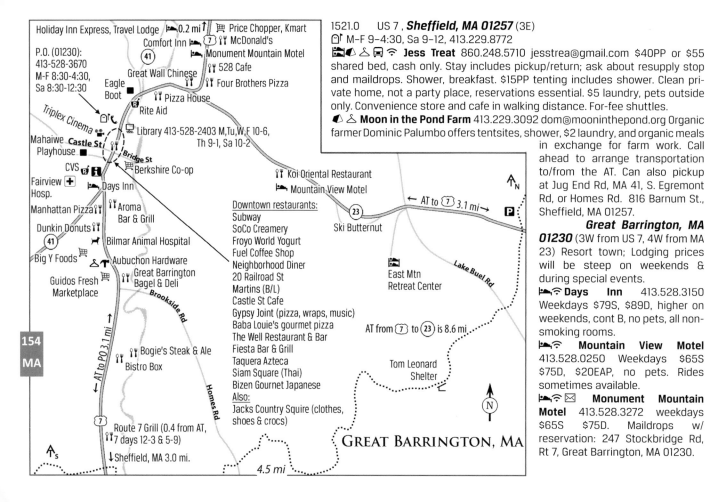

Holiday Inn Express, Travel Lodge ⛟0.2 mi↑ | ⊞ Price Chopper, Kmart

Comfort Inn ⛟ | ⊞ ♨ McDonald's

P.O. (01230): 413-528-3670 M-F 8:30-4:30, Sa 8:30-12:30

⛟ Monument Mountain Motel

♨ 528 Cafe

Great Wall Chinese | ♨ Four Brothers Pizza

Eagle Boot

♨ Pizza House

Triplex Cinema ☎ Rite Aid

Mahaiwe Playhouse **Castle St** | ▭ Library 413-528-2403 M,Tu,W,F 10-6, Th 9-1, Sa 10-2

Bridge St

CVS | ⊞ Berkshire Co-op

Fairview Hosp. ⊞ | ⛟ Days Inn

Manhattan Pizza ♨ | ♨ Aroma Bar & Grill

Dunkin Donuts ♨

41

Big Y Foods | ⚓ Aubuchon Hardware

Bilmar Animal Hospital

Guidos Fresh Marketplace | ♨ Great Barrington Bagel & Deli

Brookside Rd

↑ AT to PO 3.1 mi ↓

♨ Bogie's Steak & Ale
Bistro Box

Homes Rd

7

Route 7 Grill (0.4 from AT, ♨ 7 days 12-3 & 5-9)

↓ Sheffield, MA 3.0 mi.

4.5 mi

♨ Koi Oriental Restaurant
⛟ Mountain View Motel

AT to ⑦ 3.1 mi →

23 Ski Butternut

Downtown restaurants:
Subway
SoCo Creamery
Froyo World Yogurt
Fuel Coffee Shop
Neighborhood Diner
20 Railroad St
Martins (B/L)
Castle St Cafe
Gypsy Joint (pizza, wraps, music)
Baba Louie's gourmet pizza
The Well Restaurant & Bar
Fiesta Bar & Grill
Taquera Azteca
Siam Square (Thai)
Bizen Gourmet Japanese
Also:
Jacks Country Squire (clothes, shoes & crocs)

⊞ East Mtn Retreat Center

Lake Buel Rd

P

AT from ⑦ to 23 is 8.6 mi

Tom Leonard Shelter

N

GREAT BARRINGTON, MA

154 MA

1521.0 US 7 , **Sheffield, MA 01257** (3E)

▢ M-F 9-4:30, Sa 9-12, 413.229.8772

🏠♨⛺🚐📶 **Jess Treat** 860.248.5710 jesstrea@gmail.com $40PP or $55 shared bed, cash only. Stay includes pickup/return; ask about resupply stop and maildrops. Shower, breakfast. $15PP tenting includes shower. Clean private home, not a party place, reservations essential. $5 laundry, pets outside only. Convenience store and cafe in walking distance. For-fee shuttles.

♨⛺ **Moon in the Pond Farm** 413.229.3092 dom@mooninthepond.org Organic farmer Dominic Palumbo offers tentsites, shower, $2 laundry, and organic meals in exchange for farm work. Call ahead to arrange transportation to/from the AT. Can also pickup at Jug End Rd, MA 41, S. Egremont Rd, or Homes Rd. 816 Barnum St., Sheffield, MA 01257.

Great Barrington, MA 01230 (3W from US 7, 4W from MA 23) Resort town; Lodging prices will be steep on weekends & during special events.

⛟📶 **Days Inn** 413.528.3150 Weekdays $79S, $89D, higher on weekends, cont B, no pets, all non-smoking rooms.

⛟📶 **Mountain View Motel** 413.528.0250 Weekdays $65S $75D, $20EAP, no pets. Rides sometimes available.

⛟📶✉ **Monument Mountain Motel** 413.528.3272 weekdays $65S $75D. Maildrops w/ reservation: 247 Stockbridge Rd, Rt 7, Great Barrington, MA 01230.

⊷⚲🛰🖳✉ **Fairfield Inn & Suites** 413.644.3200 Prices seasonal. Full B, indoor heated pool & hot tub, no pets. Maildrops with advance reservation: 249 Stockbridge Rd, Rt 7, Great Barrington, MA 01230.

⊷⚲🛰 **Travel Lodge** 413.528.2340 Su-Th $50-89D + tax, $10EAP, cont B, coin laundry.

🛒 **Guido's** Organic produce, cold juices, and more.

➕ **Fairview Hospital** 413.528.0790

🚗 **All Points Driving Service** 413.429.7397 Range: Salisbury-Dalton.

1529.4   MA 23

🔋✉ (1.5W) **East Mountain Retreat Center** 413.528.6617 1.0W from MA 23 or Lake Buel Rd. and 0.5 mile up driveway (where there is a blue sign), $10PP donation, no credit cards. Shower, dryer (no washer), pizzeria delivers to hostel, 10pm curfew, 8:30am checkout.Open May 15-Oct15. Maildrops (FedEx or UPS only): 8 Lake Buel Rd, Great Barrington, MA 01230.

1540.5   Jerusalem Rd (0.6W to town)
1541.6   Main Rd (0.9W to town)
          Tyringham, MA 01264
🏤 M-F 9-12:30 & 4-5:30, Sa 8:30-12:30, 413.243.1225
🛰🖳 **Library** 413.243.1373 Adjacent to P.O. Tu 3-5, Saturday 10-12
⊷**Cobble View B&B** 413.243.2463 Mid-week discounts,includes cont B, no pets, no smoking, Visa/MC accepted.

1548.5   **Upper Goose Pond Cabin** (0.5W)
⊏(14)⚫⚫🌙 On side trail north of pond. Fireplace, covered porch, bunks with mattresses. Swimming and canoeing. Open daily Memorial Day through Columbus Day (dates subject to change). When caretaker not in residence, hikers may camp on porch (no cooking) or tent platforms. Please store food in bear box. During summer, caretaker brings water; otherwise, pond is water source. Donations welcome. ✖ A pair of geese are inside keeping warm, what color are they?

1550.1   US 20

⊷🛰✉◆ (0.1E) **Berkshire Lakeside Lodge** 413.243.9907 Weekdays $60-90, weekends $94-164 2-person room, $10EAP. Cont. breakfast. No pets. Hikers welcome to get water. Sodas for sale. No services nearby but you can get Italian & Chinese food delivered. Maildrops with reservation: 3949 Jacob's Ladder Rd, Rt 10, Becket, MA 01223

          Lee, MA 01238 (5W) Lodging busy and expensive on weekends and during Tanglewood Music Festival.
🏤 M-F 8:30-4:30, Sa 9-12, 413.243.1392
⊷🛰 **Americas Best Value Inn** 413.243.0501 Apr-May $52-55 Su-Th, $65-75 F-Sa, Jun-Oct $60-79 Su-Th, $110-$195 F-Sa, cont B.
⊷🛰 **Roadway Inn** 413.243.0813 Jul-Aug $79 weekdays $159-189 weekends, other months $55/up. Cont B.
⊷⚲🛰 **Pilgrim Inn** 413.243.1328 Peak rates Jun 15-Aug; Su-Th $95D, F-Sa $225D. Non-peak rates $85D-$110D. Cont B, micro, fridge.
⊷ **Super 8** 413.243.0143
🍴 **Dunkin Donuts, Athena's Pizza House**, **Friendly's**, **Joe's Diner**, **McDonalds**, and many more.
🛒 **Price Chopper Supermarket** 413.528.2408
💊 **Rite Aid**
🐾 **Valley Veterinary Clinic** 413.243.2414
⚲ **Lee Coin-Op Laundry**

🚌   **BRTA**   800.292.2782 Commuter bus connects ***Great Barrington***, ***Dalton***, ***Cheshire***, ***North Adams***, ***Adams***, ***Williamstown, Pittsfield***, ***Lee*** and **Berkshire Mall**. Buses run M-F 5:45am-7:20pm, Sa 7:15pm-7pm. Fare $1.75 for local routes (in-town and adjoining towns), or $4.50 systemwide. "CharlieCard", available from drivers for $5, gives you a discount per ride and allows you to make bus transfers. Drivers cannot make change. Flag bus anywhere on route.

SoBo	NoBo	Feature	Elev
648.7	1540.5	Jerusalem Rd (paved), **Tyringham, MA 01264** (0.6W). . . . . . . (pg.155)	1106
		Water 0.1W on left side of road, water also outside of P.O. 0.6W.	
648.2	1541.0	Three streams crossed by footbridges	995
647.6	1541.6	Main Rd (paved), **Tyringham, MA** (0.9W) . N42 14.125 W73 11.667 **P** ♦ (pg.155)	987
		Water, parking to west.	
646.0	1543.2	Baldy Mtn	1901
645.8	1543.4	Webster Rd (gravel).	1800
645.2	1544.0	Knee-Deep Pond to west. . . .	1687
644.2	1545.0	Spring on side trail 0.1W . . .	1780
643.4	1545.8	Goose Pond Rd (gravel) . . . . . . N42 16.459 W73 11.025 **P** (0.1E)	1650
643.0	1546.2	Cooper Brook, footbridge. . . .	1566
642.5	1546.7	Signed trail junction	1733
		⚠ NoBo: this is not the side trail to Upper Goose Pond Cabin.	
641.4	1547.8	Higley Brook, footbridge, Upper Goose Pond to west . . .	1510
640.8	1548.4	Old chimney.	1499
640.7	1548.5	**Upper Goose Pond Cabin** (0.5W). . . . . . . ⊏ (pg.155)	1570
		21.1◀15.8◀14.0▲▶8.8▶17.6▶34.5	
639.5	1549.7	MA Turnpike I-90	1400
639.2	1550.0	Greenwater Brook, footbridge . . .	1356
639.1	1550.1	US 20, **Lee, MA** (5.0W), hotel 0.1E . . . . . . N42 17.577 W73 9.684 **P** (0.1W) (pg.155)	1400
638.7	1550.5	Powerline, stream to north. . . .	1584
638.3	1550.9	Tyne Rd / Becket Rd, stream to south . .	1797
637.8	1551.4	Becket Mountain	2180
636.8	1552.4	Walling Mountain	2215
636.2	1553.0	Finerty Pond	1942
634.4	1554.8	Washington Mountain Brook . . .	1762
633.8	1555.4	County Rd (gravel)	1853
633.5	1555.7	Bald Top.	2040
631.9	1557.3	**October Mountain Shelter**, intermittent stream, cables. . . . . . . ⊃ ◁ ⊏ (12)	1923
		24.6◀22.8◀8.8▲▶8.8▶25.7▶32.3	
631.2	1558.0	West Branch Rd (gravel) . . .	1960
629.6	1559.6	At joins dirt road and crosses . . . . N42 22.618 W73 9.044 **P** (pg.158)	2001
		Washington Mtn Rd (paved), **Becket, MA 01223** (5.0E)	

SoBo	NoBo	Description		Elev
627.6	1561.6	Streams		1837
626.5	1562.7	Blotz Rd (paved), small parking lot on north side . . . . N42 24.561 W73 9.017 P		1850
625.8	1563.4	Warner Hill	(image)	2050
624.2	1565.0	Tully Mountain	(image)	2092
623.4	1565.8	Powerline		1944
623.1	1566.1	**Kay Wood Shelter** (0.2E) 31.6◀17.6◀8.8◀▶16.9▶23.5▶33.4 . . . ☾ ▲ ⊏ (10)		1775
622.8	1566.4	Grange Hall Rd		1655
622.6	1566.6	Barton Brook, footbridge		1572
621.2	1568.0	Woods road		1392
620.6	1568.6	Railroad tracks, Housatonic St + Depot St		1273
620.1	1569.1	MA 8 & 9, **Dalton, MA**	(pg.158)	1200
619.1	1570.1	AT on Gulf Rd / High St for 1.0 mile . . . . N42 28.909 W73 10.695 P		1180

✸ **Touch-Me-Not** – Also known as "jewelweed". Trumpet-shaped flowers with a short curled tail hang horizontally like a bug in flight. Yellow with splotches of orange. Salve from crushed stems is a folk remedy for poison ivy's itch.

SoBo	NoBo	Description		Elev
616.9	1572.3	Spring		1915
616.0	1573.2	Powerlines		1900
615.9	1573.3	Crystal Mountain Campsite 0.2E, water on AT just north of side trail . . ☾ ▲ ▲ (5)		1953
615.1	1574.1	Gore Brook, outlet of Gore Pond		2028
614.0	1575.2	Stream		1978
613.6	1575.6	Stream		1834
612.9	1576.3	The Cobbles, outcroppings of marble with view of Hoosic. River Valley, Mt Greylock, and the town of Cheshire.	(image)	1812
611.8	1577.4	Furnace Hill Rd (south end)		1045
611.3	1577.9	Main St + School St, **Cheshire, MA**	(pg.159)	980
610.8	1578.4	MA 8, **Cheshire, MA, Adams, MA** (4.0E)	(pg.159)	1002
609.7	1579.5	Outlook Ave (paved), stream and powerline to north		1326

1559.6   Washington Mtn Rd

◣ ◆ 🚐 ✉   Home of the "**Cookie Lady**" 100 yards east. 413.623.5859 Water spigot near the garage door, please sign register on the steps. Homemade cookies often available. Soda, ice cream, boiled eggs & pick your own blueberries. Camping allowed, ask permission first. Shuttle range from Hoyt Rd. in NY to Manchester Center, VT. Maildrops: Roy & Marilyn Wiley, 47 Washington Mountain Road, Becket, MA 01223.

     Becket, MA 01223 (5E) 🏠 M–F 8–4, Sa 9–11:30, 413.623.8845

🛏⛺📶 (6E) **Becket Motel** 413.623.8888 $95-139+tax, includes shuttle from/to US 20 or Wash Mtn Rd). Tavern next door. Guest maildrops: 29 Chester Road, Becket, MA 01223.

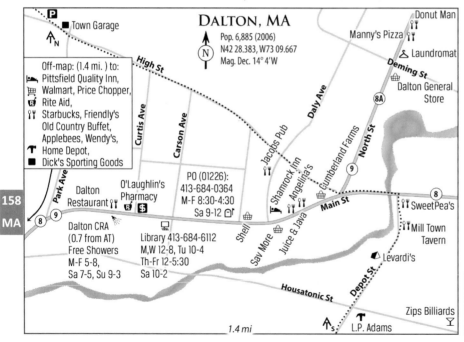

DALTON, MA

Pop. 6,885 (2006)
N42 28.383, W73 09.667
Mag. Dec. 14° 4'W

Off-map: (1.4 mi.) to:
🛏 Pittsfield Quality Inn,
🏬 Walmart, Price Chopper,
💊 Rite Aid,
🍴 Starbucks, Friendly's
   Old Country Buffet,
   Applebees, Wendy's,
🔱 Home Depot,
■ Dick's Sporting Goods

Town Garage
High St
Curtis Ave
Carson Ave
Park Ave
Daly Ave
Donut Man
Manny's Pizza
Deming St
Laundromat
Dalton General Store
8A
North St
9
Jacobs Pub
Shamrock Inn
Angelina's
Cumberland Farms
Main St
8
SweetPea's
Mill Town Tavern
Dalton Restaurant
O'Laughlin's Pharmacy
PO (01226):
413-684-0364
M-F 8:30-4:30
Sa 9-12
Shell
Sav More
Juice & Java
Levardi's
Dalton CRA
(0.7 from AT)
Free Showers
M-F 5-8,
Sa 7-5, Su 9-3
Library 413-684-6112
M,W 12-8, Tu 10-4
Th-Fr 12-5:30
Sa 10-2
Housatonic St
Depot St.
Zips Billiards
L.P. Adams
1.4 mi

158
MA

1569.1   **MA 8 & 9**   *Dalton, MA 01227*
     12% tax added to lodging prices.

◣ ✹ ◆   **Thomas Levardi** 413.684.3359, 413.212.9691. 83 Depot Street, allows hikers to use water spigot outside and, *with permission,* provides the hospitality of his front porch and back yard for tenting. Space is limited.

🛏⛺📶🖥   **Shamrock Village Inn** 413.684.0860 Hiker rates Su-Th are $66.60S, $72D, $81 king bed. Fri&Sat prices $85.50/$93.60/$99. respectively. Well-behaved pets allowed with $75 deposit. Coin laundry, free use of computer and WiFi.

🍴 **Angelina's Subs** with veggie burgers, **Dalton Restaurant** serves D Th–Sa with live entertainment.

🍴 **SweetPea's** Ice cream, summer hours M-Th 12-9, F-Sa 12-10, Su 1-8

⛺ **Dalton Laundry** M-F 9-6, Sa 10-4, Su 10-2.

🔱 **LP Adams** Coleman/denatured alcohol.

     Pittsfield, MA Many stores & restaurants approx. 2.0W from Dalton, see map.

🛏📶 **Pittsfield Quality Inn** 413.443.5661 prices seasonal.

Berkshire Mall on SR 8, 4 mi. north of Dalton & 7 mi. south of Cheshire has:
🏃 **EMS** 413.445.4967
🎦 **Regal Cinema 10** 413.499.3106

1577.9   Main St, School St
1578.4   MA 8 (4.0E)

Cheshire, MA 01225 (pronounced "chesh-er")

📧☀⊠ **St. Mary of the Assumption Church** Check in with Father David Raymond (west side door near the mailbox). Use of restrooms and outside cooking area. No laundry or showers. No smoking, alcohol or drugs on church property. Welcome to attend service in hiker attire. Please donate. Maildrops: 159 Church Street, Cheshire, MA 01225.

🛏⛺📶🖥⊠ **Harbour House Inn Bed & Breakfast** 413.743.8959 (Eva) ⟨www.harbourhouseinn.com⟩ $95D hiker rate Su-Th, sometimes available on weekends. Includes breakfast, no pets, no smoking, shuttle w/stay often available. Guest maildrops: 725 North State Rd, Cheshire, MA 01225.

🍴 **Cobble View Pub & Pizzeria** T–Su 11-10

🍴 **Diane's Twist** Limited hours, deli sandwiches, soda, ice cream.

🏪 **HD Reynolds** 413.743.9512 M-W & F 8-5, Th 8-7, Sa 8-3. General store, hiker snacks, Coleman fuel/oz.

🚌 **BRTA** (pg. 155) stops across the street from the post office; ride to outfitter or Adams, MA $1.75.

East from MA 8:

🥾 (2.2E) **Berkshire Outfitters** 413.743.5900 ⟨www.berkshireoutfitters.com⟩ M-F 10-6, Sa 10-5, Su 11-4, Full service outfitter, Coleman/alcohol/oz and canister fuel, freeze-dried foods, footwear, minor equipment repairs. Often provides return ride to Cheshire.

Adams, MA 01220 (4.2E)

📪 M-F 8:30–4:30, Sa 10–12, 413.743.5177

🛏⛺📶 **Mount Greylock Inn** 413.743.2665 ⟨www.mountgreylockinn.com⟩ Accepts major CC, open year round.

🛒 **Big Y Foods Supermarket**

💊 **Rite Aid**, **Medicine Shop**

🐕 **Adams Veterinary Clinic** 413.743.4000

⛺🔌 **Thrifty Bundle Laundromat**, **Waterworks,** fast-food outlets.

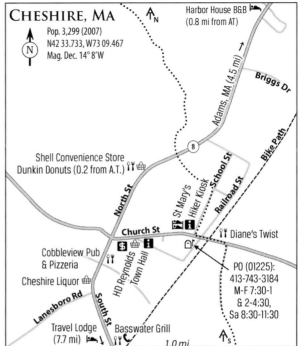

CHESHIRE, MA
Pop. 3,299 (2007)
N42 33.733, W73 09.467
Mag. Dec. 14° 8'W

Harbor House B&B
(0.8 mi from AT)

Adams, MA (4.5 mi)

Briggs Dr

Bike Path

School St

Railroad St

Shell Convenience Store
Dunkin Donuts (0.2 from A.T.)

North St

St Mary's
Hiker Kiosk

Church St

Diane's Twist

Cobbleview Pub
& Pizzeria

HD Reynolds

Town Hall

Cheshire Liquor

PO (01225):
413-743-3184
M-F 7:30-1
& 2-4:30,
Sa 8:30-11:30

Lanesboro Rd

South St

Travel Lodge
(7.7 mi)

Basswater Grill

1.0 mi

Gary Monk (trail name "Blaze") counted every white blaze he passed during his 2002 northbound thru-hike. There were 80,900. I wouldn't tell anyone about getting lost.

SoBo	NoBo	Description	Elev
607.1	1582.1	Old Adams Rd (dirt).	2364
606.2	1583.0	**Mark Noepel Shelter** (0.2E), spring to right of shelter ♪ ● ◢ ⌐ (10)	2843
		34.5◀25.7◀16.9▼▶6.6▶16.5▶23.7 Spring stronger the farther you go.	
605.7	1583.5	Jones Nose Trail to west	3249
603.9	1585.3	Rockwell Rd / Summit Rd to west N42 37.864 W73 10.696 **P**	3026
603.5	1585.7	Cross Rockwell Rd twice, side trails to east	3146
602.9	1586.3	Mt Greylock, highest peak in MA. ⛺ (pg.162)	3491
602.5	1586.7	Thunderbolt Trail and Bellows Pipe Trail, 75 yards apart, both to east.	3112
600.9	1588.3	Bernard Farm Trail	2793
600.6	1588.6	Mt Williams	2966
599.8	1589.4	Notch Rd (paved)	2335
599.6	1589.6	**Wilbur Clearing Shelter** (0.3W) On Money Brook Trail ♪ ◊ ● ⌐ (8)	2300
		32.3◀23.5◀6.6◀▼▶9.9▶17.1▶23.0 Intermittent stream.	
599.3	1589.9	Mt Prospect Trail to west.	2524
597.7	1591.5	Pattison Rd (paved) N42 41.256 W73 9.586 **P** ●	1035
597.1	1592.1	Phelps Ave (south end), on road 0.5 mile	743
596.6	1592.6	MA 2, Hoosic River. N42 41.941 W73 9.208 **P** (0.1E) (pg.162-163)	660
		footbridge and RR tracks, **Williamstown, MA** (west), **North Adams, MA** (east)	
596.5	1592.7	Massachusetts Ave / Hoosac Rd. NoBo: east on road for 0.1 mile. (pg.163)	678
596.2	1593.0	Footbridge, stream. ●	759
595.0	1594.2	Petes Spring. Sherman Brook Campsite 0.1W. ♪ ● ◢	1354
594.3	1594.9	Bad weather bypass trail.	1808
593.9	1595.3	Pine Cobble Trail to west.	2112
593.8	1595.4	'98 Trail to west.	2132
592.5	1596.7	**MA-VT** border, southern end of Long Trail (LT) ◢	2330
		The AT and LT are concurrent northbound for the next 105.2 miles.	
592.1	1597.1	Spring, stream to north. ●	2172
590.0	1599.2	Stream. ●	2089
589.7	1599.5	**Seth Warner Shelter** (0.2W) ♪ ◊ ● ⌐ (8)	2243
		33.4◀16.5◀9.9◀▼▶7.2▶13.1▶21.6 Brook 0.1 left of shelter, known to dry up.	
589.4	1599.8	Country Rd, Powerline	2290

Elev

SoBo	NoBo	Feature	Elev	
587.7	1601.5	Powerline	2872	
586.8	1602.4	Roaring Branch, pond	2478	◆
585.6	1603.6	Consultation Peak	2847	
584.5	1604.7	Woods road, Stamford Stream	2245	◆
584.1	1605.1	Stream	2195	◆
583.6	1605.6	Pond	2209	◆
583.2	1606.0	Woods road	2215	
582.5	1606.7	**Congdon Shelter**, creek is water source 23.7◄17.1◄7.2◄▶5.9▶14.4▶18.7	2104	☾◆⌐(8)
581.7	1607.5	Stream	2243	◆
580.4	1608.8	Footbridge, stream	2230	◆
580.0	1609.2	Harmon Hill	2325	
579.5	1609.7	Spring	2117	◆
578.2	1611.0	VT 9, **Bennington, VT** (5.1W) Bridge over City Stream north of road	1367	N42 53.104 W73 6.920 P ◆ (pg.164-165)
576.6	1612.6	Brook, **Melville Nauheim Shelter**, stream north of trail to shelter 23.0◄13.1◄5.9▶8.5▶12.8▶17.4	2436	⌐(8)
576.1	1613.1	Powerline	2636	
575.7	1613.5	Spring	2583	◆
575.4	1613.8	Stream	2373	◆
575.0	1614.2	Hell Hollow Brook, footbridge	2350	◆
574.0	1615.2	Porcupine Ridge	2830	
571.8	1617.4	Little Pond Mtn (wooded summit)	3313	
568.1	1621.1	**Goddard Shelter** 21.6◄14.4◄8.5◄▶4.3▶8.9▶19.3 Spring 50 yards south on AT, limited tenting.	3573	☾◆⌐(12)
567.8	1621.4	Glastenbury Mountain, lookout tower	3748	

Elev

1586.3   Mt Greylock (3,491') is Massachusetts's highest peak. Veterans War Memorial Tower is on the summit. There are views of the Green, Catskill, and Taconic mountain ranges and surrounding towns. No camping or fires on summit.

🛏️🏠🍴🚿📶 **Bascom Lodge** on summit 413.743.1591 private rooms $125/up, bunkroom $36.   Bunkroom includes use of shower and continental breakfast.   Shower & towel w/o stay $5, some snacks in gift shop, restaurant serves B/L/D.

1592.6   MA 2

Williamstown, MA 01267 (2.6W) All hotels are expensive on peak nights, 11.7% lodging tax.

🛏️🚿📶💻✉️ **Willows Motel** 413.458.5768, $58-129, fourth night free, elaborate cont. breakfast, free pickup/return with stay, discount at adjacent Olympia restaurant. Laundry $6. Pool, no pets. Maildrops: 480 Main Street, Williamstown, MA 01267.

🛏️🚿📶💻✉️ **Williamstown Motel** 413.458.5202 $59S $69D wkdays, $79S $89D wkends; prices higher on high-demand nights. Cont B. Laundry (done for you) $8. Will pickup at Route 2. Major CC accepted. Maildrops: 295 Main Street, Williamstown, MA 01267.

🛏️📶💻✉️ **Howard Johnson** 413.458.8158, Rates seasonal, cont B. Maildrops (fee for non-guests): 213 Main Street, Williamstown, MA 01267.

🛏️📶 **Maple Terrace** 413.458.9677 Prices seasonal, call for rates. Continental B, heated pool, all rooms non-smoking.

🛏️ **River Bend Farm** 413.458.3121 $120D includes breakfast. Unique experience in an authentic 1770 colonial farmhouse. Free pickup & return when available.

🛏️🍴🚿🅿️ **Williams Inn** 413.458.9371 $155D/up. Non-guests can pay $8 for use of shower, swim and sauna. Restaurant open 7 days 7am-9pm. Short term parking $2/day.

🛏️📶 **Redwood Motel** 413.664.4351 $69-$99

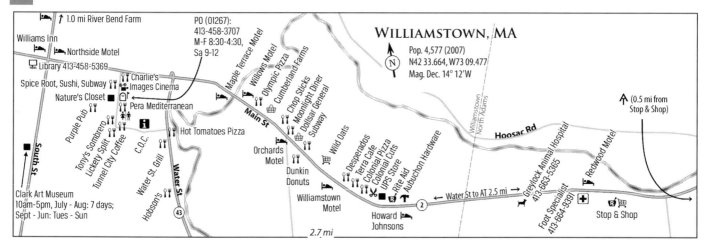

Desperado's is hiker friendly.

Spice Root Indian Cuisine 10% hiker discount.

✉ **Nature's Closet** Apparel, footwear, canister fuel and consignment sales. Maildrops: 61 Spring St, Williamstown, MA 01267.

🖳 **Milne Public Library** M-F 10-5:30, W 10-8, Sa 10-4

🚌 **Greyhound Bus Service**

North Adams, MA 01247 (services spread out east of AT)

🛏️🍴⛺📶🖳 **Holiday Inn** 413.663.6500 Summer rates $169.99/up. Pool, hot tub. **Richmond Grill** on-site.

Oriental Buffet, AYCE L/D buffet

➕ **North Adams Regional Hospital** 413.664.5000

🐾 **Greylock Animal Hospital** 413.663.5365, M-Th 8-7, F 8-5, Sa 8-3, Su 9-3, M-F doctor on call until 11pm.

🚌 **David Ackerson** 413.346.1033, 413.652.9573 daveackerson@yahoo.com Shuttles to trailheads ranging from Bear Mtn Bridge to Hanover, and to/from area airports.

1592.7   Massachusetts Ave / Hoosac Rd

🛏️⛺📶**The Birches B&B** 413.458.8134 〈www.birchesbb.com〉 $125D/up. Free pickup/return from Massachusetts Ave or MA 2 with stay, advance notice required. Two night min on weekends Jun-Oct. Swimming pond, laundry, big breakfast. Ask about slackpacking (19.3mi to Bennington).

---

*Red-spotted newt is the slow-moving red salamander that can be seen anywhere along the AT. The newt lives on land for the middle stage of its life, which lasts about two years. During this stage, it's also known as a **red eft**. It is a tadpole in its first stage. In its last stage it returns to water and turns green, but retains its red spots.*

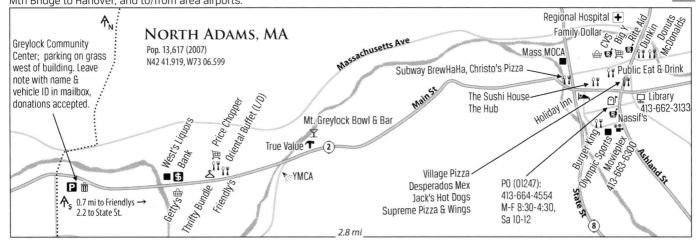

NORTH ADAMS, MA
Pop. 13,617 (2007)
N42 41.919, W73 06.599

Greylock Community Center; parking on grass west of building. Leave note with name & vehicle ID in mailbox, donations accepted.

0.7 mi to Friendlys →
2.2 to State St.

Massachusetts Ave

Main St

Mt. Greylock Bowl & Bar
True Value ②

West's Liquors
Bank
Price Chopper
Oriental Buffet (L/D)

Getty's
Thrifty Bundle
Friendly's
YMCA

Regional Hospital ➕
Family Dollar
CVS Big Y Rite Aid
Dunkin Donuts
McDonalds

Mass MOCA

Subway BrewHaHa, Christo's Pizza

Public Eat & Drink

The Sushi House
The Hub

Holiday Inn

Library
413-662-3133

Nassif's

Village Pizza
Desperados Mex
Jack's Hot Dogs
Supreme Pizza & Wings

Burger King
Olympic Sports
Movieplex
413-663-6300

State St

Ashland St

PO (01247):
413-664-4554
M-F 8:30-4:30,
Sa 10-12

⑧

2.8 mi

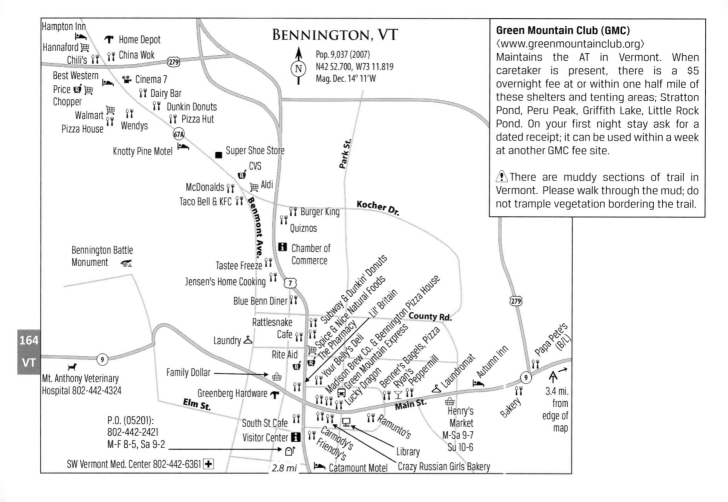

BENNINGTON, VT

Pop. 9,037 (2007)
N42 52.700, W73 11.819
Mag. Dec. 14° 11'W

Green Mountain Club (GMC)
⟨www.greenmountainclub.org⟩
Maintains the AT in Vermont. When caretaker is present, there is a $5 overnight fee at or within one half mile of these shelters and tenting areas; Stratton Pond, Peru Peak, Griffith Lake, Little Rock Pond. On your first night stay ask for a dated receipt; it can be used within a week at another GMC fee site.

⚠ There are muddy sections of trail in Vermont. Please walk through the mud; do not trample vegetation bordering the trail.

Hampton Inn
Hannaford
Chili's
Home Depot
China Wok
279
Best Western
Price Chopper
Cinema 7
Dairy Bar
Walmart
Pizza House
Wendys
Dunkin Donuts
Pizza Hut
67A
Knotty Pine Motel
Super Shoe Store
CVS
McDonalds
Taco Bell & KFC
Aldi
Bennington Battle Monument
Park St.
Kocher Dr.
Burger King
Quiznos
Chamber of Commerce
Benmont Ave.
Tastee Freeze
Jensen's Home Cooking
7
Blue Benn Diner
Subway & Dunkin' Donuts
Spice & Nice Natural Foods
The Pharmacy
Your Belly's Deli
Lil' Britain
County Rd.
Bennington Pizza House
Rattlesnake Cafe
Laundry
Rite Aid
Madison Brew Co. & Green Mountain Express
Lucky Dragon
Benner's Bagels, Pizza
Ryan's
Peppermill
279
Autumn Inn
Papa Pete's (B/L)
Mt. Anthony Veterinary Hospital 802-442-4324
9
Family Dollar
Greenberg Hardware
Elm St.
Laundromat
Bakery
9
Main St.
3.4 mi. from edge of map
Henry's Market
M-Sa 9-7
Su 10-6
P.O. (05201):
802-442-2421
M-F 8-5, Sa 9-2
South St Cafe
Visitor Center
Ramunto's
Carmody's Friendly's
Library
SW Vermont Med. Center 802-442-6361
2.8 mi
Catamount Motel
Crazy Russian Girls Bakery

164
VT

Bennington, VT 05201 (5.1W)

🛏🏕🛜 **Catamount Motel** 802.442.5977, $50S, $10EAP + tax. Laundry $4. Pets okay, accepts credit cards.

🛏🏕🖥🛜🖳✉ **Autumn Inn Motel** 802.447.7625 $60S / $70D, Pickup or return to trail $10 (each way). Pets $10. Guest maildrops: 924 Main Street, Bennington, VT 05201.

🛏🛜🖳✉ **Knotty Pine Motel** 802.442.5487 ⟨www.knottypinemotel.com⟩ 6.5 miles from the AT on VT 9, $85D/ up, $8EAP up to 4. Includes cont B, pets free, pool. Maildrops (guests only): 130 Northside Drive, Bennington, VT 05201.

🛏🏕🛜🖳 **Best Western** 802.442.6311 $99/up

🛏🏕🛜🖳 **Hampton Inn** 802.440.9862 rates seasonal, hot bfast.

🍴 **Lil' Britain** Fish & chips.

🚌 **Green Mountain Express** 802.447.0477 ⟨www.greenmtncn.org⟩ 215 Pleasant St. Free bus route "Emerald Line" passes between Bennington and Wilmington (17E) 3 times a day M-F. Board at town bus station, or flag the bus down at the trailhead. You may also request an unscheduled ride from town to trail for $3.

🚌 **Bennington Taxi** 802.442.9052

🚌 **Vermont Translines** 844.888.7267 ⟨vttranslines.com⟩ Routes cover from Albany, NY airport through towns including Bennington, VT, Wallingford, VT, Rutland, VT, and Hanover, NH.

🎞 **Cinema 7** 802.442.8170

🎞 **Bennington Battle Monument** Contains statue of Seth Warner, Revolutionary War leader of the Green Mountain Boys, for whom the shelter is named.

(3.0E) Prospect Mountain Ski Area

🏕◣🛜 **Greenwood Lodge & Campsites** 802.442.2547 bunk prices approx. $30.

🛏 **Stratton Mountain Resort** 802.297.4000 can be reached by taking a 1.0 mi. side trail from the summit to a gondola ride. Gondola has limited days/hours; don't make the walk unless you are certain of gondola operation (or are willing to walk an additional 1.5 miles down ski slopes). The resort has a restaurant, hotel rooms starting at $84 in summer, and **First Run Ski Shop** 802.297.2200 that has footwear, fuel and snacks.

Travel and Camp on Durable Surfaces

•Stay on the trail; never shortcut switchbacks. Take breaks off-trail on durable surfaces, such as rock or grass.

•Restrict activities to areas where vegetation is already absent.

•Avoid expanding existing trails and campsites by walking in the middle of the trail, and using the already-impacted core areas of campsites.

•If tree branches block the trail, move them off if possible, rather than going around and creating new trails.

•Wear gaiters and waterproof boots, so you may walk through puddles instead of walking around them and creating a wide spot in the trail.

Read more of the Leave No Trace techniques developed for the A.T.:   www.appalachiantrail.org/LNT

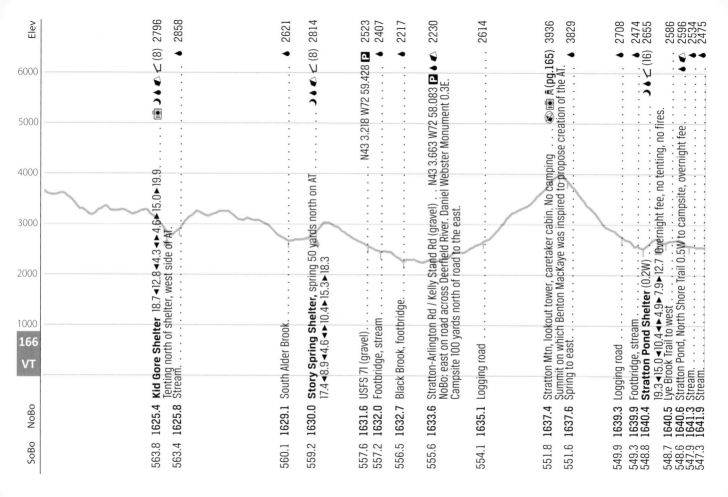

Elev

6000

4000

3000

2000

1000

166
VT

SoBo   NoBo

SoBo	NoBo	Description	Elev
563.8	1625.4	**Kid Gore Shelter** 18.7◀12.8◀4.3▶4.6▶15.0▶19.9 ⊡ ◢ ◆ △ ⊏ (8)	2796
563.4	1625.8	Tenting north of shelter, west side of AT. Stream. ◆	2858
560.1	1629.1	South Alder Brook. ◆ ◢	2621
559.2	1630.0	**Story Spring Shelter,** spring 50 yards north on AT ◗ ◢ ◆ △ ⊏ (8)	2814
		17.4◀8.9◀4.6▶10.4▶15.3▶18.3	
557.6	1631.6	USFS 71 (gravel) N43 3.218 W72 59.428 🅿	2523
557.2	1632.0	Footbridge, stream ◆	2407
556.5	1632.7	Black Brook, footbridge. ◆	2217
555.6	1633.6	Stratton-Arlington Rd / Kelly Stand Rd (gravel) N43 3.663 W72 58.083 🅿 ◢ ◆ △	2230
		NoBo: east on road across Deerfield River. Daniel Webster Monument 0.3E.	
		Campsite 100 yards north of road to the east.	
554.1	1635.1	Logging road	2614
551.8	1637.4	Stratton Mtn, lookout tower, caretaker cabin. No camping ⊛ ⊡ ⓘ ▲ (pg.165) ◆	3936
		Summit on which Benton MacKaye was inspired to propose creation of the AT.	
551.6	1637.6	Spring to east. ◆	3829
549.9	1639.3	Logging road ◆	2708
549.3	1639.9	Footbridge, stream ◆	2474
548.8	1640.4	**Stratton Pond Shelter** (0.2W) ◗ ◢ ◆ ⊏ (16)	2655
		19.3◀15.0◀10.4▶4.9▶7.9▶12.7 Overnight fee, no tenting, no fires.	
548.7	1640.5	Lye Brook Trail to west	2586
548.6	1640.6	Stratton Pond, North Shore Trail 0.5W to campsite, overnight fee ◣ ◆	2596
547.9	1641.3	Stream. ◣ ◆	2534
547.3	1641.9	Stream. ◆	2475

SoBo	NoBo	Feature	Elev
546.8	1642.4	Winhall River, footbridge, stream	2302
545.3	1643.9	Stream.	2246
543.9	1645.3	**William B. Douglas Shelter** (0.5W) 19.9◄15.3◄4.9▼3.0▶7.8▶15.9 Spring to left of shelter.	2304
543.0	1646.2	Prospect Rock to west, view. ⚠ NoBo: AT turns east off gravel road.	2150
540.9	1648.3	**Spruce Peak Shelter** (0.1W) 18.3◄7.9◄3.0▼4.8▶12.9▶17.6.	2247
540.5	1648.7	Spruce Peak 0.1W.	2040
540.1	1649.1	Stream, powerline	1833
539.9	1649.3	Stream.	1887
538.6	1650.6	Powerline, footbridge, stream	1704
538.1	1651.1	VT 11 & 30 N43 12.409 W72 58.243 **P** (pg.168-169)	1840
		Manchester Center, VT (5.4W)	
537.2	1652.0	Footbridge, stream.	2140
536.1	1653.1	**Bromley Shelter** 12.7◄7.8◄4.8▼8.1▶12.8▶14.3.	2605
535.5	1653.7	Ski slope	3088
535.1	1654.1	Bromley Mountain, no tenting or fires, okay to overnight in ski warming hut, no smoking, please keep hut clean.	3260
532.6	1656.6	Mad Tom Notch, USFS 21 (gravel)	2446
531.0	1658.2	Styles Peak	3394
529.3	1659.9	Peru Peak	3429
528.4	1660.8	Spring.	2819
528.0	1661.2	**Peru Peak Shelter** 15.9◄12.9◄8.1▼4.7▶6.2▶6.4 (fee).	2616
527.7	1661.5	Footbridge, stream (two).	2581
527.5	1661.7	Griffith Lake Tenting Area, camping only at designated sites within 0.5 mi.	2600
527.2	1662.0	Old Job Trail to east, Griffith Lake Trail to west	2614

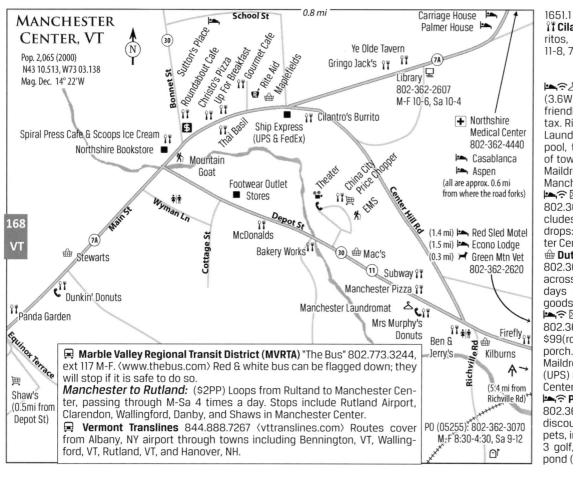

1651.1   VT 11 & 30

Cilantro Burrito (0.5E) Burritos, tacos, ice cream, sodas. 11-8, 7 days.

Manchester Center, VT (5.4W)

Red Sled Motel (3.6W) 802.362.2161. Hiker-friendly. $70/room includes tax. Ride to trail when available. Laundry for a fee, swimming pool, trout pond. Motel is 1.5E of town. Some resupply on-site. Maildrops: 2066 Depot Street Manchester Center, VT, 05255.

Econo Lodge (3.4W) 802.362.3333, $79-$109 includes cont. B. Pets $15. Maildrops: 2187 Depot St, Manchester Center, VT 05255.

Dutton Farm Stand (3.5W) 802.362.3083 Produce stand across from Red Sled Motel, 7 days 9am-7pm. Sodas, baked goods, ice cream.

Sutton's Place 802.362.1165, $70S, $80D, $99(room for 3), pets okay on porch. Accepts MC/Visa. USPS Maildrops: (USPS) PO Box 142 or (UPS) 50 School St, Manchester Center, VT 05255.

Palmer House 802.362.3600 Ask for hiker discount, $2.50 for cont B, no pets, indoor & outdoor pool. Par-3 golf, tennis courts and trout pond (equipment provided).

Green Mountain House 330.388.6478
〈www.greenmountainhouse.net〉 Jeff & Regina Taussig host hikers at their home. Open Jun 10 - Sep 7. Space is limited so reservations are essential. Clean bed with linens, shower, free laundry, WiFi, phone & well equipped hiker kitchen. Private room for couples. Free breakfast supplies; make your own pancakes, eggs, cereal, coffee. Not a party place, no alcohol. Check in from 1pm to 7pm. Free shuttles back to the trail in the morning for guests. Credit cards accepted. $30+tax per person.

Carriage House 802.362.1706 $68D and up, no pets.

Mountain Goat Outfitter 802.362.5159, M-Sa 10-6, Su 10-5, 〈www.mountaingoat.com〉 Full-service outfitter, white gas/alcohol/oz canister fuel, footwear. Maildrops: 4886 Main St, Manchester, VT 05255.

EMS 802.366.8082, 7 days 10-6, full service outfitter, Coleman/alcohol/oz, list of shuttlers and places to stay.

Leonards Taxi 802.362.7039

Northshire Taxi 802.345.9333

Peru, VT (Businesses below are to the east, toward Peru)

The Lodge at Bromley(2.1E) 802.824.6941 $99 hiker rate, no pets, tavern with light menu, indoor pool, game room, ride to/from trail w/stay. Maildrops: (non-guests $5) 4216 VT 11, Peru, VT 05152.

Bromley Market (2.5E) 802.824.4444 7 days 7am-7pm

Bromley View Inn (3.6E) on VA 30, 802.297.1459 〈www.bromleyviewinn.com〉 $85D/up, includes hot breakfast, shuttle to/from VT 11/30 trailhead w/stay. Maildrops: 522 VT 30, Bondville, VT 05340.

JJ Hapgood General Store & Eatery (4.2E) 802.824.4800 On Main St. in Peru, next to PO. Wood-fired pizza, beer and resupply. Open 7-7, extended hours on weekends.

1668.7   Danby-Landgrove Rd   *Danby, VT 05739* (3.5W)
M-F 7:15-10:15 & 1-4, Sa 7:30-10:30, 802.293.5105

Silas Griffith B&B 802.293.5567 〈www.silasgriffith.com〉 Starting at $99D midweek, 2 night min weekends & holidays. Includes full breakfast. Check-in starts at 2pm. Laundry $20/load, pets $25. Dinner with advance reservation; vegetarian/gluten free can be arranged. Hiker friendly, family friendly, pet friendly, no smoking. Maildrops with reservation: 178 South Main St, Danby, VT 05739.

Otter Creek Campground 802.293.5041 2mi. north of USFS 10 in Danby on US 7, tent sites $20PP, pets on leash, Small selection of food & camping supplies, long-term parking for fee. USPS/UPS Maildrops: 1136 US 7, Danby, VT 05739.

Mt. Tabor Country Store 802.293.5641 M-Sa 5-8, Su 5-7

Nichols Store & Deli

Silas Griffith Library 802.293.5106

Crosby Hardware 802.293.5111

1677.2   VT 140, *Wallingford, VT 05773* (2.8W)
M-F 8-4:30, Sa 9-12, 802.446.2140

Mom's Country Kitchen 802.446.2606 W-Sa 6:30-2, Su 7-1.

Sal's Italian Restaurant & Pizza

Wallingford Country Store & Deli

Cumberland Farms Bus stop for **MVRTA** (4 times daily) and **Vermont Translines** (see page 168)

Nail It Down Hardware

Gilbert Library 802.446.2685 Tu,Th,F 10-5, W 10-8, Sa 9-12.

1683.5   VT 103

Qu's Whistle Stop Restaurant (0.5W) 802.772.7012. Open Su,M, Tu 7-3, Th-Sa 7-7, closed Wed. Serves breakfast all day, hiker specials, ice cream, beer, charging stations, and bag lunches. Ask about tenting. The Bus (route to Rutland) stops here.

Cold River Veterinary Center (0.5W) 802.747.4076

Loretta's Deli (1W) 802.772.7638, M-Sa 6am-7pm, Su 8-4. Prepared meals & to-go trail foods. Fuel/oz, water filters.

MVRTA Stops near deli 4/day.

North Clarendon, VT 05759 (4.2W)
M-F 8-1 & 2-4:30, Sa 8-10, 802.773.7893

Mike's Country Store

Rutland, VT (8W of VT 103) See page 172

1694.6   Trail to Killington Peak (0.2E from Cooper Lodge Shelter)

Killington Peak Lodge (0.2E) 800.621.6867 Food service at the summit lodge, gondola ride ($15 round trip) to the ski resort. Summer hours 10am-5pm.

SoBo	NoBo		Elev
525.4	1663.8	Baker Peak Trail to west, Baker Peak 0.1N on AT	2649
523.3	1665.9	**Lost Pond Shelter** 17.6◀12.8◀4.7▶1.5▶1.7▶5.0	2210
522.8	1666.4	Spring	1975
521.8	1667.4	Old Job Trail to **Old Job Shelter** (1.0E), Lake Brook is water source	1544
521.6	1667.6	**Big Branch Shelter** 14.3◀6.2◀1.5▶0.2▶3.5▶8.3 ... 6.4◀1.7▶0.2▶3.3▶8.1▶13.2 Close to road; heavy weekend use. Water source is Big Branch. Privy uphill.	1512
520.5	1668.7	Danby-Landgrove Rd., N43 22.362 W72 57.764 **P** (pg.169)	1539
519.9	1669.3	Big Black Branch Bridge, **Danby, VT** (3.5W) ... Footbridge, stream	1667
518.4	1670.8	Homer Stone Brook Trail to west.	1880
518.3	1670.9	**Little Rock Pond Shelter & Tenting Area** 5.0◀3.5◀3.3▶4.8▶9.9▶13.6 Water source is at the caretaker's platform. Overnight fee. Tenting restricted to designated sites.	1852
517.3	1671.9	Footbridge, stream	1955
514.1	1675.1	Trail to White Rocks Cliff 0.2W	2294
513.5	1675.7	**Greenwall Shelter** (0.2E) 8.3◀8.1◀4.8▶5.1▶8.8▶14.6. Spring 0.1 mile on side trail behind shelter, prone to fail in dry seasons.	2114
512.8	1676.4	Bully Brook, Keewaydin Trail to west.	1456
512.1	1677.1	Sugar Hill Rd (gravel)	1270
512.0	1677.2	VT 140, footbridge, stream N43 27.404 W72 55.972 (0.2E) **P** (pg.169) **Wallingford, VT** (2.8W)	1160
511.0	1678.2	Short side trail to west to Domed Ledge Vista (no longer a view)	1715
510.3	1678.9	Bear Mountain	2263
509.4	1679.8	Patch Hollow	1787
509.0	1680.2	Footbridge, stream (3)	1672
508.8	1680.4	Lake Trail loop to west (yellow blazed), 100 yards north, red-blazed tr to east	1673
508.4	1680.8	**Minerva Hinchey Shelter** 13.2◀9.9◀5.1▶3.7▶9.5▶13.8 spring 75 yards in front of shelter.	1631

SoBo	NoBo	Description	Elev
506.5	1682.7	View to Rutland Airport	1371 📷
505.8	1683.4	Clarendon Gorge, suspension bridge, swimming holes in Mill River	815 ♦
505.7	1683.5	VT 103, restaurant 0.5W N43 31.286 W72 55.550 P ♦ (pg.169)	860
505.2	1684.0	**North Clarendon, VT** (4.2W) **Rutland, VT** (8.0W) View, north end of rock scramble	1326 📷
504.7	1684.5	**Clarendon Shelter** (0.1E) 13.6◄8.8◄3.7◄►5.8►10.1►12.6.) ♦ ⌐ (10)	1264
504.2	1685.0	Beacon Hill	1740
503.9	1685.3	Lottery Rd (gravel), powerline	1658
503.4	1685.8	Hermit Spring to east (unreliable)	1794 △
502.3	1686.9	Stream	1586 ♦
502.1	1687.1	Keiffer Rd (gravel)	1523 ♦
501.8	1687.4	Cold River Rd / Lower Rd (paved) Nobo east on road 75 yards	1390 ⊞
501.0	1688.2	**W.E. Pierce Groceries** in North Shrewsbury (2.4E) Gould Brook to west, AT parallel for 0.5 miles.	1480 ♦
500.3	1688.9	Upper Cold River Rd (gravel)	1630
499.6	1689.6	Gravel road, Robinson Brook	1742 ♦
498.9	1690.3	**Governor Clement Shelter** 14.6◄9.5◄5.8◄►4.3►6.8►8.7.) ♦ ⌐ (12) ⚠ Shelter's proximity to road makes it prone to use by non-hiking crowd.	1920
498.6	1690.6	At on gravel road 0.3 miles north of shelter.	2069
497.6	1691.6	Ski trail, blue diamond blazes	2582
496.6	1692.6	Spring	3342
496.2	1693.0	Shrewsbury Peak Trail to east, signed.	3512
494.6	1694.6	**Cooper Lodge Shelter** 13.8◄10.1◄4.3◄►2.5►4.4►16.3 📷) ⌐ (16) (pg.169) Spring 60 yards north on AT. Trail behind shelter 0.2 to Killington peak & view.	3928
494.5	1694.7	Bucklin Trail to west	3806
494.3	1694.9	Spring	3607

✱ **Clintonia** – Foot-tall plant with plastic-looking blue berries atop long stems.

SoBo	NoBo	Description	Elev
492.1	1697.1	**Pico Camp** (0.5E) 12.6◄6.8◄2.5◄►1.9►13.8►23.7 ♦ ⌐ (4) Shelter on Sherburne Pass Tr where it leaves the Long Tr/AT south of Pico summit.	3482
490.9	1698.3	Spring	3153 ♦
490.2	1699.0	**Churchill Scott Shelter** (0.1W) 8.7◄4.4◄1.9◄►11.9►21.8►33.4) △ ⌐ Composting privy, unreliable water at southern spur from shelter, no fires.	2620
490.0	1699.2	Stream.	2434 △
489.2	1700.0	Stream.	2062 ♦
488.3	1700.9	US 4, **Rutland, VT** (8.5W) N43 39.996 W72 50.997 P (pg.172)	1880 📷
488.2	1701.0	Stream.	1889 ♦
487.9	1701.9	Maine Junction, Tucker-Johnson camping area (0.4W) ⚠ The Long Trail is also white-blazed, it turns to the west.	2259 ♦△
487.1	1702.1	Spring, Deer Leap Trail to east.	2304 ♦
486.5	1702.7	Deer Leap Trail 0.3E to view	2438 📷

| SoBo | NoBo | | Elev |

1700.9 US 4, **Rutland, VT** (8.5W), **Killington, VT 05751** (1.8E, pg.173)

🛏️🔥🚿🍴⛺📶✉️ (0.8E) **The Inn at Long Trail** 802.775.7181 or 800.325.2540 ⟨www.innatlongtrail.com⟩ Hiker rates on rooms that include full breakfast. Limited pet rooms, reservations recommended on weekends. Overflow camping across street with no facilities. Coin laundry, outside water spigot. Closed mid-April through Mem Day. **McGrath's Irish Pub** L/D 11:30-9pm, live music Fri & Sat. Maildrops: (FedEx/UPS) 709 US 4, Killington, VT 05751.

🛏️📶✉️ (1.4W) **Mendon Mountain View Lodge** 802.773.4311 Hiker rate $59S $79D includes breakfast. No pets. Heated pool & suana, bus stops here. Maildrops: 5654 Route 4, Mendon, VT 05701.

🚶🏠🔥🍴🍽️⛺🚌📶✉️ **Hikers Hostel at the Yellow Deli** 802.683.9378 or 802.775.9800 ⟨www.hikershostel.org⟩ Run by a Twelve Tribes spiritual community. $20 Suggested donation, WFS when available. Kitchenette, coin laundry ($1 wash $1 dry). No alcohol, no smoking. Stay includes breakfast and 15% off at deli and at **Simon the Tanner** (adjacent outfitter, open 10-5 M-Th, F 10-3). Deli open 24/7 except from 3pm Friday till noon Sunday. Free showers even w/o stay. Maildrops: Hiker Hostel, 23 Center Street, Rutland, VT 05701.

🚶 **Mountain Travelers Outdoor Shop** 802.775.0814 M–F 10–6, Sa 10-5. Full line of gear, Coleman/alcohol/oz.

🍴 **Rutland Area Food Co-op** 802.773.0737 7 days

🐾 **Rutland Veterinary** 802.773.2779

🚂 **Amtrak** 800.872.7245 Daily routes Rutland to many NE cities.

🚐 **Rutland Taxi** 802.236.3133

✈️ **Rutland Airport** South of Rutland on US 7

🚐 **Marble Valley Regional Transit District (MVRTA)** "The Bus" 802.773.3244, ext 117 M-F. ⟨www.thebus.com⟩ Red & white bus can be flagged down; they will stop if it is safe to do so.
Rutland Killington Commuter (RKC) ($2PP) Loops hourly from 5:15-7:15, 7 days from Rutland to Killington, passing AT on US 4. Stops westbound at The Inn at Long Trail.

🚐 **Vermont Translines** (see page 168) Stops at Rutland bus station and at Long Trail Inn.

172
VT

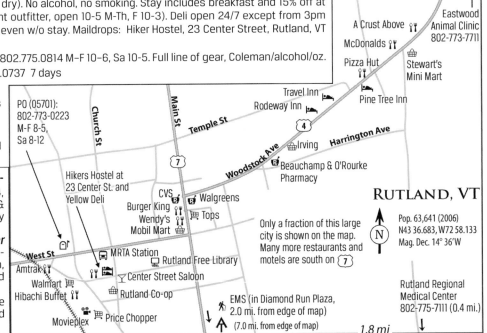

PO (05701): 802-773-0223 M-F 8-5, Sa 8-12

Church St

Main St

Temple St

Hikers Hostel at 23 Center St. and Yellow Deli

(7)

CVS

Burger King
Wendy's
Mobil Mart

West St

Amtrak

Walmart
Hibachi Buffet

Movieplex

MRTA Station

Price Chopper

Walgreens

Tops

Rutland Free Library

Center Street Saloon

Rutland Co-op

Travel Inn
Rodeway Inn

(4)

Irving

Woodstock Ave

Beauchamp & O'Rourke Pharmacy

Harrington Ave

Pine Tree Inn

(6.7 mi. from edge of map)

Home Depot
Dunkin Donuts
Mtn Traveler
Little Ceasars
Applebees

A Crust Above

McDonalds

Pizza Hut

Eastwood Animal Clinic 802-773-7711

Stewart's Mini Mart

RUTLAND, VT

N

Pop. 63,641 (2006)
N43 36.683, W72 58.133
Mag. Dec. 14° 36'W

Only a fraction of this large city is shown on the map. Many more restaurants and motels are south on (7)

Rutland Regional Medical Center 802-775-7111 (0.4 mi.)

EMS (in Diamond Run Plaza, 2.0 mi. from edge of map)
(7.0 mi. from edge of map)

1.8 mi

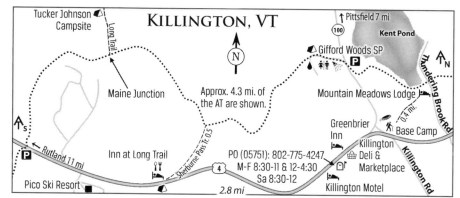

KILLINGTON, VT

Tucker Johnson Campsite

Long Trail

↑ Pittsfield 7 mi
100
Kent Pond

Gifford Woods SP
🅿

N

Maine Junction

Approx. 4.3 mi. of the AT are shown.

Mountain Meadows Lodge

Thundering Brook Rd

N

Greenbrier Inn

Base Camp

Killington Rd

Inn at Long Trail

Killington Deli & Marketplace

🅿 Rutland 11 mi

Sherburne Pass Tr. 0.5

PO (05751): 802-775-4247
M-F 8:30-11 & 12-4:30
Sa 8:30-12
4

Killington Motel

Pico Ski Resort

2.8 mi

1704.0 🔺👫🚿⛲ The AT passes thru **Gifford Woods State Park** 802.775.5354 Shelters, discounted tent sites for AT hikers in special hiker section, coin-op showers, water spigot. Open Mem Day-Columbus Day. Fills quickly in fall.

1704.2   VT 100   *Killington, VT 05751* (0.6E from VT 100, 1.8E from US 4 trailhead)
🚶✉🛹 **Base Camp Outfitters** 802.775.0166, Summer hours: 9-6 every day. Full service outfitter, alcohol/oz & canister fuel. Also accessible by side trail from Mountain Meadows Lodge. Disc golf. Maildrops: 2363 Route 4, Killington VT 05751.
🛏📶 **Greenbrier Inn** 802.775.1575 15% discount for hikers, no pets.
🛏📶💻 **Killington Motel** 802.773.9535 Rates seasonal, includes cont. B, outdoor pool.
🚐 **Apex Shuttle Service** 603.252.8294 AThikershuttle@gmail.com Inn-to-Inn hiking packages between Killington & Franconia Notch, NH. Shuttle, lodging and lunches provided for hikers who want the AT day hiking experience with a comfortable night's lodging.
🍴🍸⛺ **Scrub a Dub Pub** 802.422.5335 Eat/drink while-u-wash 0.8S of US4 on Killington Rd.
Pittsfield, VT 05762 (7W) 🏤 M-F 8-12, 2-4:30, Sa 8:30-11:30, 802.746.8953
⛪🍴🏪 **Original General Store** B/L/D

1704.8   Kent Pond, AT crosses behind lodge near pond, 0.4E trail to **Base Camp Outfitters**
🛏🔥🛖🍴⛺🅿📶💻✉ **Mountain Meadows Lodge** ⟨www.mountainmeadowslodge.com⟩

802.775.1010   Room $69D, single room sometimes available for $59. Tent/hammock site $10/PP. Occasional WFS. Lunch or dinner $10. No pets inside; barn & woodshed available. Outdoor pool, hot tub, and sauna. Parking for section hikers. Open year round. Lodging not available most weekends & events. Maildrops: 285 Thundering Brook Rd, Killington, VT 05751.

1724.2   VT 12, Barnard Gulf Rd
⛪ **On The Edge Farm** (0.2W) 802.457.4510 Mid-May-Labor Day 7 days 10-5:30; rest of year Th-M 10-5. Pies, fruit, ice cream, smoked meats and cheese, cold drinks.

Woodstock, VT 05091 (4.2E)
🏤 M-F 8:30-5, Sa 9-12, 802.457.1323 Pricey resort town, several motels & restaurants, movie theater, bookstore.
🛏📶 **Shire River View Motel** 802.457.2211 $138/up
🛏📶 **Braeside Motel** 802.457.1366
🍴 **Bentley's, Pizza Chef**
⛪ **Cumberland Farms, Gillingham & Sons**
💊 **Woodstock Pharmacy**
🐾 **Woodstock Vet. Hospital** 802.457.2229
💻 **Library** 802.457.2295 M-F 10-5

1726.1   Woodstock Stage Rd
South Pomfret, VT 05067 (1E)
🏤 M-F 10-2, Sa 8:30-11:30, 802.457.1147 located inside of Teago's
⛪ **Teago's General Store** 802.457.1626 M-Sa 7-6, Su 7-4, B&J ice cream, beer, sandwiches & salads.

SoBo	NoBo	Description	Elev
486.4	1702.8	Sherburne Pass Trail 0.5E to **Inn at Long Trail**	2440
485.6	1703.6	Spring	1854
485.2	1704.0	**Gifford Woods State Park,** coin-op showers 🏛🍴♿ ♦ (pg.173)	1656
485.0	1704.2	VT 100, **Killington, VT** (0.6E) N43 40.455 W72 48.578 🅿 (pg.173)	1615
484.4	1704.8	Kent Pond, side trail to **Killington, VT** (0.4E) ♦ (pg.173)	1561
483.1	1706.1	Thundering Brook Rd (gravel)	1407
482.9	1706.3	Thundering Falls to west	1243
482.7	1706.5	River Rd (gravel) N43 40.838 W72 46.932 🅿	1271
481.4	1707.8	Quimby Mountain	2527
480.8	1708.4	Powerline, boulder to sit on, view to Pico slopes	2342
480.5	1708.7	Gravel road	2339
478.3	1710.9	**Stony Brook Shelter** (0.1E) 16.3◄13.8◄11.9◄▸9.9▸21.5▸30.3 ☾♦⊂(8)	1779
		Tent sites behind shelter. Water from stream 0.1N on AT.	
477.7	1711.5	Stony Brook Rd (gravel), Stony Brook and footbridge. ♦	1368
475.3	1713.9	Streams ♦	2032
473.8	1715.4	Chateauguay Rd (gravel), Mink Brook ♦	2022
473.4	1715.8	Locust Creek ♦	2160
471.0	1718.2	The Lookout, 0.1W to cabin and tower, no fires ⌂	2384
468.4	1720.8	**Wintturi Shelter** (0.2W) 23.7◄21.8◄9.9◄▸11.6▸20.4▸27.7 ☾♦⌂⊂(8)	2082
467.7	1721.5	Woods road	1773

(Elevation profile chart spanning Elev 1000–6000)

SoBo	NoBo	Description	Elev
466.1	1723.1	Ascutney Mountain.	1497
465.0	1724.2	VT 12, Barnard Gulf Rd (paved). N43 39.309 W72 33.972 P ♦ (pg.173)	891
		Gulf Stream south of road crossing. **Woodstock, VT** (4.2E)	
464.3	1724.9	Dana Hill.	1551
463.1	1726.1	Woodstock Stage Rd, Barnard Brook, **South Pomfret, VT** (1E). ♦(pg.173)	820
462.8	1726.4	Stream.	1049
462.3	1726.9	Totman Hill Rd, footbridge, stream.	1038
461.5	1727.7	Bartlett Brook Rd (gravel), footbridge, stream.	1055
460.9	1728.3	Pomfret Rd (paved), Pomfret Brook south of road crossing, powerline.	980
460.5	1728.7	View.	1588
459.7	1729.5	View.	1729
459.1	1730.1	Cloudland Rd (gravel), **Cloudland Market** (0.2W) closed M & Su	1370
458.6	1730.6	Previous AT shelter (Cloudland, 0.5W) now on private land. Owners also own Cloudland Market and hikers are welcome to stay at the shelter.	1614
457.3	1731.9	Thistle Hill.	1954
456.8	1732.4	**Thistle Hill Shelter** (0.2E) stream 0.1 further (8)	1774
		33.4◄21.5◄11.6◄►8.8►16.1►25.6	
456.5	1732.7	Dimick Brook	1520
455.5	1733.7	Joe Ranger Rd (gravel)	1310
454.9	1734.3	Bunker Hill Rd (dirt).	1418

❋ Queen Anne's Lace – White flower cluster in disk shaped doily 3-5" wide on hairy stem.

SoBo	NoBo	Description	Elev
452.5	1736.7	Stream	543
452.3	1736.9	Quechee West Hartford Rd, NoBo west on road 0.4 mi, cross White River.	481
452.0	1737.2	VT 14, White River, **West Hartford, VT.** (pg.176-177)	397
		NoBo: turn west, on road 0.3 mile.	
451.6	1737.6	Tigertown Rd, NoBo: turn east, on road 0.4 mile	400
451.3	1737.9	I-89 underpass N43 43.250 W72 24.793 P	560
450.6	1738.6	Podunk Rd (gravel), Podunk Brook N43 43.006 W72 24.013 P	860
450.1	1739.1	Woods road	1052
449.7	1739.5	Woods road, stream	1006
448.0	1741.2	**Happy Hill Shelter** (0.2E) 30.3◄20.4◄8.8◄►7.3►16.8►22.5 (8)	1426
		Brook near shelter, known to run dry.	
447.7	1741.5	Tucker Trail 3.1W to Norwich	1336
446.4	1742.8	Woods road	1140

SoBo NoBo

Plan Ahead and Prepare

•Check Appalachian Trail (A.T.) guidebooks and maps for guidance and note that camping regulations vary considerably along the Trail. Travel in groups of 10 or fewer. If you are traveling in a group of more than 5, avoid using shelters, leaving them for lone hikers and smaller groups.

•Bring a lightweight trowel or wide tent stake to dig a hole for burying human waste.

•Bring a piece of screening to filter food scraps from your dishwater and pack them out with you.

•Bring a waterproof bag and at least 50 feet of rope to hang food and other scented articles. Or, carry a bear-resistant food container ("bear canister") to store these items.

•Repackage food in resealable bags to minimize waste.

•Prepare for extreme weather, hazards, and emergencies – especially the cold – to avoid impacts from searches, rescues, and campfires.

•Learn when areas are most crowded and try to avoid those times. If you are planning a northbound thru-hike, avoid starting on March 1, March 15, the first day of spring, or April 1.

Read more of the Leave No Trace techniques developed for the A.T.: www.appalachiantrail.org/LNT

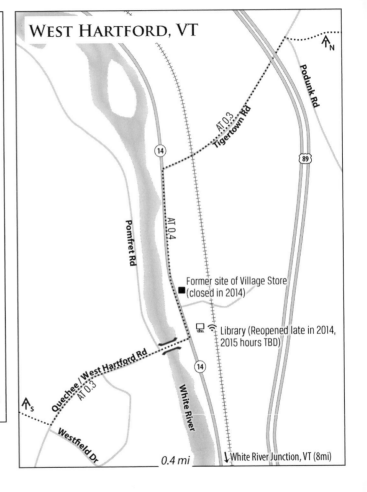

WEST HARTFORD, VT

N

Podunk Rd

AT 0.3

Tigertown Rd

14

89

AT 0.4

Pomfret Rd

■ Former site of Village Store (closed in 2014)

Library (Reopened late in 2014, 2015 hours TBD)

Quechee / West Hartford Rd

AT 0.3

14

White River

S

Westfield Dr

0.4 mi

↓ White River Junction, VT (8mi)

1737.2   VT 14, White River
West Hartford, VT 05084

🚌 **Big Yellow Taxi** 802.281.8294 Also covers Woodstock, Norwich, Hanover, Lebanon and White River Junction.

1745.6   Main St
Norwich, VT 05055 (more services on map)

🛏🍴🛜🖥✉ **Norwich Inn** 802.649.1143 ⟨www.norwichinn.com⟩ $99D includes a free beer, rooms for pets, no smoking, reservations recommended. **Jasper Murdocks Ale House** Tu–Su B/L/D, serves dinner 7 days, microbrewery. Maildrops for guests: PO Box 908, Norwich, VT 04055, or FedEx to 325 Main St.

🏪🖥 **Dan & Whits General Store** 802.649.1602, 7 days 7-9, 0.1W on Main St. Hikers get free day old sandwiches when available. Small gear items, canister fuel, batteries, ponchos, hardware and grocery.

🖥🛜 **Norwich Library** 802.649.1184, M 1-8, Tu-W-F 10-5:30, Th 10-8, Sa 10-3.

🚌 **Advance Transit** ⟨www.advancetransit.com⟩ M-F 6-6, offers FREE bus service connecting Hanover area towns. Detailed schedule and stops are available on-line and at libraries. The routes are indicated on maps, pg. 177 & 178, and primary bus stops are:
Norwich - Dan & Whits (Brown).
Hanover - Dartmouth Book Store (Orange/Blue), Hanover Inn (Brown). White River Junction - Amtrak.
West Lebanon - Main St. (Orange/Red), grocery stores, outfitters.
Lebanon - City Hall (Blue/Red).

🚌 **Vermont Translines** 844.888.7267 ⟨vttranslines.com⟩ Routes cover from Albany, NY airport through towns including Bennington, VT, Wallingford, VT, Rutland, VT, White River Junction, NH, and Hanover, NH.

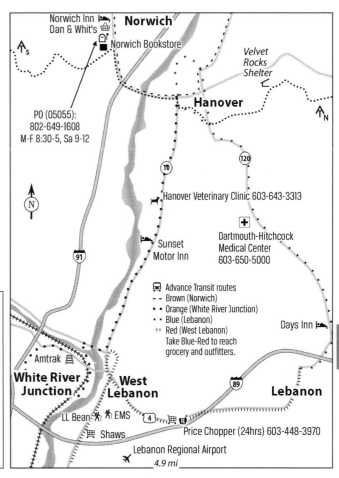

Norwich Inn 🛏
Dan & Whit's 🏪
🏠📮 Norwich Bookstore

Norwich

Velvet Rocks Shelter

Hanover

PO (05055):
802-649-1608
M-F 8:30-5, Sa 9-12

N

🔟

120

Hanover Veterinary Clinic 603-643-3313

🛏 Sunset Motor Inn

✚ Dartmouth-Hitchcock Medical Center 603-650-5000

91

🚌 Advance Transit routes
– – Brown (Norwich)
• • Orange (White River Junction)
∗ ∗ Blue (Lebanon)
▪▪ Red (West Lebanon)
Take Blue-Red to reach grocery and outfitters.

Days Inn 🛏

Amtrak 🚃

White River Junction

West Lebanon

89

Lebanon

LL Bean 🛏 🚶 EMS
4 🚃 🚌
🚃 Shaws
Price Chopper (24hrs) 603-448-3970

✈ Lebanon Regional Airport
4.9 mi

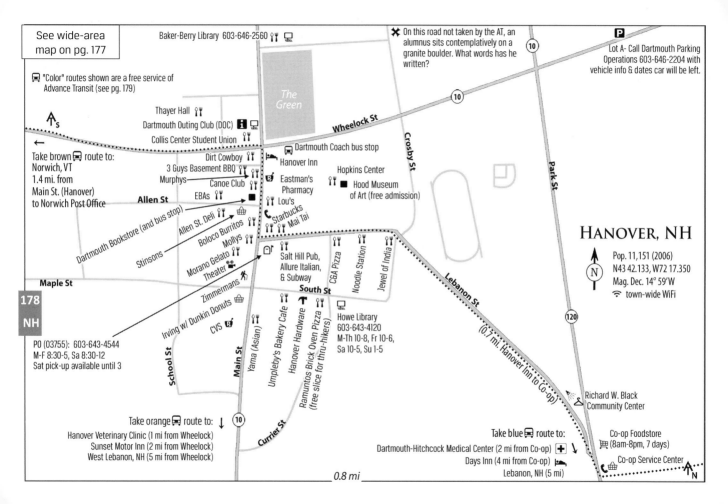

See wide-area map on pg. 177

Baker-Berry Library 603-646-2560

On this road not taken by the AT, an alumnus sits contemplatively on a granite boulder. What words has he written?

P

Lot A- Call Dartmouth Parking Operations 603-646-2204 with vehicle info & dates car will be left.

"Color" routes shown are a free service of Advance Transit (see pg. 179)

The Green

Wheelock St

10

10

Thayer Hall
Dartmouth Outing Club (DOC)
Collis Center Student Union

Crosby St

Park St

Take brown route to:
Norwich, VT
1.4 mi. from
Main St. (Hanover)
to Norwich Post Office

Dirt Cowboy
Dartmouth Coach bus stop
Hanover Inn
3 Guys Basement BBQ
Murphys
Canoe Club
EBAs
Allen St
Lou's
Starbucks
Mai Tai

Hopkins Center
Hood Museum of Art (free admission)

Eastman's Pharmacy

HANOVER, NH

Pop. 11,151 (2006)
N43 42.133, W72 17.350
Mag. Dec. 14° 59'W
town-wide WiFi

N

Dartmouth Bookstore (and bus stop)
Allen St. Deli
Boloco Burritos
Stinsons
Mollys
Morano Gelato
Theater

Maple St

Salt Hill Pub,
Allure Italian,
& Subway

C&A Pizza
Noodle Station
Jewel of India

South St

Lebanon St
(0.7 mi. Hanover Inn to Co-op)

120

178 NH

Zimmermans

Irving w/ Dunkin Donuts
CVS

School St

Main St

Yama (Asian)
Umpleby's Bakery Cafe
Hanover Hardware
Ramuntos Brick Oven Pizza (free slice for thru-hikers)

Howe Library
603-643-4120
M-Th 10-8, Fr 10-6,
Sa 10-5, Su 1-5

Richard W. Black Community Center

Co-op Foodstore
(8am-8pm, 7 days)

Co-op Service Center

PO (03755): 603-643-4544
M-F 8:30-5, Sa 8:30-12
Sat pick-up available until 3

Take orange route to:
Hanover Veterinary Clinic (1 mi from Wheelock)
Sunset Motor Inn (2 mi from Wheelock)
West Lebanon, NH (5 mi from Wheelock)

10

Currier St

Take blue route to:
Dartmouth-Hitchcock Medical Center (2 mi from Co-op)
Days Inn (4 mi from Co-op)
Lebanon, NH (5 mi)

N

0.8 mi

1747.1   Dartmouth College *Hanover, NH 03755*

🏛 **Hanover Friends of the AT** produce a brochure with complete list of hiker services, available at the DOC, PO, libraries, Co-op.

🏛 🛜 🖥 **Dartmouth Outing Club (DOC)** 603.646.2428 In Robinson Hall. Not available during Dartmouth orientation (last week of Aug and first two weeks of Sept). Unsecured room in basement for hikers to store gear while in town, cannot be left overnight. Computers for free internet use. There are no hiker accommodations on campus.

🅿 Overnight parking on Wheelock Street Lot A, see map. No parking near Connecticut River Bridge.

🛏⛺🛜✉ **Sunset Motor Inn** 603.298.8721, open 8-11, Call ahead for availability; discount for hikers. Will shuttle when bus is not running, free laundry before 6pm, quiet after 10pm, $15 pet fee. Maildrops: 305 N Main Street, West Lebanon, NH 03874.

🛏🍴 **Hanover Inn** 603.643.4300 Pricey, discount sometimes avail.

🍴 **EBA's** 603.643.6145 Full menu and beer, daily specials. Pizza buffet Tuesday night $7.95, Su brunch $11.95.

🍴 **Allen St. Deli** Open 7-4, 7 days. One free bagel for thru-hikers.

🍴 **Jewel of India** buffet Su 11:30-2:30

🏪🍴 **Stinson's** Convenience store with $5 hiker lunch special: deli sandwich, soda & small bag of chips. Good selection of beer & tobacco.

🍴🛜 **Hanover Food Co-op** 603.643.4889 8am-8pm 7 days year round. Deli and food bar in-store. Please use member #7000 at checkout to help fund AT related initiatives.

🚿⛺🛜 **Richard W. Black Recreation Center** 603.643.5315 M-F 9am-5pm. Open Saturdays Sept-June. Shower w/soap & towel $3, laundry w/soap $2, must finish either by 4:30pm. Pack storage.

🚶 **Zimmerman's** 603.643.6863 Hiker-friendly, canister fuel, Aquamira, socks & outdoor clothes.

🔧 **Hanover Hardware** Coleman/alcohol/oz

🚌 **Advance Transit** (see pg. 177)

🚌 **Big Yellow Taxi** 603.643.8294

🚌 **Dartmouth Coach** 603.448.2800 ⟨www.dartmouthcoach.com⟩ Routes to Boston, to Logan Airport, and to NY. See schedules on website.

🚌 **Apex Shuttle Service** 603.252.8294 AThikershuttle@gmail.com (Steve "Stray Cat" Lake) To/from anywhere if originating or ending in the Hanover area.

🐾 **Hanover Veterinary** 603.643.3313

White River Junction, VT

🚆 **Amtrak** 800.872.7245 Vermonter line travels north as far as St. Albans, VT, and south through New York, Philadelphia, Baltimore and Washington, DC. There is no ticket office at this station, but you can reserve on the phone and pay when you board.

Lebanon & West Lebanon, NH (see map pg. 177)

🛏🛜🖥 **Days Inn** 603.448.5070, 4 mi. south of the Co-op on Rte 120 on free bus route, cont. B, pets $20.

🚶 **EMS** 603.298.7716, **LL Bean** 603.298.6975

🛒 **Shaw's** 603.298.0388 7am-10pm, 7-9 Sunday

1752.9   Etna-Hanover Center Rd, *Etna, NH 03750* (0.8E)

🏕👐⛺ **Tiggers Tree House** 603.643.9213 Private home; not a party place. No drive-ins. Advance notice ensures a place to stay. Call from trailhead, Etna General Store (will let you use phone) or Dartmouth Outing Club for pickup. Pets allowed, donations accepted or buy laundry soap or work for stay. Rides to grocery store, Walmart, EMS.

🏪🍴 (0.8E) **Etna General Store** 603.643.1655, M-F 6-7, Sa, Su 8-7. Deli, hot meals, open 7 days. Denatured alcohol/oz.

179

NH

SoBo	NoBo	Feature	Elev
445.2	1744.0	Powerline	1174
444.7	1744.5	Stream	835
444.6	1744.6	Elm Street, NoBo: turn east, on road 1.0 mile	839
443.6	1745.6	Main St, **Norwich, VT**, NoBo: turn east, on road 1.4 miles (pg.177)	516
442.7	1746.5	**VT-NH** border, Connecticut River	380
442.1	1747.1	**Hanover, NH,** Dartmouth College ... N43 42.391 W72 16.656 P (pg.178-179) NoBo: turn east on SR 10.	527
441.4	1747.8	NH 120, trailhead near convenience store.	520
440.7	1748.5	**Velvet Rocks Shelter** (0.2W) 27.7◄16.1◄7.3◄►9.5►15.2►21.9	925
440.1	1749.1	Spring on northern access to shelter. North shelter loop trail (0.2W)	974
438.4	1750.8	Pond, boardwalk	809
437.7	1751.5	Trescott Rd (paved).	940
436.4	1752.8	Footbridge, stream (2)	852
436.3	1752.9	Etna-Hanover Center Rd (paved), **Etna, NH** (0.8E) (pg.179) Cell phone reception at cemetery to west	845
433.8	1755.4	Three Mile Rd (gravel) N43 43.077 W72 10.559 P	1416
433.6	1755.6	Mink Brook, footbridge	1347
432.0	1757.2	Moose Mountain south peak.	2290
431.2	1758.0	**Moose Mountain Shelter** (0.1E) 25.6◄16.8◄9.5◄►5.7►12.4 17.7 Loop trail to shelter, water at AT and northern leg intersection, tenting on northern leg of loop.	2131
429.9	1759.3	Moose Mountain north peak	2315
428.4	1760.8	South fork of Hewes Brook.	1059
428.2	1761.0	Goose Pond Rd (paved)	963
426.1	1763.1	Holts Ledge, precipitous drop-off, views	1937

✖ **Cattail** – A tall (head-high) plant that grows in swampy areas. Characteristic part of the plant looks like a fuzzy cigar impaled lengthwise on a spear.

SoBo	NoBo		Elev
425.5	1763.7	**Trapper John Shelter** (0.2W), priv behind shelter 0.1 mile. . . . ☽ ◆ ◀ ⌐ (6)	1517
424.6	1764.6	22.5◄15.2◄5.7▼◀6.7▲12.0►27.7	880
		Grafton Turnpike(paved), Dorchester Rd . . . . N43 47.400 W72 6.000 **P** ◆(pg.182)	
		Lyme Center, NH (1.3W), **Lyme, NH** (3.2W) ⚠ Nobo east on wedge of land	
		between fork in road, side trail to Bill Ackerly home 0.1 north of intersection.	
423.2	1766.0	Grant Brook	1212
422.9	1766.3	Concrete milepost	1128
422.6	1766.6	Lyme-Dorchester Rd (gravel) N43 47.400 W72 6.176	1110
420.9	1768.3	Lamberts Ridge	2361
419.4	1769.8	Smarts Ranger Trail to east	2729
418.9	1770.3	Campsite, weak spring to east, fire tower north of camp, west of AT . . . Å △ ◀	3246
418.8	1770.4	Smarts Mountain, **Fire Wardens Cabin** . . . . . ☽ △ ◀ ⌐ (12)	3237
		21.9◄12.4◄6.7▼◀5.3▲21.0►27.9 Shelter is cabin north of summit,	
		west of AT. Spring 0.2 in front of cabin. Clark Pond Loop Trail to east.	
414.9	1774.3	South Jacobs Brook . . . . ◆	1450
414.3	1774.9	Eastman Ledges	1899
413.9	1775.3	North Jacobs Brook . . . . . . ◆	1936
413.5	1775.7	**Hexacuba Shelter** (0.3E) 17.7◄12.0◄5.3▲15.7►22.6►31.6 ☽ △ ◀ (8)	2071
		Shelter on steep side trail, unreliable stream at intersection with side trail.	
411.9	1777.3	Mt Cube south peak, cross Rivendell Trail to west	2911
411.8	1777.4	Side trail 0.3W to Mt Cube north peak	2881
410.2	1779.0	Brackett Brook . . . . ◆	1472
409.3	1779.9	Stream . . . . ◆	1298
409.1	1780.1	Woods road . . . . . . ◆	1197
408.5	1780.7	NH 25A (paved) Nobo east on road 300 yards N43 54.078 W71 59.029 **P** (pg.186)	915
		Wentworth, NH (4.8E)	
406.7	1782.5	Cape Moonshine Rd (gravel) . . . . N43 54.950 W71 57.876 **P** (pg.186)	1432
		AT northbound joins Ore Hill Trail.	
406.0	1783.2	Ore Hill Campsite (shelter destroyed by fire in 2011) . . . . ☽ △ ◀	1883
		Muddy spring 100 yards downhill from tentsites.	

1764.6   Grafton Turnpike, Dorchester Rd, Dartmouth Skiway

◆) **Bill Ackerly** Welcomes hiker visits. Help yourself to water, rest, chat and play a game of croquet. Porta-potty on-site. Ask about camping. ✖ What does Bill have in his left hand?

Lyme Center, NH 03769 (1.3W)

⌂ M–F 8–10, Sa 8–11:30, 603.795.4037

Lyme, NH 03768 (3.2W)

⌂ M–F 7:45–12 & 1:30–5:15, Sa 7:45–12, 603.795.4421

⫲ ☎ **Stella's Italian Kitchen & Market** 603.795.4302 ⟨www.stellaslyme.com⟩, M-Th 10-9, F-Sa 10-10, Su closed.

🛏☎🖵 **Dowd's Country Inn B&B** 9 Main Street, Lyme, NH, 603.795.4712 ⟨www.dowdscountryinn.com⟩ Call in advance and let them know you are a hiker. Pickup/return available. Rates fluctuate; starting at $85S, $100D mid week, $125S, $140D weekends through Sep 20, Includes full breakfast, afternoon tea and NH taxes. Pets allowed in some rooms with surcharge.

⫲⫲☎ **Lyme Country Store** (3.3W) ice cream, produce, deli, 7 days.

🐾 **Lyme Veterinary Hospital** (2.8W) bear right onto High St and hospital is 50 yards up on the left, 603.795.2747.

Appalachian Mountain Club (AMC) 603.466.2727 ⟨www.outdoors.org⟩ Maintains the AT from Kinsman Notch, NH to Grafton Notch, ME and operates 8 huts with space for 30-90 people. There is no road access, heat, or showers. Huts use alternative energy sources and composting toilets. Huts are closed in the winter. In the spring & fall huts are open to "self-serve" use (member/nonmember rates: $26/$31 Su-F; $40/$49 Sa. See White Mtn map for dates. "Full serve" season includes bunk, dinner & breakfast, starting at $125PP for non-members. Reservations recommended and can be made by phone or with any AMC caretaker. Work-for-stay is available to the first 2 thru-hikers to arrive, no reservations. WFS hikers get floor space for sleeping, feast on leftovers, and are typically asked to work 2 hours after breakfast. Lakes of the Clouds Hut has 4 WFS spots and a $10 thru-hiker only bunkroom called "The Dungeon". Don't count on hut stays without reservations, and camping is not allowed near huts, except at Nauman Tentsite. No pets inside huts. Limit WFS to 3 nights in the Whites to give other hikers the opportunity.

🚌 **AMC Hiker Shuttle** (see pg. 187)

White Mountain National Forest (the "Whites")

Passage through the Whites should be planned carefully. It is one of the more heavily visited sections of the AT, and campsites are limited. The trail is rugged, so your pace may be slowed. Weather is dynamic, adding to the dangers of hiking on stretches of trail above treeline.

Take adequate cold-weather gear, check weather reports, carry maps, and know your options for overnighting. The AMC and Randolph Mountain Club (RMC) maintain camps, which are detailed in the following pages. Most have fees. Have cash on hand even if you do not plan to use them; your plans may change.

There are many trails in the Whites. The AT is the only white-blazed trail, but blazes are scant. There are no blazes in the Great Gulf Wilderness Area. The AT is always coincident with another named trail, and the other trail name may be the one you see on signs. Wherever the AT changes from one trail to another, this book uses the notation: "AT: Town Line Tr◄►Glencilff Tr." This means that the AT to the south of this point is coincident with the Town Line Trail; to the north, the AT joins the Glencliff Trail.

The area within a quarter mile of all AMC and RMC facilities and everything above treeline (trees 8' or less) are part of the Forest Protection Area (FPA). Trails are often marked where they enter or leave the FPA. Do not camp within a FPA, and camp at least 200' from water and trails. Rocks aligned to form a trail boundary (scree walls) are an indication that you should not leave the treadway. Doing so damages fragile plant life.

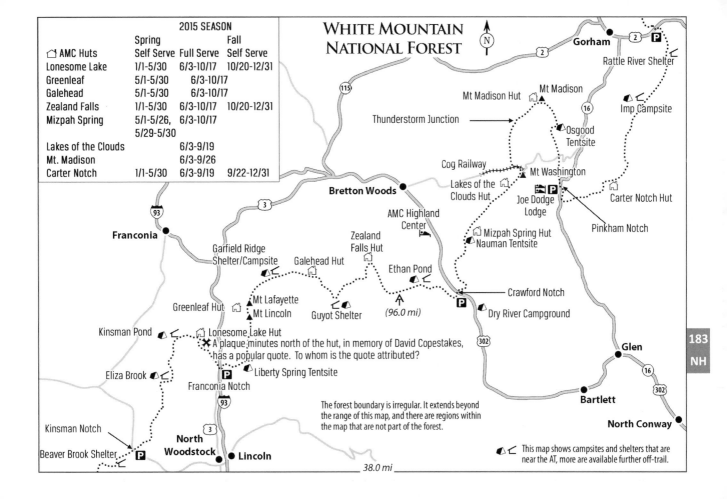

WHITE MOUNTAIN NATIONAL FOREST

N

2015 SEASON

AMC Huts	Spring Self Serve	Full Serve	Fall Self Serve
Lonesome Lake	1/1-5/30	6/3-10/17	10/20-12/31
Greenleaf	5/1-5/30	6/3-10/17	
Galehead	5/1-5/30	6/3-10/17	
Zealand Falls	1/1-5/30	6/3-10/17	10/20-12/31
Mizpah Spring	5/1-5/26, 5/29-5/30	6/3-10/17	
Lakes of the Clouds		6/3-9/19	
Mt. Madison		6/3-9/26	
Carter Notch	1/1-5/30	6/3-9/19	9/22-12/31

Gorham

Rattle River Shelter

Mt Madison Hut

Mt Madison

Thunderstorm Junction

Osgood Tentsite

Imp Campsite

Cog Railway

Mt Washington

Lakes of the Clouds Hut

Joe Dodge Lodge

Carter Notch Hut

Pinkham Notch

Bretton Woods

AMC Highland Center

Mizpah Spring Hut
Nauman Tentsite

Franconia

Garfield Ridge Shelter/Campsite

Zealand Falls Hut

Galehead Hut

Ethan Pond

Crawford Notch

Greenleaf Hut

Mt Lafayette

Mt Lincoln

Guyot Shelter

(96.0 mi)

Dry River Campground

Kinsman Pond

Lonesome Lake Hut

Glen

✖ A plaque minutes north of the hut, in memory of David Copestakes, has a popular quote. To whom is the quote attributed?

Eliza Brook

Liberty Spring Tentsite

Bartlett

Franconia Notch

Kinsman Notch

North Conway

Beaver Brook Shelter

North Woodstock

Lincoln

The forest boundary is irregular. It extends beyond the range of this map, and there are regions within the map that are not part of the forest.

This map shows campsites and shelters that are near the AT, more are available further off-trail.

38.0 mi

Elev		
1828		
1543	(pg.186)	
2200		
1874		
1683		
1055	(pg.186-187)	
1330		
1352		
1367		
1527		
1692		
2529		
3056		
4802		
4628		
4075		
3749		
1884		
1870	(pg.187-188)	
2664		
2689		

⚠ The notation "AT: Ore Hill Tr ▼►Wachipauka Pond Tr" indicates that the AT to the south is coincident with the Ore Hill Tr; the AT to the north joins the Wachipauka Pond Tr.

SoBo	NoBo	
404.0	1785.2	Ore Hill.
403.3	1785.9	Lake Tarleton Rd, NH 25C, **Warren, NH** (4E) N43 57.220 W71 56.690 🅿 (pg.186) ◆
		AT on road past parking area & power lines, Ore Hill Brook north of road.
401.3	1787.9	Mt Mist
400.9	1788.3	View
400.7	1788.5	Webster Slide Trail 0.7W to summit, view
398.7	1790.5	NH 25, Oliverian Brook north of road. N43 59.395 W71 53.971 🅿 (pg.186-187)
		AT: Ore Hill Tr ▼►Wachipauka Pond Tr, **Glencliff, NH** (0.3E), **Warren, NH** (5.0E)
397.8	1791.4	**Jeffers Brook Shelter**, Jeffers Brook, footbridge 0.1 south) ◆ ⊆ (10)
		27.7◄21.0◄15.7▶6.9▶15.9▶19.9
397.7	1791.5	Long Pond Rd ⚠ NoBo 0.1E on road AT: Wachipauka Pond Tr ▼►Town Line Tr.
397.5	1791.7	High St (paved) ⚠ NoBo: 0.2W on road. AT: Town Line Trail ▼►Glencliff Trail
397.2	1792.0	Stream.
396.9	1792.3	Hurricane Trail to east
396.0	1793.2	Stream.
395.5	1793.7	Spring
393.2	1796.0	Mt Moosilauke, Gorge Brook Trail to east
392.8	1796.4	AT: Glencliff Trail ▼►Beaver Brook Trail, Benton Trail to west
391.3	1797.9	Ridge Trail to east
390.9	1798.3	**Beaver Brook Shelter** 27.9◄22.6◄6.9▶9.0▶13.0▶28.1) ◆ ⌂ ⊆ (10)
		Shelter on Beaver Brook trail. Beaver Brook on way to shelter.
389.6	1799.6	Beaver Brook, footbridges, streams
389.4	1799.8	Lost River Rd, NH 112, Kinsman Notch. N44 2.389 W71 47.525 🅿 (pg.187-188)
		North Woodstock, NH (5.0E), **Lincoln, NH** (6.0E)
388.7	1800.5	AT: Beaver Brook Trail ▼►Kinsman Ridge Trail
		Dilly Cliff Trail to east.
386.1	1803.1	Gordon Pond Trail to east

SoBo	NoBo	Description	Elev
384.8	**1804.4**	Mt Wolf east peak, summit to west	3478
382.9	**1806.3**	Reel Brook Trail to west.	2640
382.5	**1806.7**	Powerline	2616
381.9	**1807.3**	**Eliza Brook Shelter** 31.6◄15.9◄9.0◄▶4.0▶19.1▶24.6. (8)	2408
		3 single tentpads, one double. Water source is brook.	
381.1	**1808.1**	Eliza Brook, parallel to AT for 0.8 mi	2880
380.5	**1808.7**	Harrington Pond	3430
379.4	**1809.8**	South Kinsman Mountain	4358
378.5	**1810.7**	North Kinsman Mountain	4293
378.0	**1811.2**	Mt Kinsman Trail to west.	3856
377.9	**1811.3**	**Kinsman Pond Shelter** 19.9◄13.0◄4.0◄▶15.1▶20.6▶29.6. (16)	3763
		Caretaker, fee $8PP. Treat pond water. Kinsman Ridge Tr to west, Kinsman Pond	
		Tr to east. AT: Kinsman Ridge Trail ◄▶ Fishin' Jimmy Trail	
377.0	**1812.2**	Stream.	2838
376.1	**1813.1**	Lonesome Lake Hut. (see AMC notes, pg.182-183)	2764
		AT: Fishin' Jimmy Tr ◄▶ Cascade Brook Tr (east), many other trail intersections	
375.1	**1814.1**	Kinsman Pond Trail to east.	2328
374.6	**1814.6**	Cascade Brook	2116
373.6	**1815.6**	Whitehouse Brook	1658
373.3	**1815.9**	US 3, I-93, AT underpass. Town east on US 3; better to take side trail (next entry)	1487
373.1	**1816.1**	Franconia Notch N44 6.014 W71 40.952 🅿 (pg.188-189)	1443
		Paved trail (1.0E) to Liberty Springs trailhead parking. **North Woodstock, NH**	
		(4.8S) left from parking area on US 3. **Lincoln, NH** (1.0E) of North Woodstock.	
		AT: Cascade Brook Trail ◄▶ Liberty Springs Trail	
372.4	**1816.8**	Flume side trail to east.	1852
371.9	**1817.3**	Streams.	2082
370.4	**1818.8**	Liberty Spring Campsite	3910
		Overnight fee $8PP, caretaker, 7S and 3D platforms.	
370.2	**1819.0**	AT: Liberty Springs Tr ◄▶ Franconia Ridge Tr to west	4291
368.4	**1820.8**	Little Haystack Mountain, Falling Waters Trail to west	4800
		NoBo: AT above treeline for next 2.0 miles.	
367.7	**1821.5**	Mt Lincoln, Franconia Ridge	5089
366.7	**1822.5**	Mt Lafayette, Greenleaf Hut (0.2W) (1.1W)	5291
		Greenleaf Hut visible from summit of Mt Lafayette. Located down steep Greenleaf	
		Trail. AT: Franconia Ridge Trail ◄▶ Garfield Ridge Trail	
365.9	**1823.3**	Skookumchuck Trail to west	4779

1780.7   NH 25A, Gov. Meldrim Thomson Scenic Hwy

◣ **Mt Cube Sugar Farm** (1.9W) 603.353.4709 Owned by the Thomson family, for whom the road is named. Store is not manned, but caretaker makes frequent stops. Hikers may tent outside or may be allowed to stay in the sugar house. Sometimes more is offered.

Wentworth, NH 03282 (4.3E on NH 25A, then right 0.5 on NH 25)

⌂ M–F 7-11 & 2:45-4:45, Sa 7:15-12, 603.764.9444

🛒☎ **Shawnee's General Store** 603.764.5553.

1782.5   Cape Moonshine Rd

◣💦 **Dancing Bones Intentional Community** (1.4E) Hot outdoor showers, open-air kitchen, tenting, composting toilets and good conversation.   This is a residential community, so please be respectful when using shared facilities. Smoking is permitted in designated areas. Pets are welcome on a case by case basis.

1785.9   Lake Tarleton Rd, NH 25C
Warren, NH 03279 (4E)

⌂ M-F 7:30-9:30 & 3-5, Sa 7:30-12, 603.764.5733

🍴 **Calamity Jane's Restaurant** 603.764.5288, B/L Tu-Th, B/L/D F-Sa

🍴 **Greenhouse Food & Spirits** 603.764.5708 Th,F 3-11pm, Sa 3-10, Su 3-8pm. Open mic Thursdays, band on Fridays.

🛒 **Tedeschi Food Shop** 603.764.9002 Open 7 days 5am-11pm. Grocery with produce, deli with sandwiches & pizza, deli closes 9pm M-Sa, 7pm Su.

⛉ **Laundry** M-Su 8:30-8:30

💻🛜 **Library** 603.764.9072 M-Tu 10-2, W 3-7, Sa 10-1. No WiFi password so you can use it after hours.

🔧 **Burning Bush Hardware**

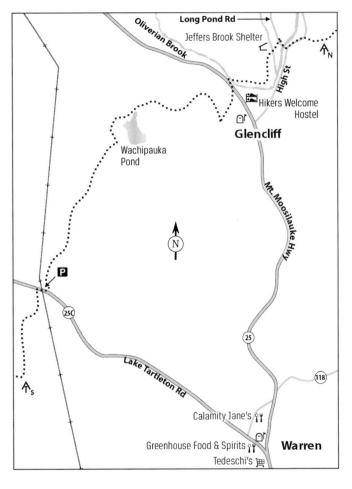

1790.5   NH 25   **Glencliff, NH 03238** (0.3E)

M-F 12-2, Sa 7-1, 603.989.5154

Hikers Welcome Hostel 603.989.0040
Bunk ($20) and camping ($15) includes shower. Shower only w/towel $2.50, laundry $2.50 wash, $2.50 dry. Snacks, sodas, and ice cream. All hikers (even non-guests) are welcome to hang out and enjoy huge DVD library. Slackpacking & shuttles (5 miles to resupply in Warren). Coleman/alcohol/oz. Tools to help with gear repair, and selection of used gear available, particularly winter wear. Pet Friendly. Both guests and non-guests are welcome to send maildrops (USPS/FedEx/UPS): c/o Hikers Welcome Hostel, 1396 NH Rt 25, PO Box 25, Glencliff, NH 03238

Warren, NH (5E) see entry pg. 186

1799.8   Lost River Rd, NH 112, Kinsman Notch

Lost River Gorge (0.5E) 603.745.8031 Tourist attraction featuring a boulder jumble similar to Mahoosuc Notch. Gift store with microwavable food (and microwave), snacks, coffee, soda. Open early May - late Oct.

Lost River Valley Campground (3.0E) 603.745.8321, 800.370.5678 ⟨www.lostriver.com⟩ cabin $59S, 69D, camping primitive sites $20, pets allowed but not in cabins. Showers, coin laundry, pay phone, open mid-May to Columbus Day 8-9, quiet 10pm-8am, owner Jim Kelly. Maildrops: 951 Lost River Rd, North Woodstock, NH 03262.

(16E) **Wise Way Wellness Center** 603.726.7600 $65 for 1 or 2 persons in cabin, includes light breakfast. $10PP for pickup and return from Franconia Notch, Kinsman Notch, North Woodstock, or Lincoln. Cabin is 10 miles south of Lincoln in Thornton, NH. This is a serene rustic cabin with no TV or phone. Bathroom and shower inside adjacent building and outdoor bathtub. Amenities include WiFi, pool, sauna, mini-fridge and grill. Epson salt bath available. Licensed Massage Therapist on-site $35/30 min.

North Woodstock, NH (5E), **Lincoln, NH** (6E)
(See pg. 188-189)

Randolph Mountain Club (RMC)

Maintains the section of the AT from Edmands Col to Madison Hut and four shelters in the Northern Presidentials. Per-person fees for non-members: Gray Knob or Crag Camp $20, The Perch or Log Cabin $10. Fees must be paid in cash for stays at Gray Knob, Crag Camp and The Perch. Persons without cash can stay at the Log Cabin and will receive a receipt to mail in their fee. There is a caretaker year-round at Gray Knob if you need assistance or have questions. During the summer months, a second caretaker is in residence at Crag Camp. A caretaker visits Crag Camp and The Perch every evening throughout the year.

Shelter use is first-come, first-served; no reservations. Weekends are busy. If space is not available, be prepared to camp. Camping is not permitted within a quarter mile of RMC shelters.

There is no trash disposal. Carry in, carry out. Please keep noise to a minimum after 10pm. The use of cell phones and portable TVs is not permitted. Group size is limited to ten. There is no smoking inside RMC facilities. When a camp is full, all guests are asked to limit their stay to two consecutive nights. Outdoor wood campfires are not allowed at any of the camps. Dogs are allowed at RMC's facilities, but they should be under voice control at all times.

AMC Hiker Shuttle 603.466.2727 Schedule on-line: ⟨www.outdoors.org/lodging/lodging-shuttle.cfm⟩ Operates June - mid Sept daily, and weekends and holidays through mid Oct. Stops at Lincoln, Franconia Notch (Liberty Springs Trailhead), Crawford Notch (Webster Cliff Trailhead), Highland Center, Pinkham Notch, and Gorham; $23 for non-members. Walk-ons if space available.

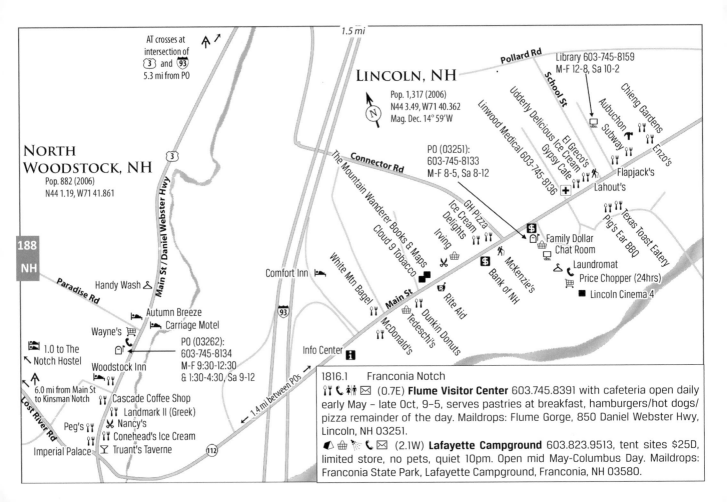

AT crosses at intersection of ③ and ⑨③ 5.3 mi from PO

1.5 mi

Pollard Rd

LINCOLN, NH

Pop. 1,317 (2006)
N44 3.49, W71 40.362
Mag. Dec. 14° 59'W

Library 603-745-8159
M-F 12-8, Sa 10-2

School St

Chieng Gardens

Aubuchon

Subway

Enzo's

Udderly Delicious Ice Cream

Linwood Medical 603-745-8136

El Greco's
Gypsy Cafe

Flapjack's

Lahout's

PO (03251):
603-745-8133
M-F 8-5, Sa 8-12

NORTH WOODSTOCK, NH

Pop. 882 (2006)
N44 1.19, W71 41.861

Connector Rd

③

The Mountain Wanderer Books & Maps

GH Pizza
Ice Cream
Delights

Irving

Family Dollar
Chat Room

Texas Toast Eatery
Pig's Ear BBQ

McKenzie's

Laundromat
Price Chopper (24hrs)

Cloud 9 Tobacco

Bank of NH

Lincoln Cinema 4

Paradise Rd

Handy Wash

Comfort Inn

White Mtn Bagel

Main St

Rite Aid

Wayne's

Autumn Breeze
Carriage Motel

Woodstock Inn

PO (03262):
603-745-8134
M-F 9:30-12:30
& 1:30-4:30, Sa 9-12

McDonald's

Dunkin Donuts
Tedeschi's

Info Center

1.0 to The
Notch Hostel

6.0 mi from Main St
to Kinsman Notch

Lost River Rd

Cascade Coffee Shop

Landmark II (Greek)

Nancy's

Peg's

Conehead's Ice Cream

Truant's Taverne

Imperial Palace

⑪②

1.4 mi between POs

1816.1   Franconia Notch

⑪📞🚹🚺✉ (0.7E) **Flume Visitor Center** 603.745.8391 with cafeteria open daily early May – late Oct, 9–5, serves pastries at breakfast, hamburgers/hot dogs/pizza remainder of the day. Maildrops: Flume Gorge, 850 Daniel Webster Hwy, Lincoln, NH 03251.

🔥🏠🚿📞✉ (2.1W) **Lafayette Campground** 603.823.9513, tent sites $25D, limited store, no pets, quiet 10pm. Open mid May-Columbus Day. Maildrops: Franconia State Park, Lafayette Campground, Franconia, NH 03580.

📶🛜✉ (1.2E) **Profile Motel & Cottages** 603.745.2759 ⟨www.profilemotel.com⟩ $49-$89, fridge & microwave in room, grills & tables outside, open 7am-10pm, closed Nov-Mar. Maildrops: 391 US 3, Lincoln, NH 03251.

📶⛺🛜✉ (3.0E) **Mt. Liberty Motel** 603.745.3600 ⟨MtLibertyMotel.com⟩ $85 or less includes pickup/return from Kinsman or Franconia Notch when available and town shuttle. No pets. Closed Nov-Apr. Maildrops: 10 Liberty Road, PO Box 422, Lincoln, NH 03251.

🚐 **AMC Hiker Shuttle** (pg. 187)

🚐⛺ **The Shuttle Connection** 603.745.3140 ⟨www.shuttleconnection.com⟩ Shuttles between town & Kinsman or Franconia Notch or to bus terminals and airports ranging from Portland, ME to NY. Can handle large groups.

🚐 **Notch Taxi Service** 603.991.8777, Reservations recommended, runs 7 days.

North Woodstock, NH (4.8S of Franconia Notch)

📶🍴⛺🚐🛜💻✉ **The Notch Hostel** 603.348.1483 ⟨www.notchhostel.com⟩ Opens July 15, 2015. Bunk in large farmhouse on Lost River Rd. 1.0W of North Woodstock. Ideally situated for slackpack between Kinsman and Franconia Notch. $30pp includes bunk, fresh linens, towel, shower, laundry service, 12oz denatured alcohol, coffee/tea. Overflow tenting available for $20pp. Basic breakfast $5. Pizza, ice cream & some supplies sold on site. WiFi, computer & printer, sauna, kitchen, large yard. Pick up from town (Lincoln or North Woodstock). Return to Kinsman Notch or Franconia Notch. Bikes available for town trips. Dogs allowed to stay outside. No liquor; beer & wine in moderation. Maildrops: c/o The Notch Hostel, 324 Lost River Rd, North Woodstock, NH 03262.

📶🍴🛜 **Woodstock Inn** 603.745.3951, 800.321.3985 ⟨www.woodstockinnnh.com⟩ 10% discount for thru-hikers, prices seasonal, stay includes full breakfast. No pets. **Woodstock Station** restaurant, outdoor bar, and a micro-brewery on-site.

📶🛜 **Autumn Breeze** 603.745.8549 ⟨www.autumnbreezemotel.com⟩ summer rates $75-90, rooms have kitchenettes, no pets.

📶🛜✉ **The Carriage Motel** 603.745.2416 ⟨www.carriagemotel.com⟩ $72/up, no pets, game room, pool, gas grills. Closed in winter. Maildrops ($5 non-guest fee): 180 Main Street, North Woodstock, NH 03262.

🏪🍴💲 **Wayne's Market** Deli, ATM, 99¢ sandwiches, large beer selection.

🛖 **Fadden's General Store** ice cream, fudge and more.

Lincoln, NH (5.8S of Franconia Notch)

📶 **Wise Way Wellness Center** 10S of Lincoln, see listing pg. 187.

🚶 **Lahout's Summit Shop** ⟨www.lahouts.com⟩ 603.745.2882 M-F 9:30-5:30, Sa 9-5:30, Su 9-5, full service outfitter, packs, Coleman/alcohol/oz, canister fuel, freeze-dried foods.

🖥 **Chat Room/Books** M-Th 10-6, F-Sa 10-8.

■ **Mountain Wanderer** 603.745.2594 Book and map store has everything you need to navigate the Whites.

Franconia, NH 03580 (11W of Franconia notch)

🏤 M-F 8:30-1 & 2-5, Sa 9-12, 603.823.5611

📶⛺🚐🛜💻✉ **Gale River Motel** 603.823.5655, 800.255.7989 ⟨www.galerivermotel.com⟩ $50–$200, pets with approval, laundry wash $1, dry $1, Coleman/oz. Free pickup/return to trail with stay, longer shuttles for a fee, open year-round. Maildrops (fee for non-guest): 1 Main Street, Franconia, NH 03580.

🏪 **Mac's Market**

🛖🍴 **Franconia Village Store** deli

🖥 **Abbie Greenleaf Library**

Littleton, NH (17W)

🚶🛜 **Badass Outdoors Gear Shop** 603.444.9445 Full service outfitter 17 miles west (compass north) from Franconia Notch. Thru-hiker discount. Hiker food, canister fuel. Open Tu-Th 11-5, F-Sa 10-6, Su 11-5. Sometimes rides are available.

190 NH

SoBo	NoBo	Feature	Elev
363.6	1825.6	Garfield Pond	3995
363.2	1826.0	Mt Garfield	4500
363.0	1826.2	Garfield Trail to west	4317
362.8	1826.4	**Garfield Ridge Shelter/Campsite** (0.2W), reliable water ☾♦◭ (7) ⊾ (12) Overnight fee $8PP, caretaker. 28.1◀19.1◀15.1▶5.5▶14.5▶56.5	3951
362.3	1826.9	Franconia Brook Trail to east goes steeply down 2.2mi to 13 Falls Campsite.	3451
360.7	1828.5	Gale River Trail to west	3425
360.1	1829.1	Frost Trail to Galehead Hut ☾ AT: Garfield Ridge Trail ▼ ▶ Twinway Trail	3800
359.3	1829.9	South Twin Mountain, North Twin Spur Trail to west	4902
357.3	1831.9	**Guyot Shelter** 0.7E on Bondcliff Tr, plus 0.3 left on spur trail. ☾♦◭ (6) ⊾ (14) Overnight fee $8PP, caretaker, 24.6◀20.6◀5.5▶9.0▶51.0▶57.1	4534
357.2	1832.0	Mt. Guyot, view to east. 🔄	4597
356.2	1833.0	Trail west to summit of Zeacliff Ridge	4056
354.9	1834.3	Zeacliff Pond to east	3807
354.7	1834.5	Zeacliff, Zeacliff Trail to east	3774
354.3	1834.9	View to east. 🔄	3681
353.8	1835.4	Whitewall Brook, many streams leading to falls	3213
353.4	1835.8	Lend-A-Hand Trail to west	2686
353.3	1835.9	Zealand Falls Hut, next to falls ♦☾ 🔄	2635
353.0	1836.2	Ethan Pond Trail to west, AT: Twinway Trail ▼ ▶ Ethan Pond Trail	2481
351.6	1837.6	Zeacliff Trail to east.	2461
350.8	1838.4	Stream, Thoreau Falls to east ♦	2483
350.6	1838.6	Footbridge, stream ♦	2483
350.3	1838.9	Stream, Shoal Pond Trail to east ♦	2528
349.6	1839.6	Footbridge, stream	2644
348.3	1840.9	**Ethan Pond Campsite** (0.2W), Ethan Pond, inlet brook to pond ☾♦◭⊾ (8) Overnight fee $8PP, caretaker, 3S and 2D platforms. 29.6◀14.5◀9.0▶42.0▶48.1▶61.8	2874
347.2	1842.0	Willey Range Trail to west, stream north on AT ♦	2632
347.0	1842.2	Kedron Flume Trail to west.	2465
345.9	1843.3	Ripley Falls 0.5E	1561
345.7	1843.5	RR tracks, parking, AT: Ethan Pond Trail ▼ ▶ road walk. N44 10.627 W71 23.167 🅿 AT follows paved parking driveway 0.3 to US 302.	1438
345.4	1843.8	Crawford Notch, US 302. AT: road walk ▶ Webster Cliff Trail (pg.192)	1277
345.3	1843.9	Saco River (treat), Saco River Trail to east, Sam Willey Trail to west. ♦	1263

SoBo	NoBo		Elev
344.6	1844.6	Stream.	◊ 1949
343.0	1846.2	Webster Cliffs, views from many spots along 0.5 mile traverse.	📷 3345
342.1	1847.1	Mt Webster, Webster Jackson Trail to west, NoBo: AT to east	📷 3910
340.7	1848.5	Mt Jackson, Webster Jackson Trail to west	📷 4052
339.0	1850.2	Mizpah cutoff to west, Mizpah Spring Hut to east, Nauman Campsite Tent site next to hut, overnight fee $8PP.	▲🏠♥ 3800
338.2	1851.0	Mt Pierce (Mt Clinton)	📷 4312
338.1	1851.1	AT: Webster Cliff Trail ◆▶ Crawford Path	4262
336.8	1852.4	Mt Eisenhower Loop Trail west to summit.	📷 4506
336.2	1853.0	Mt Eisenhower Loop Trail west to summit.	📷 4541
336.0	1853.2	Mt Eisenhower Trail to east	4582
335.4	1853.8	Mt Franklin	📷 5004
334.9	1854.3	Mt Monroe Loop Trail west to summit	📷 5163
334.3	1854.9	Mt Monroe Loop Trail west to summit	📷 5157
334.2	1855.0	Lakes of the Clouds Hut	♥🏠🔌 (pg.192) 5106
		Four trails intersect near hut. AT stays on Crawford Path.	
333.5	1855.7	Davis Path to east, Westside Trail to west.	⚠️ see map pg.193) 5617
333.0	1856.2	AT: Crawford Path ◆▶ Trinity Heights Connector	6216
332.9	1856.3	Mt Washington.	📷 (pg.192-193) 6288
332.7	1856.5	AT: Trinity Heights Connector ◆▶ Gulfside Trail	6100
332.5	1856.7	Cross Cog Railroad, stay west on Gulfside Trail.	5921
332.0	1857.2	Westside Trail to west	5476
331.7	1857.5	Mt Clay Loop Trail to east.	5402
331.2	1858.0	Mt Clay Loop Trail to east, Sphinx Trail to east	5189
330.2	1859.0	Mt Jefferson Loop Trail, summit 0.3W	📷 5315
329.8	1859.4	Six Husband Trail 0.4W to Mt Jefferson	📷 5232
329.4	1859.8	Edmands Col, Gulfside Spring 50 yards east.	4938
		Edmands Col cutoff to east, Randolph Path & Mt Jefferson loop to west.	
328.7	1860.5	Israel Ridge Path to RMC Perch Shelter (0.9W), $7 fee	♥▲ (4) ⊆ (8) 5222
328.1	1861.1	Thunderstorm Junction, RMC cabins to west.	(pg.192) 5500
327.5	1861.7	Airline Trail, King Ravine Trail to west	5149
327.2	1862.0	Madison Spring Hut, Valley Way Trail 0.6W to VW Tent Site, no fee	♥🏠▲ 4800
		AT: Gulfside Trail ◆▶ Osgood Trail	
326.7	1862.5	Mt Madison, Watson Path to west.	📷 5366
326.4	1862.8	Howker Ridge Trail to east	5116
326.1	1863.1	Parapet Trail to east, Daniel Webster Trail to west	4877

⚠️ There are no blazes in the Great Gulf Wilderness area, approx. Mt. Madison to Auto Rd.

191

NH

SoBo	NoBo	

1843.8 Crawford Notch, US 302

🍴📞 (1W) **Willey House** 603.374.0999 Snack bar open 9:30-5, 7 days, weekend before Memorial Day - weekend after Columbus Day.

◣ ⚬ ⛺ (1.8E) **Dry River Campground** 603.374.2272 ⟨www.nhstateparks.com/crawford.html⟩ Tent sites $25 for 2 adults and up to 4 children. Pets allowed, coin laundry & showers, ask about shuttles, quiet 10pm-8am. Open May-3rd week of Oct.

🛏️📷🍴🚿⚬🚌🖂 (3.5W) **AMC Highland Center** 603.278.4453 ⟨www.outdoors.org⟩ Lodge $106PP/up includes dinner & breakfast. Shapleigh Bunkhouse $81 with dinner & breakfast, $54 with B only. Rates lower for AMC members. No pets, no smoking. Coin shower for non-guests. AMC Shuttle stops daily mid-Jun to Columbus Day, afterwards only weekends and holidays. Restaurant open to all for B/L/D. Store sells snacks, sodas, some clothing and canister fuel. Maildrops: Route 302, Bretton Woods, NH 03574.

🛏️◣🚿 (E3.3) **Crawford Notch General Store & Campground** 603.374.2779 ⟨www.crawfordnotch.com⟩ Cabins $75-95, tent sites (hold 2 tents) $30. 9% lodging tax. Store carries hiker foods, ice cream and beer. Open mid May - mid Oct.

🚐 **Notch Taxi Service** 603.991.8777 Covers northern NH.

🚐 **AMC Hiker Shuttle** (pg. 187)

Bretton Woods, NH (8.0W)

🍴 **Faybans Station**

🚿 **Bretton Woods Station** 603.278.5055 convenience store, M-F 6-8, S,Su 6-9, open later in mid-summer.

🧍 **Drummonds Mountain Shop** 603.278.7547 Boots, packs, rain gear, hiking foods, stoves and fuel.

Bartlett, NH (13.0E from Crawford Notch)
Resort town has unique mountain roller coaster and water slide at **Attitash Resort** 800.223.7669 ⟨www.attitash.com⟩.

1855.0 Lakes of the Clouds Hut

🛏️📷◣) Lodging and WFS (see AMC notes, pg. 182). Also "The Dungeon," a bunkroom available to 6 thru-hikers for $10PP with access to hut restroom and the common area. When the hut is closed, The Dungeon serves as an emergency shelter.

1856.3 Mt Washington, NH

🏤 (03589) M-S 10-4 For outgoing mail; please do not send maildrops. 🍴🚿🧍📞 Second highest peak on the AT. **Summit House** open 8am-8pm Memorial Day-Columbus Day. Snack bar open 9am-6pm.

🚂 **Cog Railway** 603.278.5404 ⟨www.thecog.com⟩ Runs hourly Apr-Nov. One-way tickets $45 (if space-available) sold at summit station. Base station 3 miles away near Bretton Woods, NH.

1861.1 Thunderstorm Junction

🛏️ **Crag Camp Cabin** (1.1W) on Spur Trail, **Gray Knob Cabin** (1.2W) on Lowe Path; $20 fee for either. If you camp along these side trails, it must be at least 0.25mi. from either cabin.

1865.1 - 1866.3 Map of trail intersections

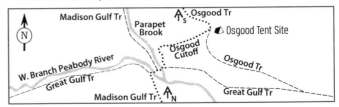

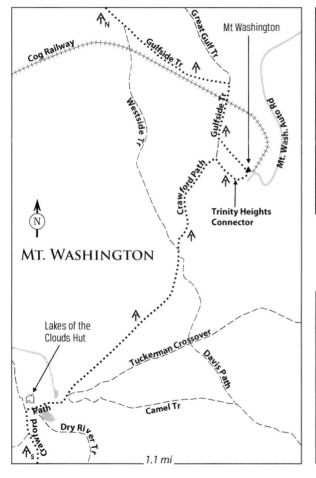

MT. WASHINGTON

Cog Railway
Gulfside Tr.
Great Gulf Tr.
Mt Washington
Westside Tr.
Gulfside Tr.
Crawford Path
Mt. Wash. Auto Rd.
Trinity Heights Connector
N
Lakes of the Clouds Hut
Tuckerman Crossover
Davis Path
Path
Camel Tr.
Crawford Path
Dry River Tr.
S
1.1 mi

American Hiking Society

Founded in 1976, American Hiking Society is the only national organization dedicated to promoting and protecting America's hiking trails, their surrounding natural areas and the hiking experience.

To learn more about American Hiking Society and our programs such as National Trails Day, National Trails Fund, and Volunteer Vacations, visit AmericanHiking.org or call 800.972.8608.

National Weather Service Wind Chill Chart

		Temperature (°F)												
		35	30	25	20	15	10	5	0	-5	-10	-15	-20	-25
Wind (mph)	5	31	25	19	13	7	1	-5	-11	-16	-22	-28	-34	-40
	10	27	21	15	9	3	-4	-10	-16	-22	-28	-35	-41	-47
	15	25	19	13	6	0	-7	-13	-19	-26	-32	-39	-45	-51
	20	24	17	11	4	-2	-9	-15	-22	-29	-35	-42	-48	-55
	25	23	16	9	3	-4	-11	-17	-24	-31	-37	-44	-51	-58
	30	22	15	8	1	-5	-12	-19	-26	-33	-39	-46	-53	-60
	35	21	14	7	0	-7	-14	-21	-27	-34	-41	-48	-55	-62
	40	20	13	6	-1	-8	-15	-22	-29	-36	-43	-50	-57	-64

SoBo	NoBo	Description	Elev
324.1	1865.1	Osgood Tent Site to west, no fee. AT: Osgood Trail ▶ Osgood Cutoff.	2554
323.9	1865.3	Stream.	2540
323.5	1865.7	AT: Osgood Cutoff ◀▶ Great Gulf Trail to east. **(see map pg.192)**	2341
323.5	1865.7	Parapet Brook, AT: Great Gulf Trail ◀▶ Madison Gulf Trail to west.	2337
323.4	1865.7	West branch of Peabody River, suspension bridge. Great Gulf Tr to east.	2300
322.9	1866.3	Stream.	2410
322.0	1867.2	Stream.	2580
321.5	1867.7	Lowes Bald Spot 0.1W	2841
321.4	1867.8	Mt Washington Auto Rd N44 16.892 W71 15.203 P	2731
321.2	1868.0	AT: Madison Gulf Trail ◀▶ Old Jackson Rd Nelson Crag Trail and Raymond Path to east	2673
320.4	1868.8	George's Gorge Trail to west.	2571
320.1	1869.1	Peabody River, four other trails cross the AT from here to Pinkham Notch	2266
319.4	1869.8	NH 16, Pinkham Notch N44 15.416 W71 15.158 P P (pg.196-197) **Gorham, NH** (10.7W), AT: Old Jackson Rd ◀▶ Lost Pond Trail	2050
318.4	1870.8	AT: Lost Pond Trail ◀▶ Wildcat Ridge Trail	2016
318.0	1871.2	View.	2851
317.4	1871.8	Rocky crevasse, stairs	3259
316.7	1872.5	Wildcat Mountain peak E.	4065
316.4	1872.8	Wildcat Mountain peak D, observation tower, ski gondola 0.1 north Gondola rides to/from the AT, $12 round trip, restaurant at base, open Jul-Oct.	3990
315.3	1873.9	Wildcat Mountain peak C.	4274
314.4	1874.8	Wildcat Mountain peak A.	4422
313.9	1875.3	Spring.	3680
313.7	1875.5	AT: Wildcat Ridge Trail ◀▶ Nineteen Mile Brook Trail to east.	3407
313.5	1875.7	AT: Nineteen Mile Brook Trail ◀▶ Carter Moriah Trail, Carter Notch Hut (0.1E)	3308
312.8	1876.4	Spring to west	4311
312.3	1876.9	Carter Dome, Rainbow Trail to east	4832
311.9	1877.3	Black Angel Trail to east, Carter Dome Trail to west.	4616
311.4	1877.8	Mt Hight, view.	4652
310.9	1878.3	Zeta Pass, two Carter Dome trailheads to west	3890
308.8	1880.4	Middle Carter Mountain, view	4610
308.2	1881.0	North Carter Mountain, North Carter Trail to west, just south of summit	4539
306.3	1882.9	**Imp Campsite** (0.2W) 56.5◀51.0◀42.0◀▶6.1▶19.8▶25.0 ♦ ⏾ (5) ⊏ (10) Overnight fee $8PP, caretaker, composting privy.	3344
305.6	1883.6	Stony Brook Trail to west, Moriah Brook Trail to east.	3143
304.2	1885.0	Mt Moriah, summit to west, AT: Carter Moriah Trail ◀▶ Kenduskeag Trail	3991

SoBo	NoBo	Description	Elev
302.9	1886.3	AT: Kenduskeag Trail ◀▶ Rattle River Trail	3387
302.5	1886.7	Stream.	2871
301.8	1887.4	Rattle River	2022
300.4	1888.8	East Rattle River, multiple streams	1349
300.2	1889.0	**Rattle River Shelter** 57.1◀48.1◀6.1◀▶13.7▶18.9▶23.3. No fee. Water source is Rattle River. Gently sloping trail from shelter to US 2.	1279
298.9	1890.3	Stream.	969
298.4	1890.4	Fork in trail, AT to east (not over bridge).	904
298.3	1890.9	AT 0.1W on US 2, **Gorham, NH** (3.6W) N44 24.048 W71 6.589 P (pg.196-197)	780
298.2	1891.0	AT east on North Rd. N44 24.386 W71 7.009 P	795
297.6	1891.6	AT west on Hogan Rd (gravel)	785
296.7	1892.5	Brook	1230
294.7	1894.5	Mt Hayes, Mahoosuc Trail to west.	2555
293.1	1896.1	View	2344
292.5	1896.7	Cascade Mountain	2631
291.4	1897.8	Trident Col Campsite (0.2W), no fee, spring on side trail	2020
291.1	1898.1	Spring	1906
290.4	1898.8	Page Pond.	2223
289.8	1899.4	Wocket Ledge, view.	2643
289.3	1899.9	Stream.	2597
288.6	1900.6	Dream Lake, Peabody Brook Trail to east	2624
286.5	1902.7	**Gentian Pond Shelter/Campsite** (0.2E) 61.8◀19.8◀13.7◀▶5.2▶9.6▶14.7 Junction of Mahoosuc Trail (AT) and Austin Brook Trail, inlet brook of Gentian Pond. 3S and 1D platforms.	2181
285.5	1903.7	Stream	2263
285.1	1904.1	Stream	2517

195
NH

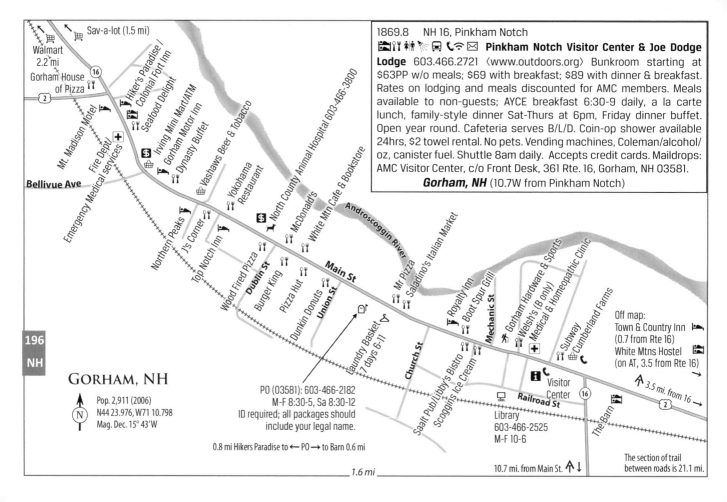

1869.8 NH 16, Pinkham Notch

Pinkham Notch Visitor Center & Joe Dodge Lodge 603.466.2721 ⟨www.outdoors.org⟩ Bunkroom starting at $63PP w/o meals; $69 with breakfast; $89 with dinner & breakfast. Rates on lodging and meals discounted for AMC members. Meals available to non-guests; AYCE breakfast 6:30-9 daily, a la carte lunch, family-style dinner Sat-Thurs at 6pm, Friday dinner buffet. Open year round. Cafeteria serves B/L/D. Coin-op shower available 24hrs, $2 towel rental. No pets. Vending machines, Coleman/alcohol/oz, canister fuel. Shuttle 8am daily. Accepts credit cards. Maildrops: AMC Visitor Center, c/o Front Desk, 361 Rte. 16, Gorham, NH 03581.

Gorham, NH (10.7W from Pinkham Notch)

196 NH

Sav-a-lot (1.5 mi)
Walmart 2.2 mi
Gorham House of Pizza
16
2
Mt. Madison Motel
Fire Dept/
Emergency Medical services
Bellivue Ave
Hiker's Paradise / Colonial Fort Inn
Seafood Delight
Irving Mini Mart/ATM
Gorham Motor Inn
Dynasty Buffet
Vashaws Beer & Tobacco
Yokohama Restaurant
North County Animal Hospital 603-466-3800
McDonald's
White Mtn Cafe & Bookstore
Androscoggin River
Mr Pizza
Saladino's Italian Market

Northern Peaks
J's Corner
Top Notch Inn
Wood Fired Pizza
Dublin St
Burger King
Pizza Hut
Dunkin Donuts
Union St
Main St
Royalty Inn
Boot Spur Grill
Mechanic St
Gorham Hardware & Sports
Welsh's (B only)
Medical & Homeopathic Clinic
Subway
Cumberland Farms

GORHAM, NH

N Pop. 2,911 (2006)
N44 23.976, W71 10.798
Mag. Dec. 15° 43'W

Laundry Basket 7 days 6-11

PO (03581): 603-466-2182
M-F 8:30-5, Sa 8:30-12
ID required; all packages should
include your legal name.

0.8 mi Hikers Paradise to ← PO → to Barn 0.6 mi

Church St
Saalt Pub/Libby's Bistro
Scoggins Ice Cream
Visitor Center
Railroad St
Library
603-466-2525
M-F 10-6
The Barn
16
2
3.5 mi. from 16

Off map:
Town & Country Inn
(0.7 from Rte 16)
White Mtns Hostel
(on AT, 3.5 from Rte 16)

10.7 mi. from Main St.

The section of trail
between roads is 21.1 mi.

1.6 mi

1890.9   US 2

🛏🍴⚠☕❄💻✉ 🅿 **White Mountains Lodge & Hostel**
603.466.5049   ⟨www.whitemountainslodgeandhostel.com⟩
DIRECTLY on AT at the northern Gorham trailhead (Rte. 2 & North Rd). Clean, B&B style rooms, some private, w/fresh linens & towels. $33PP includes, huge gourmet breakfast, laundry, loaner clothes, showers, computer, town & resupply shuttles. Liquid and canister fuel, sodas, ice cream, snacks for sale. Shuttle and slack-pack (21 mi) from Pinkham Notch (Gorham 1 exit) free w/2 nights stay. Parking for section hikers. Open June 1-Oct 8. Maildrops (also free for non-guests): 592 State Rte. 2, Shelburne, NH 03581

🛏⚠ ☕❄⚠ ✉ (1.7W) **White Birches Camping Park**
603.466.2022 ⟨www.whitebirchescampingpark.com⟩ bunks $15, tent sites $13PP, pool, air hockey, pool table, pets allowed, Coleman/ alcohol/oz and canister fuel. Free shuttle from/to trail and town with stay, open May-Oct. Guest maildrops ($5 fee for non-guest): 218 US 2, Shelburne, NH 03581.

Gorham, NH 03581 (3.6W from US 2)

⌂ ID required; all packages should include your legal name.

🛏🍴☕💻 (2.6W) **Town and Country Inn** 603.466.3315 ⟨www.townandcountryinn.com⟩ $64-120, pets $10. Breakfast 6-10:30, dinner 5-9, cocktails. Indoor pool, sauna.

🛏🛏⚠❄⚠ ✉ **The Barn** and **Libby House B&B** 603.466.2271 Bunks $27, B&B room for two $100, cont. breakfast with all stays. Serving hikers for 30 years. Kitchen, stove, microwave, refrigerator for use, no pets, laundry $5, Visa MC accepted, shuttles as time permits, free ride from Rte 2 trailhead for guests. Open year round. Maildrops ($15 fee for non-guests): 55 Main Street, Gorham, NH 03581.

🛏🛏❄🍴⚠🚌☕ **Hiker's Paradise** at Colonial Fort Inn 603.466.2732 ⟨www.hikersparadise.com⟩ bunks $23 (includes tax) with linen, tub/shower, kitchen. Private rooms available. No pets or maildrops. Coin laundry for guests. Restaurant serves breakfast. Coleman/alcohol/oz. Free shuttle with stay from/to Route 2, other limited shuttles.

🛏🍴⚠☕ **Royalty Inn** 603.466.3312 ⟨www.royaltyinn.com⟩ Hiker rate $79 (subject to change). Indoor Pool, sauna, A/C.

🛏⚠☕ **Top Notch Inn** 603.466.5496 ⟨www.topnotchinn.com⟩ Hiker discount, pool, A/C, well behaved dogs under 50 lbs allowed, no smoking, all major credit cards accepted. Open May-mid Oct.

🛏☕ **Northern Peaks Motor Inn** 603.466.2288 ⟨www.northernpeaksmotorinn.com⟩ $70/up + tax. A/C, pets $5, no smoking, all major credit cards accepted, hiker friendly.

🛏☕ **Gorham Motor Inn** 603.466.3381 $58-$158 Open May-Oct.

🚶🏪 **Gorham Hardware & Sports** 603.466.2312 Open M-F 8-5:30, Sa 8-4, Su 8-1. Hiking poles, Water treatment, hiking food, cold-weather clothes, White gas/alcohol/oz and canisters. Visa/MC/Disc.

🚌 **Trail Angels Hiker Services** 978.855.9227 Shuttles covering all of NH and ME.

🚌 **Concord Coach** 800.639.3317 Bus service 7:50am daily from Irving Mini Mart to Pinkham Notch. $6 one-way, $11 round-trip.

Berlin, NH 03570

➕ **Androscoggin Valley Hospital** 603.752.2200

SoBo	NoBo		Elev
283.7	1905.5	Mt Success	🔘 3565
283.1	1906.1	Success Trail to west	3174
		⚡ Camp fires are only allowed along the AT in ME within fireplaces at designated campsites.	
281.8	1907.4	**NH-ME border**	2972
281.3	1907.9	**Carlo Col Shelter and Campsite** (0.3W), on Carlo Col Trail . ☽♦🍴⊂(16)	3210
		25.0◀18.9◀5.2▲4.4▶9.5▶16.4 Platforms 3S and 2D, bear box, no fee.	
280.9	1908.3	Mt Carlo	🔘 3565
279.5	1909.7	Goose Eye Mountain west peak, Goose Eye Mtn Trail to west	🔘 3804
279.1	1910.1	Goose Eye Mountain east peak	🔘 3790
278.8	1910.4	Wright Trail to east.	3479
277.9	1911.3	Goose Eye Mountain north peak.	🔘 3686
276.9	1912.3	**Full Goose Shelter and Campsite** 3S and 1D platforms ☽♦🍴⊂(12)	2966
		23.3◀9.6◀4.4▲5.1▶12.0▶15.5 No Fee, stream behind shelter.	
276.4	1912.8	Fulling Mill Mountain south peak	3395
275.4	1913.8	Mahoosuc Notch south end, Mahoosuc Notch Trail to west	♦ 2494
		Most difficult or fun mile of the AT. Make way through jumbled pit of boulders.	
274.2	1915.0	Mahoosuc Notch north end, Bull Branch, campsite	♦ 2163
273.2	1916.0	Spring	♦ 3291
272.7	1916.5	Mahoosuc Arm	3770
272.0	1917.2	Speck Pond brook	♦ 3426
271.8	1917.4	**Speck Pond Shelter & Campsite**. ☽♦🍴⊂(8)	▲ 3438
		14.7◀9.5◀5.1▲6.9▶10.4▶20.9 Overnight fee $8PP, caretaker. Spring down	
		Speck Pond Trail just beyond caretaker's yurt. 3S and 3D platforms	
270.7	1918.5	Intersection, AT north on Old Speck Tr., south on Mahoosuc Tr.	🔘 📷 4033
		Side Trail 0.3E to Old Speck summit and observation tower.	
		♦ ME camping: AT hikers are encouraged to use designated campsites. Dispersed camping is permitted except for specific prohibitions. Look for local postings at signposts and shelters; prohibitions listed in this guidebook are not comprehensive. Camping at non-designated locations is prohibited above treeline (where trees are less than 8' tall).	
268.4	1920.8	Eyebrow Trail to west	♦ 2512
268.1	1921.1	Stream.	♦ 2391
267.3	1921.9	Eyebrow Trail to west	1521
267.2	1922.0	Grafton Notch, ME 26 · · · N44 35.382 W70 56.803 🅿 🏛 ☽ (pg.202)	1495
266.4	1922.8	Stream, Table Rock Trail to east	♦ 2113
264.9	1924.3	**Baldpate Lean-to** (0.1E), stream next to lean-to · · · ☽♦🍴⊂(8)	2683
		16.4◀12.0◀6.9▲3.5▶14.0▶26.8	
264.1	1925.1	Baldpate west peak	🔘 3662

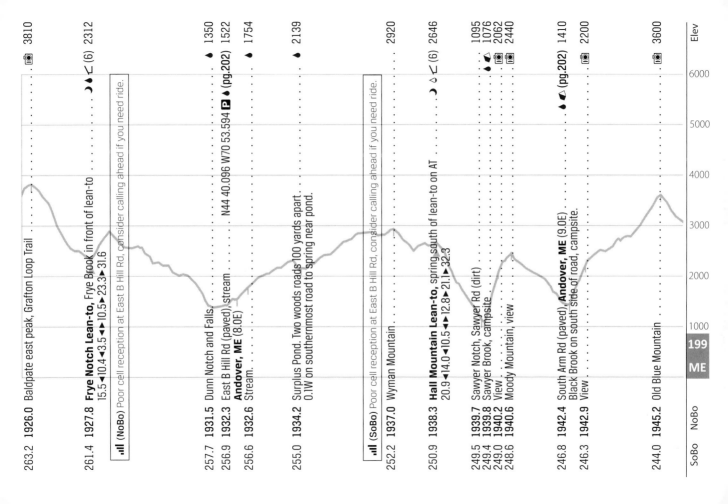

			Elev
263.2	**1926.0**	Baldpate east peak, Grafton Loop Trail	3810 🔭
261.4	**1927.8**	**Frye Notch Lean-to,** Frye Brook in front of lean-to	2312 🌙◆⊏(6)
		15.5◀10.4◀3.5◀▶10.5▶23.3▶31.6	
	.ıll (NoBo) Poor cell reception at East B Hill Rd, consider calling ahead if you need ride.		
257.7	**1931.5**	Dunn Notch and Falls	1350 ◆
256.9	**1932.3**	East B Hill Rd (paved) stream N44 40.096 W70 53.594 🅿 (pg.202)	1522 ◆
		Andover, ME (8.0E)	
256.6	**1932.6**	Stream	1754 ◆
255.0	**1934.2**	Surplus Pond. Two woods roads 100 yards apart.	2139 ◆
		0.1W on southernmost road to spring near pond.	
	.ıll (SoBo) Poor cell reception at East B Hill Rd, consider calling ahead if you need ride.		
252.2	**1937.0**	Wyman Mountain	2920
250.9	**1938.3**	**Hall Mountain Lean-to,** spring south of lean-to on AT	2646 🌙◇⊏(6)
		20.9◀14.0◀10.5◀▶12.8▶21.1▶32.3	
249.5	**1939.7**	Sawyer Notch, Sawyer Rd (dirt)	1095 ◖
249.4	**1939.8**	Sawyer Brook, campsite	1076 ◣
249.0	**1940.2**	View	2062 🔭
248.6	**1940.6**	Moody Mountain, view	2440 🔭
246.8	**1942.4**	South Arm Rd (paved) **Andover, ME** (9.0E)	1410 ◆◖(pg.202)
		Black Brook on south side of road, campsite.	
246.3	**1942.9**	View	2200 🔭
244.0	**1945.2**	Old Blue Mountain	3600 🔭

199

ME

SoBo   NoBo

SoBo	NoBo	Feature	Elev
242.4	1946.8	Unnamed Gap, mileage sign, water to west	3015
241.1	1948.1	Spring	3169
240.8	1948.4	Bemis Stream Trail to east	3350
239.8	1949.4	Bemis Mountain	3554
239.3	1949.9	View	3305
238.1	1951.1	Bemis Mountain Lean-to, small spring to left of lean-to 26.8◄23.3◄12.8◄►8.3►19.5►28.4	2845
236.8	1952.4	Bemis Mountain Second Peak	2924
234.6	1954.6	Dirt road, campsite and stream north of road	1603
234.4	1954.8	Bemis Stream (ford)	1547
233.6	1955.6	ME 17, Oquossoc, ME (11.0W) . . . N44 50.181 W70 42.602 P (pg.202) Height of Land view, bench and boulder seating	2255
232.5	1956.7	Woods road	2429
231.9	1957.3	Moxie Pond	2400
229.8	1959.4	Sabbath Day Pond Lean-to 31.6◄21.1◄8.3◄►11.2►20.1►28.1 Pond in front of lean-to. Sandy beach 0.3S on AT, swimming.	2396
229.3	1959.9	Houghton Fire Rd	2406
228.2	1961.0	Powerline	2804
225.2	1964.0	Little Swift River Pond Campsite. Spring house next to pond.	2460
224.0	1965.2	Chandler Mill Stream, pond	2186

200
ME

SoBo	NoBo		Elev
222.9	1966.3	Stream.	2305
222.5	1966.7	South Pond	2174
220.4	1968.8	ME 4, **Rangeley, ME** (9.0W) N44 53.213 W70 32.431 🅿 (pg.203)	1622
220.2	1969.0	Sandy River, footbridge	1675
219.7	1969.5	Old County Rd (gravel)	1880
218.9	1970.3	Stream	1996
218.6	1970.6	**Piazza Rock Lean-to,** stream through campsite 🌙♦◐⏢⊏ (8) (pg.203)	2109
		32.3◄19.5▼11.2▲8.9◄16.9▲35.5 Two-seat privy and cribbage board.	
217.8	1971.4	Ethel Pond	2382
217.6	1971.6	Saddleback Stream	2469
216.8	1972.4	Eddy Pond, woods road passes near north bank, no camping near pond	2654

✗ How many rebar holds are on the rock face about 0.5 north of Eddy Pond?

214.7	1974.5	Saddleback Mountain, trail 2.0W to ski lodge. 📷	4120
213.1	1976.1	The Horn. 📷	4032
212.4	1976.8	Redington Campsite to west, water 0.2W on side trail 🌙♦⏢ (8)	3172
211.1	1978.1	Saddleback Junior 📷	3655
210.8	1978.4	Stream.	3253
209.7	1979.5	**Poplar Ridge Lean-to** (1961) 🌙♦◐⏢⊏ (6)	2968
		28.4◄20.1▼8.0▲26.6▲36.8	
		Some tenting at lean-to, more on knoll to the north. Stream in front.	
207.0	1982.2	Orbeton Stream (ford)	1550
206.9	1982.3	Woods road, NoBo: walk a short distance east on road	1626
206.2	1983.0	Sluice Brook.	2086
205.6	1983.6	Woods road	2320
205.1	1984.1	Perham Stream, logging road to north (not accessible by car)	2299
203.9	1985.3	Lone Mountain	3260
202.7	1986.5	Mt Abraham Trail, 1.7E to summit above treeline, remnants of lookout tower 📷	3257

ANDOVER, ME
Pop. 910 (2009)
N44 38.128, W70 45.050
Mag. Dec. 15° 43'W

(8 mi) East B Hill Rd
Little Red Hen
Pine Ellis
Pine St

Main St
120
(9 mi) S. Arm Rd

Andover General Store
Mills Market
The Cabin (off map 2.2 mi)

Library 207-392-4841
Tu,W & Sa 1-4:30, Th 1-4:30 & 6-8

PO (04216): 207-392-4571
M-F 8:15-11:15 & 1:45-4:30, Sa 8:30-11:30

N
5
1.0 mi

1922.0   Grafton Notch, ME 26

⬥🏚🎣⛺📶✉ (12.8E) **Stony Brook Camping** 207.824.2836 ⟨www.stonybrookrec.com⟩ tent site $28 for 4, lean-to $32 for 4. Shuttles from Grafton Notch for a fee. Pool, miniature golf, zip line, rec room, campstore, Coleman fuel. 12.0E on Hwy 26, then left 0.8 mile on Route 2. Maildrops: 42 Powell Place, Hanover, ME 04237.

Bethel, ME 04217 (12E to Rt 2, right 5 miles on Rt 2)
⌂ M-F 9-4, Sa 10-12:30, 207.824.2668

🛏🏚⛺📶✉ **Chapman Inn** 207.824.2657 ⟨www.chapmaninn.com⟩ Bunk space $35 includes shower and full breakfast, $25 without breakfast. Rooms $69/up include breakfast. Kitchen privileges, $5 laundry. Maildrops: PO Box 1067, Bethel, ME 04217.

⬥⛺📶**Bethel Outdoor Adventure** 207.824.4224 About 20 minutes by car from Grafton Notch or US 2 trailheads $22 campsites near river within walking distance of Bethel stores. Shuttles for a fee.

🍴 **Pat's Pizza** 7 days 11-9

🍴 **Sudbury Inn Restaurant & Pub**, Tu-Su 5:30-9, pub 7 days 4:30-9.

🏚 **Bethel Shop 'n Save**

🚶 **True North Adventurewear** 207.824.2201 Full line of gear, M-Th 10-6. F-Sa 9-6, Su 10-5. Leki repair, Coleman/alcohol/oz & canisters, freeze-dried foods.

🐾 **Bethel Animal Hospital** 207.824.2212

1932.3   East B Hill Rd   *Andover, ME 04216* (8E)

🛏🏚🏠�⛺🚌📶🖥✉ **Pine Ellis Lodging** 207.392.4161 ⟨www.pineellislodging.com⟩ Bunks $25PP, private rooms $45S, $60D, $75 triple. Stays include kitchen privileges, laundry, and morning coffee. For a fee: trailhead pickup (call in advance), slackpack Grafton Notch to Rangeley, and shuttles to nearby towns, airport and bus station. No dogs. Extensive resupply includes on-trail snacks & meals, Coleman/denatured/oz and canister fuel. Hiker-friendly hosts Ilene Trainor and David Rousselin. Guest maildrops: (USPS) PO Box 12 or (UPS) 20 Pine Street, Andover, ME 04216.

🛏⛏ **Paul's AT Camp for Hikers** Contact Pine Ellis for stay at rustic cabin $60 for 4. Located 3 miles from Andover. Stay includes shower one round trip shuttle from the hostel.

🏚🍴💲☎ **Andover General Store** 207.392.4172 Short-order food & pizza, **Sweet Treats** ice cream. Open M-Sa 5-8, Su 6-8.

🏚🍴 **Mills Market** Open 7 days 5am-9pm.

🍴📶 **Little Red Hen** 207.392.2253 Open Tu-Su (T-Th 6:30am-2pm, F-Sat 6am-8pm, Sun 7am-2pm) closed Monday. AYCE Pizza on Sat. **Also:** Massage therapist, Donna Gifford, 207.357.5686, call for rates. Free pickup/return to Andover.

2.8 miles east of Andover:

🏚🏠📶🖥 **The Cabin** 207.392.1333 ⟨www.thecabininmaine.com⟩ By reservation only; alumni hikers welcome.

1942.4   South Arm Rd

⬥🏚⛺ (3.5W) **South Arm Campground** 207.364.5155 ⟨www.southarm.com⟩ Tent sites, camp store, no credit cards, pets okay, open May 1–Oct 1.

Andover, ME (9E from South Arm Rd)

1955.6   ME 17   *Oquossoc, ME 04964* (11W)
⌂ M-F 8-10 & 2:15–4:15, Sa 9–12, 207.864.3685

🏪☎ **Oquossoc Grocery** deli, bakery, Coleman fuel

🍴 **Gingerbread House** B/L/D, vegetarian specials.

🍴 **Four Seasons Café** 7 days 11-9 L/D vegetarian specialties.

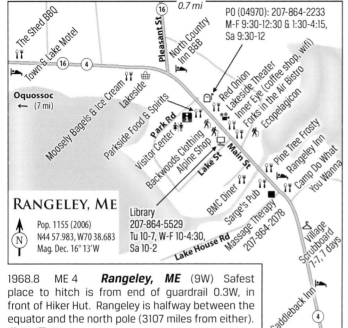

RANGELEY, ME

Pop. 1155 (2006)
N44 57.983, W70 38.683
Mag. Dec. 16° 13'W

PO (04970): 207-864-2233
M-F 9:30-12:30 & 1:30-4:15,
Sa 9:30-12

Library
207-864-5529
Tu 10-7, W-F 10-4:30,
Sa 10-2

The Shed BBQ
Town & Lake Motel
Moosely Bagels & Ice Cream
Lakeside
Oquossoc ← (7 mi)
Parkside Food & Spirits
Park Rd
Visitor Center
Backwoods Clothing
Alpine Shop
Lake St
BMC Diner
Sarge's Pub
Massage Therapy 207-864-2078
Lake House Rd
Village Scrubboard 7-7, 7 days
Saddleback Inn
(9 mi)
IGA
Main St
Red Onion
Lakeside Theater
Inner Eye (coffee shop, wifi)
Forks in the Air Bistro
Ecopelagicon
Pine Tree Frosty
Rangeley Inn
Camp Do What You Wanna
North Country Inn B&B
Pleasant St
16
0.7 mi

1968.8 ME 4 **Rangeley, ME** (9W) Safest place to hitch is from end of guardrail 0.3W, in front of Hiker Hut. Rangeley is halfway between the equator and the north pole (3107 miles from either). **The Hiker Hut** (0.3W) 207.897.8984 hikerhut@gmail.com. Quiet, restful sanctuary along the Sandy River with Artisan jewelry maker and sports massage therapist on-site. $25PP includes bunk with mattress, pillows, sheets, home cooked meal and shuttle into Rangeley. $50 private hut for couples. All shuttling available. Maildrops ($5 for non-guests) C/O Steve Lynch 2 Pine Rd. Sandy River Plantation, ME 04970.

Farmhouse Inn 207.864.3113 Hiker bunkroom for $30PP, includes shower w/towel and return to Rte 4 trailhead. Private rooms avail. Not a party place. Laundry $5. Hiker supplies, Coleman/Denatured/oz, slackpacking. Nice clean facility with use of a kitchen, bikes for riding into town. 0.5 south of IGA. Maildrops: 2057 Main St, Rangeley, ME 04970.

Town & Lake Motel 207.864.3755 Call for hiker rate. Pets $5. Canoes for guest use. Maildrops: PO Box 47, Rangeley, ME 04970.

Rangeley Inn & Tavern 207.864.3341 ⟨www.therangeleyinn.com⟩ Rates start at $135 in summer, $115 in fall (after Sept 1). Includes cont. breakfast. Senior discount, free calls to US and CA.

Saddleback Motor Inn 207.864.3434 $95, pets $10, pool.

North Country Inn B&B 207.864.2440 ⟨www.northcountrybb.com⟩ $99-149, includes full breakfast, specials in mid-week and off-season. Multi-night discount.

Camp Do What You Wanna 207.864.3000 B/L pastries.

Sarge's Sports Pub & Grub L/D and bar, 7 days 11-1, house bands on Friday and Saturday.

Moose Alley 207.864.9955 Bowling, billiards, darts, food. Just west of The Shed BBQ on Main St.

IGA Supermarket 207.864.5089 ATM 7 days 7-8.

Ecopelagicon 207.864.2771 Hiker friendly nature store White gas/alcohol/oz, canister fuel, freeze-dried foods, water filters, clothes, Leki poles and does warranty work. Ask about shuttles. Maildrops: 7 Pond St, Rangeley, ME 04970

Alpine Shop ⟨www.alpineshoprangeley.com⟩ 207.864.3741 M-S 9-7, Su 10-6, some hiking gear, Coleman/alcohol/oz.

Back Woods 207.864.2335 Gear, clothes.

Rangeley Health & Wellness Center Wellness 207.864.3055; Medical 207.864.3303 On Dallas Hill Rd south of IGA. $5 shower, towel provided. M-Th 5am-8pm, F 5am-7:30pm, Sa-Su 8-2.

1970.6 **Piazza Rock Lean-to** Two side trails north of shelter; 100 yards north: west to Piazza Rock; 0.1 north: To "The Caves", blue-blazed trail through boulders & caves.

SoBo	NoBo	Elev	Feature
201.7	1987.5	3139	**Spaulding Mountain Lean-to,** spring on north shelter loop trail . . . ⊃ ◖ ⊏ (8) — 28.1◀16.9◀8.0◀▶18.6▶28.8▶36.5
200.9	1988.3	4000	Crest NW shoulder of Spaulding Mountain — Side trail 0.1E to summit.
200.2	1989.0	3643	Bronze plaque — Completion of the last section of the AT from GA-ME.
199.0	1990.2	3645	View to east.
198.7	1990.5	3727	Sugarloaf Mountain, stream 0.2E, Sugarloaf Mountain Trail 0.6E to summit
196.6	1992.6	2195	South Branch Carrabassett River (ford), tenting on north side of river
196.5	1992.7	2264	Caribou Valley Rd (gravel)
196.1	1993.1	2475	Spring
195.5	1993.7	2757	Crocker Cirque Campsite (0.2E), stream
194.4	1994.8	4040	South Crocker Mountain, summit 50 yards west
193.4	1995.8	4228	North Crocker Mountain
192.3	1996.9	3369	Spring
188.2	2001.0	1450	ME 27 (paved), **Stratton, ME** (5.0W) . . . N45 6.201 W70 21.413 **P** (pg.208)
187.4	2001.8	1250	Stratton Brook Pond Rd
187.3	2001.9	1201	Stratton Brook, footbridge
186.5	2002.7	1279	Footbridge, stream
186.4	2002.8	1323	Cranberry Stream Campsite
185.0	2004.2	2400	Bigelow Range Trail 0.2W to Cranberry Pond
183.9	2005.3	3379	View to east
183.3	2005.9	3200	Horns Pond Trail
183.1	2006.1	3183	**Horns Pond Lean-tos** 35.5◀26.6◀18.6◀▶10.2▶17.9▶27.9
182.7	2006.5	3720	Trail 0.2W to North Horn, small boxed spring just south of this intersection
182.6	2006.6	3831	South Horn

SoBo	NoBo		Elev
180.5	2008.7	Bigelow Mountain west peak	4145
180.1	2009.1	Avery Memorial Campsite, spring 0.2N on AT, Fire Wardens Trail to east	3841
179.8	2009.4	Avery Peak	4090
178.6	2010.6	View	2810
177.9	2011.3	Safford Brook Trail to west	2260
177.8	2011.4	Safford Notch Campsite 0.3E	2224
175.6	2013.6	View	2909
174.6	2014.6	Little Bigelow Mountain, view	3010
172.9	2016.3	**Little Bigelow Lean-to** 36.8◄28.8◄10.2◄▶7.7▶17.7▶27.4 (8) Plenty of tent sites at lean-to. Swimming in "the Tubs" along AT.	1812
171.5	2017.7	East Flagstaff Rd, N45 8.073 W70 10.283 P (0.1W) ⟩(pg.208) AT east on road for 0.1 mile	1200
171.3	2017.9	Bog Brook Rd, Flagstaff Lake outlet, footbridge	1196
170.6	2018.6	Hemlock Trail to east	1256
170.3	2018.9	East Flagstaff Lake fentpads, 2 beaches, 2 firepits (9)	1207
169.8	2019.4	Two intersections with Hemlock Trail	1244
168.7	2020.5	Long Falls Dam Rd (paved) (pg.208)	1225
168.6	2020.6	Jerome Brook	1236
165.8	2023.4	Connector trail to Great Carrying Pond Portage Trail	1336
165.2	2024.0	**West Carry Pond Lean-to** 36.5◄17.9◄7.7◄▶10.0▶19.7▶28.7 (8) Swimming in pond. Water at spring house to left of lean-to or at West Carry Pond.	1345
164.5	2024.7	Unmarked trail 0.5W to Arnolds Point on West Carry Pond	1338
162.7	2026.5	Gravel road, AT to west over Sandy Stream	1288

"Carry" ponds are so named because they were used for portage.
✗ Find a commemorative orange disk nailed to a tree or post. How many men are in the boat?

205
ME

SoBo	NoBo	Feature	Elev
161.8	2027.4	Gravel road	1299
161.5	2027.7	East Carry Pond, beach at north end	1269
159.5	2029.7	Scott Rd (gravel)	1339
158.7	2030.5	North branch of Carrying Place Stream	1200
155.2	2034.0	**Pierce Pond Lean-to**, 27.9◄17.7◄10.0◄▶9.7▶18.7▶22.8 ☾ ⌐(6) (pg.208) Blue-blazed loop trail west to lean-to. From north end of loop, Harrison's is 0.3E.	1224
155.1	2034.1	Wooden dam, outlet of Pierce Pond	1152
154.8	2034.4	Trail 0.1E to Harrison's Pierce Pond Camps, boat landing to west (pg.208)	1057
154.6	2034.6	Otter Pond Rd (gravel)	979
154.1	2035.1	Pierce Pond Stream Falls 0.1E	953
154.0	2035.2	Waterfall 0.1E	
153.5	2035.7	Otter Pond Stream, footbridge	866
151.6	2037.6	Kennebec River. Do not ford. Use ferry service. ♦(pg.209)	492
151.2	2038.0	US 201, **Caratunk, ME** (0.3E). N45 14.302 W69 59.777 P (pg.209)	520
150.9	2038.3	Woods road	673
148.6	2040.6	Holly Brook	911
147.2	2042.0	Grove Rd (gravel)	1233
146.7	2042.5	Holly Brook	1309
146.0	2043.2	Boise-Cascade Logging Rd to west (gravel), Pleasant Pond Rd to east.	1447
145.5	2043.7	**Pleasant Pond Lean-to** 27.4◄19.7◄9.7◄▶9.0▶13.1▶22.0 ☾♦⌐(6)	1391
145.3	2043.9	Stream left of lean-to. Beach 0.2 on side trail beyond lean-to. Pleasant Pond Beach to east	1355
144.2	2045.0	Pleasant Pond Mountain	2470

⊘ Camping on either shore of Kennebec River is prohibited.

✱ **Blueberries** – Abundant on open summits like Pleasant Pond Mountain and north peak of Moxie Bald.

SoBo	NoBo		Elev
139.7	2049.5	Stream.	
139.3	2049.9	Moxie Pond south end (ford), road, powerlines N45 14.984 W69 49.857 [P]	1034
139.1	2050.1	Baker Stream	970
138.8	2050.4	Powerline	1014
136.5	2052.7	**Bald Mountain Brook Lean-to** (0.1E)	1329
		28.7◀18.7◀9.0◀▶4.1▶13.0▶25.0 Bald Mountain Brook in front of lean-to.	
		"AT Road" (gravel) 75 yards north of shelter.	
135.1	2054.1	Summit bypass trail to west	2156
134.5	2054.7	Moxie Bald Mountain	2629
134.2	2055.0	Summit bypass trail to west	2418
133.5	2055.7	Trail to Moxie Bald north peak (0.5W)	2221
132.4	2056.8	**Moxie Bald Mountain Lean-to**	1242
		22.8◀13.1◀4.1◀▶8.9▶20.9▶28.3	
		Bald Mountain Pond in front of lean-to.	
131.3	2057.9	Gravel road	1278
130.8	2058.4	Gravel road	1251
130.4	2058.8	Bald Mountain Stream (ford)	1234
128.5	2060.7	Bald Mountain Rd (gravel) N45 16.570 W69 41.311 [P]	1136
		bridge and stream to west	
126.9	2062.3	Marble Brook	1003
126.5	2062.7	West Branch of Piscataquis River (ford)	982
		River normally knee-deep. During heavy rain periods, fording can be dangerous.	
123.5	2065.7	**Horseshoe Canyon Lean-to** 22.0◀13.0◀8.9◀▶12.0▶19.4▶24.1	794
		On blue-blazed trail. Stream at northern AT junction or river in front and below.	
123.1	2066.1	Stream.	769

2001.0   ME 27

🛒 (2E) **Mountainside Grocers** 207.237.2248, open 7:30–8pm.

Stratton, ME 04982 (5W)

🛏️⚹🍴⚹📶✉️💲 **White Wolf Inn** 207.246.2922 $55S/D, $65 on weekends, $10EAP + tax. Pets $10. Visa, M/C accepted $20 min. Restaurant (closed Tues) serves L/D. Breakfast on weekends. Home of the 8oz Wolf Burger; Fish Fry Friday; **Wolf Den Bar** on-site. Maildrops: Main Street, PO Box 590, Stratton, ME 04982.

🛏️🚌⚹🚐📶🖥️✉️ **Stratton Motel** 207.246.4171 ⟨www.thestrattonmotel.com⟩ $25 bunk, $60 private room, Cash Only, no credit cards. Slack packing & shuttle range Gorham to Monson and to airports, train, bus and car rental hubs in Portland, Bangor, Farmington, Augusta and Waterville. Canister fuel. Maildrops: PO Box 284, Stratton, ME 04982; FEDEX & UPS 162 Main St.,Stratton,ME 04982.

🛏️✉️📶 **Spillover Motel** 207.246.6571 ⟨spillovermaine.com⟩ $79D/up. Pets $10, cont B. Full kitchen for use by guests. Maildrops: PO Box 427, Stratton, ME 04982.

🛏️⚘🍴 **Stratton Plaza Hotel** 207.246.2000 Some rooms, ask about camping.

🛒💲 **Fotter's Market** 207.246.2401 M-Th 8-7, F-Sa 8-8, Su 9-5. Coleman/alcohol/oz.

🏠🍴💲📶 **Flagstaff General Store** 207.246.2300 Deli, pizza, subs, sodas, coffee, protein bars, beer, canister fuel. M-F 5:30am-9pm, Sa 7-9, Su 7-7.

🛒💲✉️ **Northland Cash Supply** 207.246.2376 Open 7 days 5–10, groceries, beer, tobacco, hiker box, Coleman/alcohol/oz. Owner (Mark) provides rides back to the trail for free when he's available. Maildrops (no FedEx): 152 Main Street, Stratton, ME 04982.

2017.7   East Flagstaff Rd
2020.5   Long Falls Dam Rd

Kingfield, ME (18E from either Rd)

🛏️🚌📶🖥️✉️ **Mountain Village Farm B&B** 207.265.2030 Hiker rate of $40 per person for room with fridge, microwave and private bath. Includes breakfast. Round-trip shuttle $40 for up to 4 persons from either trailhead. Pets welcome. Bed & Breakfast on an organic farm; inquire about work-for-stay. Town center within walking distance has grocery, laundry, and restaurants. Slackpack the Bigelows (Stratton to East Flagstaff Rd, either direction) $40/carload. Maildrops: PO Box 216, Kingfield, ME 04947.

2034.0, 2034.4   Trails to camp

🛏️🍴 **Harrison's Pierce Pond Camps** 207.672.3625, 207.612.8184 May-Nov, 7 days. Bed, shower, and 12-pancake breakfast $40. If you only want breakfast ($9-12 served 7-7:30am), reserve a seat the day before. Cash only. Okay to get water at camp and dispose of trash. Shortest route to camp is west along the north blue-blaze shelter loop trail.

STRATTON, ME

27 16

Fotter's Market

Stratton Plaza

Pop. 368 (2006)
N45 8.450, W70 26.617
Mag. Dec. 16° 20'W

PO (04982): 207-246-6461
M-F 8:30-1 & 1:30-4, Sa 8:30-11
Limited cash-back

Old Mill Laundry

Main St

Stratton Motel & Hostel

Northland General Store

White Wolf Inn, Restaurant & Bar

School St

(5.0 mi from PO)

16   27

Flagstaff General Store

Library M,W,F 10-5; Tu,Th 1-5; Sa 9-1

Spillover Motel (0.6 mi from PO)

0.5 mi

2037.6   Kennebec River - The ferry is the official AT route (do not ford); the current is strong and unpredictable due to an upstream dam. Ferry holds 1 or 2.

Before May 1	No service
May 1 - May 21	on-call service $50 time & weather permitting
May 22 - July 9	9am-11am, 7 days
July 10 - Sept 30	9am-11am and 2pm-4pm, 7 days
Oct 1 - Oct 12	9am-11am, 7 days
Oct 13 - Oct 31	on-call service $50 time & weather permitting
After Oct 31	No service

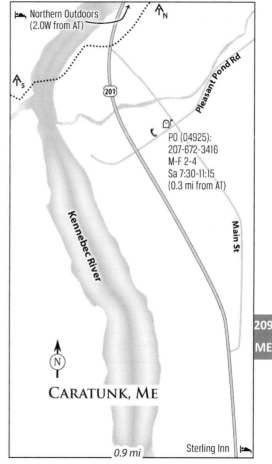

Fletcher Mountain Outfitters 207.672.4879 David Corrigan provides ferry service and shuttles when not operating ferry.

2038.0   US 201   *Caratunk, ME 04925* (0.3E)
Note limited hours (on map); consider using businesses below for maildrops. Accepts debit cards with limited cash back.

(1.3E) **The Sterling Inn** 207.672.3333
〈www.mainesterlinginn.com〉 bunk room $25, semi-private $30PP, private $40S, $55D (shared bed), $80/4. All include breakfast buffet. Multi-night discount, credit/debit cards accepted, pets welcome, open year-round. Extensive resupply including fuel/oz, canister fuel, Lipton Sides, dog food, batteries & candy bars. Ice cream, sodas, and cook-yourself options. Free shuttle to/from trail, PO, and pub. Free daily shuttle to General store for guests. Resupply, showers ($2.50) and laundry ($5) available even if you are not staying. Address: 1041 Route 201. Maildrops & shipping (also free for non-guests): PO Box 129, Caratunk Maine 04925.

(2W) **Northern Outdoors** 800.765.7238
〈www.northernoutdoors.com〉 Hikers welcome to ride free shuttle, use shower & pool with or without stay. Shuttle makes three trips a day coinciding with ferry schedule. Hikers get 25% discount on lodge rooms; prices vary by season and on weekends; peak season is July 12-Sept 1. Weekends in August are often booked. Cabin tents $17-25PP/up, tenting $11-13PP. Coin laundry, hot tub, ATM. Some resupply including Coleman/denatured/oz. No pets. Rafting trips (class IV) require reservation. Food and ale in **Kennebec River Pub & Brewery**. Maildrops: 1771 US 201, The Forks, ME 04985.

Berry's General Store (7.5W) 207.663.4461 Food, and some hardware. 5am-7pm 7 days, year-round. Open till 8 in summer.

209
ME

SoBo	NoBo	Description	Elev
121.2	2068.0	East Branch of Piscataquis River (ford)	650
120.9	2068.3	Gravel road	765
120.8	2068.4	Shirley-Blanchard Rd (paved) N45 17.072 W69 35.223 P	850
119.7	2069.5	AT on woods road for 0.5 mile	976
119.3	2069.9	Gravel road	893
117.8	2071.4	Historic AT route near Lake Hebron. N45 17.442 W69 31.995 P (pg.212) 0.2E on woods road to Pleasant St & parking, then left 1.6 mi to Monson, ME.	900
117.4	2071.8	Dirt road	1032
115.9	2073.3	Side trail to Doughty Ponds (0.1W), 180' footbridge built in 2014	1229
115.8	2073.4	Stream.	1251
115.2	2074.0	Gravel road	1386
114.5	2074.7	ME 15 (paved), Monson, ME (3.6E) N45 19.856 W69 32.122 P (pg.212-213) South end of 100-Mile Wilderness.	1215
114.4	2074.8	Spectacle Pond outlet	1179
113.6	2075.6	Old Stage Rd (dirt) Once a stagecoach road and part of the original AT	1291
113.3	2075.9	Bell Pond	1278
112.6	2076.6	Lily Pond	1130
111.5	2077.7	**Leeman Brook Lean-to.** 25.0◄20.9◄12.0▶7.4▶12.1▶16.1 Stream in front of lean-to. ⊂(6)	1077
110.7	2078.5	North Pond outlet	1023
110.4	2078.8	North Pond Tote Rd.	1094
109.3	2079.9	Mud Pond	1026
108.9	2080.3	Bear Pond Ledge	1190
108.5	2080.7	James Brook	935
108.1	2081.1	Woods road	927
108.0	2081.2	Little Wilson Falls, west 30 yards	822
107.7	2081.5	Little Wilson Stream (ford), campsite	750
107.3	2081.9	Follow gravel road for 100 yards, pond	906
105.4	2083.8	Big Wilson Tote Rd	561
105.2	2084.0	Thompson Brook	561
104.8	2084.4	Big Wilson Stream (ford)	600
104.5	2084.7	Railroad tracks	889
104.1	2085.1	**Wilson Valley Lean-to** (1993). 28.3◄19.4◄7.4▶4.7▶8.7▶15.6 Spring on opposite side of AT. ⊂(6)	972
103.4	2085.8	Woods road	1198
102.1	2087.1	Stream	942
101.8	2087.4	Stream	941

SoBo	NoBo	Feature	Elev
100.9	2088.3	Wilber Brook	614
100.8	2088.4	Vaughn Stream	633
100.2	2089.0	Bodfish Farm/Long Pond Tote Rd (gravel), ford Long Pond Stream north of road	659
99.4	2089.8	**Long Pond Stream Lean-to** 24.1◄12.1◄4.7◄►4.0►10.9►20.8 ⟂(8)	950
99.2	2090.0	Trail 0.8E to Otter Pond parking **P**	1075
98.3	2090.9	Barren Slide to east, view	1986
98.1	2091.1	Barren Ledges	2019
96.3	2092.9	Barren Mountain, remnants of tower	2660
95.4	2093.8	Side trail to **Cloud Pond Lean-to** (0.4E) 16.1◄8.7◄4.0◄►6.9►16.8►24.0 Cloud Pond is water source. ⟂(6)	2501
93.9	2095.3	Fourth Mountain Bog	1955
93.3	2095.9	Fourth Mountain	2380
92.1	2097.1	Mt Three and a Half	1970
91.7	2097.5	Third Mountain Trail to west	1812
90.8	2098.4	Third Mountain, Monument Cliff	2087
90.2	2099.0	Trail 0.1E to West Chairback Pond, stream crosses AT north of side trail	1770
89.3	2099.9	View	2148
89.2	2100.0	Spring	2234
88.9	2100.3	Columbus Mountain	2325
88.5	2100.7	**Chairback Gap Lean-to** 15.6◄10.9◄6.9◄►9.9►17.1►20.7 ⟂(6)	1979
88.0	2101.2	Spring on AT north of shelter. Chairback Mountain	2180
85.9	2103.3	0.2W to East Chairback Pond ◀(0.2W)	1722
85.3	2103.9	Spring	1498
84.7	2104.5	Katahdin Ironworks Rd (gravel) N45 28.632 W69 17.107 **P** (0.4E)	830
84.2	2105.0	West Branch Pleasant River (ford). Wide ford with slick rocky bottom. Campsites to south; no camping/fires for 2.0N.	718
83.3	2105.9	Stream	821
82.8	2106.4	Gulf Hagas Trail to west, 5.2 mile loop trail whose ends intersect the AT 0.7 mile apart. Features narrow, deep gorge with many waterfalls.	950
82.1	2107.1	Gulf Hagas Trail to west	1050

2071.4 Historic AT route, side trail 0.2E to Pleasant St., left 0.1 to cabins, 1.6 further to *Monson*

◖ ⌂ ◨ ⧖ **100 Mile Wilderness Adventures and Outfitters**
207.991.7030 ⟨www.100milewilderness.info⟩ 349 Pleasant St, Monson, ME 04464. Bunkhouse $25pp, private cabin $50 1-2 people, campsites $15 1-2 people, include full kitchen, library, WiFi & internet. Free shuttles into town & use of bicycles. Laundry (wash/dry) $5. Well stocked campstore. Mid-wilderness resupply options. Free long term parking for section hikers. Licensed/insured shuttle services from Rangeley to Baxter SP and pickup/drop off in Bangor. Open May 15-October 15 with other dates available by prior arrangement.

2074.7   ME 15   *Monson, ME 04464* (3.6E)
Strictly enforced: No stealth camping in town

◛ ◙ ◈ ⌂ ⧍ ⑂ △ ◨ ⧖ ⊡ ⊠ 🖇 **P** **Lakeshore House Lodging & Pub**
207.997.7069, 207.343.5033 ⟨www.thelakeshorehouse.com⟩ Bunkroom $30PP, private rooms $45S/$60D w/shared bath. Well-behaved dogs okay. Reservations appreciated, packs out of rooms by 10:30am; full check out/vacate by noon please. Accepts credit cards, ATM on-site. Free for guests: trailhead pickup & return (only till 11:00 AM for return), loaner laptop, loaner clothing, WiFi, kayaks, paddleboat, swimming. Parking $1/day. Laundry ($5) & shower ($5) available to non-guests. Pub hours: Tu-Sa 12-9, Su 12-8, bar open later, closed M. Live music Su 3-6pm. House quiet by 10:00 PM and NO BINGE DRINKING. Guests welcome at Shaws for breakfast. 100 Mile Wilderness food drops $25, some restrictions. Maildrops for guests (non-guests $5): PO Box 215, C/O Lakeshore House, Monson, ME 04464 or UPS/FedEx (no Sat delivery): 9 Tenney Hill Rd.

◛ ◙ ◢ ⌂ ⧍ ⑂ △ ◨ ⧖ ⊡ ⊠ **Shaw's Lodging** 207.997.3597
shawslodging@gmail.com ⟨www.shawslodging.com⟩ Mid-May-mid-Oct, $25 bunks, $35 private room, $30 semi-private, $12 tenting. Free pickup/return with stay. $9 breakfast, $5 laundry, $5 shower and towel (w/o stay), internet available. Food drops, slackpacking and shuttles all over Maine, Coleman/alcohol/oz, canister fuel & Aquamira. No credit cards. Maildrops (non-guests $5): PO Box 72 or 17 Pleasant St, Monson, ME 04464.

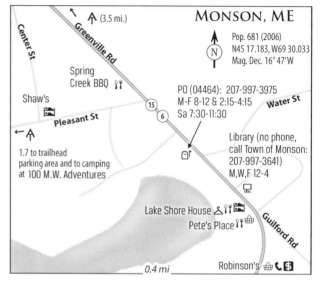

MONSON, ME

Pop. 681 (2006)
N45 17.183, W69 30.033
Mag. Dec. 16° 47'W

PO (04464): 207-997-3975
M-F 8-12 & 2:15-4:15
Sa 7:30-11:30

Library (no phone, call Town of Monson: 207-997-3641)
M,W,F 12-4

Spring Creek BBQ
Shaw's
Pleasant St
1.7 to trailhead parking area and to camping at 100 M.W. Adventures
Center St
Greenville Rd (3.5 mi.)
Water St
Lake Shore House
Pete's Place
Guilford Rd
Robinson's
0.4 mi

◨ **Charlie Anderson** 207.965.5678 or 207.997.7069 Statewide shuttles/slackpack/food drops, call for prices.

◨ **Sydney Pratt** 207.997.3221 pielady13@myfairpoint.net will shuttle from Stratton to Katahdin.

⑂ ⌂ ⌂ **Pete's Place** 207.997.3400 5am-5pm M-F, 7-5 S-Su. Open April thru Nov. Restaurant, bakery, ice cream. Resupply: hiker foods, small gear items, dog food. Coleman/denatured/oz, canisters.

⑂ ⌂ 🖇 **A.E. Robinson's** 207.997.3700 5am-10pm 7 days. ATM fee $2. Country Cafe Deli inside serves burgers, pizza, breakfast.

⑂ **Spring Creek Bar-B-Q** 207.997.7025 Th-Sa 11am-8pm, Sunday 11am-6pm.

Greenville, ME 04485 (10W from ME 15)

🛏🛜 **Kineo View Motor Lodge** 207.695.4470 $79-$99, $10EAP includes continental breakfast. Clean, quiet motel with a nice view, 7.5 mi. from trailhead.

🛏🛜 **Indian Hill Motel** 207.695.2623 $74 weekdays, $79 weekends up to 3 persons. In center of town.

🍴 **Kelly's Landing** 207.695.4438 7 days 7-9, Su AYCE breakfast.

🍴 **The Black Frog** 207.695.1100 Restaurant, pub, pizza.

🍴 **Dairy Bar** 207.695.2921 ice cream

🛒🍴 **Harris Drug Store** dining counter inside.

🚶🏪 **Indian Hill Trading Post & Supermarket** 800.675.4487

🏪 **Jamieson's Store** supplies, pizza and subs.

🚶🍴🛜💻 **Northwoods Outfitters** 207.695.3288 ⟨www.maineoutfitter.com⟩ Full service outfitter with fuel/oz and canister fuel. Expresso bar, pastries, internet. 7 days, 8-5.

➕ **Charles Dean Memorial Hospital** 207.695.5200

Also: two banks with ATMs

Guilford, ME (14E from ME 15)

🛏🍴⛺🛜💻 **Salmon's** 828.215.0834, 37 Hudson Ave, Guilford, ME 04443. Bunkroom $30, private room (1 or 2) $60, includes AYCE breakfast, evening pickup from Monson or from trailhead and return after breakfast. Please call for group pickup (up to 5) if possible. Laundry $5/load. Limited capacity in a quiet atmosphere; first-come, first serve, max 2 nights, cash only. Bikes for around-town use; grocery, restaurants, pubs, drugstore, library and post office all within a mile.

Suggestions for Providing Trail Magic. These suggestions incorporate Leave No Trace practices (www.LNT.org) to help those providing trail magic to have the most positive impact on hikers, the Trail, its plants, wildlife, and the volunteers who maintain and preserve it. The ATC and ALDHA endorse these suggestions.

Help conserve and maintain the Trail. The most essential service you can perform is to volunteer to maintain the AT & overnight sites, or to monitor boundaries and resource conditions. To find out how or where you may assist, visit www.appalachiantrail.org or check with your local trail-maintaining club.

Locate events in developed areas on durable surfaces. Large gatherings in the backcountry can lead to the disturbance of wildlife habitat. Trail towns and local parks are better locations. Keep events small. Consider whether your event may be contributing to an overabundance of trail feeds in the local area or region.

Prepare and serve food safely. If you will be cooking or preparing food, check with the landowner to find an appropriate area and learn what food-safety or other regulations apply. Permits may be required. Charging a fee or asking for donations may not be allowed.

Be present if you provide food or drink. Unattended items and their packaging can harm wildlife that consume them. Unattended items are considered litter and they detract from the wildland character of backcountry environments.

Restore the site. Leave the site as you found it—don't create a burden for Trail volunteers.

Advertise off-trail. Advertising—even noncommercial—is prohibited on the A.T.

Forgo alcoholic beverages. Don't risk the legality and liability associated with serving minors, over-serving adults, or the safety issues associated with intoxicated hikers.

Be hospitable to all. Be sure to make all trail users & volunteers feel welcome.

Visit ATC's Web site at www.appalachiantrail.org/trailmagic.

SoBo	NoBo		Elev

Elev axis: 6000, 5000, 4000, 3000, 2000, 1000

214 ME

⚠ Roads in the 100 M.W. are ambiguously named on maps and in "local use". Roads that pass near Logan Brook and Cooper Brook Shelters both may be referred to as "B Pond Road". When getting shuttles or supply drops be clear about the destination. All roads are privately owned, gated, and there are fees for using them.

SoBo	NoBo	Description	Elev
78.6	2110.6	**Carl A. Newhall Lean-to** 20.8◄16.8◄9.9◄►7.2►10.8►18.9. ♪♠♦⊂(6)	1938
		Gulf Hagas Brook, south of shelter, is water source.	
77.6	2111.6	Gulf Hagas Mountain	2713
76.8	2112.4	Sidney Tappan Campsite, water 0.1E ♠♦◁	2478
76.1	2113.1	West Peak	3178
74.5	2114.7	Hay Mountain	3244
73.7	2115.5	White Brook Trail to east	3004
72.8	2116.4	White Cap Mountain ▣	3650
71.9	2117.3	View of Katahdin from north side of mountain. ▣	2740
71.4	2117.8	**Logan Brook Lean-to** 24.0◄17.1◄7.2◄►3.6►11.7►23.1 ♪♠♦⊂(6)	2406
		Some tent sites; better sites 0.1N on AT. Logan Brook in front of lean-to; cascades upstream.	
69.8	2119.4	Logan Brook Rd (dirt). ♦	1620
		Piped spring 50 yards south of road, west of AT	
67.8	2121.4	**East Branch Lean-to,** Pleasant River in front. ♪♠♦⊂(6)	1261
		20.7◄10.8◄3.6◄►8.1►19.5►29.6	
67.5	2121.7	East branch of Pleasant River (ford). ♦	1224
65.9	2123.3	Mountain View Pond outlet ♦	1585
65.6	2123.6	Spring to east ♦	1570
64.3	2124.9	Side trail 100 yards to Little Boardman Mountain.	1980
63.0	2126.2	Cooper Brook Rd, a.k.a. Kokadjo-B Pond Rd (gravel)	1230
62.7	2126.5	West to beach on Crawford Pond (no camping) ♦	1253
62.1	2127.1	Cooper Brook ♦	1218

SoBo	NoBo		Elev
60.2	2129.0	Stream	1019
59.7	2129.5	**Cooper Brook Falls Lean-to** 18.9◄11.7◄8.1◄▶11.4▶21.5▶29.6 ⌂(6)	946
		Brook, falls, swimming hole in front of lean-to. Privy across trail and up hill.	
59.1	2130.1	Large tributary to Cooper Brook	835

> **❀ Indian pipe** – A plant without chlorophyll that grows in moist duff. Translucent white candy cane shape 3-4" tall, grows in clusters. Scale-like leaves/petals.

SoBo	NoBo		Elev
56.0	2133.2	Jo-Mary Rd .... N45 39.087 W69 1.900 **P** ♦ (pg.216)	625
54.6	2134.6	Footbridge, snowmobile trail	584
53.5	2135.7	Side trail 0.2E to north shore of Cooper Pond	520
53.1	2136.1	Mud Pond to west, footbridge over Mud Brook	508
51.8	2137.4	Antlers Campsite	500
		Campsites on edge of Jo-Mary Lake. Fort Relief two seat privy.	
50.3	2138.9	Potaywadjo Ridge Trail 1.0W	587
50.1	2139.1	East to sandy beach on lower Jo-Mary Lake	580
48.3	2140.9	**Potaywadjo Spring Lean-to** (1995) ⌂(8)	655
		23.1◄19.5◄11.4◄▶10.1▶18.2▶29.7 Potaywadjo Spring to right.	
48.0	2141.2	Tirio Access Rd (gravel)	579
47.7	2141.5	Twitchell Brook, footbridge, east to Pemadumcook Lake, view of Katahdin.	521
46.5	2142.7	Deer Brook	548
45.8	2143.4	Woods road	565
45.7	2143.5	Mahar Tote Rd (dirt)	566
45.6	2143.6	Tumbledown Dick Stream (ford)	558
45.1	2144.1	High water trail to west	561
44.5	2144.7	Ford branch of the Nahmakanta Stream	584
44.0	2145.2	Nahmakanta Stream Campsite	600
42.0	2147.2	Stream	676
41.1	2148.1	Gravel Road near south end of Nahmakanta Lake ..... N45 44.162 W69 06.208 **P**	687
		Camping on shore of Nahmakanta Lake is prohibited.	

2133.2   Jo-Mary Rd. (little traffic on road) 12.0E to ME 11.

🔥 🚿 ⛺ (9.0E) **Jo-Mary Campground** 207.723.8117 (2014 prices) Campsites $17 per person for ME residents, $22 non-residents; 2-person minimum (camping for one non-resident would cost $44). Pets welcome, coin operated showers and laundry. Open mid May - Mid Sep.

Manufacturers and Retailers

AntiGravityGear	910.794.3308	Garmont	800.943.4453	Patagonia	800.638.6464
Arc'Teryx	866.458.2473	Gossamer Gear	512.374.0133	Peak 1/Coleman	800.835.3278
Asolo/Lowe Alpine	603.448.8827	Granite Gear	218.834.6157	Petzl	877.807.3805
Backcountry.com	800.409.4502	Gregory	877.477.4292	Photon	877.584.6898
Big Agnes	877.554.8975	Hi-Tec	800.521.1698	Primus	307.857.4700
Black Diamond	801.278.5552	Hyperlite Mountain Gear	800.464.9208	Princeton Tec	800.257.9080
CamelBak	800.767.8725	Jacks 'R' Better	757.643.8908	REI	800.426.4840
Campmor	888.226.7667	JanSport	800.552.6776	Royal Robbins	800.587.9044
Camp Trails	800.345.7622	Katadyn/PUR	800.755.6701	Salomon	800.654.2668
Cascade Designs	800.531.9531	Keen	866.676.5336	Sierra Designs	800.736.8592
(MSR/Therm-a-Rest/Platypus)		Kelty	866.349.7225	Sierra Trading Post	800.713.4534
Cedar Tree (Packa)	276.780.2354	Leki	800.255.9982	Six Moon Designs	503.430.2303
Columbia	800.547.8066	Limmer	603.694.2668	Slumberjack	800.233.6283
Dana Designs	888.357.3262	LL Bean	800.441.5713	SOTO Outdoors	503.314.5119
Danner	877.432.6637	Marmont	888.357.3262	Speer Hammocks	252.619.8292
Eagle Creek	800.874.1048	Merrell	800.288.3124	Suunto	800.543.9124
Eastern Mountain Sports	888.463.6367	Montbell	877.666.8235	Tarptent / Henry Shires	650.587.1548
Etowah Outfitters	770.975.7829	Montrail	800.826.1598	Tecnica	800.258.3897
Eureka!	800.572.8822	Mountain Hardwear	800.953.8398	Teva	800.367.8382
Ex Officio	800.644.7303	Mountainsmith	800.551.5889	The Underwear Guys	570.573.0209
Feathered Friends	206.292.2210	Mystery Ranch	406.585.1428	ULA	435.753.5191
First Need	800.441.8166	NEMO	800.997.9301	Vasque	800.224.4453
Frogg Toggs	800.349.1835	North Face	866.715.3223	Warmstuff/Adventurelite	570.573.0209
Garmin	800.800.1020	Osprey	866.314.3130	Western Mountaineering	408.287.8944
		Outdoor Research	888.467.4327	Zip Stove	800.594.9046

Baxter State Park ⟨http://www.baxterstateparkauthority.com/hiking/thru-hiking.html⟩ ⟨https://www.facebook.com/baxterstatepark⟩

ℹ For information and reservations call 207.723.5140 8am-4pm, 7 days, between Memorial and Columbus Day. When driving, even as far as Medway, tune to AM 1610 for recent reports.

The hiking season is approximately May 15 through October 15. Dates vary based on weather, and trails in the park can be closed any day of the year due to weather. Weather reports are posted at **Katahdin Stream Campground** (KSC) at 7:00am every morning, along with "Trail Status and Alerts." Katahdin ascents may be disallowed even when the park is open. Consequences for hiking when the trail is closed include fines, equipment seizure and loss of park visitation privileges.

All hikers intending to climb Katahdin must sign in at KSC and sign out when leaving. Recommended cut-off times for starting hikes to Baxter Peak are noon in June and July, 11am in August, 10am in September, and 9am in October. Overnight camping above treeline is against park regulations and can damage rare alpine plants. Hikers are welcome to leave their backpack at KSC. Loaner daypacks are available at no charge from the KSC ranger's station. Northbound thru-hikers completing their hike in late summer or early fall usually have an easy time hitching from KSC into Millinocket.

There are fees for nonresidents entering the park by car and fees for use of campsites by residents and nonresidents. Fees must be paid in cash; no credit cards and no work-for-stay.

◣ ⼲ The Birches near KSC has 2 shelters and one tentsite, open to northbound long distance hikers who have hiked a minimum of "the 100 mile wilderness" immediately prior to entering the Park. Stay is limited to a single night, is limited to 12 persons (combined tenting and in the shelter) and the fee is $10 per person. ⚠ All other hikers, including flip-floppers and southbound thru-hikers, who wish to overnight in the Park should make reservations in advance. Common options, listed in order of their proximity to KSC are **Abol Campground**, **Daicey Pond Campground** (cabins $55D/ up) and **Foster Field Group Area**, just north of Katahdin. Note that Abol Campground in the Park, Abol Pines at Abol Bridge and the privately run Abol Bridge Campground are three distinct entities.

P If you are driving to Baxter: gates open 6am. Maine residents enter for free; $14 per vehicle for non-residents. KSC parking is limited to 25 cars and you will not be allowed to enter if the lots are full. Day-use parking reservations are highly recommended and can be obtained for KSC, Abol or Roaring Brook Campgrounds by phone up to three weeks in advance, for a $5 fee. There is no long-term parking in Baxter. Check with local taxi and shuttle services for info on long term parking outside the Park.

Cell phone reception is unlikely anywhere in the park other than on Katahdin, so do not count on calling for a ride from KSC. Even where there is reception, do not place calls from the summit or within earshot of other hikers. Please use a cell phone only if there is an emergency.

Pets are not allowed in the park.

🐕 Connie McManus 207.723.6795, 207.731.3111 Privately run kennel service; pickup/drop off at Abol Bridge.

SoBo	NoBo	Description	Elev
39.9	2149.3	Prentiss Brook	698
38.6	2150.6	Side trail east to sand beach on shore of Nahmakanta Lake	684
38.2	2151.0	**Wadleigh Stream Lean-to,** stream can be dry during summer. 29.6◄21.5◄10.1▼8.1►19.6►33.0	717
37.2	2152.0	Spring	809
36.3	2152.9	Nesuntabunt Mountain, short side trail east to view of Katahdin, 16 mile line-of-sight distance to Katahdin summit from here.	1520
35.8	2153.4	View	1180
35.1	2154.1	Wadleigh Pond Rd (gravel).	1028
34.4	2154.8	Crescent Pond west end	1008
33.6	2155.6	Pollywog Gorge, side trail overlooking gorge	900
32.6	2156.6	Pollywog Stream Cross stream on logging road bridge. N45 46.774 W69 10.320	681
30.6	2158.6	Outlet stream from Murphy Pond	971
30.1	2159.1	**Rainbow Stream Lean-to,** baseball bat floor. 29.6◄18.2◄8.1▼11.5►24.9►0.0 Tenting on hill behind lean-to. Excellent swimming hole upstream.	1023
28.2	2161.0	West to Rainbow Lake dam	1109
28.0	2161.2	Stream.	1071
26.3	2162.9	Rainbow Lake Campsite, spring west 30 yards.	1100
25.1	2164.1	Stream.	1080
24.8	2164.4	Unmarked trail leads 0.2W to Rainbow Lake Camps (private)	1124
24.5	2164.7	Trail 0.7E to Rainbow Mountain	1146
22.9	2166.3	Side trail 0.1E to Little Beaver Pond, 0.7E to Big Beaver Pond	1086
21.1	2168.1	Rainbow Ledges, view of Katahdin	1517

SoBo	NoBo	Description	Elev
18.6	2170.6	**Hurd Brook Lean-to,** baseball bat floor . . . . ☽ ◑ ⊏(6)	720
		29.7◀19.6◀11.5◀▶13.4▶0.0▶0.0	
18.1	2171.1	Small spring. . . . . ●	791
15.9	2173.3	Bog bridge	624
15.4	2173.8	Golden Rd (paved). Nobo east on road, **Millinocket, ME** (19E) . . . (pg.220)	609
15.1	2174.1	Abol Bridge crosses west branch . . . . N45 50.111 W68 58.158 🅿 (pg.220)	578
		of Penobscot River. Parking on east side of road between bridge and trailhead.	
14.7	2174.5	End of Golden Rd, Nobo veer left on dirt road.	620
14.6	2174.6	Abol Stream Trail to east, footbridge, Baxter State Park Boundary	606
14.3	2174.9	Information board, Abol Pond Trail east, registration for The Birches Campsites.	595
14.0	2175.2	Footbridge, Katahdin Stream, Foss and Knowlton Trail to east ●	591
13.2	2176.0	Foss and Knowlton Brook, footbridge ●	598
10.5	2178.7	Lower fork of Nesowadnehunk Stream . . . ●	626
		Both forks of this stream may require fording. There is a highwater bypass.	
9.5	2179.7	Upper fork of Nesowadnehunk Stream . . . ●	808
8.7	2180.5	Short side trail to view of Big Niagara Falls. 🄫	951
8.4	2180.8	Side trail west to Toll Dam and Little Niagara Falls.	1054
7.7	2181.5	Daicey Pond Nature Trail to west, parking area and privy north of trailhead 🅿 ☽	1096
6.9	2182.3	Tracy and Elbow Pond Trails to west, Daicey Pond Nature Trail to east ●	1119
6.2	2183.0	Grassy Pond Trail to west (two intersections). . . . ●	1082
5.8	2183.4	Footbridge, stream ●	1059
5.3	2183.9	Perimeter Rd ●	1090
5.2	2184.0	Katahdin Stream Campground. . . . ● ◭ ⊏(16)	1106
		The Birches Lean-tos & Campsite (0.2E) thru-hikers only, $10PP pay at KSC	
		ranger station or info board (9.1S). 33.0◀24.9◀13.4◀▶0.0▶0.0▶0.0	
4.0	2185.2	Owl Trail to west, footbridge, stream ●	1563
3.9	2185.3	Katahdin Stream Falls. ✗ How many benches are in the privy waiting area? ☽	1647
3.0	2186.2	Spring	2399
2.6	2186.6	Pass "The cave" small slab cave	2850
1.6	2187.6	The Gateway, The Tableland	4518
1.0	2188.2	Thoreau Spring, Abol Trail to east ●	4620
0.0	2189.2	**Katahdin,** Baxter Peak, Northern Terminus of the AT . . . (pg.220-221)	5268

SoBo | NoBo

219
ME

SoBo

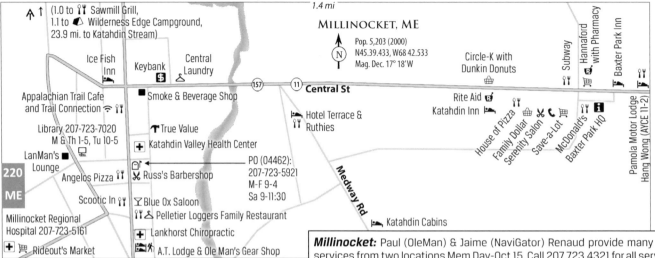

Millinocket, ME
Pop. 5,203 (2000)
N45.39.433, W68 42.533
Mag. Dec. 17° 18' W

1.4 mi

(1.0 to ↑↑ Sawmill Grill,
1.1 to ⚑ Wilderness Edge Campground,
23.9 mi. to Katahdin Stream)

Ice Fish Inn
Keybank
Central Laundry
Smoke & Beverage Shop
Appalachian Trail Cafe and Trail Connection
Library 207-723-7020 M & Th 1-5, Tu 10-5
True Value
Katahdin Valley Health Center
LanMan's Lounge
PO (04462): 207-723-5921 M-F 9-4 Sa 9-11:30
Russ's Barbershop
Angelos Pizza
Scootic In
Blue Ox Saloon
Pelletier Loggers Family Restaurant
Millinocket Regional Hospital 207-723-5161
Lankhorst Chiropractic
Rideout's Market
A.T. Lodge & Ole Man's Gear Shop

Central St

Medway Rd

Hotel Terrace & Ruthies

Katahdin Cabins

Circle-K with Dunkin Donuts
Rite Aid
Katahdin Inn
House of Pizza
Family Dollar
Serenity Salon
Save-a-Lot
McDonald's
Baxter Park HQ
Subway
Hannaford with Pharmacy
Baxter Park Inn
Pamola Motor Lodge
Hang Wong (AYCE 11-2)

220
ME

2173.8, 2174.1   Golden Rd, Abol Bridge

🛶 ↑↑ 🏪 📷 ✉ **Abol Bridge Campground & Store**
207.447.5803 ⟨www.abolcampground.com⟩ Closed in winter. Campsites (2014 prices) $16.05S, $25.68D includes tax. Shower w/o stay $5. Visa/MC accepted. Breakfast sandwiches & subs, sodas, ice cream, long-term resupply, white gas/oz and Heet. **The Northern Restaurant** on-site. ⚠ $10 maildrop fee, send well in advance: P.O. Box 536 Millinocket, ME 04462

🛶 **Abol Pines** $8+tax ($4+tax ME residents) self-register tent sites and shelters across the street from Abol Bridge Store, south of Golden Road. Provided by Maine Dept. of Conservation.

Millinocket: Paul (OleMan) & Jaime (NaviGator) Renaud provide many hiker services from two locations Mem Day-Oct 15. Call 207.723.4321 for all services in this block ⟨www.appalachiantraillodge.com⟩ credit cards accepted.

🛏🖥⚑♨🚲🅿🛜🖥✉ **The Appalachian Trail Lodge** Bunkroom $25, private room $35S, $55D, family suite $95D $10EAP. Showers for nonguests $3. Coin laundry. Free daily shuttle from Baxter park, from Sept 1, till Oct 15, between 3:30pm – 4:30pm. Licensed and insured shuttle service for hire to and from bus in Medway, into 100-Mile Wilderness or Monson, food drops. Slackpack in 100-Mile Wilderness, other shuttles by arrangement, free parking. No pets. SoBo special: pickup in Medway, bed in bunkroom, breakfast at AT Cafe, and shuttle to KSC. $70pp, by reservation. Maildrops for guests: 33 Penobscot Avenue, Millinocket, ME 04462.

🔥 **Ole Man's Gear Shop** Full line of gear at the lodge; packs, bags, fuel, stoves, poles, Southbound A.T. Guide and more. No clothing or shoes.

↑↑ ⚜ **The Appalachian Trail Cafe** Serves B/L/D

🔥🛜🖥 **Trail Connection** Above Cafe; computer, wireless, specialty coffee.

2189.2   Katahdin, Baxter Peak, **Millinocket, ME 04462** (24E)
Trail's End Festival Second weekend after Labor Day (Sept. 18-20) with vendors, food & entertainment. Hardcore trail work on Friday.

🛏️🍴📶 **Hotel Terrace & Ruthie's Restaurant** 207.723.4545 $70.15S, $80.95D. Ruthie's serves B/L/D.

🛏️⛺📶🖥️**Katahdin Inn** 207.723.4555 $70S, $80D +tax, $10EAP, indoor heated pool and hot tub.

🛏️🍴📶✉️ **Pamola Motor Lodge** 800.575.9746 $69S $10EAP up to 4. Pets $10. Cont. breakfast. **Hang Wong** Chinese restaurant on site with AYCE lunch buffet. Maildrops with reservation: 973 Central Street, Millinocket, ME 04462.

🛏️🍴📶✉️ **Katahdin Cabins** 207.723.6305 〈www.katahdincabins. com〉 Skip & Nicole Mohoff run eco-friendly cabins with continental breakfast, TV, DVD, frig & mwave. $65 up to 3 persons, $85 up to 5. Cafe on-site with coffee and baked goods. No smoking. Gas grill, bikes free for use, community room, accepts CC/cash/checks. Maildrops: 181 Medway Rd, Millinocket, ME 04462.

🛏️📶⛺ **Baxter Park Inn** 207.723.9777 $89.99D, $10EAP, pets $25, sauna, pool.

🛏️📶✉️ **Ice Fish Inn** 207.723.9999 $123-138 (double) includes full hot breakfast. Maildrops: PO Box 136, Millinocket, ME 04462.

🔌✨⛺📶🅿️ **Wilderness Edge Campground** 207.447.8485, Tent site $10PP, shower only $3, tax included. WiFi in office, coin laundry, section hiking guests park free. Campstore: soda, candy, ice cream.

🍴**Sawmill Grill** 207.447.6996 Open Tu-Sun 11am-11pm. Burgers, pizza, beer. "Mile High Club"; $20 for t-shirt, return from Katahdin with photo to get another t-shirt and a free meal.

🍴⛺ **Pelletier Loggers Family Restaurant** 207.723.6100 Open Wed-Sun 11am-9pm. Laundry adjacent open 7 days 8am-8pm.

■ ⛒ **LanMan's Lounge** Relax with TV, restroom; pack storage $5.
🚐 **Maine Quest Adventures** 207.447.5011, 207.746.9615 〈www.mainequestadventures.com〉 pick up at Medway bus station and drop off at Katahdin Stream or Abol Bridge. Shuttles to Monson

and parts of the 100- Mile Wilderness. Food Drops can be arranged.
🚐 **Bull Moose Taxi** 207.447.8079 Medway to Millinocket $18, Millinocket to KSC $57. Fares are per ride, $1 EAP up to 4 persons. Covers all of Maine.

🚐 **Millinocket Municipal Airport** 207.731.9906 Car rental available from airport on Medway Rd. one mile south of Central St.

✈ **Katahdin Air** 866.359.6246 〈www.KatahdinAir.com〉 One-way flights to many trailheads from Pemadumcook Lake to Monson. $65-135 per person, includes shuttle from Abol Bridge to seaplane base.

Getting to Katahdin

⚠️Flip-floppers and southbound hikers need a reservation to stay in Baxter State Park. See park rules on pg. 217.

Most routes to Katahdin are through Bangor, Maine, which has an airport and bus terminal. Bangor is 91 miles from Baxter SP. Shuttle services will pick you up in Bangor, but it is more economical to take **Cyr Bus Lines** to Medway, 31 miles from Baxter State Park. Hikers often layover in Millinocket, 24 miles from Katahdin Stream Campground, the closest parking area to Katahdin.

Bangor, ME - Medway, ME

🚌 **Cyr Bus Lines** 800.244.2335 〈www.cyrbustours.com〉 One-way routes 7 days $12. Cash, credit cards accepted. Routes below are to Concord Hub near airport; bus also stops at Greyhound station 20 min later (arrival) or 20 min sooner on departure.
Medway 9:30am (station at Irving store) to Bangor 10:50
Bangor 6:30pm to Medway 7:40pm
🚌 **Concord Trailways** 207.945.4000 〈www.concordtrailways.com〉 Hub near Bangor airport, service to South Station in Boston.
🚌 **The Appalachian Trail Lodge, Maine Quest Adventures, and Bull Moose Taxi,** all listed in Millinocket, provide transportation from Medway to Millinocket and Katahdin.

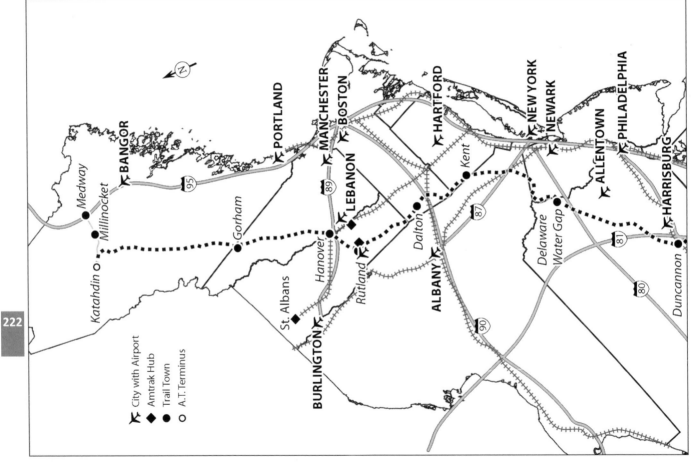

222

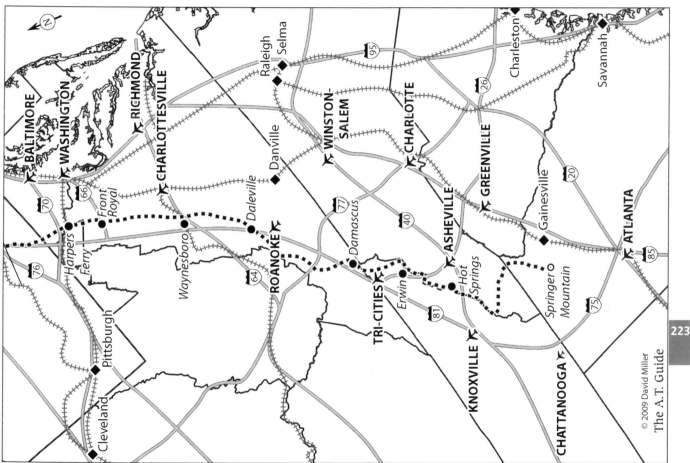

N

BALTIMORE

WASHINGTON

RICHMOND

CHARLOTTESVILLE

70

66

Front
Royal

Harpers
Ferry

76

Waynesboro

64

ROANOKE

Cleveland

Pittsburgh

Daleville

Raleigh
Selma

95

Charleston

Savannah

WINSTON-
SALEM

Danville

CHARLOTTE

26

GREENVILLE

20

Gainesville

ATLANTA

85

77

Damascus

40

ASHEVILLE

Hot
Springs

TRI-CITIES

Erwin

81

Springer
Mountain

75

KNOXVILLE

CHATTANOOGA

223

© 2009 David Miller

The A.T. Guide

The A.T. Guide is the guidebook of choice for hikes of any length on the Appalachian Trail. The book contains thousands of landmarks such as campsites, water sources, summits and gaps. The trail's elevation profile is included and every landmark is aligned to the profile. Hikers using this guide know where they are on the trail, what views, streams and campsites are ahead, and whether they'll be hiking uphill or downhill to get there.

The A.T. Guide answers all of your questions about how to get rides, where to stay, and where to get supplies. There are 80 maps of towns on or near the trail showing where to find these services and detailed listings for businesses.

The A.T. Guide is the most innovative trail guidebook ever developed.

- Mileages to trail landmarks, south-to-north and north-to-south.

- Elevation profile maps.

- Town and area maps.

- Mileages from all shelters to the next three shelters in each direction.

- GPS navigation coordinates for over 200 parking areas.

- Icons for easy identification of services.

$15.95

Jerelyn Press

www.theATguide.com

ISBN 978-0-9829808-7-3

9 780982 980873

51595>

O9-ATU-121

(800) 274-7333
Catalogue: free

Wayside Gardens
Hodges, SC 29695
(800) 845-1124
Catalogue: free

White Flower Farm
Route 63
Litchfield, CT 06759
(203) 496-9600
Catalogue: $4.00

African Violets and Other Gesneriads

Organizations

African Violet Society of America, Inc.
2375 North Street
Beaumont, TX 77702
(409) 839-4725
(800) 770-AVSA
Dues: $18.00
Publication: *African Violet*
(bimonthly magazine)

African Violet Society of Canada
c/o Bonnie Scanlan
1573 Arbourdale Avenue
Victoria, British Columbia V8N 5J1
(604) 477-7561
Dues: Canada $12.00; US $14.00
Publication: *Chatter* (quarterly)

American Gloxinia and Gesneriad
Society, Inc.
Horticultural Society of New York
128 West 58th Street
New York, NY 10019
Dues: $20.00
Publication: *The Gloxinian*
(bimonthly journal)

Gesneriad Correspondence Club
207 Wycoff Way West
East Brunswick, NJ 08816
Dues: $5.00
Publication: bimonthly newsletter

Gesneriad Hybridizers Association
Meg Stephenson
4115 Pillar Drive, Route 1
Whitmore Lake, MI 48189
Dues: $5.00
Publication: *Crosswords*

Gesneriad Research Foundation
1873 Oak Street
Sarasota, FL 34236

Gesneriad Society International
Richard Dunn
11510 124th Terrace North
Largo, FL 34648
(813) 585-4247
Dues: $16.50
Publication: *Gesneriad Journal*
(bimonthly)

Royal Saintpaulia Club
c/o Ms. A. Moffett
Box 198
Sussex, New Brunswick E0E 1P0

Saintpaulia and Houseplant Society
The Secretary
33 Church Road, Newbury Park
Ilford, Essex 1G2 7ET
England
(081) 590-3710
Dues: £5.00
Publication: quarterly bulletin

Saintpaulia International
1650 Cherry Hill Road South
State College, PA 16803
(814) 237-7410
Publication: *Saintpaulia International News*
(bimonthly)

Supplies and Tools

CMI Plastics
Box 369
Cranbury, NJ 08512
(609) 395-1920
Product: Humidi-Grow plant trays
Catalogue: free

Dyna-Gro™ Corporation
1065 Broadway
San Pablo, CA 94806
(800) DYNA-GRO
Product: Dyna-Gro™ fertilizer
Catalogue: free

Innis Violets
8 Madison Lane
Lynnfield, MA 01904
Products: growing supplies
and terrariums
Catalogue: $1.00

JF Industries
CHR 65, Box 309
Pryor, OK 74361
(918) 434-6768
Product: leaf supports
Catalogue: long SASE

Source Technology Biologicals, Inc.
(800) 356-8733
Product: Phyton® 27 fungicide

V-Base
920 Leland Avenue
Lima, OH 45805
Product: plant-finding computer database

Violet Express
1440–41 Everett Road
Eagle River, WI 54521
(715) 479-3099
Products: general supplies
Catalogue: $2.75

The Violet House
Box 1274
Gainesville, FL 32602
(904) 377-8465
Products: general supplies
Catalogue: free

The Violet Showcase
3147 South Broadway
Englewood, CO 80110
(303) 761-1770
Products: violet grooming kit;
general supplies
Catalogue: $1.00

W. F. G. & Associates
3345 Owens Brook Way
Kennesaw, GA 30152
(770) 974-0883
Product: Freedom® Planter

Plant Sources

A-mi Violettes
Box 630, 75 Marier Street
St.-Felix de Valois, Quebec J0K 2M0
(514) 889-8673
Catalogue: $2.00

African Queen
2351 Ballycastle Drive
Dallas, TX 75228
(214) 320-4944
Catalogue: $2.00

Alice's Violet Room
Route 6, Box 233
Waynesville, MO 65583
(314) 336-4763
Catalogue: long SASE

Belisle's Violet House
Box 111
Radisson, WI 54867
(715) 945-2687
Catalogue: $2.00

Big Sky Violets
10678 Schoolhouse Lane
Moiese, MT 59824
(406) 644-2296
Catalogue: $2.50

Cape Cod Violetry
28 Minot Street
Falmouth, MA 02540
(508) 548-2798
Catalogue: $2.00

Coda Gardens
Box 8417
Fredericksburg, VA 22404
Catalogue: $2.00

Florals of Fredericks
155 Spartan Drive
Maitland, FL 32751
Catalogue: $2.00

Hidden Valley Sinningias
Box 862
Indian Hills, CO 80454
(303) 697-4293
Catalogue: $1.00

JoS Violets
2205 College Drive
Victoria, TX 77901
(512) 575-1344
Catalogue: long SASE

Just Enough Sinningias
Patti Schwindt
Box 560493
Orlando, FL 32856
(407) 423-4750
Catalogue: $2.00

Karleens Achimenes
1407 West Magnolia
Valdosta, GA 31601
(912) 242-1368
Catalogue: $1.50

Kartuz Greenhouses
1408 Sunset Drive
Vista, CA 92083
(619) 941-3613
Catalogue: $2.00

Kent's Flowers
2501 East 23rd Avenue
Fremont, NE 68025
(402) 721-1478
Catalogue: 50¢

Lauray of Salisbury
432 Undermountain Road
Salisbury, CT 06068
(203) 435-2263
Catalogue: $2.00

Les Violettes Natalia
Box 206
Beecher Falls, VT 05902
(819) 889-3235
Catalogue: $2.00

Lyndon Lyon Greenhouses, Inc.
14 Mutchler Street
Dolgeville, NY 13329
(315) 429-8291
Catalogue: $2.00

McKinney's Glasshouse
89 Mission Road
Wichita, KS 67207
(316) 686-9438
Catalogue: $2.00

Mighty Minis
7318 Sahara Court
Sacramento, CA 95828
Catalogue: $2.00

Pat's Pets
Dunlap Enterprises
4189 Jarvis Road
Hillsboro, MO 63050
Catalogue: $1.00

Pleasant Hill African Violets
Route 1, Box 73
Brenham, TX 77833
(409) 836-9736
Catalogue: $1.50

Rob's Mini-o-lets
Box 9
Naples, NY 14512
(716) 374-8592
Catalogue: $1.00

Rozell Rose Nursery & Violet Boutique
12206 Highway 31 West
Tyler, TX 75709
(903) 595-5137
Catalogue: $1.00

Teas Nursery Company, Inc.
Box 1603
Bellaire, TX 77402
(800) 446-7723
Catalogue: $2.00

Tiki Nursery
Box 187
Fairview, NC 28730
(704) 628-2212
Catalogue: $2.00

Tinari Greenhouses
Box 190
2325 Valley Road
Huntington Valley, PA 19006
(215) 947-0144
Catalogue: $1.00

Travis' Violets
Box 42
Ochlocknee, GA 31773
(912) 574-5167
Catalogue: $1.00

Violet Creations
5520 Wilkins Road
Tampa, FL 33610

(813) 626-6817
Catalogue: free

Violet Express
1440–41 Everett Road
Eagle River, WI 54521
(715) 479-3099
Catalogue: $2.75

The Violet House
Box 1274
Gainesville, FL 32602
(904) 377-8465
Catalogue: free

Violets by Appointment
45 3rd Street
West Sayville, NY 11796
(516) 589-2724
Catalogue: $1.50

Violets Collectible
1571 Wise Road
Lincoln, CA 95648
(916) 645-3487
Catalogue: $2.00

The Violet Showcase
3147 South Broadway
Englewood, CO 80110
(303) 761-1770
Catalogue: $1.00

Volkmann Brothers Greenhouses
2714 Minert Street
Dallas, TX 75219
(214) 526-3484
Catalogue: $1.00

Weiss' Gesneriads
2293 South Taylor Road
Cleveland Heights, OH 44118
Catalogue: free

Jim Wildman
133 Rosemont Drive

Syracuse, NY 13205
(315) 492-2562
Catalogue: $1.00

Alpine Plants
See chapter 2, **Alpine and Rock Gardening**

Azaleas, Rhododendrons, and Woody Shrubs

Organizations

American Rhododendron Society
Barbara R. Hall, Executive Director
Box 1380
Gloucester, VA 23061
(804) 693-4433
Dues: $25.00
Publication: *Journal of the ARS* (quarterly)

Azalea Society of America, Inc.
Membership Chair
Box 34536
West Bethesda, MD 20827
(301) 585-5269
Dues: $20.00
Publication: *The Azalean* (quarterly)

Rhododendron Society of Canada
c/o R. S. Dickhout
5200 Timothy Crescent
Niagara Falls, Ontario L2E 5G3
(416) 357-5981
Note: *See* American Rhododendron Society

Rhododendron Species Foundation
Box 3798
Federal Way, WA 98063
(206) 838-4646
Dues: $30.00
Publication: *RSF Newsletter* (quarterly)

Woody Plant Society
c/o Betty Ann Mech
1315 66th Avenue NE

Minneapolis, MN 55432
(612) 574-1197
Dues: $15.00
Publication: *Bulletin* (biannual)

Plant Sources

Appalachian Gardens
Box 82
Waynesboro, PA 17268
(717) 762-4312
Catalogue: free

A Sandy Rhododendron
41610 SE Coalman Road
Sandy, OR 97055
(503) 668-4830
Catalogue: $5.00

Warren Baldsiefen
Box 88
Bellvale, NY 10912
Catalogue: $3.00

Barbour Bros., Inc.
RD 2
Stoneboro, PA 16153
Catalogue: free

Vernon Barnes & Son
Box 250
McMinnville, TN 37110
Catalogue: $3.00

Beaver Creek Nursery
Box 18243
Knoxville, TN 37928
(615) 922-3961
Catalogue: $1.00

Benjamin's Rhododendrons
Box 147
Sumner, WA 98390
Catalogue: $3.00

The Bovees Nursery
1737 SW Coronado
Portland, OR 97219
(800) 435-9250
Catalogue: $2.00

Briarwood Gardens
14 Gully Lane
East Sandwich, MA 02537
(508) 888-2146
Catalogue: $1.00

Broken Arrow Nursery
13 Broken Arrow Road
Hamden, CT 06518
(203) 288-1026
Catalogue: long SASE with three stamps

Brown's Kalmia and Azalea Nursery
8527 Semihamoo Drive
Blaine, WA 98230
(206) 371-2489
Catalogue: long SASE

Bull Valley Rhododendron Nursery
214 Bull Valley Road
Aspers, PA 17304
(717) 677-6313
Catalogue: $2.00

Camellia Forest Nursery
125 Carolina Forest
Chapel Hill, NC 27516
Catalogue: $1.00

Cape Cod Vireyas
405 Jones Road
Falmouth, MA 02540
(508) 548-1613
Catalogue: $3.00

Cardinal Nursery
Route 1, Box 316
State Road, NC 28676
Catalogue: $3.00

Carlson's Gardens
Box 305
South Salem, NY 10590
(914) 763-5958
Catalogue: $3.00

The Cummins Garden
22 Robertsville Road
Marlboro, NJ 07746
(908) 536-2591
Catalogue: $1.00

Phillip Curtis Farms
Box 640
Canby, OR 97013
Catalogue: $1.00

Eastern Plant Specialties
Box 226
Georgetown, ME 04548
(207) 371-2888
Catalogue: $3.00

Flora Lan Nursery
Route 1, Box 357
Forest Grove, OR 97116
Catalogue: $3.00

Forest Farm
990 Tetherow Road
Williams, OR 97544
(503) 846-7269
Catalogue: $3.00

Garver Gardens
Box 609
Laytonville, CA 95454
(707) 984-6724
Catalogue: free

Girard Nurseries
Box 428
Geneva, OH 44041
(216) 466-2881
Catalogue: free

Plant Sources

Gossler Farms Nursery
1200 Weaver Road
Springfield, OR 97477
(503) 746-3922
Catalogue: $2.00

The Greenery
1451 West Burdickville Road
Maple City, MI 49664
(616) 228-7037
Catalogue: free

Greer Gardens
1280 Goodpasture Island Road
Eugene, OR 97401
(800) 548-0111
Catalogue: $3.00

Hager Nurseries
RFD 5, Box 2000
Spotsylvania, VA 22553
Catalogue: 50¢

Hall Rhododendrons
1280 Quince Drive
Junction City, OR 97448
Catalogue: $1.00

Hammond's Acres of Rhodys
25911 70th Avenue NE
Arlington, WA 98223
(206) 435-9206
Catalogue: $2.00

James Harris Hybrid Azaleas
538 Swanson Drive
Lawrenceville, GA 30243
(404) 963-7463
Catalogue: long SASE

Hillhouse Nursery
90 Kresson-Gibbsboro Road
Voorhees, NJ 08043
(609) 784-6203
Catalogue: free

Holbrook Farm and Nursery
Box 368
115 Lance Road
Fletcher, NC 28732
(704) 891-7790
Catalogue: free

Homeplace Garden Nursery
Box 300
Harden Bridge Road
Commerce, GA 30529
(706) 335-2892
Catalogue: $2.00

Kellygreen Rhododendron Nursery
6924 Highway 38
Drain, OR 97435
(503) 836-2290
Catalogue: $1.25

Lamtree Farm
RR 1, Box 162
2323 Copeland Road
Warrensville, NC 28693
(910) 385-6144
Catalogue: $2.00

E. B. Nauman and Daughter
688 St. Davids Lane
Schenectady, NY 12309
(518) 276-6726
Catalogue: $1.00

North Coast Rhododendron Nursery
Box 308
Bodega, CA 94922
(707) 829-0600
Catalogue: $1.00

Nuccio's Nurseries
Box 6160
3555 Chaney Trail
Altadena, CA 91003
(818) 794-3383
Catalogue: free

Oak Hill Farm
204 Pressly Street
Clover, SC 29710
(803) 222-4245
Catalogue: $1.00

Red's Rhodies
15920 SW Oberst Lane
Sherwood, OR 97140
(503) 625-6331
Catalogue: long SASE with two stamps

Schild Azalea Gardens and Nursery
1705 Longview Street
Hixson, TN 37343
(615) 842-9686
Catalogue: $1.00

F. W. Schumacher Company, Inc.
36 Spring Hill Road
Sandwich, MA 02563
(508) 888-0659
Catalogue: free

Shepherd Hill Farm
200 Peekskill Hollow Road
Putnam Valley, NY 10579
(914) 528-5917
Catalogue: free

Sonoma Horticultural Nursery
3970 Azalea Avenue
Sebastopol, CA 95472
Catalogue: $2.00

Sorum's Nursery
18129 SW Belton Road
Sherwood, OR 97140
(503) 628-2354
Catalogue: long SASE

Southern Plants
Box 232
Semmes, AL 36575
Catalogue: $1.50

Stubbs Shrubs
23225 SW Bosky Dell Lane
West Linn, OR 97068
(503) 638-5048
Catalogue: $2.00

Sun, Wind & Rain
Box 505
Silverton, OR 97381
(503) 873-5541
Catalogue: free

Transplant Nursery
Parkertown Road
Lavonia, GA 30553
(706) 356-8947
Catalogue: $1.00

Westgate Garden Nursery
751 Westgate Drive
Eureka, CA 95503
(707) 442-1239
Catalogue: $4.00

Whitney Gardens and Nursery
Box F
31600 Highway 101
Brinnon, WA 98320
(360) 796-4411
Catalogue: $4.00

Bamboo

Organization

American Bamboo Society
666 Wagnon Road
Sebastopol, CA 95472
(518) 765-3507
Dues: $20.00
Publications: *ABS Newsletter* (bimonthly);
Journal of the ABS (irregular)

Plant Sources

Publication

Temperate Bamboo Quarterly
30 Myers Road
Summertown, TN 38483
(615) 964-4151
Frequency: quarterly
Subscription: $24.00

Plant Sources

A Bamboo Shoot
1462 Darby Road
Sebastopol, CA 95472
(707) 823-0131
Catalogue: $1.00

American Bamboo Company
345 West 2nd Street
Dayton, OH 45402
Catalogue: free

Bamboo Gardens of Washington
5015 192nd Place NE
Redmond, WA 98053
(206) 868-5166
Catalogue: $4.00

Bamboo Sourcery
666 Wagnon Road
Sebastopol, CA 95472
(707) 823-5866
Catalogue: $2.00

Kurt Bluemel, Inc.
2740 Greene Lane
Baldwin, MD 21013
(410) 557-7229
Catalogue: $3.00

Burt Associates Bamboo
Box 719
Westford, MA 01886
(508) 692-3240
Catalogue: $2.00

Endangered Species
Box 1830
Tustin, CA 92680
Catalogue: $6.00

New England Bamboo Company
Box 358
Rockport, MA 01966
(508) 546-3581
Catalogue: $2.00

Northern Groves
Box 86291
Portland, OR 97286
(503) 774-6353
Catalogue: $1.00

Raintree Nursery
393B Butts Road
Morton, WA 98356
(206) 496-6400
Catalogue: free

Steve Ray's Bamboo Gardens
909 79th Place South
Birmingham, AL 35206
(205) 833-2052
Catalogue: $2.00

Tornello Landscape
Box 788
Ruskin, FL 33570
(813)645-5445
Catalogue: $1.00

Tradewinds Nursery
28446 Hunter Creek Loop
Gold Beach, OR 97444
(503) 247-0835
Catalogue: long SASE

Upper Bank Nurseries
Box 486
670 South Ridley Creek Road
Media, PA 19063

(215) 566-0679
Catalogue: long SASE

Begonias

Organizations

American Begonia Society
c/o John Ingle, Jr.
157 Monument Road
Rio Bell, CA 95562
(707) 764-5407
Dues: $21.00
Publication: *The Begonian*
 (bimonthly magazine)

British Columbia Fuchsia and Begonia
Society
c/o Lorna Herchenson
2402 Swinburne Avenue
North Vancouver, British Columbia
V7H 1L2
(604) 929-5382
Dues: Canada $10.00
Publication: *The Eardrop*
 (11 times annually)

Canadian Begonia Society
70 Enfield Avenue
Toronto, Ontario M8W 1T9
Dues: Canada $20.00

Plant Sources

Antonelli Brothers
2545 Capitola Road
Santa Cruz, CA 95062
(408) 475-5222
Catalogue: $1.00

B & K Tropicals
5300 48th Terrace North
St. Petersburg, FL 33709
(813) 522-8691
Catalogue: $1.00

Cruickshank's, Inc.
1015 Mount Pleasant Road
Toronto, Ontario M4P 2M1
(416) 488-8292
(800) 665-5605
Catalogue: $3.00

Daisy Farm
9995 SW 66th Street
Miami, FL 33173
(305) 274-9813
Catalogue: $2.00

Fairyland Begonia and Lily Garden
1100 Griffith Road
McKinleyville, CA 95521
(707) 839-3034
Specialties: hybrid lilies
Catalogue: 50¢

Golden Hills Nursery
Box 247, Macdoel, CA 96058
(916) 398-4023
Catalogue: $2.00

Kartuz Greenhouses
1408 Sunset Drive
Vista, CA 92083
(619) 941-3613
Catalogue: $2.00

Kay's Greenhouses
207 West Southcross
San Antonio, TX 78221
Catalogue: $2.00

Lauray of Salisbury
432 Undermountain Road
Salisbury, CT 06068
(203) 435-2263
Catalogue: $2.00

Logee's Greenhouses
141 North Street
Danielson, CT 06239
Catalogue: $3.00

Paul P. Lowe
5741 Dewberry Way
West Palm Beach, FL 33415
(407) 686-9392
Catalogue: long SASE

Miree's
70 Enfield Avenue
Toronto, Ontario M8W 1T9
(416) 251-6369
Catalogue: $2.00

Palos Verdes Begonia Farm
4111 242nd Street
Torrance, CA 90505
(800) 349-9299
Catalogue: $2.00

Sunshine State Tropicals
Box 1033
Port Richey, FL 34673
(813) 841-9618
Catalogue: $1.00

Van Bourgondien Bros.
245 Farmingdale Road
Babylon, NY 11702-0598
(516) 669-3500
(800) 622-9997
Catalogue: free

Vicki's Exotic Plants
522 Vista Park Drive
Eagle Point, OR 97524
(503) 826-6318
Catalogue: $1.00

White Flower Farm
Box 63
Litchfield, CT 06759
(203) 496-9600
Catalogue: $4.00

Bog Plants
See chapter 2, **Water Gardening**

Bonsai
See chapter 2, **Bonsai**

Bromeliads and Epiphytic Plants
See also chapter 2, **Orchids**

Organizations

Bromeliad Society, Inc.
2488 East 49th Street
Tulsa, OK 74105
Dues: $20.00
Publication: *BSI Journal* (bimonthly)

The Cryptanthus Society
2355 Rusk
Beaumont, TX 77702
(409) 835-0644
Dues: $10.00
Publications: *The Cryptanthus Journal*
(quarterly); *Yearbook*

Epiphyllum Society of America
Betty Berg, Membership Secretary
Box 1395
Monrovia, CA 91017
(818) 447-9688
Dues: $10.00
Publication: *The Bulletin* (bimonthly)

Epiphytic Plant Study Group
c/o Dr. Seymour Linden
1535 Reeves Street
Los Angeles, CA 90035
(310) 556-1923
Dues: $12.50
Publication: *Epiphytes* (journal)

Plant Sources

Alberts and Merkel Brothers
2210 South Federal Highway
Boynton Beach, FL 33435
(407) 732-2071
Catalogue: $1.00

Don Beadle
First Dirt Road
Venice, FL 34292
(813) 485-1096
Specialties: billbergias
Catalogue: SASE

Bird Rock Tropicals
6523 El Camino Real
Carlsbad, CA 92009
(619) 438-9393
Specialties: tillandsias
Catalogue: long SASE

Arthur Boe Distributor
Box 6655
New Orleans, LA 70114
Specialties: tillandsias
Catalogue: SASE

City Gardens
451 West Lincoln
Madison Heights, MI 48071
(313) 398-2660
Catalogue: $2.00

Colin's Nursery
448 North Lake Pleasant Road
Apopka, FL 32712
(407) 886-2982
Specialties: cryptanthus
Catalogue: $1.00

Cornelison Bromeliads
225 San Bernardino Street
North Fort Myers, FL 33903
(813) 995-4206
Catalogue: SASE

Dane Company
4626 Lamont Street
Corpus Christi, TX 78411
(512) 852-3806
Catalogue: long SASE

Epi World
10607 Glenview Avenue
Cupertino, CA 95014
(408) 865-0566
Catalogue: $2.00

Fox Orchids, Inc.
6615 West Markham Street
Little Rock, AR 72205
(501) 663-4246
Catalogue: free

Golden Lake Greenhouses
10782 Citrus Drive
Moorpark, CA 93021
(805) 529-3620
Catalogue: $2.00

Gray/Davis Epiphyllums
Box 710443
Santee, CA 92072
(619) 448-2540
Catalogue: $2.00

Holladay Jungle
Box 5727
1602 East Fountain Way
Fresno, CA 93755
(209) 229-9858
Specialties: tillandsias
Catalogue: free

Kenner & Sons
10919 Explorer Road
La Mesa, CA 91941
(619) 660-0161
Catalogue: free

Lauray of Salisbury
432 Undermountain Road
Salisbury, CT 06068
(203) 435-2263
Catalogue: $2.00

Ann Mann's Orchids
9045 Ron-Den Lane

Plant Sources

Windermere, FL 34786
(407) 876-2625
Catalogue: $1.00

Marilyn's Garden
13421 Sussex Place
Santa Ana, CA 92705
(714) 633-1375
Catalogue: $2.00

Michael's Bromeliads
1365 Canterbury Road North
St. Petersburg, FL 33710
(813) 347-0349
Catalogue: long SASE

Northwest Epi Center
2735 SE Troutdale Road
Troutdale, OR 97060
(503) 666-4171
Catalogue: $2.00

Oak Hill Gardens
Box 25
Dundee, IL 60118
(708) 428-8500
Catalogue: $1.00

Pineapple Place
3961 Markham Woods Road
Longwood, FL 32779
(407) 333-0445
Catalogue: long SASE

Rainbow Gardens Nursery and Bookshop
1444 East Taylor Street
Vista, CA 92084
(619) 758-4290
Catalogue: $2.00

Rainforest Flora
1927 West Rosecrans Avenue
Gardena, CA 90249
(310) 515-5200
Catalogue: $2.00

Russell's Bromeliads
1690 Beardall Avenue
Sanford, FL 32771
(800) 832-5632
Specialties: tillandsias
Catalogue: SASE

Shelldance Nursery
2000 Highway 1
Pacifica, CA 94044
(415) 355-4845
Catalogue: $1.00

Southern Exposure
35 Minor Street
Beaumont, TX 77702
(409) 835-0644
Specialties: cryptanthus
Catalogue: $5.00

Tropiflora
3530 Tallevast Road
Sarasota, FL 34243
(813) 351-2267
Specialties: tillandsias
Catalogue: free

Bulbs
See also **Daffodils**

Organization

International Bulb Society
Box 4928
Culver City, CA 90230
Dues: $30.00
Publication: *Herbertia* (annual journal)

Plant Sources

Jacques Amand
Box 59001
Potomac, MD 20859
(301) 762-2942
(800) 452-5414

Specialties: spring and summer bloomers
Catalogue: $2.00

Amaryllis, Inc.
Box 318
1452 Glenmore Avenue
Baton Rouge, LA 70821
(504) 924-5560
Specialties: amaryllis
Catalogue: $1.00

Autumn Glade Botanicals
46857 West Ann Arbor Trail
Plymouth, MI 48170
Specialties: summer bloomers
Catalogue: free

Bio-Quest International
Box 5752
Santa Barbara, CA 93150
(805) 969-4072
Specialties: South African bulbs
Catalogue: $2.00

Breck's
U.S. Reservation Center
6523 North Galena Road
Peoria, IL 61656
(800) 722-9069
Specialties: spring bloomers
Catalogue: free

The Bulb Crate
2560 Deerfield Road
Riverwoods, IL 60015
(708) 317-1414
Catalogue: $1.00

Bundles of Bulbs
112 Greenspring Valley Road
Owings Mills, MD 21117
(410) 363-1371
Specialties: spring bloomers
Catalogue: $1.00

Cruickshank's, Inc.
1015 Mount Pleasant Road
Toronto, Ontario M4P 2M1
(416) 488-8292
(800) 665-5605
Specialties: spring and summer bloomers
Catalogue: $3.00

The Daffodil Mart
1004 Daffodil Lane
Route 3, Box 794
Gloucester, VA 23601
(804) 693-3966
Catalogue: free

Peter deJager Bulb Company
Box 2010
188 Asbury Street
South Hamilton, MA 01982
(508) 468-4707
Specialties: Dutch bulbs
Catalogue: free

Dick's Flower Farm
North 5028 Delaney Road
Delavan, WI 53115
(414) 724-5682
Specialties: summer bloomers
Catalogue: $1.00

Jim Duggan Flower Nursery
1817 Sheridan
Leucadia, CA 92024
(619) 943-1658
Specialties: South African bulbs
Catalogue: $2.00

Dunford Farms
Box 238
Sumner, WA 98390
Specialties: agapanthus, alstromerias,
cyclamens
Catalogue: $1.00

Plant Sources

Dutch Gardens, Inc.
Box 200
Adelphia, NJ 07710
(908) 780-2713
(800) 818-3861
Specialties: Dutch bulbs, summer
bloomers
Catalogue: free

Flowers & Greens
Box 1802
Davis, CA 95617
(916) 756-9238
Specialties: alstromerias, gladioli, freesias
Catalogue: $2.00

Howard B. French Bulb Importer
Route 100
Pittsfield, VT 05762
(802) 746-8148
Specialties: spring bloomers
Catalogue: free

Russell Graham, Purveyor of Plants
4030 Eagle Crest Road NW
Salem, OR 97304
(503) 362-1135
Specialties: species bulbs
Catalogue: $2.00

GreenLady Gardens
1415 Eucalyptus Drive
San Francisco, CA 94132
(415) 753-3332
Specialties: spring and summer bloomers
Catalogue: $3.00

Growers Service Company
10118 Crouse Street
Hartland, MI 48353
Specialties: species and exotic bulbs
Catalogue: $5.00

Holland Bulb Farm
354 Old Hook Road
Westwood, New Jersey 06765

(201) 391-3499
Catalogue: free

Holland Bulb Farm, Inc.
Box 220
Tatamy, PA 18085
(800) 283-5082
Catalogue: free

Jackson & Perkins Company
2518 South Pacific Highway
Medford, OR 97501
(800) 292-4769
Specialties: spring bloomers
Catalogue: free

Kelly's Plant World
10266 East Princeton
Sanger, CA 93657
(209) 294-7676
Specialties: summer bloomers
Catalogue: $1.00

John D. Lyon
143 Alewife Brook Parkway
Cambridge, MA 02140
Catalogue: $3.00

Mad River Imports
RR 1, Box 1695
Rankin Road
Moretown, VT 05660
(802) 496-3004
Specialties: spring bloomers
Catalogue: free

McClure & Zimmerman
Box 368
108 West Winnebago
Friesland, WI 53935
(414) 326-4220
Specialties: Dutch and species bulbs
Catalogue: free

Messelaar Bulb Company
Box 269
Ipswich, MA 01938
(508) 356-3737
Specialties: Dutch bulbs
Catalogue: free

Michigan Bulb Company
1950 Waldorf NW
Grand Rapids, MI 49550
Specialties: Dutch bulbs
Catalogue: free

Charles H. Mueller Company
7091 North River Road
New Hope, PA 18938
(215) 862-2033
Specialties: spring and summer bloomers
Catalogue: free

New Holland Bulb Company
Box 335
Rockport, IL 62370
Catalogue: free

Old House Gardens
536 3rd Street
Ann Arbor, MI 48103
(313) 995-1486
Specialties: historical bulbs
Catalogue: $1.00

Robinett Bulb Farm
Box 1306
Sebastopol, CA 95473
(707) 829-2729
Specialties: West Coast–native bulbs
Catalogue: free

John Scheepers, Inc.
Box 700
Bantam, CT 06750
(203) 567-0838
Specialties: spring and summer bloomers
Catalogue: free

Schipper & Co., USA
Box 7584
Greenwich, CT 06836-7584
(203) 625-0638
(800) 877-8637
Specialties: spring bloomers
Catalogue: free

Skolaski's Glads and Field Flowers
4821 County Highway Q
Waunakee, WI 53597
(608) 836-4822
Specialties: summer bloomers
Catalogue: free

Sunsweet Bulb Company
Box Z
Sumner, GA 31789
(912) 386-2211
Catalogue: $1.00

Ty Ty Plantation Bulbs
Box 159
Ty Ty, GA 31795
(912) 382-0404
Specialties: spring and summer bloomers
Catalogue: $2.00

Van Bourgondien Bros.
Box 1000
245 Farmingdale Road
Babylon, NY 11702
(516) 669-3500
(800) 622-9997
Specialties: spring and summer bloomers
Catalogue: free

Van Dyck's Flower Farms, Inc.
Box 430-4033
Brightwaters, NY 11718-9831
(800) 248-2852
Specialties: spring bloomers
Catalogue: free

Van Engelen, Inc.
Stillbrook Farm

Plant Sources

313 Maple Street
Litchfield, CT 06759
(203) 567-8734
Catalogue: free

VanLierop Bulb Farm
13407 80th Street East
Puyallup, WA 98372
(206) 848-7272
Catalogue: $1.00

Mary Mattison van Schaik
Box 32
Cavendish, VT 05412
(802) 226-7653
Specialties: Dutch bulbs
Catalogue: $1.00

Veldheer Tulip Gardens
12755 Quincy Street
Holland, MI 49424
(616) 399-1900
Specialties: Dutch bulbs
Catalogue: free

Mary Walker Bulb Company
Box 256
Omega, GA 31775
(912) 386-1919
Catalogue: $1.00

The Waushara Gardens
N5491 5th Drive
Plainfield, WI 54966
(715) 335-4462
Specialties: summer bloomers
Catalogue: $1.00

White Flower Farm
Route 63
Litchfield, CT 06759
(203) 469-9600
Specialties: spring and summer bloomers
Catalogue: $4.00

Wildflower Nursery
1680 Highway 25-70
Marshall, NC 28753
(704) 656-2681
Specialties: Southeast-native plants
Catalogue: $1.00

Cacti and Succulents

Organizations

British Cactus and Succulent Society
Mr. P. A. Lewis, FBCSS
Firgrove, 1 Springwoods, Courtmoor
Fleet, Hants. GU13 9SU
England
Dues: £13.00
Publications: *British Cactus and Succulent Journal* (quarterly); *Bradleya* (annual)

Cactus and Succulent Society of America
c/o Dr. Seymour Linden
1535 Reeves Street
Los Angeles, CA 90035
(310) 556-1923
Dues: $30.00
Publication: *Cactus & Succulent Journal* (bimonthly)

Desert Plant Society of Vancouver
6200 McKay Avenue, Box 145-790
Barnaby, British Columbia V5H 4MY
(604) 525-5315
Dues: Canada $15.00

Toronto Cactus and Succulent Club
David Naylor
RR 2
9091 8th Line Road
Georgetown, Ontario L7G 4S5
(416) 877-6013
Dues: Canada $20.00
Publication: *Cactus Factus*

Publications

The Amateur's Digest
Marina Welham, Editor
8591 Lochside Drive
Sidney, British Columbia V8L 1M5
Frequency: bimonthly
Subscription: US $20.00

Desert Plants
Boyce Thompson Southwestern
Arboretum
Box AB
Superior, AZ 85273
(602) 689-2723
Frequency: quarterly
Subscription: $15.00

Other Information and Sources

*A free directory of California's cactus nurseries
(wholesale and retail) is available from:*

California Cactus Growers Association
11152 Palm Terrace Lane
Riverside, CA 92505

*Software for managing your cactus collection is
available from:*

Lucio Mondolfo
6563 College Hill Road
Clinton, NY 13323
Programs: CactusBase database; Lexicon
of Cactus Names
System requirements: IBM DOS 3.1+,
4MB RAM

Plant Sources

Abbey Garden Cactus
Box 2249
La Habra, CA 90632
(805) 684-5112
Catalogue: $3.00

Arid Lands Greenhouses
3560 West Bilby Road
Tucson, AZ 85746
(520) 883-9404
Catalogue: SASE

Aztekakti/Desertland Nursery
Box 26126
11306 Gateway East
El Paso, TX 79926
(915) 858-1130
Catalogue: $1.00

B & B Cactus Farm
11550 East Speedway
Tucson, AZ 85748
(602) 721-4687
Catalogue: SASE

Betsy's Brierpatch
1610 Ellis Hollow Road
Ithaca, NY 14850
(607) 273-6266
Catalogue: long SASE

Blossom Creek Greenhouse
Box 598
North Plain, OR 97133
(503) 647-0915
Catalogue: $2.00

Cactus by Dodie
934 Mettler Road
Lodi, CA 95242
(209) 368-3692
Catalogue: $2.00

Cactus by Mueller
10411 Rosedale Highway
Bakersfield, CA 93312
(805) 589-2674
Catalogue: $2.00

Cactus Farm
Route 5, Box 1610
Nacogdoches, TX 75961

(409) 560-6406
Catalogue: free

Christa's Cactus
529 West Pima
Coolidge, AZ 85228
(602) 723-4185
Catalogue: $1.00

Desert Moon Nursery
Box 600
Veguita, NM 87062
(505) 864-0614
Catalogue: $1.00

Desert Nursery
1301 South Copper
Deming, NM 88030
(505) 546-6264
Catalogue: free

Desert Theatre
17 Behler Road
Watsonville, CA 95076
(408) 728-5513
Catalogue: $2.00

The Great Petaluma Desert
5010 Bodega Avenue
Petaluma, CA 94952
(707) 778-8278
Catalogue: $3.00

Grigsby Cactus Gardens
2326 Bella Vista
Vista, CA 92084
(619) 727-1323
Catalogue: $2.00

Henrietta's Nursery
1345 North Brawley
Fresno, CA 93722
(209) 275-2166
Catalogue: $1.00

Highland Succulents
1446 Bear Run Road
Gallipolis, OH 45631
(614) 256-1428
Catalogue: $2.00

Intermountain Cactus
1478 North 750 East
Kaysville, UT 84037
(801) 546-2006
Catalogue: long SASE

K & L Cactus and Succulent Nursery
9500 Brook Ranch Road East
Ione, CA 95640
(209) 274-0360
Catalogue: $3.00

Lauray of Salisbury
432 Undermountain Road
Salisbury, CT 06068
(203) 435-2263
Catalogue: $2.00

Living Stones Nursery
2936 North Stone
Tucson, AZ 85705
(602) 628-8773
Specialties: lithops and mesembs
Catalogue: $2.00

Loehman's Cactus Patch
Box 871
Paramount, CA 90723
(310) 428-4501
Catalogue: $1.00

Mesa Garden
Box 72
Belen, NM 87002
(505) 864-3131
Catalogue: two stamps

Midwest Cactus
Box 163
New Melle, MO 63365

(314) 828-5389
Specialties: opuntias
Catalogue: $1.00

Miles' To Go
Box 6
Cortaro, AZ 85652
Catalogue: free

Nature's Curiosity Shop
3551 Evening Canyon Road
Oceanside, CA 92056
Specialties: succulents
Catalogue: $1.00

New Mexico Cactus Research
Box 787
1132 East River Road
Belen, NM 87002
(505) 864-4027
Catalogue: $1.00

New Mexico Desert Garden
10231 Belnap NW
Albuquerque, NM 87114
(505) 898-0121
Catalogue: $2.00

Northridge Gardens
9821 White Oak Avenue
Northridge, CA 91325
(818) 349-9798
Specialties: succulents
Catalogue: $1.00

Plantasia Cactus Gardens
867 Filer Avenue West
Twin Falls, ID 83301
(208) 734-7959
Specialties: winter-hardy cacti
Catalogue:two stamps

Plants of the Southwest
Agua Fria
Route 6, Box 11
Santa Fe, NM 87505

(800) 788-SEED
Catalogue: $3.50

Rainbow Gardens Nursery and Bookshop
1444 Taylor Street
Vista, CA 92084
(619) 758-4290
Catalogue: $2.00

Rare Plant Research
13245 SE Harold
Portland, OR 97236
Specialties: rare succulents
Catalogue: $2.00

Redlo Cacti
2315 NW Circle Boulevard
Corvallis, OR 97330
(503) 752-2910
Catalogue: $2.00

Schulz Cactus Growers
1095 Easy Street
Morgan Hill, CA 95037
(408) 683-4489
Catalogue: free

Scotty's Desert Plants
Box 1017
Selma, CA 93662
(209) 891-1026
Catalogue: $1.00

The Seed Shop
Tongue River Stage
Miles City, MT 59301
Specialties: seeds
Catalogue: $2.00

Shein's Cactus
3360 Drew Street
Marina, CA 93933
(408) 384-7765
Catalogue: $1.00

Bob Smoley's Gardenworld
4038 Watters Lane
Gibsonia, PA 15044
(412) 443-6770
Catalogue: SASE

Southwestern Exposure
10310 East Fennimore
Apache Junction, AZ 85220
(602) 986-7771
Catalogue: two stamps

Strong's Alpine Succulents
Box 50115
Parks, AZ 86018
(602) 526-5784
Catalogue: $1.00

Succulenta
Box 480325
Los Angeles, CA 90048
(213) 933-1552
Catalogue: $1.00

Sunrise Nursery
13705 Pecan Hollow
Leander, TX 78641
(512) 259-1877
Catalogue: $1.00

Winter Country Cacti
Box 296
Littleton, CO 80160
Catalogue: $2.00

Caladiums

Plant Sources

Caladium World
Drawer 629
Sebring, FL 33871
(813) 385-7661
Catalogue: free

Fancy Leaf Caladiums
704 County Road 621 East
Lake Placid, FL 33852
(813) 465-0044
Catalogue: free

Rainbow Acres
Box 1362
Avon Park, FL 33825
(813) 382-4449
Catalogue: free

Spaulding Bulb Farm
1811 Howey Road
Sebring, FL 33872
Catalogue: $1.00

Camellias

Organizations

American Camellia Society
Massee Lane Gardens
1 Massee Lane
Fort Valley, GA 31030
(912) 967-2358
Dues: $20.00
Publication: *The Camellia Journal*
(quarterly)

International Camellia Society
c/o Thomas H. Perkins III
Box 750
Brookhaven, MS 39601
(601) 833-7351
Dues: $13.00
Publication: *International Camellia Journal*
(annual)

Southern California Camellia Society
c/o Mrs. Bobbie Belcher
7457 Brydon Road
La Verne, CA 91750

Plant Sources

Camellia Forest Nursery
125 Carolina Forest
Chapel Hill, NC 27516
Catalogue: $1.00

Erinon Nursery
Box 325
Plymouth, FL 32768
(407) 886-7917
Catalogue: SASE

Fairweather Gardens
Box 330
Greenwich, NJ 08323
(609) 451-6261
Catalogue: $3.00

Nuccio's Nurseries
Box 6160
3555 Chaney Trial
Altadena, CA 91003
(818) 794-3383
Catalogue: free

Valdosta Camellia Scions
2436 Meadowbrook Drive
Valdosta, GA 31602
(912) 242-1390
Catalogue: send want list

Wheelers Nursery, Inc.
Route 20
Macon, GA 31211
(912) 745-3131
Note: no shipping
Catalogue: SASE

Woodlanders, Inc.
1128 Colleton Avenue
Aiken, SC 29801
(803) 648-7522
Catalogue: $2.00

Campanulas

Plant Source

Campanula Connoisseur
702 Traver Trail
Glenwood Springs, CO 81601
Catalogue: $1.00

Cannas

Plant Sources

Brudy's Exotics
Box 820874
Houston, TX 77282
(800) 926-7333
Catalogue: free

Kelly's Plant World
10266 East Princeton
Sanger, CA 93657
(209) 294-7676
Catalogue: $1.00

Wheel View Farm
212 Reynolds Road
Shelburne, MA 01370
Catalogue: $1.00

Carnivorous Plants

Organizations

The Carnivorous Plant Society
174 Baldwins Lane
Croxley Green, Hertfordshire WD3 3LQ
England
Dues: £13.00
Publication: *Journal of the Carnivorous Plant Society* (quarterly)

International Carnivorous Plant Society
Fullerton Arboretum

Plant Sources

California State University
Fullerton, CA 92634
(714) 773-2766
Dues: $15.00
Publication: *Carnivorous Plant Newsletter* (quarterly)

Plant Sources

Acid-Wetland Flora
1705 North Quebec Street
Arlington, VA 22207
(703) 524-3181
Catalogue: $1.50

Botanique Nursery
Route 1, Box 183
Stanardsville, VA 22973
Catalogue: $1.00

California Carnivores
7020 Trenton-Healdsburg Road
Forestville, CA 95436
(707) 838-1630
Catalogue: $2.00

Carolina Exotic Gardens
Route 5, Box 238A
Greenville, NC 27834
(919) 758-2600
Catalogue: $1.00

Glasshouse Works
Box 97, Church Street
Stewart, OH 45778
(614) 662-2142
Catalogue: $2.00

Hungry Plants
1216 Cooper Drive
Raleigh, NC 27607
(919) 829-3751
Catalogue: free

Lee's Botanical Garden
Box 669

LaBelle, FL 33935
(813) 675-8728
Catalogue: free

Marie's Orchids and Carnivorous Plants
6400 Cedarbrook Drive
Pinellas Park, FL 34666
(813) 546-7882
Catalogue: $1.00

Orgel's Orchids
18950 SW 136th Street
Miami, FL 33196
(305) 233-7168
Catalogue: free

Peter Paul's Nursery
4665 Chapin Road
Canandaigua, NY 14424
(716) 394-7397
Catalogue: free

Chuck Powell
2932 Sunburst Drive
San Jose, CA 95111
(408) 363-0926
Catalogue: $1.00

Southern Carnivores
Box 864081
Marietta, GA 30060
Catalogue: $2.00

Tropiflora
3530 Tallevast Road
Sarasota, FL 34243
(813) 351-2267
Catalogue: free

Chrysanthemums

Organizations

Canadian Chrysanthemum and Dahlia Society

c/o Karen Ojaste
17 Granard Boulevard
Scarborough, Ontario M1M 2E2
(416) 269-6960
Dues: Canada $10.00

National Chrysanthemum Society (UK)
H. B. Locke
2 Lucas House, Craven Road
Rugby, Warwickshire CV21 3HY
England
(0788) 56-9039
Dues: $15.00
Publications: fall and spring bulletins;
yearbook

National Chrysanthemum Society, Inc.
(US)
Galen L. Goss
10107 Homar Pond Drive
Fairfax Station, VA 22039
(703) 978-7981
Dues: $12.50
Publication: *The Chrysanthemum* (quarterly)

Publication

Chrysanthemum Corner with Peony Highlights
Box 5635
Dearborn, MI 48128
Frequency: bimonthly
Subscription: $18.00

Plant Sources

Dooley Mum Gardens
210 North High Drive NE
Hutchinson, MN 55350
(612) 587-3050
Catalogue: $2.00

Huff's Garden Mums
710 Juniatta
Burlington, KS 66839
(316) 364-2765
(800) 279-4675

Catalogue: $2.00

King's Mums
20303 East Liberty Road
Clements, CA 95227
(209) 759-3571
Catalogue: $2.00

Mums by Paschke
12286 East Main Road
North East, PA 16428
(814) 725-9860
Catalogue: free

Sunnyslope Gardens
8638 Huntington Drive
San Gabriel, CA 91775
(818) 287-4071
Catalogue: free

Clematis

Organization

The British Clematis Society
Mrs. B. Risdon, Membership Secretary
The Tropical Bird Gardens, Rode
Bath, Somerset BA3 6QW
England
(0373) 83-0326
Dues: £12.00
Publication: *The Clematis Journal* (annual)

Plant Sources

Clifford's Perennial and Vine
Route 2, Box 320
East Troy, WI 53120
(414)968-4040

The Compleat Garden—Clematis Nursery
217 Argilla Road
Ipswich, MA 01938-2614
Catalogue: $2.00

Garden Scapes
1840 West 48th Street
Davenport, IA 52806
(800) 690-9858
Catalogue: $3.00

D. S. George Nurseries
2491 Penfield
Fairport, NY 14450
Catalogue: $1.00

Homestead Farms
Route 2, Box 31A
Owensville, MO 65066
(314) 437-4277
Catalogue: free

Arthur H. Steffen, Inc.
Box 184
Fairport, NY 14450
(716) 377-1665
Catalogue: $2.00

Coleus

Plant Source

Color Farm Growers
2710 Thornhill Road
Auburndale, FL 33823
(813) 967-9895
Catalogue: $1.00

Cyclamens
See also **Bulbs**

Organization

Cyclamen Society
Dr. D. V. Bent
Little Pilgrims, 2 Pilgrims Way East
Otford, Sevenoaks, Kent TN14 5QN
England
(0959) 52-2322

Dues: £7.00
Publication: *Cyclamen* (semiannual)

Plant Sources

Hansen Nursery
Box 446
Donald, OR 97020
(503) 678-5409
Catalogue: long SASE

Kline Nursery Company
Box 23161
Tigrad, OR 97281
(503) 244-3910
Catalogue: $2.00

Daffodils
See also **Bulbs**

Organizations

American Daffodil Society, Inc.
c/o Mary Lou Gripshover
1686 Grey Fox Trails
Milford, OH 45150
(513) 248-9137
Dues: $20.00
Publication: *Daffodil Journal* (quarterly)

The Daffodil Society (UK)
c/o Don Barnes
32 Montgomery Avenue
Sheffield S7 1NZ
England
Dues: $15.00

Plant Sources

Bonnie Brae Gardens
110 SE Christensen Road
Corbett, OR 97019
(503) 695-5190
Catalogue: long SASE

Cascade Daffodils
Box 10626
White Bear Lake, MN 55110
(612) 426-9616
Catalogue: $2.00

The Daffodil Mart
7463 Heath Trail
Gloucester, VA 23601
(804) 693-3966
Catalogue: $1.00

Grant E. Mitsch Novelty Daffodils
Box 218
Hubbard, OR 97032
(503) 651-2742
Catalogue: $3.00

Oregon Trail Daffodils
41905 SE Louden Road
Corbett, OR 97019
(503) 695-5513
Catalogue: free

Sisters' Bulb Farm
Route 2, Box 170
Gibsland, LA 71028
(318) 843-6379
Catalogue: free

Nancy R. Wilson
6525 Briceland–Thorn Road
Garberville, CA 95542
(707) 923-2407
Specialties: narcissi
Catalogue: $1.00

Dahlias

Organizations

American Dahlia Society
Terry Shaffer, Membership Chair
422 Sunset Boulevard
Toledo, OH 43612

(419) 478-4159
Dues: $20.00
Publication: *Bulletin* (quarterly)

Canadian Chrysanthemum and Dahlia
Society
c/o Karen Ojaste
17 Granard Boulevard
Scarborough, Ontario M1M 2E2
(416) 269-6960
Dues: Canada $10.00

Puget Sound Dahlia Association
Roger L. Walker
Box 5602
Bellevue, WA 98005
Dues: $15.00
Publication: *PSDA Bulletin*

Plant Sources

Almand Dahlia Gardens
2541 West Avenue 133
San Leandro, GA 94577
Catalogue: $1.00

Alpen Gardens
173 Lawrence Lane
Kalispell, MT 59901
(406) 257-2540
Catalogue: free

Bedford Dahlias
65 Leyton Road
Bedford, OH 44146
(216) 232-2852
Catalogue: one stamp

Blue Dahlia Gardens
San Jose, IL 62682
Catalogue: $1.00

Bowles Nursery
292 Terry Road
Smithtown, NY 11787
Catalogue: one stamp

Clacks Dahlia Patch
5585 North Myrtle Road
Myrtle Creek, OR 97457
Catalogue: SASE

Connell's Dahlias
10216 40th Avenue East
Tacoma, WA 98446
(206) 531-0292
Catalogue: $2.00

Dahlias by Phil Traff
10717 SR 162
Puyallup, WA 98374
Catalogue: $1.00

Dan's Dahlias
994 South Bank Road
Oakville, WA 98568
(206) 482-2607
Catalogue: $2.00

Evergreen Acres Dahlia Gardens
682 Pulaski Road
Greenlawn, NY 11740
(516) 262-9423
Catalogue: long SASE with two stamps

Ferncliff Gardens
Box 66
Sumas, WA 98295
(604) 826-2447
Catalogue: free

Frey's Dahlias
12054 Brick Road
Turner, OR 97392
(503) 743-3910
Catalogue: one stamp

Garden Valley Dahlias
406 Lower Garden Valley Road
Roseburg, OR 97470
(503) 673-8521
Catalogue: one stamp

Golden Rule Dahlia Farm
3460 Route 48 North
Lebanon, OH 45036
(513) 932-3805
Catalogue: $1.00

Heartland Dahlias
804 East Vistula
Bristol, IN 46507
Catalogue: $2.00

Homestead Gardens
125 Homestead Road
Kalispell, MT 59901
(406) 756-6631
Catalogue: free

J. T. Dahlias
Box 20967
Greenfield, WI 53220
Catalogue: long SASE

Gordon Le Roux Dahlias
5021 View Drive
Everett, WA 98023
(206) 252-4991
Catalogue: $1.00

Pleasant Valley Glads and Dahlias
Box 494
163 Senator Street
Agawam, MA 01001
(413) 789-0307
Catalogue: free

Sea-Tac Dahlia Gardens
20020 Des Moines Memorial Drive
Seattle, WA 98198
(206) 824-3846
Catalogue: long SASE

Shackleton's Dahlias
30535 Division Drive
Troutdale, OR 97060
(503) 663-7057
Catalogue: one stamp

Swan Island Dahlias
Box 700
995 NW 22nd Avenue
Canby, OR 97013
(503) 266-7711
Catalogue: $3.00

Phil Traff Dahlia Gardens
1316 132nd Avenue East
Sumner, WA 98390
Catalogue: $1.00

Wisley Dahlia Farm
9076 County Road 87
Hammondsport, NY 14840
(607) 569-3578
Catalogue: free

Daylilies

Organization

American Hemerocallis Society
c/o Elly Launius, Executive Secretary
1454 Rebel Drive
Jackson, MS 39211
(601) 366-4362
Dues: $18.00
Publication: *The Daylily Journal* (quarterly)

Plant Sources

A & D Peony and Perennial Nursery
6808 180th Street SE
Snohomish, WA 98290
(206) 485-2487
Catalogue: $1.50

Adamgrove
Route 1, Box 246
California, MO 65018
Catalogue: $3.00

Alcovy Daylily Farm
775 Cochran Road

Covington, GA 30209
(404) 787-7177
Catalogue: $1.00

Alpine Valley Gardens
2627 Calistoga Road
Santa Rosa, CA 95404
(707) 539-1749
Catalogue: long SASE

American Daylily and Perennials
Box 210
Grain Valley, MO 64029
(816) 224-2852
(800) 770-2777
Catalogue: $3.00

American Hostas, Daylilies and
Perennials
1288 Gatton Rocks Road
Bellville, OH 44813
Catalogue: $5.00

Artemis Gardens
170 Moss Bridge Road
Bozeman, MT 59715
Catalogue: $1.00

Ater Nursery
3803 Greystone Drive
Austin, TX 78731
(512) 345-3225
Specialties: diploids and tetraploids
Catalogue: one stamp

Babbette's Gardens
Babbette Sandt
40975 North 172nd Street East
Lancaster, CA 93535
Catalogue: $1.00

Balash Gardens
26595 H Drive North
Albion, MI 49224
(517) 629-5997
Catalogue: $1.00

Bayberry Row
Box 1439
Hopewell, VA 23860
Catalogue: $1.00

Bell's Daylily Garden
1305 Griffin Road
Sycamore, GA 31790
(912) 567-4284
Catalogue: free

John Benz
12195 6th Avenue
Cincinnati, OH 45249
Catalogue: $1.00

Big Tree Daylily Garden
777 General Hutchison Parkway
Longwood, FL 32750
(407) 831-5430
Catalogue: $2.00

Bloomingfields Farm
Route 55
Gaylordsville, CT 06755
(203) 345-6951
Catalogue: free

Blossom Valley Gardens
15011 Oak Creek Road
El Cajon, CA 92021
Catalogue: $1.00

Borboleta Gardens
Route 5, 15980 Canby Avenue
Faribault, MN 55021
(507) 334-2807
Catalogue: $3.00

Brookwood Gardens, Inc.
303 Fir Street
Michigan City, IN 46360
(800) 276-6593
Catalogue: $3.00

Busse Gardens
13579 10th Street NW
Cokato, MN 55321
(612) 286-2654
Catalogue: $2.00

C & C Nursery
Route 3, Box 422
Murray, KY 42071
(502) 753-2993
Catalogue: $1.00

Caprice Farm Nursery
15425 SW Pleasant Hill Road
Sherwood, OR 97140
(503) 625-7241
Catalogue: $2.00

Cascade Bulb and Seed
Box 271, 2333 Crooked Finger Road
Scotts Mills, OR 97375
Catalogue: long SASE

Chaparral Gardens
7221 Chaparral Drive
Latrobe, CA 95682
(916) 676-7918
Catalogue: $1.00

Coburg Planting Fields
573 East 600 North
Valparaiso, IN 46383
(219) 462-4288
Catalogue: $2.00

Cooper's Garden
2345 Decatur Avenue North
Golden Valley, MN 55427
(612) 591-0495
Catalogue: $1.00

Cordon Bleu Farms
Box 2033
418 Buena Creek Road
San Marcos, CA 92079
Catalogue: $1.00

Corner Oaks Garden
6139 Blanding Boulevard
Jacksonville, FL 32244
(904) 771-0417
Note: AHS display garden
Catalogue: SASE

Covered Bridge Gardens
1821 Honey Run Road
Chico, CA 95928
(916) 342-6661
Note: AHS display garden
Catalogue: $1.00

Crintonic Gardens
County Line Road
Gates Mills, OH 44040
(216) 423-3349
Catalogue: $1.00

Crochet Daylily Garden
Box 425
Prairieville, LA 70769
Catalogue: $1.00

Day Bloomers Garden
Box 869
Loughman, FL 33858
(941) 424-3949
Catalogue: $1.00

Daylilies in the Pines
1551 Cedar Street
Ramona, CA 92065
(619) 789-5790
Catalogue: SASE

Daylily Discounters
One Daylily Plaza
Alachua, FL 32615
(904) 462-1539
Catalogue: $2.00

Daylily Farms
Route 1, Box 89A
Bakersville, NC 28705-9714
Catalogue: $2.00

Daylily World
Box 1612
260 North White Cedar Road
Sanford, FL 32772
(407) 322-4034
Catalogue: $5.00

Helen Deering
2847 64th Street
Byron Center, MI 49315
Catalogue: $1.00

Edith's Daylilies
Route 1, Box 1840
Clarkesville, GA 30523
(706) 947-3683
Note: AHS display garden
Catalogue: free

Enchanted Valley Gardens
9123 North Territorial Road
Evansville, WI 53536
(608) 882-4200
Catalogue: free

Albert C. Faggard
3840 LeBleu Street
Beaumont, TX 77707
Catalogue: $1.00

Farmhouse Daylily Garden
591 Strickland Road
Whigham, GA 31797
(912) 762-3135
Catalogue: SASE

Floyd Cove Nursery
725 Longwood-Markham Road
Sanford, FL 32771
(407) 324-9229
Catalogue: $2.00

Forestlake Gardens
HC 72 LOW Box 535
Locust Grove, VA 22508
(703) 972-2890
Specialties: seeds
Catalogue: free

Four Winds Garden
Box 141
South Harpswell, ME 04079
Catalogue: $1.00

Gardenimport
Box 760
Thornhill, Ontario L3T 4A5
Catalogue: $4.00

Garden Path Daylilies
Box 8524
Clearwater, FL 34618
(813) 442-4730
Catalogue: $1.00

Garden Perennials
Route 1, Wayne, NE 68787
(402) 375-3615
Catalogue: $1.00

Gleber's Daylily Garden
17163 Swearingen Road
Kentwood, LA 70444
(504) 229-3740
Catalogue: $1.00

Goravani Growers
1730 Keane Avenue
Naples, FL 33964
(813) 455-4287
Catalogue: $2.00

G. R.'s Perennials
465 North 660 West
West Bountiful, UT 84708
(801) 292-8237
Note: AHS display garden
Catalogue: SASE

Grace Gardens North
N 3739 County Highway K
Granton, WI 54436
(715) 238-7122
Catalogue: free

Greenwood Daylily Gardens
5595 East 7th Street
Long Beach, CA 90804
(310) 494-8944
Catalogue: $5.00

Guidry's Daylily Garden
1005 East Vermilion Street
Abbeville, LA 70510
(318) 893-0812
Catalogue: free

Hahn's Rainbow Iris Garden
200 North School Street
Desloge, MO 63601
(314) 431-3342
Catalogue: $1.50

Hem'd Inn
Lucille Warner
534 Aqua Drive
Dallas, TX 75218
Catalogue: $1.00

Hermitage Gardens
Route 2
Raleigh, NC 27610
Catalogue: $1.00

Herrington Daylily Garden
204 Winfield Road
Dublin, GA 31021
Catalogue: $1.00

Hickory Hill Gardens
RR 1, Box 11
Loretto, PA 15940
Catalogue: $2.50

Howard J. Hite
370 Gallogly Road
Pontiac, MI 48055
Catalogue: $1.00

Hobby Garden, Inc.
38164 Monticello Drive
Prairieville, LA 70769
(504) 673-3623
Catalogue: free

Homestead Farms
Route 2, Box 31A
Owensville, MO 65066
(314) 437-4277
Catalogue: free

Iron Gate Gardens
Route 3, Box 250
Kings Mountain, NC 28086
(704) 435-6178
Catalogue: $3.00

Jaggers Bayou Beauties
15098 Knox Ferry Road
Bastrop, LA 71220
(318) 283-2252
Catalogue: free

Jernigan Gardens
Route 6, Box 593
Dunn, NC 28334
(919) 567-2135
Catalogue: long SASE

Johnson Daylily Garden
70 Lark Avenue
Brooksville, FL 34601
(904) 544-0330
Catalogue: SASE

Joiner Gardens
9630 Whitfield Avenue
Savannah, GA 31406
Catalogue: free

Klehm Nursery
4210 North Duncan Road
Champaign, IL 61821
(800) 553-3715
Catalogue: $4.00

Ladybug Beautiful Gardens
857 Leopard Trail
Winter Springs, FL 32708
Note: AHS display garden
Catalogue: $2.00

Lake Norman Gardens
580 Island Forest Drive
Davidson, NC 28036
Catalogue: $1.00

Lakeside Acres
8119 Roy Lane
Ooltewah, TN 37363
(615) 238-4534
Catalogue: $2.00

Larkdale Farms
4058 Highway 17 South
Green Cove Springs, FL 32043
Catalogue: $1.00

Lee's Gardens
Box 5
25986 Sauder Road
Tremont, IL 61568
(309) 925-5262
Catalogue: $2.00

Le Petit Jardin
Box 55, McIntosh, FL 32664
(904) 591-3227
Specialties: tetraploids
Catalogue: free

Little River Farm
7815 NC 39
Middlesex, NC 27557
(919) 965-9507
Catalogue: $2.00

Little River Gardens
1050 Little River Lane
Alpharetta, GA 30201
(404) 740-1371
Specialties: hybrids
Catalogue: $1.00

Louisiana Nursery
Route 7, Box 43
Opelousas, LA 70570
(318) 948-3696
Specialties: diploids and tetraploids
Catalogue: $4.00

Majestic Gardens
2100 North Preble County Line Road
West Alexandria, OH 45381
(513) 833-5100
Note: AHS display garden
Catalogue: free

Maple Tree Gardens
Box 547
Ponca, NE 68770
Catalogue: 50¢

Marietta Gardens
Box 70
Marietta, NC 28362
(910) 628-9466
Note: AHS display garden
Catalogue: SASE

McMillen's Iris Garden
RR 1
Norwich, Ontario N0J 1P0
(519) 468-6508
Catalogue: $2.00

Meadowlake Gardens
Route 4, Box 709
Walterboro, SC 29488
(803) 844-2524
Catalogue: $2.00

Mercers Garden
6215 Maude Street
Fayetteville, NC 28306
Catalogue: $1.00

Metamora Country Gardens
1945 Dryden Road
Metamora, MI 48455
(810) 678-3519
Catalogue: $1.00

Mid-America Iris Gardens
3409 North Geraldine Avenue
Oklahoma City, OK 73112
(405) 946-5743
Catalogue: $2.00

Mike's Daylilies
426 Copeland Road
Powell, TN 37849
(615) 947-9419
Catalogue: free

Bryant K. Millikan
6610 Sunny Lane
Indianapolis, IN 46220
Catalogue: $1.00

Moldovan's Gardens
38830 Detroit Road
Avon, OH 44011
Catalogue: $1.00

Monarch Daylily Garden
Route 2, Box 182
Edison, GA 31746
(912) 835-2636
Catalogue: SASE

Nicholls Gardens
4724 Angus Drive
Gainesville, VA 22065
(703) 754-9623
Catalogue: $1.00

Oakes Daylilies
8204 Monday Road
Corryton, TN 37721
(615) 687-3770
(800) 532-9545
Catalogue: $2.00

Olallie Daylily Gardens
HCR 63, Box 1
Marlboro Branch Road
South Newfane, VT 05351
(802) 348-6614
Catalogue: free

Oxford Gardens
3022 Oxford Drive
Durham, NC 27707
Catalogue: $1.00

Petree Gardens
4447 Cain Circle
Tucker, GA 30084
Catalogue: $1.00

Pinecliffe Daylily Gardens
6604 Scottsville Road
Floyds Knob, IN 47119
(812) 923-8113
Catalogue: $2.00

Powell's Gardens
9468 US Highway 70E
Princeton, NC 27569
(919) 936-4421
Catalogue: $3.00

Ramona Gardens
2178 El Paso Street
Ramona, CA 92065
(619) 789-6099
Catalogue: $2.00

Renaissance Gardens
1047 Baron Road
Weddington, NC 28173
Catalogue: $1.00

Roderick Hillview Garden
3862 Highway O
Farmington, MO 63640
(314) 431-5711
Catalogue: one stamp

Rollingwood Gardens
21234 Rollingwood Trail
Eustis, FL 32726
(904) 589-8765
Catalogue: $3.00

Roycroft Nursery
Belle Isle Road, Route 6, Box 70
Georgetown, SC 29440
Catalogue: $1.00

Sandstone Gardens
1323 Sandstone Place
Green Bay, WI 54313
(414) 498-2895
Catalogue: SASE

Saxton Gardens
1 1st Street
Saratoga Springs, NY 12866
(518) 584-4697
Catalogue: two stamps

Schmid Gardens
847 Westwood Boulevard
Jackson, MI 49203
(517) 787-5275
Catalogue: $1.00

Scott Daylily Farm
5830 Clark Road
Harrison, TN 37341
(615) 344-9113
Catalogue: SASE

Seaside Daylily Farm
Box 807I
West Tisbury, MA 02575
(508) 693-3276
Catalogue: free

R. Seawright
201 Bedford Road
Carlisle, MA 01741
(508) 369-2172
Catalogue: $2.00

Serendipity Gardens
3210 Upper Bellbrook Road
Bellbrook, OH 45305
(513) 426-6596
Catalogue: SASE

Shields Gardens
Box 92, Westfield, IN 46074
(317) 896-3925
Catalogue: $1.00

Singing Oaks Garden
Box 56, Abell Road
Blythwood, SC 29016
(803) 786-1351
Note: AHS display garden
Catalogue: free

Sir Williams Gardens
2852 Jackson Boulevard
Highland, MI 48356
(313) 887-4779
Catalogue: $2.00

Snow Creek Daylily Gardens
330 P Street
Port Townsend, WA 98368
Catalogue: $2.00

Soules Garden
5809 Rahke Road
Indianapolis, IN 46217
(317) 786-7839
Catalogue: $1.00

The Split Rail Daylily Farm
Route 1, Box 849
High Springs, FL 32643
(904) 752-4654
Catalogue: $1.00

Spring Creek Daylily Garden
25150 Gosling
Spring, TX 77389
Catalogue: free

Springlake Ranch Gardens
Route 2, Box 360
De Queen, AR 71832
Catalogue: $1.00

Starlight Daylily Gardens
2515 Scottsville Road
Borden, IN 47106
(812) 923-3735
Catalogue: $2.00

Sterrett Gardens
Box 85
Craddockville, VA 23341
(804) 442-4606
Note: AHS display garden
Catalogue: free

Sunnyridge Gardens
1724 Drinnen Road
Knoxville, TN 37914
(615) 933-0723
Catalogue: $1.00

Sunshine Hollow
198 CR 52, Athens, TN 37303
(615) 745-4289
Catalogue: $1.00

Swann's Daylily Garden
Box 7687
Warner Robins, GA 31095
(912) 953-4778
Note: AHS display garden
Catalogue: free

Dave Talbott Nursery
4038 Highway 17 South
Green Cove Springs, FL 32043
(904) 284-9874
Catalogue: $2.00

Thoroughbred Daylilies
Box 21864
Lexington, KY 40522
(606) 268-4462
Specialties: seeds
Catalogue: free

Thundering Springs Daylily Garden
1056 South Lake Drive
Thundering Springs Lake
Dublin, GA 31021
(912) 272-1526
Note: AHS display garden
Catalogue: $1.00

Tranquil Lake Nursery, Inc.
45 River Street
Rehoboth, MA 02769
(508) 242-4002
Catalogue: $1.00

Valente Gardens
RFD 2, Box 234
Dillingham Road
East Lebanon, ME 04027
(207) 457-2076
Catalogue: two stamps

Andre Viette Farm and Nursery
Route 1, Box 16
Fishersville, VA 22939
(703) 942-2118
Catalogue: $3.00

Water Mill Daylily Garden
56 Winding Way
Water Mill, NY 11976
(516) 726-9640
Catalogue: free

Gilbert H. Wild and Son, Inc.
Box 338
1112 Joplin Street
Sarcoxie, MO 64862
(417) 548-3514
Catalogue: $3.00

Wimberlyway Gardens
7024 NW 18th Avenue
Gainesville, FL 32605
(904) 331-4922
Catalogue: $3.00

Windmill Gardens
Box 351
Luverne, AL 36049
Catalogue: $1.00

Woodside Garden
824 Williams Lane
Chadds Ford, PA 19317
Catalogue: $1.00

Delphiniums

Organization

The Delphinium Society
Mrs. Shirley E. Bassett
"Takakkaw," Ice House Wood
Oxted, Surrey RH8 9DW
England
Dues: $10.00
Publication: *Delphinium Year Book*

Plant Source

Thompson & Morgan, Inc.
Box 1308
Jackson, NJ 09527
(908) 363-2225
Catalogue: free

Epimediums

Plant Sources

Collector's Nursery
1602 NE 162nd Avenue
Vancouver, WA 98684
Catalogue: $1.00

Cricklewood Nursery
11907 Nevers Road
Snohomish, WA 98290
(206) 568-2829
Catalogue: $2.00

Robyn's Nest Nursery
7802 NE 63rd Street
Vancouver, WA 98662
(206) 256-7399
Catalogue: $2.00

Siskiyou Rare Plant Nursery
2825 Cummings Road
Medford, OR 97501
(503) 772-6846
Catalogue: $2.00

We-Du Nurseries
Route 5, Box 724
Marion, NC 28752
(704) 738-8300
Catalogue: $2.00

Epiphytic Plants

See **Bromeliads and Epiphytic Plants**

Exotic and Tropical Plants

Organization

Peperomia and Exotic Plant Society
c/o Anita Baudean
100 Neil Avenue
New Orleans, LA 70131
(504) 394-4146
Dues: $7.50
Publication: *The Gazette*
(three times annually)

Plant Sources

Autumn Glade Botanicals
46857 Ann Arbor Trail

Plymouth, MI 48170
(800) 331-7969
Catalogue: free

The Banana Tree
715 Northampton Street
Easton, PA 18042
(215) 253-9589
Catalogue: $3.00

Bob's
Route 2, Box 42
Wingate, TX 79566
Catalogue: $1.00 plus SASE

Brudy's Exotics
Box 820874
HR 595
Houston, TX 77282
(800) 926-7333
Catalogue: free

Crockett's Tropical Plants
Box 389
Harlingen, TX 78551
(210) 423-1747
Catalogue: $3.00

D'anna B'nana
15-1293 Auina Road
Pahoa, HI 96778
(808) 965-6262
Catalogue: free

Endangered Species
Box 1830
Tustin, CA 92680
Catalogue: $6.00

Exotics Hawaii, Ltd.
1344 Hoakoa Place
Honolulu, HI 96821
Catalogue: SASE

Glasshouse Works
Box 97, Church Street

Stewart, OH 45778
(614) 662-2142
Catalogue: $2.00

Heliconia and Ginger Gardens
Box 79161
Houston, TX 77279
Catalogue: $2.00

Jerry Horne Rare Plants
10195 SW 70th Street
Miami, FL 33173
(305) 270-1235
Catalogue: long SASE

Olive Road Nursery
1615 Olive Road
Pensacola, FL 32514
(904) 477-9862
Catalogue: free

The Plumeria People
910 Leander Drive
Leander, TX 78641
(713) 496-2352
Catalogue: $3.00

Rainbow Tropicals
Box 4038
Hilo, HI 96720
(808) 959-4565
Catalogue: free

Southern Exposures
35 Minor Street
Beaumont, TX 77702
(409) 835-0644
Catalogue: $5.00

Stallings Nursery
910 Encinitas Boulevard
Encinitas, CA 92024
(619) 753-3079
Catalogue: $3.00

Sunshine Farms
Box 289
Mountain View, HI 96771
(808) 968-6312
Catalogue: SASE

Two Strikes
819 West Main Street
Blytheville, AR 72315
Catalogue: SASE with two stamps

Valhalla Nursery
204 Nixon Place
Chula Vista, CA 91910
(619) 425-7754
Catalogue: $2.00

Guy Wrinkle Exotic Plants
11610 Addison Street
North Hollywood, CA 91601
(310) 670-8637
Specialties: cycads
Catalogue: $1.00

Ferns

Organizations

American Fern Society
c/o Richard Hauke
456 McGill Place
Atlanta, GA 30312
(404) 525-3147
Dues: $15.00
Publications: *American Fern Journal*
(quarterly); *Fiddlehead Forum* (bimonthly
newsletter)

Hardy Fern Foundation
Box 166
Medina, WA 98039
(206) 747-2998
Dues: $20.00
Publication: quarterly newsletter

International Tropical Fern Society
8720 SW 34th Street
Miami, FL 33165
(305) 221-0502

Los Angeles International Fern Society
Box 90943
Pasadena, CA 91109
Dues: $20
Publication: *LAIFS Journal* (bimonthly)

Plant Sources

Fancy Fronds
Box 1090
Gold Bar, WA 98251
(360)793-1472
Catalogue: $1.00

Timothy D. Field Ferns and Wildflowers
395 Newington Road
Newington, NH 03801
(603) 436-0457
Catalogue: free

Foliage Gardens
2003 128th Avenue SE
Bellevue, WA 98005
(206) 747-2998
Catalogue: $2.00

Fox Orchids, Inc.
6615 West Markham Street
Little Rock, AR 72205
(501) 663-4246
Catalogue: free

Gardens of the Blue Ridge
Box 10
US 221 North
Pineola, NC 28662
(704) 733-2417
Catalogue: $3.00

Ann Mann's Orchids
9045 Ron-Den Lane

Windermere, FL 34786
(407) 876-2625
Catalogue: $1.00

Oak Hill Gardens
Box 25
West Dundee, IL 60118
(708) 428-8500
Catalogue: $1.00

Oakridge Nursery
Box 182
East Kingston, NH 03827
(603) 642-8227
Catalogue: free

Orchid Gardens
2232 139th Avenue NW
Andover, MN 55744
Catalogue: 75¢

Orgel's Orchids
18950 SW 136th Street
Miami, FL 33196
(305) 233-7168
Catalogue: free

Palestine Orchids
Route 1, Box 312
Palestine, WV 26160
(304) 275-4781
Catalogue: free

Shady Lace Nursery
Box 266
Olive Branch, MS 38654
(800) 335-8657
Catalogue: free

Shady Oaks Nursery
112 10th Avenue SE
Waseca, MN 56903
(507) 835-5033
Catalogue: $3.00

Varga's Nursery
2631 Pickertown Road
Warrington, PA 19876
(610) 343-0646
Catalogue: $1.00

Wild Earth Native Plant Nursery
49 Mead Avenue
Freehold, NJ 07728
(908)308-9777
Catalogue: $1.00

Geraniums

Organizations

British and European Geranium Society
Leyland Cox
Norwood Chine, 26 Crabtree Lane
Sheffield, Yorkshire S5 7AV
England
(0742) 426-2000
Dues: $15.00
Publications: *The Geranium Gazette*
(three times annually);
The Geranium Yearbook

British Pelargonium and Geranium
Society
c/o Carol Helyar
134 Montrose Avenue
Welling, Kent DA16 2QY
(081) 856-6137
Dues: $12.00
Publications: *Pelargonium News*
(three times annually); *Yearbook*

Canadian Pelargonium and Geranium
Society
Kathleen Gammer, Membership
Secretary
101-2008 Fullerton Avenue
North Vancouver, British Columbia
V7P 3G7
(604) 926-2190

Dues: Canada $10.00
Publication: *Storksbill* (quarterly)

The Geraniaceae Group
c/o Penny Clifton
9 Waingate Bridge Cottages
Haverigg, Cumbria LA18 4NF
England
Dues: $16.00
Publication: *The Geraniaceae Group News*
(quarterly)

International Geranium Society
Membership Secretary
Box 92734
Pasadena, CA 91109
(818) 908-8867
Dues: $12.50
Publication: *Geraniums Around the World*
(quarterly journal)

Plant Sources

A Scented Geranium
Box 123
Washington, KY 41096
Catalogue: $3.50

Brawner Geraniums
Route 4, Box 525A
Buckhannon, WV 26201
(304) 472-4203
Specialties: pelargoniums
Catalogue: $2.00

Cook's Geranium Nursery
712 North Grand
Lyons, KS 67554
(316) 257-5033
Catalogue: $1.00

Davidson-Wilson Greenhouses, Inc.
RR 2, Box 168
Crawfordsville, IN 47933-9426
(317) 364-0556
Catalogue: $3.00

Plant Sources

Fischer Geraniums
24500 SW 167th Avenue
Homestead, FL 33031
(305) 245-9464
Catalogue: $1.00

Highfield Garden
4704 NE Cedar Creek Road
Woodland, WA 98674
(800) 669-9956
Catalogue: $1.00

Holbrook Farm and Nursery
Box 368
Fletcher, NC 28732
(704) 891-7790
Catalogue: free

Lake Odessa Greenhouse
1123 Jordan Lake Street
Lake Odessa, MI 48849
(616) 374-8488
Catalogue: free

Logee's Greenhouse
141 North Street
Danielson, CT 06239
(203) 774-8038
Catalogue: $1.00

Oglevee, Ltd.
150 Oglevee Lane
Connellsville, PA 15425
(412) 628-8360
Catalogue: $1.00

Shady Hill Gardens
821 Walnut Street
Batavia, IL 60510
(708) 879-5679
Catalogue: $2.00

Shepherd Geraniums
13851 Christensen Road
Galt, CA 95632
Catalogue: $1.00

Sunnybrook Farms Nursery
Box 6
9448 Mayfield Road
Chesterland, OH 44026
(216) 729-7232
Catalogue: $1.00

Wheeler Farm Gardens
171 Bartlett Street
Portland, CT 06480
(203) 342-2374
(800) 934-3341
Catalogue: free

Willamette Valley Gardens
Box 285A
Lake Oswego, OR 97034
(503) 636-6517
Catalogue: $1.00

Gesneriad

See **African Violets and Other Gesneriads**

Gladioli

Organizations

All-America Gladiolus Selections
11734 Road 33½
Madera, CA 93638
(209) 645-5329

Canadian Gladiolus Society
c/o W. L. Turbuck
3073 Grant Road
Regina, Saskatchewan S4S 5G9
Dues: Canada $10.00
Publication: *Canadian Gladiolus Annual*

North American Gladiolus Council
c/o William Strawser
701 South Hendricks Avenue
Marion, IN 46953

(317) 664-3857
Dues: $10.00
Publication: *Bulletin* (quarterly)

Plant Sources

Pleasant Valley Glads and Dahlias
Box 494
163 Senator Street
Agawam, MA 01001
(413) 789-0307
Catalogue: free

Skolaski's Glads & Field Flowers
4821 County Highway Q
Waunakee, WI 53597
(608) 836-4822
Catalogue: free

Summerville Gladiolus
RD 1, Box 449
1330 Ellis Mill Road
Glassboro, NJ 08028
(609) 881-0704
Catalogue: free

The Waushara Gardens
5491 North 5th Drive
Plainfield, WI 54966
(715) 335-4462
Catalogue: $1.00

Ground Covers

Plant Sources

Barbour Bros. Inc.
RD 2, Stoneboro, PA 16153
Catalogue: free

Double D Nursery
2215 Dogwood Lane
Arnoldsville, GA 30619
(706) 742-7417
Catalogue: free

Gilson Gardens, Inc.
Box 277
Perry, OH 44081
(216) 259-5252
Catalogue: free

Joyce's Garden
64640 Old Bend-Redmond Highway
Bend, OR 97701
(503) 388-4680
Catalogue: $2.00

Nichols Garden Nursery
1190 North Pacific Highway
Albany, OR 97321
(503) 928-9280
Catalogue: free

Peekskill Nurseries
Box 428
Shrub Oak, NY 10588
(914) 245-5595
Catalogue: free

Pinky's Plants
Box 126
442 G Street
Pawnee City, NE 68420
(800) 94-PINKY
Catalogue: $3.50

Prentiss Court Ground Covers
Box 8662
Greenville, SC 29604
(803) 277-4037
Catalogue: $2.00

Silver Springs Nursery
HCR 62, Box 86
Moyle Springs, ID 83845
(208) 267-5753
Catalogue: 50¢

Andre Viette Farm and Nursery
Route 1, Box 16
Fishersville, VA 22939

(703) 942-2118
Catalogue: $3.00

Woodlanders, Inc.
1128 Colleton Avenue
Aiken, SC 29801
(803) 648-7522
Catalogue: $2.00

Heathers and Heaths

Organizations

The Heather Society
c/o Mrs. A. Small
Denbeigh, All Saints Road,
Creeting St. Mary
Ipswich, Suffolk 1P6 8PJ
England
(0449) 71-1220
Dues: £6.00
Publications: *Bulletin* (three times
annually); yearbook

North American Heather Society
c/o Pauline Croxton
3641 Indian Creek Road
Placerville, CA 95667
Dues: $10.00
Publication: *Heather News* (quarterly)

Northeast Heather Society
Walter K. Wornick
Box 101, Highland View
Alstead, NH 03602
(603) 835-6165
Dues: $5.00
Publication: *Heather Notes*

Plant Sources

Ericaceae
Box 293
Deep River, CT 06417
Catalogue: free

Heaths and Heathers
Box 850
1199 Monte–Elma Road
Elma, WA 98541
(206) 482-3258
Catalogue: long SASE

Rock Spray Nursery
Box 693
Depot Road
Truro, MA 02666
(508) 349-6769
Catalogue: $1.00

Hibiscus

Organization

American Hibiscus Society
Jeri Grantham, Executive Secretary
Box 321540
Cocoa Beach, FL 32932
(407) 783-2576
Dues: $17.50
Publication: *The Seed Pod* (quarterly)

Plant Sources

Air Expose
4703 Leffingwell Street
Houston, TX 77026
Catalogue: long SASE

Fancy Hibiscus
1142 SW 1st Avenue
Pompano Beach, FL 33060
(305) 782-0741
Catalogue: $2.00

Florida Colors Nursery
23740 SW 147th Avenue
Homestead, FL 33032
(305) 258-1086
Catalogue: free

Reasoner's, Inc.
Box 1881
2501 53rd Avenue East
Oneco, FL 34264
(813) 756-1881
Catalogue: $1.00

Hostas

Organization

American Hosta Society
c/o Robyn Duback
7802 NE 63rd Street
Vancouver, WA 98662
Dues: $19.00
Publication: *Hosta Journal* (semiannual)

Publication

The Hosta Digest
Meadowbrook Hosta Farm
81 Meredith Road
Tewksbury, MA 01876
(508) 851-8943
Frequency: quarterly
Subscription: $20.00

Plant Sources

A & D Peony and Perennial Nursery
6808 180th Street SE
Snohomish, WA 98290
(206) 485-2487
Catalogue: $1.50

Adrian's Flowers of Fashion Nursery
855 Parkway Boulevard
Alliance, OH 44601
(216) 823-1964
Catalogue: SASE with two stamps

Akin' Back Farm
Box 158H
Buckner, KY 40010

(502) 222-5791
Catalogue: $2.00

Ambergate Gardens
8015 Krey Avenue
Waconia, MN 55387
(612) 443-2248
Catalogue: $2.00

American Hostas, Daylilies and
Perennials
1288 Gatton Rocks Road
Bellville, OH 44813
Catalogue: $5.00

Anderson Iris Gardens
22179 Keather Avenue North
Forest Lake, MN 55025
(612) 433-5268
Catalogue: $2.00

The Azalea Patch
2010 Mountain Road
Joppa, MD 21085
(410) 679-0762
Catalogue: $1.00

Brookwood Gardens, Inc.
303 Fir Street
Michigan City, IN 46360
(800) 276-6593
Catalogue: $3.00

Busse Gardens
13579 10th Street NW
Cokato, MN 55321
(612) 286-2654
Catalogue: $2.00

C & C Nursery
Route 3, Box 422
Murray, KY 42071
(502) 753-2993
Catalogue: $1.00

Caprice Farm Nursery
15425 SW Pleasant Hill Road
Sherwood, OR 97140
(503) 625-7241
Catalogue: $2.00

Coastal Gardens and Nursery
4611 Socastee Boulevard
Myrtle Beach, SC 29575
(803) 293-2000
Catalogue: $2.00

Cooks Nursery
10749 Bennett Road
Dunkirk, NY 14048
(716) 366-8844
Catalogue: $1.00

Daylily Farms
Route 1, Box 89A
Bakersville, NC 28705-9714
Catalogue: $2.00

Donnelly's Nursery
705 Charlotte Highway
Fairview, NC 28730
Catalogue: $1.00

Hildenbrandt's Iris Gardens
HC 84, Box 4
Lexington, NE 68850
(308) 324-4334
Catalogue: $1.00

Holbrook Farm and Nursery
Box 368
115 Lance Road
Fletcher, NC 28732
(704) 891-7790
Catalogue: $1.00

Homestead Farms
Route 2, Box 31A
Owensville, MO 65066
(314) 437-4277
Catalogue: free

Honeysong Farm
51 Jared Place
Seaford, DE 19973
Catalogue: $1.00

Hosta Haven
10302 Nantucket Court
Fairfax, VA 22032
(800) 354-0503
Catalogue: $1.00

House of Hosta
2320 Elmwood Road
Green Bay, WI 54313
(414) 434-2847
Catalogue: one stamp

Iron Gate Gardens
Route 3, Box 250
Kings Mountain, NC 28086
(704) 435-6178
Catalogue: $3.00

Kuk's Forest Nursery
10174 Barr Road
Brecksville, OH 44141
(216) 526-5271
Catalogue: $2.00

Lakeside Acres
8119 Roy Lane
Ooltewah, TN 37363
(615) 238-4534
Catalogue: $2.00

Laurie's Landscaping
2959 Hobson Road
Downers Grove, IL 60517
(708) 969-1270
Catalogue: long SASE

Lee's Gardens
Box 5, 25986 Sauder Road
Tremont, IL 61568
(309) 925-5262
Catalogue: $2.00

Mary's Plant Farm
2410 Lanes Mill Road
Hamilton, OH 45013
(513) 894-0022
Catalogue: $1.00

Matterhorn Nursery Inc.
227 Summit Park Road
Spring Valley, NY 10977
(914) 354-5986
Catalogue: $5.00

Meadowbrook Hosta Farm
81 Meredith Road
Tewksbury, MA 01876
(508) 851-8943
Catalogue: free

Mid-America Iris Gardens
3409 North Geraldine Avenue
Oklahoma City, OK 73112
(405) 946-5743
Catalogue: $2.00

Piccadilly Farm
1971 Whippoorwill Road
Bishop, GA 30621
Catalogue: $1.00

Plant Delights Nursery
9241 Sauls Road
Raleigh, NC 27603
(919) 772-4794
Catalogue: $3.50

Plant Hideaway
Route 3, Box 259
Franklinton, NC 27525
(919) 494-7178
Catalogue: free

Powell's Gardens
9468 US Highway 70 E
Princeton, NC 27569
(919) 936-4421
Catalogue: $3.00

Savory's Gardens, Inc.
5300 Whiting Avenue
Edina, MN 55439
(612) 941-8755
Catalogue: $2.00

Schmid Gardens
847 Westwood Boulevard
Jackson, MI 49203
(517) 787-5275
Catalogue: $1.00

R. Seawright
201 Bedford Road
Carlisle, MA 01741
(508) 369-2172
Catalogue: $2.00

Shady Oaks Nursery
112 10th Avenue SE
Waseca, MN 56903
(507) 835-5033
Catalogue: $3.00

Silvermist
1986 Harrisville Road
Stoneboro, PA 16153
(814) 786-9219
Catalogue: free

Soules Garden
5809 Rahke Road
Indianapolis, IN 46217
(317) 786-7839
Catalogue: $1.00

Stark Gardens
631 G24 Highway
Norwalk, IA 50211
(515) 981-4780
Catalogue: one stamp

Sunnybrook Farms Nursery
Box 6
9448 Mayfield Road
Chesterland, OH 44026

(216) 729-7232
Catalogue: $1.00

Tower Perennial Gardens
3412 East 64th Court
Spokane, WA 99223
(509) 448-5837
Catalogue: free

Triple Creek Farm
8625 West Banks Mill Road
Winston, GA 30187
(404) 489-8022
Catalogue: $1.00

Walden-West
5744 Crooked Finger Road
Scotts Mills, OR 97375
(503) 873-6875
Catalogue: SASE

White Oak Nursery
6145 Oak Point Court
Peoria, IL 61614
(309) 693-1354
Catalogue: $1.00

Hydrangeas

Plant Sources

Bell Family Nursery
6543 South Zimmerman Road
Aurora, OR 97002
(503) 651-2887
Catalogue: $3.50

Wilkerson Mill Gardens
9595 Wilkerson Mill Road
Palmetto, GA 30268
Catalogue: $1.00

Irises

Organizations

American Iris Society
Marilyn Harlow, Membership Secretary
Box 8455
San Jose, CA 95155
(408) 971-0444
Dues: $12.50
Publication: *Bulletin of the AIS* (quarterly)

AMERICAN IRIS SOCIETY SECTIONS

Dwarf Iris Society of America
Lynda S. Miller
3167 East US 224
Ossian, IN 46777
(219) 597-7403
Dues: AIS dues plus $3.00
Publication: *Dwarf Iris Society Newsletter*

Historic Iris Preservation Society (HIPS)
Ada Godfrey
9 Bradford Street
Foxborough, MA 01035
Dues: AIS dues plus $5.00
Publication: *Roots Journal*

Median Iris Society
Deborah Outcalt
Route 1, Box CW 20
Spencer, IN 47460
Dues: AIS dues plus $5.00
Publication: journal

Reblooming Iris Society
Charlie Brown
3114 South FM 131
Denison, TX 75020
Dues: AIS dues plus $5.00
Publication: bulletin

Society for Japanese Irises
Carol Warner
16815 Falls Road

Upperco, MD 21155
(410) 374-4788
Dues: AIS dues plus $3.50
Publication: *The Review*

Society for Pacific Coast Native Iris
Adele Lawyer
4333 Oak Hill Road
Oakland, CA 94605
Dues: AIS dues plus $5.00
Publication: *SPCNI Almanac*

The Society for Siberian Irises
Howard L. Brookins
N 75 W14247 North Point Drive
Menomonee Falls, WI 53051
(414) 251-5292
Dues: AIS dues plus $5.00
Publication: *The Siberian Iris*

Species Iris Group of North America
(SIGNA)
Colin Rigby
18341 Paulson SW
Rochester, WA 98579
Dues: AIS dues plus $5.00
Publication: *SIGNA*

Spuria Iris Society
Floyd W. Wickenkamp
10521 Bellarose Drive
Sun City, AZ 85351
(602) 977-2354
Dues: AIS dues plus $5.00
Publication: *Spuria Newsletter*

AMERICAN IRIS SOCIETY COOPERATING SOCIETIES

Aril Society International
Audrey Roe
2816 Charleston NE
Albuquerque, NM 87110
Dues: $5.00
Publication: yearbook

Society for Louisiana Irises
Elaine Bourque
1812 Broussard Road East
Lafayette, LA 70508
Dues: $7.50
Publications: newsletter; special bulletins

OTHER ORGANIZATIONS

British Iris Society
Mrs. E. M. Wise
197 The Parkway, Iver Heath
Iver, Bucks. SL0 0RQ
England
Publication: *The Iris Year Book*

Canadian Iris Society
c/o Verna Laurin
199 Florence Avenue
Willowdale, Ontario M2N 1G5
(416) 225-1088
Dues: Canada $5.00
Publication: *CIS Newsletter* (quarterly)

Iris Products and Supplies

House of Iris
The Mills Falls Marketplace
Route 3, Box 16
Meredith, NH 03253
(603) 279-8155
Specialties: iris crafts, jewelry, gifts

Plant Sources

Abbey Gardens
32009 South Ona Way
Molalla, OR 97038
(503) 829-2928
Catalogue: $1.00

Adamgrove
Route 1, Box 246
California, MO 65018
Catalogue: $3.00

Aitken's Salmon Creek Garden
608 NW 119th Street
Vancouver, WA 98685
(206) 573-4472
Specialties: bearded irises
Catalogue: $2.00

Amberway Gardens
5803 Amberway Drive
St. Louis, MO 63128
(314) 842-6103
Catalogue: $1.00

Anderson Iris Gardens
22179 Keather Avenue North
Forest Lake, MN 55025
(612) 433-5268
Specialties: tall bearded irises
Catalogue: $2.00

Artemis Gardens
170 Moss Bridge Road
Bozeman, MT 59715
Specialties: bearded irises
Catalogue: $1.00

Babbette's Gardens
Babbette Sandt
40975 North 172nd Street East
Lancaster, CA 93535
Specialties: tall bearded irises
Catalogue: $1.00

Bay View Gardens
1201 Bay Street
Santa Cruz, CA 95060
Catalogue: $2.00

Bluebird Haven Iris Garden
6940 Fairplay Road
Somerset, CA 95684
(209) 245-5017
Catalogue: $1.00

Blue Iris Country Gardens
20791 Woodbury Drive

Grass Valley, CA 95949
(916) 346-2905
Catalogue: $1.00

Bois d'Arc Gardens
1831 Bull Run
Schriever, LA 70395
(504) 446-2329
Specialties: Louisiana irises
Catalogue: $1.00

Borboleta Gardens
Route 5
15980 Canby Avenue
Faribault, MN 55021
(507) 334-2807
Specialties: bearded and Siberian irises
Catalogue: $3.00

Borglum's Iris
2202 Austin Road
Geneva, NY 14456
Catalogue: $1.00

Bridge in Time Iris Gardens
10116 Scottsville Road
Alvaton, KY 42122
Specialties: reblooming irises
Catalogue: one stamp

George C. Bush
1739 Memory Lane Extension
York, PA 17402
(717) 755-0557
Specialties: beardless irises
Catalogue: one stamp

Cal-Dixie Iris Gardens
14115 Pear Street
Riverside, CA 92508
Specialties: bearded irises
Catalogue: two stamps

Cape Iris Gardens
822 Rodney Vista Boulevard
Cape Girardeau, MO 63701

(314) 334-3383
Catalogue: $1.00

Caprice Farm Nursery
15425 SW Pleasant Hill Road
Sherwood, OR 97140
(503) 625-7241
Specialties: Japanese and Siberian irises
Catalogue: $2.00

Cascade Bulb and Seed
Box 271
2333 Crooked Finger Road
Scotts Mills, OR 97375
Specialties: Siberian irises
Catalogue: long SASE

Chuck Chapman Iris
11 Harts Lane
Guelph, Ontario N1L 1B1
Catalogue: $2.00

Chehalem Gardens
Box 693
Newberg, OR 97132
(503) 538-8920
Specialties: spuria and Siberian irises
Catalogue: $2.00

Comanche Acres Iris Gardens
Route 1, Box 258
Gower, MO 64454
(816) 424-6436
Catalogue: $3.00

Contemporary Gardens
Box 534
Blanchard, OK 73010
Specialties: Australian imports
Catalogue: $1.00

Cooley's Gardens
Box 126
11553 Silverton Road NE
Silverton, OR 97381-0126
(503) 873-5463

(800) 225-5391
Specialties: tall bearded irises
Catalogue: $4.00

Cooper's Garden
2345 Decatur Avenue North
Golden Valley, MN 55427
(612) 591-0495
Specialties: species irises
Catalogue: $1.00

Cordon Bleu Farms
Box 2033
418 Buena Creek Road
San Marcos, CA 92079
Specialties: Louisiana and spuria irises
Catalogue: $1.00

Cottage Gardens
266 17th Avenue
San Francisco, CA 94121
(415) 387-7145
Specialties: median and tall bearded irises
Catalogue: free

C. Criscola Iris Garden
Route 2, Box 183
Walla Walla, WA 99362
(509) 525-4841
Specialties: bearded irises
Catalogue: two stamps

D. and J. Gardens
7872 Howell Prairie Road NE
Silverton, OR 97381
Catalogue: $1.00

David Iris Farm
Route 1
Fort Dodge, IA 50501
Catalogue: one stamp

Draycott Gardens
16815 Falls Road
Upperco, MD 21155
(410) 374-4788

Specialties: Siberian and Japanese irises
Catalogue: $1.00

Enchanted Iris Garden
715 Central Canyon
Nampa, ID 83651
(208) 465-5713
Specialties: tall bearded irises
Catalogue: $1.00

Ensata Gardens
9823 East Michigan Avenue
Galesburg, MI 49053
(616) 665-7500
Specialties: Japanese irises
Catalogue: $2.00

Fleur de Lis Gardens
185 NE Territorial Road
Canby, OR 97013
Specialties: tall bearded irises
Catalogue: $2.00

Foxes' Iris Patch
RR 5, Box 382
Huron, SD 57350
Catalogue: $3.00

Friendship Gardens
2590 Wellworth Way
West Friendship, MD 21794
Specialties: reblooming and
tall bearded irises
Catalogue: $1.00

Garden of the Enchanted Rainbow
Route 4, Box 439
Killen, AL 35645
Catalogue: $1.00

Grace Gardens North
N 3739 County Highway K
Granton, WI 54436
(715) 238-7122
Catalogue: free

Hahn's Rainbow Iris Garden
200 North School Street
Desloge, MO 63601
(314) 431-3342
Catalogue: $1.50

Hildenbrandt's Iris Gardens
75741 Road 431
Lexington, NE 68850
(308) 324-4334
Specialties: tall bearded and dwarf irises
Catalogue: $1.00

Holly Lane Iris Gardens
10930 Holly Lane
Osseo, MN 55369
Specialties: bearded irises
Catalogue: long SASE with two stamps

Huggins Farm Irises
Route 1, Box 348
Hico, TX 76457
(817) 796-4041
Specialties: bearded irises
Catalogue: $1.00

Illini Iris
Route 3, Box 5
Monticello, IL 61856
(217) 762-3446
Specialties: Siberian irises
Catalogue: SASE

Iris Acres
Route 4, Box 189
Winamac, IN 46996
(219) 946-4197
Specialties: bearded irises
Catalogue: $1.00

Iris City Gardens
502 Brighton Place
Nashville, TN 37205
(615) 386-3778
Catalogue: free

Iris Country
6219 Topaz Street NE
Brooks, OR 97035
(503) 393-4739
Specialties: bearded irises
Catalogue: $1.00

Iris Farm
Box 336
Ojo Caliente, NM 87539
Specialties: tall bearded irises
Catalogue: $1.00

The Iris Garden
Route 1, Box CW 20
Spencer, IN 47460
Specialties: tall bearded and median irises
Catalogue: two stamps

Iris Hill Farm
7280 Tassajara Creek Road
Santa Margarita, CA 93453
(805) 438-3070
Specialties: tall bearded irises
Catalogue: $1.00

The Iris Pond
7311 Churchill Road
McLean, VA 22101
Catalogue: $1.00

Iris Test Gardens
1010 Highland Park Drive
College Place, WA 99324
(509) 525-8804
Specialties: tall bearded irises
Catalogue: 50¢

Joni's Dance-in-the-Wind Garden
810 South 14th Street
Tekamah, NE 68061
Catalogue: $1.00

Keith Keppel
Box 18154
Salem, OR 97305

(503) 391-9241
Specialties: tall bearded and median irises
Catalogue: $2.00

Knee-Deep in June
708 North 10th Street
St. Joseph, MO 64501
Catalogue: $1.00

Laurie's Garden
41856 McKenzie Highway
Springfield, OR 97478
(503) 896-3756
Specialties: beardless irises
Catalogue: long SASE

Lee's Gardens
Box 5, 25986 Sauder Road
Tremont, IL 61568
(309) 925-5262
Catalogue: $2.00

Lone Star Iris Gardens
5637 Saddleback Road
Garland, TX 75043
Specialties: Louisiana irises
Catalogue: $2.00

Long's Gardens
Box 19
Boulder, CO 80306
(303) 442-2353
Specialties: tall bearded irises
Catalogue: free

Lorraine's Iris Patch
20272 Road 11 NW
Quincy, WA 98848
Catalogue: free

Louisiana Nursery
Route 7, Box 43
Opelousas, LA 70570
(318) 948-3696
Specialties: Louisiana irises
Catalogue: $4.00

M. A. D. Garden
4828 Jella Way
North Highland, CA 95660
Specialties: Bob and Mary Dunn intro-
ductions
Catalogue: SASE

Manchester Garden
614 Nandale Lane
Manchester, MO 63021
Catalogue: free

Maple Tree Gardens
Box 547
Ponca, NE 68770
Specialties: tall bearded and median irises
Catalogue: 50¢

Maryott's Gardens
1073 Bird Avenue
San Jose, CA 95125
(408) 971-0444
Specialties: bearded irises
Catalogue: long SASE

Maxim's Greenwood Gardens
2157 Sonoma Street
Redding, CA 96001
(916) 241-0764
Catalogue: $1.00

McAllister's Iris Gardens
Box 112
Fairacres, NM 88033
Specialties: aril irises
Catalogue: $1.00

McMillen's Iris Garden
RR 1
Norwich, Ontario N0J 1P0
(519) 468-6508
Catalogue: $2.00

Mid-America Iris Gardens
3409 North Geraldine Avenue
Oklahoma City, OK 73112

(405) 946-5743
Specialties: bearded and reblooming
irises
Catalogue: $2.00

Millar Mountain Nursery
RR 3
5086 McLay Road
Duncan, British Columbia V9L 2X1
(604) 748-0487
Catalogue: $2.00

Mill Creek Gardens
210 Parkway
Lapeer, MI 48446
(810) 664-5525
Catalogue: $1.00

Miller's Manor Gardens
3167 East US 224
Ossian, IN 46777
(219) 597-7403
Catalogue: $1.00

Misty Hill Farms—Moonshine Gardens
5080 West Soda Rock Lane
Healdsburg, CA 95448
(707) 433-8408
Specialties: reblooming irises
Catalogue: free

Monument Iris Garden
50029 Sunflower Road
Mitchell, NE 69357
Specialties: tall bearded irises
Catalogue: $1.00

Mountain View Gardens
2435 Middle Road
Columbia Falls, MT 59912
Specialties: Siberian irises
Catalogue: one stamp

Mountain View Iris Gardens
6307 Irwin Avenue
Lawton, OK 73503

(405) 492-5183
Catalogue: $1.50

Napa Country Iris Gardens
9087 Steele Canyon Road
Napa, CA 94558
Specialties: tall bearded irises
Catalogue: one stamp

Newburn's Iris Gardens
1415 Meadow Dale Drive
Lincoln, NE 68505
Specialties: tall bearded irises
Catalogue: free

Nicholls Gardens
4724 Angus Drive
Gainesville, VA 22065
(703) 754-9623
Catalogue: $1.00

Nicholson's Woodland Iris Gardens
2405 Woodland Avenue
Modesto, CA 95358
(209) 578-4184
Catalogue: $1.00

North Forty Iris
93 East 100 South
Logan, UT 84321
Specialties: tall bearded irises
Catalogue: $1.00

North Pine Iris Gardens
Box 595
Norfolk, NE 68701
Specialties: tall bearded and median irises
Catalogue: $1.00

O'Brien Iris Garden
3223 Canfield Road
Sebastopol, CA 95472
Catalogue: two stamps

Ohio Gardens
102 Laramie Road

Marietta, OH 45750
Catalogue: $1.00

Pacific Coast Hybridizers
Box 972, 1170 Steinway Avenue
Campbell, CA 95009
(408) 370-2955
Catalogue: $1.00

Pederson's Iris Patch
Sibley Road
Dazey, ND 58429
Catalogue: one stamp

Pine Ridge Gardens
832 Sycamore Road
London, AR 72847
(501) 293-4359
Specialties: beardless irises
Catalogue: $1.00

Pleasure Iris Gardens
425 East Luna
Chaparral, NM 88021
(505) 824-4299
Specialties: aril irises
Catalogue: $1.00

Portable Acres
2087 Curtis Drive
Penngrove, CA 94951
Specialties: Pacific Coast native irises
Catalogue: long SASE with two stamps

Powell's Gardens
9468 US Highway 70 E
Princeton, NC 27569
(919) 936-4421
Catalogue: $3.00

Ramona Gardens
2178 El Paso Street
Ramona, CA 92065
(619) 789-6099
Specialties: bearded irises
Catalogue: $2.00

Rancho de los Flores
8000 Balcom Canyon Road
Moorpark, CA 93021
Specialties: reblooming irises
Catalogue: free

Riverdale Iris Gardens
Box 524
Rockford, MN 55373
(612) 477-4859
Specialties: dwarf and median irises
Catalogue: $1.00

Roderick Hillview Garden
3862 Highway 0
Farmington, MO 63640
(314) 431-5711
Specialties: tall bearded irises
Catalogue: one stamp

Roris Gardens
8195 Bradshaw Road
Sacramento, CA 95829
(916) 689-7460
Specialties: tall bearded irises
Catalogue: $3.00

Royal Rainbow Gardens
2311 Torquay
Royal Oak, MI 48073
Catalogue: two stamps

Ruth's Iris Garden
1621 Adams Road
Yuba City, CA 95993
Catalogue: two stamps

Schreiner's Iris Gardens
3629 Quinaby Road
Salem, OR 97303
(800) 525-2367
Catalogue: $4.00

Shepard Iris Garden
3342 West Orangewood
Phoenix, AZ 85051

(602) 841-1231
Specialties: bearded and spuria irises
Catalogue: two stamps

Shiloh Gardens
Route 1, Box 77
Pawnee, IL 62558
Catalogue: two stamps

Sir Williams Gardens
2852 Jackson Boulevard
Highland, MI 48356
(313) 887-4779
Catalogue: $2.00

Sourdough Iris Gardens
109 Sourdough Ridge Road
Bozeman, MT 59715
Catalogue: long SASE

Spruce Gardens
2317 3rd Road
Wisner, NE 68791
(402) 529-6860
Specialties: tall bearded irises
Catalogue: $1.00

Stanley Iris Garden
3245 North Wing Road
Star, ID 83669
(208) 286-7079
Specialties: tall bearded irises
Catalogue: $1.00

Stephens Lane Gardens
Route 1, Box 136
Bells, TN 38006
Catalogue: $1.00

Sunnyridge Gardens
1724 Drinnen Road
Knoxville, TN 37914
(615) 933-0723
Catalogue: $1.00

Superstition Iris Gardens
2536 Old Highway
Cathey's Valley, CA 95306
Specialties: bearded irises
Catalogue: $1.00

Sutton's Green Thumber
16592 Road 208
Porterville, CA 93257
Catalogue: $1.00

TB's Place
1513 Ernie Lane
Grand Prairie, TX 75052
Catalogue: SASE

Tranquil Lake Nursery, Inc.
45 River Street
Rehoboth, MA 02769-1395
(508) 242-4002
Specialties: Japanese and Siberian irises
Catalogue: $1.00

Uranium Country Gardens
728 1675 Road
Delta, CO 81416
Catalogue: $1.00

Valley Gardens
4896 Granada Lane
Linden, CA 95236
Specialties: tall bearded and reblooming
irises
Catalogue: $1.00

York Hill Farm
18 Warren Street
Georgetown, MA 01833
Specialties: Japanese and Siberian irises
Catalogue: $1.00

Zebra Gardens
2511 West 10950 South
South Jordan, UT 84095
(801) 254-2536
Catalogue: $1.00

Ivies

Organization

American Ivy Society
Daphne Pfaff, Membership Chair
696 16th Avenue South
Naples, FL 33940
(813) 261-0388
Dues: $15.00
Publications: *The Ivy Journal* (annual);
Between the Vines (semiannual newsletter)

Plant Sources

Ivies of the World
Box 408
Weirsdale, FL 32195
(904) 821-2201
Catalogue: $1.50

Sunnybrook Farms Nursery
Box 6
9448 Mayfield Road
Chesterland, OH 44026
(216) 729-7232
Catalogue: $1.00

Lilacs

Organization

International Lilac Society
The Holden Arboretum
9500 Sperry Road
Mentor, OH 44060
(216) 946-4400
Dues: $15.00
Publication: *Lilac Journal* (quarterly)

Plant Sources

Ameri-Hort Research
Box 1529
Medina, OH 44258

(216) 723-4966
Catalogue: $2.00

Fox Hill Nursery
347 Lunt Road
Freeport, ME 04032
(207) 729-1511
Catalogue: $2.00

Heard Gardens, Ltd.
5355 Merle Hay Road
Johnston, IA 50131
(515) 276-4533
Catalogue: $2.00

Wedge Nursery
Route 2, Box 144
Albert Lea, MN 56007
(507) 373-5225
Catalogue: free

Lilies

Organizations

American Calochortus Society
c/o H. P. McDonald
Box 1128
Berkeley, CA 94701
Dues: $4.00
Publication: *Mariposa* (quarterly)

British Columbia Lily Society
Del Knowlton, Secretary/Treasurer
5510 239th Street
Langley, British Columbia V3A 7N6
(604) 534-4729
Dues: Canada $5.00
Publication: *BCLS Newsletter* (quarterly)

Canadian Prairie Lily Society
M. E. Driver, Secretary
22 Red River Road
Saskatoon, Saskatchewan S7K 1G3
(306) 242-5329

Dues: Canada $5.00
Publication: *Newsletter* (quarterly)

International Aroid Society
Box 43-1853
Miami, FL 33143
(305) 271-3767
Dues: $18.00
Publications: *IAS Newsletter* (bimonthly);
Aroideana (annual)

North American Lily Society, Inc.
Dr. Robert Gilman, Executive Secretary
Box 272
Owatonna, MN 55060
(507) 451-2170
Dues: $12.50
Publications: *Lily Yearbook;* quarterly bulletin

Pacific Northwest Lily Society
Dick Malpass
10804 NW 11th Avenue
Vancouver, WA 98685
(503) 656-1575
Dues: $8.00
Publication: bulletin

Plant Sources

Ambergate Gardens
8015 Krey Avenue
Waconia, MN 55387
(612) 443-2248
Specialties: Martagnon lilies
Catalogue: $2.00

B & D Lilies
330 P Street
Port Townsend, WA 98368
(206) 385-1738
Catalogue: $3.00

Borboleta Gardens
Route 5
15980 Canby Avenue

Faribault, MN 55021
(507) 334-2807
Catalogue: $3.00

Fairyland Begonia and Lily Garden
1100 Griffith Road
McKinleyville, CA 95521
(707) 839-3034
Specialties: hybrid lilies
Catalogue: 50¢

Hartle-Gilman Gardens
RR 4, Box 14
Owatona, MN 55060-9416
(507) 451-3191
Specialties: hybrid lilies
Catalogue: free

Honeywood Lilies
Box 68
Parkside, Saskatchewan S0J 2A0
(306) 747-3296
Catalogue: $2.00

The Lily Garden
36752 SE Bluff Road
Boring, OR 97009
(503) 668-5291
Catalogue: free

The Lily Nook
Box 657
Rolla, ND 58367
(204) 476-3225
Catalogue: $2.00

The Lily Pad
5102 Scott Road
Olympia, WA 98502
(206) 866-0291
Catalogue: $2.00

Lindel Lilies
5510 239th Street
Langley, British Columbia V3A 7N6
(604) 534-4729

Specialties: hybrid lilies
Catalogue: free

Olympic Coast Garden
84 Eaton Lane
Sequim, WA 98382
Catalogue: $1.00

Rex Bulb Farms
Box 774
Port Townsend, WA 98368
Catalogue: $1.00

Riverside Gardens
RR 5
Saskatoon, Saskatchewan S7K 3J8
Specialties: hybrid Asiatic lilies
Catalogue: $1.00

Native Plants
See also **Prairie Plants; Wildflowers**

Organizations
See chapter 8, **Native Plant Societies and Botanical Clubs**

Plant Sources

A High Country Garden
2902 Rufina Street
Santa Fe, NM 87505
(800) 925-9387
Specialties: xeric plants
Catalogue: free

Alplains
32315 Pine Crest Court
Kiowa, CO 80117
(303) 621-2247
Specialties: Rocky Mountains
Catalogue: $1.00

Amanda's Garden
8410 Harpers Ferry Road
Springwater, NY 14560

Specialties: perennials
Catalogue: free

Cherokee Rose
9382 Island Road
St. Francisville, LA 70775
Specialties: Southeast
Catalogue: $1.00

Comstock Seed
8520 West 4th Street
Reno, NV 89523
(702) 746-3681
Specialties: Great Basin
Catalogue: free

Desert Moon Nursery
Box 600
Veguita, NM 87062
(505) 864-0614
Specialties: desert plants
Catalogue: $1.00

Edge of the Rockies
133 Hunna Road
Bayfield, CO 81122
Specialties: Rocky Mountains
Catalogue: $2.00

Frosty Hollow
Box 53
Langley, WA 98260
(206) 221-2332
Specialties: Northwest
Catalogue: long SASE

Goodness Grows
Box 311
Lexington, GA 30648
(706) 743-5055
Specialties: Southeast
Catalogue: free

Great Basin Natives
770 West 400 South
Provo, UT 84601

Specialties: Great Basin
Catalogue: $1.00

Wallace W. Hansen
2158 Bower Court SE
Salem, OR 97301
(503) 581-2638
Specialties: Pacific Northwest
Catalogue: $2.00

High Altitude Gardens
Box 419
Ketchum, ID 83340
(800) 874-7333
Specialties: high-altitude plants
Catalogue: $3.00

Holman Brothers Seed
Box 337
Glendale, AZ 85311
(602) 244-1650
Specialties: Sonoran and Mojave Desert
Catalogue: two stamps

Kiowa Creek Botanicals
520 North Grant Avenue
Fort Collins, CO 80521
Specialties: Plains and prairies seeds
Catalogue: $1.00

Las Pilitas Nursery
Star Route, Box 23X
Las Pilitas Road
Santa Margarita, CA 93453
(805) 438-5992
Specialties: California
Catalogue: $1.00

Little Valley Farm
Route 3, Box 544
Spring Green, WI 53588
(608) 935-3324
Specialties: Midwest
Catalogue: one stamp

Mostly Natives Nursery
Box 258, 27235 Highway 1
Tomales, CA 94971
(707) 878-2009
Specialties: West Coast and xeric plants
Catalogue: $3.00

Native Gardens
5737 Fisher Lane
Greenback, TN 37742
(615) 856-0220
Catalogue: $2.00

Native Plants, Inc.
417 Wakara Way
Salt Lake City, UT 84108
(800) 533-8498
Catalogue: $1.00

Niche Gardens
1111 Dawson Road
Chapel Hill, NC 27516
(919) 967-0078
Specialties: Southeast
Catalogue: $3.00

Northwest Native Seed
915 Davis Place South
Seattle, WA 98144
(206) 329-5804
Specialties: Northwest
Catalogue: $1.00

NWN Nursery
Box 1143
DeFuniak Springs, FL 32433
(904) 638-7572
Specialties: Southeast
Catalogue: free

Ben Pace Nursery
Route 1, Box 925
Pine Mountain, GA 31822
(706) 663-2346
Specialties: Southeast
Catalogue: free

Theodore Payne Foundation Nursery
10459 Tuxford Street
Sun Valley, CA 91352
(818) 768-1802
Specialties: California
Catalogue: $3.00

Pine Ridge Gardens
832 Sycamore Road
London, AR 72847
Catalogue: $1.00

Plants of the Southwest
Agua Fria
Route 6, Box 11
Santa Fe, NM 87505
(800) 788-SEED
Specialties: Southwest
Catalogue: $3.50

Rouge House Seed
250 Maple Street
Central Point, OR 97502
Specialties: Pacific Northwest
Catalogue: $1.00

Sharp Brothers Seed Company
Box 140
Healy, KS 67850
(316) 398-2231
Specialties: Midwest
Catalogue: $5.00

Shooting Star Nursery
444 Bates Road
Frankfort, KY 40601
(502) 223-1679
Specialties: east of the Rockies
Catalogue: $2.00

Southwestern Exposure
10310 East Fennimore
Apache Junction, AZ 85220
(602) 986-7771
Specialties: Southwest
Catalogue: two stamps

Southwestern Native Seeds
Box 50503
Tucson, AZ 85703
Specialties: Southwest
Catalogue: $1.00

Tripple Brook Farm
37 Middle Road
Southampton, MA 01073
(413) 527-4626
Specialties: Northeast
Catalogue: free

Western Native Seed
Box 1281
Canon City, CO 81215
(719) 275-8414
Specialties: West
Catalogue: long SASE

Wild Earth Native Plant Nursery
49 Mead Avenue
Freehold, NJ 07728
(908) 780-5661
Catalogue: $2.00

Wild Seed
Box 27751
Tempe, AZ 85285
(602) 345-0669
Specialties: Southwest
Catalogue: free

Yucca Du Nursery
Box 655
Waller, TX 77484
(409) 826-6363
Specialties: Texas and Mexico
Catalogue: $4.00

Orchids
See chapter 2

Ornamental Grasses

Plant Sources

Ambergate Gardens
8015 Krey Avenue
Waconia, MN 55387
(612) 443-2248
Catalogue: $2.00

Baylands Nursery
2835 Temple Court
East Palo Alto, CA 94303
Catalogue: $1.00

Kurt Bluemel, Inc.
2740 Greene Lane
Baldwin, MD 21013
(410) 557-7229
Catalogue: $3.00

Coastal Gardens and Nursery
4611 Socastee Boulevard
Myrtle Beach, SC 29575
(803) 293-2000
Catalogue: $2.00

Endangered Species
Box 1830
Tustin, CA 92681
Catalogue: $6.00

Flowerplace Plant Farm
Box 4865
Meridian, MS 39304
(601) 482-5686
Catalogue: $3.00

Garden Place
Box 388
6780 Heisley Road
Mentor, OH 44061
(216) 255-3705
Catalogue: $1.00

Gardens North
34 Helena Street
Ottawa, Ontario K1Y 3M8
Catalogue: $3.00

Greenlee Nursery
301 East Franklin Avenue
Pomona, CA 91766
(714) 629-9045
Catalogue: $5.00

Holbrook Farm and Nursery
Box 368
115 Lance Road
Fletcher, NC 28732
(704) 891-7790
Catalogue: free

Landscape Alternatives
1465 North Pascal Street
St. Paul, MN 55108
(612) 488-1342
Specialties: Minnesota wildflowers
Catalogue: $1.00

Limerock Ornamental Grasses, Inc.
RD 1, Box 111C
Port Matilda, PA 16870
(814) 692-2272
Catalogue: $3.00

Matterhorn Nursery, Inc.
227 Summit Park Road
Spring Valley, NY 10977
(914) 354-5986
Catalogue: $5.00

Neufeld Nursery
1865 California Street
Oceanside, CA 92054
Catalogue: $1.00

Pacific Coast Seed
7074D Commerce Circle
Pleasanton, CA 94566
Catalogue: $1.00

Paradise Water Gardens
14 May Street
Whitman, MA 02382
(617) 447-4711
Catalogue: $3.00

Pinky's Plants
Box 126
442 G Street
Pawnee City, NE 68420
(800) 94-PINKY
Catalogue: $3.50

Rice Creek Gardens
11506 Highway 65
Blaine, MN 55434
Catalogue: $1.00

Sunlight Gardens
174 Golden Lane
Andersonville, TX 77805
Catalogue: $3.00

Wavecrest Nursery and Landscaping
Company
2509 Lakeshore Drive
Fennville, MI 49408
(616) 542-4175
Catalogue: $1.00

Wildlife Nurseries
Box 2724
Oshkosh, WI 54903
(414) 231-3780
Catalogue: $1.00

Wildwood Nursery
3975 Emerald Avenue
LaVerne, CA 91750
Catalogue: $1.00

Woodlanders, Inc.
1128 Colleton Avenue
Aiken, SC 29801
(803) 648-7522
Catalogue: $2.00

Ya-Ka-Ama Nursery
6215 Eastside Road
Forestville, CA 95436
Catalogue: $1.00

Peonies

Organizations

American Peony Society
c/o Greta Kessenich
250 Interlachen Road
Hopkins, MN 55343
(612) 938-4706
Dues: $10.00
Publication: *Bulletin* (quarterly)

Canadian Peony Society
1246 Donlea Crescent
Oakville, Ontario L6J 1V7
(416) 845-5380

Publication

Chrysanthemum Corner with Peony Highlights
Box 5635
Dearborn, MI 48128
Frequency: bimonthly
Subscription: $18.00

Plant Sources

A & D Peony and Perennial Nursery
6808 180th Street SE
Snohomish, WA 98290
(206) 485-2487
Catalogue: $1.50

Bigger Peony Farm
201 Northeast Rice Road
Topeka, KS 66616
Catalogue: free

Brand Peony Farm
Box 842

St. Cloud, MN 56302
Catalogue: $1.00

C & C Nursery
Route 3, Box 422
Murray, KY 42071
(502) 753-2993
Catalogue: $1.00

Caprice Farm Nursery
15425 SW Pleasant Hill Road
Sherwood, OR 97140
(503) 625-7241
Catalogue: $2.00

Cricket Hill Garden
670 Walnut Hill Road
Thomaston, CT 06787
(203) 283-4707
Specialties: tree peonies
Catalogue: $2.00

Ellery Nurseries
Box 68
Smyrna, DE 19977
Catalogue: free

Don Hollingsworth Peonies
RR 3, Box 27
Maryville, MO 64468
(816) 562-3010
Catalogue: $1.00

Homestead Farms
Route 2, Box 31A
Owensville, MO 65066
(314) 437-4277
Catalogue: free

Klehm Nursery
4210 North Duncan Road
Champaign, IL 61821
(800) 553-3715
Catalogue: $4.00

Laurie's Landscaping
2959 Hobson Road
Downers Grove, IL 60517
(708) 969-1270
Catalogue: long SASE

The New Peony Farm
Box 18235
St. Paul, MN 55118
(612) 457-8994
Catalogue: free

Nicholls Gardens
4724 Angus Drive
Gainesville, VA 22065
(703) 754-9623
Catalogue: $1.00

Reath's Nursery
County Road 577, Box 247
Vulcan, MI 49892
(906) 563-9777
Catalogue: $1.00

Sevald Nursery
4937 3rd Avenue South
Minneapolis, MN 55409
(612) 822-3279
Specialties: herbaceous peonies
Catalogue: $1.00

Gilbert H. Wild and Son, Inc.
Box 338
1112 Joplin Street
Sarcoxie, MO 64862-0338
(417) 548-3514
Catalogue: $3.00

Perennials

Organization

The Perennial Plant Association
Department of Horticulture
Ohio State University

2001 Fyffe Court
Columbus, OH 43210

Plant Sources

Ambergate Gardens
8015 Krey Avenue
Waconia, MN 55387
(612) 443-2248
Catalogue: $2.00

Bluestone Perennials, Inc.
7211 Middle Ridge Road
Madison, OH 44057
(800) 852-5243
Catalogue: free

Busse Gardens
13579 10th Street NW
Cokato, MN 55321
(612) 286-2654
Catalogue: $2.00

Burch Estate
650 Dodds Lane
Gladwyne, PA 19035
(215) 649-8944
Catalogue: $1.00

Canyon Creek Nursery
3527 Dry Creek Road
Oroville, CA 95965
(916) 533-2166
Catalogue: $2.00

Carroll Gardens
Box 310
Westminster, MD 21157
(800) 638-6334
Catalogue: $3.00

Coastal Gardens and Nursery
4611 Socastee Boulevard
Myrtle Beach, SC 29575
(803) 293-2000
Catalogue: $2.00

The Crownsville Nursery
Box 797
1241 Generals Highway
Crownsville, MD 21032
(410) 923-2212
Catalogue: $2.00

Daisy Fields
12635 SW Brighton Lane
Hillsboro, OR 97123
Catalogue: $1.00

Digging Dog Nursery
Box 471
Albion, CA 95410
(707) 937-1130
Catalogue: $3.00

Donaroma's Nursery
Box 2189
Edgartown, MA 02539
(508) 627-3036
Catalogue: $1.00

Englearth Gardens
2461 22nd Street
Hopkins, MI 49328
(616) 793-7196
Catalogue: 50¢

Fieldstone Gardens, Inc.
620 Quaker Lane
Vassalboro, ME 04989
(207) 923-3826
Catalogue: $2.00

Fir Grove Perennial Nursery
19917 NE 68th Street
Vancouver, WA 98682
(206) 944-8384
Catalogue: $2.00

Flowerplace Plant Farm
Box 4865, Meridian, MS 39304
(601) 482-5686
Catalogue: $3.00

Foothill Cottage Gardens
13925 Sontag Road
Grass Valley, CA 95945
(916) 272-4362
Catalogue: $3.00

Forestfarm
990 Tetherow Road
Williams, OR 97544
(503) 846-7269
Catalogue: $3.00

Garden Perennials
Route 1
Wayne, NE 68787
(402) 375-3615
Catalogue: $1.00

Garden Place
Box 388
6780 Heisley Road
Mentor, OH 44061
(216) 255-3705
Catalogue: $1.00

The Gathering Garden
Route 1, Box 41E
Efland, NC 27243
Catalogue: $1.00

Goodwin Creek Gardens
Box 83, Williams, OR 97544
(503) 846-7357
Catalogue: $1.00

Hauser's Superior View Farm
Route 1, Box 199
Bayfield, WI 54814
(715) 779-5404
Catalogue: free

Heronswood Nursery
7530 288th Street NE
Kingston, WA 98346
(360) 297-4172
Catalogue: $4.00

Hillary's Garden
Box 378
Sugar Loaf, NY 10981
Catalogue: $2.00

Hillside Gardens
515 Litchfield Road
Norfolk, CT 06058
(203) 542-5345
Note: No mail order
Catalogue: $3.00

Holbrook Farm and Nursery
Box 368
115 Lance Road
Fletcher, NC 28732
(704) 891-7790
Catalogue: $1.00

Indigo Marsh Nursery
2236 Iseman Road
Darlington, SC 29532
Catalogue: $2.00

International Growers Exchange, Inc.
17142 Lasher Road
Detroit, MI 48219
Catalogue: $3.00

Ivy Garth
Box 606
Gates Mills, OH 44040
Catalogue: free

Joy Creek Nursery
20300 NW Watson Road
Scappoose, OR 97056
(503) 543-7474
Catalogue: $2.00

Judy's Perennials
1206 Maple Avenue
Downers Grove, IL 60615
(708) 969-6514
Catalogue: free

Klehm Nursery
4210 North Duncan Road
Champaign, IL 61821
(800) 553-3715
Catalogue: $4.00

Lamb Nurseries
Route 1, Box 460B
Long Beach, WA 98631
(360) 642-4856
Catalogue: $1.50

Ledgecrest Greenhouses
1029 Storrs Road
Storrs, CT 06268
(203) 487-1661
Catalogue: free

Mary's Plant Farm
2410 Lanes Mill Road
Hamilton, OH 45013
(513) 894-0022
Catalogue: $1.00

Matterhorn Nursery
227 Summit Park Road
Spring Valley, NY 10977
(914) 354-5986
Catalogue: $5.00

Meadow View Farms
Box 3146
Central Point, OR 97502
Catalogue: $3.00

Milaeger's Gardens
4838 Douglas Avenue
Racine, WI 53402
(414) 639-2371
Catalogue: $1.00

Montrose Nursery
Box 957
Hillsborough, NC 27278
(919) 732-7787
Catalogue: $2.00

Niche Gardens
111 Dawson Road
Chapel Hill, NC 27516
(919) 967-0078
Catalogue: $1.00

Owen Farms
RR 3, Box 158
2951 Curve-Nankipoo Road
Ripley, TN 38063
(901) 635-1588
Catalogue: $2.00

The Perennial Connection
Box 3002-115
Newburyport, MA 01950
Catalogue: $1.00

The Perfect Season
Box 191
McMinnville, TN 37110
(615) 668-3225
Catalogue: $2.00

Pine Ridge Gardens
832 Sycamore Road
London, AR 72847
Catalogue: $1.00

Pinky's Plants
Box 126, 442 G Street
Pawnee City, NE 68420
(800) 94-PINKY
Catalogue: $3.50

Plant Delights Nursery
9241 Sauls Road
Raleigh, NC 27603
(919) 772-4794
Catalogue: $3.50

Powell's Gardens
9468 US Highway 70 E
Princeton, NC 27569
(919) 936-4421
Catalogue: $3.00

The Primrose Path
RD 2, Box 110
Scottdale, PA 15683
(412) 887-6756
Catalogue: $2.00

Riverhead Perennials
5 Riverhead Lane
East Lyme, CT 06333
(203) 437-7828
Catalogue: $2.00

Rolling Green Landscaping and Nursery
Box 760
64 Breakfast Hill Road
Greenland, NH 03840
(603) 436-2732
Catalogue: SASE

Roslyn Nursery
211 Burrs Lane
Dix Hills, NY 11746
(516) 543-9347
Catalogue: $3.00

Sunlight Gardens
174 Golden Lane
Andersonville, TX 77805
Catalogue: $3.00

Sunset Ridge Farm
Box 131
Sharptown, MD 21861
(410) 883-2347
Catalogue: $1.00

Surry Gardens
Box 145
Route 172
Surry, ME 04684
(207) 667-4493
Catalogue: free

H. R. Talmage & Sons
Horticultural Goddess
36 Sound Avenue

Riverhead, NY 11901
(516) 727-0124
Catalogue: $1.00

Andre Viette Farm and Nursery
Route 1, Box 16
Fishersville, VA 22939
(703) 942-2118
Catalogue: $3.00

Wayside Gardens
Box 1
Hodges, SC 29695
(800) 845-1124
Catalogue: $1.00

We-Du Nurseries
Route 5, Box 724
Marion, NC 28752
(704) 738-8300
Catalogue: $2.00

Weiss Brothers Perennial Nursery
11690 Colfax Highway
Grass Valley, CA 95945
(916) 272-7657
Catalogue: free

White Flower Farm
Route 63, Litchfield, CT 06759
(203) 469-9600
Catalogue: $4.00

Woodside Gardens
1191 Egg & I Road
Chimcum, WA 98325
(206) 732-4754
Catalogue: $2.00

Prairie Plants
See also **Native Plants; Wildflowers**

Organizations
See chapter 8, **Native Plant Societies and Botanical Clubs**

Plant Sources

Bamert Seed Company
Route 3, Box 1120
Muleshoe, TX 79347
(800) 262-9892
Catalogue: free

Bluestem Prairie Nursery
Route 2, Box 106A
Hillsboro, IL 62049
(217) 532-6344
Catalogue: free

Dyck Arboretum of the Plains
Seed Exchange
Hesston College
Box 3000
Hesston, KS 67062
(316) 327-8127
Catalogue: long SASE

Holland Wildflower Farms
290 O'Neal Lane
Elkins, AR 72727
(501) 643-2622
Catalogue: long SASE with two stamps

Kiowa Creek Botanicals
520 North Grant Avenue
Fort Collins, CO 80521
Catalogue: $1.00

LaFayette Home Nursery
RR #1, Box 1A
LaFayette, IL 61449
(309) 995-3311
Catalogue: free

Landscape Alternatives
1465 North Pascal Street
St. Paul, MN 55108
(612) 488-1342
Catalogue: $1.00

Milaeger's Gardens
4838 Douglas Avenue
Racine, WI 53402
(414) 639-2371
Catalogue: $1.00

The Natural Garden
38 W443 Highway 64
St. Charles, IL 60174
(708) 584-0150
Catalogue: $2.00

Nesta Prairie Perennials
1019 Miller Road
Kalamazoo, MI 49001
(800) 233-5025
Catalogue: free

Prairie Moon Nursery
Route 3, Box 163
Winona, MN 55987
(507) 452-1362
Catalogue: $2.00

Prairie Nursery
Box 306
Westfield, WI 53964
(608) 296-3679
Catalogue: $3.00

Prairie Restoration, Inc.
Box 327
Princeton, MN 55371
(612) 389-4342
Catalogue: free

Prairie Ridge Nursery
9738 Overland Road
Mount Horeb, WI 53572
(608) 437-5245
Catalogue: $3.00

Prairie Seed Source
Box 83
North Lake, WI 53064
Catalogue: $1.00

Shooting Star Nursery
444 Bates Road
Frankfort, KY 40601
(502) 223-1679
Catalogue: $2.00

Stock Seed Farms, Inc.
28008 Mill Road
Murdock, NE 68407
(402) 867-3771
Catalogue: free

Rare and Unusual Plants and Seeds

Plant Sources

Dr. A. N. Berkutenko
c/o Louise Ann Zurbrick
Box 210562
Anchorage, AK 99521
Specialties: seeds from Siberia
and the Russian far east
Catalogue: $1.00

J. L. Hudson, Seedsman
Box 1058
Redwood City, CA 94064
Specialties: rare seeds
Catalogue: $1.00

Karmix Exotix Nursery
Box 146
Shelburne, Ontario L0N 1S0
Specialties: wild-collected
international seeds
Catalogue: $2.00

Rare Plant Research
13245 SE Harold
Portland, OR 97236
Specialties: caudiciforms
Catalogue: $2.00

Rare Seed Locators, Inc.
Drawer 2479

2140 Shattuck Avenue
Berkeley, CA 94704
Catalogue: long SASE

SBE Seeds
3421 Bream Street
Gautier, MS 39553
(601) 497-6544
Catalogue: three stamps

Siskiyou Rare Plant Nursery
2825 Cummings Road
Medford, OR 97501
(503) 772-6846
Catalogue: $2.00

Sunquest Seed Company
2411 Aquarius Road
Orange Park, FL 32073
Catalogue: free

Rhododendrons
See **Azaleas, Rhododendrons,
and Woody Shrubs**

Rock Garden Plants
See chapter 2

Roses
See chapter 2

Shade Plants

Plant Sources

Busse Gardens
13579 10th Street NW
Cokato, MN 55321
(612) 286-2654
Catalogue: $2.00

Heronswood Nursery
7530 288th Street NE
Kingston, WA 98436
(360) 297-4172
Catalogue: $4.00

Nature's Garden
40611 Highway 226
Scio, OR 97374
Catalogue: long SASE with two stamps

Pinky's Plants
Box 126
442 G Street
Pawnee City, NE 68420
(800) 94-PINKY
Catalogue: $3.50

Rainforest Gardens
13139 224th Street
Maple Ridge, British Columbia V2X 7E7
(604) 467-4218
Catalogue: $2.00

Shady Oaks Nursery
112 10th Avenue SE
Waseca, MN 56903
(507) 835-5033
Catalogue: $3.00

Spring Hill Gardens
110 West Elm Street
Tipp City, OH 45371
(800) 582-8527
Catalogue: $3.00

Stocklein's Nursery
135 Critchlow Road
Renfrew, PA 16053
(412) 586-7882
Catalogue: $1.00

Sunlight Gardens
174 Golden Lane
Andersonville, TX 77805
Catalogue: $3.00

Underwood Shade Nursery
Box 1386
North Attleboro, MA 02763
Catalogue: $2.00

Succulents
See **Cacti and Succulents**

Tulips
See **Bulbs**

Violas

Plant Source

Canyon Creek Nursery
3527 Dry Creek Road
Oroville, CA 95965
(916) 533-2166
Catalogue: $2.00

Water Garden Plants
See Chapter 2

Wildflowers

Organizations
See also chapter 8, **Native Plant Societies**
and Botanical Clubs

National Wildflower Research Center
4801 La Crosse Boulevard
Austin, TX 78739
(512) 292-4100
Dues: $25.00
Publications: *Wildflower Journal; Wildflower*
newsletter

New England Wild Flower Society
Garden in the Woods
180 Hemenway Road

Framingham, MA 01701
(508) 877-7630
Dues: $35.00
Publication: *From the Garden* newsletter
(three times annually)

Plant Sources

Agua Fria Nursery
1409 Agua Fria Street
Santa Fe, NM 87501
Specialties: western wildflowers
Catalogue: free

Agua Viva Seed Ranch
Route 1, Box 8
Taos, NM 87571
(800) 248-9080
Specialties: xeric plants
Catalogue: free

Appalachian Wildflower Nursery
Route 1, Box 275A
Reedsville, PA 17804
(717) 667-6998
Catalogue: $2.00

Applewood Seed Company, Inc.
Box 10761, Edgemont Station
Golden, CO 80401
(303) 431-6283
Catalogue: free

Bentley Seeds, Inc.
16 Railroad Avenue
Cambridge, NY 12816
(518) 677-2603
Catalogue: $1.00

Boothe Hill Wildflower Seeds
23B Boothe Hill
Chapel Hill, NC 27514
(919) 967-4091
Catalogue: $2.00

Brookside Wildflowers
Route 3, Box 740
Boone, NC 28607
(704) 963-5548
Catalogue: $2.00

Cattail Meadows, Ltd.
Box 39391
Solon, OH 44139
Catalogue: free

Donaroma's Nursery
Box 2189
Edgartown, MA 02539
(508) 627-3036
Catalogue: $1.00

Earthly Goods, Ltd.
903 East 15th Street
New Albany, IN 47150
Catalogue: $2.00

Ernst Crownvetch Farms
RD 5, Box 806
Meadville, PA 16335
(800) 873-3321
Specialties: Northeast
Catalogue: free

Timothy D. Field Ferns and Wildflowers
395 Newington Road
Newington, NH 03801
(603) 436-0457
Catalogue: free

Flowerplace Plant Farm
Box 4865
Meridian, MS 39304
(601) 482-5686
Catalogue: $3.00

Gardens of the Blue Ridge
Box 10, US 221 North
Pineola, NC 28662
(704) 733-2417
Catalogue: $3.00

Green Horizons
218 Quinland
Kerrville, TX 78028
(210) 257-5141
Specialties: Texas
Catalogue: long SASE

Groveland Botanicals
422 Clymer
Penwater, MI 49449
Catalogue: $1.00

High Altitude Gardens
Box 419
Ketchum, ID 83340
(800) 874-7333
Specialties: Northwest
Catalogue: $3.00

Holbrook Farm and Nursery
Box 368
115 Lance Road
Fletcher, NC 28732
(704) 891-7790
Catalogue: $1.00

J. L. Hudson, Seedsman
Box 1058
Redwood City, CA 94064
Specialties: California
Catalogue: $1.00

Landscape Alternatives
1465 North Pascal Street
St. Paul, MN 55108
(612) 488-1342
Specialties: Minnesota wildflowers
Catalogue: $1.00

Larner Seeds
Box 407
Bolinas, CA 94924
(415) 868-9407
Specialties: western wildflowers
Catalogue: $3.00

Midwest Wildflowers
Box 64
Rockton, IL 61072
Catalogue: $1.00

Missouri Wildflowers Nursery
9814 Pleasant Hill Road
Jefferson City, MO 65109
Catalogue: $1.00

Moon Mountain Wildflowers
Box 725
Carpinteria, CA 93014
(805) 684-2565
Catalogue: $2.00

Native Gardens
5737 Fisher Lane
Greenback, TN 37742
(615) 856-0220
Catalogue: $2.00

Native Seeds, Inc.
14590 Triadelphia Mill Road
Dayton, MD 21036
(301) 596-9818
Catalogue: free

New England Wild Flower Society
Garden-in-the-Woods Gift Shop
180 Hemenway Road
Framingham, MA 01701
(617) 237-4924
Catalogue: $2.50

Niche Gardens
1111 Dawson Road
Chapel Hill, NC 27516
(919) 967-0078
Specialties: southeastern wildflowers
Catalogue: $3.00

Northwest Native Seed
915 Davis Place South
Seattle, WA 98144
(206) 329-5804

Specialties: Northwest
Catalogue: $1.00

Oakridge Nursery
Box 182
East Kingston, NH 03827
(603) 642-8227
Catalogue: free

Orchid Gardens
2232 139th Avenue NW
Andover, MN 55744
Catalogue: 75¢

Theodore Payne Foundation Nursery
10459 Tuxford Street
Sun Valley, CA 91352
(818) 768-1802
Specialties: California
Catalogue: $3.00

Plants of the Southwest
Agua Fria
Route 6, Box 11
Santa Fe, NM 87505
(800) 788-SEED
Specialties: Southwest
Catalogue: $3.50

Clyde Robin Seed Company, Inc.
Box 2366
Castro Valley, CA 94546
(510) 785-0425
Catalogue: $2.00

Rocky Mountain Rare Plants
Box 20483
Denver, CO 80220
Specialties: drought-tolerant seeds and plants
Catalogue: $1.00

Seeds of Alaska
Box 3127
Kenai, AK 99611
(907) 262-5267

Specialties: Alaska wildflowers
Catalogue: $3.00

Shooting Star Nursery
444 Bates Road
Frankfort, KY 40601
(502) 223-1679
Specialties: east of the Rockies
Catalogue: $2.00

Sunlight Gardens
174 Golden Lane
Andersonville, TX 77805
Catalogue: $3.00

The Vermont Wildflower Farm
Route 7, Box 5
Charlotte, VT 05445
(802) 425-3500
Catalogue: $1.00

We-Du Nurseries
Route 5, Box 724
Marion, NC 28752
(704) 738-8300
Catalogue: $2.00

Wild and Crazy Seed Company
Box 895
Durango, CO 81302
(303) 780-5661
Specialties: Southwest
Catalogue: $2.00

Wild Earth Native Plant Nursery
49 Mead Avenue
Freehold, NJ 07728
(908) 780-5661
Catalogue: $2.00

Wildflower Seed Company
Box 406
St. Helena, CA 94574
Catalogue: $1.00

Wild Seed
Box 27751
Tempe, AZ 85285
(602) 345-0669
Specialties: Southwest
Catalogue: free

Wildseed Farms
Box 308
1101 Campo Rosa Road
Eagle Lake, TX 77434
(800) 848-0078
Catalogue: $2.00

The Wildwood Flower
Route 3, Box 165
Pittsboro, NC 27312
(919) 542-4344
Catalogue: long SASE

Zinnias

Plant Source

Van Dyke Zinnias
5910 Corey Road
Perry, MI 48872
Catalogue: $1.00

Specialty Gardening

THIS SECTION OF THE GARDENER'S SOURCEBOOK *contains listings for specialty garden areas: alpine and rock gardens, bonsai, butterfly gardening, fragrance gardens, historical gardens, orchids, roses, and water gardens. A section on rare-seed exchanges is also included. As in chapter 1, the sections for the different specialty garden types start with organizations and other sources of information and products; they go on to list plant sources alphabetically by nursery. With very few exceptions, only nurseries that specialize in these areas and can ship their plants are listed. Specialty nurseries that don't sell by mail often do exhibit at local and regional plant and flower shows. If you join an organization dedicated to your area of interest, you'll be kept informed about upcoming exhibits.*

Alpine and Rock Gardening
See also **Bonsai**

Organizations

Alpine Garden Club of British Columbia
Main Post Office Box 5161
Vancouver, British Columbia V6B 4B2
Publication: *Alpine Garden Club Bulletin*
(five times annually)

Alpine Garden Society
The Secretary
AGS Centre
Avon Bank, Pershore
Worcestershire WR10 3JP
England
(0386) 55-4790
Dues: £18.00
Publications: quarterly bulletin;
newsletter

American Rock Garden Society

Secretary
Box 67
Millwood, NY 10546
(914) 762-2948
Dues: $25.00
Publication: *Rock Garden Quarterly*

Newfoundland Alpine and
Rock Garden Club
Memorial University Botanical Garden
University of Newfoundland
St. John's, Newfoundland A1C 5S7
(709) 737-8590

Ontario Rock Garden Society
c/o Andrew Osyany
Box 146
Shelburne, Ontario L0N 1S0

Saxifrage Society
Adrian Young, Secretary
31 Eddington Road
London SW16 5BS

England
Dues: £10.00

Scottish Rock Garden Club
c/o Mrs. J. Thomlinson
1 Hillcrest Road
Bearsden, Glasgow G61 2EB
Scotland
Dues: $28.00
Publication: *The Rock Garden*
(semiannual journal)

Supplies

Dorothy Bonitz
Herb & Flower Thyme
146 Great Oak Drive
Hampstead, NC 28443
Product: trough kit
Catalogue: free

Earthworks
Box 67
Hyattville, WY 82428
Product: hypertufa troughs
Catalogue: long SASE

Karen Harris
200 East Genesee Street
Fayetteville, NY 13066
Product: hypertufa troughs
Catalogue: SASE

Old World Garden Troughs®
Box 1253
Carmel, IN 46032
Product: troughs
Catalogue: $2.00

Plant Sources

Alpenflora Gardens
17985 40th Avenue
Surrey, British Columbia V3S 4N8
Catalogue: $1.00

Alpine Gardens
12446 County F
Stitzer, WI 53825
(608) 822-6382
Catalogue: $2.00

Alplains
32315 Pine Crest Court
Kiowa, CO 80117
(303) 621-2247
Catalogue: $1.00

Appalachian Wildflower Nursery
Route 1, Box 275A
Reedsville, PA 17084
(717)667-6998
Catalogue: $2.00

Arrowhead Alpines
Box 857, Fowlerville, MI 48836
(517) 223-3581
Catalogue: $2.00

Bijou Alpines
13921 240th Street East
Graham, WA 98338
(206) 893-6191
Catalogue: $1.00

Boulder Wall Gardens
McLean Road
Walpole, NH 03608
(603) 756-9056
Catalogue: $1.00

The Bovees Nursery
1737 SW Coronado
Portland, OR 97219
(800) 435-9250
Catalogue: $2.00

Sam Bridge Nursery N' Greenhouses
437 North Street
Greenwich, CT 06830
(203) 869-3418
Note: No shipping

Chehalis Rare Plant Nursery
Route 3, Box 363
Lebanon, MO 65536
(206) 748-7627
Specialties: auricula seed
Catalogue: $1.00

Collector's Nursery
1602 NE 162nd Avenue
Vancouver, WA 98684
Catalogue: $1.00

Colorado Alpines
Box 2708
Avon, CO 81620
(303) 949-6464
Catalogue: $2.00

Country Cottage
10502 North 135th Street West
Sedgwick, KS 67135
Catalogue: 50¢

Cricklewood Nursery
11907 Nevers Road
Snohomish, WA 98290
(206) 568-2829
Catalogue: $2.00

The Cummins Garden
22 Robertsville Road
Marlboro, NJ 07746
(908) 536-2591
Catalogue: $2.00

Daystar
Route 2, Box 250
Litchfield, ME 04350
(207) 724-3369
Catalogue: $1.00

Dilworth Nursery
1200 Election Road
Oxford, PA 19363
(610) 932-0347
Catalogue: $1.00

Eastern Plant Specialties
Box 226
Georgetown, ME 04548
(207) 371-2888
Catalogue: $3.00

Ericaceae
Box 293
Deep River, CT 06417
Catalogue: free

Evergreen Gardenworks
430 North Oak Street
Ukiah, CA 95482
(707) 462-8909
Catalogue: $2.00

Field House Alpines
6730 West Mercer Way
Mercer Island, WA 98040
Catalogue: $2.00

Fieldstone Gardens, Inc.
620 Quaker Lane
Vassalboro, ME 04989
(207) 923-3826
Catalogue: $2.00

Fir Grove Perennial Nursery
19917 NE 68th Street
Vancouver, WA 98682
(206) 944-8384
Catalogue: $2.00

Joy Creek Nursery
20300 NW Watson Road
Scappoose, OR 97056
(503) 543-7474
Catalogue: $2.00

Lamb Nurseries
East 101 Sharp Avenue
Spokane, WA 99202
(509) 328-7956
Catalogue: $1.00

Miniature Plant Kingdom
4125 Harrison Grade Road
Sebastopol, CA 95472
(707) 874-2233
Catalogue: $2.50

Montrose Nursery
Box 957
Hillsborough, NC 27278
(919) 732-7787
Catalogue: $2.00

Mt. Tahoma Nursery
28111 112th Avenue East
Graham, WA 98338
(206) 847-9827
Catalogue: $1.00

Nature's Garden
40611 Highway 226
Scio, OR 97374
Catalogue: one stamp

Porterhowse Farms
41370 SE Thomas Road
Sandy, OR 97055
(503) 668-5834
Catalogue: $6.00

The Primrose Path
RD 2, Box 110
Scottdale, PA 15683
(412) 887-6756
Catalogue: $2.50

Rare Plant Research
13245 SE Harold
Portland, OR 97236
(503) 762-0289
Specialties: lewisia
Catalogue: $2.00

Rice Creek Gardens
11506 Highway 65
Minneapolis, MN 55434
Catalogue: $1.00

Robyn's Nest Nursery
7802 NE 63rd Street
Vancouver, WA 98662
(206) 256-7399
Catalogue: $2.00

Rocknoll Nursery
7812 Mad River Road
Hillsboro, OH 45133
(513) 393-5545
Catalogue: $1.00

Rocky Mountain Rare Plants
Box 20483
Denver, CO 80220
Catalogue: $1.00

Roslyn Nursery
211 Burrs Lane
Dix Hills, NY 11746
(516) 543-9347
Catalogue: $3.00

Siskiyou Rare Plant Nursery
2825 Cummings Road
Medford, OR 97501
(503) 772-6846
Catalogue: $2.00

Skyline Nursery
4772 Sequim-Dungeness Way
Sequim, WA 98382
Catalogue: $2.00

Springvale Farm Nursery
Mozier Hollow Road
Hamburg, IL 62045
(618) 232-1108
Catalogue: $2.00

Squaw Mountain Gardens
36212 SE Squaw Mountain Road
Estacada, OR 97023
(503) 630-5458
Catalogue: $2.00

Strong's Alpine Succulents
Box 2264
Flagstaff, AZ 86003
(602) 526-5784
Catalogue: $1.00

Surry Gardens
Box 145
Route 172
Surry, ME 04684
(207) 667-4493
Catalogue: free

Trennoll Nursery
3 West Page Avenue
Trenton, OH 45067
(513) 988-6121
Catalogue: $2.00

We-Du Nurseries
Route 5, Box 724
Marion, NC 28752
(704) 738-8300
Catalogue: $2.00

Wildginger Woodlands
Box 1091
Webster, NY 14580
Catalogue: $1.00

Willamette Valley Gardens Nursery
Box 285
Lake Oswego, OR 97034
(503) 636-6517
Catalogue: one stamp

Woodland Rockery
6210 Klam Road
Otter Lake, MI 48464
Catalogue: $1.00

Wrightman Alpines
RR 3
Kerwood, Ontario N0M 2B0
(519) 247-3751
Catalogue: $2.00

Bonsai

Organizations

The American Bonsai Society
Executive Office
2901 31st Court SE
Puyallup, WA 98374
Dues: $20.00
Publications: BONSAI: *Journal of The
American Bonsai Society*; *ABStracts newsletter*

Bonsai Canada
12 Beardmore Crescent
Willowdale, Ontario M2K 2P5
Publication: *Bonsai Canada*

Bonsai Clubs International
c/o Virginia Ellermann
2636 West Mission Road
Tallahassee, FL 32304
(904) 575-1442
Dues: $25.00
Publication: *Bonsai*
(bimonthly magazine)

Bonsai Society of Greater New York
Membership Secretary
Box 565
Glen Oaks, NY 11004
(516) 293-9246
Dues: $17.00
Publication: *The Bonsai Bulletin*
(quarterly)

Toronto Bonsai Society
Eva Rae Davidson
190 McAllister Road
Downsview, Ontario M3H 2N9
(416) 590-9969
Dues: Canada $10.00
Publication: journal

Publications

Bonsai Today
Stone Lantern Publishing Company
Box 816, Sudbury, MA 01776
Frequency: bimonthly
Subscription: $42.00

International Bonsai
International Bonsai Arboretum
Box 23894
Rochester, NY 14692
(716) 334-2595
Frequency: quarterly
Subscription: $24.00

Bonsai Institute of California
Box 6268
Whittier, CA 90609
Note: Publisher of books on bonsai

Tools and Supplies

Artistic Plants
608 Holly Drive
Burleson, TX 76028
(817) 295-0802
Catalogue: $1.00

Jim Barrett
480 Oxford Drive
Arcadia, CA 91006
(818) 445-4529
Catalogue: free

Bennett's Bonsai Nursery
1816 Fairfax Avenue
Metairie, LA 70003
(504) 888-7994
Catalogue: free

Bonsai Associates, Inc.
3000 Chestnut Avenue
Baltimore, MD 21211
(410) 235-5336
Catalogue: $2.00

Bonsai Mountain Garden
Box 241
Helotes, TX 78023
Catalogue: $5.00

Bonsai Northwest
5021 South 144th Street
Seattle, WA 98168
(206) 242-8244
Catalogue: $2.00

Dallas Bonsai Garden
Box 801565
Dallas, TX 75380
(800) 982-1223
Catalogue: free

Dave's Aquarium and Greenhouse
RR 1, Box 97
Kelley, IA 50134
(515) 769-2446
Catalogue: four stamps

Fujiyama^{TM} Tool Company
Box 830384
Richardson, TX 75083
(800) 842-5523
Product: Fujiyama^{TM} brand bonsai tools

J & J Landscaping
Bonsai International Division
Box 21683
Tampa, FL 33622
(813) 645-8777
Catalogue: $3.00

Living Sculpture Bonsai
Box 257
Princeton Junction, NJ 08550
(609) 275-9270
(800) 941-0888
Product: humidity trays
Catalogue: free

Masakuni Company USA
Box 18290

Encino, CA 91416
(818) 345-7614
Product: Masakuni brand bonsai tools
Catalogue: free

Nature's Way Nursery
1451 Pleasant Hill Road
Harrisburg, PA 17112
(717) 545-4555
Catalogue: free

Niwa Tool Company
2661 Bloomfield Court
Fairfield, CA 94533
(800) 443-5512
Catalogue: $2.00

John Palmer Bonsai
Box 29
Sudbury, MA 01776
(617) 443-5084
Catalogue: free

Raska Sales
Route 2, Box 38
Skiatook, OK 74070
(918) 396-2663
Catalogue: free

Rosade Bonsai Studio
6912 Ely Road
New Hope, PA 18938
(215) 862-5925
Catalogue: $1.00

Joshua Roth Limited
9901 SW 25th Avenue
Portland, OR 97219
(800) 624-4635
Catalogue: free

Bonsai Containers

Bonsai by the Monastery
Box B
2625 Highway 212 SW

Conyers, GA 30208
(770) 918-9661
Catalogue: $3.00

Bonsai Northwest
5021 South 144th Street
Seattle, WA 98168
(206) 242-8244
Catalogue: $2.00

DuPont Bonsai
Box 375
Newberg, OR 97132
(503) 538-6071
Catalogue: $4.00

Flowertown Bonsai
207 East Luke Street
Summerville, SC 29483
(800) 774-0003
Catalogue: free

Little Trees
Box 41
Carlotta, CA 95528
(707) 768-3450
Product: planting stones and slabs
Catalogue: 50¢

Midwest Bonsai Pottery
8311 Racine Trail
Austin, TX 78717
Catalogue: $1.00

Oregon Outcroppings
Box 178
Trail, OR 97541
(503) 878-3313
Catalogue: $2.00

Pine Garden Bonsai Company
20331 State Route 530 NE
Arlington, WA 98223
(360) 435-5995
Catalogue: $2.00

Sara Rayner Pottery
1025 West 4th Street
Red Wing, MN 55066
Catalogue: $3.00

Sosaku Bonsai Potter
Box 520476
Salt Lake City, UT 84152
Catalogue: SASE

Tokonoma Bonsai
87 Old Trolley Road
Summerville, SC 29485
(803) 875-6567
Catalogue: free

Other Information and Supplies

*An extensive annual directory of bonsai growers
and suppliers is available from:*

Equinox, Inc.
Box 550
Nicholasville, KY 40356
(606) 887-2671
Cost: $6.00

The Bonsai Manager database program is available from:

Phillip Adams
140 Riverside Drive
New York, NY 10024
System requirements: DOS
Catalogue: free

Bonsai wood-carving burrs are available from:

Nippon Art Forms
Box 4975
Laguna Beach, CA 92652
(714) 497-5626
Catalogue: free

Flumes (kakeki) are available from:

I-Ten
124 Johnston Boulevard
Lexington, KY 40503
Catalogue: SASE

Bonsai notepaper is available from:

Jennie Popeleski
96 Greenlawn Road
Huntington, NY 11743
Catalogue: free

Bonsai jewelry is available from:

Lucille Lee Roberts
445 South Los Robles, Suite 207
Pasadena, CA 91101
(818) 568-8161
Catalogue: free

Plant Sources

Allshapes Bonsai Nursery
Box 337
230 Everitts Road
Ringoes, NJ 08551
(908) 788-1938
Catalogue: SASE

Artistic Plants
608 Holly Drive
Burleson, TX 76028
(817) 295-0802
Catalogue: $1.00

Bennett's Bonsai Nursery
1816 Fairfax Avenue
Metairie, LA 70003
(504) 888-7994
Catalogue: free

Bonsai Farm
Box 130
Lavernia, TX 78121

(210) 649-2109
Catalogue: $1.00

Bonsai of Brooklyn
2443 McDonald Avenue
Brooklyn, NY 11223
(718) 339-8252
(800) 8-BONSAI
Catalogue: free

The Bonsai Shop
43 William Street
Smithtown, NY 11787
(516) 724-3055
Catalogue: $2.00

The Bonsai Tree
609 Shallowford Road
Gainesville, GA 30504
(404) 535-2991
Catalogue: free

Bonsai West
Box 1291, 100 Great Road
Littleton, MA 01460
(508) 486-3556
Catalogue: $2.00

Brussel's Bonsai Nursery
8365 Center Hill Road
Olive Branch, MS 38654
(601) 895-7457
(800) 582-2593
Catalogue: $2.00

The Cummins Garden
22 Robertsville Road
Marlboro, NJ 07746
(908) 536-2591
Catalogue: $2.00

Dallas Bonsai Garden
Box 801565
Dallas, TX 75380
(800) 982-1223
Catalogue: free

Evergreen Gardenworks
430 North Oak Street
Ukiah, CA 95482
(707) 462-8909
Catalogue: $2.00

Flowertown Bonasi
207 East Luke Street
Summerville, SC 29483
(800) 774-0003
Catalogue: free

Green Gardens Nursery
16 Burr Road
East Northport, NY 11731
(516) 499-4235
Catalogue: $1.00

Grove Way Bonsai Nursery
1239 Grove Way
Hayward, CA 94541
(510) 537-1157
Catalogue: SASE

Japan Nursery Florida, Inc.
5300 Orange Boulevard
Sanford, FL 32771
(407) 328-9793
Catalogue: $4.00

Jiu-San Bonsai
1243 Melville Road
Farmingdale, NY 11735
(516) 293-9246
Note: no mail order

Jope's Bonsai Nursery
Box 594
Wenham, MA 10984
Catalogue: $2.00

Kyodai Bonsai
5485 Riversedge
Milford, MI 48383
(800) 513-5995
Catalogue: free

Lone Pine Connection
Box 1338
Forestville, CA 95436
Catalogue: $3.00

The Maine Bonsai Gardens
Old Stage Road
Woolwich, ME 04579
(800) 532-3983
Catalogue: SASE

Marrs Tree Farm
Box 375
Puyallup, WA 98371
Catalogue: $1.00

Matsu-Momiji Nursery
Box 11414
410 Borbeck Street
Philadelphia, PA 19111
(215) 722-6286
Catalogue: $2.00

McLain's Garden Center and Bonsai
Nursery
5776 Buncomb Road
Shreveport, LA 71129
(318) 688-1640
Catalogue: $1.00

Miami Tropical Bonsai
14775 SW 232nd Street
Homestead, FL 33170
(305) 258-0865
Catalogue: free

MicroFolia Bonsai Nursery
Box 265, Camp Hill, PA 17001
(717) 691-0286
Catalogue: $1.00

Miniature Plant Kingdom
4125 Harrison Grade Road
Sebastopol, CA 95472
(707) 874-2233
Catalogue: $2.50

Mountain Maples
5901 Spyrock Road
Laytonville, CA 95454
Specialties: Japanese maple cultivars
Catalogue: $1.00

Mt. Si Bonsai
43321 SE Mt. Si Road
North Bend, WA 98045
(206) 888-0350
Catalogue: SASE

Nature's Way Nursery
1451 Pleasant Hill Road
Harrisburg, PA 17112
(717) 545-4555
Catalogue: free

New England Bonsai
914 South Main Street
Bellingham, MA 02019
(508) 883-2666
Catalogue: $1.00

Northland Gardens
315A West Mountain Road
Queensbury, NY 12804
(518) 798-4277
Catalogue: $2.00

Oriental Garden
307 Disbrow Hill Road
Perrineville, NJ 08535
(609) 490-0705
Catalogue: $2.00

Pen Y Bryn Nursery
RR 1, Box 1313, Forksville, PA 18616
(717) 924-3377
Catalogue: free

Pine Garden Bonsai Company
20331 State Route 530 NE
Arlington, WA 98223
(360) 435-5995
Catalogue: $2.00

Porterhowse Farms
41370 SE Thomas Road
Sandy, OR 97055
(503) 668-5834
Catalogue: $6.00

The Potted Forest
805 Dickens Road
Lilburn, GA 30247
(404) 564-0292
Catalogue: SASE

Rarafolia
16 Beverly Drive
Kintnersville, PA 18930
(215) 847-8208
Catalogue: $3.00

Roots 'n All Bonsai Gardens
RR 1, Box 586, Warner, NH 03278
(800) 223-3050
Catalogue: free

Royal Bonsai Garden, Inc.
1297 Park Street
Stoughton, MA 02072
(617) 344-6358
Catalogue: SASE

Shanti Bithi Nursery
3047 High Ridge Road
Stamford, CT 06903
(203) 329-0768
Catalogue: $3.00

Tom's Tiny Trees
14318 State Road
North Royalton, OH 44133
(216) 582-9411
Catalogue: free

Wildwood Gardens
14488 Rock Creek Road
Chardon, OH 44024
(216) 286-3714
Catalogue: $1.00

Wright's Nursery
1285 Southeast Township Road
Canby, OR 97013
(503) 266-8895
Catalogue: $1.00

Butterfly Gardening

Organizations

The Butterfly Gardeners Association
1021 North Main Street
Allentown, PA 18104

The Xerces Society
10 SW Ash Street
Portland, OR 97204
(503) 222-2788
Dues: $25.00
Publication: *Wings*
(three times annually)

Butterfly Boxes

Old Beach
416 Brookcliff Lane
Cary, NC 27511
Catalogue: free

Treetop Designs
1117 East Webb Avenue
Burlington, NC 27215
(919) 229-9111
Catalogue: $2.00

Butterfly Gardens

Butterfly World
Tradewinds Park South
3600 West Sample Road
Coconut Creek, FL 33063
(305) 977-4400

Butterfly World at Marine World
Marine World Parkway

Vallejo, CA 94589
(707) 644-4000

Callaway Gardens
Cecil B. Day Butterfly Center
Pine Mountain, GA 31822
(404) 663-2281

Cincinnati Zoo
3400 Vine Street
Cincinnati, OH 45220
(513) 281-4701

Des Moines Botanical Center
909 East River Drive
Des Moines, IA 50316
(515) 283-4148

Vancouver Island Butterfly World
341 West Crescent Road
Qualicum Beach, British Columbia
V0R 2T0
(604) 752-9319

Plant Source

Brudy's Exotics
Box 820874
HR 595
Houston, TX 77282
(800) 926-7333
Products: plants; seeds; eggs; larvae;
books
Catalogue: free

Fragrance Gardening

Plant Sources

Flower Scent Gardens
14820 Moine Road
Doylestown, OH 44230
Catalogue: $2.00

The Fragrant Bower
11 Maya Loop
Santa Fe, NM 87505
(505) 983-6317
Catalogue: $5.00

The Fragrant Path
Box 328
Fort Calhoun, NE 68023
Catalogue: $1.00

Select Seeds—Antique Flowers
180 Stickney Hill Road
Union, CT 06076
(203) 684-9310
Catalogue: $2.00

Historical Gardening

Organizations

Agricultural History Society
1301 New York Avenue NW, Room 1232
Washington, DC 20005
(202) 447-8183
Publication: *Agricultural History* (quarterly)

Alliance for Historic Landscape
Preservation
82 Wall Street, Suite 1105
New York, NY 10005

Association for Living Historical Farms
and Agricultural Museums
Route 14, Box 214
Santa Fe, NM 87505
(505) 471-2261
Publication: *Living Historical Farms Bulletin*
(quarterly)

Centre for Canadian Historical
Horticultural Studies
Library, Box 399
Royal Botanical Gardens
Hamilton, Ontario L8N 3H8

(416) 527-1158
Publication: *Canadian Horticultural History*

Cottage Garden Society
c/o Mrs. C. Tordorff
5 Nixon Close, Thornhill
Dewsbury, West Yorkshire WF12 0JA
England
(0924) 46-8469
Dues: $20.00
Publication: *CGS Newsletter* (quarterly)

The Garden Conservancy
Box 219
Cold Spring, NY 10516
(914) 265-2029
Dues: $35.00
Publication: newsletter

Garden History Society
Mrs. Anne Richards
5 The Knoll
Hereford HR1 1RU
England
(0432) 35-4479
Dues: £18.00
Publications: *Garden History* (semiannual);
Newsletter (three times annually)

Heritage Rose Foundation
1512 Gorman Street
Raleigh, NC 27606
(919) 834-2591
Publication: *Heritage Rose Foundation News*
(quarterly)

Historic Iris Preservation Society (HIPS)
Ada Godfrey
9 Bradford Street
Foxborough, MA 01035
Dues: AIS dues plus $5.00
Publication: *Roots Journal*

Historic Preservation Committee
American Society of
Landscape Architects

4401 Connecticut Ave NW
Washington, DC 20008
(202) 686-ASLA

National Association for Olmstead Parks
5010 Wisconsin Avenue NW, Suite 308
Washington, DC 20016
(202) 363-9511

New England Garden History Society
Massachusetts Horticultural Society
300 Massachusetts Avenue
Boston, MA 02115
(617) 536-9280
Dues: $25.00
Publications: *Journal* (annual);
Belvedere (occasional newsletter)

Pioneer Plant Society
c/o Mrs. P. A. Puryear
708 Holland Street
Navasota, TX 77868
(409) 825-3220
Dues: $7.00
Publication: *PPS Newsletter* (quarterly)

Southern Garden History Society
Old Salem, Inc.
Drawer F, Salem Station
Winston-Salem, NC 27101
(919) 724-3125
Dues: $20.00
Product: *Magnolia* (quarterly)

Texas Rose Rustlers
c/o Margaret Sharpe
9246 Kerrwood Lane
Houston, TX 77080
(713) 464-8607
Publication: *Old Texas Rose* (quarterly)

The Thomas Jefferson Center for
Historic Plants
Monticello, Box 316
Charlottesville, VA 22902
(804) 979-5283

Publications

The Historical Gardener
1910 North 35th Place
Mount Vernon, WA 98273
(206) 424-3154
Frequency: quarterly
Subscription: $12.00

Journal of Garden History
Taylor & Francis, Inc.
1900 Frost Road, Suite 101
Bristol, PA 19007
Frequency: quarterly
Subscription: $70.00

Plant Sources

The Thomas Jefferson Center
for Historic Plants
Monticello
Box 316
Charlottesville, VA 22902
(804) 296-4800
Catalogue: $1.00

Old House Gardens
536 3rd Street
Ann Arbor, MI 48103
(313) 995-1486
Specialties: historical bulbs
Catalogue: $1.00

Perennial Pleasures Nursery
2 Brickhouse Road
East Hardwick, VT 05836
(802) 472-5512
Specialties: plants for historical
restoration
Catalogue: $2.00

Select Seeds—Antique Flowers
180 Stickney Hill Road
Union, CT 06076
(203) 684-9310
Catalogue: $2.00

Sisters' Bulb Farm
Route 2, Box 170
Gibsland, LA 71028
(318) 843-6379
Specialties: heirloom daffodils
Catalogue: free

Orchids

Organizations

American Orchid Society
6000 South Olive Avenue
West Palm Beach, FL 33405
(407) 585-8666
Dues: $30.00
Publication: *Orchids* (monthly journal)

Canadian Orchid Congress
c/o Peter Root
Box 241
Goodwood, Ontario L0C 1A0
(416) 640-5643
Publication: *Canadian Orchid Journal*
(annual)

Cymbidium Society of America
533 South Woodland
Orange, CA 92669
(714) 532-4719
Dues: $25.00
Publication: *The Orchid Advocate*
(bimonthly magazine)

Orchid Society of Great Britain
120 Crofton Road
Orpington, Kent BR6 8HZ
England

Victoria Orchid Society
Ingrid Ostrander
Box 6538, Depot 1
Victoria, British Columbia
V8P 5M4
(604) 652-6133

Dues: Canada $15.00
Publication: monthly bulletin

Publications

Orchid Digest
Orchid Digest Corporation
Box 916
Carmichael, CA 95609
Frequency: quarterly
Subscription: $18.00

The Orchid Hunter
Terry Ferrar, Editor
RR 1, Box 62A
Adamsville, PA 16110
Frequency: monthly
Subscription: $17.00

Orchid Information Exchange
1230 Plum Avenue
Simi Valley, CA 93065
Frequency: monthly
Subscription: $15.00

The Orchid Review
The Royal Horticultural Society
80 Vincent Square
London SW1P 2PE
England
Frequency: bimonthly
Subscription: £20.00

Phalaenopsis Fancier
Doreen Vander Tuin, Editor
1230 Plum Avenue
Simi Valley, CA 93065
Frequency: monthly newsletter
Subscription: $15.00

Growing Supplies

Dr. James D. Brasch
Box 354
McMaster University
Hamilton, Ontario L8S 1C0

(416) 335-1713
Product: Keikigrow plant growth
regulators
Catalogue: $2.00

Classic Stone Corporation
4044 West Lower Buckeye Road
Phoenix, AZ
(800) 644-0827
Product: media planting kits
Catalogue: free

CMI Plastics
Box 369
Cranbury, NJ 08512
(609) 395-1920
Product: Humidi-Grow® plant trays
Catalogue: free

Dyna-Gro™ Corporation
1065 Broadway
San Pablo, CA 94806
(800) DYNA-GRO
Product: liquid nutrient formula
Catalogue: free

G & B Orchid Laboratory and Nursery
2426 Cherimoya Drive
Vista, CA 92084
(619) 727-2611
(800) 786-1569
Product: propagation media
Catalogue: free

G & S Laboratories
645 Stoddard Lane
Santa Barbara, CA 93108
(805) 969-5991
Product: propagation media
Catalogue: free

M & M Orchid Supply
Box 306
Whippany, NJ 07981
(201) 515-5209
Catalogue: free

The Nova Company
Box 2192
Kearney, NE 68847
(308) 237-0971
Product: Ag-Tonic foliar feed
Catalogue: free

OFE International, Inc.
Box 161302
Miami, FL 33186
(305) 253-7080
Catalogue: $2.00

Plant Collectibles
103 Kenview Avenue
Buffalo, NY 14217
(716) 875-1221
Catalogue: $2.00

Sigma Chemical Company
Box 14508
St. Louis, MO 63178
(314) 771-5765
Product: propagation media
Catalogue: free

Stewart Orchids
Box 550
3376 Foothill Road
Carpinteria, CA 93013
(805) 684-5448
(800) 621-2450
Catalogue: $2.00

Sunshine Growers' Supply, Inc.
4760 Taylor Road
Punta Gorda, FL 33950
(800) 954-6735
Catalogue: free

Teas Nursery Company, Inc.
Box 1603
Bellaire, TX 77402
(800) 446-7723
Catalogue: $2.00

Tropical Plant Products
Box 547754
Orlando, FL 32854
(407) 293-2451
Catalogue: long SASE

Wilder Agriculture Products
Company, Inc.
4188 Bethel-Wilmington Road
New Wilmington, PA 16142
(800) 462-8102
Catalogue: free

Worm's Way, Inc.
3151 South Highway 446
Bloomington, IN 47401
(812) 331-0300
(800) 274-9676
Catalogue: free

Tissue Culture and Other Services

Bastrop Botanical
Box 628
Bastrop, TX 78602
(512) 321-7161
Services: species flasking
Catalogue: free

Critter Creek Laboratory
400 Critter Creek Road
Lincoln, CA 95648
(916) 645-7111
Services: virus testing
Catalogue: free

G & B Orchid Laboratory and Nursery
2426 Cherimoya Drive
Vista, CA 92084
(619) 727-2611
(800) 786-1569
Services: species flasking
Catalogue: free

Halcyon Laboratories
2627 North Baldwin

Portland, OR 97217
(503) 240-1724
Services: seed flasking and tissue culture
Catalogue: free

Orchis Laboratories
4820 Mason Road
Burdett, NY 14818
(607) 546-2072
Services: tissue culture and virus testing
Catalogue: free

Stewart Orchids Micropropagation
100 Hawthorne Road
Conroe, TX 77301
(409) 760-3433
Services: seed sowing, replating,
tissue culture

Orchid Software

Computer/Management Services
1426 Medinah Court
Arnold, MD 21012
Product: record-keeping and collection
management software
System requirements: Windows 3.1+
or DOS 6.0+
Catalogue: free

Wildcatt Database Company
5614 Valley Road
Ames, IA 50014
(515) 232-4720
Product: orchid database
System requirements: 386+,
Windows 3.1+
Catalogue: free

Orchid-of-the-Month Clubs

Carter & Holmes Orchids
Box 668
629 Mendenhall Road
Newberry, SC 29108
(803) 276-0579

Interior Water Gardens
615 Long Beach Boulevard
Surf City, NJ 08008
(609) 494-1900
(800) 874-4937

Orchid Club
Box 463
Baldwinsville, NY 13027
(800) 822-9411

R. F. Orchids, Inc.
28100 SW 182nd Avenue
Homestead, FL 33030
(305) 245-4570

Other Information and Services

*This nonprofit conservation organization offers
an international orchid locating and information
service, species flasking program, and orchid
inventory software:*

OrchidNet™
626 Humboldt Street
Richmond, CA 94805
(510) 235-8815

*This firm offers flasking services and a computer
bulletin-board service (BBS) for locating orchids:*

The Orchid Database, Inc.
626 Humboldt Street
Richmond, CA 94805
(510) 235-8815
Services: orchid locating
and species flasking
Catalogue: free

Wardian cases for orchids are available from:

Design North
1500 New Brighton Boulevard
Minneapolis, MN 55413
(612) 789-3373
Catalogue: free

Test tubes for display, transport, and shows are available from:

Lee's Botanical Supply
351 Buttonwood Lane
Cinnaminson, NJ 08077
(609) 829-6557
Catalogue: SASE

Plant Sources

A & P Orchids
110 Peters Road
Swansea, MA 02777
(508) 675-1717
Specialties: paphiopedilums
and phalaenopsis
Catalogue: $5.00

Adagent Acres
2245 Floral Way
Santa Rosa, CA 95403
(707) 575-4459
Catalogue: 50¢

Adams & Foster Orchids
Box 1195
Apopka, FL 32704
(800) 884-4230
Catalogue: free

Adkins Orchids
Box 4417
Fort Lauderdale, FL 33338
(305) 563-6823
Catalogue: free

Alberts and Merkel Brothers
2210 South Federal Highway
Boynton Beach, FL 33435
(407) 732-2071
Catalogue: $1.00

Charles Alford Plants
Box 772025
Winter Garden, FL 34777

(407) 877-1007
Catalogue: free

The Angraecum House
Box 976
Grass Valley, CA 95945
(916) 273-9426
Specialties: angraecums and aeranthes
Catalogue: free

Baker & Chantry Orchids
Box 554
18611 132nd Street NE
Woodinville, WA 98072
(206) 483-0345
Specialties: hybrids
Catalogue: long SASE with two stamps

Bergstrom Orchids Nursery
Box 1502
Keaau, HI 96749
Catalogue: $1.00

Blietz-Wailea Orchids
3456 Akala Drive
Kihei, Maui, HI 96753
(808) 874-0034
Catalogue: free

Bloomfield Orchids
251 West Bloomfield Road
Pittsford, NY 14534
(716) 381-4206
Specialties: paphiopedilums
and phragmipediums
Catalogue: free

Breckinridge Orchids
6201 Summit Avenue
Brown Summit, NC 27214
(910) 656-7591
Catalogue: long SASE

Brighton Farms
Poplar & Shore Roads
Linwood, NJ 08221

(609) 927-4131
Specialties: cattleyas
Catalogue: $1.00

Cal-Orchid
1251 Orchid Drive
Santa Barbara, CA 93111
(805) 967-1312
Catalogue: $1.00

Camp Lot-A-Noise Tropicals
4084 47th Street
Sarasota, FL 34235
(813) 351-2483
(800) 351-2483
Catalogue: SASE

Carmela Orchids, Inc.
Box H
Hakalau, HI 96710
(808) 963-6189
Specialties: phalaenopsis
Catalogue: free

Carter & Holmes Orchids
Box 668
629 Mendenhall Road
Newberry, SC 29108
(803) 276-0579
Catalogue: $2.00

The Cedar Tree Nursery
2825 Allen
Kelso, WA 98626
Specialties: pleione species and hybrids
Catalogue: SASE

Chaotic Exotics
4314 West Ocean Avenue
Lompoc, CA 93436
(805) 736-0040
Specialties: laelias
Catalogue: free

Chieri Orchids
2913 9th Street North

Tacoma, WA 98406
(206) 752-5510
Catalogue: free

City Gardens
451 West Lincoln
Madison Heights, MI 48071
(313) 398-2660
Catalogue: $2.00

Clackamas Orchids
7920 South Zimmerman Road
Canby, OR 97013
(503) 651-3438
Catalogue: free

Clargreen Gardens, Ltd.
814 Southdown Road
Mississauga, Ontario L5J 2Y4
(905) 822-0992
Catalogue: $2.00

Cloud Forest Orchids
Box 370, Honokaa, HI 96727
(808) 775-9850
Catalogue: free

Coes' Orchid Acres
4647 Winding Way
Sacramento, CA 95841
(916) 482-6719
Catalogue: free

Jeff Corder
1257 Hall Road
North Fort Myers, FL 33903
(941) 997-1637
Specialties: species orchids
Catalogue: free

Creole Orchids
Box 24458
New Orleans, LA 70184
(504) 282-5191
Specialties: hybrids
Catalogue: $2.00

Drago Orchid Corporation
4601 Southwest 127th Avenue
Miami, FL 33175
(305) 554-1021
Specialties: cattleyas
Catalogue: free

Elmore Orchids
324 Watt Road
Knoxville, TN 37922
(615) 966-5294
(800) 553-3528
Specialties: phalaenopsis
Catalogue: free

Eric's Exotics
6782 Belevedere Road
West Palm Beach, FL 33413
(800) ORCHIDS
Specialties: hybrids
Catalogue: $3.00

Everglades Orchids, Inc.
1101 Tabit Road
Belle Glade, FL 33430
(407) 996-9600
Specialties: odonts and cymbidiums
Catalogue: free

John Ewing Orchids, Inc.
Box 1318
Soquel, CA 95073
(408) 684-1111
Specialties: phalaenopsis
Catalogue: free

Exotic Orchids of Maui
3141 Ua Noe Place
Haiku, HI 96708
(808) 575-2255
Catalogue: free

Fantasy Orchids, Inc.
Box 516, Louisville, CO 80027
(303) 666-5432
Catalogue: free

Fender's Flora, Inc.
4315 Plymouth Sorrento Road
Apopka, FL 32712
(407) 886-2464
Specialties: phalaenopsis
Catalogue: free

Floridel Gardens, Inc.
330 George Street
Port Stanley, Ontario N5L 1C6
(519) 782-4015
Specialties: phalaenopsis
Catalogue: $2.00

Fordyce Orchids
1330 Isabel Avenue
Livermore, CA 94550
(510) 447-7171
Specialties: miniature cattleyas
Catalogue: free

Fox Orchids, Inc.
6615 West Markham Street
Little Rock, AR 72205
(501) 663-4246
Catalogue: free

Fox Valley Orchids, Ltd.
1980 Old Willow Road
Northbrook, IL 60062
(708) 205-9660
Catalogue: free

Fuchs Orchids
26600 SW 147th Avenue
Naranja, FL 33032
(305) 258-4876
Catalogue: free

Gemstone Orchids
5750 East River Road
Minneapolis, MN 55432
(612) 571-3300
Specialties: phalaenopsis
Catalogue: free

Gold Country Orchids
390 Big Ben Road
Lincoln, CA 95648
(916) 645-8600
(800) 451-8558
Specialties: phalaenopsis
Catalogue: free

Green Plant Research
Box 735
Kaawa, HI 96730
(808) 237-8672
Catalogue: free

Green Valley Orchids
77200 Green Valley Road
Folsom, LA 70437
Specialties: phalaenopsis and cattleya
orchids
Catalogue: $1.00

H & R Nurseries
41-240 Hihimanu Street
Waimanalo, HI 96795
(808) 259-9626
Catalogue: free

Hawaiian Island Orchids, Inc.
Box 493
Waimanalo, HI 96795
(808) 259-7410
Catalogue: free

Hoosier Orchid Company
8440 West 82nd Street
Indianapolis, IN 46278
(317) 291-6269
Specialties: seed-grown species orchids
Catalogue: $1.00

Spencer M. Howard Orchid Imports
11802 Huston Street
North Hollywood, CA 91607
(818) 762-8275
Specialties: species orchids
Catalogue: long SASE with two stamps

Interior Water Gardens
615 Long Beach Boulevard
Surf City, NJ 08008
(609) 494-1900
(800) 874-4937
Catalogue: $1.00

J & L Orchids
20 Sherwood Road
Easton, CT 06612
(203) 261-3772
Specialties: species orchids
Catalogue: $1.00

J. E. M. Orchids
2595 Morikami Park Road
Delray Beach, FL 33446
(407) 498-4308
Specialties: hybrids and
lady's slippers
Catalogue: $2.00

Jungle Gems, Inc.
300 Edgewood Road
Edgewood, MD 21040
(410) 676-0672
Specialties: phalaenopsis
Catalogue: free

Kawamoto Orchid Nursery
2630 Waiomao Road
Honolulu, HI 98616
(808) 732-5808
Catalogue: $2.00

Kenner & Sons
10919 Explorer Road
La Mesa, CA 91941
(619) 660-0161
(800) 582-9933
Specialties: Australian orchids
Catalogue: free

Kensington Orchids
3301 Plyers Mill Road
Kensington, MD 20895

(301) 933-0036
Catalogue: $1.00

Khuong Orchids, Ltd.
470 Mason Road
Vista, CA 92084
(619) 941-3093
Catalogue: two stamps

Kilworth Orchids
RR 3
County Road 14
Komoka, Ontario N0L 1R0
(519) 471-9787
Catalogue: $1.00

Arnold J. Klehm Grower, Inc.
44 West 637
State Route 72
Hampshire, IL 60140
(708) 683-4761
Catalogue: free

I. N. Komoda Orchids
Box 576
Makawao, HI 96768
(808) 572-0756
Specialties: masdevallias
Catalogue: SASE

Krull-Smith Orchids
2815 Ponkan Road
Apopka, FL 32712
(407) 886-0915
Specialties: phalaenopsis and
paphiopedilums
Catalogue: free

Lauray of Salisbury
432 Undermountain Road
Salisbury, CT 06068
(203) 435-2263
Catalogue: $2.00

Lenette Greenhouses
1440 Pom Orchid Lane

Kannapolis, NC 28081
(704) 938-2042
Specialties: hybrids
Catalogue: free

Lines Orchids, Inc.
1823 Taft Highway
Signal Mountain, TN 37377
(615) 886-2111
Catalogue: free

Lion's Den Orchids
275 Olive Hill Lane
Woodside, CA 94062
(415) 851-3303
Specialties: zygo petalums
Catalogue: free

Majestic Orchids
11701 SW 80th Road
Miami, FL 33156
(305) 233-7270
Catalogue: free

Makai Farms Orchids
Box 93
Kauai, HI 96754
(808) 828-1874
Catalogue: free

Ann Mann's Orchids
9045 Ron-Den Lane
Windermere, FL 34786
(407) 876-2625
Catalogue: $1.00

Manor Hill Orchids
Box 370
Pocono Pines, PA 18350
(717) 646-4400
Specialties: rare species
Catalogue: free

James McCully Orchidculture
Box 355
Hakalau, HI 96710

(808) 963-6233
Catalogue: $1.00

Rod McLellan Company
1450 El Camino Real
South San Francisco, CA 94080
(415) 871-5655
(800) 237-4089
Catalogue: $2.00

MCM Orchids
Box 4626
Wheaton, IL 60189
(708) 668-4588
Catalogue: free

Miami Orchids
22150 SW 147th Avenue
Miami, FL 33170
(305) 258-2664
(800) 516-5348
Specialties: vanda and vadaceous hybrids
Catalogue: free

Miskimens Orchids
13420 Borden Avenue
Sylmar, CA 91342
(818) 367-8525
Specialties: phalaenopsis
Catalogue: SASE

Mohawk Valley Orchid Estate
143 East Main Street
Amsterdam, NY 12010
(518) 843-4889
Catalogue: $2.00

Motes Orchids
25000 Farmlife Road
Homestead, FL 33031
(305) 247-4398
Specialties: vandas and ascocendas
Catalogue: free

Mountain View Orchids, Inc.
Box 4235

Hilo, HI 96720
(808) 968-8029
Specialties: phalaenopsis, cattleyas, ondiciums
Catalogue: free

Oak Hill Gardens
Box 25
West Dundee, IL 60118
(708) 428-8500
Specialties: cymbidiums, cattleyas
Catalogue: $1.00

Oceanside Orchids
3015 Skyline Drive
Oceanside, CA 92054
(619) 721-5661
Specialties: phalaenopsis
Catalogue: SASE

Odom's Orchids, Inc.
1611 South Jenkins Road
Fort Pierce, FL 34947
(407) 467-1386
Specialties: phalaenopsis
Catalogue: free

Orchid Acres, Inc.
4159 120th Avenue South
Lake Worth, FL 33467
(407) 795-9190
Specialties: dendrobiums
Catalogue: free

Orchidanica
Box 13151
Oakland, CA 94661
(510) 482-0408
Catalogue: free

Orchid Art
1433 Kew Avenue
Hewlett, NY 11557
(516) 374-6426
Catalogue: free

The Orchid House
1699 Sage Avenue
Los Osos, CA 93402
(805) 528-1417
(800) 235-4139
Catalogue: free

Orchid Gardens
6700 Splithand Road
Grand Rapids, MN 55744
(218) 326-6975
Catalogue: $2.00

Orchid Magic
Box 3475
Morristown, TN 37815
(423) 581-9222
Catalogue: $1.00

Orchids by Hausermann
2N 134 Addison Road
Villa Park, IL 60181
(708) 543-6855
Catalogue: $1.00

Orchids Limited
4630 North Fernbrook Lane
Plymouth, MN 55446
(612) 559-6425
(800) 669-6006
Specialties: phragmipediums
Catalogue: free

Orchid Species Specialties
42314 Road 415
Raymond Road
Coarsegold, CA 93614
(209) 683-3239
Specialties: species orchids
Catalogue: $1.00

Orchid Thoroughbreds
731 West Siddonsburg Road
Dillsburg, PA 17019
(717) 432-8100
Catalogue: free

Orchid World International, Inc.
10885 SW 95th Street
Miami, FL 33176
(305) 271-0268
(800) 367-6720
Catalogue: free

Our Orchids
23113 SW 156th Avenue
Miami, FL 33170
(305) 852-1824
Specialties: species orchids
Catalogue: long SASE with two stamps

Owens Orchids
Box 365
Pisgah Forest, NC 18768
(704) 877-3313
Specialties: phalaenopsis
Catalogue: free

Palestine Orchids
Route 1, Box 312
Palestine, WV 26160
(304) 275-4781
Specialties: fragrant orchids
Catalogue: free

Peach State Orchids, Inc.
920 Homer Road
Woodstock, GA 30188
(404) 751-8770
Specialties: phalaenopsis
Catalogue: free

Penn Valley Orchids
239 Old Gulph Road
Wynnewood, PA 19096
(610) 642-9822
Specialties: hybrid orchids
Catalogue: $1.00

Pretty Orchids, Inc.
Box 772887, Houston, TX 77215
Specialties: phalaenopsis
Catalogue: free

R. J. Rands Orchids
421 Westlake Boulevard
Malibu, CA 90265
(818) 707-3410
Specialties: paphiopedilums
Catalogue: $1.00

Rare Orchids
Box 6332
Malibu, CA 90265
(818) 597-1389
Catalogue: free

R. F. Orchids, Inc.
28100 SW 182nd Avenue
Homestead, FL 33030
(305) 245-4570
Catalogue: free

Riverbend Orchids
14220 Lorraine Road
Biloxi, MS 39532
(601) 392-2699
Specialties: phalaenopsis
Catalogue: free

R. K. S. Orchids
RD 3, Box 56
Glen Rock, PA 17327
(717) 235-2421
(800) 206-8092
Specialties: paphiopedilums
Catalogue: free

Rolling Knolls Orchids
Route 104
Bristol, NH 03222
(603) 744-8579
Catalogue: free

Alan C. Salzman,Orchids
1806 Jackson Road
Penfield, NY 14526
(716) 377-3213
Specialties: paphiopedilums
Catalogue: free

Santa Barbara Orchid Estate
1250 Orchid Drive
Santa Barbara, CA 93111
(800) 553-3387
Specialties: cymbidium and species
orchids
Catalogue: $2.00

Seagulls Landing Orchids
Box 388
Glen Head, NY 11545
(516) 367-6336
Specialties: cattleyas
Catalogue: $2.50

George Shorter Orchids
Box 16952
Mobile, AL 36616
(205) 443-7469
Catalogue: free

South Shore Orchids
87 Pine Road
Mastic Beach, NY 11951
(516) 281-0097
Catalogue: free

Stewart Orchids, Inc.
Box 550
3376 Foothill Road
Carpinteria, CA 93013
(805) 684-5448
(800) 621-2450
Specialties: hybrids
Catalogue: $2.00

Sunset Orchids
2709 Hillside Drive
Burlingame, CA 94010
(415) 342-3092
Catalogue: SASE

Sunswept Laboratories
Box 1913
Studio City, CA 91614
(818) 506-7271

Specialties: rare and endangered species
from seed
Catalogue: free

Sweetwater Orchids, Inc.
2467 Ridgeway Drive
National City, CA 91950
(619) 472-1226
Catalogue: free

Tropical Orchid Farm
Box 354
Haiku, HI 96708
(808) 572-8569
Catalogue: free

Tropic 1 Orchids, Inc.
3710 North Orchid Drive
Haines City, FL 33844
(813) 422-4750
Specialties: phalaenopsis
Catalogue: free

Venamy Orchids
Route 22 North
Brewster, NY 10509
(800) 362-3612
Catalogue: $2.00

Venger's Orchids
1220 Pando Avenue
Colorado Springs, CO 80906
(719) 576-7686
(800) 483-6437
Catalogue: free

Wacahoota Orchids
Route 1, Box 354
County Road 320
Micanopy, FL 32667
(800) 833-3747
Catalogue: free

We-Du Nurseries
Route 5, Box 724
Marion, NC 28752

(704) 738-8300
Specialties: bletillas
Catalogue: $2.00

Ken West Orchids
Box 1332
Pahoa, HI 96778
(808) 965-9895
Specialties: cattleyas
Catalogue: free

Whippoorwill Orchids
9790 Larkin Lane
Rogers, AR 72756
(501) 925-1885
Catalogue: free

Wilk Orchid Specialties
Box 1177
45-212 Nohonani Place
Kaneohe, HI 96744
(808) 247-6733
Catalogue: free

Windsong Orchids
14N456 Factly Road
Sycamore, IL 60178
(708) 683-2139
Catalogue: free

Woodland Orchids
1816 Hart Road
Charlotte, NC 28214
(704) 394-6530
Catalogue: SASE

A World of Orchids
2501 Old Lake Wilson Road
Kissimmee, FL 34747
(407) 396-1887
Catalogue: free

Andrew Zarauskas Orchids
144 Indian Run Parkway
Union, NJ 07083
(908) 964-5763

Specialties: phaphiopedilums
and phragmipediums
Catalogue: free

Zuma Canyon Orchids
5949 Bonsall Drive
Malibu, CA 90265
(310) 457-9771
Catalogue: free

Roses

Organizations

American Rose Society
Box 30,000
Shreveport, LA 71130
(318) 938-5402
Dues: $32.00
Publication: *The American Rose Magazine*
(eleven times annually)
Special interest quarterlies: *Marvelous
Miniatures; Rose Arranger's Bulletin; Rose
Exhibitor's Forum; The Old Garden Roses and
Shrubs Gazette;* all $10.00 annually

Canadian Rose Society
Anne Graber, Secretary
10 Fairfax Crescent
Scarsborough, Ontario M1L 1Z8
(416) 757-8809
Dues: Canada $18.00
Publications: *The Rosarian*
(three times annually);
Canadian Rose Annual

Heritage Rose Foundation
1512 Gorman Street
Raleigh, NC 27606
(919) 834-2591
Publication: *Heritage Rose Foundation* News
(quarterly)

Heritage Rose Group
Miriam Wilkins

925 Galvin Drive
El Cerrito, CA 94530
(510) 526-6960
Dues: $5.00
Publication: *Heritage Rose Letter* (quarterly)

Rose Hybridizers Association
c/o Larry D. Peterson
3245 Wheaton Road
Horseheads, NY 14845
(607) 562-8592
Dues: $7.00
Publication: quarterly newsletter

The Royal National Rose Society
The Secretary
Chiswell Green
St. Albans, Herts. AL2 3NR
England
(0727) 50-461
Dues: £13.50
Publication: *The Rose* (quarterly journal)

Texas Rose Rustlers
c/o Margaret Sharpe
9246 Kerrwood Lane
Houston, TX 77080
(713) 464-8607
Publication: *Old Texas Rose* (quarterly)

World Federation of Rose Societies
c/o Jill Bennell
46 Alexandra Road
St. Albans, Herts. AL1 3AZ
England
(0727) 833-648
Dues: £25.00
Publication: *World Rose News* (semiannual)

All-America Rose Selections

All-America Rose Selections is a nonprofit organization dedicated to maintaining
high standards for rose introductions.
AARS tests new varieties and reports the
results to the public; only outstanding

new roses become selections.
Nationwide, AARS maintains twenty-four
rose test gardens and 135 public rose gardens. These public gardens serve as
showcases for AARS award winners over
the years. For more information and a
free list of AARS accredited public rose
gardens, write to:

All-America Rose Selections
221 North LaSalle Street, Suite 3900
Chicago, IL 60601
(312) 372-7090

Tools and Growing Supplies

Harlane Company, Inc.
266 Orangeburgh Road
Old Tappan, NJ 07675
Catalogue: free

Other Services and Supplies

Well-known rosarian Bev Dobson pub-
lishes an invaluable newsletter for the
rose lover; she also puts out an annual
source guide to help you find any rose
variety available in North America and
abroad. For information, write to:

Bev Dobson's Rose Letter/The Combined
Rose List
Beverly Dobson
215 Harriman Road
Irvington, NY 10533
Subscription: $12.00
Frequency: bimonthly

Rose database software is available from:

Mach Rose Farm
27646 13th Avenue
Aldergrove, British Columbia V4W 2S4
(604) 856-2631
Catalogue: free

Rosebud
3707 SW Coronado Street
Portland, OR 97219
(503) 245-0546
Catalogue: free

*Gifts and collectibles featuring roses are
available from:*

Everything Roses
189 Berdan Avenue
Wayne, NJ 07474
(800) 787-6739
Catalogue: free

Plant Sources

The Antique Rose Emporium
Route 5, Box 143
Brenham, TX 77833
(409) 836-9051
(800) 441-0002
Specialties: old roses
Catalogue: $5.00

Arena Rose Company
536 West Cambridge Avenue
Phoenix, AZ 85003
(602) 266-2223
Specialties: old roses for hot climates
Catalogue: free

Blossoms & Bloomers
11415 East Krueger Lane
Spokane, WA 99207
(509) 922-1344
Specialties: hardy old roses
Catalogue: $1.00

Bridges Roses
2734 Toney Road
Lawndale, NC 28090
(704) 538-9412
Specialties: miniature roses
Catalogue: free

Butner's Old Mill Nursery
806 South Belt Highway
St. Joseph, MO 64507
(816) 279-7434
Catalogue: free

Carlton Rose Nurseries
Box 366
Carlton, OR 97111
(503) 852-7135
Specialties: modern roses
Catalogue: free

Carroll Gardens
Box 310
Westminster, MD 21157
(800) 638-6334
Catalogue: $3.00

Chamblee's Rose Nursery
10926 US Highway 69 North
Tyler, TX 75706
(800) 256-7673
Specialties: old and miniature roses
Catalogue: free

Conard-Pyle Company
372 Rose Hill Road
West Grove, PA 19390
(800) 458-6559
Catalogue: $1.00

Corn Hill Nursery, Ltd.
RR 5
Petitcodiac, New Brunswick E0A 2H0
(506) 756-3635
Catalogue: free

Country Bloomers Nursery
Route 2, Box 33
Udall, KS 67146
(316) 986-5518
Specialties: old and miniature roses
Catalogue: free

Donovan's Roses
Box 37800
Shreveport, LA 71133
(318) 861-6693
Catalogue: long SASE

Edmunds' Roses
6235 SW Kahle Road
Wilsonville, OR 97070
(503) 682-1476
Specialties: modern roses
Catalogue: free

Forestfarm
990 Tetherow Road
Williams, OR 97544
(503) 846-7269
Specialties: antique roses
Catalogue: $3.00

Forevergreen Farm
70 New Gloucester Road
North Yarmouth, ME 04097
(207) 829-5830
Catalogue: $1.00

Garden Valley Nursery
Box 750953
498 Pepper Road
Petaluma, CA 94975
(707) 795-5266
Catalogue: $1.00

Giles' Ramblin' Roses
2968 State Road 710
Okeechobee, FL 34974
(813) 763-6611
Catalogue: SASE

Gloria Dei Nursery
36 East Road
High Falls, NY 12440
(914) 687-9981
Specialties: miniature roses
Catalogue: free

Greenmantle Nursery
3010 Ettersburg Road
Garberville, CA 95442
(707) 986-7504
Catalogue: long SASE

Hardy Roses for the North
Box 273, Danville, WA 99121
(604) 442-8442
(800) 442-8122
Specialties: hardy roses
Catalogue: $2.00

Heirloom Old Garden Roses
24062 North Riverside
St. Paul, OR 97137
(503) 538-1576
Specialties: old roses
Catalogue: $5.00

Heritage Rosarium
211 Haviland Mill Road
Brookeville, MD 20833
(301) 774-2806
Specialties: old roses
Catalogue: $1.00

Heritage Rose Gardens
16831 Mitchell Creek Drive
Fort Bragg, CA 95437
(707) 984-6959
Specialties: old roses
Catalogue: $1.50

Hidden Garden Nursery, Inc.
13515 SE Briggs
Milwaukie, OR 97222
Specialties: miniature roses
Catalogue: long SASE

High Country Rosarium
1717 Downing Street
Denver, CO 80218
(303) 832-4026
Specialties: old and hardy roses
Catalogue: free

Historical Roses
1657 West Jackson Street
Painesville, OH 44077
(216) 357-7270
Specialties: old roses
Catalogue: long SASE

Hortico, Inc.
RR 1
723 Robson Road
Waterdown, Ontario L0R 2H1
(905) 689-3002
Catalogue: $3.00

Howertown Rose Nursery
1657 Weaversville Road
Northampton, PA 18067
Catalogue: free

Ingraham's Cottage Garden Roses
Box 126
Scotts Mills, OR 97375
(503) 873-8610
Specialties: old and modern roses
Catalogue: $1.00

Jackson & Perkins Company
1 Rose Lane
Medford, OR 97501
(503) 776-2000
(800) USA-ROSE
Catalogue: free

Justice Miniature Roses
5947 SW Kahle Road
Wilsonville, OR 97070
(503) 682-2370
Specialties: miniature roses
Catalogue: free

Kimbrew-Walter Roses
Route 2, Box 172
Grand Saline, TX 75140
Catalogue: free

V. Kraus Nurseries
Box 180
1380 Centre Road
Carlisle, Ontario L0R 1H0
(416) 689-4022
Catalogue: $1.00

Lowe's Own-Root Roses
6 Sheffield Road
Nashua, NH 03062
(603) 888-2214
Specialties: old roses
Catalogue: $2.00

Magic Moment Miniatures
Box 499
Rockville Centre, NY 11571
Specialities: miniature roses
Catalogue: free

McDaniel's Miniature Roses
7323 Zemco Street
Lemon Grove, CA 91945
(619) 469-4669
Specialties: miniature roses
Catalogue: free

Mendocino Heirloom Roses
Box 670
Mendocino, CA 95460
(707) 877-1888
Specialties: old roses
Catalogue: $1.00

Michigan Miniature Roses
45951 Hull Road
Belleville, MI 48111
Specialties: miniature roses
Catalogue: free

Milaeger's Gardens
4838 Douglas Avenue
Racine, WI 53402
(414) 639-2371
Catalogue: $1.00

Miniature Plant Kingdom
4125 Harrison Grade Road
Sebastopol, CA 95472
(707) 874-2233
Specialties: miniature roses
Catalogue: $2.50

The Mini-Rose Garden
Box 203
Cross Hill, SC 29332
(864) 998-4331
Specialties: miniature roses
Catalogue: free

Nor'East Miniature Roses, Inc.
Box A
Rowley, MA 01969
(508) 948-7964
Specialties: miniature roses
Catalogue: free

Oregon Miniature Roses, Inc.
8285 SW 185th Avenue
Beaverton, OR 97007
(503) 649-4482
Specialties: miniature roses
Catalogue: free

Richard Owen Nursery
2300 East Lincoln Street
Bloomington, IL 61701
Catalogue: $2.00

Carl Pallek & Son Nurseries
Box 137
Virgil, Ontario L0S 1T0
Specialties: tea roses
Catalogue: free

Petaluma Rose Company
Box 750953
581 Gossage Avenue
Petaluma, CA 94975
(707) 769-8862
Catalogue: free

Pickering Nurseries, Inc.
670 Kingston Road
Pickering, Ontario L1V 1A6
(905) 839-2111
Catalogue: $3.00

Pixie Treasures Miniature Roses
4121 Prospect Avenue
Yorba Linda, CA 92686
(714) 993-6780
Specialties: miniature roses
Catalogue: $1.00

Rabbit Shadow Farm
2880 East Highway 402
Loveland, CO 80538
(303) 667-5531
Catalogue: $1.00

Rennie Roses International
RR 2
Elora, Ontario N0B 1SO
(519) 846-0329
Specialties: miniature roses
Catalogue: free

Roseberry Gardens
Box 933, Postal Station F
Thunder Bay, Ontario P7C 4X8
Catalogue: free

Rosehaven Nursery
8617 Tobacco Lane SE
Olympia, WA 98503
Catalogue: free

Rosehill Farm
Box 188
Gregg Neck Road
Galena, MD 21635
(410) 648-5538
Specialties: miniature roses
Catalogue: free

The Roseraie at Bayfields
Box R

Waldboro, ME 04572
Catalogue: $5.00

The Rose Ranch
Box 10087
240 Cooper Road
Salinas, CA 93912
(408) 758-6965
Catalogue: $3.00

Roses & Wine
6260 Fernwood Drive
Shingle Springs, CA 95682
(916) 677-9722
Specialties: old roses
Catalogue: long SASE

Roses of Yesterday and Today
802 Brown's Valley Road
Watsonville, CA 95076
(408) 724-3537
Specialties: old, rare, and new roses
Catalogue: $3.00

Roses Unlimited
Route 1, Box 587
Laurens, SC 29360
(803) 682-ROSE
Catalogue: SASE

Rozell Rose Nursery & Violet Boutique
12206 Highway 31 West
Tyler, TX 75709
(903) 595-5137
Catalogue: $1.00

Royall River Roses
70 New Gloucester Road
North Yarmouth, ME 04097
(207) 829-5830
Catalogue: $1.00

Schumacher's Hill Country Gardens
588 FM Highway 1863
New Braunfels, TX 78132
Catalogue: $1.00

Sequoia Nursery/
Moore Miniature Roses
2519 East Noble Avenue
Visalia, CA 93277
(209) 732-0190
Specialties: miniature roses
Catalogue: $1.00

Spring Hill Nursery
Box 1758
Peoria, IL 61632
(309) 689-3849
Catalogue: $1.00

Stanek's Garden Center
2929 27th Avenue East
Spokane, WA 99223
(509) 535-2939
Specialties: hybrid roses
Catalogue: free

Tate Rose Nursery
10306 FM Road 2767
Tyler, TX 75708
(903) 593-1020
Specialties: hybrid roses
Catalogue: free

Taylor's Roses
Box 11272
Chicasaw, AL 36671
Specialties: miniature roses
Catalogue: free

Texas Mini Roses
Box 267
Denton, TX 76202
(817) 566-3034
Catalogue: $1.00

Thomasville Nurseries
Box 7
1842 Smith Avenue
Thomasville, GA 31792

(912) 226-5568
Specialties: modern roses
Catalogue: free

Tiny Petals Miniature Rose Nursery
489 Minot Avenue
Chula Vista, CA 91910
(619) 422-0385
Specialties: miniature roses
Catalogue: free

Vintage Gardens
2227 Gravenstein Highway South
Sebastopol, CA 95472
(707) 829-2035
Specialties: old roses
Catalogue: $4.00

Witherspoon's Roses
Box 51655
Durham, NC 27717
Catalogue: $3.00

Wayside Gardens
One Garden Lane
Hodges, SC 29695
(800) 845-1124
Catalogue: free

A World of Roses
Box 90332
Gainesville, FL 32607
Catalogue: $1.00

York Hill Farm
271 North Haverhill Road
Kensington, NH 03833
(603) 772-8567
Catalogue: $1.00

Young's American Rose Nursery
Route 2, Box 112
Elsberry, MO 63343
Catalogue: $3.00

Seed Exchanges

Organizations

Heritage Seed Program
RR 3
Uxbridge, Ontario L0C 1K0
(416) 852-7965
Dues: $18.00
Publication: *Heritage Seed Program*
(three times annually)

Seed Savers Exchange
3076 North Winn Road
Decorah, IA 52101
(319) 382-5990
Dues: $25.00
Publications: yearbook; newsletter

Publications

Gardeners' Seed Swap
703 Church Street
Scott City, KS 67871
Frequency: monthly newsletter
Subscription: $14.00

Seed Exchange Monthly
Peter Collier
56 Red Willow
Harlow, Essex CM19 5PD
England
Frequency: monthly
Subscription: write for information

Seed Traders' Companion
222 New Elizabeth Street
Wilkes-Barre, PA 18702
Frequency: monthly newsletter
Subscription: write for information

Seed Supplies

V.L. Price Horticultural
506 Grove Avenue
Catawissa, PA 17820

Products: seed-saving supplies
Catalogue: free

Seed Saver®/KLACK Company
Box 2726
Idaho Falls, ID 83403
(208) 522-2224
Products: seed files and storage
equipment
Catalogue: free

Twinholly's
3633 NE 19th Avenue
Portland, OR 97212
Product: seed storage envelopes
Catalogue: free

Seed Exchanges

Abundant Life Seed Foundation
Box 772
Port Townsend, WA 98368
(206) 385-5660
Catalogue: $1.00

AHS Seed Exchange Program
7931 East Boulevard Drive
Alexandria, VA 22308
Catalogue: free

Alberene Seed Foundation
Box 271
Keene, VA 22946
Catalogue: $1.00

Blue Ridge Seed Savers
Box 106
Batesville, VA 22924
Catalogue: $1.00

Central Prairie Seed Exchange
7949 SW 21st Street
Topeka, KS 66604
(913) 478-4944
Catalogue: $1.00

Dyck Arboretum of the Plains
Seed Exchange
Hesston College
Box 3000
Hesston, KS 67062
(316) 327-8127
Specialties: prairie plants
Catalogue: long SASE

Kusa Research Foundation
Box 761
Ojai, CA 93023
Catalogue: $1.00

Liberty Seed Company
Box 806
New Philadelphia, OH 44663
(216) 364-1611
Catalogue: $1.00

National Heirloom Flower Seed
Exchange
136 Irving Street
Cambridge, MA 02138
(617) 576-5065
Catalogue: $1.00

Native Seeds/SEARCH
2509 North Campbell Avenue
Tucson, AZ 85719
(602) 327-9123
Catalogue: $1.00

Peace Seeds
2385 SE Thompson Street
Corvallis, OR 97333
Catalogue: $1.00

Seed Savers Exchange
Kent Wheatly
RR 3, Box 239
Decorah, IA 52101
Catalogue: $1.00

Southern Exposure Seed Exchange
Box 158

North Garden, VA 22959
(804) 973-4703
Catalogue: $3.00

Seeds Blüm
Idaho City Stage
Boise, ID 83707
Catalogue: $2.00

Water Gardening

Organizations

Aquatic Gardeners Association
c/o Dorothy Reimer, Membership
83 Cathcart Street
London, Ontario N6C 3L9
Dues: $15.00
Publication: *The Aquatic Gardener*
(bimonthly journal)

International Water Lily Society
c/o Dr. Edward Schneider
Santa Barbara Botanic Gardens
Santa Barbara, CA 93105
(805) 682-4726
Dues: $18.00
Publication: *Water Garden Journal*
(quarterly)

Publications

Pondscapes
National Pond Society
Box 449
Acworth, GA 30101
(800) 742-4701
Frequency: ten times annually
Subscription: $24.00

The Practical Pondkeeper
1670 South 900 East
Zionsville, IN 46077
Frequency: ten times annually
Subscription: $20.00

The Water Gardener
East-West Specialties
Box 6004, Norfolk, VA 23508
(804) 461-0665
Frequency: bimonthly newsletter
Subscription: $15.00

Pond Supplies—General

Cherryhill Aquatics, Inc.
2627 North County Line Road
Sunbury, OH 43074
(614) 965-2798
Catalogue: free

Discount Pond Supplies
Box 423371
Kissimmee, FL 34742
(407) 847-7937
Catalogue: free

Hardwicke Gardens
254A Boston Turnpike Road
Westboro, MA 01581
Catalogue: $2.00

Henri Water Gardening
Wauconda, IL 60084
(800) 92-HENRI
Catalogue: free

Lilypons Water Gardens
6800 Lilypons Road
Buckeystown, MD 21717
(301) 428-0686
(800) 723-7667
Catalogue: $5.00

Paradise Water Gardens
14 May Street
Whitman, MA 02382
(617) 447-4711
Catalogue: $3.00

Patio Garden Ponds
7919 South Shields

Oklahoma City, OK 73149
(800) 487-LILY
Catalogue: free

Perry's Water Gardens
191 Leatherman Gap Road
Franklin, NC 28734
(704) 524-3264
Catalogue: free

Pets Unlimited
1888 Drew
Clearwater, FL 34625
(813) 442-2197
Catalogue: $2.00

S. Scherer & Sons
104 Waterside Road
Northport, NY 11768
(516) 261-7432
Catalogue: $1.00

Slocum Water Gardens
1101 Cypress Gardens Boulevard
Winter Haven, FL 33880
(813) 293-7151
Catalogue: $3.00

Stigall Water Gardens
7306 Main Street
Kansas City, MO 64114
(816) 822-1256
Catalogue: $1.00

Tetra Pond
3001 Commerce Street
Blacksburg, VA 20460
(703) 951-5400
Catalogue: free

William Tricker, Inc.
7125 Tanglewood Drive
Independence, OH 44131
(800) 524-3492
Catalogue: $3.50

West Kentucky Ornamental Water
Gardens
(800) 705-5509
Catalogue: free

Al Zimmer Ponds & Supplies
(215) 582-9714
(800) 722-8877
Catalogue: free

Pond Supplies—Products

Adams & Adkins, Inc.
104 South Early Street
Alexandria, VA 22304
(703) 823-3404
(800) 928-3588
Product: Water Flute™ fountain pond
Catalogue: free

Aquarium Pharmaceuticals, Inc.
50 East Hamilton Street
Chalfont, PA 18914
(215) 822-8181
Product: pond maintenance supplies
Catalogue: $1.00

Aquarium Products, Inc.
180-L Penrod Court
Glen Burnie, MD 21061
(410) 761-2100
Product: pond maintenance supplies
Catalogue: free

Beckett Corporation
2521 Willowbrook Road
Dallas, TX 75220
Product: pumps
Catalogue: free

E. G. Danner Manufacturing, Inc.
160 Oval Drive
Central Islip, NY 11722
(516) 234-5261
Product: pumps
Catalogue: free

Hermitage Gardens
Box 361
Canastoga, NY 13032
(315) 697-9093
Products: pumps; submersible lighting
Catalogue: $1.00

Little Giant Pump Company
Box 12010
Oklahoma City, OK 73157
(405) 947-2511
Products: pumps; submersible lighting
Catalogue: free

Northwest Landscape Supply, Inc.
12500 132nd Avenue NE
Kirkland, WA 98034
(206) 820-9325
Product: pond liners
Catalogue: free

Plantabbs Products
Box 397
Timonium, MD 21093
(800) 227-4340
Product: aquatic plant food
Catalogue: free

Pondfiltration, Inc.
501 West Travelers Trail
Burnsville, MN 55337
(800) 882-5327
Product: filters
Catalogue: free

Remanoid Lawn Ponds
3001 Rouse Avenue
Pittsburg, KS 66762
(316) 232-2400
Product: pond maintenance supplies
Catalogue: free

Resource Conservation Technology
2633 North Calvert Street
Baltimore, MD 21218
(410) 366-1146

Product: pond liners
Catalogue: free

SeaChem
1939 C Parker Court
Stone Mountain, GA 30087
(404) 972-5999
Product: pond maintenance supplies
Catalogue: free

Unit Liner Company
(800) 633-4603
Product: pond liners
Catalogue: free

Waterscapes
155 Washington
Kingston, NY 12401
(914) 339-8382
Product: custom pond kits
Catalogue: free

Winston Company, Inc.
Box 636
Bixby, OK 74008
(800) 331-9099
Product: water treatment products
Catalogue: free

Aquatic, Pond, and Bog Plants

Aquatics and Exotics
Box 693
Indian Rocks Beach, FL 34635
(813) 595-3075
Catalogue: free

Bee Fork Water Gardens
Box 440037
Brentwood, MO 63144
(314) 962-1583
Specialties: water lilies
Catalogue: $1.00

Country Wetlands Nursery
South 75 West 20755
Field Drive
Muskego, WI 53150
(414) 679-1268
Specialties: wetland plants
Catalogue: $2.00

Crystal Palace Perennials
Box 154
St. John, IN 46373
(219) 374-9419
Specialties: water plants
Catalogue: free

Hemlock Hollow Nursery
Box 125
Sandy Hook, KY 41171
(606) 738-6285
Specialties: water lilies and lotus
Catalogue: free

J's Custom Koi Ponds
14050 FM Road 848
Whitehouse, TX 75791
Catalogue: $3.00

Green & Hagstrom, Inc.
Box 658
Fairview, TN 37062
(615) 799-0708
Catalogue: free

Japonica
36484 Camp Creek Road
Springfield, OR 97478
Catalogue: SASE

Lilyblooms Water Gardens
(800) 921-0005
Specialties: water lilies
Catalogue: free

Lilypons Water Gardens
6800 Lilypons Road
Buckeystown, MD 21717

(301) 428-0686
(800) 723-7667
Catalogue: $5.00

Maryland Aquatic Nurseries
3427 North Furnace Road
Jarrettsville, MD 21084
(410) 557-7615
Catalogue: $5.00

Miami Water Lilies
22150 SW 147th Avenue
Miami, FL 33170
(305) 258-2664
Specialties: water lilies
Catalogue: free

Moore Water Gardens
Box 70
Port Stanley, Ontario N5L 1J4
(519) 782-4052
Catalogue: free

Perry's Water Gardens
191 Leatherman Gap Road
Franklin, NC 28734
(704) 524-3264
Catalogue: free

Picov Greenhouses
380 Kingston Road East
Ajax, Ontario L1S 4S7
(416) 686-2151
(800) 663-0300
Catalogue: free

Pond Doctor
HC 65, Box 265
Kingston, AR 72742
(501) 665-2232
Catalogue: $2.00

Reed Water Lilies
Box 9154
College Station, TX 77842
(409) 361-2378

Specialties: water lilies
Catalogue: free

Renrick's
Box 1383
Chickasha, OK 7303
Specialties: water lilies
Catalogue: SASE

Santa Barbara Water Gardens
160 East Mountain Drive
Santa Barbara, CA 93108
(805) 969-5129
Catalogue: $2.00

S. Scherer & Sons
104 Waterside Road
Northport, NY 11768
(516) 261-7432
Catalogue: $1.00

Scottsdale Fishponds
6915 East Oak Street
Scottsdale, AZ 85257
(602) 946-8025
Catalogue: $2.00

Slocum Water Gardens
1101 Cypress Gardens Boulevard
Winter Haven, FL 33880
(813) 293-7151
Specialties: water lilies
Catalogue: $3.00

Stigall Water Gardens
7306 Main Street
Kansas City, MO 64114
(816) 822-1256
Catalogue: $1.00

Tilley's Nursery/The WaterWorks
111 East Fairmount Street
Coopersburg, PA 18036
(215) 282-4784
Catalogue: $2.00

Trees by Touliatos
202 Brooks Road
Memphis, TN 38116
(901) 345-7361
Catalogue: long SASE

William Tricker, Inc.
7125 Tanglewood Drive
Independence, OH 44131
(800) 524-3492
Specialties: water lilies
Catalogue: $3.50

Tropical Pond and Garden
17888 61st Place North
Loxahutchee, FL 33470
Specialties: water lilies
Catalogue: free

Van Ness Water Gardens
2460 North Euclid Avenue
Upland, CA 91786
(909) 982-2425
Catalogue: $4.00

Waterford Gardens
74 East Allendale Road
Saddle River, NJ 07458
(201) 327-0721
Catalogue: $5.00

Water's Edge
2775 Hardin Road
Choctaw, OK 73020
Catalogue: free

Water Ways Nursery
Route 2, Box 247
Lovettsville, VA 22080
(703) 822-5994
Catalogue: $2.00

Wicklein's Water Gardens
Box 9780
Baldwin, MD 21013
(410) 823-1335
Catalogue: $2.00

Wildlife Nurseries, Inc.
Box 2724
Oshkosh, WI 54903
(414) 231-3780
Catalogue: $3.00

Windy Oaks Daylilies & Aquatics
West 377 South 10677
Betts Road
Eagle, WI 53119
(414) 594-2803
Catalogue: free

Indoor Gardening

INDOOR GARDENING can go far, far beyond a few potted plants on a windowsill. *This section lists organizations, publications, and manufacturers of home greenhouses and solariums, along with retailers of greenhouse and propagation supplies, grow lights, and other indoor essentials. Many of the manufacturers listed here will sell directly to home gardeners. In many cases, however, the manufacturer will provide descriptive catalogues, brochures, and the like, and refer you to a dealer in your area to make your purchase.*

Organizations

Hobby Greenhouse Association
18517 Kingshill Road
Germantown, MD 20874
(410) 275-0377
Dues: $15.00
Publications: *Hobby Greenhouse*
(quarterly magazine);
HGA News (quarterly); annual directory
of greenhouse manufacturers

Hydroponic Society of America
2819 Crow Canyon Road, Suite 218
San Ramon, CA 94583
(510) 743-9605
Dues: $30.00
Publication: *Soilless Grower*
(bimonthly)

Indoor Gardening Society of America
Sharon Zentz, Membership Secretary
944 South Munro Road
Tallmadge, OH 44278
(216) 733-8414

Dues: $20.00
Publication: *The Indoor Garden*
(bimonthly)

International Society of Greenhouse
Gardeners
Box 7567
Olympia, WA 98507
Publication: newsletter

Publications

The Growing EDGE Magazine
New Moon Publishing
Box 1027
Corvallis, OR 97339
(800) 888-6785
Frequency: quarterly
Subscription: $18.00

The Twenty-First Century Gardener
Growers Press, Inc.
Box 189
Princeton, British Columbia V0X 1W0

Frequency: bimonthly
Subscription: Canada $26.00

Greenhouses

Amdega Machin Conservatories
Box 7, Glenview, IL 60025
(800) 922-0110
Catalogue: $10.00

Charley's Greenhouse Supply
1569 Memorial Highway
Mount Vernon, WA 98273
(800) 322-4707
Product: traditional English greenhouses
Catalogue: free

Everlite Greenhouses, Inc.
9515 Gerwig Lane, Suite 115
Columbia, MD 20146
(301) 381-3881
Products: greenhouses and conservatories
Catalogue: free

Farm Wholesale, Inc.
2396 Perkins Street NE
Salem, OR 97303
(503) 393-3973
(800) 825-1925
Product: stretch Quonset greenhouses
Catalogue: free

Four Seasons Solar Products
5005 Veterans Highway
Holbrook, NY 11741
(516) 694-4400
(800) FOURSEA
Catalogue: free

Fox Hill Farm
1358 Bridge Street
South Yarmouth, MA 02664
(800) 760-5192
Product: Hoop House greenhouses
Catalogue: $1.00

Gardener's Supply Company
128 Intervale Road
Burlington, VT 05401
(800) 863-1700
Catalogue: free

GardenStyles
Box 50670
Minneapolis, MN 55405
(800) 356-8890
Product: Juliana greenhouses
Catalogue: free

Garden Trends, Inc.
Box 22960
Rochester, NY 114692
(800) 514-4441
Product: Elite greenhouses
Catalogue: free

Gothic Arch Greenhouses
Box 1564
Mobile, AL 36633
(205) 432-7529
(800) 628-4974
Catalogue: $5.00

Hobby Gardens
Box 83
Grand Isle, VT 05458
(802) 372-4041
Catalogue: free

Janco Greenhouses
9390 Davis Avenue
Laurel, MD 20723
(301) 498-5700
(800) 323-6933
Catalogue: free

National Greenhouses
400 East Main Street
Pana, IL 62557
(800) 826-9314
Product: residential greenhouses
Catalogue: free

Northwest Eden Sales, Inc.
15103 NE 68th Street
Redmond, WA 98052
(800) 545-3336
Catalogue: free

Pacific Coast Greenhouse
Manufacturing Company
Box 2130
Petaluma, CA 94953
(800) 227-7061
Product: redwood greenhouses
Catalogue: $2.00

Pacific Greenhouse
25550 Rio Vista Drive
Carmel, CA 93923
(408) 622-9233
Product: redwood greenhouse kits
Catalogue: free

Powell & Powell Supply Company
1206 Broad Street
Fuquay-Varina, NC 27526
(919) 552-9708
Product: The Little Greenhouse
Catalogue: free

Progressive Building Products
Box 453
Exeter, NH 03833
(603) 679-1208
(800) 776-2534
Catalogue: free

Santa Barbara Greenhouses
721 Richmond Avenue
Oxnard, CA 93030
(805) 483-4288
(800) 544-5276
Product: redwood greenhouses
Catalogue: free

Simpson Strong-Tie Company
4637 Chabot Drive
Pleasanton, CA 94588

(800) 999-5099
Product: GardenHouse kits
Catalogue: free

Solar Components Corporation
121 Valley Street
Manchester, NH 03103
(603) 668-8186
Products: greenhouses and greenhouse
kits
Catalogue: $2.00

Solar Prism Manufacturing Inc.
Box 29
McMinnville, OR 97128
(503) 472-1285
Catalogue: free

Sturdi-Built Greenhouse
Manufacturing Company
11304 SW Boones Ferry Road
Portland, OR 97219
(503) 244-4100
(800) 722-4115
Product: redwood greenhouses
Catalogue: free

Sundance Greenhouses
1813 Cedar Street
Berkeley, CA 94703
Catalogue: $2.00

Sunglo Solar Greenhouses
4441 26th Avenue West
Seattle, WA 98199
(206) 284-8900
(800) 647-0606
Product: kit greenhouses
Catalogue: free

Sun 'N Rain Greenhouses
45 Dixon Avenue
Amityville, NY 11701
(800) 999-9459
Product: Clicker 2000
Catalogue: free

Sunspot, Inc.
5030 40th Avenue
Hudsonville, MI 49426
(616) 669-9400
(800) 635-4786
Catalogue: free

Turner Greenhouses
Box 1260
Goldsboro, NC 27533
(800) 672-4770
Products: greenhouses and accessories
Catalogue: free

Under Glass Manufacturing Corporation
Box 323
Wappingers Falls, NY 12590
(914) 298-0645
Products: greenhouses and solariums
Catalogue: $3.00

Solariums and Conservatories

Amdega Machin Conservatories
Box 7
Glenview, IL 60025
(800) 922-0110
Products: conservatories and garden
buildings
Catalogue: $10.00

Pella
Box 308
Moline, IL 61265
(800) 524-3700
Product: solariums
Catalogue: $2.00

Sun-Porch
Vegetable Factory, Inc.
Box 1353
Stamford, CT 06904
Product: solariums
Catalogue: $2.00

Sun Room Company, Inc.
322 East Main Street
Leola, PA 17540
(800) 426-2737
Product: solariums
Catalogue: free

Sunspot, Inc.
5030 40th Avenue
Hudsonville, MI 49426
(616) 669-9400
(800) 635-4786
Product: solariums
Catalogue: free

Tanglewood Conservatories
Silver Spring, MD
(800) 229-2925
Product: period glasshouses
Catalogue: $1.00

Texas Greenhouse Company
2524 White Settlement Road
Fort Worth, TX 76107
(800) 227-5447
Catalogue: $4.00

Turner Greenhouses
Box 1260
Goldsboro, NC 27533
(800) 672-4770
Catalogue: free

Under Glass Manufacturing Corporation
Box 323
Wappingers Falls, NY 12590
(914) 298-0645
Products: greenhouses and solariums
Catalogue: $3.00

Victory Garden Supply Company
1428 East High Street
Charlottesville, VA 22902
(804) 293-2298
Product: aluminum greenhouses
Catalogue: free

Minigreenhouses, Cold Frames, and Plant Stands

Day-Dex Company
4725 NW 36th Avenue
Miami, FL 33142
(305) 635-5241
Product: galvanized steel tiered benches
Catalogue: free

Floralight Gardens
6-620 Supertest Road
North York, Ontario M3J 2M5
(416) 665-4000
(800) 665-4000
Product: plant stands
Catalogue: free

Florist Products, Inc.
2242 North Palmer Drive
Schaumburg, IL 60173
(312) 885-2242
Product: Wonder Garden lighted plant
stand
Catalogue: free

Green Thumb Industries
2400 Easy Street
San Leandro, CA 94578
(510) 276-0252
Product: English RollHouse cold frames
Catalogue: free

Home Gardener Manufacturing
Company
30 Wright Avenue
Lititz, PA 17543
(800) 880-2345
Product: RotoGro growing shelves
Catalogue: free

Humbug Manufacturing Company
Box 541
North Hampton, NH 03862
(603) 964-1115
Product: minigreenhouses
Catalogue: free

Mason-Kemp Associates, Inc.
Box 1371
Madison, CT 06443
(203) 245-2734
Product: Gro Mate minigreenhouses
Catalogue: free

Northern Tier
Box 5083, Sheridan, WY 82801
(800) 443-7467
Product: Window Shelter minigreen
houses
Catalogue: free

Radco
120 Plant Avenue
Wayne, PA 19087
(610) 688-8989
Products: plant shelves
Catalogue: free

Silver Creek Supply
RR 1, Box 70
Port Trevorton, PA 17864
(717) 374-8010
Products: Hot Kaps cold frames
Catalogue: free

Volkmann Brothers Greenhouses
2714 Minert Street
Dallas, TX 75219
(214) 526-3484
Product: plant stands
Catalogue: $1.00

Greenhouse and Propagation Supplies

General Supplies

Alternative Garden Supply, Inc.
297 North Barrington Road
Streamwood, IL 60107
(708) 885-8282
(800) 444-2837
Catalogue: free

American Hydroponics
186 South G Street
Arcata, CA 95521
(800) 458-6543
Catalogue: $1.00

Aqua Culture, Inc.
700 West 1st Street
Tempe, AZ 85281
(800) 633-2137
Catalogue: free

Aquaducts Hydroponics Systems
Box 99
Mill Valley, CA 94942
(415) 388-0838
Catalogue: free

Aqua-Ponics International
121A North Harbor Boulevard
Fullerton, CA 92632
(800) 426-1261
Catalogue: free

Brighton By-Products Company, Inc.
Box 23, New Brighton, PA 15066
(800) 245-3502
Catalogue: free

Cascade Greenhouse Supply
4441 26th Avenue West
Seattle, WA 98199
(206) 428-2626
Catalogue: $2.00

Charley's Greenhouse Supply
1569 Memorial Road
Mount Vernon, WA 98273
(800) 322-4707
Catalogue: free

Chicago Indoor Garden Supply
297 North Barrington Road
Streamwood, IL 60107
(708) 885-8282
Catalogue: free

CropKing, Inc.
Box 310
Medina, OH 44258
(216) 725-5656
(800) 321-5211
Catalogue: free

Eco Enterprises
1240 NE 175th Street
Seattle, WA 98155
(800) 426-6937
Catalogue: free

Foothill Hydroponics
10705 Burbank Boulevard
North Hollywood, CA 91601
(801) 760-0688
Catalogue: free

Garden District
5160 Commerce Drive
Baldwin Park, CA 91706
(800) 677-9977
Catalogue: free

E. C. Geiger, Inc.
Box 285
Harleysville, PA 19438
(800) 443-4437
Catalogue: free

Greentrees Hydroponics
2244 South Santa Fe Avenue
Vista, CA 92084
(619) 598-7551
(800) 772-1997
Catalogue: free

The Growing Experience
1901 NW 18th Street
Pompano Beach, FL 33069
(305) 960-0822
(800) 273-6092
Catalogue: free

Hamilton Technology Corporation
14902 South Figueroa Drive
Gardena, CA 90248
(800) 458-7474
Catalogue: free

Heartland Hydroponics
115 Townline Road
Vernon Hills, IL 60061
(701) 816-4769
Catalogue: free

Hollister's Hydroponics
Box 16601
Irvine, CA 92713
(714) 551-3822
Catalogue: $1.00

Home Harvest Garden Supply, Inc.
13426 Occoquan Road
Woodbridge, VA 22191
(800) 348-4769
Catalogue: free

Hydrofarm Gardening Products
3135 Kerner Boulevard
San Rafael, CA 94901
(800) 634-9999
Catalogue: free

Hydro-Gardens, Inc.
Box 25845
Colorado Springs, CO 80936
(800) 634-6362
Catalogue: free

Indoor Garden Supplies
914 164th Street SE
Mill Creek, WA 98012
(800) 335-4707
Catalogue: free

Indoor Gardening Supplies
Box 40567, Detroit, MI 48240
(313) 426-9080
Catalogue: free

M. A. H.
115 Commerce Drive
Hauppauge, NY 11788
(516) 434-6872
Catalogue: free

New Earth Indoor Garden Center
3623 East Highway 44
Shepherdsville, KY 40165
(800) 462-5953
Catalogue: free

Northwest Agriculture
12414 Highway 99 South
Everett, WA 98204
(800) 335-4707
Catalogue: free

Plant Collectibles
103 Kenview Avenue
Buffalo, NY 14217
(716) 875-1221
Catalogue: $2.00

Rain or Shine
13126 NE Airport Way
Portland, OR 97230
(800) 248-1981
Catalogue: free

Season Extenders
Box 312
971 Nichols Avenue
Stratford, CT 06497
(203) 375-1317
Catalogue: free

Smith Greenhouse & Supply
Box 618
603 14th Street
Mendota, IL 61342
(800) 255-4906
Catalogue: free

Texas Greenhouse Company
2524 White Settlement Road

Fort Worth, TX 76107
(800) 227-5447
Catalogue: $4.00

Worm's Way, Inc.
3151 South Highway 446
Bloomington, IN 47401
(812) 331-0300
(800) 274-9676
Catalogue: free

Specialized Supplies and Products

Aquamonitor
Box 327
Huntington, NY 11743
(516) 427-5664
Product: greenhouse mist
irrigation systems
Catalogue: free

Back To Nature Filtration
3837 Cedarbend Drive
Glendale, CA 91214
(818) 248-7133
Product: reverse osmosis
water purification systems
Catalogue: free

BioTherm Hydronic, Inc.
Box 750967
Petaluma, CA 94975
(800) GET-HEAT
Product: greenhouse heating systems
Catalogue: $2.00

Bramen Company, Inc.
Box 70
Salem, MA 01970
(508) 745-7765
Product: window ventilation controllers
Catalogue: free

Discus Haven Ultra Pure Water Systems
539 Diana Avenue
Morgan Hills, CA 95037

(408) 779-8482
(800) 407-8734
Product: reverse osmosis
water purification systems
Catalogue: free

Eco Enterprises
1240 NE 175th Street
Seattle, WA 98155
(800) 426-6937
Product: liquid nutrient formulas
Catalogue: free

Environmental Concepts
710 SW 57th Street
Fort Lauderdale, FL 33309
(305) 491-4490
Product: greenhouse meters
Catalogue: free

EZ Soil Company
Route 3, Box 176
Idabel, OK 74745
(405) 286-9447
(800) 441-3672
Product: compressed potting mixes
Catalogue: free

Florist Products, Inc.
2242 North Palmer Drive
Schaumburg, IL 60173
(312) 885-2242
Product: Wonder Garden
lighted plant stand
Catalogue: free

GreenTech Environmental Systems
(800) 844-3665
Product: computerized
greenhouse controls
Catalogue: free

Jaybird Manufacturing, Inc.
RD 1, Box 489A
Center Hall, PA 16828
(814) 364-1810

Products: environmental and humidity
control systems
Catalogue: free

Malley Supply
7439 La Palma Avenue, Suite 514
Buena Park, CA 90620
Products: plastic pots and
growing containers
Catalogue: $1.00

Ann Mann's Orchids
9045 Ron-Den Lane
Windermere, FL 34786
(407) 876-2625
Product: micro-foggers
Catalogue: $1.00

Dan Mattern
267 Filbert Street
San Francisco, CA 94133
(415) 781-6066
Product: HERRmidifier greenhouse
humidifiers
Catalogue: free

Northern Greenhouse Sales
Box 42
Neche, ND 58265
(204) 327-5540
Product: polyethylene for greenhouses
Catalogue: $1.00

Plastic Specialties, Ltd.
Box 168
Ventura, IA 50482
(515) 829-4464
Product: plastic trellises for potted plants
Catalogue: free

Retrac Gifts and Collectables
6305 Hoovers Gap Road
Christiana, TN 37037
(615) 896-8449
Product: moisture meter
Catalogue: free

Rodco Products Company, Inc.
2565 16th Avenue
Columbus, NE 68601
(800) 323-2799
Product: temperature monitors
Catalogue: free

Southern Burner Company
Box 885
Chickasha, OK 73023
(405) 224-5000
(800) 375-5001
Product: vented greenhouse heaters
Catalogue: free

Spiral Filtration, Inc.
747 North Twin Oaks Valley Road
San Marcos, CA 92069
(619) 744-3012
Product: reverse osmosis
water purification systems
Catalogue: free

Superior Autovents
17422 La Mesa Lane
Huntington Beach, CA 92647
Product: automatic vent openers
Catalogue: free

Tamarack Technologies, Inc.
Box 490
West Wareham, MA 02576
(800) 222-5932
Products: The Turbulator™ air circulator
Catalogue: free

Yonah Manufacturing Company
Box 280
Cornelia, GA 30531
(800) 972-8057
Product: shade cloth
Catalogue: free

Grow Lights

Diamond Lights
628 Lindaro Street
San Rafael, CA 94901
(800) 331-3994
Catalogue: free

Duro-Lite Lamps, Inc.
9 Law Drive
Fairfield, NJ 07004
(800) 526-7193
Catalogue: free

Energy Technics
3925 Ridgewood Road
York, PA 17402
(717) 755-5642
Catalogue: free

Environmental Lighting Concepts, Inc.
3923 Coconut Palm Drive
Tampa, FL 33619
(800) 842-8848
Product: OTT-Lite®
Catalogue: free

Floralight Gardens
6-620 Supertest Road
North York, Ontario M3J 2M5
(416) 665-4000
(800) 665-4000
Catalogue: free

Full Spectrum Lighting
27 Clover Lane
Burlington, VT 05401
(800) 261-3101
Product: Wonderlite®
Catalogue: free

GTE Sylvania
100 Endicott Street
Danvers, MA 01923
(800) 544-4828
Catalogue: free

Hamilton Technology Corporation
14902 South Figueroa Street
Gardena, CA 90248
(800) 458-7474
Products: metal halide and HPS lights
Catalogue: free

Light Manufacturing Company
1634 SE Brooklyn Street
Portland, OR 97202
(800) NOW-LITE
Catalogue: $3.00

Lumenarc Lighting USA
37 Fairfield Place
West Caldwell, NJ 07006
(800) 845-4815
(800) 8-SODIUM
Products: Super Agro lamp
and other lights
Catalogue: free

Phillips Lighting
Box 200
Somerset, NJ 08875
(201) 563-3000
Products: Son Agro lamps
and other lights
Catalogue: free

Public Service Lamp Corporation
410 West 16th Street
New York, NY 10011
(800) 221-4392
Product: Wonderlite®
Catalogue: free

Verilux, Inc.
Box 2937
Stamford, CT 06906
(203) 921-2430
(800) 786-6850
Product: Verilux® lights
Catalogue: free

Voight Lighting Industries, Inc.
135 Fort Lee Road
Leonia, NJ 07605
(201) 461-2493
Product: lighting fixtures
Catalogue: free

Tools for Gardeners

T HE RIGHT TOOL MAKES any gardening job easier. Most local garden centers carry a reasonably good selection of gardening tools, but the mail-order tool suppliers listed below offer extensive selections that often include hard-to-find specialty items. Also listed are manufacturers and retailers of watering equipment, garden carts, and gardening gloves and clothing.

The decision to purchase a large, expensive item such as a lawn tractor, chipper, or tiller should not be made lightly. The manufacturers listed below will gladly help you make an informed choice by sending you catalogues, brochures, and other information about their products. They will usually refer you to a local dealer for making your purchase.

Hand Tools

Tool Emporiums

Alsto's Handy Helpers
Box 1267
Galesburg, IL 61401
(309) 343-6181
(800) 447-0048
Catalogue: free

American Arborist Supplies, Inc.
882 South Matlack Street
West Chester, PA 19382
(610) 430-1214
(800) 352-3458
Catalogue: $4.00

Berry Hill Limited
75 Burwell Road
St. Thomas, Ontario N5P 3R5
(519) 631-0480
Catalogue: free

Brookstone Hard-to-Find Tools
1655 Bassford Drive
Mexico, MO 65265
(800) 926-7000
Catalogue: free

Denman & Company
187 West Orangethorpe Avenue
Placentia, CA 92670
(714) 524-0668
Catalogue: free

de Van Koek Dutch Traders, Ltd.
9400 Business Drive
Austin, TX 78758
(800) 992-1220
Catalogue: free

The English Garden Emporium
Box 222, Manchester, VT 05254
(800) 347-8130
Catalogue: free

Gardener's Supply Company
128 Intervale Road
Burlington, VT 05401
(800) 863-1700
Catalogue: free

The Garden Pantry
Box 1145
Folsom, CA 95673
(800) 916-3332
Catalogue: free

Gates English Garden Tools
Box 24196
Ventura, CA 93002
(805) 645-5439
Catalogue: free

Harmony Farm Supply
Box 460
3244 Highway 116 North
Graton, CA 95444
(707) 823-9125
Catalogue: $2.00

Kinsman Company, Inc.
River Road
Point Pleasant, PA 18950
(800) 733-4146
Catalogue: free

Langenbach Fine Garden Tools
Box 1140
El Segundo, CA 90245
(800) 362-1991
Catalogue: free

Lee Valley Tools, Ltd.
Box 1780
Ogdensburg, NY 13669
(800) 871-8158
Catalogue: free

Lehman Hardware & Appliances
Box 41
Kidron, OH 44636

(216) 857-5441
Catalogue: $2.00

A. M. Leonard, Inc.
Box 816, Piqua, OH 45356
(513) 773-2694
(800) 543-8955
Catalogue: $1.00

MacKenzie Nursery Supply, Inc.
Box 322
Perry, OH 44081
(216) 259-3004
(800) 777-5030
Catalogue: free

Milestone-Windsor, Ltd.
446 Ellis Place
Wyckoff, NJ 07481
(800) 262-3334
Catalogue: free

MNS, Inc.
3891 Shepard Road
Perry, OH 44081
(800) 777-5030
Catalogue: free

The Natural Gardening Company
217 San Anselmo Avenue
San Anselmo, CA 94960
(415) 456-5060
Catalogue: free

Walt Nicke Company
36 McLeod Lane
Topsfield, MA 01983
(508) 887-3388
(800) 822-4114
Catalogue: free

Niwa Tool Company
2661 Bloomfield Court
Fairfield, CA 94533
(800) 443-5512
Catalogue: $2.00

Peaceful Valley Farm Supply
Box 2209
Grass Valley, CA 95945
(916) 272-4769
Catalogue: free

Seasons Change
19–21 Aubrey Terrace
Malden, MA 02148
(800) 222-0606
Catalogue: free

Smith & Hawken
117 East Strawberry Drive
Mill Valley, CA 94941
(800) 776-3336
Catalogue: free

Vermont Garden Shed
RR 2, Box 180
Wallingford, VT 05773
(800) 288-SHED
Catalogue: free

Specialized Hand Tools

American Standard Company
157 Water Street
Southington, CT 06489
(800) 275-3618
Product: Florian Ratchet-Cut™ pruning
tools
Catalogue: free

Beaco, Inc.
Box 1168, Glenside, PA 19038
Product: Cutly shears
Catalogue: free

Corona Clipper Company
1540 East 6th Street
Corona, CA 91719
(714) 737-6515
(800) 234-CLIP
Product: edged hand tools
Catalogue: free

Craftech Industries
Box 636
Hudson, NY 12534
Product: dibbles
Catalogue: free

Creative Enterprises
Box 3452
Idaho Falls, ID 83403
(800) 388-4539
Product: Wing Weeder tools
Catalogue: free

Edge-a-Lawn Tool Company
Box 7028
Jacksonville, NC 28540
(910) 347-6292
(800) 533-7027
Product: edgers
Catalogue: free

Fiskars®
(800) 500-4849
Products: Softouch™ and Power-Lever®
pruning tools
Catalogue: free

Genuine Ratchet Cut
674 Meriden-Waterbury Road
Southington, CT 06489
(203) 621-2004
Product: ratchet-action pruning tools
Catalogue: free

Handy Forks
6223 Knollwood Road
Springfield, OH 45502
(800) 467-3398
Product: Handy Forks pickup tools
Catalogue: free

Hilltop Enterprises
4 Lisa Court
Red Hook, NY 12571
Product: ratchet-action garden shears
Catalogue: free

Marugg Company
Box 1418
Tracy City, TN 37387
Products: Austrian scythes and cutting
tools
Catalogue: free

MTP
Box 1049
Chino, CA 91710
Product: Handy Rakes pickup tools
Catalogue: free

RMN Sales
Box 666
Jacksonville, OR 97530
(503) 899-7117
Product: Weed Twist weeders
Catalogue: free

Rudon International Trading Company
Box 331104
Fort Worth, TX 76163
(817) 292-8485
Product: EZ-Diggers
Catalogue: free

Snow & Nealley
Bangor, ME 04401
(207) 947-6642
Catalogue: free

Sonoran Horticultural
6049 West Grandview
Glendale, AZ 83506
(602) 843-0027
Product: Shark Saw pruning tools
Catalogue: free

UnionTools
500 Dublin Avenue
Columbus, OH 43216
(614) 222-4400
Product: long-handled tools
Catalogue: free

Valley Oak Tool Company
448 West 2nd Avenue
Chico, CA 95926
(916) 342-6188
Products: wheel hoes; cultivators
Catalogue: free

Wonder Hoe
Box 11618
Prescott, AZ 86304
Product: Wonder Hoe multipurpose tools
Catalogue: free

Power Tillers

Ariens Company
655 West Ryan Street
Brillon, WI 54110
(414) 756-2141
(800) 678-5443
Catalogue: free

BCS America, Inc.
Box 7162
Charlotte, NC 28241
(800) 227-8791
Catalogue: free

Echo, Inc.
400 Oakwood Road
Lake Zurich, IL 60047
(708) 540-8400
(800) 432-3246
Catalogue: free

Hoffco®, Inc.
358 NW F Street
Richmond, IN 47374
(800) 999-8161
Product: Li'L Hoes
Catalogue: free

Homelite
14401 Carowinds Boulevard
Charlotte, NC 28241

(704) 588-3200
Catalogue: free

Honda Power Equipment
4475 River Green Parkway
Duluth, GA 30136
(404) 497-6000
Catalogue: free

Husqvarna Forest and Garden Company
9006 Perimeter Woods Drive
Charlotte, NC 28216
(800) 438-7297
Catalogue: free

Kubota Tractor Corporation
550 West Artesia Boulevard
Compton, CA 90220
(213) 537-2531
Catalogue: free

MacKissic, Inc.
Box 111
Parker Ford, PA 19457
(610) 495-7181
Catalogue: free

Mainline Tillers
Box 526
London, OH 43140
(614) 852-9733
(800) 837-2097
Catalogue: free

Mantis
1028 Street Road
Southampton, PA 18966
(800) 366-6268
Catalogue: free

MTD Yard Machine
Box 368022
Cleveland, OH 44136
(800) 800-7310
Catalogue: free

Poulan Pro
5020 Flournoy-Lucas Road
Shreveport, LA 71129
(318) 687-0100
(800) 554-6723
Catalogue: free

Ryobi America Corporation
5201 Pearman Dairy Road
Anderson, SC 29625
(800) 525-2579
Catalogue: free

Snapper Power Equipment
535 Macon Highway
McDonough, GA 30253
(404) 954-2500
Catalogue: free

Troy-Bilt Manufacturing Company
102nd Street and 9th Avenue
Troy, NY 12180
(800) 828-5500
Catalogue: free

Shredders and Chippers

Atlas Power Equipment Company
Box 70
Harvard, IL 60033
(815) 943-7417
Catalogue: free

Baker™ Corporation
500 North Spring Street
Port Washington, WI 53074
(414) 284-8669
(800) 945-0235
Catalogue: free

BCS America, Inc.
Box 7162
Charlotte, NC 28241
(800) 227-8791
Catalogue: free

Billy Goat Industries, Inc.
Box 308
Lees Summit, MO 64063
(816) 524-9666
Product: The Termite
Catalogue: free

Crary Company
Box 849
West Fargo, ND 58078
(701) 282-5520
(800) 247-7335
Products: Bear Cat™ line
Catalogue: free

Cub Cadet Power Equipment
Box 368023
Cleveland, OH 44136
(216) 273-9723
Catalogue: free

John Deere
Box 29533, Raleigh, NC 27626
(800) 537-8233
Catalogue: free

Easy Rake
1001 South Ransdell Road
Lebanon, IN 46052
(800) 777-6074
Catalogue: free

Echo, Inc.
400 Oakwood Road
Lake Zurich, IL 60047
(708) 540-8400
(800) 432-3246
Catalogue: free

Flowtron Outdoor Products
2 Main Street
Melrose, MA 02176
(617) 321-2300
(800) 343-3280
Product: Leafeater mulcher
Catalogue: free

Goossen Industries
Box 705
Beatrice, NE 68310
(800) 228-6542
Catalogue: free

Ingersoll Equipment Company
Box 5001
Winneconne, WI 54986
(414) 582-5021
Catalogue: free

Kemp Company
160 Koser Road
Lititz, PA 17543
(717) 627-7979
(800) 441-5367
Catalogue: free

Lambert Corporation
117 South 3rd Street
Ansonia, OH 45303
(513) 337-3641
Catalogue: free

Little Wonder
Box 38
Southampton, PA 18966
(215) 357-5110
Catalogue: free

MacKissic, Inc.
Box 111
Parker Ford, PA 19457
(610) 495-7181
Product: Might Mac chippers
Catalogue: free

The Patriot Company
944 North 45th Street
Milwaukee, WI 53208
(800) 798-2447
Catalogue: free

Parker Sweeper Company
Box 1758

Springfield, OH 45501
(513) 323-9420
Products: Minuteman line
Catalogue: free

Roto-Hoe
345 15th Street NW
Barberton, OH 44203
(216) 753-2320
Catalogue: free

Ryobi America Corporation
5201 Pearman Dairy Road
Anderson, SC 29625
(800) 525-2579
Catalogue: free

Salsco, Inc.
105 School House Road
Cheshire, CT 06410
(800) 8-SALSCO
Catalogue: free

Simplicity Manufacturing, Inc.
Box 997
Port Washington, WI 53074
(414) 284-8789
Catalogue: free

Steiner Turf Equipment, Inc.
289 North Kurzen Road
Dalton, OH 44618
(216) 828-0200
Catalogue: free

Tilton Equipment Company
Box 68
Rye, NH 03870
(800) 447-1152
Catalogue: free

Trim-Rite, Inc.
Box 1506
Weatherford, TX 76086
(800) 553-2100
Catalogue: free

Troy-Bilt Manufacturing Company
102nd Street and 9th Avenue
Troy, NY 12180
(800) 828-5500
Catalogue: free

White Outdoor Products Company
Box 361131
Cleveland, OH 44136
(216) 273-7786
(800) 94-WHITE
Catalogue: free

Mowers and Lawn Tractors

Push Mowers

Agri-Fab, Inc.
303 West Raymond Street
Sullivan, IL 61951
(217) 728-8388
Catalogue: free

American Lawn Mower Company/Great
States Corporation
830 Webster Street
Shelbyville, IN 46176
(317) 392-3615
Catalogue: free

McLane Manufacturing, Inc.
7110 East Rosecrans Avenue
Paramount, CA 90723
(213) 633-8158
Catalogue: free

C. K. Petty & Company
203 Wildemere Drive
South Bend, IN 46615
(219) 232-4095
Catalogue: free

Power Mowers and Lawn Tractors

Ariens Company
655 West Ryan Street
Brillon, WI 54110
(414) 756-2141
(800) 678-5443
Catalogue: free

Cub Cadet Power Equipment
Box 368023
Cleveland, OH 44136
(216) 273-9723
Catalogue: free

John Deere
Box 29533
Raleigh, NC 27626
(800) 537-8233
Catalogue: free

The Grasshopper Company
Box 637
Moundridge, KS 67107
(316) 345-8621
Catalogue: free

Gravely International, Inc.
1 Gravely Lane
Clemmons, NC 27012
(919) 766-4721
Catalogue: free

Honda Power Equipment
4475 River Green Parkway
Duluth, GA 30136
(404) 497-6000
Catalogue: free

Husqvarna Forest and Garden Company
9006 Perimeter Woods Drive
Charlotte, NC 28216
(800) 438-7297
Catalogue: free

Ingersoll Equipment Company
Box 5001
Winneconne, WI 54986
(414) 582-5021
Catalogue: free

Kubota Tractor Corporation
550 West Artesia Boulevard
Compton, CA 90220
(213) 537-2531
Catalogue: free

Poulan Pro
5020 Flournoy-Lucas Road
Shreveport, LA 71129
(318) 687-0100
(800) 554-6723
Catalogue: free

Power King Products Company
1100 Green Valley Road
Beaver Dam, WI 53916
(800) 262-1191
Catalogue: free

Simplicity Manufacturing, Inc.
Box 997
Port Washington, WI 53074
(414) 284-8789
Catalogue: free

Snapper Power Equipment
535 Macon Highway
McDonough, GA 30253
(404) 954-2500
Catalogue: free

Steiner Turf Equipment, Inc.
289 North Kurzen Road
Dalton, OH 44618
(216) 828-0200
Catalogue: free

The Toro Company
8111 Lyndale Avenue South
Minneapolis, MN 55420

(612) 888-8801
(800) 321-TORO
Catalogue: free

Walker Manufacturing Company
5925 East Harmony Road
Fort Collins, CO 80525
(303) 221-5614
Catalogue: free

White Outdoor Products Company
Box 361131
Cleveland, OH 44136
(216) 273-7786
(800) 94-WHITE
Catalogue: free

Yard-Man Outdoor Power Products
Box 360940
Cleveland, OH 44136
(216) 273-3600
Catalogue: free

Yazoo Manufacturing Company
3650 Bay Street
Jackson, MS 39206
(800) 354-6562
Catalogue: free

Sprayers

Dramm Corporation
Box 1960
Manitowoc, WI 54221
(414) 684-0227
(800) 258-0808
Catalogue: free

K & G Manufacturing, Inc.
Box 350
Duke, OK 73532
(405) 679-3955
Product: Spray Boss
Catalogue: free

PeCo, Inc.
100 Airport Road
Arden, NC 28704
(704) 684-1234
(800) 438-5823
Catalogue: free

Wheelbarrows and Garden Carts

Carts Vermont
1890 Airport Parkway
South Burlington, VT 05403
(802) 862-6304
Product: garden carts
Catalogue: free

Cart Warehouse
Box 3
Point Arena, CA 95468
(800) 852-2588
Product: garden carts
Catalogue: free

Catamount Cart
Box 365
Shelburne Falls, MA 01370
(413) 625-0284
(800) 444-0056
Product: Catamount garden carts
Catalogue: free

Country Home Products
Box 89
Ferry Road
Charlotte, VT 05445
(800) 641-8008
Product: DR® Powerwagon™
Catalogue: free

DuCART
(800) 360-2278
Product: utility carts
Catalogue: free

Homestead Carts
2396 Perkins Street NE
Salem, OR 97303
(503) 393-3973
(800) 825-1925
Product: Homestead carts
Catalogue: free

Kadco USA
27 Jumel Place
Saratoga Springs, NY 12866
(518) 587-2224
(800) 448-5503
Product: Carry-It garden carts
Catalogue: free

Norway Industries
41 East 9237 Highway O
Sauk City, WI 53583
(608) 544-5000
Product: Carry-All carts
Catalogue: free

Roll'Erg North America, Inc.
970 Golden Hills Road
Colorado Springs, CO 80919
(719) 598-5274
Product: Roll'Erg™ wheelbarrow

S.A.N. Associates, Inc.
Box 88
Greendell, NJ 07839
(908) 852-4612
Product: Big Daddy™ garden caddy
Catalogue: free

Scenic Road Manufacturing
3539 Scenic Road
Gordonville, PA 17529
(717) 768-3364
Product: wheelbarrows
Catalogue: free

True Engineering, Inc.
999 Roosevelt Trail
Windham, ME 04062

(207) 892-0200
Product: Muller's Smart Carts
Catalogue: free

WheelAround Corporation
241 Grandview Avenue
Bellevue, KY 41073
(800) 335-CART
Product: WheelAround® carts
Catalogue: free

Wisconsin Wagon Co.
507 Laurel Avenue
Janesville, WI 53545
(608) 754-0026
Products: wagons and wheelbarrows
Catalogue: free

Watering Supplies

Ames
Box 1774
Parkersburg, WV 26102
(304) 424-3000
(800) 624-2654
Products: hoses and hose reels
Catalogue: fee

Aquapore Moisture Systems
610 South 80th Avenue
Phoenix, AZ 85043
(800) 635-8379
Product: Moisture Master™ soaker hoses
Catalogue: free

D. I. G. Corporation
130 Bosstick Boulevard
San Marcos, CA 92082
(619) 727-0914
(800) 322-9146
Product: drip irrigation supplies
Catalogue: free

Dramm Corporation
Box 1960

Manitowoc, WI 54221
(414) 684-0227
(800) 258-0808
Products: Dramm Water Breaker
nozzles; watering cans
Catalogue: free

Dripworks-Everliner
380 Maple Street
Willits, CA 95490
(707) 459-6323
(800) 522-3747
Product: drip irrigation systems
Catalogue: free

Environmental Concepts, Inc.
710 NW 57th Street
Fort Lauderdale, FL 33309
(305) 491-4490
Product: moisture meters
Catalogue: free

Gardener's Supply Company
128 Intervale Road
Burlington, VT 05401
(800) 863-1700
Product: drip irrigation supplies
Catalogue: free

Gilmour Manufacturing Company
Box 838
Somerset, PA 15501
(814) 443-4802
(800) 458-0107
Product: Flexogen hoses
Catalogue: free

The Great American Rain Barrel
Company, Inc.
295 Maverick Street
East Boston, MA 02120
(617) 569-3690
(800) 251-2352
Product: plastic rain barrels
Catalogue: free

Grosoke, Inc.
7415 Whitehall Street
Fort Worth, TX 76118
(817) 284-0696
(800) 522-0696
Product: Agrosoke hydrogels
Catalogue: free

Harmony Farm Supply
3244 Highway 116 North
Graton, CA 95444
(707) 823-9125
Product: drip irrigation supplies
Catalogue: $2.00

International Irrigation Systems
Box 360
Niagara Falls, NY 14304
(905) 688-4090
Product: IRRIGRO® drip
irrigation systems
Catalogue: free

Janziker
Box 957
Davis, CA 95617
Product: SuperSorb water-absorbing
crystals
Catalogue: free

Jasco Distributing
Box 520
Lancaster, NH 03584
(603) 788-4744
Product: Aqua Spike slow-release
watering reservoirs
Catalogue: free

Magnalawn 2000
2935 Bayberry Road
Hatboro, PA 19040
(800) 699-1102
Product: Magnalawn 2000®
water purification devices
Catalogue: free

Multiple Concepts
Box 4248
Chattanooga, TN 37405
(615) 266-3967
Product: Moisture Mizer hydrogels
Catalogue: long SASE with two stamps

Northern Tier
Box 5083
Sheridan, WY 82801
(800) 443-7467
Product: Big Dripper™ tank drip
irrigation systems
Catalogue: free

Plant Collectibles
103 Kenview Avenue
Buffalo, NY 14217
(716) 875-1221
Products: Aquamatic hose waterers;
nozzles
Catalogue: $2.00

Plastic Plumbing Products, Inc.
Box 186
Grover, MO 63040
(314) 458-2226
Product: drip irrigation supplies
Catalogue: $1.00

Rain Control
Box 662
Adrian, MI 49221
(517) 263-5226
Product: Irri-Gator drip irrigation systems
Catalogue: free

Raindrip, Inc.
2250 Agate Court
Simi Valley, CA 93065
(800) 367-3747
(800) 544-3747
Product: drip irrigation systems
Catalogue: free

Submatic Irrigation Systems
Box 246
Lubbock, TX 79408
(800) 692-4100
Product: drip irrigation supplies
Catalogue: free

Swan Garden Hose
Box 509
Worthington, OH 43085
(614) 548-6511
Product: Perfect Gardener hoses
Catalogue: free

Teknor Apex Company
Pawtucket, RI 02861
(800) 556-3864
Product: garden hoses
Catalogue: free

TFS Injector Systems
211 West Maple Avenue
Monrovia, CA 91016
(818) 358-5507
Product: drip irrigation supplies
Catalogue: long SASE

Universal Products
Box 4293, Reading, PA 19606
Product: garden hose guides
Catalogue: free

The Urban Farmer Store
2833 Vicente Street
San Francisco, CA 94116
(415) 661-2204
Product: drip irrigation systems
Catalogue: $1.00

Wade Manufacturing Company
Box 23666
Portland, OR 97281
(800) 222-7246
Product: Acu-Drip® System EZ
drip irrigation systems
Catalogue: free

Waterboy Garden Trellis
23 McKinley Street
Uniontown, PA 15401
Product: self-watering garden trellises
Catalogue: free

Watermiser Drip Irrigation
Box 18157
Reno, NV 89511
(800) 332-1570
Product: drip irrigation supplies
Catalogue: free

Witherspoon-Pike Enterprises, Inc.
Box 51655
Durham, NC 27717
(800) 643-0315
Product: Shur-Flo™ water savers
Catalogue: free

Clothing and Gloves

Calo Enterprises
4625 Broadway
Union City, NJ 07087
Product: gloves
Catalogue: free

Carolina Glove Company
Drawer 820
Newton, NC 28658
(704) 464-1132
(800) 438-6888
Product: gardening gloves
Catalogue: free

Clothcrafters, Inc.
Box 176
Elkhart Lake, WI 53020
(414) 876-2112
Products: gloves; aprons
Catalogue: free

Denman & Company
187 West Orangethorpe Avenue
Placentia, CA 92670
(714) 524-0668
Product: Greenknee™ gardening trousers
Catalogue: free

Little's Good Gloves
Box 808
Johnstown, NY 12095
(518) 736-5014
Product: gardening gloves
Catalogue: free

MN Productions
Box 577
Freeland, WA 98249
(206) 331-7995
Product: Iron-Neezers™
gardening trousers
Catalogue: free

Womanswork
Box 543
York, ME 03909
(207) 363-0804
Product: gardening gloves
Catalogue: free

Composting, Fertilizers, and Soil Care

T AKING GOOD CARE *of your garden soil pays off handsomely in stronger, healthier plants with better blooms. Adding compost to your soil is an inexpensive, ecologically sound way to add nutrients and improve the tilth. The retailers and manufacturers below sell composters, composting supplies, organic fertilizers, and other organic supplies. For the sake of completeness, some manufacturers of chemical fertilizers and plant foods are also listed. Soil-testing laboratories, which can provide detailed information about your soil, end the listings.*

Organic Supplies Emporiums

Bozeman Bio-Tech, Inc.
Box 3146
Bozeman, MT 59772
(800) 289-6656
Catalogue: free

Charley's Greenhouse Supply
1569 Memorial Highway
Mount Vernon, WA 98273
(800) 322-4707
Catalogue: free

Gardener's Supply Company
128 Intervale Road
Burlington, VT 05401
(800) 863-1700
Catalogue: free

Garden-Ville of Austin
8648 Old Bee Cave Road

Austin, TX 78735
(512) 288-6115
(800) 320-0724
Catalogue: free

Harmony Farm Supply
Box 460, 3244 Highway 116 North
Graton, CA 95444
(707) 823-9125
Catalogue: $2.00

Peaceful Valley Farm Supply
Box 2209
Grass Valley, CA 95945
(916) 272-4769
Catalogue: free

Richters
357 Highway 47
Goodwood, Ontario L0C 1A0
(416) 640-6677
Catalogue: $2.00

Worm's Way, Inc.
3151 South Highway 446
Bloomington, IN 47401
(812) 331-0300
(800) 274-9676
Catalogue: free

Composters

A & N Enterprises
Box 537
Bethany, OK 73008
Product: composter construction plans
Catalogue: free

Blue Planet, Ltd.
Box 1500
Princeton, NJ 08542
(800) 777-9201
Product: Composift composters
Catalogue: free

Compost and Recycling Systems
Box 265
Fox River Grove, IL 60021
(800) 848-3829
Product: The Composter
Catalogue: free

Gardner Equipment Company
(800) 393-0333
Product: No-Turn™ composters
Catalogue: free

Gear Up Technologies Corporation
12900 Eckel Junction Road
Perrysburg, OH 43551
Product: The Compost Corral™
composters
Catalogue: free

Home Gardener Manufacturing
Company
30 Wright Avenue
Lititz, PA 17543

(800) 880-2345
Product: ComposTumbler® composters
Catalogue: free

Kemp Company
160 Koser Road
Lititz, PA 17543
(717) 627-7979
(800) 441-5367
Product: compost tumblers
Catalogue: free

Master Garden Products, Inc.
(800) 949-6620
Product: Mulch Master® composters
Catalogue: free

Morco Products
Box 160
Dundas, MN 55019
(507) 645-4277
Product: Turn Easy composters
Catalogue: free

Nature's Backyard, Inc.
126 Duchaine Boulevard
New Bedford, MA 02745
(800) 853-2525
Product: Brave New Composter
Catalogue: free

Northwest Toolbox
12808 North Point Lane
Laurel, MD 20708
(301) 604-0090
Product: aerobic composting systems
Catalogue: free

Palmor Products
Box 38
Thorntown, IN 46071
(800) 872-2822
Product: rotary composters
Catalogue: free

Rivendell Company
Box 174
Old Saybrook, CT 06475
(800) 690-0899
Product: The Best Little Composter in
America®
Catalogue: free

Solarcone, Inc.
Box 67
Seward, IL 61077
(815) 247-8454
(800) 80-SOLAR
Product: The Green Keeper™
composters
Catalogue: free

The Toro Company
8111 Lyndale Avenue South
Minneapolis, MN 55420
(612) 888-8801
(800) 321-TORO
Product: YardCycler™ composters
Catalogue: free

Tumblebug
2029 North 23rd Street
Boise, ID 83702
(800) 531-0102
Product: Tumblebug® rolling composters
Catalogue: free

Composting Supplies

Bronwood Worm Gardens
Box 28
Bronwood, GA 31726
(912) 995-5994
Product: redworms
Catalogue: long SASE

Cape Cod Worm Farm
30 Center Avenue
Buzzards Bay, MA 02532
(508) 759-5664

Product: redworms
Catalogue: free

The Crafter's Garden
Box 3194
Peabody, MA 01961
(508) 535-1142
Product: composting supplies
Catalogue: free

Morning Mist Worm Farm
Box 1155
Davis, CA 95617
(707) 448-6836
Product: redworms
Catalogue: free

Ratskee Worm Farm
Box 764
Bolinas, CA 94924
(415) 868-9556
Product: redworms
Catalogue: free

Smith Worms
Boston, GA 31626
(912) 498-1605
Product: redworms
Catalogue: free

The Worm Czar
Amherst Junction, WI 54407
(715) 824-3868
Product: redworms
Catalogue: long SASE with two stamps

Organic Fertilizers

Age-Old Organics
Box 1556
Boulder, CO 80306
(303) 499-0201
Catalogue: free

A Natural Way to Grow
39 East Main Street
Sykesville, PA 15865
(800) 685-4769
Catalogue: free

Arbico, Inc.
Box 4247
Tucson, AZ 85712
(602) 825-9785
(800) 827-2847
Catalogue: free

Astoria-Pacific, Inc.
Box 830
Clackamas, OR 97015
(800) 536-3111
Product: Dip 'n Grow® rooting
hormones
Catalogue: free

Avant Horticultural Products
5755 Balfrey Drive
West Palm Beach, FL 33414
(800) 334-7979
Product: reacted liquid plant foods
Catalogue: free

Bio-Gard Agronomics
Box 4477
Falls Church, VA 22044
(800) 673-8502
Product: foliar fertilizers
Catalogue: free

BioResource Recovery Systems, Inc.
Box 255
Lone Tree, IA 52755
(319) 629-4407
(800) 299-1898
Catalogue: free

Cape Cod Worm Farm
30 Center Avenue
Buzzards Bay, MA 02532
(508) 759-5664

Product: worm castings
Catalogue: free

Cotton, Inc.
Box 30067
Raleigh, NC 27622
Product: cottonseed meal
Catalogue: free

Dirt Cheap Organics
5645 Paradise Drive
Corte Madera, CA 94925
(415) 924-0369
Catalogue: free

Earlee, Inc.
2002 Highway 62
Jeffersonville, IN 47130
(812) 282-9134
Catalogue: free

Elgin Landscape and Garden Center
1881 Larkin Avenue
Elgin, IL 60123
(708) 697-8733
Catalogue: $2.00

EnP, Inc.
Box 618
Mendota, IL 61342
(800) 255-4906
Catalogue: free

Erth-Rite, Inc.
RD 1, Box 243
Gap, PA 17527
(717) 442-4171
Catalogue: free

Gardens Alive!
5100 Schenley Place
Lawrenceburg, IN 47025
(812) 537-8650
Catalogue: free

Green Growers Supply
Box 3168
Framingham, MA 01701
Product: liquid fish fertilizers
Catalogue: free

Guano Company International, Inc.
3562 East 80th Street
Cleveland, OH 44105
(216) 641-1200
(800) 424-8266
Product: seabird guano
Catalogue: free

Integrated Fertility Management
333 Ohme Gardens Road
Wenatchee, WA 98801
(509) 662-3179
(800) 332-3179
Catalogue: free

Johnny's Selected Seeds
Foss Hill Road
Albion, ME 04910
(207) 437-9294
Catalogue: free

Liquid Fish, Inc.
Box 99
Bonduel, WI 54107
(715) 758-2280
(800) 448-2280
Catalogue: free

Maestro-Gro
Box 6670
Springdale, AR 72766
(501) 361-9155
Catalogue: free

Milorganite
Box 3049
Milwaukee, WI 53201
(414) 225-2222
Catalogue: free

Mother Nature's Worm Castings
Box 1055
Avon, CT 06001
(203) 673-3029
Product: worm castings
Catalogue: long SASE

Natural Products, Inc.
1000 Oak Street
Grinnell, IA 50112
(800) 238-4634
Product: alfalfa meal
Catalogue: free

The Necessary Trading Company
1 Natures Way
New Castle, VA 24127
(703) 864-5103
Product: CONCERN® plant foods
Catalogue: free

New Earth
3623 East Highway 44
Shepherdsville, KY 40165
(800) 462-5953
Catalogue: free

Nitron Industries, Inc.
Box 1447
Fayetteville, AR 72702
(800) 835-0123
Catalogue: $1.00

North American Kelp
Box 279A
Waldoboro, ME 04572
(207) 832-7506
Product: seaweed fertilizers
Catalogue: free

Ohio Earth Food, Inc.
5488 Swamp Street NE
Hartville, OH 44632
(216) 877-9356
Catalogue: free

Primary Products
100E Tower Office Park
Woburn, MA 01801
(617) 932-8509
Product: MegaBoost™ growth stimulants
Catalgue: free

Rainbow Red Worms
Box 278
Lake Elsinor, CA 92531
(909) 674-7041
Product: worm castings
Catalogue: free

Saltwater Farms
102 South Freeport Road
Freeport, ME 04032
(207) 865-9066
(800) 293-KELP
Product: seaweed fertilizers
Catalogue: free

Sea Born/Lane, Inc.
Box 204
Charles City, IA 50616
(800) 457-5013
Product: seaweed fertilizers
Catalogue: free

Spray-N-Grow, Inc.
20 Highway 35 South
Rockport, TX 78382
(512) 790-9033
Product: Spray-N-Grow growth stimulants
Catalogue: free

Territorial Seed Company
Box 157
Cottage Grove, OR 97424
(503) 942-9547
Catalogue: free

Chemical Fertilizers

Crystal Company
Box 220055
St. Louis, MO 63122
(314) 966-5999
(800) 845-4777
Product: Throw & Grow™ plant foods
Catalogue: free

Dyna-Gro™ Corporation
1065 Broadway
San Pablo, CA 94806
(800) DYNA-GRO
Product: Dyna-Gro™ nutrient formulas
Catalogue: free

JRP International, Inc.
17 Forest Avenue
fond du Lac, WI 54936
Product: Nutri-Pak® time-release fertilizer packets

Miracle-Gro
(800) 4-PRO-SOL
Product: Pro-Sol Plant Food
Catalogue: free

Schultz Company
14090 Riverport Drive
St. Louis, MO 63043
(314) 298-3045
(800) 325-3045
Product: Schultz-Instant fertilizers

Wilt-Pruf® Products, Inc.
Box 469
Essex, CT 06426
Product: Wilt-Pruf® antitranspirants

Soil-Testing Laboratories

Inexpensive home soil-testing kits are easily available at any garden center, but they usually test only for the pH of your soil. While knowing the acidity or alkalinity of your soil is an important first step, more extensive testing is needed to get detailed information about nutrient levels and recommendations for soil amendments. Your local USDA extension agent (see chapter 9) can provide some additional testing, usually for a nominal fee. For thorough testing and recommendations, try one of the professional soil-testing laboratories listed below.

A & L Analytical Laboratories, Inc.
411 North Third Street
Memphis, TN 38105
(901) 527-2780

A & L Eastern Agricultural
Laboratories, Inc.
7621 Whitepine Road
Richmond, VA 23237
(804) 743-9401

Biosystem Consultants
Box 43
Lorane, OR 97451

Cook's Consulting
RD 2, Box 13
Lowville, NY 13367
(315) 376-3002

Harmony Farm Supply
Box 460
3244 Highway 116 North
Graton, CA 95472
(707) 823-9125

Integrated Fertility Management
333 Ohme Gardens Road
Wenatchee, WA 98801
(509) 662-3179
(800) 332-3179

LaRamie Soils Service
Box 255
Laramie, WY 82070
(307) 742-4185

Ohio Earth Food, Inc.
5488 Swamp Street, NE
Hartville, OH 44632
(216) 877-9356

Peaceful Valley Farm Supply
Box 2209
Grass Valley, CA 95945
(916) 272-4769

Timberleaf
5569 State Street
Albany, OH 45710
(614) 698-3861

Wallace Laboratories
365 Coral Circle
El Segundo, CA 90245
(310) 615-0116

Pest and Weed Control

D*AMAGING INSECTS, hungry deer, and weeds are all constant headaches for gardeners. Environmentally aware gardeners prefer to deal with these and other pests through nonchemical means. Many harmful insects, for example, can be controlled by introducing their natural insect predators to your garden. The retailers and manufacturers listed below sell beneficial insects, landscape fabrics, and other supplies for controlling garden pests. For the sake of completeness, the manufacturers of some popular herbicides and insecticides are listed as well. Although there are some rare instances when use of these products may be justified, their drawbacks almost always far outweigh their advantages. Responsible home gardeners should consider carefully before applying chemical herbicides and pesticides.*

Beneficial Insects

Publications

The Bio-Integral Resource Center
Box 7414
Berkeley, CA 94707
(415) 524-2567
Products: IPM publications
and newsletters
Catalogue: free

Sources

A Natural Way to Grow
39 East Main Street
Sykesville, PA 15865
(800) 685-4769
Catalogue: free

Arbico, Inc.
Box 4247
Tucson, AZ 85712

(602) 825-9785
(800) 827-2847
Catalogue: free

Bob Bauer
311 Ford Road
Howell, NJ 07731
Product: praying mantis egg clusters
Catalogue: free

The Beneficial Insect Company
244 Forrest Street
Fort Mill, SC 29715
(803) 547-2301
Catalogue: free

Beneficial Resources, Inc.
Box 34
Turbotville, PA 17772
(717) 649-6289
Catalogue: free

Better Yield Insects
RR 3, Site 4, Box 48
Belle River, Ontario N5P 3R5
(519) 727-6108
Catalogue: $1.00

BioLogic
Box 177
Springtown Road
Willow Hill, PA 17271
(717) 349-2789
Product: nematodes
Catalogue: long SASE

Biological Control of Weeds
1418 Maple Drive
Bozeman, MT 59715
(406) 586-5111
Catalogue: free

Biosys
1057 East Meadow Circle
Palo Alto, CA 94303
(800) 821-8448
Product: nematodes
Catalogue: free

Bozeman Bio-Tech, Inc.
Box 3146
Bozeman, MT 59772
(800) 289-6656
Catalogue: free

The Bug Store
4472 Shaw Boulevard
St. Louis, MO 63110
(314) 773-7374
Catalogue: free

Charley's Greenhouse Supply
1569 Memorial Highway
Mount Vernon, WA 98273
(800) 322-4707
Catalogue: free

Cyline Biotic
Box 48
Goodyears Bar, CA 95944
(916) 289-3122
Product: ladybugs
Catalogue: free

Dirt Cheap Organics
5645 Paradise Drive
Corte Madera, CA 94925
(415) 924-0369
Catalogue: free

Foothill Agricultural Research, Inc.
510½ West Chase Drive
Corona, CA 91720
(714) 371-0120
Catalogue: free

GB Systems, Inc.
Box 19497
Boulder, CO 80308
(303) 863-1700
Catalogue: free

Gardener's Supply Co.
128 Intervale Road
Burlington, VT 05401
(800) 873-1700
Catalogue: free

Garden-Ville of Austin
8648 Old Bee Cave Road
Austin, TX 78735
(512) 288-6115
(800) 320-0724
Catalogue: free

Gardens Alive!
5100 Schenley Place
Lawrenceburg, IN 47025
(812) 537-8650
Catalogue: free

Great Lakes IPM
10220 Church Road NE

Vestaburg, MI 48891
(517) 268-5693
Catalogue: free

The Green Spot
93 Priest Road
Barrington, NH 03825
(603) 942-8925
Catalogue: $2.00

Harmony Farm Supply
Box 460
3244 Highway 116 North
Graton, CA 95444
(707) 823-9125
Catalogue: $2.00

Hydro-Gardens, Inc.
Box 25845
Colorado Springs, CO 80936
(800) 634-6362
Catalogue: free

Integrated Fertility Management
333 Ohme Gardens Road
Wenatchee, WA 98801
(509) 662-3179
(800) 332-3179
Catalogue: free

IPM Laboratories, Inc.
Box 300, Locke, NY 13092
(315) 497-2063
Catalogue: free

Johnny's Selected Seeds
Foss Hill Road
Albion, ME 04910
(207) 437-9294
Catalogue: free

Kunafin Trichogramma
Route 1, Box 39
Quemado, TX 78877
(800) 832-1113
Catalogue: free

The Lady Bug Company
8706 Oro-Quincy Highway
Berry Creek, CA 95916
(916) 589-5227
Catalogue: free

Land Steward
434 Lower Road
Souderton, PA 18964
Catalogue: free

M & R Durango
Box 886
Bayfield, CO 81122
(303) 259-3521
Catalogue: free

Natural Insect Control
RR 2
Stevensville, Ontario L0S 1S0
(905) 382-2904
Catalogue: $1.00

Nature's Alternative Insectary, Ltd.
Box 19, Dawson
Nanoose Bay, British Coumbia V0R 2R0
(604) 468-7912
Catalogue: free

Nature's Control
Box 35
Medford, OR 97501
(503) 899-8318
Catalogue: free

The Necessary Trading Company
1 Natures Way
New Castle, VA 24127
(703) 864-5103
Catalogue: free

Ohio Earth Food, Inc.
5488 Swamp Street NE
Hartville, OH 44632
(216) 877-9356
Catalogue: free

Organic Control, Inc.
Box 781147
Los Angeles, CA 90016
(213) 937-7444
Catalogue: free

Peaceful Valley Farm Supply
Box 2209
Grass Valley, CA 95945
(916) 272-4769
Catalogue: free

Pest Management Supply
311 River Drive
Hadley, MA 01035
(800) 272-7672
Catalogue: free

Richters
357 Highway 47
Goodwood, Ontario L0C 1A0
(416) 640-6677
Catalogue: $2.00

Rincon-Vitova Insectaries, Inc.
Box 95
Oak View, CA 93022
(800) 248-2847
Catalogue: free

Territorial Seed Company
Box 157
Cottage Grove, OR 97424
(503) 942-9547
Catalogue: free

Unique Insect Control
5504 Sperry Drive
Citrus Heights, CA 95621
(916) 961-7945
Catalogue: free

Worm's Way, Inc.
3151 South Highway 446
Bloomington, IN 47401
(812) 331-0300

(800) 274-9676
Catalogue: free

Insect Control

*Many of the beneficial insect companies listed
above also sell pheromone traps for insect control.
The companies listed below sell additional insect
control products.*

Bargyla Rateaver
9049 Covina Street
San Diego, CA 92126
(619) 566-8994
Product: organic pesticides
Catalogue: long SASE

Bonide Products, Inc.
2 Wurz Avenue
Yorkville, NY 13495
(315) 736-8233
Product: organic pesticides
Catalogue: $2.00

Dow Elanco
9002 Purdue Road
Indianapolis, IN 46268
(317) 875-8618
Product: Dursban insecticides
Catalogue: free

Enviro-Chem, Inc.
Box 1298
Walla Walla, WA 99362
(800) 247-9011
Product: Slug-Fest slug and snail control
Catalogue: free

Fairfax Biological Laboratory, Inc.
Box 300
Clinton Corners, NY 12514
(914) 266-3705
Product: organic pest control for
Japanese beetles
Catalogue: free

Garlic Research Labs
3550 Wilshire Boulevard
Los Angeles, CA 90010
(800) 424-7990
Product: garlic liquid insect repellents
Catalogue: free

Great Lakes IPM
10220 Church Road NE
Vestaburg, MI 48891
(517) 268-5911
Products: insect traps and pheromones
Catalogue: free

Naturally Scientific
726 Holcomb Bridge Road
Norcross, GA 30071
(800) 248-9970
Products: slug and snail baits
Catalogue: free

Phero Tech, Inc.
7572 Progress Way
Delta, British Columbia V4G 1E9
Products: insect traps and pheromones
Catalogue: free

Slugbuster™
827 Albemarle Avenue
Cuyahoga Falls, OH 44221
(216) 923-0631
Products: slug and snail killers
Catalogue: free

Sterling International, Inc.
Box 220
Liberty Lake, WA 99019
(800) 666-6766
Products: Rescue! insect control products
Catalogue: free

Bird Control

Bird-X
(800) 662-5021

Product: bird repellents
Catalogue: free

InterNet, Inc.
2730 Nevada Avenue North
Minneapolis, MN 55427
(800) 328-8456
Product: bird netting
Catalogue: free

Reed-Joseph International
Box 894
Greenville, MS 38702
(800) 647-5554
Product: bird frightening balloons
Catalogue: free

Rice Lake Products
100 27th Street NE
Minot, ND 58701
(800) 998-7450
Product: scare owls
Catalogue: free

The Tanglefoot Company
314 Straight Avenue SW
Grand Rapids, MI 49504
(616) 459-4139
Products: crawling insect and
animal protectants
Catalogue: free

Deer Control

Benner's Gardens
6974 Upper York Road
New Hope, PA 18938
(800) 753-4660
Product: mesh barriers
Catalogue: free

Bobbex, Inc.
52 Hattertown Road
Newtown, CT 06470
(203) 426-9696

Product: foliar repellent sprays
Catalogue: free

Burlington Scientific Corporation
222 Sherwood Avenue
Farmingdale, NY 11735
(516) 694-9000
Product: Ro-Pel animal repellents
Catalogue: free

Bye Deer
Stoll Road Associates
Box 1223
Woodstock, NY 12498
Product: deer repellents
Catalogue: free

Deer-B-Gone
Leticia Duenas
Box 4195
Santa Rosa, CA 95402
(707) 829-5872
Product: deer repellent containers
Catalogue: free

Deerbusters
(800) 248-DEER
Product: deer repellents
Catalogue: free

Deer No No
Box 112
West Cornwall, CT 06796
(800) 484-7107
Product: deer repellents
Catalogue: free

IntAgra, Inc.
8500 Pillsbury Avenue South
Minneapolis, MN 55420
(612) 881-5535
(800) 468-2472
Product: Deer-Away^{TM} deer repellents
Catalogue: free

Tenax Corporation
8291 Patuxent Range Road
Jessup, MD 20794
(301) 725-5910
(800) 356-8495
Product: Tenax$^{®}$ deer fencing
Catalogue: free

Uniroyal Chemical Company, Inc.
Benson Road
Middlebury, CT 06749
(203) 573-2000
Product: Hinder$^{®}$ deer and rabbit
repellents
Catalogue: free

Varmint Guard
Box 8317
Portland, ME 04104
Product: deer repellents
Catalogue: free

Fungus Control

Source Technology Biologicals, Inc.
(800) 356-8733
Products: Phyton$^{®}$ 27 bactericides
and fungicides
Catalogue: free

Weed Control

AgrEvo Environmental Health
95 Chestnut Ridge Road
Montvale, NJ 07645
(800) 843-1702
Product: Finale^{TM} and InterCept H&G^{TM}
weed killers
Catalogue: free

Agri-Tex, Inc.
Box 1106
Danbury, CT 06813
(800) 243-0989

Product: MagicMat™landscape fabrics
Catalogue: free

American Agrifabrics, Inc.
1122D Cambridge Square
Alpharetta, GA 30201
(404) 664-7820
Product: landscape fabrics
Catalogue: free

DeWitt®
Route 3, Box 31
Sikeston, MO 63801
(800) 888-9669
Product: landscape fabrics
Catalogue: free

Dow Elanco
9002 Purdue Road
Indianapolis, IN 46268
(317) 875-8618
Product: Team and Gallery herbicides
Catalogue: free

Easy Gardener, Inc.
Box 21025
Waco, TX 76702
(817) 753-5353
(800) 327-9462
Product: landscape fabrics
Catalogue: free

Greenview®
1600 East Cumberland
Lebanon, PA 17042
(800) 233-0626
Product: Preen® weed preventers
Catalogue: free

Landmaster Products, Inc.
2395 West 4th Avenue
Denver, CO 80222
(303) 571-4636
Product: landscape fabrics
Catalogue: free

Monsanto Company
(800) 225-2883
Product: Roundup® weed killers
Catalogue: free

Reemay, Inc.
Box 511
Old Hickory, TN 37138
(800) 321-6271
Product: Typar landscape fabrics
Catalogue: free

Warp Brothers
4647 West Augusta Boulevard
Chicago, IL 60651
(312) 261-5200
(800) 621-3345
Product: No-Hoe landscape fabrics
Catalogue: free

Garden Furnishings

GARDEN FURNISHINGS are every bit as important to an enjoyable garden as the plants. An artfully placed garden bench or other ornament can add just the right touch; arbors and trellises can add height and interest. The retailers and manufacturers listed below sell garden furnishings and ornaments of all sorts, including benches, trellises, arbors, gazebos, lights, fencing, and plant markers.

Garden Furnishings Emporiums

Alsto's Handy Helpers
Box 1267
Galesburg, IL 61401
(309) 343-6181
(800) 447-0048
Catalogue: free

A Proper Garden
225 South Water Street
Wilmington, NC 28401
(800) 626-7177
Catalogue: $1.00

The Decorated Garden
5850 Bowcroft Street
Los Angeles, CA 90016
(310) 815-1077
Catalogue: free

The English Garden Emporium
Box 222
Manchester, VT 05254
(800) 347-8130
Catalogue: free

The Garden Concepts Collection
Box 241233
Memphis, TN 38124
(901) 756-1649
Catalogue: $5.00

Gardeners Eden
Box 7037
San Francisco, CA 94120
(800) 822-9600
Catalogue: free

The Garden Pantry
Box 1145
Folsom, CA 95673
(800) 916-3332
Catalogue: free

David Kay Garden & Gift Catalog
1 Jenni Lane
Peoria, IL 61614
(800) 535-9917
Catalogue: free

Kinsman Company
River Road
Point Pleasant, PA 18950

(800) 733-5613
Catalogue: free

Kenneth Lynch & Sons, Inc.
Box 488, Wilton, CT 06897
(203) 762-8363
Catalogue: $10.00

The Plow & Hearth
Box 830
Orange, VA 22960
(800) 627-1712
Catalogue: free

Elizabeth Schumacher's Garden Accents
4 Union Hill Road
West Conshohocken, PA 19428
(610) 825-5525
(800) 296-5525
Catalogue: $3.00

Smith & Hawken
25 Corte Madera
Mill Valley, CA 94941
(415) 383-2000
Catalogue: free

Winterthur Museum & Gardens
100 Enterprise Place
Dover, DE 19901
(800) 767-0500
Catalogue: free

Gazebos and Other Garden Structures

Bow Bends™
Box 900
Bolton, MA 01740
(508) 779-2271
Products: gazebos and follies
Catalogue: $3.00

Dalton Pavilions, Inc.
20 Commerce Drive
Telford, PA 18969

(215) 721-1492
Product: red cedar garden pavilions
Catalogue: free

Garden Structures
5603 Friendly Avenue, Suite 102
Greensboro, NC 27410
Product: garden shed plans
Catalogue: free

Heritage Garden Houses
311 Seymour Avenue
Lansing, MI 48933
(517) 372-3385
Products: gazebos and other
garden structures
Catalogue: $3.00

Ivywood Gazebos
Box 9
Fairview Village, PA 19403
(215) 584-0206
Product: gazebos
Catalogue: $3.00

Oregon Timberframe
1389 Highway 99 North
Eugene, OR 97402
(503) 688-4940
Products: gazebos and other
garden structures
Catalogue: free

Vintage Wood Works
Box R
Quinlan, TX 78624
(903) 356-2158
Product: Victorian gazebos
Catalogue: $2.00

Vixen Hill Manufacturing Company
Main Street
Elverson, PA 19520
(800) 423-2766
Product: gazebos
Catalogue: $4.00

Arbors, Arches, and Trellises

Anderson Design
Box 4057
Bellingham, WA 98227
(800) 947-7697
Products: red cedar arbors and trellises
Catalogue: $2.00

Architectural Brick Paving, Ltd.
1187 Wilmette Avenue
Wilmette, IL 60091
(708) 256-8432
Product: copper trellises
Catalogue: free

Bow Bends™
Box 900
Bolton, MA 01740
(508) 779-2271
Product: arbors
Catalogue: $3.00

Cross Industries, Inc.
3174 Marjan Drive
Atlanta, GA 30340
(770) 451-4531
(800) 521-9878
Product: vinyl arbors
Catalogue: free

Dr. TLC Greenthumb
1935 Yosemite Street
Denver, CO 80220
(303) 756-5286
Product: topiary frames
Catalogue: $1.00

Dulik Manufacturing
23 McKinley Street
Uniontown, PA 15401
Product: Waterboy trellises
Catalogue: free

Cliff Finch's Zoo
Box 54

Friant, CA 93626
(209) 822-2315
Product: topiary frames
Catalogue: SASE

French Wyres
Box 131655
Tyler, TX 75713
(903) 597-8322
Products: trellises and topiary frames
Catalogue: $3.00

Garden Architecture
719 South 17th Street
Philadelphia, PA 19146
(215) 545-5442
Product: tuteur trellises
Catalogue: free

The Garden Architecture Group
631 North 3rd Street
Philadelphia, PA 19123
(215) 627-5552
Product: cedar trellises
Catalogue: $3.00

Garden Trellises
Box 105
LaFayette, NY 13084
(315) 489-9003
Product: galvanized-steel trellises
Catalogue: free

Island Arbors
732 Sunrise Highway
West Babylon, NY 11704
(516) 669-3886
Product: red cedar arbors
Catalogue: free

M. R. Labbe, Company
Box 467
Biddeford, ME 04005
(207) 282-3420
Product: red cedar arbor kits
Catalogue: free

Moonstruck Designs
Box 177
Uniontown, OH 44685
(216) 699-7419
Product: latticed trellises
Catalogue: free

Nebraska Plastics, Inc.
Box 45
Cozad, NE 69130
(800) 445-2887
Products: Country Manor PVC arbors
and trellises
Catalogue: free

New England Garden Ornaments
38 East Brookfield Road
North Brookfield, MA 01535
(508) 867-4474
Product: Agriframes garden structures
Catalogue: free

Poly Concepts, Inc.
9176 Red Branch Road
Columbia, MD 21045
(800) 474-POLY
Product: PVC trellises
Catalogue: free

Rivertown Products
Box 5174
St. Joseph, MO 64505
(816) 232-8822
Product: handcrafted arbors
Catalogue: $1.00

Taylor Ridge Farm
Box 222
Saluda, NC 28773
(704) 749-4756
Products: steel and copper trellises
Catalogue: $3.00

Topiaries Unlimited
RD 2, Box 40C
Pownal, VT 05261

(802) 823-5536
Product: topiary frames
Catalogue: long SASE

Topiary, Inc.
41 Bering Street
Tampa, FL 33606
Product: topiary frames
Catalogue: long SASE

Valcovic Cornell Design
Box 380
Beverly, MA 01915
Product: sculptured trellises
Catalogue: $1.00

Westcoast Topiary
Box 20422, Portland, OR 97220
(503) 257-8340
Product: topiary frames
Catalogue: $1.00

Landscape Lights

Copper Craft Lighting, Inc.
5100-1B Clayton Road, Suite 291
Concord, CA 94521
(510) 672-4337
Products: copper and bronze landscape
lights
Catalogue: free

Doner Design, Inc.
2175 Beaver Valley Pike
New Providence, PA 17560
(717) 786-8891
Product: copper landscape lights
Catalogue: free

Escort Lighting
201 Sweitzer Road
Sinking Spring, PA 19608
Fax: (610) 670-5170
Product: copper garden lights
Catalogue: free

Genie House
Box 2478
Vincentown, NJ 08088
(609) 859-0600
(800) 634-3643
Product: reproduction garden lights
Catalogue: $3.00

Great American Salvage Company
34 Cooper Square
New York, NY 10003
(212) 505-0070
Product: reproduction lighting
Catalogue: free

Hanover Lanterns
470 High Street
Hanover, PA 17331
(717) 632-6464
Product: Terralight® lighting fixtures
Catalogue: free

Heritage Lanterns
70A Main Street
Yarmouth, ME 04096
(207) 846-3911
(800) 544-6070
Product: garden lights
Catalogue: $3.00

Idaho Wood
Box 488
Sandpoint, ID 83864
(208) 263-9521
(800) 635-1100
Product: wooden garden lights
Catalogue: free

Landscape Resources
(800) 934-1448
Products: landscape lighting fixtures
and parts
Catalogue: free

Liteform Designs
Box 3316

Portland, OR 97208
(503) 257-8464
(800) 458-2505
Product: landscape lighting fixtures
Catalogue: free

Popovitch Associates, Inc.
346 Ashland Avenue
Pittsburgh, PA 15228
(412) 344-6097
Product: ornamental garden lighting
Catalogue: $2.00

Stonelight Corporation
2701 Gulf Shore Boulevard North
Naples, FL 33940
(813) 263-2208
Product: Vermont granite
lighting fixtures
Catalogue: free

Benches and Other Garden Furniture

Acorn Services Corporation
Box 2854, Brewster, MA 02631
(508) 240-0072
(800) 472-4957
Product: redwood garden furniture
Catalogue: free

Adirondack Designs
350 Cypress Street
Fort Bragg, CA 95437
(707) 964-4940
(800) 222-0343
Product: redwood garden furniture
Catalogue: free

Alpine Millworks Company
1231 West Lehigh Place
Englewood, CO 80110
(303) 761-6334
Products: teak and mahogany garden
furniture
Catalogue: free

Ballard Designs
1670 DeFoor Avenue NW
Atlanta, GA 30318
(404) 351-5099
Products: metal and glass furniture
Catalogue: free

Barlow Tyrie, Inc.
1263 Glen Avenue
Moorestown, NJ 08067
(609) 273-1631
Product: English teak furniture
Catalogue: free

The BenchSmith
Box 86
Warrington, PA 18976
(800) 48-CEDAR
Products: cedar benches; planters
Catalogue: free

Celestial Creations
1427 Centre Circle
Downers Grove, IL 60515
(708) 629-9999
Product: cast-aluminum angel benches
Catalogue: free

The Chair That Fits
2628 Ridgewood Avenue
Charleston, SC 29414
(803) 766-6758
Product: wooden outdoor chairs
Catalogue: free

Charleston Battery Bench, Inc.
191 King Street
Charleston, SC 29401
(803) 722-3842
Product: cast-iron benches
Catalogue: free

Country Casual
17317 Germantown Road
Germantown, MD 20874
(301) 540-0040

Product: teak garden furniture
Catalogue: free

Country Wood™
Box 314
Sugar Loaf, NY 10981
Products: Adirondack rockers and chairs
Catalogue: free

Florentine Craftsmen, Inc.
46-24 28th Street
Long Island City, NY 11101
(718) 937-7632
Product: metal garden furniture
Catalogue: $5.00

The Garden Concepts Collection
Box 241233
Memphis, TN 38124
(901) 756-1649
Product: wooden garden furniture
Catalogue: $5,00

Kelly Grayson Woodcarving & Design
5111 Todd Road
Sebastopol, CA 95472
(707) 829-7764
Product: redwood garden furniture
Catalogue: $1.00

Green Enterprises
43 South Rogers Street
Hamilton, VA 22068
(703) 338-3606
Product: Victorian oak garden furniture
Catalogue: free

Hemlock Shop
RD 1, Box 273
Olyphant, PA 18447
(717) 586-8809
Product: Adirondack chairs
Catalogue: free

Heritage Garden Furniture
1209 East Island Highway

Parksville, British Columbia V9P 1R5
(604) 248-9598
Product: cedar garden furniture kits
Catalogue: free

Homeward
1007 Wisconsin Avenue
Washington, DC 20007
(800) 616-3667
Product: wooden garden benches
Catalogue: free

Kelly Pacific, Inc.
10260 SW Nimbus Avenue
Portland, OR 97223
(800) 999-3845
Product: wooden garden furniture
Catalogue: free

Kingsley-Bate
5587B Guinea Road
Fairfax, VA 22032
(703) 978-7222
Product: teak garden furniture
Catalogue: free

McKinnon and Harris, Inc.
Box 4885
Richmond, VA 23220
(804) 358-2385
Product: metal garden furniture
Catalogue: $4.00

Park Place
2251 Wisconsin Avenue NW
Washington, DC 20007
(202) 342-6294
Product: bentwood garden furniture
Catalogue: free

Reed Brothers
Turner Station
Sebastopol, CA 95472
(707) 795-6261
Product: redwood garden furniture
Catalogue: free

Richardson Allen Furniture
Box 701
Cape Porpoise, ME 04014
(207) 967-8482
Product: wooden garden furniture
Catalogue: free

Seth Rolland
HCR 74, Box 22203
El Prado, NM 87529
(800) 858-9053
Product: redwood garden furniture
Catalogue: free

Sloan Designs
Route 1, Box 183A
Linden, VA 22642
(703) 636-1626
Products: wooden benches;
Adirondack chairs
Catalogue: free

Southerlands
10 Biltmore Avenue
Asheville, NC 28801
(704) 252-0478
(800) 968-5596
Product: garden furniture
Catalogue: free

The Thaxted Cottage Gardener
121 Driscoll Way
Gaithersburg, MD 20878
(301) 330-6211
Product: historic English benches
Catalogue: $2.00

Tidewater Workshop
Oceanville, NJ 08231
(800) 666-TIDE
Product: cedar Classic English
Garden Bench^{TM}
Catalogue: free

Vermont Outdoor Furniture
Box 375

East Barre, VT 05649
(800) 588-8834
Product: white cedar garden furniture
Catalogue: free

The Virginia Bench Company
Keswick, VA 22947
(804) 295-7299
Product: pine folding garden bench
Catalogue: free

Wetherend Estate Furniture
Box 648
Rockland, ME 04841
(207) 596-6483
Product: wooden garden furniture
Catalogue: free

Wikco Industries, Inc.
4931 North 57th Street
Lincoln, NE 68507
(402) 464-2070
(800) 872-8864
Product: wrought-iron garden benches
Catalogue: free

Willsboro Wood Products
Box 509
Keesville, NY 12944
(518) 834-5200
(800) 342-3373
Product: cedar Adirondack
garden furniture
Catalogue: free

Windsor Designs
37 Great Valley Parkway
Malvern, PA 19355
(215) 640-5896
(800) 722-5434
Products: wooden and cast-aluminum
garden furniture
Catalogue: free

Wood Classics, Inc.
Osprey Lane
Gardiner, NY 12525
(914) 255-5599
Product: wooden garden furniture
Catalogue: free

Woodbrook Furniture
Manufacturing Company
Box 175
Trussville, AL 35173
(800) 828-3607
Product: cypress garden furniture
Catalogue: free

Garden Ornaments

Adams & Adkins, Inc.
104 South Early Street
Alexandria, VA 22304
(703) 823-3404
(800) 928-3588
Product: Water Flute? fountain-pond
Catalogue: free

American Weather Enterprises
Box 1383
Media, PA 19063
(215) 565-1232
Products: weather instruments; sundials
Catalogue: free

The Artisans Group
1039 Main Street
Dublin, NH 03444
(603) 563-8782
(800) 528-2035
Product: handcrafted garden ornaments
Catalogue: $1.00

Asian Artifacts
Box 2494
Oceanside, CA 92051
(619) 723-3039
Product: Japanese garden ornaments
Catalogue: $2.00

Baker's Lawn Ornaments
RD 5, Box 265
Somerset, PA 15501
(814) 445-7028
Product: gazing globes
Catalogue: free

Bridgeworks
306 East Lockwood Street
Covington, LA 70433
(504) 893-7933
Product: bridges
Catalogue: free

Carruth Studio, Inc.
1178 Farnsworth Road
Waterville, OH 43566
(800) 225-1178
Product: cast-limestone garden art
Catalogue: free

Claycraft
807 Avenue of the Americas
New York, NY 10001
(212) 242-2903
Product: fiberglass planters
Catalogue: $2.00

Robert Compton, Ltd.
RD 3, Box 3600
Bristol, VT 05443
(802) 453-3778
Product: fountains
Catalogue: $2.00

Design Toscano, Inc.
17 East Campbell Street
Arlington Heights, IL 60005
(800) 525-0733

Product: historical reproduction
outdoor sculptures
Catalogue: $4.00

Elizabeth Street
210 Elizabeth Street
New York, NY 10012
(212) 941-4800
Products: garden ornaments; fountains
Catalogue: free

Florentine Craftsmen, Inc.
46-24 28th Street
Long Island City, NY 11101
(718) 937-7632
Products: ornaments; statuary; fountains
Catalogue: $5.00

French Wyres
Box 131655
Tyler, TX 75713
(903) 597-8322
Product: planters
Catalogue: $3.00

Granite Impressions
342 Carmen Road
Talent, OR 97540
(503) 535-6190
Product: Japanese garden ornaments
Catalogue: $1.00

Haddonstone (USA), Ltd.
201 Heller Place
Interstate Business Park
Bellmawr, NJ 08031
(609) 931-7011
Product: ornamental cast stonework
Catalogue: $10.00

Hollowbrook Pottery and Tile
26 Anton Place
Lake Peekskill, NY 10537
Product: stoneware planters
Catalogue: free

The Joiner's Workshop
2006 43rd Avenue
San Francisco, CA 94116
(415) 681-7271
Product: planters
Catalogue: free

Made in the Shade Umbrellas
810 West 6th Street, Suite 2
Chico, CA 95928
(916) 342-3025
Product: garden umbrellas
Catalogue: free

D. F. Mangum Company
5311 Acoma SE
Albuquerque, NM 87108
(800) 859-6399
Product: garden bridge kits
Catalogue: free

MDT-Muller Design, Inc.
971 Dogwood Trail
Tyrone, GA 30290
(404) 631-9074
Product: garden umbrellas
Catalogue: $2.00

Mister Boardwalk
Box 789
Point Pleasant, NJ 08742
(908) 341-4800
Product: wooden walkways
Catalogue: free

Mitchells & Son
13558 Sunrise Drive NE
Bainbridge Island, WA 98110
(206) 842-9827
Product: cedar planters
Catalogue: free

New England Garden Ornaments
38 East Brookfield Road
North Brookfield, MA 01535
(508) 867-4474

Products: ornaments; statuary; fountains
Catalogue: free

P & R International, Inc.
Box 939
Norwalk, CT 06852
(203) 846-2989
Products: ornaments; planters; fountains
Catalogue: $3.00

Pennoyer Castings Company
Box 597
Locust Valley, NY 11560
(516) 676-1920
Product: classic garden ornaments
Catalogue: free

Pompeian Studios
90 Rockridge Road
Bronxville, NY 10708
(914) 337-5595
(800) 457-5595
Products: stone and wrought-iron
garden ornaments
Catalogue: $10.00

Redwood Arts
Box 419
Airway Heights, WA 99001
(509) 244-9669
Product: redwood planters
Catalogue: free

Salt Creek Traders
Route 1, Box 189W
Effingham, IL 62401
(800) 360-1512
Product: sundials
Catalogue: free

Seibert & Rice
Box 365
Short Hills, NJ 07078
(201) 467-8266
Product: terra-cotta planters
Catalogue: free

Spademan Pottery
218 Chestnut Street
Cambridge, MA 02139
(617) 354-1704
Product: terra-cotta planters
Catalogue: free

Stone Forest
Box 2840
Santa Fe, NM 87504
(505) 986-8883
Product: granite garden ornaments
Catalogue: $3.00

Stoneworks Gallery
Box 35
Tuxedo, NY 10987
(800) STONE-08
Product: Riverstones™
Catalogue: free

Sun Garden Specialties
Box 52382
Tulsa, OK 74152
Product: Japanese garden ornaments
Catalogue: free

Utopian Designs
Box 1434
Eugene, OR 97440
(503) 683-5530
Product: gazing globes
Catalogue: free

Wind & Weather
Box 2320
Mendocino, CA 95460
(800) 922-9463
Products: weather instruments; sundials;
gazing globes
Catalogue: free

Wood Classics, Inc.
Osprey Lane
Gardiner, NY 12525
(914) 255-5599

Product: market umbrellas
Catalogue: free

Wood Garden
11 Fitzrandolph Street
Green Brook, NJ 08812
(201) 968-4325
Product: wooden planters
Catalogue: free

Wundrella, Inc.
8239 SW 64th Street
Miami, FL 33143
(305) 598-8202
Product: market umbrellas
Catalogue: free

Fencing

Architectural Iron Company
Route 6 West, Box 126
Milford, PA 18337
(717) 296-7722
Product: wrought-iron fences
Catalogue: free

Bamboo & Rattan Works
470 Oberlin Avenue South
Lakewood, NJ 08701
(908) 370-0220
(800) 4-BAMBOO
Products: bamboo and reed fencing
Catalogue: free

Bamboo Fencer
31 Germania Street
Jamaica Plain, MA 02130
(617) 524-6137
(800) 775-8641
Product: bamboo fencing
Catalogue: $3.00

Bufftech
2525 Walden Avenue
Buffalo, NY 14225

(800) 333-0569
Product: polyvinyl fencing
Catalogue: free

Country Estate Fence
Nebraska Plastics, Inc.
Box 45
Cozad, NE 69130
(800) 445-2887
Product: polyvinyl fencing
Catalogue: free

Invisible Fence Company
355 Phoenixville Pike
Malvern, PA 19355
(800) 538-DOGS
Product: pet containment fencing
Catalogue: free

Jerith Manufacturing Company
3939 G Street
Philadelphia, PA 19124
Product: aluminum fencing
Catalogue: free

Materials Unlimited
2 West Michigan Avenue
Ypsilanti, MI 48197
(313) 483-6980
IProduct: wrought-iron fencing
Catalogue: free

Moultrie Manufacturing Company
Drawer 1179, Moultrie, GA 31768
(912) 985-1312
(800) 841-8674
Product: metal fencing
Catalogue: free

Stewart Iron Works Company
20 West 18th Street
Covington, KY 41012
(606) 431-1985
Products: Victorian and Edwardian
fences and gates
Catalogue: free

Walpole Woodworkers
767 East Street
Walpole, MA 02081
(508) 668-2800
(800) 343-6948
Product: cedar fencing
Catalogue: free

Garden Gates

Fine Architectural Metalsmiths
Box 30, Chester, NY 10918
(914) 651-7550
Product: wrought-iron gates
Catalogue: $3.50

The Timeless Garden
Box 500998
Atlanta, GA 31150
(404) 518-9127
Product: historic garden gate replicas
Catalogue: free

Edging

Proline Edging
13505 Barry Street
Holland, MI 49424
(800) 356-9660
Product: aluminum edging
Catalogue: free

The Victoriana Collection
(905) 627-4035
Product: terra-cotta edging
Catalogue: free

Warp Brothers
4647 West Augusta Boulevard
Chicago, IL 60651
(312) 261-5200
(800) 621-3345
Product: Easy Edge landscape borders
Catalogue: free

Plant Markers

AAA Quality Engravers
5754 Oxford Place
New Orleans, LA 70131
(504) 391-2225
Products: engraved markers
Catalogue: free

Amaranth Stoneware
Box 243
Sydenham, Ontario K0H 2T0
(800) 465-5444
Products: stoneware and terra-cotta
garden signs
Catalogue: free

Art Line, Inc.
600 North Kibourn
Chicago, IL 60624
(312) 722-8100
Catalogue: free

Beason Engraving
731 Springhill Avenue
Spartanburg, SC 29303
(803) 583-8913
Product: custom engraved markers
Catalogue: free

Berkshire Brass
162 Chipman Road
Chester, MA 01011
(413) 623-5649
Product: brass markers
Catalogue: free

Blackburn Manufacturing Company
Box 86
Neligh, NE 68756
(402) 887-4161
Catalogue: free

Brass Butterfly, Inc.
58 Garin Mill Park
Poultney, VT 05764

(802) 287-9818
Product: brass markers
Catalogue: free

Eon Industries
Box 11
Liberty Center, OH 43532
(419) 533-4961
Product: metal markers
Catalogue: free

Evergreen Garden Plant Labels
Box 922
Cloverdale, CA 95425
Product: galvanized-steel markers
Catalogue: one stamp

Forget-Me-Not Marker Company
1917 Kenneth Street
Urbana, IL 61801
Product: metal markers
Catalogue: long SASE

Garden Expressions
Box 1358
Loveland, CO 80539
(303) 663-7989
Catalogue: $1.00

Garden Fonts
RFD 1, Box 54
Barnstead, NH 03218
Product: custom printed peel-and-stick
labels
Catalogue: free

Garden Graphics
17 Woodfield Road
Pomona, NY 10970
(914) 354-3981
Product: custom engraved markers
Catalogue: free

Harlane Company, Inc.
266 Orangeburgh Road
Old Tappan, NJ 07675

Product: plastic markers
Catalogue: free

Mark Kit Company
Box 1667
San Pedro, CA 90733
Catalogue: free

MIS-Q
1865 Laraway Lake Drive SE
Grand Rapids, MI 49546
Product: custom engraved terra-cotta
markers
Catalogue: SASE

Permanent Metal Labels
Box 93
Paw Paw, MI 49070
Product: metal markers
Catalogue: SASE

S & D Enterprises
1280 Quince Drive
Junction City, OR 97448
(503) 998-2060
Product: anodized aluminum markers
Catalogue: long SASE

Spring Valley Roses
7637 330th Street
Spring Valley, WI 54767
Product: rose plaques
Catalogue: $1.00

TK Company
Box 610
Walker, MN 56484
(218) 547-1530
Product: custom markers
Catalogue: free

F. R. Unruh
37 Oaknoll Road
Wilmington, DE 19808
(302) 994-2328
Product: metal markers
Catalogue: SASE

Versamax Company
Box 918
East Troy, WI 53120
(800) 642-4408
Product: large plastic markers
Catalogue: free

Wingfoot Studios
Box 951
Langley, WA 98260
(360) 321-3974
Product: porcelain herb tags; custom tags
Catalogue: SASE

The Wood Rapture
6369 SW 10th Street
Topeka, KS 66615
Catalogue: free

Organizations for Gardeners

GARDENERS ARE a well-organized group, both by geography and by interest. General gardening organizations that promote the hobby overall are active at the national, state, and provincial levels, while gardening clubs and societies exist in almost every state and municipality. In the interest category, many national organizations—such as the American Orchid Society—have local chapters that sponsor get-togethers and flower shows. Native plant societies are active in many states and provinces.

The listings below start with national gardening organizations and go on to state and provincial organizations. They are followed by listings of specialty gardening organizations and native plants groups, organized first nationally, then by state or province. A listing of professional organizations ends this section.

Most organizations put out some sort of publication for their members—the subscription price is part of your annual dues. Publications can range from sophisticated magazines with paid advertising to simple newsletters produced at the local copy shop. In any case, these publications generally provide a lot of information and give schedules of upcoming events.

An enjoyable and interesting feature of some plant societies is the chance to participate in round-robins. A round-robin is basically a sort of circulating bulletin board that travels around a small group of gardeners (usually no more than ten) with common interests—orchid fanciers with an interest in cattleyas, for example. One member agrees to be the volunteer director. The director writes a letter about cattleyas, perhaps describing something interesting about them or asking a cultivation question. The letter is then mailed to the next person on the list, who reads it and writes his or her own letter, perhaps answering the question. The two letters are mailed on to the next person on the list, who repeats the process. The entire packet of letters eventually arrives back at the director, who removes the original letter, writes a new one, and starts the process all over again.

At the state and local level, many plant societies are run on a shoestring by volunteers. Membership dues are usually nominal. The headquarters of the organization is often the home of whoever is president or membership chair that year, so the contact addresses change rapidly. Your inquiry will almost certainly be forwarded to the proper person, but it may take a little time—be patient. Be considerate as well. Don't call very early in the morning or late at night, bear time zone differences in mind, and send a stamped, self-addressed envelope when you write for information.

National Organizations

American Community Gardening
Association
325 Walnut Street
Philadelphia, PA 19106
(215) 625-8280
Dues: $25.00
Publication: *Journal of Community Gardening*
(quarterly)

American Horticultural Society
7931 East Boulevard Drive
Alexandria, VA 22308
(703) 768-5700
(800) 777-7931
Dues: $35.00
Publication: *American Horticulturist*
(monthly magazine)

The Garden Club of America
598 Madison Avenue
New York, NY 10022
(212) 753-8287
Publications: GCA *Bulletin* (biannual);
GCA Newsletter (bimonthly)

Garden Clubs Canada
6 Compton Place
London, Ontario N6C 4G4
(519) 681-7089
Publication: *Garden Clubs Canada Newsletter*
(three times annually)

Indoor Gardening Society
of America, Inc.
1082 Hillstone Road
Cleveland Heights, OH 44121
(800) 892-7594
Dues: $22.00
Publication: *House Plant Magazine*
(bimonthly)

Men's Garden Club of America, Inc.
5560 Merle Hay Road
Johnston, IA 50131

(515) 278-0295
Publication: *The Gardener* (bimonthly)

National Arbor Day Foundation
100 Arbor Avenue
Nebraska City, NE 68410
(402) 474-5655
Dues: $15.00
Publication: *Arbor Day* (bimonthly)

National Council for
State Garden Clubs, Inc.
4401 Magnolia Avenue
St. Louis, MO 63110
(314) 776-7574
Publication: *The National Gardener*
(bimonthly)

National Gardening Association
1800 Flynn Avenue
Burlington, VT 05401
(802) 863-1308
(800) LETSGRO
Dues: $18.00
Publication: *National Gardening*
(bimonthly magazine)

National Junior Horticultural Association
401 North 4th Street
Durant, OK 74701
(405) 924-0771
Publication: *Going & Growing*
(three times annually)

National Xeriscape Council
Box 163172
Austin, TX 78716
(512) 392-6225
Publication: *Xeriscape News* (bimonthly)

The Royal Horticultural Society
Membership Secretary
80 Vincent Square
London SW1P 2PE
England
(071) 834-4333

Publication: *The Garden*
(monthly magazine)

Women's National Farm and Garden
Association, Inc.
2402 Clearview Drive
Glenshaw, PA 15116
(412) 486-7964

State and Provincial Organizations

Alabama

Garden Club of Alabama
c/o Mrs. Gene Castleberry
124 Highland Place
Sheffield, AL 35660

South Alabama Botanical and
Horticultural Society
c/o John Bowen
Box 8382
Mobile, AL 36608

Alaska

Alaska Federation of Garden Clubs
c/o Mrs. Albert Silk
2801 Bennett Drive
Anchorage, AK 99517

Alaska Horticultural Association
Box 1909
Palmer, AK 99645

Arizona

Arizona Federation of Garden Clubs
c/o Mrs. Harry Wagner
508 Highland Drive
Prescott, AZ 86303

Arkansas

Arkansas State Horticultural Society
University of Arkansas
Plant Science Building, Room 306
Fayetteville, AR 72701
(501) 575-2603

California

California Garden Clubs, Inc.
c/o Mrs. Allan Nielsen
7540 Granite Avenue
Orangeville, CA 95662

The California Horticultural Society
California Academy of Sciences
Elsie Mueller, Secretary
1847 34th Avenue
San Francisco, CA 94122
(415) 566-5222
Dues: $35.00
Publication: *Pacific Horticulture* (quarterly)

Southern California Horticultural Society
c/o Joan DeFato
Box 41080
Los Angeles, CA 90041
(818) 567-1496
Dues: $20.00
Publications: *Pacific Horticulture* (quarterly);
monthly bulletin

Western Horticultural Society
Treasurer
Box 60507
Palo Alto, CA 94306
(415) 941-1332
Dues: $25.00
Publications: *Pacific Horticulture* (quarterly);
newsletter (ten times annually)

Colorado

Colorado Federation of Garden Clubs, Inc.
c/o Mrs. Dode Mehrer

Box 186
Idaho Springs, CO 80452

Connecticut

Connecticut Horticultural Society
150 Main Street
Wethersfield, CT 06109
(203) 529-8713
Publication: *CHS Newsletter* (ten times
annually)

Federated Garden Clubs of Connecticut
c/o Lee Bauerfield
Box 672
Wallingford, CT 06492

Delaware

Delaware Federation of
Garden Clubs, Inc.
c/o Mrs. Robert Weeks
2306 Jamaica Drive
Wilmington, DE 19810

Florida

Florida Federation of Garden Clubs
c/o Mrs. Kenton Haymans
Box 1604
Winter Park, FL 32790
(407) 647-7016

Georgia

Garden Club of Georgia, Inc.
c/o Mrs. E. Carl White
7 Woodland Drive
Cartersville, GA 30120

Hawaii

Hawaii Federation of Garden Clubs, Inc.
c/o Mrs. John Johnson
Box 25401
Honolulu, HI 96825

Idaho

Idaho State Federation of
Garden Clubs, Inc.
c/o F. Ruth Thacker
1218 North 25th Street
Boise, ID 83702

Illinois

Garden Clubs of Illinois, Inc.
c/o Mrs. William Laycock
23W163 Blackberry Lane
Glen Ellyn, IL 60137

Indiana

Garden Club of Indiana
c/o Barbara Yoder
Route 1, Box 34
Geneva, IN 46740
(219) 334-5453

Iowa

Federated Garden Clubs of Iowa
c/o Mrs. G. B. Cox
Windsong
Route 4, Box 223
Marshalltown, IA 50158

Iowa State Horticultural Society
Wallace State Office Building
Des Moines, IA 50319
(515) 281-5402
Publication: *Horticulturist* (quarterly)

Kansas

Kansas Associated Garden Clubs
c/o Mrs. Vernon Carlsen
811 Sunset Drive
Lawrence, KS 66044

Kentucky

Garden Club of Kentucky
c/o Mrs. Charles Huddleston
Box 1653
Middleboro, KY 40965

Louisiana

Federated Council of New Orleans
Garden Clubs, Inc.
c/o Mrs. Donald Miester
787 Jewell Street
New Orleans, LA 70124
(540) 282-5077

Louisiana Garden Club Federation
c/o Mrs. E. Massa
139 Citrus Road
River Ridge, LA 70123

New Orleans Garden Society
3914 Prytania Street
New Orleans, LA 70115

Maine

Garden Club Federation of Maine, Inc.
c/o Mrs. Steen Meryweather
Box 56
Salisbury Cove, ME 04672

Maine Federated Garden Club
c/o Mrs. Phillip Burril
RFD 1, Box 1040
Corinna, ME 04928
(207) 278-5994

Maryland

Federated Garden Clubs
of Maryland, Inc.
c/o Mrs. Hal Tray
128 Round Bay Road
Severna Park, MD 21146

Horticultural Society of Maryland
1563 Sherwood Avenue
Baltimore, MD 21239
(301) 352-7863

Massachusetts

Garden Club Federation of
Massachusetts, Inc.
c/o Mrs. George Dennett
547 Central Avenue
Needham, MA 01294

Massachusetts Horticultural Association
300 Massachusetts Avenue
Boston, MA 02115
(617) 536-9280
Dues: $45.00
Publication: Horticulture
(monthly magazine)

Worcester County Horticultural Society
Tower Hill Botanic Garden
11 French Drive
Boylston, MA 01505
(508) 869-6111
Dues: $25.00
Publication: Grow With Us (bimonthly)

Michigan

Federated Garden Club of Michigan
c/o Mrs. Peter Butus
1509 Orchard Lane
Niles, MI 49120
(616) 683-3030

Garden Club of Michigan
c/o Mrs. Douglas Roby
7113 Greer Road
Howell, MI 48843
(517) 546-2649

Michigan Botanical Club
Dorothy Sibley
7951 Walnut Avenue

Newaygo, MI 49337
(616) 652-2036
Dues: $17.00
Publication: *The Michigan Botanist*
(quarterly)

Minnesota

Federated Garden Clubs of Minnesota
c/o Mrs. Herbert Larson
1295 Dodd Road West
St. Paul, MN 55118

Minnesota State Horticultural Society
1755 Prior Avenue North
Falcon Heights, MN 55113
(612) 645-7066
Dues: $25.00
Publication: *Minnesota Horticulturalist*
(nine times annually)

Mississippi

Garden Clubs of Mississippi
c/o Mrs. H. T. Miller
Box 265
Drew, MS 38737

Missouri

Federated Garden Clubs of Missouri, Inc.
c/o Mrs. J. Herman Belz
10 Chipper Road
St. Louis, MO 63131

Garden Club of St. Louis
c/o Peggy Jones
33 Granada Way
St. Louis, MO 63124
(314) 997-5185

Montana

Montana Federation of Garden Clubs
c/o Mrs. Anthony Hanic
Box 356, Ashland, MT 59003

Nebraska

Federated Garden Clubs of Nebraska
c/o Mrs. Robert Keating
Route 1, Box 70
Palisade, NE 69040

Omaha Council of Garden Clubs
4014 South 14th Street
Omaha, NE 68107

Nevada

Nevada Garden Clubs, Inc.
c/o Mrs. Charles Gorley
Box 27624
Las Vegas, NV 89126

New Hampshire

New Hampshire Federation
of Garden Clubs
c/o Mrs. William Murdock
Box 10
Windham, NH 03087

New Jersey

Garden Club of New Jersey
c/o Mrs. Carmine Grossi
Box 622
West Milford, NJ 07480

New Jersey State Horticultural Society
Box 116
Clayton, NJ 08312
(609) 863-0110

New Mexico

New Mexico Garden Clubs, Inc.
c/o Mrs. Donald Wood
7000 Seminole Road NE
Albuquerque, NM 87110

New York

Federated Garden Clubs of New York
State, Inc.
5432 Collett Road
Shortsville, NY 14548
(716) 289-3539
(518) 869-6311

Horticultural Society of New York
128 West 58th Street
New York, NY 10019
(212) 757-0915
Dues: $35.00
Publication: *HSNY Newsletter* (quarterly)

Long Island Horticultural Society
c/o David Carrody
9 Anita Avenue
Syosset, NY 11791
(516) 921-4661
Publication: monthly newsletter

North Carolina

Garden Club of North Carolina, Inc.
c/o Mrs. E. L. Swaim
848 Shoreline Road
Winston-Salem, NC 27106

North Dakota

North Dakota Federation of Garden
Clubs
c/o Lois Forrest
RR 3
Jamestown, ND 58401

North Dakota State Horticultural Society
Box 5658
North Dakota State University
Fargo, ND 58105
(701) 237-8161
Publication: *North Dakota Horticulture*
(monthly)

Ohio

Garden Club of Ohio, Inc.
c/o Mrs. Donald De Cessna
883 Bexley Drive
Perrysburg, OH 43551

Ohio Association of Garden Clubs
c/o Jan Harman
402 Craggy Creek Drive
Chippewa Lake, OH 44215
(216) 769-2210

Ohio Horticulture Council
c/o David Kelly
4680 Indianola Avenue
Columbus, OH 43314
(614) 261-6834

Ohio Junior Horticulture Association
Dennis Waldman, Executive Officer
5759 Sandalwood NE
North Canton, OH 44721
(216) 492-3252

Oklahoma

Oklahoma Garden Clubs, Inc.
c/o Mrs. W. A. Williams
115 West 1st
Atoka, OK 74525

Oklahoma Horticulture Society
OSU Technical Branch
900 North Portland
Oklahoma City, OK 73107
(405) 945-3358
Publication: Horizons (quarterly)

Oregon

Oregon State Federation of Garden
Clubs, Inc.
c/o Mrs. Sam Roller
820 NW Elizabeth Drive
Corvallis, OR 97330

Pennsylvania

Garden Club Federation of Pennsylvania
c/o Mrs. Henry Hermani
445 North Front Street
Milton, PA 17847

Horticultural Society of Western
Pennsylvania
Box 5126
Pittsburgh, PA 15206
(412) 392-8540

The Pennsylvania Horticultural Society
325 Walnut Street
Philadelphia, PA 19106
(215) 625-8250
Dues: $40.00
Publications: Green Scene (bimonthly
journal); PHS News (monthly newsletter)

Rhode Island

Rhode Island Federation of Garden Clubs
c/o Mrs. G. Dickson Kenney
130 Waterway
Saunderstown, RI 02874

South Carolina

Garden Club of South Carolina
c/o Mrs. John F. C. Hunter
912 Santee Drive
Florence, SC 29501

South Dakota

South Dakota Federation of Garden Clubs
c/o Catherine Hladky
Box 540
Yankton, SD 57078

Tennessee

Tennessee Federation of Garden Clubs
c/o Mrs. D. V. Pennington

958 Brownlee Road
Memphis, TN 38116

Texas

Rio Grande Valley Horticultural Society
Box 107
Weslaco, TX 78596
(512) 968-5000

Texas Garden Clubs, Inc.
c/o Mrs. Ben P. Denman
7173 Kendallwood
Dallas, TX 75240

Texas State Horticultural Society
4348 Carter Creek Parkway
Bryan, TX 77802
(409) 846-1752
Publication: The Texas Horticulturist
(monthly)

Utah

Utah Associated Garden Clubs, Inc.
c/o Mrs. Arlan Headman
4060 South 1500 East
Salt Lake City, UT 84124

Utah Horticulture Association
Chad Rowley, President
Box 567
Santaquin, UT 48655
(801) 754-5601

Vermont

Federated Garden Clubs of Vermont
c/o Mrs. Howard A. Allen
Overlake #15
545 South Prospect Street
Burlington, VT 05401

Virginia

Virginia Federation of Garden Clubs, Inc.
c/o Mrs. Dewitt B. Casler
205 Culpepper Road
Richmond, VA 23229

Virginia Horticulture Council, Inc.
383 Coal Hollow Road
Christiansburg, VA 24073
(703) 382-0904

Washington

Northwest Horticultural Society
c/o Yoosun Park
Isaacson Hall, University of Washington
Seattle, WA 98195
(206) 527-1794
Dues: $35.00
Publication: *Pacific Horticulture*

Washington State Federation
of Garden Clubs, Inc.
c/o Mrs. Ralph Swenson
2314 108th Street SE
Bellevue, WA 98004

West Virginia

West Virginia Garden Club, Inc.
c/o Mrs. Robert L. Swoope
1978 Smith Road
Charleston, WV 25314

Wisconsin

Milwaukee Horticultural Soceity
c/o Boerner Gardens
5879 South 92nd Street
Hales Corners, WI 53130

Wisconsin Garden Club Federation, Inc.
c/o Mrs. Walter Seeliger
75 East Water Street
Markesan, WI 53946

Wyoming

Wyoming Federation
of Garden Clubs, Inc.
c/o Mrs. Harry Pelliccione
Box 1208
Pinedale, WY 82941

CANADA

Alberta

Alberta Horticultural Association
Box 223
Lacombe, Alberta T0C 1S0
(403) 782-3053

Calgary Horticultural Society
2405 9th Avenue SE
Calgary, Alberta T2G 4T4
(403) 262-5609
Dues: Canada $20.00
Publication: *CHS Newsletter*
(eight times annually)

Edmonton Horticultural Society
Arlene Smith, Director
11707 150th Avenue
Edmonton, Alberta T5X 1C1
(403) 456-7986

Lethbridge and District
Horticultural Society
D. L. Weightman, Secretary
74 Eagle Road North
Lethbridge, Alberta T1H 4S5

St. Albert and District Garden Club
25 Lombard Crescent
St. Albert, Alberta T8N 3N1

Western Canadian Society
for Horticulture
University of Alberta
Devonian Botanic Garden

Edmonton, Alberta T6G 2E1
(403) 987-3054
Publication: *WCSH Grapevine* (quarterly)

British Columbia

Garden Club of Vancouver
3185 West 45th Avenue
Vancouver, British Columbia V6N 3L9

Victoria Horticultural Society
Box 5081, Station B
Victoria, British Columbia V8R 6N3

New Brunswick

Fredericton Garden Club
107 Summer Street
Fredericton, New Brunswick E3A 1X7

Newfoundland

Newfoundland Horticultural Society
Box 10099
St. John's, Newfoundland A1A 4L5
(709) 712-4604
Publication: *Down to Earth*
(eleven times annually)

Nova Scotia

Nova Scotia Association of Garden Clubs
Box 550
Truro, Nova Scotia B2N 5E3

Ontario

Garden Club of Ancaster
50 Academy Street
Ancaster, Ontario L9G 2Y1

Garden Club of Burlington
c/o Mrs. R. D. Shots
RR 3
Campbelville, Ontario L0P L8O

Garden Club of Hamilton
2070 Watson Drive
Burlington, Ontario L7R 3X4

Garden Club of Kitchener-Waterloo
284 Shakespeare Drive
Waterloo, Ontario N2L 2T6

Garden Club of London
34 Bromleigh Avenue
London, Ontario N6G 1T9

Garden Club of Ontario
c/o Mrs. W. J. E. Spence
228 Dunvegan Road
Toronto, Ontario M5P 2P2

Garden Club of Toronto
777 Lawrence Avenue East
Don Mills, Ontario M3C 1P2

Garden Research Exchange
536 MacDonnell Street
Kingston, Ontario K7K 4W7
(613) 542-6547

Men's Garden Club
173 Joycey Boulevard
Toronto, Ontario M5M 2V3

Ontario Horticultural Association
c/o Bonnie Warner
RR 3
Englehart, Ontario P0J 1H0
(705) 544-2474

Woodstock Horticultural Society
c/o Mary Yeoman
RR 2
Burgessville, Ontario N0J 1C0

Quebec

Diggers and Weeders Garden Club
20 Thornhill Avenue
Westmount, Quebec K3Y 2E2

Garden Club of Montreal
66 St. Sulpice Road
Montreal, Quebec M3Y 2B7

La Société d'Animation du Jardin
et de l'Institut Botaniques
Botanical Garden
4101 East Sherbrooke Avenue
Montreal, Quebec H1X 2B2
(514) 872-1493

Saskatchewan

Evergreen Garden Club
13 Kootenay Drive
Saskatoon, Saskatchewan S7K 1T2

Prairie Flower Club
Box 35
White City, Saskatchewan S9G 5B0

Prairie Garden Guild
Monty Zary, Treasurer
Box 211
Saskatoon, Saskatchewan S7K 3K4

Saskatoon Horticultural Society
Box 161
Saskatoon, Saskatchewan S7K 3K4

Plant Species Organizations

See also chapter 1, **Plant Sources,** *and*
chapter 2, **Specialty Gardening**

African Violet Society of America, Inc.
2375 North Street
Beaumont, TX 77702
(409) 839-4725
(800) 770-AVSA
Dues: $18.00
Publication: *African Violet* (bimonthly
magazine)

African Violet Society of Canada
c/o Bonnie Scanlan

1573 Arbourdale Avenue
Victoria, British Columbia V8N 5J1
(604) 477-7561
Dues: Canada $12.00; US $14.00
Publication: *Chatter* (quarterly)

Alpine Garden Society
The Secretary
AGS Centre
Avon Bank, Pershore
Worcestershire WR10 3JP
England
(0386) 55-4790
Dues: £18.00
Publications: quarterly bulletin;
newsletter

American Bamboo Society
666 Wagnon Road
Sepastopol, CA 95472
(518) 765-3507
Dues: $20.00
Publications: *ABS Newsletter* (bimonthly);
Journal of the ABS (irregular)

American Begonia Society
c/o John Ingles Jr.
157 Monument Road
Rio Bell, CA 95562
(707) 764-5407
Dues: $21.00
Publication: *The Begonian*
(bimonthly magazine)

American Calochortus Society
c/o H. P. McDonald
Box 1128
Berkeley, CA 94701
Dues: $4.00
Publication: *Mariposa* (quarterly)

American Camellia Society
Massee Lane Gardens
1 Massee Lane
Fort Valley, GA 31030
(912) 967-2358

Dues: $20.00
Publication: *The Camellia Journal*
(quarterly)

American Conifer Society
827 Brooks Street
Ann Arbor, MI 48103
(313) 665-1871
Dues: $25.00
Publication: quarterly bulletin

American Daffodil Society, Inc.
c/o Mary Lou Gripshover
1686 Grey Fox Trails
Milford, OH 45150
(513) 248-9137
Dues: $20.00
Publication: *Daffodil Journal* (quarterly)

American Dahlia Society
Terry Shaffer, Membership Chair
422 Sunset Boulevard
Toledo, OH 43612
(419) 478-4159
Dues: $20.00
Publication: *Bulletin* (quarterly)

The American Dianthus Society
c/o Rand B. Lee
Box 22232
Santa Fe, NM 87502
(505) 438-7038
Dues: $15.00
Publication: *The Gilliflower Times*
(quarterly newsletter)

American Fern Society
c/o Richard Hauke
456 McGill Place
Atlanta, GA 30312
(404) 525-3147
Dues: $15.00
Publications: *American Fern Journal*
(quarterly); *Fiddlehead Forum*
(bimonthly newsletter)

American Fuchsia Society
County Fair Building
9th Avenue and Lincoln Way
San Francisco, CA 94122
(707) 643-0449
Dues: $15.00
Publication: *American Fuchsia Society*
Bulletin (bimonthly)

American Ginger Society
Box 100
Archer, FL 32618
(904) 495-9168
Publication: *Zingiber* (irregular)

American Gloxinia and Gesneriad
Society, Inc.
New York Horticultural Society
128 West 58th Street
New York, NY 10019
(212) 757-0915
Dues: $20.00
Publication: *The Gloxinian*
(bimonthly journal)

American Hemerocallis
(Daylilies) Society
c/o Elly Launius, Executive Secretary
1454 Rebel Drive
Jackson, MS 39211
(601) 366-4362
Dues: $18.00
Publication: *The Daylily Journal* (quarterly)

American Hepatica Association
c/o Paul Held
195 North Avenue
Westport, CT 06880
Dues: $20.00
Publication: newsletter

American Hibiscus Society
Jeri Grantham, Executive Secretary
Box 321540
Cocoa Beach, FL 32932
(407) 783-2576

Dues: $17.50
Publication: The Seed Pod (quarterly)

American Hosta Society
c/o Robyn Duback
7802 NE 63rd Street
Vancouver, WA 98662
Dues: $19.00
Publication: *Hosta Journal* (semiannual)

American Iris Society
Marilyn Harlow, Membership Secretary
Box 8455
San Jose, CA 95155
(408) 971-0444
Dues: $12.50
Publication: *Bulletin of the AIS* (quarterly)

American Ivy Society
Daphne Pfaff, Membership Chair
696 16th Avenue South
Naples, FL 33940
(813) 261-0388
Dues: $15.00
Publications: *The Ivy Journal* (annual);
Between the Vines (semiannual newsletter)

American Orchid Society
6000 South Olive Avenue
West Palm Beach, FL 33405
(407) 585-8666
Dues: $30.00
Publication: *Orchids* (monthly journal)

American Penstemon Society
Ann W. Bartlett, Membership Secretary
1569 South Holland Court
Lakewood, CO 80232
(303) 986-8096
Dues: $10.00
Publication: *APS Bulletin* (semiannual)

American Peony Society
c/o Greta Kessenich
250 Interlachen Road
Hopkins, MN 55343

(612) 938-4706
Dues: $10.00
Publication: *Bulletin* (quarterly)

American Primrose, Primula,
and Auricula Society
c/o Addaline Robinson
9705 SE Spring Crest Drive
Portland, OR 97225
Dues: $15.00
Publication: *Primroses* (quarterly)

American Rhododendron Society
Barbara R. Hall, Executive Director
Box 1380
Gloucester, VA 23061
(804) 693-4433
Dues: $25.00
Publication: *Journal of the ARS* (quarterly)

American Rose Society
Box 30,000
Shreveport, LA 71130
(318) 938-5402
Dues: $32.00
Publication: *The American Rose Magazine*
(eleven times annually); special interest
quarterlies

Azalea Society of America, Inc.
Membership Chair
Box 34536
West Bethesda, MD 20827
(301) 585-5269
Dues: $20.00
Publication: *The Azalean* (quarterly)

British Cactus and Succulent Society
Mr. P. A. Lewis, FBCSS
Firgrove, 1 Springwoods, Courtmoor
Fleet, Hants. GU13 9SU
England
Dues: £13.00
Publications: *British Cactus and Succulent
Journal* (quarterly); *Bradleya* (annual)

The British Clematis Society
Mrs. B. Risdon, Membership Secretary
The Tropical Bird Gardens, Rode
Bath, Somerset BA3 6QW
England
(0373) 83-0326
Dues: £12.00
Publication: *The Clematis Journal* (annual)

British and European Geranium Society
Leyland Cox
Norwood Chine, 26 Crabtree Lane
Sheffield, Yorkshire S5 7AY
England
(0742) 426-2000
Dues: $15.00
Publication: *The Geranium Gazette* (three
times annually);*The Geranium Yearbook*

British Fuchsia Society
Membership Secretary
20 Brodawel, Llannon
Llanelli, Dyfed SA14 6BJ
Wales
Dues: £5.00
Publication: *Bulletin* (semiannual)

British Iris Society
Mrs. E. M. Wise
197 The Parkway, Iver Heath
Iver, Bucks. SL0 0RQ
England
Publication: *The Iris Year Book*

British Pelargonium and Geranium
Society
c/o Carol Helyar
134 Montrose Avenue
Welling, Kent DA16 2QY
England
(081) 856-6137
Dues: £12.00
Publications: *Pelargonium News*
(three times annually);*Yearbook*

Bromeliad Society, Inc.
2488 East 49th Street
Tulsa, OK 74105
Dues: $20.00
Publication: *BSI Journal* (bimonthly)

Cactus and Succulent Society of America
c/o Dr. Seymour Linden
1535 Reeves Street
Los Angeles, CA 90035
(310) 556-1923
Dues: $30.00
Publication: *Cactus & Succulent Journal*
(bimonthly)

Canadian Begonia Society
70 Enfield Avenue
Toronto, Ontario M8W 1T9
Dues: Canada $20.00

Canadian Chrysanthemum
and Dahlia Society
c/o Karen Ojaste
17 Granard Boulevard
Scarborough, Ontario M1M 2E2
(416) 269-6960
Dues: Canada $10.00

Canadian Gladiolus Society
c/o W. L. Turbuck
3073 Grant Road
Regina, Saskatchewan S4S 5G9
Dues: Canada $10.00
Publication: *Canadian Gladiolus Annual*

Canadian Iris Society
c/o Verna Laurin
199 Florence Avenue
Willowdale, Ontario M2N 1G5
(415) 225-1088
Dues: Canada $5.00
Publication: *CIS Newsletter* (quarterly)

Canadian Orchid Congress
c/o Peter Root
Box 241

Goodwood, Ontario L0C 1A0
(416) 640-5643
Publication: *Canadian Orchid Journal*
(annual)

Canadian Pelargonium
and Geranium Society
Kathleen Gammer, Membership
Secretary
101-2008 Fullerton Avenue
North Vancouver, British Columbia
V7P 3G7
(604) 926-2190
Dues: Canada $10.00
Publication: *Storksbill* (quarterly)

Canadian Peony Society
1246 Donlea Crescent
Oakville, Ontario L6J 1V7
(416) 845-5380

Canadian Prairie Lily Society
M. E. Driver, Secretary
22 Red River Road
Saskatoon, Saskatchewan S7K 1G3
(306) 242-5329
Dues: Canada $5.00
Publication: *Newsletter* (quarterly)

Canadian Rose Society
Anne Graber, Secretary
10 Fairfax Crescent
Scarborough, Ontario M1L 1Z8
(416) 757-8809
Dues: Canada $18.00
Publications: *The Rosarian* (three times
annually); *Canadian Rose Annual*

The Cryptanthus Society
2355 Rusk
Beaumont, TX 77702
(409) 835-0644
Dues: $15.00
Publications: *The Cryptanthus Journal*
(quarterly); *Yearbook*

The Cycad Society
c/o David Mayo
1161 Phyllis Court
Mountain View, CA 94040
(415) 964-7898
Dues: $15.00
Publication: *The Cycad Newsletter*
(three times annually)

Cyclamen Society
Dr. D. V. Bent
Little Pilgrims, 2 Pilgrims Way East
Otford, Sevenoaks, Kent TN14 5QN
England
(0959) 52-2322
Dues: £7.00
Publication: *Cyclamen* (semiannual)

Cymbidium Society of America
533 South Woodland
Orange, CA 92669
(714) 532-4719
Dues: $25.00
Publication: *The Orchid Advocate*
 (bimonthly magazine)

The Daffodil Society (UK)
c/o Don Barnes
32 Montgomery Avenue
Sheffield S7 1NZ
England
Dues: £15.00

The Delphinium Society
Mrs. Shirley E. Bassett
"Takakkaw," Ice House Wood
Oxted, Surrey RH8 9DW
England
Dues: £10.00
Publication: *Delphimium Year Book*

Epiphyllum Society of America
Betty Berg, Membership Secretary
Box 1395
Monrovia, CA 91017
(818) 447-9688

Dues: $10.00
Publication: *The Bulletin* (bimonthly)

Gardenia Society of America
c/o Lyman Duncan
Box 879
Atwater, CA 95301
(209) 358-2231
Dues: $5.00
Publication: *Gardenia News*
(3 times annually)

The Geraniaceae Group
c/o Penny Clifton
9 Waingate Bridge Cottages
Haverigg, Cumbria LA18 4NF
England
Dues: $16.00
Publication: *The Geraniaceae Group News*
(quarterly)

Gesneriad Society International
Richard Dunn
11510 124th Terrace North
Largo, FL 34648
(813) 585-4247
Dues: $16.50
Publication: *Gesneriad Journal* (bimonthly)

Hardy Fern Foundation
Box 166
Medina, WA 98039
(206) 747-2998
Dues: $20.00
Publication: quarterly newsletter

The Heather Society
c/o Mrs. A. Small
Denbeigh, All Saints Road,
Creeting St. Mary
Ipswich, Suffolk 1P6 8PJ
England
(0449) 71-1220
Dues: £6.00
Publications: *Bulletin* (three times
annually); yearbook

Heliconia Society International
Flamingo Gardens
3750 Flamingo Road
Fort Lauderdale, FL 33330
(305) 473-2955
Dues: $35.00
Publication: HSI Bulletin (quarterly)

Herb Research Foundation
1007 Pearl Street, Suite 200
Boulder, CO 80301
(303) 449-2265
Dues: $35.00
Publication: HerbalGram (quarterly)

Herb Society of America, Inc.
9019 Kirtland Chardon Road
Mentor, OH 44060
(216) 256-0514
Dues: $35.00
Publications: *HSA News* (quarterly);
The Herbalist (annual)

Heritage Rose Group
Miriam Wilkins
925 Galvin Drive
El Cerrito, CA 94530
(510) 526-6960
Dues: $5.00
Publication: *Heritage Rose Letter* (quarterly)

Holly Society of America, Inc.
c/o Linda Parsons
11318 West Murdock
Wichita, KS 67212
(301) 825-8133
Dues: $15.00
Publication: *Holly Society Journal*
(quarterly)

The Hoya Society International
Box 1043
Porterdale, GA 30270
Dues: $20.00
Publication: *The Hoyan* (quarterly)

International Aroid Society
Box 43-1853
Miami, FL 33143
(305) 271-3767
Dues: $18.00
Publications: *IAS Newsletter* (bimonthly);
Aroideana (annual)

International Bulb Society
Box 4928
Culver City, CA 90230
Dues $30.00
Publication: *Herbertia* (annual journal)

International Camellia Society
c/o Thomas H. Perkins III
Box 750
Brookhaven, MS 39601
(601) 833-7351
Dues: $13.00
Publication: *International Camellia Journal*
(annual)

International Carnivorous Plant Society
Fullerton Arboretum
California State University
Fullerton, CA 92634
(714) 773-2766
Dues: $15.00
Publication: *Carnivorous Plant Newsletter*
(quarterly)

International Geranium Society
Membership Secretary
Box 92734
Pasadena, CA 91109
(818) 908-8867
Dues: $12.50
Publication: *Geraniums Around the World*
(quarterly journal)

International Lilac Society
The Holden Arboretum
9500 Sperry Road
Mentor, OH 44060
(216) 946-4400

Dues: $15.00
Publication: *Lilac Journal* (quarterly)

International Oleander Society
Elizabeth Head, Corresponding
Secretary
Box 3431
Galveston, TX 77552
(409) 762-9334
Dues: $10.00
Publication: *Nerium News* (quarterly)

International Ornamental Crabapple
Society
c/o Thomas L. Green
Department of Agriculture
Western Illinois University
Macomb, IL 61455
Dues: $15.00
Publication: *Malus* (semiannual)

The International Palm Society
Box 1897
Lawrence, KS 66044
(913) 843-1235
Dues: $25.00
Publication: *Principes* (quarterly)

International Tropical Fern Society
8720 SW 34th Street
Miami, FL 33165
(305) 221-0502

International Violet Association
c/o Elaine Kudela
8604 Main Road
Berlin Heights, OH 44814
(419) 588-2616
Dues: $15.00
Publication: *Sweet Times* (quarterly)

International Water Lily Society
c/o Dr. Edward Schneider
Santa Barbara Botanic Gardens
Santa Barbara, CA 93105
(805) 682-4726

Dues: $18.00
Publication: *Water Garden Journal*
(quarterly)

Los Angeles International Fern Society
Box 90943
Pasadena, CA 91109
Dues: $20.00
Publication: *LAIFS Journal*
(bimonthly)

Marigold Society of America, Inc.
c/o Jeannette Lowe
Box 5112
New Britain, PA 18901
(215) 348-5273
Dues: $12.00
Publication: *Amerigold Newsletter* (quarterly)

National Auricula and Primula Society
Mr. D. G. Hadfield
146 Queens Road, Cheadle Hulme
Cheadle, Cheshire SK8 5HY
England
Publication: yearbook

National Chrysanthemum Society (UK)
H. B. Locke
2 Lucas House, Craven Road
Rugby, Warwickshire CV21 3HY
England
(0788) 56-9039
Dues: $15.00
Publications: fall and spring bulletins;
yearbook

National Chrysanthemum Society, Inc.
(US)
Galen L. Goss
10107 Homar Pond Drive
Fairfax Station, VA 22039
(703) 978-7981
Dues: $12.50
Publication: *The Chrysanthemum*
(quarterly)

National Fuchsia Society
c/o Agnes Rietkerk
11507 East 187th Street
Artesia, CA 90701
(213) 865-1806
Dues: $15.00
Publication: *Fuchsia Fan* (bimonthly)

North American Gladiolus Council
c/o William Strawser
701 South Hendricks Avenue
Marion, IN 46953
(317) 664-3857
Dues: $10.00
Publication: *Bulletin* (quarterly)

North American Heather Society
c/o Pauline Croxton
3641 Indian Creek Road
Placerville, CA 95667
Dues: $10.00
Publication: *Heather News* (quarterly)

North American Lily Society, Inc.
Dr. Robert Gilman, Executive Secretary
Box 272
Owatonna, MN 55060
(507) 451-2170
Dues: $12.50
Publications: *Lily Yearbook;*
quarterly bulletin

Passiflora Society International
c/o Anna Zinno
Butterfly World
3900 West Sample Road
Coconut Creek, FL 33073
(305) 977-4434
Dues: $15.00
Publication: quarterly newsletter

Peperomia and Exotic Plant Society
c/o Anita Baudean
100 Neil Avenue
New Orleans, LA 70131
(504) 394-4146

Dues: $7.50
Publication: *The Gazette*
(three times annually)

The Plumeria Society of America, Inc.
Box 22791
Houston, TX 77227
Dues: $15.00
Publication: *Plumeria Potpourri* (quarterly newsletter)

Rare Conifer Foundation
Box 100
Potter Valley, CA 95469
Dues: $25.00
Publications: newsletter, yearbook

Rhododendron Society of Canada
c/o R. S. Dickhout
5200 Timothy Crescent
Niagara Falls, Ontario L2E 5G3
(416) 357-5981
Note: See American Rhododendron Society

Rhododendron Species Foundation
Box 3798
Federal Way, WA 98063
(206) 838-4646
Dues: $30.00
Publication: *RSF Newsletter* (quarterly)

Rose Hybridizers Association
c/o Larry D. Peterson
3245 Wheaton Road
Horseheads, NY 14845
(607) 562-8592
Dues: $7.00
Publication: quarterly newsletter

The Royal National Rose Society
The Secretary
Chiswell Green
St. Albans, Herts. AL2 3NR
England
(0727) 50-461

Dues: £13.50
Publication: *The Rose* (quarterly journal)

Royal Saintpaulia Club
c/o Ms. A. Moffett
Box 198
Sussex, New Brunswick E0E 1P0

Saintpaulia and Houseplant Society
The Secretary
33 Church Road, Newbury Park
Ilford, Essex 1G2 7ET
England
(081) 590-3710
Dues: £5.00
Publication: quarterly bulletin

Saintpaulia International
1650 Cherry Hill Road South
State College, PA 16803
(814) 237-7410
Publication: *Saintpaulia International News* (bimonthly)

Saxifrage Society
Adrian Young, Secretary
31 Eddington Road
London SW16 5BS
England
Dues: £10.00

The Sedum Society
c/o Micki Crozier
10502 North 135th Street West
Sedgwick, KS 67135
(316) 796-0496
Dues: $17.50
Publication: quarterly newsletter

Sempervivum Fanciers Association
37 Ox Bow Lane
Randolph, MA 02368
(617) 963-6737
Dues:
Publication: *SFA Newsletter* (quarterly)

The Sempervivum Society
The Secretary
11 Wingle Tye Road
Burgess Hill, West Sussex RH15 9HR
England
(0444) 23-6848
Dues: £2.50
Publication: *Newsletter*
(three times annually)

Solanaceae Enthusiasts
3370 Princeton Court
Santa Clara, CA 95051
(408) 241-9440
Publication: *Solanaceae Enthusiasts*
(quarterly)

Woody Plant Society
c/o Betty Ann Mech
1315 66th Avenue NE
Minneapolis, MN 55432
(612) 574-1197
Dues: $15.00
Publication: *Bulletin* (biannual)

World Federation of Rose Societies
c/o Jill Bennell
46 Alexandra Road
St. Albans, Herts. AL1 3AZ
England
(0727) 833-648
Dues: £25.00
Publication: *World Rose News* (semiannual)

Specialty Garden Organizations

Alpine Garden Club of British Columbia
Main Post Office Box 5161
Vancouver, British Columbia V6B 4B2
Publication: *Alpine Garden Club Bulletin*
(five times annually)

American Rock Garden Society
Secretary
Box 67

Millwood, NY 10546
(914) 762-2948
Dues: $25.00
Publication: *Rock Garden Quarterly*

Aquatic Gardeners Association
c/o Dorothy Reimer, Membership
83 Cathcart Street
London, Ontario N6C 3L9
Dues: $15.00
Publication: *The Aquatic Gardener*
(bimonthly journal)

Bonsai Clubs International
c/o Virginia Ellermann
2636 West Mission Road
Tallahassee, FL 32304
(904) 575-1442
Dues: $25.00
Publication: *Bonsai* (bimonthly magazine)

Cottage Garden Society
c/o Mrs. C. Tordorff
5 Nixon Close, Thornhill
Dewsbury, West Yorkshire. WF12 0JA
England
(0924) 46-8469
Dues: $20.00
Publication: *CGS Newsletter* (quarterly)

Desert Plant Society of Vancouver
Box 145-790
6200 McKay Avenue
Barnaby, British Columbia V5H 4MY
(604) 525-5315
Dues: Canada $15.00

Hardy Plant Society (UK)
Little Orchard, Great Comberton
Pershore WR10 3DP
England
(0386) 71-0317
Dues: £8.50
Publications: *The Hardy Plant*
(semiannual);
Newsletter (three times annually)

Hardy Plant Society (US)
c/o Betty Mackey
440 Louella Avenue
Wayne, PA 19087
Dues: $12.00
Publication: *The Newsletter* (quarterly)

Hobby Greenhouse Association
18517 Kingshill Road
Germantown, MD 20874
(410) 275-0377
Dues: $12.00
Publications: *Hobby Greenhouse* (quarterly);
HGA News (quarterly)

Hydroponic Society of America
2819 Crow Canyon Road, Suite 218
San Ramon, CA 94583
(510) 743-9605
Dues: $30.00
Publication: *Soilless Grower* (bimonthly)

Indoor Gardening Society of America
Sharon Zentz, Membership Secretary
944 South Munro Road
Tallmadge, OH 44278
(216) 733-8414
Dues: $20.00

International Society of Greenhouse
Gardeners
Box 7567
Olympia, WA 98507
Publication: newsletter

Northern Horticultural Society
Harlow Carr Gardens, Crag Lane
Harrogate, North Yorkshire HG3 1QB
England
(0423) 56-5418
Dues: £19.00
Publication: *Northern Gardener* (quarterly)

Pioneer Plant Society
c/o Ms. P. A. Puryear
708 Holland Street

Navasota, TX 77868
(409) 825-3220
Dues: $7.00
Publication: *PPS Newsletter* (quarterly)

Scottish Rock Garden Club
c/o Mrs. J. Thomlinson
1 Hillcrest Road
Bearsden, Glasgow G61 2EB
Scotland
Dues: $28.00
Publication: *The Rock Garden* (semiannual
journal)

The Terrarium Association
c/o Robert C. Baur
Box 276
Newfane, VT 05345
(802) 365-4721

Native Plant Societies and Botanical Clubs

National and Regional Organizations

American Association of Field Botanists
Box 23542
Chattanooga, TN 37422

American Floral Meadow Society
c/o John M. Krouse
University of Maryland
Cherry Hill Turf Research Facility
3120 Gracefield Road
Silver Spring, MD 20904
(301) 572-7247
Dues: $35.00
Publication: quarterly newsletter

American Wildflower Society
c/o John Rough, Treasurer
11 Johnson Avenue
Chicopee, MA 02138

Center for Plant Conservation
The Missouri Botanical Garden

4344 Shaw Boulevard
St. Louis, MO 63166
(314) 577-5100

Eastern Native Plant Alliance
Box 6101
McLean, VA 22106

National Wildflower Research Center
4801 La Crosse Avenue
Austin, TX 78739
(512) 292-4100
Dues: $25.00
Publication: bimonthly newsletter;
semiannual journal

New England Wild Flower Society, Inc.
Garden in the Woods
180 Hemenway Road
Framingham, MA 01701
(508) 877-7630
Dues: $35.00
Publication: newsletter
(three times annually)

Operation Wildflower
National Council of State Garden Clubs
9516 Glenbrook Drive
Charlotte, NC 28175

Southern Appalachian Botanical Club
c/o Charles N. Horn, Secretary/Treasurer
Biology Department
Newberry College
2100 College Street
Newberry, SC 29108

Alabama

Alabama Wildflower Society
c/o Dottie Elam, Treasurer
240 Ivy Lane
Auburn, AL 36830

Alaska

Alaska Native Plant Society
Box 141613
Anchorage, AK 99514

Arizona

Arizona Native Plant Society
Box 41206, Sun Station
Tucson, AZ 85717

Arkansas

Arkansas Native Plant Society
Route 2, Box 256BB
Mena, AR 71953
(501) 394-4666

California

California Native Grass Association
Box 566
Dixon, CA 95620
(916) 678-6282
Dues: $35.00
Publication: *Grasslands* (quarterly)

California Native Plant Society
1722 J Street, Suite 17
Sacramento, CA 95814
(916) 447-2677
Dues: $25.00
Publications: *Fremontia*
(quarterly magazine); *Bulletin* (newsletter)

Regional Parks Botanic Garden
Tilden Regional Park
Berkeley, CA 94708
(510) 841-8732
Publication: *The Four Seasons* (quarterly)

Southern California Botanists
c/o Alan Romspert
Department of Biology
Fullerton State University

Fullerton, CA 92634
(714) 449-7034
Dues: $8.00
Publication: *Crossosoma* (semiannual)

Colorado

Colorado Native Plant Society
Box 200
Fort Collins, CO 80522
Dues: $12.00
Publication: *Aquilegia*
(four to six times annually)

Connecticut

Connecticut Botanical Society
c/o Margaret Taylor, Secretary
10 Hillside Circle
Storrs, CT 06268

District of Columbia

Botanical Society of Washington
Department of Botany, NHB 166
Smithsonian Institution
Washington, DC 20560

Florida

Florida Native Plant Society
Box 680008
Orlando, FL 32868
(407) 299-1472
Dues: $20.00
Publication: *The Palmetto* (quarterly)

Georgia

Georgia Botanical Society
c/o Ted Reissing, President
5102 Hidden Branches Drive
Atlanta, GA 30338

Hawaii

Hawaii Botanical Society
Botany Department
University of Hawaii
3190 Maille Way
Honolulu, HI 96822

Hawaii Plant Conservation Center
National Tropical Botanical Garden
Box 340, Lawai
Kauai, HI 96765
(808) 332-7324

Idaho

Idaho Native Plant Society
Box 9451
Boise, ID 83707
Dues: $8.00
Publications: *Sage Notes* (bimonthly);
Sage Briefs (bimonthly)

Illinois

Illinois Native Plant Society
Forest Glen Preserve
20301 East 900 North Road
Westville, IL 61883

Indiana

Indiana Native Plant and
Wildflower Society
c/o Caroline Harstad
5952 Lieber Road
Indianapolis, IN 46208

Kansas

Kansas Wildflower Society
c/o R. L. McGregor Herbarium
University of Kansas
2045 Constant Avenue
Lawrence, KS 66047

Kentucky

Kentucky Native Plant Society
c/o Dr. Douglas N. Reynolds
Department of Natural Sciences
East Kentucky University
Richmond, KY 40475

Louisiana

Louisiana Native Plant Society
c/o Ella Price
Box 393
Blanchard, LA 71009
Dues: $10.00
Publication: *LNPS Newsletter* (quarterly)

Louisiana Project Wildflower
Lafayette Natural History Museum
637 Girard Park Drive
Lafayette, LA 70503

Maine

Josselyn Botanical Society
c/o Marilyn Dwelley, Treasurer
Box 41
China, ME 04926

Maryland

Maryland Native Plant Society
Box 4877
Silver Spring, MD 20914

Massachusetts

New England Botanical Club
22 Divinity Avenue
Cambridge, MA 02138

Michigan

Michigan Botanical Club
c/o Dr. Peter Kaufman
Biology Department

University of Michigan
Ann Arbor, MI 48109

Wildflower Association of Michigan
Box 80527
6011 West St. Joseph, Suite 403
Lansing, MI 48908

Minnesota

Friends of the Eloise Butler Wildflower
Garden
Box 11592
Minneapolis, MN 55412

Minnesota Native Plant Society
220 BioScience Center
University of Minnesota
1445 Gortner Avenue
St. Paul, MN 55108

Mississippi

Mississippi Native Plant Society
c/o Victor Rudis
Box 2151
Starkville, MS 38759
(601) 324-0430
Dues: $7.50
Publication: quarterly newsletter

Missouri

Missouri Native Plant Society
Box 20073
St. Louis, MO 63144
(314) 577-9522
Dues: $9.00
Publications: *Petal Pusher*
(bimonthly newsletter);
Missouriensis (semiannual journal)

Montana

Montana Native Plant Society
Box 8783, Missoula, MT 59807

Nevada

The Mohave Native Plant Society
8180 Placid Street
Las Vegas, NV 89123

Northern Nevada Native Plant Society
c/o Loring Williams
Box 8965
Reno, NV 89507
(702) 358-7759
Dues: $10.00
Publication: newsletter (nine times
annually)

New Jersey

Native Plant Society of New Jersey
Box 231
Cook College
New Brunswick, NJ 08903

New Mexico

Native Plant Society of New Mexico
443 Live Oak Loop NE
Albuquerque, NM 87122
(505) 356-3942
Dues: $10.00
Publication: bimonthly newsletter

New York

Amherst Museum Wildflower Society
3755 Tonawanda Creek Road
East Amherst, NY 14501

Long Island Botanical Society
45 Sandy Hill Road
Oyster Bay, NY 11771

New York Flora Association
New York State Museum
3132 CEC
Albany, NY 12230

Niagara Frontier Botanical Society
Buffalo Museum of Science
1020 Humboldt Parkway
Buffalo, NY 14211

Syracuse Botanical Club
c/o Janet Holmes
101 Ambergate Road
DeWitt, NY 13214

Torrey Botanical Club
c/o Margaret Basile, Treasurer
Department of Biological Science
Herbert H. Lehman College
Bronx, NY 10468

North Carolina

North Carolina Wild Flower
Preservation Society
UNC Botanical Garden
Chapel Hill, NC 27517
(919) 962-0522
Dues: $15.00
Publication: semiannual newsletter

Western Carolina Botanical Club
c/o Dick Smith
6 Tenequa Drive
Connestee Falls
Brevard, NC 28712

University Botanical Gardens at Asheville
151 W. T. Weaver Boulevard
Asheville, NC 28804

Ohio

Native Plant Society of Northeastern
Ohio
2651 Kerwick Road
University Heights, OH 44118

Ohio Native Plant Society
c/o A. K. Malmquist
6 Louise Drive

Chagrin Falls, OH 44022
(216) 338-6622
Publication: *Trillium* (bimonthly)

Oklahoma

Oklahoma Native Plant Society
Tulsa Garden Center
2435 South Peoria
Tulsa, OK 74114

Oregon

Native Plant Society of Oregon
c/o Jan Dobak, Membership Chair
2584 NW Savier Street
Portland, OR 97210
(503) 248-9242
Dues: $12.00
Publications: *Kalmiopsis* (annual);
Bulletin (monthly)

Pennsylvania

Botanical Society of Western
Pennsylvania
c/o Robert F. Bahl, Secretary
401 Clearview Avenue
Pittsburgh, PA 15205

Delaware Valley Fern and
Wildflower Society
c/o Dana Cartwright
263 Hillcrest Road
Wayne, PA 19087

Muhlenberg Botanical Society
North Museum
Franklin and Marshall College
Box 3003
Lancaster, PA 17604

Pennsylvania Native Plant Society
1806 Commonwealth Building
316 4th Avenue
Pittsburgh, PA 15222

Philadelphia Botanical Club
Academy of Science
19th and Parkway
Philadelphia, PA 19103

Rhode Island

Rhode Island Wild Plant Society
12 Sanderson Road
Smithfield, RI 01917

South Dakota

Great Plains Botanical Society
Box 461
Hot Springs, SD 57747

Tennessee

Tennessee Native Plant Society
Department of Botany
University of Tennessee
Knoxville, TN 37996
(615) 691-0077
Dues: $15.00
Publication: bimonthly newsletter

The Wildflower Society
c/o Goldsmith Civic Garden Center
750 Cherry Road
Memphis, TN 38119

Texas

El Paso Native Plant Society
7760 Maya Avenue
El Paso, TX 79912

Native Plant Society of Texas
c/o Dana Tucker
Box 891
Georgetown, TX 78627
(512) 863-7794
Dues: $20.00
Publication: *Texas Native Plant Society News*
(bimonthly)

Native Prairies Association of Texas
301 Nature Center Drive
Austin, TX 78746
(512) 327-8181
Dues: $15.00
Publication: quarterly journal

Utah

Utah Native Plant Society
c/o Pam Poulson
Box 520041
Salt Lake City, UT 84152
Dues: $10.00
Publication: *Sego Lily* (bimonthly)

Vermont

Vermont Botanical and Bird Clubs
c/o Deborah Benjamin, Secretary
Box 327
Warren Road
Eden, VT 05652

Virginia

Virginia Native Plant Society
c/o Nicky Staunton
Box 844
Annandale, VA 22003
Dues: $15.00
Publication: *Bulletin* (quarterly)

Washington

Washington Native Plant Society
c/o Shirly Post
Box 576
Woodinville, WA 98072
(206) 485-2193
Dues: $12.00
Publication: *Douglasia* (quarterly)

West Virginia

West Virginia Native Plant Society
Corresponding Secretary
Box 2755
Elkins, WV 26241
Dues: $8.00
Publication: *Native Notes*

Wisconsin

Botanical Club of Wisconsin
Wisconsin Academy of Arts,
Sciences, and Letters
1922 University Avenue
Madison, WI 53705

Wild Ones Natural Landscapers, Ltd.
c/o Judy Crane
Box 23576
Milwaukee, WI 53223
(414) 251-2185
Dues: $15.00
Publication: bimonthly newsletter

Wyoming

Wyoming Native Plant Society
3165 University Station
Laramie, WY 82071
Publication: newsletter

Canada

The Canadian Wildflower Society
John Craw, Business Secretary
Unit 12A, Box 228
4981 Highway 7 East
Markham, Ontario L3R 1N1
(416) 294-9075
Dues: $30.00
Publication: *Wildflower* (quarterly)

Newfoundland Chapter
Canadian Wildflower Society
c/o Sue Meades

633 Pouch Cove Highway
Flatrock, Newfoundland A1K 1C8

Nova Scotia Wild Flora Society
Nova Scotia Museum
1747 Summer Street
Halifax, Nova Scotia B3H 3A6
Dues: Canada $12.00
Publication: *NSWFS Newsletter*

Wellington/Waterloo Chapter
Canadian Wildflower Society
c/o Allan Anderson
Botany Department
University of Guelph
Guelph, Ontario N1G 2W1

Professional Organizations

American Association of
Nurserymen/Garden Centers of America
1250 I Street, Suite 500
Washington, DC 20005
(202) 789-2900

American Seed Trade Association
1030 15th Street NW, Suite 964
Washington, DC 20005
(202) 223-4080

American Society of Consulting Arborists
5130 West 101st Circle
Westminster, CO 80030
(303) 466-2722

American Society for Horticultural
Science
113 South West Street, Suite 400
Alexandria, VA 22314
(703) 836-4606

American Society of
Landscape Architects
4401 Connecticut Avenue NW
Washington, DC 20008
(202) 686-2752

Canadian Horticultural Council
1101 Prince of Wales Drive, Suite 310
Ottawa, Ontario K2C 3W7
(613) 226-4187

Canadian Nursery Trades Association
1293 Matheson Boulevard
Mississauga, Ontario L4W 1R1
(416) 629-1367

Garden Writers Association of America
c/o J. C. McGowan
10210 Leatherleaf Court
Manassas, VA 22111
(703) 257-1032

Mailorder Association of Nurseries, Inc.
8683 Doves Fly Way
Laurel, MD 20723
(301) 490-9143

National Garden Bureau/All-America
Selections
1311 Butterfield Road, Suite 310
Downers Grove, IL 60515
(708) 963-0770

Perennial Plant Association
3383 Schirtzinger Road
Hilliard, OH 43026
(614) 771-8431

Professional Plant Growers Association
Box 27517
Lansing, MI 48909
(800) 647-7742

Government Sources for Gardeners

THE UNITED STATES Department of Agriculture provides a number of valuable services to gardeners, at little or no cost, through the Cooperative Extension Service. Extension Service offices are located in over three thousand counties in all fifty states. For obvious reasons of space, only the horticulture specialists at state headquarters offices are listed here. Check the government blue pages of your local phone book or call the USDA Information Office (see below) for your local county extension office. For a list of on-line USDA information servers, see chapter 11.

Extension Service agents provide information and advice on all aspects of gardening. Through them, you can arrange for soil and water testing, have your garden pests identified, receive pamphlets and other publications, get cultivation advice, attend classes, organize a 4-H club, and participate in many other activities and services. The Cooperative Extension Service also sponsors the Master Gardener program (see below) and operates the National Agricultural Library (see chapter 10).

United States Department of Agriculture

Infomation Office
United States Department of Agriculture
Washington, DC 20250
(202) 447-8005

For information regarding permits to import plants from abroad, and regarding plant inspection stations, contact:

United States Department of Agriculture
Animal and Plant Health Inspection Service
Permit Unit
Federal Building
Hyattsville, MD 20782

USDA Cooperative Extension Service

Alabama

Dr. Ronald Shumack
Extension Horticulture Department
Auburn University
Auburn, AL 36849
(205) 826-4985

Alaska

Wayne G. Vandre
Extension Horticulturist
2221 East Northern Lights Boulevard
University of Alaska
Anchorage, AK 99508
(907) 279-6576

Arizona

Dr. Michael Kilby
Extension Horticulturist
University of Arizona
Tucson, AZ 85721
(602) 621-1400

Arkansas

Kenneth R. Scott
Extension Horticulturist
Box 391
Little Rock, AR 72203
(501) 376-6301

Dr. Gerald Klingaman
Extension Horticulturist
316 Plant Science Building
University of Arkansas
Fayetteville, AR 72701
(501) 575-2603

California

William B. Davis
Extension Environmental Horticulturist
University of California
Davis, CA 95616
(916) 752-0412

Dr. Tokuji Furuta
Extension Environmental Horticulturist
4114 Batchelor Hall
University of California
Riverside, CA 92521
(714) 787-3318

Colorado

Dr. Kenneth W. Knutson
Extension Associated Professor
Department of Horticulture
University of Colorado
Fort Collins, CO 80523
(303) 491-7068

Connecticut

Edmond L. Marotte
Consumer Horticulturist
Department of Plant Science
University of Connecticut
Storrs, CT 06268
(203) 486-3435

Delaware

Susan Barton
Extension Horticulturist
Townsend Hall
University of Delaware
Newark, DE 19711
(302) 451-2532

District of Columbia

Pamela Marshall
Extension Horticulturist
1351 Nicholson Street NW
Washington, DC 20011
(202) 282-7410

Florida

Dr. Robert J. Black
Extension Urban Horticulture Specialist
Ornamental Horticulture Department
University of Florida
Gainesville, FL 32611
(904) 392-1835

Georgia

Dr. A. Jefferson Lewis
Extension Horticulturist
University of Georgia
Athens, GA 30602
(404) 542-2340

Hawaii

Dr. Harry Bittenbender
Extension Horticulturist
University of Hawaii
Honolulu, HI 96822
(808) 948-6043

Idaho

Larry O'Keeffe
Department of Plant, Soil and
Entomological Sciences
University of Idaho
Moscow, ID 83843
(208) 885-6277

Illinois

James Schmidt
Extension Specialist
104 Ornamental Horticulture Building
University of Illinois
Urbana, IL 61801
(217) 333-2125

Indiana

B. R. Lerner
Extension Horticulturist
Department of Horticulture
Purdue University
West Lafayette, IN 47907
(317) 494-1311

Iowa

Dr. Michael L. Agnew
Extension Horticulturist
Department of Horticulture
Iowa State University
Ames, IA 50011
(515) 294-0027

Kansas

Dr. Frank Morrison
Extension Program Leader
Water Hall 227
Kansas State University
Manhattan, KS 66506
(913) 532-6173

Kentucky

Dr. John Strang
Extension Horticulturist
Agriculture Science Center North
University of Kentucky
Lexington, KY 40546
(606) 257-5685

Louisiana

Dr. Thomas Pope
Horticulture Specialist
J. C. Miller Horticulture Building
Louisiana State University
Baton Rouge, LA 70803
(504) 388-2222

Maine

Dr. Lois Berg Stack
Ornamental Horticulture Specialist
University of Maine
Orono, ME 04469
(207) 581-2949

Maryland

Dr. Francis Gouin
Department of Horticulture
University of Maryland
College Park, MD 20742
(301) 454-3143

Massachusetts

Kathleen Carool
Extension Specialist, Horticulture
French Hall
University of Massachusetts
Amherst, MA 01003
(413) 545-0895

Michigan

Dr. Jerome Hull Jr.
Department of Horticulture
Michigan State University
East Lansing, MI 48824
(517) 355-5194

Minnesota

Deborah L. Brown
Extension Horticulturist
1970 Folwell Avenue
University of Minnesota
St. Paul, MN 55108
(612) 624-7419

Mississippi

Dr. Richard Mullenax
Extension Horticulturist
Department of Horticulture
Box 5446
Mississippi Valley State College, MS
39762

Missouri

Dr. Gary C. Long
Extension Ornamental Plant Specialist
University of Missouri
Columbia, MO 65211
(314) 882-9625

Montana

Dr. James W. Bauder
Extension Specialist
Plant and Soil Science Department
Montana State University
Bozeman, MT 59717
(406) 994-4605

Nebraska

Dr. Donald Steinegger
Extension Horticulturist
377 Plant Science Building
University of Nebraska
Lincoln, NE 68503
(402) 472-2550

Nevada

William J. Carlos
Extension Horticulturist
1001 East 9th Street
Reno, NV 89520
(702) 328-2650

New Hampshire

Dr. Charles Williams
Extension Ornamentals Specialist
Plant Science Department
University of New Hampshire
Durham, NH 03824
(603) 862-3207

New Jersey

Lawrence D. Little Jr.
Extension Horticulturist
Blake Hall
Rutgers—The State University
New Brunswick, NJ 08903
(201) 932-9559

New Mexico

George Dickerson
Extension Horticulturist
9301 Indian School Road
New Mexico State University
Albuquerque, NM 87112
(505) 292-0097

New York

Robert Kozlowski
Senior Extension Associate
Homes and Grounds
17 Plant Science Building
Cornell University
Ithaca, NY 14853
(607) 255-1791

North Carolina

Dr. Joseph Love
Extension Horticulturist
Department of Horticultural Science
North Carolina State University
Raleigh, NC 27695
(919) 737-3322

North Dakota

Dr. Ronald Smith
Extension Horticulturist
North Dakota State University
Fargo, ND 58105
(701) 237-8161

Ohio

Barbara J. Williams
Extension Horticulturist
2001 Fyffe Court
Ohio State University
Columbus, OH 43210
(614) 292-3852

Oklahoma

Paul J. Mitchell
Extension Horticulturist
Oklahoma State University
Stillwater, OK 74078
(405) 624-6593

Oregon

Dr. James L. Green
Extension Ornamentals Specialist
Department of Horticulture
Oregon State University
Corvallis, OR 97331
(503) 754-3464

Pennsylvania

Dr. J. Robert Nuss
Extension Horticulturist
Department of Horticulture
Pennsylvania State College
102 Tyson Building
University Park, PA 16802
(814) 863-2196

Rhode Island

Kathy Mallon
Extension Specialist
Department of Plant Science
University of Rhode Island
Kingston, RI 02881
(401) 792-5999

South Carolina

Dr. Alta Kingman
Extension Horticulturist
173 Plant and Agriculture Science
Building
Clemson University
Clemson, SC 29634
(803) 656-4962

South Dakota

Dean M. Martin
Extension Horticulturist
South Dakota State University
Brookings, SD 57007
(605) 688-5136

Tennessee

Dr. Elmer Ashburn
Department of Plant and Soil Science
Box 1071
University of Tennessee
Knoxville, TN 37901
(615) 974-7208

Texas

Dr. William Welch
Extension Horticulturist
225 Horticulture Building
Texas A & M University
College Station, TX 77843
(409) 845-7341

Utah

Dr. Gerald Olson
UMC 4900
Utah State University
Logan, UT 84322
(801) 750-2194

Vermont

Dr. Leonard Perry
Extension Horticulturist
Hills Building
University of Vermont
Burlington, VT 05405
(802) 656-2630

Virginia

Dr. Paul Smeal
Extension Horticulturist
Virginia Polytechnical Institute
Blacksburg, VA 24061
(703) 961-5609

Washington

Dr. Robert Thornton
Extension Horticulturist
Washington State University
Pullman, WA 99164
(509) 335-2811

West Virginia

Dr. Richard Zimmerman
Extension Horticulturist
2088 Agricultural Sciences Building
West Virginia University
Morgantown, WV 26506
(304) 293-4801

Wisconsin

Dr. R. C. Newman
Extension Horticulturist
University of Wisconsin
Madison, WI 53706
(608) 262-1624

Wyoming

Dr. James Cook
Extension Horticulturist
University of Wyoming
Laramie, WY 82071
(307) 766-2243

Master Gardener Program

*The Master Gardener program has been sponsored
by the USDA Extension Service since 1972. This
valuable program provides free or inexpensive horticultural training to volunteers, who then repay
the training costs—through volunteer service in
their communities—by participating in local
beautification efforts, answering plant information
hotlines, or working with local gardening groups,
for example. The training programs vary considerably, especially in length and focus, from state
to state. For more information about participating
in the program, contact the Master Gardener
Coordinator at your state extension office (see
above) or:*

Master Gardeners International
Corporation (MaGIC)
Membership Services
2904 Cameron Mills Road
Alexandria, VA 22302
(703) 920-6677
Dues: $10.00
Publication: MaGIC Lantern (quarterly)

Canada

For information about government programs regarding horticulture, contact:

Agriculture Canada
Communications Branch
Ottawa, Ontario K1A 0C7
(613) 995-5222

The Well-Read Gardener

As A GROUP, *gardeners are big readers. They read lots of plant catalogues, of course, but they also read pretty much anything else they can find about gardens, gardening, and other gardeners. This section lists commercial magazines and newsletters about general, regional, and specialty gardening. (See chapter 8 for the interesting publications put out by gardening organizations.) Also listed here are dealers in new and old gardening books, book clubs, and libraries with significant horticultural collections.*

Magazines and Newsletters

If you're looking for articles about a particular aspect of gardening, these two indexes (often carried by large public libraries and specialized horticultural libraries—see below) may help you find what you need:

Gardener's Index
CompuDex Press
Box 27041
Kansas City, MO 64110
Frequency: annual
Subscription: $18.00

Garden Literature
Garden Literature Press
398 Columbus Avenue, Suite 181
Boston, MA 02116
Frequency: quarterly
Subscription: $50.00

General Gardening

Allen Lacy's Homeground
Allen Lacy

Box 271
Linwood, NJ 08221
Frequency: quarterly newsletter
Subscription: $38.00

The Avant Gardener
Horticultural Data Processors
Box 489
New York, NY 10028
Frequency: monthly newsletter
Subscription: $18.00

Baer's Garden Newsletter
John Baer's Sons
Box 328
Lancaster, PA 17608
Frequency: quarterly
Subscription: $5.00

Backyard Gardener Idea Letter
James J. Martin
Box 605
Winfield, IL 60190

Beautiful Gardens
CMK Publishing

350 Brannan Street
San Francisco, CA 94107
(800) 677-6411
Frequency: bimonthly
Subscription: $17.00

Canadian Gardening
Camar Publications, Ltd.
130 Spy Court
Markham, Ontario L3R 5H6
Frequency: bimonthly
Subscription: Canada $23.00

Country Home Country Gardens
Meredith Corporation
Box 55154
Boulder, CO 80322
(800) 677-0484
Frequency: quarterly
Subscription: $15.00

Country Journal
Box 8200
Harrisburg, PA 17105
(717) 657-9555
(800) 435-9610
Frequency: bimonthly
Subscription: $20.00

Country Living
Hearst Corporation
Box 10557
Des Moines, IA 50340
(800) 777-0102
Frequency: monthly
Subscription: $28.00

Country Living Gardener
Hearst Corporation
Box 10557
Des Moines, IA 50340
(800) 777-0102
Frequency: quarterly
Subscription: $10.00

Fine Gardening
The Taunton Press
Box 5506
Newtown, CT 06470
(203) 426-8171
Frequency: bimonthly
Subscription: $28.00

Flower & Garden
KC Publishing
700 West 47th Street, Suite 310
Kansas City, MO 64112
(816) 531-5730
Frequency: bimonthly
Subscription: $15.00

Garden Clippin's
Gene E. Bush
323 Woodside Drive
Depauw, IN 47115
(812) 633-4858
Frequency: monthly
Subscription: $15.00

Garden Design
Evergreen Publishing Company
Box 55458
Boulder, CO 80322
(800) 234-5118
Frequency: bimonthly
Subscription: $28.00

Garden Gate
Woodsmith Corporation
2200 Grand Avenue
Des Moines, IA 50312
(800) 341-4769
Frequency: bimonthly
Subscription: $20.00

Gardens and Nature
Box 394
Sound Beach, NY 11789
Frequency: bimonthly
Subscription: $12.00

Gardens Illustrated
John Brown Publishing, Ltd.
Frome, Somerset 8A11 1YA
England
US phone: (516) 627-3836
Frequency: bimonthly
Subscription: $50.00

Green Prints: The Weeder's Digest
Pat Stone
Box 1355
Fairview, NC 28730
(800) 569-0602
Frequency: quarterly
Subscription: $14.00

Grow America
Ames Lawn and Garden Tools
Box 1485
Mansfield, OH 44901
Frequency: bimonthly
Subscription: free

Harrowsmith Country Life
Camden House Publishing
Ferry Road
Charlotte, VT 05445
Frequency: bimonthly
Subscription: $18.00

Home Garden
Meredith Corporation
1716 Locust Street
Des Moines, IA 50309
(800) 413-9748
Frequency: bimonthly
Subscription: $20.00

Horticulture: The Magazine of American Gardening
Horticulture, Inc.
Box 53879
Boulder, CO 80321
(617) 742-5600
Frequency: ten times annually
Subscription: $26.00

Hortideas
Greg and Pat Williams
460 Black Lick Road
Gravel Switch, KY 40328
Frequency: monthly
Subscription: $15.00

Hortus
David Wheeler
The Neuadd
Rhayader, Powys LD6 5HH
Wales
Frequency: quarterly
Subscription: £35.00

HousePlant Magazine
HousePlant, Inc.
Route 1, Box 271–2
Elkins, WV 26241
Frequency: bimonthly
Subscription: $20.00

Indoor & Patio Gardening
Box 1182
Fort Washington, PA 19034
Frequency: bimonthly
Subscription: $17.85

National Gardening
National Gardening Association
180 Flynn Avenue
Burlington, VT 05401
(802) 863-1308
(800) 727-9097
Frequency: bimonthly
Subscription: $18.00

On the Garden Line®
The YardenCare Company
Box 6047
Wixom, MI 48393
(800) 336-5885
Frequency: eight times annually
Subscription: $28.00

Organic Flower Gardening
Rodale Press, Inc.
33 East Minor Street
Emmaus, PA 18098
(800) 666-2206
Frequency: semiannual
Subscription: $2.95/issue; newsstand sales
only

Organic Gardening
Rodale Press, Inc.
33 East Minor Street
Emmaus, PA 18098
(800) 666-2206
Frequency: nine times annually
Subscription: $25.00

Plant & Garden
Gardenvale Publishing Company, Ltd.
1 Pacifique
Ste. Anne de Bellevue, Quebec H9X 1C5
(514) 457-2744
Frequency: quarterly
Subscription: $17.00

Plants & Gardens
Brooklyn Botanic Garden
1000 Washington Avenue
Brooklyn, NY 11225
Frequency: quarterly
Subscription: $25.00

The Plantsman
Maxwell Publishing
80 Vincent Square
London SW1P 2PE
England
Frequency: quarterly
Subscription: £19.50

Weekend Gardening
Harris Publications, Inc.
1115 Broadway
New York, NY 10010
Frequency: monthly
Subscription: $20.00

Regional Gardening Periodicals

John E. Bryan Gardening Newsletter
John E. Bryan, Inc.
300 Valley Street, Suite 206
Sausalito, CA 94965
Region: northern California
Frequency: monthly
Subscription: $30.00

California Garden
San Diego Floral Association
Casa del Prado
Balboa Park
San Diego, CA 92101
Region: California
Frequency: bimonthly
Subscription: $7.00

Carolina Gardener
Carolina Gardener, Inc.
Box 4504
Greensboro, NC 27404
(800) 245-0142
Region: North and South Carolina
Frequency: bimonthly
Subscription: $15.00

The Four Seasons
Regional Parks Botanic Garden
Tilden Regional Park
Berkeley, CA 94708
(510) 841-8732
Region: California-native plants
Frequency: quarterly
Subscription: $12.00

The Gardener's Gazette
Michael Henry
Box 786
Georgetown, CT 06829
Region: New England
Frequency: ten times annually
Subscription: $15.00

Gardening Newsletter by Bob Flagg
Morningside Associates
5002 Morningside
Houston, TX 77005
Region: Sun Belt and Gulf Coast
Frequency: monthly
Subscription: $16.00

Gardens West
Dorothy Horton
Box 2690
Vancouver, British Columbia V6B 3W8
Region: western Canada
Frequency: nine times annually
Subscription: Canada $20.00

Growing Native
Growing Native Research Institute
Box 489
Berkeley, CA 94701
Region: western US
Frequency: bimonthly
Subscription: $30.00

The Island Grower
Greenheart Publications
RR 4
Sooke, British Columbia V0S 1N0
Region: Pacific Northwest
Frequency: ten times annually
Subscription: Canada $19.00

*Minnesota Horticulturist: The Magazine of
Northern Gardening*
Minnesota State Horticultural Society
1970 Folwell Avenue
St. Paul, MN 55108
(800) 676-6747
Frequency: nine times annually
Subscription: $25.00

Native Notes
Joseph L. Collins
Route 2, Box 550
Heiskell, TN 37754
Region: eastern US

Frequency: quarterly
Subscription: $17.00

New England Farm Bulletin and Garden Gazette
Jacob's Meadow, Inc.
Box 67
Taunton, MA 02780
Region: New England
Frequency: twenty-four times annually
Subscription: $17.00

Pacific Horticulture
Pacific Horticulture Foundation
Circulation Department
Box 485
Berkeley, CA 94701
(510) 849-1627
Region: California/Pacific Northwest
Frequency: quarterly
Subscription: $15.00

Rocky Mountain Gardener
Box 1230
Gunnison, CO 81230
Region: Rocky Mountain states
Frequency: quarterly
Subscription: $12.00

The Southern California Gardener
610 20th Street
Santa Monica, CA 90402
Region: southern California
Frequency: bimonthly
Subscription: $20.00

Southern Living
Box 830219
Birmingham, AL 35283
Region: Southeast and Texas
Frequency: monthly
Subscription: $25.00

Neil Sperry's Gardens
Gardens South
Box 864
McKinney, TX 75070

Region: Texas and Gulf Coast
Frequency: ten times annually
Subscription: $21.50

Sundew Garden Reports
Tom Carey
Box 214
Oviedo, FL 32765
Region: Florida and Southeast
Frequency: bimonthly
Subscription: $15.00

Sunset Magazine
Sunset Publishing Company
80 Willow Road
Menlo Park, CA 94025
(800) 777-0117
Region: western US
Frequency: monthly
Subscription: $21.00

Texas Gardener
Chris S. Corby
Box 9005
Waco, TX 76714
Region: Texas
Frequency: bimonthly
Subscription: $15.00

The Weedpatch Gazette
229 Gage Road
Riverside, IL 60546
Region: Chicago area
Frequency: quarterly
Subscription: $18.00

Specialty Gardening Periodicals

The American Cottage Gardener
131 East Michigan Street
Marquette, MI 49855
Frequency: quarterly
Subscription: $35.00

Birds & Blooms
5400 South 60th Street
Greendale, WI 53129
(414) 423-0100
Frequency: bimonthly
Subscription: $17.00

Garden Railways
Sidestreet Bannerworks
Box 61461
Denver, CO 80206
Frequency: bimonthly
Subscription: $21.00

Hardy Enough: Experimental Gardeners Journal
351 Pleasant Street
Northampton, MA 01060
Frequency: bimonthly
Subscription: $27.00

HerbalGram
American Botanical Council
Box 201660
Austin, TX 78720
(512) 331-8868
Frequency: quarterly
Subscription: $25.00

The Herb Companion
Interweave Press, Inc.
201 East 4th Street
Loveland, CO 80537
(970) 669-7672
(800) 645-3675
Frequency: bimonthly
Subscription: $24.00

The Herb Quarterly
Long Mountain Press, Inc.
Box 689
San Anselmo, CA 94960
Frequency: quarterly
Subscription: $24.00

Gardening Book Dealers

Most large bookstores carry a good selection of recent horticulture titles, but not many carry specialized titles, serious reference works, or books that are more than a few years old. Fortunately, a number of specialized book dealers are available to help you find both new and old titles. Most issue catalogues on a more or less regular basis. Most dealers in used and rare titles will search for out-of-print books for you for a modest fee or even for free.

ABT Books
6673 Chadbourne Drive
North Olmsted, OH 44070
Specialties: used and out-of-print

Acres U.S.A. Book Sales
Box 9547
Kansas City, MO 64133
Specialties: general organic gardening

agAccess
Box 2008
603 4th Street
Davis, CA 95616
(916) 756-7177
Specialties: agriculture and horticulture

Agave Books
Box 2539
Providence, RI
(401) 831-3833
Specialties: used, rare, and out-of-print

The American Botanist
Box 532
1103 West Truitt
Chillicothe, IL 61523
(309) 274-5254
Specialties: used, rare, and out-of-print

Anchor & Dolphin Books
Box 823
30 Franklin Street

Newport, RI 02840
(401) 846-6890
Specialties: used, rare, and out-of-print
garden history

Andover Books & Prints
68 Park Street
Andover, MA 01810
(508) 475-1645
Specialties: used, rare, and out-of-print
herbs

Carol Barnett Books
3562 NE Liberty Street
Portland, OR 97211
(503) 282-7036
Specialties: used, rare, and out-of-print

J. F. Beattie Book Company
105 North Wayne Avenue
Wayne, PA 19087
(215) 687-3347
Specialties: used, rare, and out-of-print

Bell's Book Store
536 Emerson Street
Palo Alto, CA 94301
(415) 323-7822
Specialties: new, used, rare, and out-of-print

B. L. Bibby Books
1225 Sardine Creek Road
Gold Hill, OR 97525
(503) 855-1621
Specialties: used, rare, and out-of-print

Robin Bledsoe, Bookseller
1640 Massachusetts Avenue
Cambridge, MA 02138
(617) 576-3634
Specialties: used, rare, and out-of-print

Book Arbor
Box 20885
Baltimore, MD 21215

(410) 367-0338
Specialties: used, rare, and out-of-print

Book Orchard
1379 Park Western Drive
San Pedro, CA 90732
(310) 548-4279
Specialties: western gardening

The Bookpress, Ltd.
Box KP
411 West Duke of Gloucester Street
Williamsburg, VA 23187
(804) 229-1260

The Book Tree
12 Pine Hill Road
Englishtown, NJ 07726
(908) 446-3853
Specialties: general gardening

The Botana Collection
Box 085756
Racine, WI 53408
(414) 633-2772
(800) 723-8502
Specialties: orchids

Warren F. Broderick Books
Box 124
Lansingburgh, NY 12182
(518) 235-4041
Specialties: used, rare, and out-of-print

Brooks Books
Box 21473
Concord, CA 94521
(510) 672-4566
Specialties: new, used, rare, and out-of-print

Builders Booksource
1817 4th Street
Berkeley, CA 94710
(800) 843-2028
Specialties: general gardening

A. C. Burke & Company
2554 Lincoln Boulevard, Suite 1058
Marina Del Ray, CA 90291
(310) 574-2770
Specialties: general gardening

Calendula Horticultural Books
Box 930
Picton, Ontario K0K 2T0
(613) 476-3521
Specialties: used, rare, and out-of-print

Capability's Books
2379 Highway 48
Deer Park, WI 54007
(800) 247-8154
Specialties: general gardening

Cape Cod Book Center
Box 1380
Mashpee, MA 02649
Specialties: general gardening

The Captain's Bookshelf, Inc.
Box 2258
Asheville, NC 28802
(704) 253-6631
Specialties: used, rare, and out-of-print

Cascadia Company
375 Candalaria Boulevard South
Salem, OR 97302
(503) 364-5127
Specialties: general gardening

Chimney Sweep Books
419 Cedar Street
Santa Cruz, CA 95060
Specialties: general gardening

Copper Fox Farm Books
Box 763
Millbrook, NY 12545
Specialties: general gardening

Cover to Cover
5499 Belfast Road
Batavia, OH 45103
Specialties: general gardening

Discount Garden Books
Box 8354
Portland, OR 97207
(800) 327-1828
Specialties: general gardening

Exeter Rare Books
200 High Street
Exeter, NH 03833
(603) 772-0618
Specialties: used, rare, and out-of-print

Barbara Farnsworth, Bookseller
Box 9
West Cornwall, CT 06796
(203) 672-6571
Specialties: used, rare, and out-of-print

Flora & Fauna Books
121 1st Avenue South
Seattle, WA 98104
(206) 623-4727
Specialties: new, used, rare, and out-of-print

Footnote
179 Washington Park
Brooklyn, NY 11205
Specialties: new and used general gardening

Fortner Books
155 Winslow Way
Bainbridge Island, WA 98110
Specialties: general gardening

Gardeners Bookshelf
Box 16416
Hooksett, NH 03106
Specialties: general gardening

The Gardener's Bookshop
Route 9
Rhinebeck, NY 10572
(914) 876-3786
Specialties: new and used general gardening

Garden Works
31 Old Winter Street
Lincoln, MA 01773
Specialties: used, rare, and out-of-print

V. L. T. Gardner Botanical Books
625 East Victoria Street
Santa Barbara, CA 93103
(805) 966-0256
Specialties: used, rare, and out-of-print

Greenfield Herb Garden
Box 9
Shipshewana, IN 46565
(219) 768-7110
Specialties: herbs

Hannon House
5310 Mountain Road
Cheyenne, WY 82009
Specialties: general gardening

Hortulus
139 Marlborough Place
Toronto, Ontario M5R 3J5
(416) 920-5057
Specialties: used, rare, and out-of-print

Hurley Books
RR 1, Box 160
Westmoreland, NH 03467
(603) 399-4342
Specialties: used, rare, and out-of-print

Ian Jackson
Box 9075
Berkeley, CA 94709
(415) 548-1431
Specialties: used, rare, and out-of-print

John Johnson, Natural History Books
RD 1, Box 513
North Bennington, VT 05257
(802) 442-6738
Specialties: used, rare, and out-of-print
botany

Myron Kimnach
5508 North Astell Avenue
Azusa, CA 91702
(818) 334-7349
Specialties: cacti and succulents

J. Kramer
Box 243, Whitehall, PA 18052
Specialties: used, rare, and out-of-print

Landscape Architecture Bookstore
4401 Connecticut Avenue NW
Washington, DC 20008
(800) 787-2665
Specialties: gardening and landscape
architecture

Landscape Books
Box 483
Exeter, NH 03833
(603) 964-9333
Specialties: landscape architecture,
garden history

Laurelbrook Book Services
5468 Dundas Street West
Toronto, Ontario M9B 6E3
Specialties: general gardening

Diane Lewis Associates
4747 Hollywood Boulevard
Hollywood, FL 33021
Specialties: general gardening

Limberlost Roses
7304 Forbes Avenue
Van Nuys, CA 91406
(818) 901-7798
Specialties: roses

Linden House
148 Sylvan Avenue
Scarborough, Ontario M1M 1K4
(416) 261-0732
Specialties: general gardening

Timothy Mawson Books
New Preston, CT 06777
(203) 868-0732
Specialties: used, rare, and out-of-print

McQuerry Orchid Books
5700 West Salerno Road
Jacksonville, FL 32244
(904) 387-5044
Specialties: new, used, rare, and out-of-
print books about orchids

Nelson Books
RR 2, Box 212
Newport, NH 03773
Specialties: new and used general
gardening

New Moon Gardening Books
Box 1027
Corvallis, OR 97339
(503) 757-0027
Specialties: hydroponics and high-tech
gardening

Mary Odette Books
3831 North Cherry Creek Place
Tucson, AZ 85749
(520) 749-2285
Specialties: cacti and succulents

Pomona Book Exchange
Box 111
Rockton, Ontario L0R 1X0
(519) 621-8897
Specialties: new, used, rare, and out-of-
print

Larry W. Price Books
353 NW Maywood Drive
Portland, OR 97210
(503) 221-1410
Specialties: used, rare, and out-of-print

Quest Rare Books
774 Santa Ynez
Stanford, CA 94305
(415) 324-3119
Specialties: used, rare, and out-of-print

Rainbow Gardens Bookshop
1444 East Taylor Street
Vista, CA 92084
(619) 758-4290
Specialties: cacti and succulents

Savoy Books
Box 271
Lanesboro, MA 01237
(413) 499-9968
Specialties: used, rare, and out-of-print

Robert Shuhi Books
Box 268
Morris, CT 06763
(203) 567-5231
Specialties: used, rare, and out-of-print

Edward F. Smiley Bookseller
43 Liberty Hill Road
Bedford, NH 03110
(603) 472-5800
Specialties: used, rare, and out-of-print

Spectrum
Box 891617
Oklahoma City, OK 73189
Specialties: bonsai

Sperling Books
160 East 38th Street
New York, NY 10016
Specialties: African violets

Storey's Books for Country Living
Schoolhouse Road
Pownal, VT 05261
(800) 441-5700

Stroud Booksellers
Star Route Box 94
Williamsburg, WV 24991
(304) 645-7169
Specialties: used, rare, and out-of-print

Stubbs Books and Prints
835 Madison Avenue
New York, NY 10021
(212) 772-3120
Specialties: used, rare, and out-of-print

Raymond M. Sutton Jr.
Box 330
430 Main Street
Williamsburg, KY 40769
(606) 549-3464
Specialties: new, used, rare, and out-of-print

Tiny Trees Book, Sales
Box 5834
Hauppauge, NY 11788
Specialties: bonsai

Tools and Books, Ltd.
16 High Street
Westerly, RI 02891
Specialties: general gardening

Gary Wayner Bookseller
Route 3, Box 18
Fort Payne, AL 35967
(205) 845-7828
Specialties: used, rare, and out-of-print

Wilkerson Books
31 Old Winter Street
Lincoln, MA 01773
(617) 259-1110

Elizabeth Woodburn
Box 398
Booknoll Farm
Hopewell, NJ 08525
(609) 466-0522
Specialties: new, used, rare, and out-of-print

Wood Violet Books
3814 Sunhill Drive
Madison, WI 53704
(608) 837-7207
Specialties: new, used, rare, and out-of-print

Gary W. Woolson Bookseller
RR 1, Box 1576
Hampden, ME 04444
(207) 234-4931
Specialties: used, rare, and out-of-print

Gardening Book Clubs

Country Homes & Gardens Book Club
Box 11436
1716 Locust Street
Des Moines, IA 50336

The Garden Book Club
3000 Cendel Drive
Delran, NJ 08370
(609) 786-1000

Organic Gardening Book Club
Box 4515
Des Moines, IA 50336

Libraries with Significant Horticultural Collections

With over two million books and more than 27,000 periodical titles, the National Agricultural Library is the largest horticultural library in the country. It's open to the public for reference only; many titles are available through interlibrary loan.

National Agricultural Library
United States Department of Agriculture
10301 Baltimore Boulevard
Beltsville, MD 20705
(301) 504-5204

A number of horticultural libraries at botanical gardens, universities, museums, and organizations are open to the public for research. Indeed, free access to the library is often one of the privileges of membership in a botanical garden. These libraries are an excellent way to look at back issues of horticultural journals, hard-to-find or rare volumes, and big, expensive scholarly reference books. Contact the library well in advance to check on the hours and to arrange permission to visit. As a rule, permission to use the collection is granted if you have an area of serious research, but there may be a small fee and some restrictions. If you can't get to a distant library, speak to your local librarian about interlibrary loan programs.

Alabama

Horace Hammond Memorial Library
Birmingham Botanical Gardens
2612 Lane Park Road
Birmingham, AL 35223
(205) 879-1227
Note: interlibrary loans

Arizona

Boyce Thompson Southwestern
Arboretum
37615 US Highway 60
Superior, AZ 85273
(602) 689-2723

Desert Botanical Garden
Richter Memorial Library
1201 North Galvin Parkway
Phoenix, AZ 85008
(602) 941-1225

California

Fullerton Arboretum
California State University
1900 Associated Road
Fullerton, CA 92631
(714) 773-3579

Los Angeles Arboretum
Plant Sciences Library
301 North Baldwin Avenue
Arcadia, CA 91007
(818) 821-3213
Note: interlibrary loans

Rancho Santa Ana Botanic Garden
1500 North College Avenue
Claremont, CA 91711
(909) 625-8767

San Diego Floral Association
Library and Information Center
Casa del Prado, Balboa Park
San Diego, CA 92101
(619) 232-5762

Santa Barbara Botanic Garden
1212 Mission Canyon Road
Santa Barbara, CA 93105
(805) 682-4726

Strybing Arboretum and Botanical Gardens
Helen Crocker Russell Library of
Horticulture
9th Avenue and Lincoln Way
San Francisco, CA 94122
(415) 661-1514

Colorado

Denver Botanic Gardens
Helen Fowler Library
1005 York Street
Denver, CO 80206
(303) 370-8014
Note: interlibrary loans

Connecticut

Bartlett Arboretum
George E. Bye Library
University of Connecticut
151 Brookdale Road
Stamford, CT 06903
(203) 322-6971
Note: interlibrary loans

Connecticut Horticultural Society
150 Main Street
Wethersfield, CT 06109
(203) 529-8713

Nurserymen's Gardens
Connecticut Agricultural Experiment
Station
Box 1106
123 Huntington
New Haven, CT 06504
(203) 789-7272

Delaware

Delaware Center for Horticulture
1810 North DuPont Street
Wilmington, DE 19806
(302) 658-1913

District of Columbia

Dumbarton Oaks Garden
1703 32nd Street NW
Washington, DC 20007
(202) 342-3280

Smithsonian Institution
Botany Library
10th and Constitution
Washington, DC 20560
(202) 357-2715

Smithsonian Institution
Horticulture Branch Library
Arts & Industries Building, Room 2282

Washington, DC 20560
(202) 357-1544
Note: interlibrary loans

United States National Arboretum
USDA Agricultural Research Service
3501 New York Avenue NE
Washington, DC 20002
(202) 475-4815
Note: interlibrary loans

Florida

Fairchild Tropical Garden
Montgomery Library
10901 Old Cutler Road
Miami, FL 33156
(305) 667-1651

Marie Selby Botanical Garden
811 South Palm Avenue
Sarasota, FL 34236
(941) 366-5730

Georgia

Atlanta Botanical Garden
Sheffield Botanical Library
Piedmont Park
Atlanta, GA 30309
(404) 876-5859

Cherokee Garden Club
Atlanta Historical Society
3101 Andrews Drive NW
Atlanta, GA 30305
(404) 814-4040

Fernbank Science Center
156 Heaton Park Drive NE
Atlanta, GA 30307
(404) 378-4311

Hawaii

Bernice Pauani Bishop Museum
1525 Bernice Street
Honolulu, HI 96817
(808) 848-4148
Note: interlibrary loans

Honolulu Botanic Gardens
Rock Library
50 North Vineyard Boulevard
Honolulu, HI 96817
(808) 533-3406

National Tropical Botanical Garden
Halima Road
Lawai, HI 96765
(808) 332-7324
Note: interlibrary loans

Illinois

Chicago Botanic Garden Library
Lake–Cook Road
Glencoe, IL 60022
(708) 835-8200
Note: interlibrary loans

Field Museum of Natural History
Roosevelt Road and Lake Shore Drive
Chicago, IL 60605
(312) 922-9410
Note: interlibrary loans

Morton Arboretum
Sterling Morton Library
Route 53, Lisle, IL 60532
(708) 968-0074
Note: interlibrary loans

University of Illinois
Agricultural Library
1301 West Gregory Drive
Urbana, IL 61801
(217) 333-2416
Note: interlibrary loans

Indiana

Indianapolis Museum of Art Horticultural
Society
Horticultural Science Library
1200 West 38th Street
Indianapolis, IN 46208
(317) 923-1331

Iowa

Dubuque Arboretum and Botanical
Gardens
3125 West 32nd Street
Dubuque, IA 52001
(319) 556-2100

Kansas

Botanica, The Wichita Gardens
Frank Good Library
701 North Amidon
Wichita, KS 67203
(316) 264-0448

Maryland

Brookside Gardens
1500 Glenallan Avenue
Wheaton, MD 20902
(301) 949-8231

Cylburn Garden Center
Horticultural Library
4915 Greenspring Avenue
Baltimore, MD 21209
(410) 367-2217

Massachusetts

Arnold Arboretum of Harvard University
125 Arborway
Jamaica Plain, MA 02130
(617) 524-1718

Berkshire Garden Center
Routes 102 and 183, Box 826
Stockbridge, MA 01262
(413) 298-3926

The Botany Libraries
Harvard University Herbaria Building
22 Divinity Avenue
Cambridge, MA 02138
(617) 495-2366
Note: interlibrary loans

Massachusetts Horticultural Library
300 Massachusetts Avenue
Boston, MA 02155
(617) 536-9280

New England Wild Flower Society, Inc.
Lawrence Newcomb Library
180 Hemenway Road
Framingham, MA 01701
(508) 877-7630

Worcester County Horticultural Society
Tower Hill Botanic Garden
11 French Hill Drive
Boylston, MA 01505
(508) 869-6111

Michigan

Chippewa Nature Center
400 South Badour Road
Midland, MI 48640
(517) 631-0803

Detroit Garden Center
1460 East Jefferson Avenue
Detroit, MI 48207
(313) 259-6363

Detroit Public Library
5201 Woodward Avenue
Detroit, MI 48202
(313) 833-1400
Note: interlibrary loans

The Dow Gardens
1018 West Main Street
Midland, MI 48640
(517) 631-2677

Fernwood Garden and Nature Center
13988 Range Line Road
Niles, MI 49120
(616) 683-8653

Hidden Lake Gardens
Michigan State University
Tipton, MI 49287
(517) 431-2060

Matthaei Botanical Gardens
University of Michigan
1800 North Dixboro Road
Ann Arbor, MI 48105
(313) 763-7061

Minnesota

Minnesota Landscape Arboretum
Andersen Horticultural Library
University of Minnesota
3675 Arboretum Drive
Box 39
Chanhassen, MN 55317
(612) 443-2460

Minnesota State Horticultural Society
1970 Folwell Avenue
St. Paul, MN 55108
(612) 624-7752

Missouri

The Missouri Botanical Garden
4344 Shaw Boulevard
St. Louis, MO 63110
(314) 577-5155
Note: interlibrary loans

New Jersey

Deep Cut Park Horticultural Center
Elvin McDonald Horticultural Library
352 Red Hill Road
Middletown, NJ 07748
(908) 671-6050

George Griswold Frelinghuysen
Arboretum
Elizabeth Donnell Kay Botanical Library
53 East Hanover Avenue
Morristown, NJ 07962
(201) 326-7600

New York

Liberty Hyde Bailey Hortorium
462 Mann Library
Cornell University
Ithaca, NY 14853
(607) 255-2131

Brooklyn Botanic Garden
1000 Washington Avenue
Brooklyn, NY 11225
(718) 941-4044

Mary Flagler Cary Arboretum
Institute of Ecosystem Studies
Box AB
Millbrook, NY 12545
(914) 677-5343

Garden Center of Rochester
5 Castle Park
Rochester, NY 14620
(716) 473-5130

Garden Club of America Library
598 Madison Avenue
New York, NY 10022
(212) 753-8287

Horticultural Society of New York
128 West 58th Street

New York, NY 10019
(212) 757-0915
Note: interlibrary loans

New York Botanical Garden
200th Street and Kazimiroff Boulevard
Bronx, NY 10458
(718) 817-8604
Note: interlibrary loans

Planting Fields Arboretum Garden Library
Planting Fields Road
Oyster Bay, NY 11771
(516) 922-9024

North Carolina

North Carolina Botanical Garden
Addie Williams Totten Library
University of North Carolina
Chapel Hill, NC 27599
(919) 962-0522

Ohio

Civic Garden Center of Cincinnati
Hoffman Horticultural Library
2715 Reading Road
Cincinnati, OH 45206
(513) 221-0981

Cox Arboretum
6733 Springboro Pike
Dayton, OH 45449
(513) 434-9005

Dawes Arboretum
7770 Jacksontown Road SE
Newark, OH 43056
(614) 323-2355

Garden Center of Greater Cleveland
Eleanor Squire Library
11030 East Boulevard
Cleveland, OH 44106
(216) 721-1600

Gardenview Horticultural Park Library
16711 Pearl Road
Strongsville, OH 44136
(216) 238-6653

Holden Arboretum
Warren H. Corning Library
9500 Sperry Road
Mentor, OH 44060
(216) 256-1110

Kingwood Center Library
900 Park Avenue West
Mansfield, OH 44906
(419) 522-0211
Note: interlibrary loans

Lloyd Library
917 Plum Street
Cincinnati, OH 45202
(513) 721-3707

Oklahoma

Tulsa Garden Center
2435 South Peoria Avenue
Tulsa, OK 74114
(918) 749-6401

Oregon

Berry Botanic Garden
11505 SW Summerville Avenue
Portland, OR 97219
(503) 636-4112

Pennsylvania

Academy of Natural Sciences of
Philadelphia
Stewart Memorial Library
1900 Benjamin Franklin Parkway
Philadelphia, PA 19103
(215) 299-1140
Note: interlibrary loans

Carnegie Museum of Natural History
4400 Forbes Avenue
Pittsburgh, PA 15213
(412) 622-3264
Note: interlibrary loans

Delaware Valley College
Joseph Krauskopf Memorial Library
Route 202
Doylestown, PA 18901
(215) 345-1500

Hunt Institute for Botanial
Documentation
Hunt Botanical Library
Carnegie Mellon University
Frew Street
Pittsburgh, PA 15213
(412) 268-2436
Note: interlibrary loans

Longwood Gardens
Route 1
Kennett Square, PA 19348
(215) 388-6745
Note: interlibrary loans

Pennsylvania Horticultural Society
325 Walnut Street
Philadelphia, PA 19106
(215) 625-8261
Note: interlibrary loans

Pittsburgh Civic Garden Center
1059 Shady Avenue
Pittsburgh, PA 15232
(412) 441-4442

University of Pennsylvania
Morris Arboretum Library
9414 Meadowbrook Avenue
Philadelphia, PA 19118
(215) 247-5777
Note: interlibrary loans

Tennessee

Memphis Botanic Garden
Sybil G. Malloy Memorial Library
750 Cherry Road
Memphis, TN 38117
(901) 685-1566

Tennessee Botanical Gardens at
Cheekwood
Minnie Ritchey and Joel Owsley Cheek
Library
1200 Forrest Park Drive
Nashville, TN 37205
(615) 353-2148

Texas

Fort Worth Botanical Garden
3220 Botanic Garden Boulevard
Fort Worth, TX 76107
(817) 870-7682

Virginia

American Horticultural Society
Harold B. Tukey Memorial Library
7931 East Boulevard Drive
Alexandria, VA 22308
(703) 768-5700

Norfolk Botanical Gardens
Huette Horticultural Library
Azalea Garden Road
Norfolk, VA 23158
(804) 441-5380
Note: interlibrary loans

Washington

University of Washington
Center for Urban Horticulture
Elisabeth C. Miller Library
Seattle, WA 98195
(206) 543-8616

Yakima Area Arboretum
Walker Horticultural Library
1207 Arboretum Drive
Yakima, WA 98901
(509) 248-7337

West Virginia

Wheeling Civic Garden Center
Oglebay Park
Wheeling, WV 26003
(304) 242-0665

Wisconsin

Boerner Botanical Gardens
Whitnall Park
5879 South 92nd Street
Hales Corners, WI 53130
(414) 425-1131

Olbrich Botanical Gardens
Schumacher Library
3330 Atwood Avenue
Madison, WI 53704
(608) 246-5805

CANADA

British Columbia

University of British Columbia
Botanical Garden Library
6804 SW Marine Drive
Vancouver, British Columbia V6T 1W5
(604) 822-3928

VanDusen Botanical Garden
5251 Oak Street
Vancouver, British Columbia V6M 4H1
(604) 266-7194

Ontario

Canadian Agriculture Library
Agriculture Canada
Ottawa, Ontario K1A 0C5
(613) 995-7829
Note: interlibrary loans

Civic Garden Centre
777 Lawrence Avenue East
North York, Ontario M3C 1P2
(416) 397-1340
Note: interlibrary loans

Niagara Parks Commission
School of Horticulture Library
Niagara Parkway North
Niagara Falls, Ontario L2E 6T2
(416) 356-8554

Royal Botanical Gardens
680 Plains Road West
Hamilton, Ontario L8N 3H8
(416) 527-1158
Note: interlibrary loans

Quebec

Montreal Botanical Garden
4101 Sherbrooke Road East
Montreal, Quebec H1X 2B2
(514) 872-1824
Note: interlibrary loans

Computer Gardening

11

GARDENING SOFTWARE and on-line services for the home computer have opened up a new world for gardeners. Numerous plant databases and software packages for keeping garden records, designing your garden, and other applications are now available. Improvements to existing programs and new programs come along all the time.

The dynamic new world of on-line services provides some fascinating sources of free information for gardeners. The major on-line services such as Compuserve, Prodigy, and America Online offer gardening forum areas where gardeners—from all over the country and the world—can "meet" to discuss their favorite pastime and share information. Depending on which service you subscribe to, you can also access the texts of some gardening magazines and check garden reference works.

The Internet and the World Wide Web provide numerous sites from all over the world, both general and specific, for gardeners to visit. These sites often have links to other, related sites that can send you off on an interesting journey through cyberspace in search of information, fellow gardeners, and fun.

The listings below for on-line sites are as current as possible. Cyberspace changes fast, however. The sites listed may no longer be accessible by the time you read this, and there will doubtless be new sites that are not listed here.

Software

Software Emporiums

A. C. Burke & Company
2554 Lincoln Boulevard, Suite 1058
Marina Del Rey, CA 90291
(310) 574-2770
Products: software; CD-ROMs; videos; books
Catalogue: free

Cascadia Company
375 Candalaria Boulevard South
Salem, OR 97302
(503) 364-5127

Products: software; CD-ROMs; books
Catalogue: free

Software

Abracadata
Box 2440
Eugene, OR 97402
(503) 342-3030
(800) 451-4871
Programs: Sprout!™ vegetable garden design program; Design Your Own Home landscaping program
System requirements: DOS 3.3+, Windows 3.1+, or Macintosh

Autodesk
18911 North Creek Parkway, Suite 105
Bothell, WA 98011
(206) 487-2233
(800) 228-3601
Program: Home Series Landscape
CAD program
System requirements: DOS 3.0+

Books That Work
2300 Geng Road
Palo Alto, Ca 94303
(800) 242-4546
CD-ROMs: 3D Landscape;
The Garden Encyclopedia
System requirements: IBM 386+,
Windows 3.1+, 4 MB RAM

Capstan Distributing Company
Box 245
Manchester, IA 52057
(319) 927-5948
Program: English Country Garden
design program
System requirements: IBM DOS 3.1+,
VGA, 640K RAM

Cornucopia Publishing
Box 307
West Boxford, MA 01885
Program: Garden Designer's Helper
design program

The Designing Gardener
Box 837
Harrison, NY 10528
(914) 698-7425
Program: Enter the Perennial database
System requirements: IBM DOS 3.1+

Double-Pawed Software
432 Bigelow Hollow
Eastford, CT 06242
Program: perpetual garden
calendar/journal
System requirements: IBM DOS 3.1+

Elemental Software
2218 North 1200 Street East
Logan, UT 84321
(801) 755-0701
Program: The Plant Doctor
plant disorder diagnosis program
System requirements: IBM 386+,
DOS 3.1+

FLOWERscape
(800) 258-2088 (Windows)
(800) 248-0800 (Macintosh)
Program: FLOWERscape design program
System requirements: IBM: Windows
3.0+, VGA, 4MB RAM; Mac: System
6.0.4+, 256 color driver, 1.5MB

Garden in Time
(800) 228-0705
Program: Garden in Time flower garden
design program
System requirements: IBM 386DX+,
Windows 3.1+, 4MB RAM,
VGA color monitor

Green Thumb Software, Inc.
75 Manhattan Drive
Boulder, CO 80303
(303) 499-1388
(800) 336-3127
Programs: LandDesigner® for Windows
(DOS available); LandDesigner
Multimedia CD-ROM; plant libraries
for LandDesigner
System requirements: IBM: 386SX+,
VGA, 4MB RAM; CD-ROM: IBM
386SX+, Windows 3.1+ VGA,
4MB RAM

J & L Bluebonnet Plantation
Box 559
Hempstead, TX 77445
(409) 826-8975
(800) 204-5614
Program: Gardner Pardner™
record-keeping program

System requirements: IBM 386+,
Windows 3.1+, 4MB RAM

Lifestyle Software Group
63 Orange Street
St. Augustine, FL 32084
(800) 289-1157
Program: Garden Companion CD
System requirements: Windows 3.1

Look Systems
105 Cascadilla Park Road
Ithaca, NY 14850
(607) 277-5665
(800) 698-LOOK
Program: Look Into The Garden
design program
System requirements: IBM 386+,
Windows 3.1+, 4MB RAM,
VGA color monitor

Mindsun
RD 2, Box 710
Andover, NJ 07821
(201) 398-8082
Program: Gardenviews 5.3 plant database
System requirements: IBM EGA/VGA

MoonOwl Software, Inc.
Box 693
Chelsea, Quebec J0X 1N0
(800) 228-0705
Program: Garden in Time design program
System requirements: IBM 386DX+,
Windows 3.1+, 4MB RAM,
VGA color monitor

Paradise Information, Inc.
Box 1701
East Hampton, NY 11937
(516) 324-2334
(800) 544-2721
Program: CHIP2 computerized
horticultural information planner

Plant Care Information Systems, Inc.
500 SE 17th Street
Ft. Lauderdale, FL 33316
(954) 522-1334
(800) 498-8383
Program: Plant Care 2000 for house-
plants care

Saroh
Box 8375
Springfield, IL 62791
Program: plant care and propagation
database
System requirements: DOS 3.1+,
10MB hard disk storage

Shapeware Corporation
520 Pike Street, Suite 1800
Seattle, WA 98101
(206) 521-4500
Program: Visio Home 3.0
System requirements: Windows 3.1

Sierra Online
Box 3403
Salinas, CA 93912
(800) 757-7707
Program: LandDesigner 3D
System requirements: 486, Windows
5.0+, VGA, CD-ROM, at least 8 MB
RAM

Surgicad Corporation
115 Etna Road
Lebanon, NH 03766
(800) 522-6695
Program: InfoSavers' floral screen saver
System requirements: Windows 3.1+

Terrace Software
Box 271
Medford, MA 02155
(617) 396-0382
Programs: Mum's the Word (Mac) design
program; Florafile (IBM) plant database

World Wide Web and Other On-Line Sources

General World Wide Web and Internet Sites

The sites listed below are general gardening areas that contain a lot of useful gardening information. Most offer book reviews, new product information, seasonal advice, areas for posting and answering queries, and the like. Some sites also offer unique information. For example, within the GardenNet site you can jump to useful state listings of public gardens and garden events. General gardening sites also include many hypertext links to other Web pages and Internet gardening sites. Some of these sites are sponsored by commercial entities, while others are put together by individuals or volunteers.

Garden Gate
http://www.prairienet.org/ag/garden/
homepage.html

Garden Gate at SunSITE
http://sunsite.unc.edu/garden-gate/

Gardening (Leisure and Recreation)
http://www.einet.net/galaxy/Leisure-and-
Recreation/Gardening.html

Gardening Launch Pad
http://www.tpoint.net/neighbor/

Gardening List WWW
http://www.cog.brown.edu/gardening/

GardenNet from Wayside Gardens
http://www.olympus.net/gardens/
welcome.html

The Garden Patch
http://mirror.wwa.com/mirror/garden/
patch/htm

The Garden Spider's Web
http://www.gardenweb.com/spdrsweb/

GardenWeb
http://www.gardenweb.com/

General Gardening Sites
http://www.btw.com/urls/garden/
general.htm

Links to Gardening-Related Home Pages
http://weber.u.washington.edu/~trav/
garden_links.html

Master Gardener files at Texas A&M
http://leviathan.tamu.edu:70/1s/mg

My Garden
http://www.hal-
pc.org/~trobb/horticul.html

The Trellis: Garden Links on the Internet
http://wormsway.com/trellis.html

The Virtual Garden from Time-Life Inc.
http://www.timeinc.com/vg/

Interesting Web Pages

The sites listed below are Web pages oriented directly to specific interests, such as bonsai. Many of these pages are linked to the general areas listed above; many also contain links to other Web sites. Most of the sites listed below are run by volunteers or organizations. Some are commercial or sponsored areas that provide interesting information along with advertising. This list is by no means complete—new sites arise daily. For reasons of space, local and personal home pages have not been listed. However, there are separate listings below of sites for books and magazines, botanic gardens, flower photos, bulletin boards, mailing lists, newsgroups, and USDA Cooperative Extension Service information servers.

SPECIAL INTEREST WEB PAGES

American Bamboo Society Home Page
http://www.halcyon.com/plrabbit/
bamboo/abs.html

American Bonsai Society Home Page
http://www.paonline.com/abs

American Rose Society Home Page
http://www.ars.org

Bonsai Home Page
http://www.pass.wayne.edu/~dan/

Books That Work Complete Guide to
Garden Stuff
http://www.btw.com/garden.htm

Botany Department at the University of
Georgia
http://dogwood.botany.uga.edu/

The Carnivorous Plant Archive Page
http://randomaccess.unm.edu/www/cp/
cparchive.html

Carnivorous Plants Database
http://www.hpl.hp.com/bot/cp_home

City Farmer: Canada's Office of Urban
Agriculture
http://unixg.ubc.ca:880/cityfarm/
gardsites65.html

Cornell University Fruit and Vegetable
Information
gopher://gopher.cce.cornell.edu/11/cenet/
submenu/fruit-veg/

The Cyber-Plantsman
http://mirror.www.com/mirror/garden/
cyberplt.htm

Designing Gardens for Butterflies
http://www.gardenweb.com/bbg/
butterfl.html

Don't Panic Eat Organic
http://www/rain.org/~sals/my.html

Daylilies Growing along the Information
Highway
http://www.daylilies.com/daylilies

Earth Matters
http://192.216.191.71/ng/earth/earth.htm

Expo Garden Tours
http://www.olympus.net/gardens/
expotour.htm

Friends of the Daylilies
http://www.primenet.com/utilehr/daylily.
html

Garden Catalogs List
http://www.cog.brown.edu/gardening

Garden Earth
http://www.interworld.com.au/garden/

Gardening for Vegetarians
http://www.veg.org/veg/Orgs/VegSocUK/
Info/gardenin.html

Garden South Africa
http://www.pix.za/garden/

Gardens & Gardening
http://www.cfn.cs.dal.ca/Recreation/Gard
ening/G_G_Home.html

General Gardening Catalogs and
Supplies
http://www.btw.com/urls/garden/
vendors.htm

Herbs & Spices
http://www.teleport.com/~ronl/herbs/
herbs.html

Horticulture Solutions
http://www.ag.uiuc.edu/~robsond/
solutions/hort.html

International Camellia Society Home
Page
http://www.med_rzuni–sb.de/med_fak/
physiol2/camellia/home.htm

Irises
http://alepho.clarke.edu/~djoyce/Iris

Hortus—A Gardening Journal
http://www.kc3ltd.co.uk/business/hortus.
html

National Museum of Natural History,
Smithsonian Institution, Department of
Botany
http://nmnhwww.si.edu/departments/
botany.html

New York Botanical Garden Library catalogue on Telnet
librisc.nybg.org

Northern Gardening
http://www/geocities.com/BainForest/1329

The Orchid House
http://cougar.uwaterloo.co/orchids.html

OrchidWeb
http://www.pathfinder.com/vg/Gardens/
AOS

Ortho Online
http://www.ortho.com

Palm trees information
http://www.geopages.com/TheTropics/
1811/

Pinetree Garden Seeds
http://www.olympus.net/gardens/
pinetree.htm

PrairieNet
http://sunsite.unc.edu/gardengate/www.
hort.htm

Pukeiti Rhododendron Trust
http://pluto.taranaki.ac.nz/pukeiti/
welcome.html

The Rhododendron Page
http://haven.los.com/~mckenzie/rhodo05
.html

Rooftop Gardens
http://unixg.ubc.ca:880/cityfarm/rooftop5
9.html

The Rose Page
http://www.mc.edu/~nettles/rofaq/
rofaq-top.html

The Seven Wonders: The Hanging
Gardens of Babylon
http://ce.ecn.purdue/edu/~ashmawy/
7WW/gardens.html

The Succulent Plant Page
http://www.graylab.oc.uk/usr/hogkiss/
succule.htm

Sunshine Farm & Gardens
http://mirror.wwwa.com/mirror/busdir/
sunshine/sunshine.htm

Tele-Garden Robotic Gardening Project
http://www.usc.edu/dept/garden

Time-Life Complete Gardener Encyclopedia
http://www.timeinc.com/vg/TimeLife/CG/
vg-search.html

USDA Growing Zone Finder
http://www.timeinc.com/cgibin/
vgzonefinder

University of Connecticut
http://florawww.eeb.uconn.edu/
homepage.htm

University of Florida Herbarium
http://nabalu.flas.ufl.edu/flashome.html

The Weekend Gardener
http://www.chestnut-sw.com

BOOKS AND GARDENING MAGAZINES ON LINE

*A number of Web sites offer book reviews; some
also provide ordering information. The magazines
listed here include both the on-line versions of print
gardening magazines and some new "e-zines"
available only on line.*

The American Cottage Gardener Home
Page
http://www.olympus.net/gardens/acg.htm

The Cyber-Plantsman magazine on
Garden Web
http://www.gardenweb.com/cyberplt/

The Garden Bookshelf of the Virtual
Garden
http://www.timeinc.com/vg/
or
http://pathfinder.com/@@91Z2X2HbdAI
AQLRr/vg/Bookshelf/index.html

The Garden Gate: The Gardener's
Reading Room
http://prairienet.org/ag/garden/
readroom.htm

The Gardening Bookshelf Page
http://www.atlgarden.com/books.html

Garden Literature Press
http://www.olympus.net/gardens/gardlit.
htm

GardenNet Book Reviews
http://www.olympus.net/gardens/review.
htm

GardenNet's *The Ardent Gardener* magazine
http://www.olympus.net/gardens/gmg.htm

GardenNet's *The Ardent Gardener Over The
Fence* e-zine
http://www.olympus.net/gardens/otf.htm

The Gourmet Gardener—Books
http://metroux.tetrobbs.com/tgg/books.htm

Homeground Newsletter on the
Virtual Garden
http://pathfinder.com/@@95CA29Flc
QIAQG9s/vg/Magazine-
Rack/Homeground

Hortus—A Gardening Journal
http://www.ke3ltd.co.uk/business/hortus.
html

Southern Garden Gate for Florida Gardeners
http://www.gate.net/good-green-fun/
ggp_1.htm

Southern Living magazine on the
Virtual Garden
http://pathfinder.com/@@1UflcBFEdAIA
QHdv/vg/Magazine-Rack/SoLiving

Sunset magazine on the Virtual Garden
http://pathfinder.com/@@@soLSlFbdwIA
QNZu/vg/Magazine-Rack/Sunset

BOTANIC GARDENS ON LINE

American Association of Botanical
Gardens and Arboreta (AABGA)
http://192.104.39.4/AABGA/aabga1.html

Australian National Botanic Gardens
http://155.187.10.12:80/anbg.html

Brooklyn Botanic Garden
http://mirror.wwa.com/mirror/orgs/bbg/
bbg.htm

Devonian Botanic Garden
http://gause.biology/ualberta.ca/
devonian.hp/dbg.html

Directory of Australian Botanic Gardens
and Arboreta
http://osprey.erin.gov.au/chabg/bg-dir/
bg-dir.html

Georgeson Botanical Garden
http://www.lter.alaska.edu/html/gbg.html

Hello Riviera #2: The Hambury Botanic
Gardens
http://www.doit.it/News/HelloRiviera/
Giugno/hambury.uk.html

Missouri Botanic Garden
http://straylight.tamu.edu/MoBot/
welcome.html

Claude Monet's Garden at Giverny
http://www.monash.edu.au/visarts/diva/
monet.html

New York Botanical Garden
http://www.pathfinder.com/vg/Gardens/
NYBG/index.html

Park and Tilford Gardens, North Vancouver
http://www.fleethouse.com/fhcanada/
ptg_home.htm

Royal Botanic Gardens, Kew
http://www.rbgkew.org.uk/

University of Delaware Botanic Gardens
gopher://bluehen.ags.udel.edu:71/hh/.
botanic_garden/botanicg.html

GARDENING PHOTOS ON LINE

The Armchair Gardener
http://www.mailer.fsu.edu/~dansley

Australian flora and fauna
http://rs306.ccs.bbk.ac.uk/flora/
welcome.html

Botany Image Archive
http://muse.bio.cornell.edu/images/

Daylilies Online (experimental project)
http://www.assumption.edu/HTML/
daylilies/about.html

DIVA (Digital Images for the Visual Arts)
gardens and landscape design
http://www.monash.edu.au/diva/gardens.
htm

Electronic Orchid Greenhouse
http://yakko.cs.wmich.edu/~charles/
orchids/greenhouse.html

Flowers pictures archive
http://sunsite.sut.ac.jp/multimed/pics/
flowers/

Hungarian flora and fauna
http://www.unigiessen.de/~gdg3/mud/
firstl.html

Madagascar flora and fauna
http://lalo.inria.fr/~andry/Mada.html

The Rose Gallery
http://www.halcyon.com/cirsium/
rosegal/welcom.htm

WWW Server of the University of Costa
Rica
http://www.ucr.ac.cr/

Bulletin Boards, Mailing Lists, Discussion Lists, and Newsgroups

Alpines and rock gardening (ALPINE-L)
LISTSERV@hearn.nic.surfnet.nl

Aroids (AROID-L)
LISTPROC@MOBOT.ORG

Gesneriad bulletin board
listproc@lists.Colorado.edu
Greenhouses (HGA-L)
LISTSERV@ULKYVM.LOUISVILLE.EDU

Herbs
LISTSERV@vm.ege.edu.tr
LISTSERV@trearn.bitnet

Home Composting discussion list
(COMPOST)
LISTPROC@listproc.wsu.edu

Home gardening e-mail list
LISTSERV@UKCC.UKY.EDU

Residential gardening (RES-GARD)
LISTSERV@TAMVM1.TAMU.EDU

Gardening newsgroups via Usenet
rec.gardens
red.gardens.orchids
rec.gardens.roses

USDA COOPERATIVE EXTENSION SERVICE INFORMATION SERVERS

This listing is adapted from USDA listings. The detailed list is available from the USDA at: http://eos.esusda.gov/partners/ceslocs.htm.

USDA Extension Service
gopher://esusda.gov/1/

Alabama Extension System
http://www.acenet.auburn.edu

Arizona Agriculture and Resource Economics Extension
http://ag.arizona.edu/AREC/exthome.html

Colorado State Cooperative Extension On Line
http://www.colostate.educ/Depts/CoopExt/

Delaware College of Agricultural Sciences (AGINFO)
http://bluehen.ags.undel.edu

Florida Institute of Food and Agricultural Sciences (IFAS)
http://bnv.ifas.ufl.edu

Illinois Cooperative Extension Service
http://www.ag.uiuc.edu

Indiana—Purdue University Cooperative Extension
gopher://hermes.ecn.purdue.edu

Iowa State University Cooperative Extension
http://www.exnex.iastate.edu/

Kansas State University, Extension Systems and Agricultural Research Programs (ESARP)
http://www.oznet.ksu.edu/

Kentucky—University of Kentucky College of Agriculture
http://www.uky.edu/CampusGuide/uk.html

Michigan State University
http://lep.cl.msu.edu/msueimp/

Minnesota National Extension
gopher://tinman.mes.umn.edu

Mississippi—University Extension, Mississippi State University
http://www.ces.msstate.edu/

Missouri—University Extension, Missouri
http://etcs.ext.missouri.edu:70/

Nebraska Institute of Agriculture and
Natural Resources (IANR)
http://unlvm.unl.edu

New Jersey—Rutgers Cooperative
Extension
http://aesop.rutgers.edu/~huntzinger/rce.
htm
New York—Cornell University
Cooperative Extension Service
http://empire.cse.cornell.edu/

North Carolina Cooperative Extension
Service
http://www.ces.ncsu.edu

North Dakota State University Extension
Service
gopher://ndsuext.nodak.edu

Oregon Extension Service Information
System
http://gopher://gopher.oes.orst.edu

Pennsylvania—PENPages
gopher://penpages.psu.edu

Texas A&M University (DOS)
http://leviathan.tamu.edu

Utah State University Extension
http://ext.us.edu:80/

Virginia Cooperative Extension (VCE)
gopher://gopher.ext.vt.edu

Washington State University College of
Agriculture and Home Economics
gopher://cru1.cahe.wsu.edu

Wisconsin—University of Wisconsin
Extension
gopher://wisdom.uwex.edu:70/1

Botanical Gardens and Arboretums

THE LISTING BELOW is a somewhat arbitrary compilation of large or notable botanical, estate, and display gardens. For reasons of space, only arboretums with extensive or very unusual display gardens have been included. (Information about All-America Rose Selections display gardens is in chapter 2.) If you're planning a visit to any botanical garden, be sure to call ahead. Hours and admission fees (if any) vary seasonally, as do peak displays.

For an extensive and detailed listing of many North American gardens open to the public, see the two invaluable volumes by Everitt L. Miller and Jay S. Cohen: The American Garden Guidebook (NY: M. Evans, 1987) and The American Garden Guidebook West (NY: M. Evans, 1989).

Botanical Gardens and Arboretums by State and Province

Alabama

Bellingrath Gardens and Home
12401 Bellingrath Gardens Road
Theodore, AL 36582
(205) 973-2217
Notable plantings: azaleas; camellias; chrysanthemums; roses; tulips

Birmingham Botanical Gardens
2612 Lane Park Road
Birmingham, AL 35223
(205) 879-1227
Notable plantings: roses; lilies

Arizona

The Arizona–Sonora Desert Musuem
2021 North Kinney Road
Tucson, AZ 85743
(520) 883-2702
Notable plantings: plants of the Sonoran Desert

The Boyce Thompson Southwestern Arboretum
Box AB
Superior, AZ 85273
(602) 689-2811
Notable plantings: plants of the Sonoran Desert

The Desert Botanical Garden
1201 North Galvin Parkway
Phoenix, AZ 85008
(602) 941-1225
Notable plantings: plants
of the Sonoran Desert

Arkansas

Arkansas State Capitol Rose Garden
Information Services Division
State Capitol
Little Rock, AR 72201
(501) 371-5164
Notable plantings: All-American Rose
Selections garden; over 1,200 rosebushes

California

All-America Gladiolus Selections
11734 Road 33 $^1/_2$
Madera, CA 93638
(209) 645-5329
Notable plantings: gladioli

Balboa Park
Laurel Street and 6th Avenue
San Diego, CA 92101
(619) 236-5984
Notable plantings: Casa del Rey Moro
garden; Alcazar garden

Berkeley Rose Garden
Euclid Avenue and Bayview Place
Berkeley, CA 94720
(415) 644-6530
Notable plantings: 4,000 rosebushes

Descanso Gardens
1418 Descanso Drive
La Cañada Flintridge, CA 91011
(818) 952-4400
Notable plantings: camellias; roses

Exposition Park Rose Garden
701 State Drive

Los Angeles, CA 90012
(213) 748-4772
Notable plantings: over 12,000
rosebushes

Filoli
Cañada Road
Woodside, CA 94062
(415) 364-2880
Notable plantings: rhododendrons;
roses; spring bulbs

Golden Gate Park. See Strybing
Arboretum

Hearst San Simeon State Historical
Monument
Micheltorena and Santa Barbara Streets
San Simeon, CA 93452
(619) 452-1950
Notable plantings: formal gardens

The Huntington Botanical Gardens
1151 Oxford Road
San Marino, CA 91108
(818) 405-2100
Notable plantings: fifteen
specialty gardens

Los Angeles State and County Arboretum
301 North Baldwin Avenue
Arcadia, CA 91007
(818) 446-8251
Notable plantings: begonias; tropical
plants; Australian plants; water garden

Mildred E. Mathias Botanical Garden
University of California at Los Angeles
405 Hilgard Avenue
Los Angeles, CA 90024
(213) 835-3620
Notable plantings: desert plants

Hortense Miller Garden
3035 Bert Drive
Laguna Beach, CA 92651

(714) 497-7692
Notable plantings: over 1,200
subtropical and native species

Moorten Botanic Garden
1702 South Palm Canyon Drive
Palm Springs, CA 92264
(619) 327-6555
Notable plantings: desert plants

Morcom Amphitheater of Roses
1520 Lakeside Drive
Oakland, CA 94612
(415) 273-3090
Notable plantings: over 8,000 rosebushes

Pageant of Roses Garden
3900 South Workman Mill Road
Whittier, CA 90608
(213) 699-0921
Notable plantings: over 7,000 rosebushes

Theodore Payne Foundation
10459 Tuxford Street
Sun Valley, CA 91352
(818) 768-1802
Notable plantings: wildflowers

Quail Botanical Gardens
230 Quail Gardens Drive
Encinitas, CA 92024
(619) 436-3036
Notable plantings: bamboos;
cycads; palms

Rancho Santa Ana Botanic Garden
1500 North College Avenue
Claremont, CA 91711
(909) 625-8767
Notable plantings: California-native
plants

San Diego Zoo
Box 551
Balboa Park
San Diego, CA 92112

(619) 231-1515
Notable plantings: over 6,500 exotic
species

Santa Barbara Botanic Garden
1212 Mission Canyon Road
Santa Barbara, CA 93105
(805) 682-4726
Notable plantings: California-native
plants

South Coast Botanical Garden
26300 Crenshaw Boulevard
Palos Verdes Peninsula, CA 90274
(310) 544-6815
Notable plantings: over 2,000 species

Strybing Arboretum and Botanical
Gardens
Golden Gate Park
9th Avenue and Lincoln Way
San Francisco, CA 94122
(415) 661-1316
Notable plantings: geographic collections
from Australia, New Zealand, Chile, and
Cape Province

University of California at Berkeley
Botanical Garden
200 Centennial Drive
Berkeley, CA 94720
(510) 642-3343
Notable plantings: California-native
plants

University of California at Irvine
Arboretum
Irvine, CA 92717
(714) 856-5833
Notable plantings: flowering bulbs

Colorado

Denver Botanic Gardens
1005 York Street
Denver, CO 80206

(303) 331-4000
Notable plantings: alpine and
rock garden plants

Connecticut

Audubon Fairchild Garden of the
National Audubon Society
613 Riversville Road
Greenwich, CT 06831
(203) 869-5272
Notable plantings: wildflowers;
medicinal plants

Bartlett Arboretum
University of Connecticut
151 Brookdale Road
Stamford, CT 06903
(203) 322-6971
Notable plantings: dwarf conifers;
flowering shrubs; ericaceous plants

Connecticut College Arboretum
5625 Connecticut College
New London, CT 06320
(203) 447-7700
Notable plantings: northeastern-
native plants

Elizabeth Park
25 Stonington Street
Hartford, CT 06106
(203) 722-6541
Notable plantings: over 15,000 rosebushes

Delaware

Nemours Mansion and Gardens
1600 Rockland Road
Wilmington, DE 19803
(302) 651-6905
Notable plantings: formal gardens

Winterthur Museum and Gardens
Winterthur, DE 19735
(302) 888-4600

(800) 448-3883
Notable plantings: azaleas; daffodils;
rhododendrons; tulips

District of Columbia

Dumbarton Oaks Gardens
1703 32nd Street NW
Washington, DC 20007
(202) 342-3200
Notable plantings: Italian gardens

Kenilworth Aquatic Gardens
National Park Service
Anacostia Avenue and Douglass Street
NE
Washington, DC 20019
(202) 426-6905
Notable plantings: aquatic gardens

United States Botanic Garden
245 1st Street SW
Washington, DC 20024
(202) 225-8333
Notable plantings: begonias; orchids;
annuals

United States National Arboretum
3501 New York Avenue NE
Washington, DC 20002
(202) 475-4815
Notable plantings: herbs; Japanese garden; bonsai; azaleas; rhododendrons

Florida

Fairchild Tropical Garden
10901 Old Cutler Road
Miami, FL 33156
(305) 667-1651
Notable plantings: tropical plants;
bromeliads; ferns; orchids; palms

Flamingo Gardens
3750 Flamingo Road
Fort Lauderdale, FL 33330

(305) 473-2955
Notable plantings: Heliconia species

Florida Cypress Gardens
State Route 540
Cypress Gardens, FL 33880
(813) 324-2111
Notable plantings: over 8,000 plant
species

H. P. Leu Botanical Gardens
1730 North Forest Avenue
Orlando, FL 32803
(407) 849-2620
Notable plantings: camellias

Orchid Jungle
26715 SW 157th Avenue
Homestead, FL 33030
(305) 247-4824
Notable plantings: orchids

Marie Selby Botanical Garden
811 South Palm Avenue
Sarasota, FL 34236
(941) 366-5731
Notable plantings: tropical plants;
epiphytes

Sunken Gardens
1825 4th Street North
St. Petersburg, FL 33704
(813) 896-3186
Notable plantings: tropical and
subtropical species

Vizcaya
3251 South Miami Avenue
Miami, FL 33129
(305) 854-6559
Notable plantings: classical Italian garden

Georgia

Atlanta Botanical Garden
Piedmont Park

Atlanta, GA 30309
(404) 876-5859
Notable plantings: over 3,500 species

Callaway Gardens
Pine Mountain, GA 31822
(404) 663-5186
(800) 282-8181
Notable plantings: azaleas; hollies;
chrysanthemums

State Botanical Garden of Georgia
2450 South Milledge Avenue
Athens, GA 30605
(404) 542-1244
Notable plantings: roses; wildflowers;
spring bulbs; azaleas

Hawaii

Hawaii Tropical Botanical Garden
Onomea Bay
Hilo, HI 96721
(808) 964-5233
Notable plantings: over 1,800
tropical species

Honolulu Botanic Gardens
50 North Vineyard Boulevard
Honolulu, HI 96817
(808) 533-3406
Notable plantings: five separate
gardens; orchids

Harold Lyon Arboretum
University of Hawaii, Manoa
3860 Manoa Road
Honolulu, HI 96822
(808) 988-3177
Notable plantings: over 4,200
tropical species

National Tropical Botanical Garden
Halima Road
Lawai, HI 96765
(808) 332-7324

Notable plantings: Hawaii-native plants;
rare and endangered tropical plants

Waimea Falls Park Arboretum and
Botanical Garden
59-864 Kamehameha Highway
Haleiwa, Oahu, HI 96712
(808) 638-8655
Notable plantings: over 5,000 Hawaii-
native plants; thirty specialty gardens

Illinois

Chicago Botanic Garden
Box 400, Lake–Cook Road
Glencoe, IL 60022
(708) 835-5440
Notable plantings: Illinois oak woodland;
greenhouse displays

Garfield Park Conservatory
300 North Central Park Boulevard
Chicago, IL 60605
(312) 533-1281
Notable plantings: over 5,000
plant varieties

Lincoln Memorial Garden and Nature
Center
2301 East Lake Drive
Springfield, IL 62707
(217) 529-1111
Notable plantings: Illinois-native plants

Morton Arboretum
Route 53
Lisle, IL 60532
(708) 968-0074
Notable plantings: flowering crab apples;
magnolias; lilacs

Washington Park Botanical Garden
Fayette and Chatham Road
Springfield, IL 63705
(217) 787-2540
Notable plantings: over 1,200 species

Indiana

Christie Woods of Ball State University
200 West University Avenue
Muncie, IN 47306
(317) 285-8838
Notable plantings: orchids

Eli Lilly Botanical Garden of the
Indianapolis Museum of Art
1200 West 38th Street
Indianapolis, IN 46208
(317) 923-1331
Notable plantings: perennials and annuals

Iowa

Arie den Boer Arboretum
Des Moines Water Works Park
408 Fleur Drive
Des Moines, IA 50321
(515) 283-8791
Notable plantings: flowering crab apples

Des Moines Botanical Center
909 East River Drive
Des Moines, IA 50316
(515) 283-4148
Notable plantings: begonias; bonsai;
orchids

Dubuque Arboretum and Botanical
Gardens
3125 West 32nd Street
Dubuque, IA 52001
(319) 556-2100
Notable plantings: All-America
Selections displays

Ewing Park Lilac Arboretum
3226 University
Des Moines, IA 50311
(515) 271-4700
Notable plantings: over 200 lilac varieties

Iowa Arboretum
Route 1, Box 44A
Madrid, IA 50156
(515) 795-3216
Notable plantings: rare and endangered
plants

Iowa State University Horticultural
Garden
Elwood Drive and Haber Road
Iowa State University
Ames, IA 50001
(515) 294-2751
Notable plantings: All-American Rose
Selections test garden

Stampe Lilac Garden
2816 Eastern Avenue
Davenport, IA 52803
(319) 326-7812
Notable plantings: over 170 lilac varieties

Kansas

Bartlett Arboretum
301 North Line
Belle Plaine, KS 67013
(316) 488-3451
Notable plantings: tulips

Botanica, The Wichita Gardens
701 North Amidon
Wichita, KS 67203
(316) 264-0448
Notable plantings: Shakespeare garden;
xeriscape garden; juniper collection

Dyck Arboretum of the Plains
Hesston College
Box 3000
Hesston, KS 67062
(316) 327-8127
Notable plantings: prairie plants and
wildflowers

Meade Park Botanic Gardens
124 North Fillmore
Topeka, KS 66606
(913) 232-5493
Notable plantings: 6,000 annuals

E. F. A. Reinisch Rose and Test Gardnes
Gage Park
4320 West 10th Street
Topeka, KS 66604
(913) 272-6150
Notable plantings: All American Rose
Selection display and test garden; over
6,500 rosebushes

Kentucky

The Bernheim Forest, Arboretum, and
Nature Center
Route 245
Clermont, KY 40110
(502) 543-2451
Notable plantings: azaleas; crab apples;
viburnums; redbuds

Louisiana

American Rose Society Garden
8877 Jefferson Paige Road
Box 3000
Shreveport, LA 71130
(318) 938-5402
Notable plantings: old roses; camellias

Hodges Gardens
Box 900
Many, LA 71449
(318) 586-3523
Notable plantings: old roses;
herb garden

Jungle Gardens
General Delivery
Avery Island, LA 70513
(318) 365-8173

Notable plantings: azaleas; bamboos; camellias; water lilies

Live Oaks Gardens and Joseph Jefferson Home
284 Rip Van Winkle Road
New Iberia, LA 70561
(318) 367-3485
Notable plantings: Alhambra fountain garden; camellias

Longue Vue House and Gardens
7 Bamboo Road
New Orleans, LA 70124
(504) 488-5488
Notable plantings: Spanish Court water garden

Rosedown Plantation
State Highway 10
St. Francisville, LA 70775
(504) 635-3332
Notable plantings: formal French gardens

Zemurray Gardens
Route 1, Box 201
Loranger, LA 70446
(504) 878-6731
Notable plantings: azaleas

Maine

Merryspring
Merryspring Foundation
Box 893
Camden, ME 04843
(207) 236-9046
Notable plantings: Maine-native plants

Wild Gardens of Acadia
Acadia National Park
Sieur de Monts Spring
Mount Desert Island
Bar Harbor, ME 04609
(207) 228-3338
Notable plantings: wildflowers

Maryland

Baltimore Conservatory
Druid Hill Park
Gwynns Falls Parkway and McCulloh Street
Baltimore, MD 21217
(301) 396-0180
Notable plantings: aroids; orchids; tropicals

Brookside Gardens
1500 Glenallan Avenue
Wheaton, MD 20902
(301) 949-8231
Notable plantings: 2,000 taxa; 10,000 woody specimens

Cylburn Garden Center
4915 Greenspring Avenue
Baltimore, MD 21209
(410) 367-2217
Notable plantings: wildflowers; perennials

Ladew Topiary Gardens
3535 Jarretsville Pike
Monkton, MD 21111
(410) 557-9570
Notable plantings: topiary

Massachusetts

Arnold Arboretum of Harvard University
125 Arborway
Jamaica Plain, MA 02130
(617) 524-1718
Notable plantings: 15,000 north temperate zone trees and shrubs

Ashumet Holly Reservation
Massachusetts Audubon Society
286 Ashumet Road
East Falmouth, MA 02536
(508) 563-6390
Notable plantings: hollies

Barnard's Inn Farm
Route 1, Box 538
Vineyard Haven, MA 02568
(508) 693-0925
Notable plantings: over 1,400 species

Berkshire Garden Center
Routes 102 and 183
Box 826
Stockbridge, MA 01262
(413) 298-3926
Notable plantings: daylilies; primroses;
perennials

Garden in the Woods
New England Wild Flower Society, Inc.
180 Hemenway Road
Framingham, MA 01701
(508) 877-7630
(617) 237-4924
Notable plantings: wildflowers

The Lyman Estate
185 Lyman Street
Waltham, MA 02154
(617) 891-7095
Notable plantings: greenhouses

Newbury Perennial Gardens
65 Orchard Street
Byfield, MA 01922
(508) 462-1144
Notable plantings: perennials

Sedgwick Gardens
572 Essex Street
Beverly, MA 01915
(617) 922-1536
Notable plantings: hostas; peonies

Michigan

W. J. Beal—Garfield Botanical Gardens
Michigan State University
East Lansing, MI 48823
(517) 355-0348

Notable plantings: over 5,500
plant varieties

Cranbrook House and Gardens
380 Lone Pine Road
Bloomfield Hills, MI 48013
(313) 645-3149
Notable plantings: formal gardens

Fernwood Garden and Nature Center
13988 Range Line Road
Niles, MI 49120
(616) 695-6491
Notable plantings: prairie plants

Grand Hotel
Mackinac Island, MI 49757
(906) 847-3331
Notable plantings: Victorian gardens

Matthaei Botanical Gardens
University of Michigan
1800 North Dixboro Road
Ann Arbor, MI 48105
(313) 998-7061
Notable plantings: roses; herbs; rock
garden; perennials

Anna Scripps Whitcomb Conservatory
Belle Isle
Detroit, MI 48207
(313) 267-7133
Notable plantings: formal gardens;
orchids

Minnesota

Eloise Butler Wildflower Garden and Bird
Sanctuary
3800 Bryant Avenue South
Minneapolis, MN 55409
(612) 348-5702
Notable plantings: over 500 species

Minnesota Landscape Arboretum
3675 Arboretum Drive

Box 39
Chanhassen, MN 55317
(612) 443-2460
Notable plantings: hostas

Schell Mansion and Gardens
Jefferson Street South
New Ulm, MN 56073
(507) 354-5528
Notable plantings: formal
Victorian gardens

Mississippi

Beauvoir
200 West Beach Boulevard
Biloxi, MS 39531
(601) 388-1313
Notable plantings: azaleas; camellias

Crosby Arboretum
1801 Goodyear Boulevard
Picayune, MS 39466
(501) 798-6961
Notable plantings: regional native plants

Mynelle Gardens
4738 Clinton Boulevard
Jackson, MS 39209
(601) 922-4011
Notable plantings: azaleas; camellias;
daylilies; roses; water lilies

Missouri

The Missouri Botanical Garden
4344 Shaw Boulevard
St. Louis, MO 63166
(314) 577-5100
Notable plantings: roses; Japanese garden; water lilies

Shaw Arboretum
State Highway 100
Box 38
Gray Summit, MO 63039

(314) 742-3512
Notable plantings: prairie plants

Laura Conyers Smith Municipal Rose
Garden
5605 East 63rd Street
Kansas City, MO 64130
(816) 561-9710
Notable plantings: All American Rose
Selections garden; 4,000 rosebushes

New Hampshire

Fuller Gardens
10 Willow Avenue
North Hampton, NH 03862
(603) 964-5414
Notable plantings: roses; hostas

New Jersey

Leonard J. Buck Gardens
Somerset County Park Commission
Layton Road
Farills, NJ 07931
(201) 234-2677
Notable plantings: rock garden

Colonial Park
RD 1, Box 49B
Mettler's Road
Somerset, NJ 08873
(201) 873-2459
Notable plantings: 4,000 rosebushes

Duke Gardens
State Route 206 South
Somerville, NJ 08876
(201) 722-3700
Notable plantings: 11 greenhouse
gardens

George Griswold Frelinghuysen
Arboretum
53 East Hanover Avenue
Morristown, NJ 07962

(201) 326-7600
Notable plantings: azaleas; bulbs; ferns;
peonies; rhododendrons

Presby Memorial Iris Gardens
474 Upper Mountain Avenue
Montclair, NJ 07043
(201) 783-5974
Notable plantings: irises

Skylands Botanical Gardens
Sloatsburg Road
Ringwood, NJ 07456
(201) 962-7031
Notable plantings: daffodils; tulips

New Mexico

Living Desert Botanical State Park
1504 Skyline Drive
Carlsbad, NM 88220
(505) 887-5516
Notable plantings: Chihuahuan
desert-native plants

New York

Boscobel Restoration
Route 9D
Garrison, NY 10524
(914) 265-3638
Notable plantings: English garden; herbs;
orangery; roses

Brooklyn Botanic Garden
1000 Washington Avenue
Brooklyn, NY 11225
(718) 622-4433
Notable plantings: Japanese garden;
flowering cherry trees; roses

Mary Flagler Cary Arboretum
Institute of Ecosystem Studies
Box AB, Millbrook, NY 12545
(914) 677-5343
Notable plantings: ferns; perennials

The Cloisters
Fort Tryon Park
New York, NY 10040
(212) 923-3700
Notable plantings: three cloister gardens

Cornell Plantations
One Plantations Road
Ithaca, NY 14850
(607) 255-3020
Notable plantings: New York-native
plants

Highland Botanical Park
180 Reservoir Avenue
Rochester, NY 14620
(716) 244-8079
Notable plantings: lilacs; hollies

International Bonsai Arboretum
1070 Martin Road
West Henrietta, NY 14586
(716) 334-2595
Notable plantings: bonsai

New York Botanical Garden
200th Street and Kazimiroff Boulevard
Bronx, NY 10458
(718) 817-8700
Notable plantings: begonias; daylilies;
ferns; orchids; rock garden; roses

Old Westbury Gardens
70 Old Westbury Road
Old Westbury, NY 11568
(516) 333-0048
Notable plantings: cottage garden; 300
European beeches; evergreen garden

Planting Fields Arboretum
Planting Fields Road
Oyster Bay, NY 11771
(516) 922-9206
Notable plantings: azaleas;
rhododendrons; conservatories

Sonnenberg Gardens
151 Charlotte Street
Canandaigua, NY 14424
(716) 394-4922
Notable plantings:
ten turn-of-the-century gardens

Wave Hill
675 West 252nd Street
Bronx, NY 10471
(718) 549-3200
Notable plantings: English garden;
aquatic garden

North Carolina

Biltmore Estate
One Biltmore Plaza
Asheville, NC 28803
(704) 274-1776
Notable plantings: formal gardens

Coker Arboretum
University of North Carolina
Chapel Hill, NC 27514
(919) 962-8100
Notable plantings: native plants; spring
bulbs

Sarah P. Duke Gardens
Duke University
Durham, NC 27706
(919) 684-3968
Notable plantings: Asian collection

Elizabethan Gardens
Manteo, NC 27954
(919) 473-3234
Notable plantings: Shakespeare garden;
camellias

North Carolina Botanical Garden
3375 Totten Center
University of North Carolina
Chapel Hill, NC 27599
(919) 962-0522

Notable plantings: native plants of the
Southeast, carnivorous plants, ferns

Sandhills Horticultural Gardens
Sandhill Community College
2200 Airport Road
Pinehurst, NC 28374
(919) 692-6185
Notable plantings: hollies

Tryon Palace Restoration
610 Pollock Street
New Bern, NC 28563
(919) 638-1560
Notable plantings: 18th-century ornamental gardens

North Dakota

International Peace Garden, Inc.
Box 116, Route 1
Dunseith, ND 58329
(701) 263-4390
Notable plantings: perennials; orchids

Ohio

Cox Arboretum
6733 Springboro Pike
Dayton, OH 45449
(513) 434-9005
Notable plantings: cacti and succulents

Falconskeape Gardens
7359 Branch Road
Medina, OH 44256
(216) 723-4966
Notable plantings: lilacs

Franklin Park Conservatory and Garden
Center
1777 East Broad Street
Columbus, OH 43203
(614) 222-7447
Notable plantings: orchids

Garden Center of Greater Cleveland
11030 East Boulevard
Cleveland, OH 44106
(216) 721-1600
Notable plantings: Japanese garden;
terrace garden

Stan Hywet Hall Foundation
714 North Portage Path
Akron, OH 44303
(216) 836-0576
Notable plantings: Japanese garden;
elliptical garden

Holden Arboretum
9500 Sperry Road
Mentor, OH 44060
(216) 256-1110
Notable plantings: lilacs

Kingwood Center
900 Park Avenue West
Mansfield, OH 44906
(419) 522-0211
Notable plantings: peonies;
daylilies; daffodils

Irwin M. Krohn Conservatory
950 Eden Park Drive
Cincinnati, OH 45202
(513) 352-4080
Notable plantings: rare and exotic plants

Toledo Botanical Garden
5403 Elmer Drive
Toledo, OH 43615
(419) 536-8365
Notable plantings: pioneer garden

Whetstone Park of Roses
4015 Olentangy Boulevard
Columbus, OH 43214
(614) 645-6648
Notable plantings: over 10,000
rosebushes and woody ornamentals

Oklahoma

Will Rogers Horticultural Gardens
3500 NW 36th Street
Oklahoma City, OK 73102
(405) 943-0827
Notable plantings: over 1,000 varieties

Tulsa Garden Center
2435 South Peoria Avenue
Tulsa, OK 74114
(918) 749-6401
Notable plantings: roses;
chrysanthemums; irises; rock garden

Oregon

Berry Botanic Garden
11505 SW Summerville Avenue
Portland, OR 97219
(503) 636-4112
Notable plantings: alpine and rock
garden plants; rhododendrons

Crystal Springs Rhododendron Garden
SE 28th and Woodstock
Portland, OR 97202
(503) 771-8386
Notable plantings: rhododendrons

Hendricks Park Rhododendron Garden
Summit Avenue and Skyline Drive
Eugene, OR 97401
(503) 687-5334
Notable plantings: rhododendrons

International Rose Test Garden
400 SW Kingston Avenue
Portland, OR 97201
(503) 248-4302
Notable plantings: roses

Leach Botanical Garden
6704 SE 122nd Avenue
Portland, OR 97236
(503) 761-9503

Notable plantings: Pacific
Northwest-native plants

Cecil and Molly Smith Garden
5065 Ray Bell Road
St. Paul, OR 97137
(503) 246-3710
Notable plantings: rhododendrons

Pennsylvania

Arboretum of the Barnes Foundation
57 Lapsley Lane
Merion Station, PA 19066
(215) 664-8880
Notable plantings: peonies

Bartram's Garden
54th Street and Lindbergh Boulevard
Philadelphia, PA 19143
(215) 729-5281
Notable plantings: oldest botanical
garden in the US

Bowman's Hill Wildflower Preserve
Washington Crossing Historic State Park
Washington Crossing, PA 18977
(215) 862-2924
Notable plantings: Pennsylvania-
native plants

Hershey Rose Gardens and Arboretum
Hotel Road
Hershey, PA 17033
(717) 534-3493
Notable plantings: roses

Longwood Gardens
Route 1, Kennett Square, PA 19348
(215) 388-6741
Notable plantings: 350 acres of formal
gardens; water gardens

Pennsbury Manor
400 Pennsbury Memorial Road
Morrisville, PA 19067

(215) 946-0400
Notable plantings: ornamental courts;
herbaceous perennials

Phipps Conservatory
Schenley Park
Pittsburgh, PA 15219
(412) 255-2370
Notable plantings: orchids

Rhode Island

Blithewold Mansion and Gardens
101 Ferry Road
Bristol, RI 02809
(401) 253-2707
Notable plantings: roses; rock
garden; water garden

Green Animals Topiary Gardens
380 Cory's Lane
Portsmouth, RI 02871
(401) 683-1267
Notable plantings: topiary

Roger Williams Park Greenhouse
and Gardens
Broad Street
Providence, RI 02905
(401) 785-9450
Notable plantings: Japanese garden; roses

South Carolina

Brookgreen Gardens
US 17 South
Murrells Inlet, SC 29576
(803) 237-4218
Notable plantings: over 2,000 species

Cypress Gardens
Hampton Park
Charleston, SC 29403
(803) 553-0515
Notable plantings: over 8,000 varieties
of flowering subtropical plants

Magnolia Plantation and Gardens
Highway 61
Charleston, SC 29414
(803) 571-1266
Notable plantings: camellias

Middleton Place
Route 4
Charleston, SC 29407
(803) 556-6020
Notable plantings: oldest landscaped garden in US; camellias; formal gardens

Swan Lake Iris Gardens
West Liberty Street
Sumter, SC 29150
(803) 775-5811
Notable plantings: irises

South Dakota

McCrory Gardens
South Dakota State University
Brookings, SD 57007
(605) 688-5136

Tennessee

Memphis Botanic Garden
750 Cherry Road
Memphis, TN 38117
(901) 685-1566
Notable plantings: twenty plant collections

Tennesse Botanical Gardens at Cheekwood
1200 Forrest Park Drive
Nashville, TN 37205
(615) 353-2148
Notable plantings: roses; daffodils; perenniels; boxwoods

Texas

Bayou Bend Garden
1 Westcott Street
Houston, TX 77219
(713) 529-8773
Notable plantings: eight gardens

The Dallas Arboretum and Botanical Garden
8525 Garland Road
Dallas, TX 75218
(214) 327-3990
Notable plantings: perennials; azaleas

Dallas Civic Garden Center
Martin Luther King Jr. Boulevard
Fair Park
Dallas, TX 75226
(214) 428-7476
Notable plantings: watergarden; bog garden; wildflowers

Fort Worth Botanical Garden
3220 Botanic Garden Boulevard
Fort Worth, TX 76107
(817) 870-7686
Notable plantings: begonias; roses; Texas-native plants

McMurry College Iris Garden
Sayles Boulevard and South 16th Street
c/o Abilene Chamber of Commerce
325 Hickory Street
Abilene, TX
(915) 692-3938
Notable plantings: over 650 iris varieties

National Wildflower Research Center
4801 La Crosse Avenue
Austin, TX 78739
(512) 292-4100
Notable plantings: rare wildflowers

San Antonio Botanical Center
555 Funston Place

San Antonio, TX 78209
(512) 821-5115
Notable plantings: Texas-native plants

Tyler Municipal Rose Garden
420 South Rose Park Drive
Tyler, TX 75710
(214) 531-1212
Notable plantings: 30,000 rosebushes

Vermont

Shelburne Museum
Route 7
Shelburne, VT 05482
(802) 985-3344
Notable plantings: lilacs; herbs

Virginia

Bryan Park Azalea Gardens
900 East Broad Street
Richmond, VA 23219
(804) 780-8785
Notable plantings: 45,000 azaleas

Lewis Ginter Botanical Garden
7000 Lakeside Avenue
Richmond, VA 23228
(804) 262-9887
Notable plantings: seasonal floral displays

Gunston Hall
10709 Gunston Road
Mason Neck, VA 22079
(703) 550-9220
Notable plantings: 18th-century garden

Maymont Foundation
1700 Hampton Street
Richmond, VA 23220
(804) 358-7166
Notable plantings: Italian garden;
daylilies

Monticello
Thomas Jefferson Memorial Foundation
Box 316
Charlottesville, VA 22902
(804) 296-4800
Notable plantings: historic flowers

Mount Vernon
Mount Vernon Ladies Association
Mount Vernon, VA 22121
(703) 780-7262
Notable plantings: 18th-century gardens

Norfolk Botanical Gardens
Airport Road
Norfolk, VA 23158
(804) 853-6972
Notable plantings: azaleas; tulips;
camellias

Oatlands Plantation
Route 2, Box 352
Leesburg, VA 22075
(703) 777-3174
Notable plantings: roses; early-
nineteenth-century gardens

Washington

Bellevue Botanical Garden
Box 7081
12001 Main Street
Bellevue, WA 98008
(206) 541-3755
Notable plantings: perennials;
rhododendrons

Bloedel Reserve
7571 NE Dolphin Drive
Bainbridge Island, WA 98110
(206) 842-7631
Notable plantings: Japanese garden

Ohme Gardens
3327 Ohme Road
Wenatchee, WA 98801

(509) 662-5785
Notable plantings: alpine and
rock garden plants

Pacific Rim Bonsai
Collection/Rhododendron Species
Botanical Garden
Weyerhauser Corporate Headquarters
2525 South 336th Street
Federal Way, WA 98063
(206) 661-9377
Notable plantings: bonsai; rhododendrons

Wisconsin

Boerner Botanical Gardens
Whitnall Park
5879 South 92nd Street
Hales Corners, WI 53130
(414) 425-1130
Notable plantings: roses; forty-acre
English garden

Mitchell Park Conservatory
524 South Layton Boulevard
Milwaukee, WI 53215
(414) 649-9830
Notable plantings: orchids

Olbrich Botanical Gardens
3330 Atwood Avenue
Madison, WI 53704
(608) 246-4551
Notable plantings: All-America
Selections display garden

University of Wisconsin Arboretum
1207 Seminole Highway
Madison, WI 53711
(608) 262-2746
Notable plantings: prairie trees; viburnum
garden

CANADA

Alberta

Calgary Zoo, Botanical Garden,
and Prehistoric Park
St. George's Island
Calgary, Alberta T2M 4R8
(403) 232-9342
Notable plantings: hardy perennials;
conservatory

Devonian Botanic Garden
University of Alberta
Edmonton, Alberta T6G 2E1
(403) 987-3054
Notable plantings: alpine garden;
irises; peonies

British Columbia

The Butchart Gardens
Box 4010
800 Benvento Avenue
Brentwood Bay
Victoria, British Columbia V8M 1J8
(604) 652-4422
Notable plantings: flowering plants

University of British Columbia
Botanical Garden
6804 SW Marine Drive
Vancouver, British Columbia V6T 1W5
(604) 822-4208
Notable plantings: alpines;
rhododendrons

VanDusen Botanical Garden
5251 Oak Street
Vancouver, British Columbia V6M 4H1
(604) 266-7194
Notable plantings: Sino-Himalayan flora

Nova Scotia

Annapolis Royal Historic Gardens
Box 278
Annapolis Royal, Nova Scotia B0S 1A0
(902) 532-7018
Notable plantings: roses;
Victorian garden

Ontario

Allan Gardens
19 Horticultural Avenue
Toronto, Ontario M5A 2P2
(416) 392-7288
Notable plantings: orchids; roses

Floral Clock and Lilac Gardens
River Road
Niagara Falls, Ontario L2E 6T2
(416) 356-2241
Notable plantings: 25,000
flowering plants

Royal Botanical Gardens
680 Plains Road West
Hamilton, Ontario L8N 3H8
(416) 527-1158
Notable plantings: clematis; climbing
plants; scented garden

Quebec

Montreal Botanical Garden
4101 Sherbrooke Road East
Montreal, Quebec H1X 2B2
(514) 872-1400
Notable plantings: thirty gardens

The Traveling Gardener

THE NEXT-BEST THING to looking at your own garden is looking at someone else's. Gardeners enjoy traveling to see gardens and visit flower shows and other events. Travel agents who specialize in organizing trips for gardeners are listed alphabetically below. A state-by-state listing of the largest and best-known annual garden events in the United States and Canada follows. Of course, there are numerous smaller, local shows and festivals throughout the country, and local and regional plant clubs hold shows and plant sales throughout the year, but space does not permit listing them here. Contact the organizations listed in chapter 8 for information.

The exact dates of the flower shows and festivals listed below vary somewhat from year to year. The phone number listed for an event is generally that of the sponsoring organization or a professional exposition company. You can get additional information by contacting the Chamber of Commerce or Convention and Visitors Bureau for the appropriate state or locality (call the local information operator to get the phone numbers—the number is often toll-free). These organizations will happily send you free details about the particular event, along with free maps and other information about visiting the area. If you mention your interest in gardening, you'll also be sent free information about nearby botanical gardens, arboretums, display gardens, and other sites and events.

An excellent annual guide to gardening events is a paperback volume called The Garden Tourist, edited by Lois G. Rosenfeld. It's available from:

THE GARDEN TOURIST
330 West 72nd Street, Suite 12B
New York, NY 10023
Price: $12.95 plus $2.55 shipping and handling

Garden Tour Operators

Border Discoveries
2117 Bobbyber Drive
Vienna, VA 22182
(703) 356-2826
Destinations: England

Coopersmith's England
Box 900

Inverness, CA 94937
(415) 669-1914
Destinations: Europe and elsewhere

Creative Travel Arrangers
36 Linaria Way
Portola Valley, CA 94028
(415) 854-4412
Destinations: worldwide

Elite Connections
(800) 354-7506
Destinations: London and the United
Kingdom

English Adventures
803 Front Range Road
Littleton, CO 80120
(303) 797-2365
Destinations: Lake District

Expo Garden Tours
101 Sunrise Hill Road
Norwalk, CT 06851
(203) 840-1441
(800) 448-2685
Destinations: worldwide

Family Society Tours, Ltd.
62 Weston Road
Weston, CT 06883
(203) 846-8486
Destinations: worldwide

Fugazy Travel
(800) 221-7181
Destinations: worldwide

Garden Adventures, Ltd.
(610) 444-6161
Destinations: worldwide

Geostar Travel
1240 Century Court
Santa Rosa, CA 95403
(707) 579-2420
(800) 624-6633
Destinations: worldwide

Horizon Travel
3520 South Osprey Avenue
Sarasota, FL 34239
(941) 955-6567
(800) 352-1036
Destinations: worldwide with
Dr. Ellen Henke

Horticulture Travel Programs
98 North Washington Street
Boston, MA 02114
(800) 334-2733
Destinations: worldwide

Ingatours
169 Bedford Road
Greenwich, CT 06831
(800) 786-5311
Destinations: Europe

J. E. G. Enterprises
26810 County Road 98
Davis, CA 95616
(800) 757-0404
Destinations: Scotland

Koelzer Travel
16971 Woodstream Drive
Huntington Beach, CA 92647
(800) 858-2742
Destinations: China

Limewalk Tours
444 South Union Street
Burlington, VT 05401
(802) 864-5720
(800) 426-5720
Destinations: the United Kingdom and
Europe

Lucas & Randall
(800) 505-2505
Destinations: France

New Zealand Australia Reservations
Office
6033 West Century Boulevard, Suite
1270
Los Angeles, CA 90045
(800) 351-2317
(800) 352-2323
Destinations: Australia and New Zealand

Port of Travel
9515 Soquel Drive
Aptos, CA 95003
(408) 688-6004
Destinations: worldwide

Reeve Garden Holidays, Inc.
Box 527
Hanover, NH 03755
(603) 643-5002
Destinations: worldwide

Sander Travel & Tours, Inc.
2760 Caraway Drive
Tucker, GA 30084
(404) 939-7818
Destinations: Europe

TOC
4208 North Freeway Boulevard
Sacramento, CA 95834
(800) 505-2505
Destinations: Europe

Travelworld
(800) 969-4194
Destinations: worldwide

Gardening Shows, Flower Festivals, and Other Annual Events

Alabama

Azalea Trail and Festival
Mobile
(205) 476-8828
Date: month of May

Birmingham Home and Garden Show
Birmingham
(800) 226-3976
Date: mid-March

Gulf Coast Home and Garden Show
Mobile
(800) 226-3976
Date: early February

North Alabama Home and Garden Show
Huntsville
(800) 226-3976
Date: mid-February

Arkansas

Magnolia Blossom Festival
Magnolia
(501) 234-4352
Date: second week in May

California

Alameda Country Home and Garden Show
Pleasanton
(800) 222-9351

Camellia Festival
Sacramento
(916) 442-7673
Date: first two weeks of March

Contra Costa Home and Garden Show
Concord
(800) 222-9351
Date: end of April

Easter in July Lily Festival
Smith River
(707) 487-3443
Date: second weekend in July

Pacific Orchid Exposition
San Francisco
(415) 665-2468
Date: end of February

Pier 39's Tulipmania
San Francisco
(415) 705-5500

San Francisco Garden and Landscape
Show
San Francisco
(415) 750-5108
Date: end of April

Southern California Home
and Garden Show
Anaheim
(714) 978-8888
Date: mid-August

Ventura County Home and Garden Show
Ventura
(800) 222-9351
Date: mid-March

Colorado

Colorado Garden and Home Show
Denver
(303) 696-6100
Date: end of January

Connecticut

Hartford Flower Show
Hartford
(203) 727-8010
Date: end of February

Wildflower Festival
Storrs
(203) 486-4460
Date: second Sunday in June

District of Columbia

Cherry Blossom Festival
Washington, DC
(202) 737-2599
Date: first week in April

Georgetown Garden Tour
Washington, DC
(202) 333-4953
Date: second weekend in May

U.S. Botanic Garden Spring Flower Show
Washington, DC
(202) 226-4082
Date: end of March–end of April

Washington DC Flower and Garden
Show
Washington, DC
(703) 569-7141
Date: early March

Florida

Chrysanthemum Festival
Cypress Gardens (Winter Haven)
Date: month of November

Jacksonville Home and Patio Show
Jacksonville
(904) 730-3356
Date: end of February

Pensacola Home and Garden Show
Pensacola
(800) 226-3976
Date: end of March

Georgia

Atlanta Flower Show
Atlanta
(404) 876-5859
Date: early March

Dogwood Festival
Atlanta
(404) 525-6145
Date: mid-April

Savannah Home and Garden Tour
Savannah
(912) 234-8054
Date: end of March–early April

Southeastern Flower Show
Atlanta
(404) 888-5638
Date: end of February

Illinois

Chicagoland Home and Garden Show
Chicago
(800) 395-1350
Date: mid-February

Marigold Festival
Pekin
(309) 346-2106

Indiana

Indiana Flower and Patio Show
Indianapolis
(317) 576-9933
Date: mid-March

Indianapolis Home Show
Indianapolis
(317) 298-7111
Date: end of January–early February

Iowa

Des Moines Home and Garden Show
Des Moines
(612) 933-3850
Date: mid-February

Pella Tulip Time Festival
Pella
(515) 628-4311
Date: second weekend in May

Kansas

Wichita Lawn, Flower and Garden Show
Wichita
(316) 721-8740
Date: mid-March

Kentucky

Metropolitan Louisville Home, Garden
and Flower Show
Louisville
(502) 637-9737
Date: early March

Louisiana

American Rose Society National Show
American Rose Center
Shreveport
(318) 938-5402
Date: mid-June–end of August

Christmas in Roseland
American Rose Center
Shreveport
(318) 938-5402
Date: month of December

First Bloom Festival
American Rose Center
Shreveport
(318) 938-5402
Date: end of April–start of May

Spring Garden Show at the Botanical
Garden
New Orleans
(504) 486-3736
Date: second week in April

Maryland

Landon Azalea Garden Festival
Bethesda
(301) 320-3200
Date: first weekend in May

Maryland Home and Garden Show
Timonium
(410) 969-8585
Date: mid-March

Massachusetts

Daffodil Festival
Nantucket Island
(508) 288-1700
Date: end of April

New England Spring Flower Show
Boston
(617) 536-9280
(617) 474-6200
Date: mid-March

Michigan

Ann Arbor Flower and Garden Show
Ann Arbor
(313) 998-7002
Date: end of March

International Builders Home and Garden
Show
Detroit
(810) 737-4477
Date: mid-March

Kalamazoo County Flowerfest
Kalamazoo
(616) 381-3597
Date: third weekend in July

Meadow Brook Landscape and Garden
Show
Rochester

(810) 646-4992
Date: early June

Michigan Home and Garden Show
Pontiac
(616) 530-1919
Date: end of February

Spring Home and Garden Show
Novi
(810) 737-4477
Date: early February

Trillium Festival
Muskegon
(616) 798-3573
Date: second weekend in May

Tulip Time Festival
Holland
(616) 396-4221
(800) 822-2770
Date: mid-May

Minnesota

Minneapolis Home and Garden Show
Minneapolis
(612) 933-3850
Date: early March

Missouri

Builders Home and Garden Show
St. Louis
(314) 994-7700
Date: mid-March

Kansas City Flower, Lawn and Garden
Show
Kansas City
(816) 871-5600
Date: early February

St. Louis Flower Show
St. Louis

(314) 569-3117
Date: end of January or early February

New Jersey

New Jersey Flower and Garden Show
Somerset
(908) 919-7660
Date: end February–early March

New York

Buffalo Home and Garden Show
Buffalo
(800) 274-6948
Date: mid-March

Capital District Garden and Flower Show
Albany
(518) 356-6410
Date: mid-March

Central New York Flower and Garden Show
Syracuse
(315) 487-7711
Date: mid-March

Greater Rochester Flower and Garden Show
Henrietta
(716) 225-8091
Date: mid-March

Lilac Festival
Rochester
(716) 546-3070
(716) 256-4960
Date: last two weeks of May

Long Island Flower Show
Nassau Coliseum
(516) 293-4242
Date: early March

New York Flower Show
New York City
(212) 757-0915
(914) 421-3293
Date: early March

Rockefeller Center Flower and Garden Show
New York City
(212) 632-3975
Date: mid-April

Tulip Festival
Albany
(800) 258-3582
Date: Mother's Day weekend

North Carolina

Festival of Flowers
Biltmore Estate
Asheville
(800) 543-2961
Date: mid-April–mid-May

Southern Spring Show
Charlotte
(704) 376-6594
(800) 849-0248
Date: end of February–early March

North Dakota

Sunflower Festival
Wahpeton
(701) 642-8559
Date: mid-August

Ohio

Akron-Canton Home and Garden Show
Akron
(216) 865-6700
Date: end of February

Carnation City Festival
Alliance
(216) 823-6260
Date: first week in August

Central Ohio Home and Garden Show
Columbus
(614) 461-5257
Date: end of February–early March

Cincinnati Flower Show
Cincinnati
(513) 762-3390
(513) 579-0259
Date: end of April–start of May

Cincinnati Home and Garden Show
Cincinnati
(513) 281-0022
Date: end of February–early March

Greater Cincinnati Flower and Garden
Show
Cincinnati
(513) 579-0346
Date: end of April

Miami Valley Home and Garden Show
Dayton
(513) 258-2999
Date: end of February

National Home and Garden Show
Cleveland
(216) 529-1300
Date: mid-February

Oklahoma

Azalea Fest
Muskogee
(918) 682-2401

Oregon

Mother's Day Annual Rhododendron
Show
Crystal Springs Rhododendron Garden
Portland
(503) 771-8386
Date: Mother's Day weekend

Portland Home and Garden Show
Portland
(800) 343-6973
Date: end of February

Rhododendron Festival
Florence
(503) 997-3128
Date: mid-May

Rose Festival
Portland
(503) 227-2681
Date: month of June

Yard, Garden and Patio Show
Portland
(503) 653-8733
Date: end of February

Pennsylvania

Acres of Spring Festival
Longwood Gardens
Kennett Square
(610) 388-1000
Date: month of April

Chrysanthemum Festival
Longwood Gardens
Kennett Square
(610) 388-1000
Date: month of November

May Market
Pittsburgh
(412) 441-4442
Date: mid-May

Philadelphia Flower Show
Philadelphia
(215) 625-8253
Date: early March

Pittsburgh Home and Garden Show
Pittsburgh
(412) 922-4900
Date: mid-March

Rhode Island

Rhode Island Spring Flower and Garden
Show
Providence
(401) 421-7811
Date: end of February

South Carolina

Charleston Festival of Houses and
Gardens
Charleston
(803) 723-1623
Date: third week in March–third week
in April

Charleston Garden Festival
Charleston
(803) 722-7527
Date: early October

Festival of Flowers
Greenwood
(803) 223-8431
Date: end of June

South Carolina Festival of Roses
Orangeburg
(803) 534-6821
Date: last weekend in April

Tennessee

Dogwood Festival
Knoxville
(615) 637-4561
Date: mid-April

Home and Garden Show
Knoxville
(615) 637-4561
Date: end of February

Nashville Lawn and Garden Show
Nashville
(615) 352-3863
Date: early March

Spring Wildflower Pilgrimage
Gatlinburg
(800) 568-4748
Date: last weekend in April

Texas

Abilene Iris Tour
Abilene
(915) 677-7241
Date: April

Bluebonnet Trail and Festival
Austin
(512) 478-9085
Date: first two weeks of April

Dallas Home and Garden Show
Dallas
(214) 680-9995
Date: early March

Fort Worth Home and Garden Show
Fort Worth
(214) 680-9995
Date: mid-February

State Garden Show of Texas
Waco
(817) 772-1270
Date: mid-March

Vermont

Stowe Flower Festival
Stowe
(800) 247-8693
Date: end of June

Virginia

Apple Blossom Festival
Winchester
(703) 662-3863
Date: early May

Dogwood Festival
Charlottesville
(804) 358-5511
Date: mid-April

Historic Garden Week in Virginia
Richmond and statewide
(804) 644-7776
Date: third week in April

Maymont Flower and Garden Show
Richmond
(804) 358-7166
Date: end of February

Washington

Daffodil Festival
Tacoma
(206) 627-6176
Date: third Saturday in April

Northwest Flower and Garden Show
Seattle
(206) 789-5333
Date: second week in February

Skagit Valley Tulip Festival
Mount Vernon
(206) 428-8547
Date: first two weeks in April

Tacoma
(206) 756-2121
Date: end of January–early February

Wisconsin

Milwaukee Landscape and Garden Show
Milwaukee
(414) 778-4929
Date: end of March

CANADA

Ontario

Canadian Tulip Festival
Ottawa
(613) 567-4447
Date: third week in May

Garden Club of Toronto Flower Show
Toronto
(416) 447-5218
Date: early March

A Gardening Miscellany

T*HIS SECTION contains, in no particular order, an assortment of interesting gardening sources and information that didn't quite fit elsewhere in this book.*

Garden Designs

For software that lets you design your garden on your computer, see chapter 11.

Beckett Corporation
2521 Willowsbrook Road
Dallas, TX 75220
(214) 357-6421
Product: garden design kits
Catalogue: free

Design Works
6510 Page Boulevard
St. Louis, MO 63133
(314) 862-1709
Product: Gardener's Guide design kits
Catalogue: free

Garden Solutions
1950 Waldorf NW
Grand Rapids, MI 49550
(616) 771-9500
Product: garden designs
Catalogue: $1.00

Great American Green, Inc.
2981 Lower Union Hill Road
Canton, GA 30115

(404) 475-5537
Product: custom garden designs
Catalogue: $3.00

Landscape Design
15345 Terrace Road NE
Ham Lake, MN 55304
Product: landscape design kit
Catalogue: free

Perennial Graphics
Box 89B Hansen Road
Schaghticoke, NY 12154
(518) 753-7771
Product: custom garden designs
Catalogue: free

SeedScapes
Box 295
Edwardsburg, MI 49112
(616) 663-8601
Product: garden designs
Catalogue: $1.00

Silverbells & Cockleshells
Box 25244, Providence, RI 02905
(401) 941-6400
Product: garden designs
Catalogue: free

Springhill Nurseries
110 West Elm Street
Tipp City, OH 45371
(309) 689-3849
(800) 582-8527
Products: garden designs and plants
Catalogue: free

Swamp Fox Farm
Box 218
Gaylordsville, CT 06755
(203) 354-2659
Product: garden designs
Catalogue: free

TV for Gardeners

Home and Garden Television (HGTV) is a 24-hour cable network that started in January 1995. The network offers extensive gardening programming. For information on how to get the network through your cable provider, call (800) HGTV-ASK.

A syndicated half-hour program called Backyard America often deals with gardening topics. Check your local television listings for stations and times in your area.

Popular garden writer Derek Fell is the host of a gardening show on QVC-TV. Contact your cable provider or check local television listings for stations and times in your area.

The Victory Garden, *hosted by Bob Thomson, is a long-running weekly program produced by WGBH, a public television station in Boston. Check with your local public television station for times in your area.*

Plant-Finding Services

If you can't find the plant you want from the sources listed in chapter 1, chapter 2, and elsewhere in this book, these fee-based plant-finding services may be able to help:

Greenlist Info Services
12 Dudley Street
Randolph, VA 05060
Catalogue: long SASE

Inscape, Inc.
Box 1231
Brigantine, NJ 08203
(609) 822-6517
Catalogue: free

Rare Seed Locators, Inc.
Drawer 2479
2140 Shattuck Avenue
Berkeley, CA 94704
Catalogue: long SASE

Gardening for Kids

The GrowLab™ program from the nonprofit National Gardening Association consists of innovative resources for classroom instruction in gardening and botany. Funded by the National Science Foundation, this program offers a complete curriculum for grades K through 8. The NGA also sponsors the Youth Garden Grants program. For more information, contact:

GrowLab™
National Gardening Association
180 Flynn Avenue
Burlington, VT 05401
(802) 863-1308
(800) 538-7476

Another organization that promotes youth gardening is:

National Junior Horticultural Association
401 North 4th Street
Durant, OK 74701
(405) 924-0771
Publication: *Going & Growing* (three times annually)

Two good sources for children's gardening supplies and backyard nature study are:

Gardens for Growing People
Box 630
Point Reyes Station, CA 94956
(415) 663-9433
Catalogue/quarterly newsletter: $4.00

Let's Get Growing
1900 Commercial Way
Santa Cruz, CA 95065
(408) 464-1868
Catalogue: free

The Nature Company stores carry an extensive line of children's nature-study products. For the location of a store near you, contact:

The Nature Company
75 Hearst Avenue
Berkeley, CA 94710
(510) 644-1337

Horticultural Therapy

Horticultural therapists are occupational therapists specially trained to work with people with disabilities and older adults. They help their clients enjoy the physical and psychological benefits of gardening. For information about becoming certified as a horticultural therapist, contact:

American Horticultural Therapy
Association

362A Christopher Avenue
Gaithersburg, MD 20879
(800) 634-1603

Canadian Horticultural Therapy
Association
Royal Botanical Garden
Box 399
Hamilton, Ontario L8N 3H8
(416) 529-7618

Flower Photography

Slides of flowers, plants, gardens, and landscaping for private use only (not for reproduction in any way) are available from:

Harper Horticultural Slide Library
219 Robanna Shores
Seaford, VA 23696
Catalogue: long SASE with two stamps

The workshops listed below can help you move beyond garden snapshots to the specialized skills needed for serious flower photography. Costs, dates, and locations vary.

California Natural Wonders
Photographic Workshop Series
Noella Ballenger & Associates
Box 457
La Cañada-Flintridge, CA 91012
(818) 954-0933

Center for Nature Photography
Allen Rokach and Anne Millman
Box 118
Riverdale, NY 10471
(914) 968-7163

Latigo Ranch Photography Workshops
Box 237
Kremmling, CO 80459
(303) 724-9008
(800) 227-9655

Lepp and Associates Seminars
Box 6240
Los Osos, CA 93412
(805) 528-7385

Natural Image Expeditions
13785 West 68th Drive
Arvada, CO 8004
(303) 420-7893
(800) 259-8771

The Nature Place
Colorado Outdoor Education Center
Florrisant, CO 80816
(719) 748-3475

Nature Photography Workshops
Edward and Lee Mason
8410 Madeline Drive
St. Louis, MO 63114
(314) 427-6311

Rocky Mountain Nature Association
Seminar Coordinator
Rocky Mountain National Park
Estes Park, CO 80517
(303) 586-1258

Botanic Art

A natural corollary to gardening is producing, looking at, and sometimes collecting botanic art. There are too many dealers in both contemporary and antique botanic art to list here, however. For information on finding a reputable botanic art dealer, contact:
National Antique and Art Dealers
Association of America
12 East 56th Street
New York, NY 10022
(212) 826-9707

Professional botanic illustrators may join:
Guild of Natural Science Illustrators
Box 652

Ben Franklin Station
Washington, DC 20044

The Hunt Institute for Botanical Documentation is a research center that studies the history of plant science, including iconography and art. The institute has an extensive collection of botanical illustrations.
Hunt Institute for Botanical
Documentation
Carnegie-Mellon University
Pittsburgh, PA 15213
(412) 268-2434

Software containing horticultural clip art is available from:
Wheeler Arts
66 Lake Park
Champaign, IL 61821
(217) 359-6816
Program: Quick Art
Catalogue: $3.00

Backyard Wildlife Habitat

Your gardening efforts can make your backyard both more beautiful and more beneficial to wildlife. The organizations listed below provide information about creating backyard wildlife habitats and award certificates of merit:
Backyard Wildlife Habitat Program
National Wildlife Federation
1400 16th Street NW
Washington, DC 20036
(202) 797-6800
(800) 432-6564

Urban Wildlife Sanctuary Program
National Institute for Urban Wildlife
10921 Trotting Ridge Way
Columbia, MD 21044
(301) 596-3311

National Register of Big Trees

Hundreds of champion big trees and their locations are listed on the National Register of Big Trees. To get a free copy, contact:
National Register of Big Trees
American Forestry Association
Box 2000
Washington, DC 20013
(202) 667-3300

Seeds from Famous Trees

Kits containing seeds from famous trees (including those from the homes of presidents and other historic sites) and all you need to grow them are available from:
Famous and Historic Trees
Box 7040
Jacksonville, FL 32238
(904) 765-0727
Catalogue: free

Special Gardening Days

April is National Garden Month. For information on events, contact the sponsor:
Garden Council
10210 Bald Hill Road
Mitchellville, MD 20721
(301) 577-4073

The second week of April is National Garden Week. For information on events, contact the sponsor:
National Garden Bureau
1311 Butterfield Road
Downers Grove, IL 60515

The first full day of spring is Master Gardener Day (see chapter 9 for more information about the

Master Gardener program). For information on events, contact:
Jim Arnold, Master Gardener
543 Wagner Street
Fort Wayne, IN 46805
(219) 426-9904

The last Friday in April is National Arbor Day. For information on events, contact the sponsor:
Committee for National Arbor Day
Box 333
West Orange, NJ 07052
(201) 731-0840

The second week in May is National Wildflower Week. For information on events, contact the sponsor:
National Ecology Committee
107 Jensen Circle
West Springfield, MA 01089
(413) 737-7600

Flowers of the Month

Who decides this stuff, anyway?

January: carnation
February: violet
March: jonquil
April: sweet pea
May: lily of the valley
June: rose
July: larkspur
August: gladiolus
September: aster
October: calendula
November: chrysanthemum
December: narcissus

State and Provincial Flowers and Trees

State	State Flower	State Tree
Alabama	camellia	southern pine (longleaf)
Alaska	forget–me–not	Sitka spruce
Arizona	saguaro	paloverde
Arkansas	apple blossom	pine
California	golden poppy	California redwood
Colorado	Rocky Mountain columbine	blue spruce
Connecticut	mountain laurel	white oak
Delaware	peach blossom	American holly
Florida	orange blossom	sabal palm
Georgia	Cherokee rose	live oak
Hawaii	hibiscus	kukui
Idaho	syringa	western white pine
Illinois	native violet	white oak
Indiana	peony	tulip tree
Iowa	wild rose	oak
Kansas	sunflower	cottonwood
Kentucky	goldenrod	Kentucky coffeetree
Louisiana	magnolia	bald cypress
Maine	white pinecone and tassel	white pine
Maryland	black-eyed Susan	white oak
Massachusetts	mayflower	American elm
Michigan	apple blossom	white pine
Minnesota	pink-and-white lady's slipper	red pine
Mississippi	magnolia	magnolia
Missouri	hawthorn	flowering dogwood
Montana	bitterroot	ponderosa pine
Nebraska	goldenrod	cottonwood
Nevada	sagebrush	single–leaf piñon
New Hampshire	purple lilac	white birch
New Jersey	purple violet	red oak
New Mexico	yucca flower	piñon pine
New York	rose	sugar maple
North Carolina	dogwood	pine
North Dakota	wild prairie rose	American elm
Ohio	scarlet carnation	buckeye
Oklahoma	mistletoe	redbud
Oregon	Oregon grape	Douglas fir
Pennsylvania	mountain laurel	hemlock
Rhode Island	violet	red maple
South Carolina	Carolina jessamine	palmetto
South Dakota	American pasqueflower	Black Hills spruce
Tennessee	iris	tulip poplar
Texas	bluebonnet	pecan
Utah	sego lily	blue spruce
Vermont	red clover	sugar maple
Virginia	dogwood	dogwood
Washington	coast rhododendron	western hemlock
West Virginia	rhododendron	sugar maple
Wisconsin	wood violet	sugar maple
Wyoming	Indian paintbrush	cottonwood

Province/Territory	Flower
Alberta	wild rose
British Columbia	Pacific dogwood
Manitoba	prairie crocus
New Brunswick	purple violet
Newfoundland	pitcher plant
Northwest Territories	mountain avens
Nova Scotia	mayflower
Ontario	white trillium
Prince Edward Island	lady's slipper
Quebec	white garden lily
Saskatchewan	red lily
Yukon Territory	fireweed

THE INFORMATION

THE INFORMATION

by MARTIN AMIS

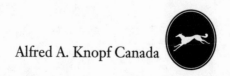

Alfred A. Knopf Canada

PUBLISHED BY ALFRED A. KNOPF CANADA

Copyright © 1995 by Martin Amis

All rights reserved under International and Pan American Copyright Conventions.
Published in Canada by Alfred A. Knopf Canada, Toronto, and simultaneously in
the United States by Harmony Books, a division of Crown Publishers Inc., New
York. Distributed by Random House of Canada Limited, Toronto

Canadian Cataloguing in Publication Data

Amis, Martin, 1949–
The information

ISBN 0-394-28111-X

I. Title
PR6051.M515   1995   823'.914   C95-930490-8

First Canadian Edition

Printed and bound in the United States of America

To Louis and Jacob

And to the memory of
Lucy Partington
(1952–1973)

PART ONE

Cities at night, I feel, contain men who cry in their sleep and then say Nothing. It's nothing. Just sad dreams. Or something like that . . . Swing low in your weep ship, with your tear scans and your sob probes, and you would mark them. Women—and they can be wives, lovers, gaunt muses, fat nurses, obsessions, devourers, exes, nemeses—will wake and turn to these men and ask, with female need-to-know, "What is it?" And the men say, "Nothing. No it isn't anything really. Just sad dreams."

Just sad dreams. Yeah: oh sure. Just sad dreams. Or something like that.

Richard Tull was crying in his sleep. The woman beside him, his wife, Gina, woke and turned. She moved up on him from behind and laid hands on his pale and straining shoulders. There was a professionalism in her blinks and frowns and whispers: like the person at the poolside, trained in first aid; like the figure surging in on the blood-smeared macadam, a striding Christ of mouth-to-mouth. She was a woman. She knew so much more about tears than he did. She didn't know about Swift's juvenilia, or Wordsworth's senilia, or how Cressida had variously fared at the hands of Boccaccio, of Chaucer, of Robert Henryson, of Shakespeare; she didn't know Proust. But she knew tears. Gina had tears cold.

"What is it?" she said.

Richard raised a bent arm to his brow. The sniff he gave was complicated, orchestral. And when he sighed you could hear the distant seagulls falling through his lungs.

"Nothing. It isn't anything. Just sad dreams."

Or something like that.

3

After a while she too sighed and turned over, away from him.

There in the night their bed had the towelly smell of marriage.

He awoke at six, as usual. He needed no alarm clock. He was already comprehensively alarmed. Richard Tull felt tired, and not just underslept. Local tiredness was up there above him—the kind of tiredness that sleep might lighten—but there was something else up there over and above it. And beneath it. That greater tiredness was not so local. It was the tiredness of time lived, with its days and days. It was the tiredness of gravity—gravity, which wants you down there in the center of the earth. That greater tiredness was here to stay: and get heavier. No nap or cuppa would ever lighten it. Richard couldn't remember crying in the night. Now his eyes were dry and open. He was in a terrible state—that of consciousness. Some while ago in his life he had lost the knack of choosing what to think about. He slid out of bed in the mornings just to find some peace. He slid out of bed in the mornings just to get a little rest. He was forty tomorrow, and reviewed books.

In the small square kitchen, which stoically awaited him, Richard engaged the electric kettle. Then he went next door and looked in on the boys. Dawn visits to their room had been known to comfort him after nights such as the one he had just experienced, with all its unwelcome information. His twin sons in their twin beds. Marius and Marcus were not identical twins. And they weren't fraternal twins either, Richard often said (unfairly, perhaps), in the sense that they showed little brotherly feeling. But that's all they were, brothers, born at the same time. It was possible, theoretically (and, Richard surmised, their mother being Gina, also practically) that Marcus and Marius had different fathers. They didn't look alike, especially, and were strikingly dissimilar in all their talents and proclivities. Not even their birthdays were content to be identical: a sanguinary summer midnight had interposed itself between the two boys and their (again) very distinctive parturitional styles, Marius, the elder, subjecting the delivery room to a systematic and intelligent stare, its negative judgment suspended by decency and disgust, whereas Marcus just clucked and sighed to himself complacently, and seemed to pat himself down, as if after a successful journey through freak weather. Now in the dawn, through the window and through the rain, the streets of London looked like the insides of an old plug. Richard contemplated his sons, their motive bodies reluctantly arrested in sleep, and reef-knotted to their bedware, and he thought, as an artist might: but the young sleep in another country, at once very dangerous and out of harm's way, perennially humid with innocuous libido—there are neutral eagles out on the windowsill, waiting, offering protection and threat.

Sometimes Richard did think and feel like an artist. He was an artist when he saw fire, even a match head (he was in his study now, lighting his first cigarette): an instinct in him acknowledged its elemental status. He was an artist when he saw society: it never crossed his mind that society had to be like this, had any right, had any business being like this. A car in the street. Why? Why *cars*? This is what an artist has to be: harassed to the point of insanity or stupefaction by first principles. The difficulty began when he sat down to write. The difficulty, really, began even earlier. Richard looked at his watch and thought: I can't call him yet. Or rather: Can't call him yet. For the interior monologue now waives the initial personal pronoun, in deference to Joyce. He'll still be in bed, not like the boys and their abandonment, but lying there personably, and smugly sleeping. For *him*, either there would be no information, or the information, such as it was, would all be good.

For an hour (it was the new system) he worked on his latest novel, deliberately but provisionally entitled *Untitled*. Richard Tull wasn't much of a hero. Yet there was something heroic about this early hour of flinching, flickering labor, the pencil sharpener, the Wite-Out, the vines outside the open window sallowing not with autumn but with nicotine. In the drawers of his desk or interleaved by now with the bills and summonses on the lower shelves on his bookcases, and even on the floor of the car (the terrible red Maestro), swilling around among the Ribena cartons and the dead tennis balls, lay other novels, all of them firmly entitled *Unpublished*. And stacked against him in the future, he knew, were yet further novels, successively entitled *Unfinished, Unwritten, Unattempted,* and, eventually, *Unconceived.*

Now came the boys—in what you would call a flurry if it didn't go on so long and involve so much inanely grooved detail, with Richard like the venerable though tacitly alcoholic pilot in the cockpit of the frayed shuttle: his clipboard, his nine-page checklist, his revving hangover—socks, sums, cereal, reading book, shaved carrot, face wash, teeth brush. Gina appeared in the middle of this and drank a cup of tea standing by the sink . . . Though the children were of course partly mysterious to Richard, thank God, he knew their childish repertoire and he knew the flavor of their hidden lives. But Gina he knew less and less about. Little Marco, for instance, believed that the sea was the creation of a rabbit who lived in a racing car. This you could discuss. Richard didn't know what Gina believed. He knew less and less about her private cosmogony.

There she stood, in light lipstick and light pancake and light woolen suit, holding her teacup in joined palms. Other working girls whose beds Richard had shared used to get up at around eleven at night to interface themselves for the other world. Gina did it all in twenty minutes. Her body threw no difficulties in her way: the wash-and-go drip-dry hair, the candid orbits that needed only the mildest of emphasis, the salmony tongue, the ten-second bowel movement, the body that all clothes loved. Gina worked two days a week, sometimes three. What she did, in public relations, seemed to him much more mysterious than what he did, or failed to do, in the study next door. Like the sun, now, her face forbade any direct address of the eyes, though of course the sun glares crazily everywhere at once and doesn't mind who is looking at it. Richard's dressing gown bent round him as he fastened Marius's shirt buttons with his eaten fingertips.

"Can you fasten it?" said Marius.

"Do you want a cup of tea making?" said Gina, surprisingly.

"Knock knock," said Marco.

Richard said, in order, "I am fastening it. No thanks, I'm okay. Who's there?"

"You," said Marco.

"No, *fasten* it. Come on, Daddy!" said Marius.

Richard said, "You who? You don't mean *fasten* it. You mean do it faster. I'm trying."

"Are they ready?" said Gina.

"Who are you calling! Knock knock," said Marco.

"I think so. Who's there?"

"What about macks?"

"Boo."

"They don't need macks, do they?"

"Mine aren't going out in that without macks."

"*Boo,*" said Marco.

"Are you taking them in?"

"Boo who? Yeah, I thought so."

"Why are you crying!"

"Look at you. You aren't even dressed yet."

"I'll get dressed now."

"Why are you crying!"

"It's ten to nine. I'll take them."

"No, I'll take them."

"Daddy! Why are you *crying?*"

"What? I'm not."

"In the night you were," said Gina.

"Was I?" said Richard.

Still in his dressing gown, and barefoot, Richard followed his family out into the passage and down the four flights of stairs. They soon out-speeded him. By the time he rounded the final half-landing the front door was opening—was closing—and with a whip of its tail the flurry of their life had gone.

Richard picked up his *Times* and his low-quality mail (so brown, so unwelcome, so slowly moving through the city). He sifted and then thrashed his way into the newspaper until he found Today's Birthdays. There it stood. There was even a picture of him, cheek to cheek with his wife: Lady Demeter.

At eleven o'clock Richard Tull dialed the number. He felt the hastening of excitement when Gwyn Barry himself picked up the telephone.

"Hello?"

Richard exhaled and said measuredly, ". . . You fucking old *wreck.*"

Gwyn paused. Then the elements came together in his laugh, which was gradual and indulgent and even quite genuine. "Richard," he said.

"Don't laugh like that. You'll pull a muscle. You'll break your neck. Forty years old. I saw your obit in *The Times.*"

"Listen, are you coming to this thing?"

"I am, but I don't think you'd better. Sit tight, by the fire. With a rug on your lap. And an old-boy pill with your hot drink."

"Yes, all right. Enough," said Gwyn. "Are you coming to this thing?"

"Yeah, I suppose so. Why don't I come to you around twelve-thirty and we'll get a cab."

"Twelve-thirty. Good."

"You fucking old *wreck.*"

Richard sobbed briefly and then paid a long and consternated visit to the bathroom mirror. His mind was his own and he accepted full respon-sibility for it, whatever it did or might do. But his *body.* The rest of the morning he spent backing his way into the first sentence of a seven-hundred-word piece about a seven-hundred-page book about Warwick Deeping. Like the twins, Richard and Gwyn Barry were only a day apart in time. Richard would be forty tomorrow. The information would not be carried by *The Times: The Times,* the newspaper of record. Only one celebrity lived at 49E Calchalk Street; and she wasn't famous. Gina was a *genetic* celebrity. She was beautiful, every inch, and she didn't change. She got older, but she didn't change. In the gallery of the old photographs she was always the same, staring out, while everyone else seemed disgracefully protean, kaftaned Messiahs, sideburned Zapatas. He sometimes wished she wasn't: wasn't beautiful. In his present travail. Her brother and sister were ordinary. Her dead dad had been ordinary. Her mother was still around for the time being, fat and falling apart and still mountainously pretty somehow, in a bed somewhere.

We are agreed—come *on*: we are agreed—about beauty in the flesh. Consensus is possible here. And in the mathematics of the universe, beauty helps tell us whether things are false or true. We can quickly agree about beauty, in the heavens and in the flesh. But not everywhere. Not, for instance, on the page.

In the van, Scozzy looked at 13 and said,

"Morrie goes to the doctor, right?"

"Right," said 13.

13 was eighteen and he was black. His real name was Bently. Scozzy was thirty-one, and he was white. His real name was Steve Cousins.

Scozzy said, "Morrie tells the doc, he says, 'I can't raise it with my wife. My wife Queenie. I can't raise it with Queenie.' "

Hearing this, 13 did something that white people have stopped really doing. He grinned. White people used to do it, years ago. "Yeah," said 13 expectantly. Morrie, Queenie, he thought: all Jews is it.

Scozzy said, "The doc goes, 'Unlucky. Listen. We got these pills in from Sweden. The latest gear. Not cheap. Like a *carpet* a pill. Okay?' "

13 nodded. "Or whatever," he said.

They were sitting in the orange van, drinking cans of Ting: pineapple-grapefruit crush. 13's fat dog Giro sat erectly between them on the handbrake section, keeping still but panting as if in great lust.

" 'Take one of them and you'll have a stiffy for four hours. A bonk with a capital O.' Morrie goes home, right?" Scozzy paused and then said thoughtfully, "Morrie rings up the doc and he's like, 'I just took one of them pills but guess what.' "

13 turned and frowned at Scozzy.

" 'Queenie's gone shopping! Won't be back for four hours!' The doc says, 'This is serious, mate. Is there anybody else indoors?' Morrie says, 'Yeah. The au pair.' The doc says, 'What she like?' 'Eighteen with big tits.' So the doc goes, 'Okay. Stay calm. You'll have to do it with the au pair. Tell her it's an emergency. Medical matter.' "

"Medical matter whatever," murmured 13.

" 'Ooh I don't know,' says Morrie. 'I mean a *carpet* a pill? Seems like an awful waste. I can get a stiffy with the au pair anyway.' "

There was silence.

Giro gulped and started panting again.

13 leaned back in his seat. Grin and frown now contested for the suzerainty of his face. The grin won. "Yeah," said 13. "Do it on the carpet is it."

". . . What fucking carpet?"

"You said carpet."

"When?"

"Pill on the carpet."

"Jesus Christ," said Scozzy. "The pills *cost* a carpet. Each."

13 looked mildly unhappy. A mere nothing. It would pass.

"A *carpet*. Jesus. You know: half a stretch."

Nothing—a mere nothing.

"*Fucking* hell. A stretch is six months. A carpet is half a stretch. Three hundred quid."

It had passed. 13 grinned weakly.

Scozzy said, "You're the one who's always in fucking prison."

With fright-movie suddenness (Giro stopped panting) Richard Tull appeared in the left foreground of the van's glass screen and fixed them with a wince before reeling on by. Giro gulped, and started panting again.

"Woe," said Scozzy.

"The man," 13 said simply.

"He's not the man. The man's the other one. He's his mate." Scozzy nodded and smiled and shook his head with all these things coming together: he loved it. "And Crash does his wife."

"The man," said 13. "Of TV fame." 13 frowned, and added, "I never seen him on the telly."

Steve Cousins said, "You just watch fucking Sky."

Richard rang the bell on Holland Park and, momentarily haggard in his bow tie, presented himself to the security camera—which jerked round affrontedly at him in its compact gantry above the door. He also made mental preparations. The state Richard sought was one of disparity readiness. And he never found it. Gwyn's setup always flattened him. He was like the chinless cadet in the nuclear submarine, small-talking with one of the guys as he untwirled the bolt (routine check) on the torpedo bay—and was instantly floored by a frothing phallus of seawater. Deep down out there, with many atmospheres. The pressure of all that Gwyn had.

To take a heftily looming instance, the house itself. Its mass and scope, its particular reach and sweep he knew well: for a year he had gone to school in an identical building across the street. The school, a cosmopolitan crammer, which was dead now, like Richard's father, who had scrimped to send him there, used to accommodate a staff of twenty-five and over two hundred pupils—an ecology of estrogen and testosterone, bumfluff, flares, fights, fancyings, first loves. That tiered rotating world was vanished. But now in a place of the same measurements, the same volume, lived Gwyn and Demeter Barry. Oh yeah. And the help . . . Richard moved his head around as if to relieve neck pain. The camera continued to stare at him incredulously. He tried to stare back at it, with mad pride. Richard wasn't guilty of covetousness, funnily enough. In the shops he seldom saw anything that looked much fun to buy. He liked the space but he didn't want the stuff you put in it. Still, everything had been so much nicer, he thought, in the old days, when Gwyn was poor.

Allowed entry, Richard was shown upstairs, not of course by Demeter (who at this hour would be unguessably elsewhere down the great passages), nor by a maid (though there were maids, called things like Ming and Atrocia, shipped here in crates from São Paolo, from Vientiane), nor by any representative of the home-improvement community (and they were always about, the knighted architect, the overalled stiff with a mouthful of nails): Richard was shown upstairs by a new type of auxiliary, an American coed or sophomore or grad student, whose straightness of hair, whose strictness of mouth, whose brown-eyed and black-browed intelligence was saying that whatever else Gwyn might be he was now an *operation*, all fax and Xerox and preselect. In the hall Richard saw beneath the broad mirror a shelf so infested with cardboard or even plywood invitations . . . He thought of the van outside, a month of tabloids wedged between dash and windscreen. And the two guys within, one white, one black, and the fat German Shepherd, more like a bear than a dog, with its scarf of tongue.

Gwyn Barry was nearing the climax of a combined interview and photo session. Richard entered the room and crossed it in a diagonal with one hand effacingly raised, and sat on a stool, and picked up a magazine. Gwyn was on the window seat, in his archaeologist's suit, also with archaeologist's aura of outdoor living, rugged inquiry, suntan. He filled his small lineaments neatly, just as his hair filled the lineaments (only a rumor, for now) of male-pattern recession. Gwyn's hair was actually gray, but bright gray: not the English gray of eelskin and wet slates; nor yet the gray that comes about through tiredness of pigment, and dryness. Bright gray hair—the hair (Richard thought) of an obvious charlatan. Richard himself, by the way, was going bald too, but anarchically. No steady shrinkage, with the flesh stealing crownwards like rising water; with him, hair loss happened in spasms, in hanks and handfuls. Visits to the barber were now as fearful and apparently hopeless as visits to the bank manager, or the agent—or the garage, in the tomato-red Maestro.

"Have you any thoughts," the interviewer was saying, "on turning forty?"

"Happy birthday," said Richard.

"Thanks. It's just a number," said Gwyn. "Like any other."

The room—Gwyn's study, his library, his lab—was very bad. When in this room it was Richard's policy to stare like a hypnotist into Gwyn's greedy green eyes, for fear of what he might otherwise confront. He didn't really mind the furniture, the remoteness of the ceiling, the good proportion of the three front windows. He *really* didn't mind the central space-platform of floppy discs and X-ray lasers. What he minded were Gwyn's books: Gwyn's books, which multiplied or ramified so crazily now. Look on the desk, look on the table, and what do you find? The lambent horror of Gwyn in Spanish (sashed with quotes and reprint updates) or an American book-club or supermarket paperback, or something in Hebrew or Mandarin or cuneiform or pictogram that seemed blameless enough but had no reason to be there if it wasn't one of Gwyn's. And then Gallimard and Mondadori and Livro Aberto and Zsolnay and Uitgeverij Contact and Kawade Shobo and Magveto Konyvkiado. In the past Richard had enjoyed several opportunities to snoop around Gwyn's study—his desk, his papers. Are snoopers snooping on their own pain? Probably. I expect you get many young girls who. You will be delighted to hear that the air tickets will be. The judges reached their decision in less than. These terms are, we feel, exceptionally. I am beginning to be translating your. Here is a photograph of the inside of my. Richard stopped flipping through the magazine on his lap (he had come to an interview with Gwyn Barry), and stood, and surveyed the bookshelves. They were fiercely alphabetized. Richard's bookshelves weren't alphabetized. He never had time to alphabetize them. He was always too busy—looking for books he couldn't find. He had books heaped under tables, under beds. Books heaped on windowsills so they closed out the sky.

Interviewer and interviewee were winding up some guff about the deceptive simplicity of the interviewee's prose style. Unlike the interviewer, the photographer was a woman, a girl, black-clad, Nordic, leggy—how she crouched and teetered for her images of Gwyn! Richard looked on with a frowsy sigh. Being photographed, as an activity, was in itself clearly not worth envying. What was enviable, and unbelievable, was that Gwyn should be worth photographing. What *happened* inside the much-photographed face—what happened to the head within? The Yanomano or the Ukuki were surely onto something. One shot wouldn't do it, but the constant snatch of the camera's mouth—it would take your reality, in the end. Yes, probably, the more you were photographed, the thinner it went for your inner life. Being photographed was dead time for the soul. Can the head think, while it does the same half smile under the same light frown? If this was all true, then Richard's soul was in great shape. No one photographed him anymore, not even Gina. When the photographs came back from the chemist's, after an increasingly infrequent Tull holiday, Richard was never there: Marius, Marco, Gina, some peasant or lifeguard or donkey—and Richard's elbow or earlobe on the edge of the frame, on the edge of life and love . . . Now the interviewer said, "A lot of people think that, because you're the figure you now are, that the next step is politics. What do you . . . Do you . . . ?"

"Politics," said Gwyn. "Gosh. Well I can't say I've given it that much thought. Thus far. Let's say I wouldn't want to rule it out. As yet."

"You sound like a politician already, Gwyn."

This was Richard. The remark went down well—because, as is often pointed out, we are all of us in need of a good laugh. Or any kind of laugh at all. The need is evidently desperate. Richard dropped his head and turned away. No, that really wasn't the kind of thing he wanted to be saying. Ever. But Gwyn's world was partly public. And Richard's world was dangerously and increasingly private. And some of us are slaves in our own lives.

"I think writing'll do me," said Gwyn. "They're not incompatible, though, are they? Novelist and politician are both concerned with human potential."

"This would be Labour, of course."

"Obviously."

"Of course."

"Of course."

Of course, thought Richard. Yeah: of course Gwyn was Labour. It was obvious. Obvious not from the ripply cornices twenty feet above their heads, not from the brass lamps or the military plumpness of the leather-topped desk. Obvious because Gwyn was what he was, a writer, in England, at the end of the twentieth century. There was nothing else for such a person to be. Richard was Labour, equally obviously. It often